THE COMPI AIR FRYER COOKBOOK FOR BEGINNERS

by Elena M. Rose

Contents

INTRODUCTION

We all love the taste of popular fatty foods. French fries, chicken nuggets, burgers, mmm... that is oh so delicious! The mere mention of these foods makes my mouths water. I am a home cook and I must admit that frying is one of the most convenient cooking methods. It is an easy, practical, and quick way to prepare everyday meals for my family. They love to gorge themselves on fatty burgers, deep-fried crispy chicken nuggets, and oily donuts. Accordingly, restaurants and fast-food chains use deep-frying as the most common technique to prepare foods. Generally speaking, fried foods are significantly higher in calories and fat than baked and boiled foods. For instance, 100 grams of French fries contain about 320 calories and 15 grams of fat, while the same amount of boiled potatoes contains about 95 calories and 0.1 grams of fat. Obviously, calories add up easily when cooking in a standard way. The healthiest ingredients in the world actually lose their nutrients when they are deep-fried in oil.

We can't deny the fact that deep-fried foods are not good for our health and beauty. Fried foods tend to be high in fats, salt, sugar, and extra calories. Moreover, deep-fried foods are typically loaded with trans-fats that are linked with an increased risk of heart disease, obesity, and other serious diseases. Trans fats occur in processed foods, baked goods, and animal products, too. Bakery goods, such as donuts, crackers, pies and cakes are just some of the examples of foods that may contain trans-fats or saturated fats i.e. partially hydrogenated vegetable oils. Thus, you should limit margarine, common frying oils, palm oil, safflower oil, and so forth. Also, avoid fried red meat, snacks, pastries, sugary foods and beverages. In fact, a few studies have found the connection between eating fried foods and early death. It means that giving up fried foods could significantly reduce the risk of obesity, diabetes, and cancer. Thus, I decided to limit fried foods and started cooking healthier meals. It was very, very difficult to achieve. I couldn't neglect the fact that fried foods are pleasing to our taste-buds, but, on the other hand, healthy meals are usually believed to be boring. I have struggled hard to try to find a solution until one day I discovered an Air Fryer!

The good news is that you don't have to sacrifice flavor when trying to eat healthier. There is a revolutionary cooking method that will change the way we eat forever. It is air frying! Yes, you read that correctly – hot air is a new oil! Instead of soaking your foods in hot cooking oil, you can cook it with a teaspoon of healthy olive oil, and achieve the same results. Moreover, you can achieve even better results since your food won't taste like fat. Thus, you will cut calories and toxic fats, not flavor and texture! An Air Fryer is a unique kitchen tool designed to cook fried food in a healthy way. How does it work? A super-heated air circulates inside the cooking chamber, producing delicious foods that are moist on the inside and crispy on the outside. An Air Fryer makes frying and baking at home faster, easier, and most importantly – healthier! Make your healthy food less boring, save your time and improve the quality of your life. Sounds impossible? Then, keep on reading!

The Benefits of Using an Air Fryer

Is an Air Fryer worth buying? Well, there are numerous benefits you can get from using an Air Fryer but it is your decision. In my opinion, here are the top three benefits of using an Air Fryer.

Healthy eating and weight loss. When it comes to healthy eating habits, choosing the right kitchen equipment is a key to success. Air frying requires less fat compared to standard frying and deep-frying, making your healthy eating goals more achievable. Needless to say, fats and oils become harmful under the high heat; in fact, deep-fried foods speed up aging, cause inflammation and increase the amount of harmful LDL cholesterol. Researches have hypothesized that even small amounts of trans-fats can increase the risk of obesity and cardiovascular disease by 20%. If you are thinking of cutting down on fat consumption and losing weight, you are in the right place. I don't know about you, but being happy with my body is my top priority. It is more important that all cheeseburgers, chips, and cakes in the world!

The Air Fryer is fast and convenient. An Air Fryer saves me time in the kitchen. Unlike a convection oven, it heats up in a few minutes; further, hot air circulates around my food evenly, cooking it quickly and perfectly. The Air Fryer is a great solution for one-pot meals; in addition, some Air Fryer models come with dividers. The Air Fryer is versatile kitchen appliance. Besides frying, you have the opportunity to bake, roast and grill your food using this high-end technology.

Further, my Air Fryer doesn't smoke up my kitchen, delivering great results with minimal hands-on time. I think I get a win-win solution! With a simple touch operation, an automatic temperature control, preset buttons, and a user-friendly design, an Air Fryer is a space and time-saving solution!

Air-fried foods are really delicious. The best part is – you can still enjoy your favorite fried foods such as fish fillets, chicken wings, and desserts. And your foods taste amazing! You can have great results without submerging your food in hot oil. Simply brush your cooking basket with healthy oils with high smoke point and you will be amazed by results. Healthy fats include olive oil, coconut oil, sesame oil, flaxseed oil, peanut oil, avocado oil, butter, and ghee The Air Fryer is a real game-changer – it promotes healthy eating that does not compromise flavor!

8 Air Fryer Tips You Should Know

You can improve the quality of your eating by making a few small adjustments to your cooking habits. If you are new to air frying, please follow these tips that I have learned during my Air Fryer journey. Once you get into air frying, delicious foods are just minutes away!

1. Most of the manufactures specify that the unit should be preheated before adding food to the cooking basket. I realized that it is not necessary in most cases but it is helpful since it can reduce the cooking time.

2. How to achieve that crispy texture? I always pat my foods dry before adding spices. Then, I brush my food with a teaspoon or two of high-quality vegetable oil; I highly recommend using misters or oil sprays. A pro tip: when cooking vegetables, remove the cooking basket from the Air Fryer and let your vegetables cool for a few minutes. Set temperature to 390 degrees F and continue to cook for 2 to 3 minutes more. The crunchiness is guaranteed! When it comes to cruciferous vegetables, I like to boil them for about 5 minutes; then, I toss my veggies with oil and put into the Air Fryer basket; and last but not least, make sure to move your vegetables around occasionally.

3. Keep food from sticking by simply brushing the bottom of the cooking basket with a little bit of oil or melted butter. If you tend to use olive oil, avoid extra-virgin olive oils, which have smoke points between 350 degrees and 410 degrees F. Simply use regular varieties with higher smoke points (up to 470 degrees F).

4. Do not over-fill the cooking basket. Although it's tempting to cook all of your foods at once, you do not want to end up with soggy or undercooked ingredients. On the other hand, avoid cooking too small amounts of food and lightweight items. Your Air Fryer has powerful fans so it is not suitable for lightweight, freeze-dried foods in most cases.

5. Do not forget to brush your food with oil. To illustrate, I usually use 1 teaspoon of oil for 2 pounds of potatoes. I realized that oils with a high smoke point work really well in my Air Fryer. On the other hand, using too much oil can cause excess oil to burn and it doesn't smell good. To keep the rendered fat drippings from burning, you can pour a little water into the bottom of the Air Fryer drawer. You do not have to add extra oil to foods that naturally have some fat such as fatty cuts of meat and fish.

6. As for cooking times, they may vary depending on the manufacturer, so always test your food for doneness. As for meats, play safe and always use a meat thermometer. There are a lot of factors that may affect actual cooking time such as the quantity of food, its quality, thickness or density. I would recommend that you should cook food in smaller batches and check your food halfway through the cooking time. Most foods need to be checked and shaken several times during the cooking time. I included approximate cooking time in every recipe but keep in mind that it is intended as a guide only.

7. You can use your Air Fryer to reheat leftovers; simply set the temperature to 300 degrees F for up to 10 minutes and your dinner is ready right on time!

8. If your food turned out dry and tasteless, this is a timing issue in most cases. If you are not sure about cooking time, simply go 50 degrees F below and cut the time by 30 percent. You can increase the cooking time easily but you can't save mushy and dry food. However, read the entire recipe before you start cooking in your Air Fryer. Remember – mistakes are natural, they are a big part of how we learn. Thus, do not be afraid to experiment with your Air Fryer.

When it comes to chewy, crumbly and mouth-watering foods, it's hard to beat an Air Fryer. This recipe collection features favorite fried foods of all time such as poultry, fish, vegetables, pastries, snacks, eggs, dairy products, and desserts. Every recipe includes approximate cook time, suggested serving size, nutritional analysis, the ingredient list, and detailed instructions. This collection is designed to help you re-create restaurant-quality meals at your home. They are pretty simple to prepare but it's all just going to take little bit of practice. I hope you won't run out of inspiration with these 400 Air Fryer recipes!

Air Fryer Cooking Guide

CHICKEN	Temperature	Time (minutes)		Temperature	Time (minutes)
Breasts, bone in	370°F	20-25	Nuggets	390°F	6-10
Chicken wings	360°F	15-20	Whole chicken	360°F	70-75
Game Hen	390°F	20-22	Tenders	360°F	8-10
Legs	370°F	20-22	Thighs, boneless	380°F	18-20
Legs, bone in	380°F	28-30	Thighs, bone in	380°F	20-22
BEEF					
Burger	370°F	16-20	Meatballs (big)	380°F	10-12
Filet mignon	400°F	18	Ribeye	400°F	10-15
Flank steak	400°F	12-15	Round roast	390°F	45-55
London broil	400°F	20-28	Sirloin steaks	400°F	9-15
Meatballs (1-inch)	380°F	7-10			
PORK and LAMB					
Bacon	400°F	5-7	Rack of lamb	380°F	22
Bacon (thick cut)	400°F	6-10	Sausages	380°F	12-15
Lamb loin chops	400°F	6-10	Spare ribs	400°F	18-25
Loin	360°F	50-55	Tenderloin	400°F	5-8
Pork chops	400°F	12-15			
FISH					
Calamari	400°F	4-5	Swordfish steak	400°F	10-12
Fish sticks	390°F	6-10	Tuna steak	400°F	8-10
Fish fillet	400°F	10-12	Scallops	400°F	5-7
Salmon (fillet)	380°F	12	Shrimp	400°F	5-6
Shellfish	400°F	12-15			
VEGETABLES					
Asparagus	400°F	5-7	Mushrooms	400°F	5
Beets	400°F	40	Onions	400°F	8-10
Broccoli	400°F	6	Parsnip	380°F	15
Brussels Sprouts	380°F	15	Peppers	400°F	15
Carrots	380°F	13-15	Potatoes	400°F	12
Cauliflower	400°F	12-15	Potatoes (baby)	400°F	15
Corn on the cob	390°F	6-10	Squash	400°F	12-15
Eggplant	400°F	15	Sweet potato	380°F	35
Fennel	370°F	15	Tomato (cherry)	380°F	20-22
Green beans	400°F	5-7	Tomato	350°F	10
Kale	250°F	12	Zucchini	400°F	10
FROZEN FOOD					
Breaded shrimp	400°F	10-12	Mozzarella stick	400°F	8-10
Fish fillets	400°F	14-20	Onion rings	400°F	8
Fish sticks	400°F	10-12	Pot stickers	400°F	8-10
French fries (thin)	400°F	15-20			

POULTRY

1. Festive Turkey with Chili Mayo

(Ready in about 45 minutes | Servings 4)

Ingredients

3 teaspoons olive oil
1/2 teaspoon marjoram
1 teaspoon basil
1/2 teaspoon garlic powder
1 teaspoon shallot powder
Coarse salt and ground black pepper, to taste

2 pounds turkey breast, boneless
Chili mayo:
1/4 cup mayonnaise
1/4 cup sour cream
1 tablespoon chili sauce
1/2 teaspoon stone-ground mustard

Directions

Start by preheating your Air Fryer to 360 degrees F.

In a mixing bowl, thoroughly combine the olive oil with spices. Rub the turkey breast with the spice mixture until it is well coated on all sides.

Air fry for 40 minutes, turning them over halfway through the cooking time. Your instant-read thermometer should read 165 degrees.

Meanwhile, mix all of the ingredients for the chili mayo. Place in your refrigerator until ready to serve.

Place the turkey breast skin-side up on a cutting board and slice it against the grain; serve with chili mayo and enjoy!

Per serving: 409 Calories; 19.2g Fat; 3.4g Carbs; 49.2g Protein; 1.3g Sugars

2. Homemade Chicken Burgers

(Ready in about 20 minutes | Servings 4)

Ingredients

1 ¼ pounds chicken white meat, ground
1/2 white onion, finely chopped
1 teaspoon fresh garlic, finely chopped
Sea salt and ground black pepper, to taste
1 teaspoon paprika

1/2 cup cornmeal
1 ½ cups breadcrumbs
4 burger buns
4 lettuce leaves
2 small pickles, sliced
2 tablespoons ketchup
1 teaspoon yellow mustard

Directions

Thoroughly combine the chicken, onion, garlic, salt and black pepper in a mixing dish. Form the mixture into 4 equal patties.

In a shallow bowl, mix paprika with cornmeal and breadcrumbs. Dip each patty in this mixture, pressing to coat well on both sides.

Spritz a cooking basket with a nonstick cooking spray. Air fry the burgers at 370 degrees F for about 11 minutes or to your desired degree of doneness.

Place your burgers on burger buns and serve with toppings. Bon appétit!

Per serving: 509 Calories; 9.8g Fat; 34g Carbs; 39.2g Protein; 7.3g Sugars

3. Italian-Style Turkey Meatballs

(Ready in about 20 minutes | Servings 5)

Ingredients

1 ½ pounds ground turkey
1/2 cup parmesan cheese, grated
1/2 cup tortilla chips, crumbled
1 yellow onion, finely chopped
2 tablespoons Italian parsley, finely chopped

1 egg, beaten
2 cloves garlic, minced
1 tablespoon soy sauce
1 teaspoon Italian seasoning mix
1 teaspoon olive oil

Directions

Thoroughly combine all of the above ingredients until well incorporated.

Shape the mixture into 10 equal meatballs.

Spritz a cooking basket with a nonstick cooking spray. Cook at 360 degrees F for about 10 minutes or to your desired degree of doneness.

Bon appétit!

Per serving: 327 Calories; 18.7g Fat; 6.9g Carbs; 32.2g Protein; 1.7g Sugars

4. Hot Chicken Drumettes with Peppers

(Ready in about 45 minutes | Servings 3)

Ingredients

1/2 cup all-purpose four
1 teaspoon kosher salt
1 teaspoon shallot powder
1/2 teaspoon dried basil
1/2 teaspoon dried oregano
1/2 teaspoon smoked paprika

1 tablespoon hot sauce
1/4 cup mayonnaise
1/4 cup milk
1 pound chicken drumettes
2 bell peppers, sliced

Directions

In a shallow bowl, mix the flour, salt, shallot powder, basil, oregano and smoked paprika.

In another bowl, mix the hot sauce, mayonnaise and milk.

Dip the chicken drumettes in the flour mixture, then, coat them with the milk mixture; make sure to coat well on all sides.

Cook in the preheated Air Fryer at 380 degrees F for 28 to 30 minutes; turn them over halfway through the cooking time. Reserve chicken drumettes, keeping them warm.

Then, cook the peppers at 400 degrees F for 13 to 15 minutes, shaking the basket once or twice. Eat warm.

Per serving: 397 Calories; 18.8g Fat; 20.6g Carbs; 34.2g Protein; 3.1g Sugars

5. Chicken Nuggets with Turnip Chips

(Ready in about 35 minutes | Servings 3)

Ingredients

1 egg
1/2 teaspoon cayenne pepper
1/3 cup panko crumbs
1/4 teaspoon Romano cheese, grated
2 teaspoons canola oil

1 pound chicken breast, cut into slices
1 medium-sized turnip, trimmed and sliced
1/2 teaspoon garlic powder
Sea salt and ground black pepper, to taste

Directions

Beat the egg with the cayenne pepper until frothy. In another shallow bowl, mix the panko crumbs with the cheese until well combined.

Dip the chicken slices into the egg mixture; then, coat the chicken slices on all sides with the the panko mixture. Brush with 1 teaspoon of canola oil. Season with salt and pepper to taste.

Cook in the preheated Air Fryer at 380 degrees F for 12 minutes, shaking the basket halfway through the cooking time; an instant-read thermometer should read 165 degrees F. Reserve, keeping them warm.

Drizzle the turnip slices with the remaining teaspoon of canola oil. Season with garlic powder, salt and pepper to taste.

Cook the turnips slices at 370 degrees F for about 20 minutes. Serve with the warm chicken nuggets. Bon appétit!

Per serving: 361 Calories; 19.1g Fat; 9.6g Carbs; 35g Protein; 1.1g Sugars

6. Turkey Sausage with Brussels Sprouts

(Ready in about 20 minutes | Servings 2)

Ingredients

4 turkey sausages
1/2 pound Brussels sprouts, trimmed and halved
1 teaspoon olive oil

Sea salt and ground black pepper, to taste
1/2 teaspoon cayenne pepper
1/2 teaspoon shallot powder
1/4 teaspoon dried dill weed

Directions

Place the sausages in the Air Fryer cooking basket.

Now, toss the Brussels sprouts with olive oil and spices. Scatter the Brussels sprouts around the the sausages.

Cook in the preheated Air Fryer at 380 degrees F for 15 minutes, shaking the basket halfway through the cooking time. Bon appétit!

Per serving: 601 Calories; 40.1g Fat; 16g Carbs; 39.1g Protein; 3.4g Sugars

7. Garlicky Duck with Potato Rösti

(Ready in about 30 minutes | Servings 2)

Ingredients

1/2 pound duck breast, skin-on, boneless
1 clove garlic, halved
Coarse sea salt and ground black pepper, to taste
1/2 teaspoon marjoram
1/4 teaspoon mustard seeds
1/4 teaspoon fennel seeds

Potato Rösti:
1/2 pound potatoes, grated
2 tablespoons butter, melted
1 teaspoon fresh rosemary, chopped
Coarse sea salt and ground black pepper, to taste

Directions

Score the duck breast to render the fat and rub with fresh garlic on all sides. Season the duck with salt, pepper, marjoram, mustard seeds and fennel seeds.

Place the duck, skin side up, into the cooking basket. Cook at 400 degrees F for 10 minutes. Turn the duck breast over and cook an additional 5 minutes.

Allow it to rest for 5 to 8 minutes before carving and serving.

Meanwhile, make the potato rösti by mixing all the ingredients in a bowl. Mix to combine well and shape the mixture into two equal patties.

Cook in your Air Fryer at 400 degrees F for 15 minutes. Serve with the warm duck breast. Enjoy!

Per serving: 356 Calories; 16.1g Fat; 24.4g Carbs; 26.1g Protein; 3.3g Sugars

8. Famous Buffalo Wings

(Ready in about 25 minutes | Servings 4)

Ingredients

1 ½ pounds chicken wings
Coarse salt and ground black pepper, to season
1/2 teaspoon onion powder
1/2 teaspoon cayenne pepper
1 teaspoon granulated garlic

4 tablespoons butter, at room temperature
2 tablespoons hot pepper sauce
1 (1-inch) piece ginger, peeled and grated
2 tablespoons soy sauce
2 tablespoons molasses

Directions

Pat dry the chicken wings with kitchen towels and set them aside.

Toss the chicken wings with the salt, pepper, onion powder, cayenne pepper and granulated garlic; toss until they're well coated on all sides.

Arrange the spiced chicken wings in the cooking basket and cook at 380 degrees F for 22 minutes until golden brown on all sides.

In the meantime, whisk the butter, hot pepper sauce, ginger, soy sauce and molasses. Pour the sauce over the chicken wings and serve hot. Bon appétit!

Per serving: 385 Calories; 19.1g Fat; 13.2g Carbs; 38.8g Protein; 10.7g Sugars

9. Garlic-Basil Turkey Breast

(Ready in about 45 minutes | Servings 4)

Ingredients

1 ½ pounds turkey breast
2 tablespoons olive oil
2 cloves garlic, minced

Sea salt and ground black pepper, to taste
1 teaspoon basil
2 tablespoons lemon zest, grated

Directions

Pat the turkey breast dry with paper towels.

Rub the turkey breast with olive oil, garlic, salt, pepper, basil and lemon zest.

Cook in the preheated Air Fryer at 380 degrees F for 20 minutes. Turn the turkey breast over and cook an additional 20 to 22 minutes.

Bon appétit!

Per serving: 355 Calories; 18.7g Fat; 2.1g Carbs; 38g Protein; 0.7g Sugars

10. Chicken Drumsticks with Blue Cheese Sauce

(Ready in about 25 minutes | Servings 4)

Ingredients

1/2 teaspoon shallot powder
1/2 teaspoon garlic powder
1/2 teaspoon coriander
1/4 teaspoon red pepper flakes
Sea salt and ground black pepper, to season

2 chicken drumsticks, skinless and boneless
1/4 cup blue cheese, softened
4 tablespoons mayonnaise
4 tablespoons sour cream
1 teaspoon fresh garlic, pressed
1 teaspoon fresh lime juice

Directions

In a resealable bag, place the shallot powder, garlic powder, coriander, red pepper, salt and black pepper; add in the chicken drumsticks and shake until they are well coated.

Spritz the chicken drumsticks with a nonstick cooking oil and place in the cooking basket.

Air fry the chicken drumsticks at 370 degrees F for 20 minutes, turning them over halfway through the cooking time.

Meanwhile, make the sauce by whisking the remaining ingredients. Place the sauce in your refrigerator until ready to serve.

Serve the chicken drumsticks with blue cheese sauce. Bon appétit!

Per serving: 246 Calories; 20g Fat; 1.5g Carbs; 14.2g Protein; 0.2g Sugars

11. Thanksgiving Turkey with Gravy

(Ready in about 55 minutes | Servings 4)

Ingredients

1 ½ pound turkey breast
1 tablespoon Dijon mustard
2 tablespoons butter, at room temperature
Sea salt and ground black pepper, to taste
1 teaspoon cayenne pepper

1/2 teaspoon garlic powder
Gravy:
2 cups vegetable broth
1/4 cup all-purpose flour
Freshly ground black pepper, to taste

Directions

Brush Dijon mustard and butter all over the turkey breast. Season with salt, black pepper, cayenne pepper and garlic powder.

Cook in the preheated Air Fryer at 360 degrees F for about 50 minutes, flipping them halfway through the cooking time.

Place the fat drippings from the cooked turkey in a sauté pan. Pour in 1 cup of broth and 1/8 cup of all-purpose flour; continue to cook, whisking continuously, until a smooth paste forms.

Add in the remaining ingredients and continue to simmer until the gravy has reduced by half. Enjoy!

Per serving: 356 Calories; 18g Fat; 7.8g Carbs; 34.2g Protein; 0.6g Sugars

12. Chicken and Cheese Stuffed Mushrooms

(Ready in about 15 minutes | Servings 4)

Ingredients

9 medium-sized button mushrooms, cleaned and steams removed
1/2 pound chicken white meat, ground
2 ounces goat cheese, room temperature

2 ounces cheddar cheese, grated
1 teaspoon soy sauce
2 tablespoons scallions, finely chopped
1 teaspoon fresh garlic, finely chopped
Sea salt and red pepper, to season

Directions

Pat the mushrooms dry and set them aside.

Thoroughly combine all ingredients, except for the cheddar cheese, in a mixing bowl. Stir to combine well and stuff your mushrooms.

Bake in your Air Fryer at 370 degrees F for 5 minutes. Top with cheddar cheese and continue to cook an additional 3 to 4 minutes or until the cheese melts. Bon appétit!

Per serving: 166 Calories; 8.2g Fat; 3.4g Carbs; 19.1g Protein; 2.3g Sugars

13. Tortilla Chip-Crusted Chicken Tenders

(Ready in about 15 minutes | Servings 3)

Ingredients

1 pound chicken tenders
Sea salt and black pepper, to taste
1/2 teaspoon shallot powder
1/2 teaspoon porcini powder
1/2 teaspoon dried rosemary
1/3 cup tortilla chips, crushed

Directions

Toss the chicken tenders with salt, pepper, shallot powder, porcini powder, dried rosemary and tortilla chips.

Spritz the cooking basket with a nonstick cooking spray. Cook in the preheated Air Fryer at 360 degrees F for 10 minutes, flipping them halfway through the cooking time.

Serve warm with your favorite sauce for dipping. Enjoy!

Per serving: 391 Calories; 25.2g Fat; 9.6g Carbs; 29.2g Protein; 0.9g Sugars

14. Turkey and Bacon Casserole

(Ready in about 15 minutes | Servings 5)

Ingredients

4 tablespoons bacon bits
1 pound turkey sausage, chopped
1/2 cup sour cream
1 cup milk
5 eggs
1/2 teaspoon smoked paprika
Sea salt and ground black pepper, to your liking
1 cup Colby cheese, shredded

Directions

Add the bacon bits and chopped sausage to a lightly greased baking dish.

In a mixing dish, thoroughly combine the sour cream, milk, eggs, paprika, salt and black pepper.

Pour the mixture into the baking dish.

Cook in your Air Fryer at 310 degrees F for about 10 minutes or until set. Top with Colby cheese and cook an additional 2 minutes or until the cheese is bubbly. Bon appétit!

Per serving: 444 Calories; 27.2g Fat; 17.4g Carbs; 31.2g Protein; 3.3g Sugars

15. Turkey Sausage Breakfast Cups

(Ready in about 20 minutes | Servings 2)

Ingredients

1 smoked turkey sausage, chopped
4 eggs
4 tablespoons cream cheese
4 tablespoons cheddar cheese, shredded
4 tablespoons fresh scallions, chopped
1/2 teaspoon garlic, minced
1/4 teaspoon mustard seeds
1/4 teaspoon chili powder
Salt and red pepper, to taste

Directions

Divide the chopped sausage between four silicone baking cups.

In a mixing bowl, beat the eggs until pale and frothy. Then, add in the remaining ingredients and mix to combine well.

Pour the egg mixture into the cups.

Cook in your Air Fryer at 330 degrees F for 10 to 11 minutes. Transfer the cups to wire racks to cool slightly before unmolding. Enjoy!

Per serving: 619 Calories; 48.2g Fat; 5.9g Carbs; 37.2g Protein; 2.6g Sugars

16. Xiang Su Ya (Chinese Duck)

(Ready in about 25 minutes | Servings 3)

Ingredients

2 tablespoons peanuts, chopped
1 tablespoon honey
1 tablespoon olive oil
1 tablespoon hoisin sauce
1 pound duck breast
1 small-sized white onion, sliced
1 teaspoon garlic, chopped
1 celery stick, diced
1 thumb ginger, sliced
4 baby potatoes, diced

Directions

Mix the peanuts, honey, olive oil and hoisin sauce; spread the mixture all over duck breast. Place the duck breast in a lightly oiled cooking basket. Scatter white onion, garlic, celery, ginger and potatoes over the duck breasts.

Cook in your Air Fryer at 400 degrees F for 20 minutes.

Serve with Mandarin pancakes and enjoy!

Per serving: 512 Calories; 15.4g Fat; 55g Carbs; 38.2g Protein; 11.5g Sugars

17. Mexican-Style Taco Chicken

(Ready in about 25 minutes | Servings 3)

Ingredients

1 pound chicken legs, skinless, boneless
1/2 cup mayonnaise
1/2 cup milk
1/3 cup all-purpose flour
Sea salt and ground black pepper, to season
1/2 teaspoon cayenne pepper
1/3 cup tortilla chips, crushed
1 teaspoon Taco seasoning blend
1/2 teaspoon dried Mexican oregano

Directions

Pat dry the chicken legs and set them aside.

In a mixing bowl, thoroughly combine the mayonnaise, milk, flour, salt, black pepper and cayenne pepper.

In another shallow bowl, mix the crushed tortilla chip, taco seasoning blend and Mexican oregano.

Dip the chicken legs into the mayonnaise mixture. Then, coat them with the tortilla chip mixture, shaking off any excess crumbs.

Cook in the preheated Air Fryer at 385 degrees F for 20 minutes, flipping them halfway through the cooking time. Enjoy!

Per serving: 522 Calories; 35.4g Fat; 16.8g Carbs; 32.2g Protein; 3.5g Sugars

18. Japanese Chicken Teriyaki

(Ready in about 40 minutes | Servings 3)

Ingredients

1 pound chicken cutlets
1 teaspoon sesame oil
1 tablespoon lemon juice
1 tablespoon Mirin
1 tablespoon soy sauce
1 teaspoon ginger, peeled and grated
2 garlic cloves, minced
1 teaspoon cornstarch

Directions

Pat dry the chicken cutlets and set them aside.

In a mixing dish, thoroughly combine the remaining ingredients until everything is well incorporated.

Brush the mixture oil over the chicken cutlets and place it in your refrigerator for 30 to 40 minutes.

Cook in the preheated Air Fryer at 360 degrees F for 10 minutes, flipping them halfway through the cooking time. Serve with shirataki noodles and enjoy!

Per serving: 222 Calories; 4.9g Fat; 3.2g Carbs; 34.1g Protein; 1.1g Sugars

19. Roasted Turkey Thighs with Cheesy Cauliflower

(Ready in about 55 minutes | Servings 4)

Ingredients

1 tablespoon butter, room temperature
2 pounds turkey thighs
1/2 teaspoon smoked paprika
1/2 teaspoon dried marjoram
1/4 teaspoon dried dill
Sea salt and ground black pepper, to taste
1 pound cauliflower, broken into small florets
1/3 cup Pecorino Romano cheese, freshly grated
1 teaspoon garlic, minced

Directions

Rub the butter all over the turkey thighs; sprinkle with smoked paprika, marjoram, dill, salt and black pepper.

Roast in the preheated Air Fryer at 360 degrees F for about 20 minutes. Flip the turkey thighs and continue to cook an additional 20 minutes. Reserve.

Toss the cauliflower florets with the Pecorino Romano and garlic; salt to taste.

Cook at 400 degrees F for 12 to 13 minutes. Serve the warm turkey thighs with the cauliflower on the side. Bon appétit!

Per serving: 315 Calories; 7.6g Fat; 7.5g Carbs; 53.9g Protein; 2.9g Sugars

20. Farmhouse Chicken Roulade

(Ready in about 20 minutes | Servings 4)

Ingredients

4 slices smoked bacon, chopped
4 slices Monterey-Jack cheese, sliced
1 ½ pounds chicken fillets
1 celery stick, chopped
1 small sized onion, chopped
1 teaspoon hot sauce
Sea salt and ground black pepper, to season
1 lemon, cut into slices

Directions

Place 1 slice of bacon and 1 slice of cheese on each chicken fillet. Divide the celery and onion between chicken fillets.

Top with hot sauce and season with salt and black pepper to your liking. Then, roll them up and tie with kitchen twine.

Roast in the preheated Air Fryer at 380 degrees F for 8 minutes; turn them over and continue to cook for 5 to 6 minutes more. Serve with lemon slices and eat warm.

Per serving: 384 Calories; 21.1g Fat; 2.8g Carbs; 43.4g Protein; 1.4g Sugars

21. Greek-Style Chicken Salad

(Ready in about 20 minutes | Servings 2)

Ingredients

1/2 pound chicken breasts, boneless and skinless
1 cup grape tomatoes, halved
1 Serrano pepper, deveined and chopped
2 bell peppers, deveined and chopped
2 tablespoons olives, pitted and sliced
1 cucumber, sliced
1 red onion, sliced
1 cup arugula
1 cup baby spinach
1/4 cup mayonnaise
2 tablespoons Greek-style yogurt
1 teaspoon lime juice
1/4 teaspoon oregano
1/4 teaspoon basil
1/4 teaspoon red pepper flakes, crushed
Sea salt and ground black pepper, to taste

Directions

Spritz the chicken breasts with a nonstick cooking oil.

Cook in the preheated Air Fryer at 380 degrees F for 12 minutes. Transfer to a cutting board to cool slightly before slicing.

Cut the chicken into bite-sized strips and transfer them to a salad bowl.

Toss the chicken with the remaining ingredients and place in your refrigerator until ready to serve. Enjoy!

Per serving: 391 Calories; 21.3g Fat; 24g Carbs; 28.4g Protein; 16g Sugars

22. Authentic Indian Chicken with Raita

(Ready in about 15 minutes | Servings 2)

Ingredients

2 chicken fillets
Sea salt and ground black pepper, to taste
2 teaspoons garam masala
1 teaspoon ground turmeric
1/2 cup plain yogurt
1 English cucumber, shredded and drained
1 tablespoon fresh cilantro, coarsely chopped
1/2 red onion, chopped
A pinch of grated nutmeg
A pinch of ground cinnamon

Directions

Sprinkle the chicken fillets with salt, pepper, garam masala and ground turmeric until well coated on all sides.

Cook in the preheated Air Fryer at 380 degrees F for 12 minutes, turning them over once or twice.

Meanwhile, make traditional raita by mixing the remaining ingredients in a bowl. Serve the chicken fillets with the raita sauce on the side. Enjoy!

Per serving: 324 Calories; 15.6g Fat; 10.4g Carbs; 33.8g Protein; 6.6g Sugars

23. Asian-Style Chicken Drumettes

(Ready in about 15 minutes + marinating time | Servings 3)

Ingredients

1/4 cup soy sauce
1 teaspoon brown mustard
1 teaspoon garlic paste
2 tablespoons tomato paste
2 tablespoons sesame oil
1 tablespoon brown sugar
2 tablespoons rice vinegar
1 pound chicken drumettes

Directions

Place the chicken drumettes and the other ingredients in a resalable bag; allow it to marinate for 2 hours.

Discard the marinade and transfer the chicken drumettes to the Air Fryer cooking basket.

Cook at 400 degrees F for 12 minutes, shaking the basket halfway through the cooking time to ensure even cooking.

In the meantime, bring the reserved marinade to a boil in a small saucepan. Immediately turn the heat to low and let it simmer until the sauce has reduced by half.

Spoon the sauce over the chicken drumettes and serve immediately.

Per serving: 333 Calories; 17.6g Fat; 10.4g Carbs; 32.8g Protein; 8.1g Sugars

24. Easy Chicken Taquitos

(Ready in about 20 minutes | Servings 3)

Ingredients

1 pound chicken breast, boneless
Sea salt and ground black pepper, to taste
1/2 teaspoon cayenne pepper
1/2 teaspoon onion powder
1/2 teaspoon garlic powder
1/2 teaspoon mustard powder
1 cup Cotija cheese, shredded
6 corn tortillas

Directions

Season the chicken with salt, black pepper, cayenne pepper, onion powder, garlic powder and mustard powder.

Cook in the preheated Air Fryer at 380 degrees F for 12 minutes; turn the chicken over halfway through the cooking time to ensure even cooking.

Transfer the chicken to a cutting board and shred with two forks.

Assemble your taquitos with the chicken and Cotija cheese; roll them up.

Bake your taquitos at 390 degrees F for 5 to 6 minutes; serve immediately.

Per serving: 533 Calories; 27.6g Fat; 24g Carbs; 45g Protein; 1.5g Sugars

25. Huli-Huli Turkey

(Ready in about 35 minutes | Servings 2)

Ingredients

2 turkey drumsticks
Sea salt and ground black pepper, to season
1 teaspoon paprika
1 teaspoon hot sauce
1 teaspoon garlic paste
1 teaspoon olive oil
1/2 teaspoon rosemary
1/2 small pineapple, cut into wedges
1 teaspoon coconut oil, melted
2 stalks scallions, sliced

Directions

Toss the turkey drumsticks with salt, black pepper, paprika, hot sauce, garlic paste, olive oil and rosemary.

Cook in the preheated Air Fryer at 360 degrees F for 25 minutes. Reserve.

Turn the temperature to 400 degrees F, place pineapple wedges in the cooking basket and brush them with coconut oil.

Cook your pineapple for 8 to 9 minutes. Serve the turkey drumsticks garnished with roasted pineapple and scallions. Enjoy!

Per serving: 533 Calories; 25.3g Fat; 33.4g Carbs; 46.9g Protein; 23.5g Sugars

26. Southwest Buttermilk Chicken Thighs

(Ready in about 15 minutes + marinating time | Servings 2)

Ingredients

1 pound chicken thighs	Sea salt and ground black pepper,
1 cup buttermilk	to taste
1/2 teaspoon garlic paste	1 teaspoon cayenne pepper
1/4 cup Sriracha sauce	1/4 cup cornflour
	1/4 cup all-purpose flour

Directions

Pat dry the chicken thighs with kitchen towels.

Now, thoroughly combine the buttermilk, garlic paste, Sriracha sauce, salt, black pepper and cayenne pepper.

Dredge the chicken into the mixture until well coated. Place in your refrigerator for 2 hours.

Place the flour in another shallow bowl. Coat the chicken thigs with the flour mixture.

Cook in your Air Fryer at 395 degrees F for 12 minutes. Bon appétit!

Per serving: 449 Calories; 12g Fat; 33.4g Carbs; 49g Protein; 8.5g Sugars

27. Traditional Greek Keftedes

(Ready in about 15 minutes | Servings 2)

Ingredients

1/2 pound ground chicken	1 teaspoon olive oil
1 egg	1/2 teaspoon dried oregano
1 slice stale bread, cubed and	1/2 teaspoon dried basil
soaked in milk	1/8 teaspoon grated nutmeg
1 teaspoon fresh garlic, pressed	Sea salt and ground black pepper,
2 tablespoons Romano cheese,	to taste
grated	2 pita bread
1 bell pepper, deveined and	
chopped	

Directions

Thoroughly combine all ingredients, except for the pita bread, in a mixing bowl. Stir until everything is well incorporated.

Roll the mixture into 6 meatballs and place them in a lightly oiled cooking basket.

Air fry at 380 degrees F for 10 minutes, shaking the basket occasionally to ensure even cooking. Place the keftedes in a pita bread and serve with tomato and tzatziki sauce if desired. Enjoy!

Per serving: 493 Calories; 27.9g Fat; 27.1g Carbs; 32.6g Protein; 4.2g Sugars

28. Italian Chicken Parmigiana

(Ready in about 15 minutes | Servings 2)

Ingredients

2 chicken fillets	1 tablespoon fresh cilantro,
1 egg, beaten	chopped
2 tablespoons milk	1/2 cup seasoned breadcrumbs
1 teaspoon garlic paste	4 tablespoons marinara sauce
	4 slices parmesan cheese

Directions

Spritz the cooking basket with a nonstick cooking oil.

Whisk the egg, milk, garlic paste and cilantro in a shallow bowl. In another bowl, place the seasoned breadcrumbs.

Dip each chicken fillet in the egg mixture, then, coat them with breadcrumbs. Press to coat well.

Cook in the preheated Air Fryer at 380 degrees F for 6 minutes; turn the chicken over.

Top with marinara sauce and parmesan cheese and continue to cook for 6 minutes. Enjoy!

Per serving: 570 Calories; 34.6g Fat; 13.1g Carbs; 50.1g Protein; 3.2g Sugars

29. Balsamic Marjoram Chicken

(Ready in about 35 minutes | Servings 3)

Ingredients

3 chicken drumsticks	1/2 teaspoon onion powder
Sea salt and ground black pepper,	1/2 teaspoon garlic powder
to season	1 teaspoon dried marjoram
1/2 teaspoon red pepper flakes,	1/4 cup cornstarch
crushed	2 tablespoons balsamic vinegar
1/2 teaspoon shallot powder	2 tablespoons milk

Directions

Pat dry the chicken with paper towels. Toss the chicken drumsticks with all seasonings.

In a shallow bowl, mix the cornstarch, balsamic vinegar and milk until well combined.

Roll the chicken drumsticks onto the cornstarch mixture, pressing to coat well on all sides; shake off any excess pieces of the mixture.

Cook in the preheated Air Fryer at 380 degrees F for 30 minutes, turning them over halfway through the cooking time. Bon appétit!

Per serving: 275 Calories; 12.6g Fat; 14.1g Carbs; 24.3g Protein; 2.9g Sugars

30. Classic Chicken Fajitas

(Ready in about 35 minutes | Servings 3)

Ingredients

1 pound chicken breast, skinless	1/2 teaspoon red pepper flakes,
and boneless	crushed
1 teaspoon butter, melted	1/2 teaspoon Mexican oregano
Sea salt and ground black pepper,	1/2 teaspoon garlic powder
to taste	3 bell peppers, thinly sliced
	1 red onion, sliced

Directions

Brush the chicken with melted butter on all sides. Season the chicken with salt, black pepper, red pepper, oregano and garlic powder.

Cook in the preheated Air Fryer at 380 degrees F for 12 minutes until golden and cooked through; turn the chicken over halfway through the cooking time.

Let the chicken rest for 10 minutes, then, slice into strips. Reserve, keeping it warm.

Place the onions and peppers in the cooking basket; cook at 400 degrees F for 10 minutes. Taste and adjust the seasonings.

Transfer the vegetables to a serving bowl; stir in the chicken and serve immediately.

Per serving: 299 Calories; 15.3g Fat; 6.4g Carbs; 32.3g Protein; 3.2g Sugars

31. Keto Chicken Quesadillas

(Ready in about 25 minutes | Servings 2)

Ingredients

1/2 pound chicken breasts,	4 ounces Ricotta cheese
boneless and skinless	2 tablespoons flaxseed meal
Salt to taste	1 teaspoon psyllium husk powder
3 eggs	Black pepper, to taste

Directions

Cook the chicken in the preheated Air Fryer at 380 degrees F for 12 minutes; turn the chicken over halfway through the cooking time. Salt to taste and slice into small strips.

In a mixing bowl, beat the eggs, cheese, flaxseed meal, psyllium husk powder and black pepper. Spoon the mixture into a lightly oiled baking pan.

Bake at 380 degrees F for 9 to 10 minutes.

Spoon the chicken pieces onto your quesadilla and fold in half. Cut your quesadilla into two pieces and serve.

Per serving: 401 Calories; 20.5g Fat; 5.7g Carbs; 48.3g Protein; 0.6g Sugars

32. Garlic Butter Chicken Wings

(Ready in about 20 minutes | Servings 3)

Ingredients

1 pound chicken wings
Salt and black pepper, to taste
2 tablespoons butter

1 teaspoon garlic paste
1 lemon, cut into slices

Directions

Pat dry the chicken wings with a kitchen towel and season all over with salt and black pepper.

In a bowl, mix together butter and garlic paste. Rub the mixture all over the wings.

Cook in the preheated Air Fryer at 380 degrees F for 18 minutes.

Serve garnished with lemon slices. Bon appétit!

Per serving: 270 Calories; 13.1g Fat; 2.9g Carbs; 33.6g Protein; 1.5g Sugars

33. Crispy Chicken Fingers

(Ready in about 15 minutes | Servings 3)

Ingredients

1 pound chicken tenders
1/4 cup all-purpose flour
1/2 teaspoon onion powder
1/2 teaspoon garlic powder
1/2 teaspoon cayenne pepper

Sea salt and ground black pepper, to taste
1/2 cup breadcrumbs
1 egg
1 tablespoon olive oil

Directions

Pat dry the chicken with kitchen towels and cut into bite-sized pieces.

In a shallow bowl, mix the flour, onion powder, garlic powder, cayenne pepper, salt and black pepper. Dip the chicken pieces in the flour mixture and toss to coat well on all sides.

In the second bowl, place breadcrumbs.

In the third bowl, whisk the egg; now, dip the chicken in the beaten egg. Afterwards, roll each piece of chicken in the breadcrumbs until well coated on all sides.

Spritz the chicken fingers with olive oil. Cook in your Air Fryer at 360 degrees F for 8 to 10 minutes, turning it over halfway through the cooking time.

Serve with your favorite sauce for dipping. Enjoy!

Per serving: 314 Calories; 12.1g Fat; 13.4g Carbs; 35.6g Protein; 1.4g Sugars

34. Chicken Alfredo with Mushrooms

(Ready in about 15 minutes | Servings 3)

Ingredients

1 pound chicken breasts, boneless
1 medium onion, quartered
1 teaspoon butter, melted

1/2 pound mushrooms, cleaned
12 ounces Alfredo sauce
Salt and black pepper, to taste

Directions

Start by preheating your Air Fryer to 380 degrees F. Then, place the chicken and onion in the cooking basket. Drizzle with melted butter.

Cook in the preheated Air Fryer for 6 minutes. Add in the mushrooms and continue to cook for 5 to 6 minutes more.

Slice the chicken into strips. Chop the mushrooms and onions; stir in the Alfredo sauce. Salt and pepper to taste.

Serve with hot cooked fettuccine. Bon appétit!

Per serving: 334 Calories; 15.1g Fat; 13.4g Carbs; 36g Protein; 7.5g Sugars

35. Grandma's Chicken with Rosemary and Sweet Potatoes

(Ready in about 35 minutes | Servings 2)

Ingredients

2 chicken legs, bone-in
2 garlic cloves, minced
1 teaspoon sesame oil
Sea salt and ground black pepper, to taste

2 sprigs rosemary, leaves picked and crushed
1/2 pound sweet potatoes

Directions

Start by preheating your Air Fryer to 380 degrees F. Now, rub garlic halves all over the chicken legs.

Drizzle the chicken legs and sweet potatoes with the sesame oil. Sprinkle them with salt and rosemary. Place the chicken and potatoes in the cooking basket.

Cook in the preheated Air Fryer for 30 minutes until the potatoes are thoroughly cooked. The chicken must reach an internal temperature of 165 degrees F.

Serve the chicken legs garnished with the sweet potatoes. Bon appétit!

Per serving: 604 Calories; 36.1g Fat; 23.4g Carbs; 44.5g Protein; 2.5g Sugars

36. Authentic Spanish Chicken Drumstick

(Ready in about 25 minutes | Servings 2)

Ingredients

2 chicken drumsticks, boneless
1 teaspoon Spanish paprika
1/2 teaspoon mustard seeds, ground
1/2 teaspoon fennel seeds, ground
1/2 teaspoon cumin seeds, ground

Sea salt and ground black pepper, to taste
1/4 cup all-purpose flour
1 egg
1 tablespoon buttermilk

Directions

Pat the chicken dry and sprinkle it with spice until well coated on all sides.

Add the flour to a rimmed plate. Dredge the chicken into the flour.

In a shallow bowl, beat the egg with buttermilk until frothy and well combined. Dip each chicken drumstick into the egg mixture.

Cook in the preheated Air Fryer at 380 degrees F for 10 minutes. Turn them over and cook for a further 10 minutes. Eat warm.

Per serving: 354 Calories; 17.1g Fat; 16.3g Carbs; 31.5g Protein; 2.1g Sugars

37. Chicken Tostadas with Nacho Cheese Sauce

(Ready in about 20 minutes | Servings 2)

Ingredients

1/2 pound chicken fillets
1 egg, beaten
1/4 cup all-purpose flour
Kosher salt and ground black pepper, to taste
1/4 cup tortilla chips, crushed
1 teaspoon corn oil

2 tostada shells
Sauce:
1/2 cup nacho cheese, melted according to package instructions
1 tablespoon lime juice
2 pickled jalapenos, chopped
1/2 teaspoon Mexican oregano

Directions

Pat the chicken fillets dry with paper towels.

Then, beat the egg in a shallow bowl. In another bowl, mix the flour, salt and black pepper. In the third bowl, place crushed tortilla chips.

Dip the chicken fillets in the flour mixture, then the egg, then, roll in the crushed tortilla chips.

Drizzle the chicken fillets with corn oil. Cook in the preheated Air Fryer at 380 degrees F for 12 minutes, turning them over once or twice; an instant thermometer should read 165 degrees F.

Heat the tostada shells at 350 degrees F for about 5 minutes. Meanwhile, make the sauce by mixing all ingredients.

Working one at a time, place a chicken fillet in the center of each tostada shell. Serve with nacho sauce on the side! Enjoy!

Per serving: 444 Calories; 20.8g Fat; 26.3g Carbs; 37.5g Protein; 1.7g Sugars

38. Thanksgiving Turkey with Mint Sauce

(Ready in about 1 hour | Servings 3)

Ingredients

1 ½ pounds turkey tenderloin
1 teaspoon olive oil
Sea salt and black pepper, to season
1 teaspoon dried thyme
1/2 teaspoon garlic powder
1/2 teaspoon dried sage

Sauce:
2 slices white bread
3/4 ounce fresh mint leaves
1 tablespoon extra-virgin olive oil
1 tablespoon white wine vinegar
1 teaspoon garlic, minced

Directions

Toss the turkey tenderloin with olive oil, salt, pepper, thyme, garlic powder and sage.

Cook in the preheated Air Fryer at 350 degrees F for about 55 minutes, turning it over halfway through the cooking time.

Meanwhile, make the mint sauce; pulse the bread slices in a food processor until coarsely crumbled.

Add in the mint, olive oil, vinegar and garlic; blend again until everything is well incorporated; make sure to add water slowly and gradually until your desired consistency is reached.

Let it rest on a wire rack to cool slightly before carving and serving. Spoon the sauce over warm turkey and serve. Bon appétit!

Per serving: 368 Calories; 11.8g Fat; 11.3g Carbs; 54g Protein; 1.8g Sugars

39. Punjabi Tandoori Murgh

(Ready in about 15 minutes + marinating time | Servings 1)

Ingredients

1/2 pound chicken tenderloin
1/4 cup Raita
1 garlic clove, pressed
1 tablespoon fresh cilantro, minced

Salt and black pepper, to taste
1 teaspoon turmeric powder
1/2 teaspoon Garam Masala

Directions

Place all ingredients in a ceramic dish; stir well and cover. Place in your refrigerator for 1 hour.

Transfer the chicken tenderloin to the cooking basket, discarding the marinade.

Cook at 360 degrees F for 6 minutes. Turn the chicken over, baste with the reserved marinade and cook for 6 minutes on the other side.

Serve with lemon wedges and enjoy!

Per serving: 294 Calories; 8g Fat; 3.8g Carbs; 48.4g Protein; 2.8g Sugars

40. Nagoya-Style Tebasaki

(Ready in about 25 minutes + marinating time | Servings 2)

Ingredients

4 chicken drumettes
1 tablespoon sesame oil
1 tablespoon black vinegar
2 tablespoons soy sauce

1 tablespoon ginger juice
2 tablespoons sake
1 tablespoon sesame seeds, lightly toasted

Directions

Place all ingredients, except for the sesame oil, in a glass bowl. Cover, transfer to your refrigerator and let it marinate for 1 hour.

Cook in the preheated Air Fryer at 370 degrees F for 22 minutes until golden brown; baste and turn them over halfway through the cooking time.

Serve garnished with toasted sesame seeds.

Per serving: 344 Calories; 18.8g Fat; 8.4g Carbs; 28.4g Protein; 3.7g Sugars

41. Pretzel Crusted Chicken with Spicy Mustard Sauce

(Ready in about 20 minutes | Servings 6)

Ingredients

2 eggs
1 ½ pound chicken breasts, boneless, skinless, cut into bite-sized chunks
1/2 cup crushed pretzels
1 teaspoon shallot powder
1 teaspoon paprika
Sea salt and ground black pepper, to taste
1/2 cup vegetable broth

1 tablespoon cornstarch
3 tablespoons Worcestershire sauce
3 tablespoons tomato paste
1 tablespoon apple cider vinegar
2 tablespoons olive oil
2 garlic cloves, chopped
1 jalapeno pepper, minced
1 teaspoon yellow mustard

Directions

Start by preheating your Air Fryer to 390 degrees F.

In a mixing dish, whisk the eggs until frothy; toss the chicken chunks into the whisked eggs and coat well.

In another dish, combine the crushed pretzels with shallot powder, paprika, salt and pepper. Then, lay the chicken chunks in the pretzel mixture; turn it over until well coated.

Place the chicken pieces in the air fryer basket. Cook the chicken for 12 minutes, shaking the basket halfway through.

Meanwhile, whisk the vegetable broth with cornstarch, Worcestershire sauce, tomato paste, and apple cider vinegar.

Preheat a cast-iron skillet over medium flame. Heat the olive oil and sauté the garlic with jalapeno pepper for 30 to 40 seconds, stirring frequently.

Add the cornstarch mixture and let it simmer until the sauce has thickened a little. Now, add the air-fried chicken and mustard; let it simmer for 2 minutes more or until heated through.

Serve immediately and enjoy!

Per serving: 357 Calories; 17.6g Fat; 20.3g Carbs; 28.1g Protein; 2.8g Sugars

42. Chinese-Style Sticky Turkey Thighs

(Ready in about 35 minutes | Servings 6)

Ingredients

1 tablespoon sesame oil
2 pounds turkey thighs
1 teaspoon Chinese Five-spice powder
1 teaspoon pink Himalayan salt
1/4 teaspoon Sichuan pepper

6 tablespoons honey
1 tablespoon Chinese rice vinegar
2 tablespoons soy sauce
1 tablespoon sweet chili sauce
1 tablespoon mustard

Directions

Preheat your Air Fryer to 360 degrees F.

Brush the sesame oil all over the turkey thighs. Season them with spices.

Cook for 23 minutes, turning over once or twice. Make sure to work in batches to ensure even cooking

In the meantime, combine the remaining ingredients in a wok (or similar type pan) that is preheated over medium-high heat. Cook and stir until the sauce reduces by about a third.

Add the fried turkey thighs to the wok; gently stir to coat with the sauce.

Let the turkey rest for 10 minutes before slicing and serving. Enjoy!

Per serving: 279 Calories; 10.1g Fat; 19g Carbs; 27.7g Protein; 17.9g Sugars

43. Easy Hot Chicken Drumsticks

(Ready in about 40 minutes | Servings 6)

Ingredients

6 chicken drumsticks
Sauce:
6 ounces hot sauce
3 tablespoons olive oil

3 tablespoons tamari sauce
1 teaspoon dried thyme
1/2 teaspoon dried oregano

Directions

Spritz the sides and bottom of the cooking basket with a nonstick cooking spray.

Cook the chicken drumsticks at 380 degrees F for 35 minutes, flipping them over halfway through.

Meanwhile, heat the hot sauce, olive oil, tamari sauce, thyme, and oregano in a pan over medium-low heat; reserve.

Drizzle the sauce over the prepared chicken drumsticks; toss to coat well and serve. Bon appétit!

Per serving: 280 Calories; 18.7g Fat; 2.6g Carbs; 24.1g Protein; 1.4g Sugars

44. Crunchy Munchy Chicken Tenders with Peanuts

(Ready in about 25 minutes | Servings 4)

Ingredients

1 ½ pounds chicken tenderloins
2 tablespoons peanut oil
1/2 cup tortilla chips, crushed
Sea salt and ground black pepper, to taste

1/2 teaspoon garlic powder
1 teaspoon red pepper flakes
2 tablespoons peanuts, roasted and roughly chopped

Directions

Start by preheating your Air Fryer to 360 degrees F.

Brush the chicken tenderloins with peanut oil on all sides.

In a mixing bowl, thoroughly combine the crushed chips, salt, black pepper, garlic powder, and red pepper flakes. Dredge the chicken in the breading, shaking off any residual coating.

Lay the chicken tenderloins into the cooking basket. Cook for 12 to 13 minutes or until it is no longer pink in the center. Work in batches; an instant-read thermometer should read at least 165 degrees F.

Serve garnished with roasted peanuts. Bon appétit!

Per serving: 343 Calories; 16.4g Fat; 10.6g Carbs; 36.8g Protein; 1g Sugars

45. Tarragon Turkey Tenderloins with Baby Potatoes

(Ready in about 50 minutes | Servings 6)

Ingredients

2 pounds turkey tenderloins
2 teaspoons olive oil
Salt and ground black pepper, to taste
1 teaspoon smoked paprika

2 tablespoons dry white wine
1 tablespoon fresh tarragon leaves, chopped
1 pound baby potatoes, rubbed

Directions

Brush the turkey tenderloins with olive oil. Season with salt, black pepper, and paprika.

Afterwards, add the white wine and tarragon.

Cook the turkey tenderloins at 350 degrees F for 30 minutes, flipping them over halfway through. Let them rest for 5 to 9 minutes before slicing and serving.

After that, spritz the sides and bottom of the cooking basket with the remaining 1 teaspoon of olive oil.

Then, preheat your Air Fryer to 400 degrees F; cook the baby potatoes for 15 minutes. Serve with the turkey and enjoy!

Per serving: 317 Calories; 7.4g Fat; 14.2g Carbs; 45.7g Protein; 1.1g Sugars

46. Mediterranean Chicken Breasts with Roasted Tomatoes

(Ready in about 1 hour | Servings 8)

Ingredients

2 teaspoons olive oil, melted
3 pounds chicken breasts, bone-in
1/2 teaspoon black pepper, freshly ground
1/2 teaspoon salt
1 teaspoon cayenne pepper

2 tablespoons fresh parsley, minced
1 teaspoon fresh basil, minced
1 teaspoon fresh rosemary, minced
4 medium-sized Roma tomatoes, halved

Directions

Start by preheating your Air Fryer to 370 degrees F. Brush the cooking basket with 1 teaspoon of olive oil.

Sprinkle the chicken breasts with all seasonings listed above.

Cook for 25 minutes or until chicken breasts are slightly browned. Work in batches.

Arrange the tomatoes in the cooking basket and brush them with the remaining teaspoon of olive oil. Season with sea salt.

Cook the tomatoes at 350 degrees F for 10 minutes, shaking halfway through the cooking time. Serve with chicken breasts. Bon appétit!

Per serving: 315 Calories; 17.1g Fat; 2.7g Carbs; 36g Protein; 1.7g Sugars

47. Thai Red Duck with Candy Onion

(Ready in about 25 minutes | Servings 4)

Ingredients

1 ½ pounds duck breasts, skin removed
1 teaspoon kosher salt
1/2 teaspoon cayenne pepper
1/3 teaspoon black pepper

1/2 teaspoon smoked paprika
1 tablespoon Thai red curry paste
1 cup candy onions, halved
1/4 small pack coriander, chopped

Directions

Place the duck breasts between 2 sheets of foil; then, use a rolling pin to bash the duck until they are 1-inch thick.

Preheat your Air Fryer to 395 degrees F.

Rub the duck breasts with salt, cayenne pepper, black pepper, paprika, and red curry paste. Place the duck breast in the cooking basket.

Cook for 11 to 12 minutes. Top with candy onions and cook for another 10 to 11 minutes.

Serve garnished with coriander and enjoy!

Per serving: 362 Calories; 18.7g Fat; 4g Carbs; 42.3g Protein; 1.3g Sugars

48. Rustic Chicken Legs with Turnip Chips

(Ready in about 30 minutes | Servings 3)

Ingredients

1 pound chicken legs
1 teaspoon Himalayan salt
1 teaspoon paprika

1/2 teaspoon ground black pepper
1 teaspoon butter, melted
1 turnip, trimmed and sliced

Directions

Spritz the sides and bottom of the cooking basket with a nonstick cooking spray.

Season the chicken legs with salt, paprika, and ground black pepper.

Cook at 370 degrees F for 10 minutes. Increase the temperature to 380 degrees F.

Drizzle turnip slices with melted butter and transfer them to the cooking basket with the chicken. Cook the turnips and chicken for 15 minutes more, flipping them halfway through the cooking time.

As for the chicken, an instant-read thermometer should read at least 165 degrees F.

Serve and enjoy!

Per serving: 207 Calories; 7.8g Fat; 3.4g Carbs; 29.5g Protein; 1.6g Sugars

49. Old-Fashioned Chicken Drumettes

(Ready in about 30 minutes | Servings 3)

Ingredients

1/3 cup all-purpose flour
1/2 teaspoon ground white pepper
1 teaspoon seasoning salt
1 teaspoon garlic paste
1 teaspoon rosemary
1 whole egg + 1 egg white
6 chicken drumettes
1 heaping tablespoon fresh chives, chopped

Directions

Start by preheating your Air Fryer to 390 degrees.

Mix the flour with white pepper, salt, garlic paste, and rosemary in a small-sized bowl.

In another bowl, beat the eggs until frothy.

Dip the chicken into the flour mixture, then into the beaten eggs; coat with the flour mixture one more time.

Cook the chicken drumettes for 22 minutes. Serve warm, garnished with chives.

Per serving: 347 Calories; 9.1g Fat; 11.3g Carbs; 41g Protein; 0.1g Sugars

50. Easy Ritzy Chicken Nuggets

(Ready in about 20 minutes | Servings 4)

Ingredients

1 ½ pounds chicken tenderloins, cut into small pieces
1/2 teaspoon garlic salt
1/2 teaspoon cayenne pepper
1/4 teaspoon black pepper, freshly cracked
4 tablespoons olive oil
1/3 cup saltines (e.g. Ritz crackers), crushed
4 tablespoons Parmesan cheese, freshly grated

Directions

Start by preheating your Air Fryer to 390 degrees F.

Season each piece of the chicken with garlic salt, cayenne pepper, and black pepper.

In a mixing bowl, thoroughly combine the olive oil with crushed saltines. Dip each piece of chicken in the cracker mixture.

Finally, roll the chicken pieces over the Parmesan cheese. Cook for 8 minutes, working in batches.

Later, if you want to warm the chicken nuggets, add them to the basket and cook for 1 minute more. Serve with French fries, if desired.

Per serving: 355 Calories; 20.1g Fat; 5.3g Carbs; 36.6g Protein; 0.2g Sugars

51. Asian Chicken Filets with Cheese

(Ready in about 50 minutes | Servings 2)

Ingredients

4 rashers smoked bacon
2 chicken filets
1/2 teaspoon coarse sea salt
1/4 teaspoon black pepper, preferably freshly ground
1 teaspoon garlic, minced
1 teaspoon black mustard seeds
1 (2-inch) piece ginger, peeled and minced
1 teaspoon mild curry powder
1/2 cup coconut milk
1/3 cup tortilla chips, crushed
1/2 cup Pecorino Romano cheese, freshly grated

Directions

Start by preheating your Air Fryer to 400 degrees F. Add the smoked bacon and cook in the preheated Air Fryer for 5 to 7 minutes. Reserve.

In a mixing bowl, place the chicken fillets, salt, black pepper, garlic, ginger, mustard seeds, curry powder, and milk. Let it marinate in your refrigerator about 30 minutes.

In another bowl, mix the crushed chips and grated Pecorino Romano cheese.

Dredge the chicken fillets through the chips mixture and transfer them to the cooking basket. Reduce the temperature to 380 degrees F and cook the chicken for 6 minutes.

Turn them over and cook for a further 6 minutes. Repeat the process until you have run out of ingredients.

Serve with reserved bacon. Enjoy!

Per serving: 376 Calories; 19.6g Fat; 12.1g Carbs; 36.2g Protein; 3.4g Sugars

52. Paprika Chicken Legs with Brussels Sprouts

(Ready in about 30 minutes | Servings 2)

Ingredients

2 chicken legs
1/2 teaspoon paprika
1/2 teaspoon kosher salt
1/2 teaspoon black pepper
1 pound Brussels sprouts
1 teaspoon dill, fresh or dried

Directions

Start by preheating your Air Fryer to 370 degrees F.

Now, season your chicken with paprika, salt, and pepper. Transfer the chicken legs to the cooking basket. Cook for 10 minutes.

Flip the chicken legs and cook an additional 10 minutes. Reserve.

Add the Brussels sprouts to the cooking basket; sprinkle with dill. Cook at 380 degrees F for 15 minutes, shaking the basket halfway through.

Serve with the reserved chicken legs. Bon appétit!

Per serving: 355 Calories; 20.1g Fat; 5.3g Carbs; 36.6g Protein; 0.2g Sugars

53. Chinese Duck (Xiang Su Ya)

(Ready in about 30 minutes + marinating time | Servings 6)

Ingredients

2 pounds duck breast, boneless
2 green onions, chopped
1 tablespoon light soy sauce
1 teaspoon Chinese 5-spice powder
1 teaspoon Szechuan peppercorns
3 tablespoons Shaoxing rice wine
1 teaspoon coarse salt
1/2 teaspoon ground black pepper
Glaze:
1/4 cup molasses
3 tablespoons orange juice
1 tablespoon soy sauce

Directions

In a ceramic bowl, place the duck breasts, green onions, light soy sauce, Chinese 5-spice powder, Szechuan peppercorns, and Shaoxing rice wine. Let it marinate for 1 hour in your refrigerator.

Preheat your Air Fryer to 400 degrees F for 5 minutes.

Now, discard the marinade and season the duck breasts with salt and pepper. Cook the duck breasts for 12 to 15 minutes or until they are golden brown. Repeat with the other ingredients.

In the meantime, add the reserved marinade to the saucepan that is preheated over medium-high heat. Add the molasses, orange juice, and 1 tablespoon of soy sauce.

Bring to a simmer and then, whisk constantly until it gets syrupy. Brush the surface of duck breasts with glaze so they are completely covered.

Place duck breasts back in the Air Fryer basket; cook an additional 5 minutes. Enjoy!

Per serving: 403 Calories; 25.3g Fat; 16.4g Carbs; 27.5g Protein; 13.2g Sugars

54. Turkey Bacon with Scrambled Eggs

(Ready in about 25 minutes | Servings 4)

Ingredients

1/2 pound turkey bacon
4 eggs
1/3 cup milk
2 tablespoons yogurt
1/2 teaspoon sea salt
1 bell pepper, finely chopped
2 green onions, finely chopped
1/2 cup Colby cheese, shredded

Directions

Place the turkey bacon in the cooking basket.

Cook at 360 degrees F for 9 to 11 minutes. Work in batches. Reserve the fried bacon.

In a mixing bowl, thoroughly whisk the eggs with milk and yogurt. Add salt, bell pepper, and green onions.

Brush the sides and bottom of the baking pan with the reserved 1 teaspoon of bacon grease.

Pour the egg mixture into the baking pan. Cook at 355 degrees F about 5 minutes. Top with shredded Colby cheese and cook for 5 to 6 minutes more.

Serve the scrambled eggs with the reserved bacon and enjoy!

Per serving: 456 Calories; 38.3g Fat; 6.3g Carbs; 21.4g Protein; 4.5g Sugars

55. Italian Chicken and Cheese Frittata

(Ready in about 25 minutes | Servings 4)

Ingredients

1 (1-pound) fillet chicken breast
Sea salt and ground black pepper, to taste
1 tablespoon olive oil
4 eggs

1/2 teaspoon cayenne pepper
1/2 cup Mascarpone cream
1/4 cup Asiago cheese, freshly grated

Directions

Flatten the chicken breast with a meat mallet. Season with salt and pepper.

Heat the olive oil in a frying pan over medium flame. Cook the chicken for 10 to 12 minutes; slice into small strips, and reserve.

Then, in a mixing bowl, thoroughly combine the eggs, and cayenne pepper; season with salt to taste. Add the cheese and stir to combine.

Add the reserved chicken. Then, pour the mixture into a lightly greased pan; put the pan into the cooking basket.

Cook in the preheated Air Fryer at 355 degrees F for 10 minutes, flipping over halfway through.

Per serving: 329 Calories; 25.3g Fat; 3.4g Carbs; 21.1g Protein; 2.3g Sugars

56. Summer Meatballs with Cheese

(Ready in about 15 minutes | Servings 4)

Ingredients

1 pound ground turkey
1/2 pound ground pork
1 egg, well beaten
1 cup seasoned breadcrumbs
1 teaspoon dried basil
1 teaspoon dried rosemary
1/4 cup Manchego cheese, grated

2 tablespoons yellow onions, finely chopped
1 teaspoon fresh garlic, finely chopped
Sea salt and ground black pepper, to taste

Directions

In a mixing bowl, combine all the ingredients until everything is well incorporated.

Shape the mixture into 1-inch balls.

Cook the meatballs in the preheated Air Fryer at 380 degrees for 7 minutes. Shake halfway through the cooking time. Work in batches.

Serve with your favorite pasta. Bon appétit!

Per serving: 497 Calories; 24g Fat; 20.7g Carbs; 41.9g Protein; 4.1g Sugars

57. Dijon Roasted Sausage and Carrots

(Ready in about 20 minutes | Servings 3)

Ingredients

1 pound chicken sausages, smoked
1 pound carrots, trimmed and halved lengthwise

1 tablespoon Dijon mustard
2 tablespoons olive oil
1/2 teaspoon sea salt
1/4 teaspoon ground black pepper

Directions

Start by preheating your Air Fryer to 380 degrees F. Pierce the sausages all over with a fork and add them to the cooking basket.

Add the carrots and the remaining ingredients; toss until well coated.

Cook for 10 minutes in the preheated Air Fryer. Shake the basket and cook an additional 5 to 7 minutes. Serve warm.

Per serving: 313 Calories; 13.6g Fat; 14.7g Carbs; 32.3g Protein; 7.2g Sugars

58. Ranch Parmesan Chicken Wings

(Ready in about 25 minutes | Servings 3)

Ingredients

1/2 cup seasoned breadcrumbs
2 tablespoons butter, melted
6 tablespoons parmesan cheese, preferably freshly grated

1 tablespoon Ranch seasoning mix
2 tablespoons oyster sauce
6 chicken wings, bone-in

Directions

Start by preheating your Air Fryer to 370 degrees F.

In a resealable bag, place the breadcrumbs, butter, parmesan, Ranch seasoning mix, and oyster sauce. Add the chicken wings and shake to coat on all sides.

Arrange the chicken wings in the Air Fryer basket. Spritz the chicken wings with a nonstick cooking spray.

Cook for 11 minutes. Turn them over and cook an additional 11 minutes. Serve warm with your favorite dipping sauce, if desired. Enjoy!

Per serving: 521 Calories; 34.2g Fat; 17.3g Carbs; 33.7g Protein; 1.4g Sugars

59. Lemon-Basil Turkey Breast

(Ready in about 1 hour | Servings 4)

Ingredients

2 tablespoons olive oil
2 pounds turkey breasts, bone-in skin-on
Coarse sea salt and ground black pepper, to taste

1 teaspoon fresh basil leaves, chopped
2 tablespoons lemon zest, grated

Directions

Rub olive oil on all sides of the turkey breasts; sprinkle with salt, pepper, basil, and lemon zest.

Place the turkey breasts skin side up on a parchment-lined cooking basket.

Cook in the preheated Air Fryer at 330 degrees F for 30 minutes. Now, turn them over and cook an additional 28 minutes.

Serve with lemon wedges, if desired. Bon appétit!

Per serving: 416 Calories; 22.6g Fat; 0g Carbs; 49g Protein; 0g Sugars

60. Agave Mustard Glazed Chicken

(Ready in about 30 minutes | Servings 4)

Ingredients

1 tablespoon avocado oil
2 pounds chicken breasts, boneless, skin-on
1 tablespoon Jamaican Jerk Rub

1/2 teaspoon salt
3 tablespoons agave syrup
1 tablespoon mustard
2 tablespoons scallions, chopped

Directions

Start by preheating your Air Fryer to 370 degrees F.

Drizzle the avocado oil all over the chicken breast. Then, rub the chicken breast with the Jamaican Jerk rub.

Cook in the preheated Air Fryer approximately 15 minutes. Turn them over and cook an additional 8 minutes.

While the chicken breasts are roasting, combine the salt, agave syrup, and mustard in a pan over medium heat. Let it simmer until the glaze thickens.

After that, brush the glaze all over the chicken breast. Air-fry for a further 6 minutes or until the surface is crispy. Serve garnished with fresh scallions. Bon appétit!

Per serving: 471 Calories; 24.6g Fat; 13.1g Carbs; 47.4g Protein; 12.7g Sugars

61. Thanksgiving Turkey Tenderloin with Gravy

(Ready in about 40 minutes | Servings 4)

Ingredients

2 ½ pounds turkey tenderloin, sliced into pieces
1/2 head of garlic, peeled and halved
1 dried marjoram
Sea salt and ground black pepper, to taste

1 teaspoon cayenne pepper
Gravy:
3 cups vegetable broth
1/3 cup all-purpose flour
Sea salt and ground black pepper, to taste

Directions

Start by preheating your Air Fryer to 350 degrees F.

Rub the turkey tenderloins with garlic halves; add marjoram, salt, black pepper, and cayenne pepper.

Cook the turkey tenderloins at 350 degrees F for 30 minutes or until an instant-read thermometer inserted into the center of the breast reaches 165 degrees F; flip them over halfway through.

In a saucepan, place the drippings from the roasted turkey. Add 1 cup of broth and 1/6 cup of flour to the pan; whisk until it makes a smooth paste.

Once it gets a golden brown color, add the rest of the chicken broth and flour. Sprinkle with salt and pepper to taste.

Let it simmer over medium heat, stirring constantly for 6 to 7 minutes. Serve with warm turkey tenderloin and enjoy!

Per serving: 374 Calories; 8.1g Fat; 20.5g Carbs; 52g Protein; 10.2g Sugars

62. Roasted Citrus Turkey Drumsticks

(Ready in about 55 minutes | Servings 3)

Ingredients

3 medium turkey drumsticks, bone-in skin-on
1/2 butter stick, melted
Sea salt and ground black pepper, to taste
1 teaspoon cayenne pepper

1 teaspoon fresh garlic, minced
1 teaspoon dried parsley flakes
1 teaspoon onion powder
Zest of one orange
1/4 cup orange juice

Directions

Rub all ingredients onto the turkey drumsticks.

Preheat your Air Fryer to 400 degrees F. Cook the turkey drumsticks for 16 minutes in the preheated Air Fryer.

Loosely cover with foil and cook an additional 24 minutes.

Once cooked, let it rest for 10 minutes before slicing and serving. Bon appétit!

Per serving: 352 Calories; 23.4g Fat; 5.2g Carbs; 29.3g Protein; 2.6g Sugars

63. Garden Vegetable and Chicken Casserole

(Ready in about 30 minutes | Servings 4)

Ingredients

2 teaspoons peanut oil
2 pounds chicken drumettes
1 garlic clove, minced
1/2 medium-sized leek, sliced
2 carrots, sliced
1 cup cauliflower florets

1 tablespoon all-purpose flour
2 cups vegetable broth
1/4 cup dry white wine
1 thyme sprig
1 rosemary sprig

Directions

Preheat your Air Fryer to 370 degrees F. Then, drizzle the chicken drumettes with peanut oil and cook them for 10 minutes. Transfer the chicken drumettes to a lightly greased pan.

Add the garlic, leeks, carrots, and cauliflower.

Mix the remaining ingredients in a bowl. Pour the flour mixture into the pan. Cook at 380 degrees F for 15 minutes.

Serve warm.

Per serving: 333 Calories; 10.7g Fat; 5.4g Carbs; 50g Protein; 1.2g Sugars

64. Creole Turkey with Peppers

(Ready in about 35 minutes | Servings 4)

Ingredients

2 pounds turkey thighs, skinless and boneless
1 red onion, sliced
2 bell peppers, deveined and sliced
1 carrot, sliced

1 habanero pepper, deveined and minced
1 tablespoon Creole seasoning mix
1 tablespoon fish sauce
2 cups chicken broth

Directions

Preheat your Air Fryer to 360 degrees F. Now, spritz the bottom and sides of the casserole dish with a nonstick cooking spray.

Arrange the turkey thighs in the casserole dish. Add the onion, pepper, and carrot. Sprinkle with Creole seasoning.

Afterwards, add the fish sauce and chicken broth. Cook in the preheated Air Fryer for 30 minutes. Serve warm and enjoy!

Per serving: 426 Calories; 15.4g Fat; 12.4g Carbs; 51g Protein; 6.1g Sugars

65. Peanut Chicken and Pepper Wraps

(Ready in about 25 minutes | Servings 4)

Ingredients

1 ½ pounds chicken breast, boneless and skinless
1/4 cup peanut butter
1 tablespoon sesame oil
1 tablespoon soy sauce
2 teaspoons rice vinegar
1 teaspoon fresh garlic, minced

1 teaspoon fresh ginger, peeled and grated
1 teaspoon brown sugar
2 tablespoons lemon juice, freshly squeezed
4 tortillas
1 bell pepper, julienned

Directions

Start by preheating your Air Fryer to 380 degrees F.

Cook the chicken breasts in the preheated Air Fryer approximately 6 minutes. Turn them over and cook an additional 6 minutes.

Meanwhile, make the sauce by mixing the peanut butter, sesame oil, soy sauce, vinegar, ginger, garlic, sugar, and lemon juice.

Slice the chicken crosswise across the grain into 1/4-inch strips. Toss the chicken into the sauce.

Decrease temperature to 390 degrees F. Spoon the chicken and sauce onto each tortilla; add bell peppers and wrap them tightly.

Drizzle with a nonstick cooking spray and bake about 7 minutes. Serve warm.

Per serving: 529 Calories; 25.5g Fat; 31.5g Carbs; 40.1g Protein; 6.8g Sugars

66. Sausage, Ham and Hash Brown Bake

(Ready in about 45 minutes | Servings 4)

Ingredients

1/2 pound chicken sausages, smoked
1/2 pound ham, sliced
6 ounces hash browns, frozen and shredded
2 garlic cloves, minced
8 ounces spinach
1/2 cup Ricotta cheese

1/2 cup Asiago cheese, grated
4 eggs
1/2 cup yogurt
1/2 cup milk
Salt and ground black pepper, to taste
1 teaspoon smoked paprika

Directions

Start by preheating your Air Fryer to 380 degrees F. Cook the sausages and ham for 10 minutes; set aside.

Meanwhile, in a preheated saucepan, cook the hash browns and garlic for 4 minutes, stirring frequently; remove from the heat, add the spinach and cover with the lid.

Allow the spinach to wilt completely. Transfer the sautéed mixture to a baking pan. Add the reserved sausage and ham.

In a mixing dish, thoroughly combine the cheese, eggs, yogurt, milk, salt, pepper, and paprika. Pour the cheese mixture over the hash browns in the pan.

Place the baking pan in the cooking basket and cook approximately 30 minutes or until everything is thoroughly cooked. Bon appétit!

Per serving: 509 Calories; 20.1g Fat; 40g Carbs; 41.2g Protein; 3.9g Sugars

67. The Best Chicken Burgers Ever

(Ready in about 20 minutes | Servings 4)

Ingredients

1 tablespoon olive oil
1 onion, peeled and finely chopped
2 garlic cloves, minced
Sea salt and ground black pepper, to taste
1/2 teaspoon paprika
1/2 teaspoon ground cumin
1 pound chicken breast, ground
4 soft rolls
4 tablespoons ketchup
4 tablespoons mayonnaise
2 teaspoons Dijon mustard
4 tablespoons green onions, chopped
4 pickles, sliced

Directions

Heat the olive oil in a skillet over high flame. Then, sauté the onion until golden and translucent, about 4 minutes.

Add the garlic and cook an additional 30 seconds or until it is aromatic. Season with salt, pepper, paprika, and cumin; reserve.

Add the chicken and cook for 2 to 3 minutes, stirring and crumbling with a fork. Add the onion mixture and mix to combine well.

Shape the mixture into patties and transfer them to the cooking basket. Cook in the preheated Air Fryer at 360 degrees F for 6 minutes. Turn them over and cook an additional 5 minutes. Work in batches.

Smear the base of the roll with ketchup, mayo, and mustard. Top with the chicken, green onions, and pickles. Enjoy!

Per serving: 507 Calories; 26.5g Fat; 37.6g Carbs; 30g Protein; 12.8g Sugars

68. Marinated Chicken Drumettes with Asparagus

(Ready in about 30 minutes + marinating time | Servings 6)

Ingredients

6 chicken drumettes
1 ½ pounds asparagus, ends trimmed
Marinade:
3 tablespoons canola oil
3 tablespoons soy sauce
3 heaping tablespoons shallots, minced
3 tablespoons lime juice
1 heaping teaspoon fresh garlic, minced
1 (1-inch) piece fresh ginger, peeled and minced
1 teaspoon Creole seasoning
Coarse sea salt and ground black pepper, to taste

Directions

In a ceramic bowl, mix all ingredients for the marinade. Add the chicken drumettes and let them marinate at least 5 hours in the refrigerator.

Now, drain the chicken drumettes and discard the marinade.

Cook in the preheated Air Fryer at 370 degrees F for 11 minutes. Turn the chicken drumettes over and cook for a further 11 minutes.

While the chicken drumettes are cooking, add the reserved marinade to the preheated skillet. Add the asparagus and cook for approximately 5 minutes or until cooked through. Serve with the air-fried chicken and enjoy!

Per serving: 356 Calories; 22.1g Fat; 7.8g Carbs; 31.4g Protein; 4.1g Sugars

69. Easy Chicken Sliders

(Ready in about 30 minutes | Servings 3)

Ingredients

1/2 cup all-purpose flour
1 teaspoon garlic salt
1/2 teaspoon black pepper, preferably freshly ground
1 teaspoon celery seeds
1/2 teaspoon mustard seeds
1/2 teaspoon dried basil
1 egg
2 chicken breasts, cut in thirds
6 small-sized dinner rolls

Directions

In mixing bowl, thoroughly combine the flour and seasonings.

In a separate shallow bowl, beat the egg until frothy.

Dredge the chicken through the flour mixture, then into egg; afterwards, roll them over the flour mixture again.

Spritz the chicken pieces with a cooking spray on all sides. Transfer them to the cooking basket.

Cook in the preheated Air Fryer at 380 degrees F for 15 minutes; turn them over and cook an additional 10 to 12 minutes.

Test for doneness and adjust the seasonings. Serve immediately on dinner rolls.

Per serving: 479 Calories; 17.9g Fat; 43g Carbs; 34.4g Protein; 1.3g Sugars

70. Turkey and Sausage Meatloaf with Herbs

(Ready in about 45 minutes | Servings 4)

Ingredients

1/2 cup milk
4 bread slices, crustless
1 tablespoon olive oil
1 onion, finely chopped
1 garlic clove, minced
1/2 pound ground turkey
1/2 pound ground breakfast sausage
1 duck egg, whisked
1 teaspoon rosemary
1 teaspoon basil
1 teaspoon thyme
1 teaspoon cayenne pepper
Kosher salt and ground black pepper, to taste
1/2 cup ketchup
2 tablespoons molasses
1 tablespoon brown mustard

Directions

In a shallow bowl, pour the milk over the bread and let it soak in for 5 to 6 minutes.

Heat 1 tablespoon of oil over medium-high heat in a nonstick pan. Sauté the onions and garlic until tender and fragrant, about 2 minutes.

Add the turkey, sausage, egg, rosemary, basil, thyme, cayenne pepper, salt, and ground black pepper. Stir in the milk-soaked bread. Mix until everything is well incorporated.

Shape the mixture into a loaf and transfer it to a pan that is lightly greased with an olive oil mister.

Next, lower the pan onto the cooking basket.

In a mixing bowl, whisk the ketchup with molasses and mustard. Spread this mixture over the top of your meatloaf.

Cook approximately 27 minutes or until the meatloaf is no longer pink in the middle. Allow it to sit 10 minutes before slicing and serving. Bon appétit!

Per serving: 431 Calories; 22.3g Fat; 32.6g Carbs; 25.9g Protein; 18.5g Sugars

71. Turkey Wings with Butter Roasted Potatoes

(Ready in about 55 minutes | Servings 4)

Ingredients

4 large-sized potatoes, peeled and cut into 1-inch chunks
1 tablespoon butter, melted
1 teaspoon rosemary
1 teaspoon garlic salt
1/2 teaspoon ground black pepper
1 ½ pounds turkey wings
2 tablespoons olive oil
2 garlic cloves, minced
1 tablespoon Dijon mustard
1/2 teaspoon cayenne pepper

Directions

Add the potatoes, butter, rosemary, salt, and pepper to the cooking basket.

Cook at 400 degrees F for 12 minutes. Reserve the potatoes, keeping them warm.

Now, place the turkey wings in the cooking basket that is previously cleaned and greased with olive oil. Add the garlic, mustard, and cayenne pepper.

Cook in the preheated Air Fryer at 350 degrees f for 25 minutes. Turn them over and cook an additional 15 minutes.

Test for doneness with a meat thermometer. Serve with warm potatoes.

Per serving: 567 Calories; 14.3g Fat; 65.7g Carbs; 46.1g Protein; 2.9g Sugars

72. Smoked Duck with Rosemary-Infused Gravy

(Ready in about 30 minutes | Servings 4)

Ingredients

1 ½ pounds smoked duck breasts, boneless
1 tablespoon yellow mustard
2 tablespoons ketchup
1 teaspoon agave syrup
12 pearl onions peeled
1 tablespoon flour
5 ounces chicken broth
1 teaspoon rosemary, finely chopped

Directions

Cook the smoked duck breasts in the preheated Air Fryer at 365 degrees F for 15 minutes.

Smear the mustard, ketchup, and agave syrup on the duck breast. Top with pearl onions. Cook for a further 7 minutes or until the skin of the duck breast looks crispy and golden brown.

Slice the duck breasts and reserve. Drain off the duck fat from the pan.

Then, add the reserved 1 tablespoon of duck fat to the pan and warm it over medium heat; add flour and cook until your roux is dark brown.

Add the chicken broth and rosemary to the pan. Reduce the heat to low and cook until the gravy has thickened slightly. Spoon the warm gravy over the reserved duck breasts. Enjoy!

Per serving: 485 Calories; 19.7g Fat; 24.1g Carbs; 51.3g Protein; 15.6g Sugars

73. Farmhouse Roast Turkey

(Ready in about 50 minutes | Servings 6)

Ingredients

2 pounds turkey
1 tablespoon fresh rosemary, chopped
1 teaspoon sea salt
1/2 teaspoon ground black pepper
1 onion, chopped
1 celery stalk, chopped

Directions

Start by preheating your Air Fryer to 360 degrees F. Spritz the sides and bottom of the cooking basket with a nonstick cooking spray.

Place the turkey in the cooking basket. Add the rosemary, salt, and black pepper. Cook for 30 minutes in the preheated Air Fryer.

Add the onion and celery and cook an additional 15 minutes. Bon appétit!

Per serving: 316 Calories; 24.2g Fat; 2.5g Carbs; 20.4g Protein; 1.1g Sugars

74. Chicken with Golden Roasted Cauliflower

(Ready in about 30 minutes | Servings 4)

Ingredients

2 pounds chicken legs
2 tablespoons olive oil
1 teaspoon sea salt
1/2 teaspoon ground black pepper
1 teaspoon smoked paprika
1 teaspoon dried marjoram
1 (1-pound) head cauliflower, broken into small florets
2 garlic cloves, minced
1/3 cup Pecorino Romano cheese, freshly grated
1/2 teaspoon dried thyme
Salt, to taste

Directions

Toss the chicken legs with the olive oil, salt, black pepper, paprika, and marjoram.

Cook in the preheated Air Fryer at 380 degrees F for 11 minutes. Flip the chicken legs and cook for a further 5 minutes.

Toss the cauliflower florets with garlic, cheese, thyme, and salt.

Increase the temperature to 400 degrees F; add the cauliflower florets and cook for 12 more minutes. Serve warm.

Per serving: 388 Calories; 18.9g Fat; 5.6g Carbs; 47.3g Protein; 1.3g Sugars

75. Adobo Seasoned Chicken with Veggies

(Ready in about 1 hour 30 minutes | Servings 4)

Ingredients

2 pounds chicken wings, rinsed and patted dry
1 teaspoon coarse sea salt
1/4 teaspoon ground black pepper
1/2 teaspoon red pepper flakes, crushed
1 teaspoon ground cumin
1 teaspoon paprika
1 teaspoon granulated onion
1 teaspoon ground turmeric
2 tablespoons tomato powder
1 tablespoon dry Madeira wine
2 stalks celery, diced
2 cloves garlic, peeled but not chopped
1 large Spanish onion, diced
2 bell peppers, seeded and sliced
4 carrots, trimmed and halved
2 tablespoons olive oil

Directions

Toss all ingredients in a large bowl. Cover and let it sit for 1 hour in your refrigerator.

Add the chicken wings to a baking pan.

Roast the chicken wings in the preheated Air Fryer at 380 degrees F for 7 minutes.

Add the vegetables and cook an additional 15 minutes, shaking the basket once or twice. Serve warm.

Per serving: 427 Calories; 15.3g Fat; 18.5g Carbs; 52.3g Protein; 9.4g Sugars

76. Spice Lime Chicken Tenders

(Ready in about 20 minutes | Servings 6)

Ingredients

1 lime
2 pounds chicken tenderloins cut up
1 cup cornflakes, crushed
1/2 cup Parmesan cheese, grated
1 tablespoon olive oil
Sea salt and ground black pepper, to taste
1 teaspoon cayenne pepper
1/3 teaspoon ground cumin
1 teaspoon chili powder
1 egg

Directions

Squeeze the lime juice all over the chicken.

Spritz the cooking basket with a nonstick cooking spray.

In a mixing bowl, thoroughly combine the cornflakes, Parmesan, olive oil, salt, black pepper, cayenne pepper, cumin, and chili powder.

In another shallow bowl, whisk the egg until well beaten. Dip the chicken tenders in the egg, then in cornflakes mixture.

Transfer the breaded chicken to the prepared cooking basket. Cook in the preheated Air Fryer at 380 degrees F for 12 minutes. Turn them over halfway through the cooking time. Work in batches. Serve immediately.

Per serving: 422 Calories; 29.2g Fat; 6.1g Carbs; 32.9g Protein; 2.4g Sugars

77. Quick and Easy Chicken Mole

(Ready in about 35 minutes | Servings 4)

Ingredients

8 chicken thighs, skinless, bone-in
1 tablespoon peanut oil
Sea salt and ground black pepper, to taste
Mole sauce:
1 tablespoon peanut oil
1 onion, chopped
1 ounce dried negro chiles, stemmed, seeded, and chopped
2 garlic cloves, peeled and halved
2 large-sized fresh tomatoes, pureed
2 tablespoons raisins
1 ½ ounces bittersweet chocolate, chopped
1 teaspoon dried Mexican oregano
1/2 teaspoon ground cumin
1 teaspoon coriander seeds
A pinch of ground cloves
4 strips orange peel
1/4 cup almonds, sliced and toasted

Directions

Start by preheating your Air Fryer to 380 degrees F. Toss the chicken thighs with the peanut oil, salt, and black pepper.

Cook in the preheated Air Fryer for 12 minutes; flip them and cook an additional 10 minutes; reserve.

To make the sauce, heat 1 tablespoon of peanut oil in a saucepan over medium-high heat. Now, sauté the onion, chiles and garlic until fragrant or about 2 minutes.

Next, stir in the tomatoes, raisins, chocolate, oregano, cumin, coriander seeds, and cloves. Let it simmer until the sauce has slightly thickened.

Add the reserved chicken to the baking pan; add the sauce and cook in the preheated Air Fryer at 360 degrees F for 10 minutes or until thoroughly warmed.

Serve garnished with orange peel and sliced almonds. Enjoy!

Per serving: 453 Calories; 17.5g Fat; 25.1g Carbs; 47.5g Protein; 12.9g Sugars

78. Chicken Sausage Frittata with Cheese

(Ready in about 15 minutes | Servings 2)

Ingredients

1 tablespoon olive oil
2 chicken sausages, sliced
4 eggs
1 garlic clove, minced
1/2 yellow onion, chopped

Sea salt and ground black pepper, to taste
4 tablespoons Monterey-Jack cheese
1 tablespoon fresh parsley leaves, chopped

Directions

Grease the sides and bottom of a baking pan with olive oil.

Add the sausages and cook in the preheated Air Fryer at 360 degrees F for 4 to 5 minutes.

In a mixing dish, whisk the eggs with garlic and onion. Season with salt and black pepper.

Pour the mixture over sausages. Top with cheese. Cook in the preheated Air Fryer at 360 degrees F for another 6 minutes.

Serve immediately with fresh parsley leaves. Bon appétit!

Per serving: 475 Calories; 34.2g Fat; 5.3g Carbs; 36.2g Protein; 2.6g Sugars

79. Traditional Chicken Teriyaki

(Ready in about 50 minutes | Servings 4)

Ingredients

1 ½ pounds chicken breast, halved
1 tablespoon lemon juice
2 tablespoons Mirin
1/4 cup milk
2 tablespoons soy sauce
1 tablespoon olive oil

1 teaspoon ginger, peeled and grated
2 garlic cloves, minced
1/2 teaspoon salt
1/2 teaspoon ground black pepper
1 teaspoon cornstarch

Directions

In a large ceramic dish, place the chicken, lemon juice, Mirin, milk, soy sauce, olive oil, ginger, and garlic. Let it marinate for 30 minutes in your refrigerator.

Spritz the sides and bottom of the cooking basket with a nonstick cooking spray. Arrange the chicken in the cooking basket and cook at 370 degrees F for 10 minutes.

Turn over the chicken, baste with the reserved marinade and cook for 4 minutes longer. Taste for doneness, season with salt and pepper, and reserve.

Mix the cornstarch with 1 tablespoon of water. Add the marinade to the preheated skillet over medium heat; cook for 3 to 4 minutes. Now, stir in the cornstarch slurry and cook until the sauce thickens.

Spoon the sauce over the reserved chicken and serve immediately.

Per serving: 362 Calories; 21.1g Fat; 4.4g Carbs; 36.6g Protein; 2.4g Sugars

80. Loaded Chicken Burgers

(Ready in about 30 minutes | Servings 5)

Ingredients

2 tablespoons olive oil
1 onion, finely chopped
2 green garlic, chopped
6 ounces mushrooms, chopped
1 ½ pounds ground chicken
1/3 cup parmesan cheese

1/4 cup pork rinds, crushed
1 tablespoon fish sauce
1 tablespoon tamari sauce
1 teaspoon Dijon mustard
5 soft hamburger buns
5 lettuce leaves

Directions

Heat a nonstick skillet over medium-high heat; add olive oil. Once hot, sauté the onion until tender and translucent, about 3 minutes.

Add the garlic and mushrooms and cook an additional 2 minutes, stirring frequently.

Add the ground chicken, cheese, pork rind, fish sauce, and tamari sauce; mix until everything is well incorporated.

Form the mixture into 5 patties. Transfer the patties to the lightly greased cooking basket.

Cook in the preheated Air Fryer at 370 degrees F for 8 minutes; then, flip them over and cook for 8 minutes on the other side.

Serve on burger buns, garnished with mustard and lettuce. Bon appétit!

Per serving: 476 Calories; 25.9g Fat; 29.9g Carbs; 31.7g Protein; 2.5g Sugars

81. Chicken and Brown Rice Bake

(Ready in about 50 minutes | Servings 3)

Ingredients

1 cup brown rice
2 cups vegetable broth
1/2 cup water
1 tablespoon butter, melted
1 onion, chopped
2 garlic cloves, minced

Kosher salt and ground black pepper, to taste
1 teaspoon cayenne pepper
3 chicken fillets
1 cup tomato puree
1 tablespoon fresh chives, chopped

Directions

Heat the brown rice, vegetable broth and water in a pot over high heat. Bring it to a boil; turn the stove down to simmer and cook for 35 minutes.

Grease a baking pan with butter.

Spoon the prepared rice mixture into the baking pan. Add the onion, garlic, salt, black pepper, cayenne pepper, and chicken. Spoon the tomato puree over the chicken.

Cook in the preheated Air Fryer at 380 degrees F for 12 minutes. Serve garnished with fresh chives. Enjoy!

Per serving: 508 Calories; 18.3g Fat; 61g Carbs; 24.5g Protein; 7.2g Sugars

82. Sticky Exotic Chicken Drumettes

(Ready in about 25 minutes | Servings 4)

Ingredients

2 tablespoons peanut oil
2 tablespoons honey
1 tablespoon tamari sauce
1 tablespoon yellow mustard
1 clove garlic, peeled and minced
2 tablespoons fresh orange juice

1/2 teaspoon sambal oelek
1 ½ pounds chicken drumettes, bone-in
Salt and ground white pepper, to taste
1/4 cup chicken broth
1/2 cup raw onion rings, for garnish

Directions

Start by preheating your Air Fryer to 380 degrees F.

Line the cooking basket with parchment paper. Lightly grease the parchment paper with 1 tablespoon of peanut oil.

In a mixing bowl, thoroughly combine the remaining 1 tablespoon of oil, honey, tamari sauce, mustard, garlic, orange juice, and sambal oelek. Whisk to combine well.

Arrange the chicken drumettes in the prepared cooking basket. Season with salt and white pepper.

Spread 1/2 of the honey mixture evenly all over each breast. Pour in the chicken broth. Cook for 12 minutes.

Turn them over, add the remaining 1/2 of the honey mixture, and cook an additional 10 minutes.

Garnish with onion rings and serve immediately.

Per serving: 317 Calories; 12.5g Fat; 11.5g Carbs; 38.4g Protein; 10.1g Sugars

83. Spanish Chicken with Golden Potatoes

(Ready in about 25 minutes | Servings 4)

Ingredients

2 tablespoons butter, melted
4 chicken drumsticks, bone-in
1 pound Yukon Gold potatoes, peeled and diced
1 lemon, 1/2 juiced, 1/2 cut into wedges
1 teaspoon fresh garlic, minced

1 teaspoon dried rosemary, crushed
1 teaspoon dried thyme, crushed
1 teaspoon cayenne pepper
1/3 teaspoon freshly ground black pepper
Kosher salt, to taste
2 tablespoons sherry

Directions

Start by preheating your Air Fryer to 370 degrees F. Then, grease a baking pan with the melted butter. Arrange the chicken drumsticks in the baking pan.

Bake in the preheated Air Fryer for 8 minutes. Add the diced potatoes. Drizzle chicken and potatoes with lemon juice. Sprinkle with garlic, rosemary, thyme, cayenne pepper, black pepper, and salt.

Turn the temperature to 400 degrees F and cook for a further 12 minutes. Make sure to shake the basket once or twice.

Remove from the Air Fryer basket and sprinkle sherry on top. Serve with the lemon wedges.

Enjoy!

Per serving: 382 Calories; 17.9g Fat; 26.1g Carbs; 26.7g Protein; 1.6g Sugars

84. Turkey Breakfast Frittata

(Ready in about 50 minutes | Servings 4)

Ingredients

1 tablespoon olive oil
1 pound turkey breasts, slices
6 large-sized eggs
3 tablespoons Greek yogurt
3 tablespoons Cottage cheese, crumbled
1/4 teaspoon ground black pepper

1/4 teaspoon red pepper flakes, crushed
Himalayan salt, to taste
1 red bell pepper, seeded and sliced
1 green bell pepper, seeded and sliced

Directions

Grease the cooking basket with olive oil. Add the turkey and cook in the preheated Air Fryer at 350 degrees F for 30 minutes, flipping them over halfway through. Cut into bite-sized strips and reserve.

Now, beat the eggs with Greek yogurt, cheese, black pepper, red pepper, and salt. Add the bell peppers to a baking pan that is previously lightly greased with a cooking spray.

Add the turkey strips; pour the egg mixture over all ingredients.

Bake in the preheated Air Fryer at 360 degrees F for 15 minutes. Serve right away!

Per serving: 327 Calories; 13.4g Fat; 3.5g Carbs; 45.4g Protein; 2.3g Sugars

85. Nana's Turkey Chili

(Ready in about 1 hour | Servings 4)

Ingredients

1/2 medium-sized leek, chopped
1/2 red onion, chopped
2 garlic cloves, minced
1 jalapeno pepper, seeded and minced
1 bell pepper, seeded and chopped
2 tablespoons olive oil
1 pound ground turkey, 85% lean 15% fat

2 cups tomato puree
2 cups chicken stock
1/2 teaspoon black peppercorns
Salt, to taste
1 teaspoon chili powder
1 teaspoon mustard seeds
1 teaspoon ground cumin
1 (12-ounce) can kidney beans, rinsed and drained

Directions

Start by preheating your Air Fryer to 365 degrees F.

Place the leeks, onion, garlic and peppers in a baking pan; drizzle olive oil evenly over the top. Cook for 4 to 6 minutes.

Add the ground turkey. Cook for 6 minutes more or until the meat is no longer pink.

Now, add the tomato puree, 1 cup of chicken stock, black peppercorns, salt, chili powder, mustard seeds, and cumin to the baking pan. Cook for 24 minutes, stirring every 7 to 10 minutes.

Stir in the canned beans and the remaining 1 cup of stock; let it cook for a further 9 minutes; make sure to stir halfway through. Bon appétit!

Per serving: 327 Calories; 13.4g Fat; 3.5g Carbs; 45.4g Protein; 2.3g Sugars

86. Delicious Turkey Sandwiches

(Ready in about 45 minutes | Servings 4)

Ingredients

1 pound turkey tenderloins
1 tablespoon Dijon-style mustard
1 tablespoon olive oil
Sea salt and ground black pepper, to taste
1 teaspoon Italian seasoning mix
1/4 cup all-purpose flour

1 cup turkey stock
8 slices sourdough, toasted
4 tablespoons tomato ketchup
4 tablespoons mayonnaise
4 pickles, sliced

Directions

Rub the turkey tenderloins with the mustard and olive oil. Season with salt, black pepper, and Italian seasoning mix.

Cook the turkey tenderloins at 350 degrees F for 30 minutes, flipping them over halfway through. Let them rest for 5 to 7 minutes before slicing.

For the gravy, in a saucepan, place the drippings from the roasted turkey. Add 1/8 cup of flour and 1/2 cup of turkey stock; whisk until it makes a smooth paste.

Once it gets a golden brown color, add the rest of the stock and flour. Season with salt to taste. Let it simmer over medium heat, stirring constantly for 6 to 7 minutes.

Assemble the sandwiches with the turkey, gravy, tomato ketchup, mayonnaise, and pickles. Serve and enjoy!

Per serving: 427 Calories; 18g Fat; 33.5g Carbs; 32.8g Protein; 6.1g Sugars

87. Traditional Chicken Tetrazzini

(Ready in about 55 minutes | Servings 4)

Ingredients

10 ounces noodles, cooked
2 tablespoons olive oil
1 pound chicken breast
Sea salt and pepper, to taste
1 onion, sliced
2 garlic cloves, minced

1 can cream of chicken soup
1 can cream of mushroom soup
1 cup sour cream
1/2 cup mozzarella cheese, shredded

Directions

Bring a large pot of lightly salted water to a boil. Cook your noodles for 10 minutes or until al dente; drain and reserve, keeping warm.

Preheat your Air Fryer to 370 degrees F. Brush the cooking basket with 1 teaspoon of olive oil.

Sprinkle the chicken breasts with salt and pepper. Cook for 25 minutes or until the chicken breasts are slightly browned.

Preheat your Air Fryer to 370 degrees F. Lightly grease the bottom and sides of the baking pan with the remaining 1 tablespoon of olive oil.

Add the onion, garlic, chicken soup, mushroom soup, and sour cream. Add the reserved noodles and the chicken.

Cook for 12 minutes in the preheated Air Fryer. Top with mozzarella and cook an additional 6 minutes until it is bubbling. Serve warm.

Per serving: 427 Calories; 18g Fat; 33.5g Carbs; 32.8g Protein; 6.1g Sugars

88. Chicken Egg Rolls with Hot Dipping Sauce

(Ready in about 35 minutes | Servings 5)

Ingredients

2 teaspoons olive oil
1 pound ground chicken
Salt and ground pepper, to taste
2 scallions, sliced thinly
2 cloves garlic, finely chopped
2 cups Napa cabbage, shredded
2 tablespoons soy sauce
1 teaspoon Dijon mustard
10 egg roll wrappers
Dipping Sauce:
1/3 cup lite soy sauce
1/3 cup Champagne vinegar
2 tablespoons molasses
1 tablespoon sesame oil
1/2 teaspoon chili powder

Directions

In a cast-iron skillet, heat the oil until sizzling; now, add the ground chicken and cook for 3 to 4 minutes, crumbling with a fork. Season with salt and pepper.

Stir in the scallions, garlic, and cabbage. Continue to sauté for 4 minutes more. Remove from the heat; add the soy sauce and mustard and stir again.

Fill the egg roll wrappers, using 1 to 2 tablespoons of filling. Place the filling in the center of the wrapper. Roll the corner over the filling and brush it with water.

Fold in the sides of the wrapper and continue rolling until it is closed. Press to seal and brush it with water.

Cook in the preheated Air Fryer at 375 degrees F for 13 to 16 minutes, turning over halfway through. Work in batches.

In the meantime, combine all of the sauce ingredients in a mixing bowl. Serve immediately with the warm egg rolls.

Per serving: 350 Calories; 19.7g Fat; 20.6g Carbs; 21.2g Protein; 8.1g Sugars

89. Easy Thanksgiving Crunchwrap

(Ready in about 1 hour 15 minutes | Servings 4)

Ingredients

2 tablespoons sesame oil
1 pound turkey breasts
1 tablespoon taco seasoning
2 onions, sliced
2 bell peppers, sliced
1 habanero pepper, sliced
8 corn tortillas, approx. 7-8-inch diameter
1/2 cup queso quesadilla
1 cup Manchego cheese, grated
1 ½ cups tortilla chips
1/2 cup mayonnaise
2 tablespoons lemon juice
1 teaspoon yellow mustard
1 1/2 cup pickled jalapenos, chopped
1/4 teaspoon dried dill weed
1/2 teaspoon Mexican oregano

Directions

Start by preheating your Air Fryer to 350 degrees F. Drizzle 1 tablespoon of sesame oil all over the turkey breasts and cook for 30 minutes, flipping them over halfway through.

Let them rest for 7 minutes; then, slice the turkey breast into strips, add the taco seasoning, and reserve.

Place the onions and peppers in the cooking basket. Cook in the preheated Air Fryer at 400 degrees F for 13 minutes; reserve.

Spritz the base of a baking pan with cooking oil. Divide the roasted turkey, pepper mixture and cheese between the tortillas. Top with tortilla chips.

Fold over your tortillas, then, arrange them in the baking pan. Drizzle the remaining 1 tablespoon of sesame oil over each tortilla. Bake at 185 degrees F for 24 minutes.

Meanwhile, make the sauce by mixing the mayonnaise with lemon juice, mustard, jalapeno, dill, and oregano. Serve with the warm tortillas. Enjoy!

Per serving: 706 Calories; 59.5g Fat; 14.9g Carbs; 27.4g Protein; 4.4g Sugars

90. Double Cheese and Chicken Crescent Bake

(Ready in about 20 minutes | Servings 4)

Ingredients

8 ounces regular-sized crescent rolls
1 ½ cups cooked turkey, shredded
1/4 cup prepared warm gravy
1 teaspoon garlic powder
1/4 teaspoon cayenne pepper
Salt and black pepper, to taste
1/2 cup cream of mushroom soup with herbs
1 can milk
1/2 teaspoon freshly ground black pepper
1 cup Colby cheese, shredded
1/4 cup Parmesan cheese grated
2 tablespoons fresh cilantro leaves, roughly chopped

Directions

Start by preheating your Air Fryer to 350 degrees F. Now, spritz the sides and bottom of a baking pan with a nonstick cooking spray.

Roll out the crescent rolls. Top with the turkey and gravy. Sprinkle with the garlic powder, cayenne pepper, salt, and black pepper.

Roll up and arrange them in the prepared baking pan. Mix the soup, milk and 1/2 teaspoon of black pepper to make the sauce. Pour the sauce around the crescents. Top with the cheese.

Bake for 12 minutes or until the top is golden brown. Serve garnished with fresh cilantro leaves. Bon appétit!

Per serving: 518 Calories; 25.4g Fat; 38.3g Carbs; 32.7g Protein; 8.6g Sugars

91. Authentic Chicken-Fajitas with Salsa

(Ready in about 30 minutes | Servings 4)

Ingredients

1 pound chicken tenderloins, chopped
Sea salt and ground black pepper, to your liking
1 teaspoon shallot powder
1 teaspoon fajita seasoning
2 bell peppers, seeded and diced
4 flour tortillas
Salsa
1 ancho chili pepper, seeded and finely chopped
2 ripe tomatoes, crushed
1 bunch fresh coriander, roughly chopped
1 lime
2 tablespoons extra-virgin olive oil

Directions

Toss the chicken with salt, pepper, shallot powder, and fajita seasoning mix.

Roast in the preheated Air Fryer at 390 degrees F for 9 minutes. Add the bell peppers and roast an additional 8 minutes.

For the salsa, mix the chilli, tomatoes and coriander. Squeeze over the juice of 1 lime; add olive oil and stir to combine well.

Warm the tortillas in your Air Fryer at 200 degrees F for 10 minutes.

Serve the chicken fajitas with tortilla and salsa. Enjoy!

Per serving: 433 Calories; 14.5g Fat; 44.9g Carbs; 30.2g Protein; 6.6g Sugars

92. Pizza Spaghetti Casserole

(Ready in about 30 minutes | Servings 4)

Ingredients

8 ounces spaghetti
1 pound smoked chicken sausage, sliced
2 tomatoes, pureed
1/2 cup Asiago cheese, shredded
1 tablespoon Italian seasoning mix
3 tablespoons Romano cheese, grated
1 tablespoon fresh basil leaves, chiffonade

Directions

Bring a large pot of lightly salted water to a boil. Cook your spaghetti for 10 minutes or until al dente; drain and reserve, keeping warm.

Stir in the chicken sausage, tomato puree, Asiago cheese, and Italian seasoning mix.

Then, spritz a baking pan with cooking spray; add the spaghetti mixture to the pan. Bake in the preheated Air Fryer at 325 degrees F for 11 minutes.

Top with the grated Romano cheese. Turn the temperature to 390 degrees F and cook an additional 5 minutes or until everything is thoroughly heated and the cheese is melted.

Garnish with fresh basil leaves. Bon appétit!

Per serving: 472 Calories; 23.1g Fat; 28.6g Carbs; 38.2g Protein; 7.6g Sugars

93. Vermouth Bacon and Turkey Burgers

(Ready in about 30 minutes | Servings 4)

Ingredients

2 tablespoons vermouth
1 tablespoon honey
2 strips Canadian bacon, sliced
1 pound ground turkey
1/2 shallot, minced
2 garlic cloves, minced
2 tablespoons fish sauce

Sea salt and ground black pepper, to taste
1 teaspoon red pepper flakes
4 soft hamburger rolls
4 tablespoons tomato ketchup
4 tablespoons mayonnaise
4 (1-ounce) slices Cheddar cheese
4 lettuce leaves

Directions

Start by preheating your Air Fryer to 400 degrees F.

Whisk the vermouth and honey in a mixing bowl; brush the Canadian bacon with the vermouth mixture.

Cook for 3 minutes. Flip the bacon over and cook an additional 3 minutes.

Then, thoroughly combine the ground turkey, shallots, garlic, fish sauce, salt, black pepper, and red pepper. Form the meat mixture into 4 burger patties.

Bake in the preheated Air Fryer at 370 degrees F for 10 minutes. Flip them over and cook another 10 minutes.

Spread the ketchup and mayonnaise on the inside of the hamburger rolls and place the burgers on the rolls; top with bacon, cheese and lettuce; serve immediately.

Per serving: 564 Calories; 30.6g Fat; 32.9g Carbs; 37.7g Protein; 11.1g Sugars

94. Chicken Taquitos with Homemade Guacamole

(Ready in about 35 minutes | Servings 4)

Ingredients

1 tablespoon peanut oil
1 pound chicken breast
Seasoned salt and ground black pepper, to taste
1 teaspoon chili powder
1 teaspoon garlic powder
1 teaspoon ground cumin
1 cup Colby cheese, shredded
8 corn tortillas
1/2 cup sour cream

Guacamole:
1 ripe avocado, pitted and peeled
1 tomato, crushed
1/2 onion, finely chopped
1 tablespoon fresh cilantro, chopped
1 chili pepper, seeded and minced
1 teaspoon fresh garlic, minced
1 lime, juiced
Sea salt and black pepper, to taste

Directions

Start by preheating your Air Fryer to 370 degrees F.

Drizzle the peanut oil all over the chicken breast. Then, rub the chicken breast with salt, black pepper, chili powder, garlic powder, and ground cumin.

Cook in the preheated Air Fryer approximately 15 minutes. Turn them over and cook an additional 8 minutes.

Then, increase the temperature to 380 degrees F.

Divide the roasted chicken and cheese between tortillas. Now, roll up the tortilla and transfer them to the lightly greased cooking basket. Spritz a nonstick cooking spray over the tortillas.

Cook approximately 10 minutes, turning them over halfway through.

Mash the avocado with a fork and add the remaining ingredients for the guacamole. Serve the chicken taquitos with the guacamole sauce and sour cream. Enjoy!

Per serving: 512 Calories; 35.2g Fat; 15.9g Carbs; 34.9g Protein; 4.7g Sugars

95. Pilaf with Chicken and Beer

(Ready in about 45 minutes | Servings 4)

Ingredients

1 tablespoon peanut oil
1 ½ cups white rice
5 cups chicken stock
1 cup beer

1 pound chicken tenders
Salt and pepper, to taste
6 tablespoons grated parmesan

Directions

Preheat your Air Fryer to 350 degrees F. Place the peanut oil in the baking pan and heat it for 1 to 2 minutes. Then, add the rice and cook for 3 minutes until the rice is lightly toasted.

Pour in the chicken stock and beer; cook for 20 minutes. Add the chicken tenders and cook for a further 10 minutes. Season with salt and pepper.

Check the rice for doneness. Top with the grated parmesan and cook an additional 5 minutes. Spoon the warm pilaf into individual bowl and serve warm.

Per serving: 529 Calories; 9.6g Fat; 65.5g Carbs; 37.9g Protein; 0.9g Sugars

PORK

96. Ground Pork and Wild Rice Casserole

(Ready in about 25 minutes | Servings 3)

Ingredients

1 teaspoon olive oil
1 small-sized yellow onion, chopped
1 pound ground pork (84% lean)
Salt and black pepper, to taste
1/2 cups cooked wild rice, uncooked

1/2 cup cream of mushroom soup
1/2 tomato paste
1 jalapeno pepper, minced
1 teaspoon Italian spice mix
1/2 cup Asiago cheese, shredded

Directions

Start by preheating your Air Fryer to 350 degrees F.

Heat the olive oil in a nonstick over medium-high heat. Then, sauté the onion and ground pork for 6 to 7 minutes, crumbling with a spatula. Season with salt and black pepper to your liking.

Spoon the pork mixture into a lightly greased baking dish.

Spoon the cooked rice over the pork layer. In a mixing dish, thoroughly combine the remaining ingredients.

Bake for 15 minutes or until bubbly and heated through. Bon appétit!

Per serving: 506 Calories; 34.7g Fat; 13.4g Carbs; 34.7g Protein; 2.3g Sugars

97. Dijon Mustard and Honey Roasted Pork Cutlets

(Ready in about 15 minutes | Servings 2)

Ingredients

1 pound pork cutlets
1 teaspoon cayenne pepper
Kosher salt and ground black pepper, to season

1/2 teaspoon garlic powder
1 tablespoon honey
1 teaspoon Dijon mustard

Directions

Spritz the sides and bottom of the cooking basket with a nonstick cooking spray.

Place the pork cutlets in the cooking basket; sprinkle with cayenne pepper, salt, black pepper and garlic powder.

In a mixing dish, thoroughly combine the honey and Dijon mustard.

Cook the pork cutlets at 390 degrees F for 6 minutes. Flip halfway through, rub with the honey mixture and continue to cook for 6 minutes more. Serve immediately.

Per serving: 326 Calories; 12.7g Fat; 15.1g Carbs; 38.7g Protein; 13g Sugars

98. Fried Pork Loin Chops

(Ready in about 15 minutes | Servings 2)

Ingredients

1 egg
1/4 cup cornmeal
1/4 cup crackers, crushed
1/2 teaspoon garlic powder

1/2 teaspoon cayenne pepper
Salt and black pepper, to taste
2 boneless pork loin chops, about 1-inch thick, 6 ounces each

Directions

In a shallow mixing bowl, whisk the egg until pale and frothy.

In another bowl, mix the cornmeal, crushed crackers, garlic powder, cayenne pepper, salt and black pepper.

Dip each pork loin chop in the beaten egg. Then, roll them over the cornmeal mixture.

Spritz the bottom of the cooking basket with cooking oil. Add the breaded pork cutlets and cook at 395 degrees F for 6 minutes.

Flip and cook for 6 minutes on the other side. Serve warm.

Per serving: 379 Calories; 12g Fat; 19.1g Carbs; 45.5g Protein; 2.3g Sugars

99. Pork Loin with Roasted Peppers

(Ready in about 55 minutes | Servings 3)

Ingredients

3 red bell peppers
1 ½ pounds pork loin
1 garlic clove, halved
1 teaspoon lard, melted
1/2 teaspoon cayenne pepper

1/4 teaspoon cumin powder
1/4 teaspoon ground bay laurel
Kosher salt and ground black pepper, to taste

Directions

Roast the peppers in the preheated Air Fryer at 395 degrees F for 10 minutes, flipping them halfway through the cooking time.

Let them steam for 10 minutes; then, peel the skin and discard the stems and seeds. Slice the peppers into halves and add salt to taste.

Rub the pork with garlic; brush with melted lard and season with spices until well coated on all sides.

Place in the cooking basket and cook at 360 digress F for 25 minutes. Turn the meat over and cook an additional 20 minutes. Serve with roasted peppers. Bon appétit!

Per serving: 409 Calories; 20.1g Fat; 4.3g Carbs; 49g Protein; 2.4g Sugars

100. BBQ-Glazed Meatloaf Muffins

(Ready in about 45 minutes | Servings 3)

Ingredients

1 pound lean ground pork
1 small onion, chopped
2 cloves garlic, crushed
1/4 cup carrots, grated
1 serrano pepper, seeded and minced

1 teaspoon stone-ground mustard
1/4 cup crackers, crushed
1 egg, lightly beaten
Sea salt and ground black pepper, to taste
1/2 cup BBQ sauce

Directions

Mix all ingredients, except for the BBQ sauce, until everything is well incorporated.

Brush a muffin tin with vegetable oil. Use an ice cream scoop to spoon the meat mixture into the cups. Top each meatloaf cup with a spoonful of BBQ sauce.

Bake in the preheated Air Fryer at 395 degrees F for about 40 minutes. Transfer to a cooling rack.

Wait for a few minutes before unmolding and serving. Bon appétit!

Per serving: 269 Calories; 9.7g Fat; 9.1g Carbs; 36.6g Protein; 4.4g Sugars

101. Pork Tenderloin with Brussels Sprouts

(Ready in about 20 minutes | Servings 3)

Ingredients

1 pound Brussels sprouts, halved
1 ½ pounds tenderloin
1 teaspoon peanut oil
1 teaspoon garlic powder

1 tablespoon coriander, minced
1 teaspoon smoked paprika
Sea salt and ground black pepper, to taste

Directions

Toss the Brussels sprouts and pork with oil and spices until well coated.

Place in the Air Fryer cooking basket. Cook in the preheated Air Fryer at 370 degrees F for 15 minutes.

Taste and adjust seasonings. Eat warm.

Per serving: 381 Calories; 11.7g Fat; 14.1g Carbs; 56g Protein; 3.4g Sugars

102. Meatballs with Sweet and Sour Sauce

(Ready in about 20 minutes | Servings 3)

Ingredients

Meatballs:
1/2 pound ground pork
1/4 pound ground turkey
2 tablespoons scallions, minced
1/2 teaspoon garlic, minced
4 tablespoons tortilla chips, crushed
1 egg, beaten

4 tablespoons parmesan cheese, grated
Salt and red pepper, to taste
Sauce:
6 ounces jellied cranberry
2 ounces hot sauce
2 tablespoons molasses
1 tablespoon wine vinegar

Directions

In a mixing bowl, thoroughly combine all ingredients for the meatballs. Stir to combine well and roll the mixture into 8 equal meatballs.

Cook in the preheated Air Fryer at 400 degrees F for 7 minutes. Shake the basket and continue to cook for 7 minutes longer.

Meanwhile, whisk the sauce ingredients in a nonstick skillet over low heat; let it simmer, partially covered, for about 20 minutes. Fold in the prepared meatballs and serve immediately. Bon appétit!

Per serving: 486 Calories; 14.8g Fat; 54.1g Carbs; 33.6g Protein; 20.4g Sugars

103. Perfect Pork Wraps

(Ready in about 55 minutes | Servings 2)

Ingredients

1/2 pound pork loin
1 teaspoon butter, melted
Salt and black pepper, to season
1/2 teaspoon marjoram
1/2 teaspoon hot paprika
2 tortillas
Sauce:
2 tablespoons tahini

1 tablespoon sesame oil
2 tablespoons soy sauce
1 tablespoon lime juice
1 tablespoon white vinegar
1 teaspoon fresh ginger, peeled and grated
2 garlic cloves, pressed
1 teaspoon honey

Directions

Rub the pork with melted butter and season with salt, pepper, marjoram and hot paprika.

Place in the cooking basket and cook at 360 digress F for 25 minutes. Turn the meat over and cook an additional 20 minutes.

Place the roasted pork loin on a cutting board. Slice the roasted pork loin into strips using a sharp kitchen knife.

In the meantime, mix the sauce ingredients with a wire whisk.

Turn the temperature to 390 degrees F. Spoon the pork strips and sauce onto each tortilla; wrap them tightly.

Drizzle with a nonstick cooking spray and bake about 6 minutes. Serve warm.

Per serving: 558 Calories; 25.7g Fat; 44.1g Carbs; 34.3g Protein; 7.2g Sugars

104. Easy Munchy Pork Bites

(Ready in about 15 minutes + marinating time | Servings 2)

Ingredients

1 pound pork stew meat, cubed
2 garlic cloves, crushed
1/4 cup dark rum
1/4 cup soy sauce
1 tablespoon lemon juice

1 tablespoon white vinegar
1 tablespoon olive oil
1/2 teaspoon sea salt
1 teaspoon mixed peppercorns
1/2 cup corn flakes, crushed

Directions

Place all ingredients, except for the cornflakes, in a ceramic dish. Stir to combine, cover and transfer to your refrigerator. Let it marinate at least 3 hours in your refrigerator.

Discard the marinade and dredge the pork cubes in the crushed cornflakes, shaking off any residual coating.

Now, cook the pork in your Air Fryer at 400 degrees F for 12 minutes. Shake the basket halfway through the cooking time. Bon appétit!

Per serving: 612 Calories; 24.4g Fat; 35.1g Carbs; 54.3g Protein; 6.4g Sugars

105. Authentic Balkan-Style Cevapi

(Ready in about 55 minutes | Servings 3)

Ingredients

1/2 pound lean ground pork
1/2 pound ground chuck
2 cloves garlic, minced
2 tablespoons green onions, chopped
1 tablespoon parsley, finely chopped

1 tablespoon coriander, finely chopped
1/2 teaspoon smoked paprika
Sea salt and ground black pepper, to taste
2 ciabatta bread

Directions

Mix the ground meat with the garlic, green onion, herbs and spices.

Roll the mixture into small sausages, about 3 inches long.

Spritz a cooking basket with a nonstick cooking spray. Cook cevapi at 380 degrees F for 10 minutes, shaking the basket periodically to ensure even cooking.

Serve in ciabatta bread with some extra onions, mustard or ketchup. Bon appétit!

Per serving: 278 Calories; 7.4g Fat; 23.1g Carbs; 27.5g Protein; 2.6g Sugars

106. Rustic Ground Pork-Stuffed Peppers

(Ready in about 20 minutes | Servings 4)

Ingredients

1 pound lean ground pork
1 small-sized shallot, chopped
2 cloves garlic, minced
2 tablespoons ketchup
Sea salt and ground black pepper, to season

1/2 teaspoon cayenne pepper
4 bell peppers, tops and cores removed
1 teaspoon olive oil
1/2 cup Colby cheese, shredded

Directions

Preheat a nonstick skillet over medium-high flame. Then, cook the pork and shallot for 3 minutes or until the meat is no longer pink.

Add in the garlic and continue to cook until fragrant for 1 minute or so. Stir the ketchup into the skillet; season the meat mixture with salt, black pepper and cayenne pepper.

Place the bell peppers cut side-up in the Air Fryer cooking basket and drizzle with oil. Spoon the meat mixture into each pepper.

Cook in your Air Fryer at 360 degrees F for 12 minutes. Top with cheese and continue to bake for 4 minutes longer. Enjoy!

Per serving: 258 Calories; 11.4g Fat; 9.3g Carbs; 25g Protein; 5g Sugars

107. Sunday Meatball Sliders

(Ready in about 15 minutes | Servings 2)

Ingredients

1/2 pound lean ground pork
1 shallot, chopped
1 teaspoon garlic, pressed
1 tablespoon soy sauce
1/2 cup quick-cooking oats
1 tablespoon Italian parsley, minced

1/2 teaspoon fresh ginger, ground
1/4 teaspoon ground bay laurel
1/2 teaspoon red pepper flakes, crushed
Sea salt and ground black pepper, to taste
4 dinner rolls

Directions

In a mixing bowl, thoroughly combine the ground pork, shallot, garlic, soy sauce, oats, parsley, ginger and spices; stir until everything is well incorporated.

Shape the mixture into 4 meatballs.

Add the meatballs to the cooking basket and cook them at 360 degrees for 10 minutes. Check the meatballs halfway through the cooking time.

Place one meatball on top of the bottom half of one roll. Top with the other half of the roll and serve immediately. Bon appétit!

Per serving: 413 Calories; 11.1g Fat; 48.3g Carbs; 33.5g Protein; 6.3g Sugars

108. Country-Style Pork Goulash

(Ready in about 45 minutes | Servings 2)

Ingredients

1/2 pound pork stew meat, cut into bite-sized chunks
2 pork good quality sausages, sliced
1 small onion, sliced into rings
2 Italian peppers, sliced
1 Serrano pepper, sliced
2 garlic cloves, minced
1 tablespoon soy sauce
1/2 teaspoon ground cumin
1 bay leaf
Salt and black pepper, to taste
1 cup beef stock

Directions

Place the pork and sausage in the Air Fryer cooking basket. Cook the meat at 380 degrees F for 15 minutes, shaking the basket once or twice; place in a heavy-bottomed pot.

Now, add the onion and peppers to the cooking basket; cook your vegetables at 400 degrees F for 10 minutes and transfer to the pot with the pork and sausage.

Add in the remaining ingredients and cook, partially covered, for 15 to 20 minutes until everything is cooked through.

Spoon into individual bowls and serve. Enjoy!

Per serving: 474 Calories; 27.1g Fat; 10g Carbs; 44.5g Protein; 5.7g Sugars

109. Korean Pork Bulgogi Bowl

(Ready in about 20 minutes | Servings 2)

Ingredients

2 pork loin chops
1 teaspoon stone-ground mustard
1 teaspoon cayenne pepper
Kosher salt and ground black pepper, to taste
2 stalks green onion
1/2 teaspoon fresh ginger, grated
1 garlic clove, pressed
1 tablespoon rice wine
2 tablespoons gochujang chili paste
1 teaspoon sesame oil
1 tablespoon sesame seeds, lightly toasted

Directions

Toss the pork loin chops with the mustard, cayenne pepper, salt and black pepper.

Cook in the preheated Air Fryer at 400 degrees F for 10 minutes. Check the pork chops halfway through the cooking time.

Add the green onions to the cooking basket and continue to cook for a further 5 minutes.

In the meantime, whisk the fresh ginger, garlic, wine, gochujang chili paste and sesame oil. Simmer the sauce for about 5 minutes until thoroughly warmed.

Slice the pork loin chops into bite-sized strips and top with green onions and sauce. Garnish with sesame seeds. Enjoy!

Per serving: 317 Calories; 13.1g Fat; 8.7g Carbs; 42.1g Protein; 2.4g Sugars

110. Mexican Pork Quesadillas

(Ready in about 25 minutes | Servings 2)

Ingredients

1/2 pound pork tenderloin, cut into strips
1 teaspoon peanut oil
1/2 teaspoon onion powder
1/2 teaspoon garlic powder
1/2 teaspoon red pepper flakes
1/4 teaspoon dried basil
1/2 teaspoon Mexican oregano
1/2 teaspoon dried marjoram
Sea salt and ground black pepper, to taste
2 flour tortillas
Pico de Gallo:
1 tomato, diced
3 tablespoons onion, chopped
3 tablespoons cilantro, chopped
3 tablespoons lime juice

Directions

Toss the pork tenderloin strips with peanut oil and spices.

Cook in the preheated Air Fryer at 370 degrees F for 15 minutes, shaking the cooking basket halfway through the cooking time.

Meanwhile, make the Pico de Gallo by whisking the ingredients or it.

Assemble your tortillas with the meat mixture and Pico de Gallo; wrap them tightly. Turn the temperature to 390 degrees F.

Drizzle the tortillas with a nonstick cooking spray and bake about 6 minutes. Eat warm.

Per serving: 517 Calories; 11.8g Fat; 67g Carbs; 34.5g Protein; 7.8g Sugars

111. Pork and Mushroom Kabobs

(Ready in about 20 minutes | Servings 2)

Ingredients

1 pound pork butt, cut into bite-sized cubes
8 button mushrooms
1 red bell pepper, sliced
1 green bell pepper, sliced
2 tablespoons soy sauce
2 tablespoons lime juice
Salt and black pepper, to taste

Directions

Toss all ingredients in a bowl until well coated.

Thread the pork cubes, mushrooms and peppers onto skewers.

Cook in the preheated Air Fryer at 395 degrees F for 12 minutes, flipping halfway through the cooking time. Bon appétit!

Per serving: 385 Calories; 16.2g Fat; 11.9g Carbs; 47.5g Protein; 7.2g Sugars

112. Warm Pork Salad

(Ready in about 20 minutes | Servings 3)

Ingredients

1 pound pork shoulder, cut into strips
1/4 teaspoon fresh ginger, minced
1 teaspoon garlic, pressed
1 tablespoon olive oil
1 tablespoon honey
2 teaspoons fresh cilantro, chopped
1 tablespoon Worcestershire sauce
1 medium-sized cucumber, sliced
1 cup arugula
1 cup baby spinach
1 cup Romaine lettuce
1 tomato, diced
1 shallot, sliced

Directions

Spritz the Air Fryer cooking basket with a nonstick spray. Place the pork in the Air Fryer cooking basket.

Cook at 400 degrees F for 13 minutes, shaking the basket halfway through the cooking time.

Transfer the meat to a serving bowl and toss with the remaining ingredients.

Bon appétit!

Per serving: 315 Calories; 13.3g Fat; 15.5g Carbs; 30.5g Protein; 10.2g Sugars

113. Delicious Chifa Chicharonnes

(Ready in about 1 hour 10 minutes | Servings 3)

Ingredients

1/2 pound pork belly
2 cloves garlic, chopped
1 rosemary sprig, crushed
1 thyme sprig, crushed
1 teaspoon coriander
3 tablespoons kecap manis
Salt and red pepper, to taste

Directions

Put the pork belly, rind side up, in the cooking basket; add in the garlic, rosemary, thyme and coriander.

Cook in the preheated Air Fryer at 350 degrees F for 20 minutes; turn it over and cook an additional 20 minutes.

Turn the temperature to 400 degrees F, rub the pork belly with the kecap manis and sprinkle with salt and red pepper. Continue to cook for 15 to 20 minutes more.

Let it rest on a wire rack for 10 minutes before slicing and serving. Enjoy!

Per serving: 415 Calories; 40g Fat; 5.3g Carbs; 7.3g Protein; 3.6g Sugars

114. Classic Fried Bacon

(Ready in about 10 minutes | Servings 4)

Ingredients

1/2 pound bacon slices
1/2 cup tomato ketchup
1/4 teaspoon cayenne pepper
1/4 teaspoon dried marjoram
1 teaspoon Sriracha sauce

Directions

Place the bacon slices in the cooking basket.

Cook the bacon slices at 400 degrees F for about 8 minutes.

Meanwhile, make the sauce by mixing the remaining ingredients. Serve the warm bacon with the sauce on the side. Bon appétit!

Per serving: 235 Calories; 23g Fat; 1.3g Carbs; 7.3g Protein; 1.1g Sugars

115. Chinese Five-Spice Pork Ribs

(Ready in about 35 minutes | Servings 3)

Ingredients

2 ½ pounds country-style pork ribs
1 teaspoon mustard powder
1 teaspoon cumin powder
1 teaspoon shallot powder
1 tablespoon Five-spice powder
Coarse sea salt and ground black pepper
1 teaspoon sesame oil
2 tablespoons soy sauce

Directions

Toss the country-style pork ribs with spices and sesame oil and transfer them to the Air Fryer cooking basket.

Cook at 360 degrees F for 20 minutes; flip them over and continue to cook an additional 14 to 15 minutes.

Drizzle with soy sauce just before serving. Bon appétit!

Per serving: 591 Calories; 25g Fat; 6.3g Carbs; 73g Protein; 3.1g Sugars

116. Honey and Herb Roasted Pork Tenderloin

(Ready in about 20 minutes + marinating time | Servings 3)

Ingredients

1 garlic clove, pressed
2 tablespoons honey
2 tablespoons Worcestershire sauce
2 tablespoons tequila
2 tablespoons yellow mustard
1 pound pork tenderloin, sliced into 3 pieces
1 teaspoon rosemary
1 teaspoon basil
1/2 teaspoon oregano
1/2 teaspoon parsley flakes
Salt and black pepper, to taste

Directions

In a glass bowl, thoroughly combine the garlic, honey, Worcestershire sauce, tequila and mustard.

Add in the pork tenderloin pieces, cover and marinate in your refrigerator for about 1 hour.

Transfer the pork tenderloin to the cooking basket, discarding the marinade. Sprinkle the pork tenderloin with herbs, salt and black pepper.

Cook in your Air Fryer at 370 degrees F for 15 minutes, checking periodically and basting with the reserved marinade. Serve warm.

Per serving: 231 Calories; 3.6g Fat; 15.3g Carbs; 32.2g Protein; 13.4g Sugars

117. Pork Loin with Greek-Style Sauce

(Ready in about 55 minutes | Servings 2)

Ingredients

1/2 pound boneless pork loin, well-trimmed
1 garlic clove, halved
1 teaspoon grainy mustard
Kosher salt and ground black pepper, to taste
1/2 teaspoon lard, melted
1/4 cup mayonnaise
1/4 cup Greek-style yogurt
1/4 teaspoon dried dill
1/2 teaspoon garlic, pressed

Directions

Rub the pork with garlic halves on all sides; then, rub the pork with mustard. Season it with salt and pepper and drizzle with melted lard.

Transfer to the Air Fryer cooking basket and cook at 360 degrees F for 45 minutes, turning over halfway through the cooking time.

In the meantime, make the sauce by whisking all ingredients.

Let it rest for 8 to 10 minutes before carving and serving. Serve the warm pork loin with the sauce on the side.

Per serving: 361 Calories; 26.4g Fat; 3.3g Carbs; 26.3g Protein; 1.4g Sugars

118. Pork Cutlets with Pearl Onions

(Ready in about 20 minutes | Servings 2)

Ingredients

2 pork cutlets
1 teaspoon onion powder
1/2 teaspoon cayenne pepper
Sea salt and black pepper, to taste
1/4 cup flour
1/4 cup Pecorino Romano cheese, grated
1 cup pearl onions

Directions

Toss the pork cutlets with the onion powder, cayenne pepper, salt, black pepper, flour and cheese.

Transfer the pork cutlets to the lightly oiled cooking basket. Scatter pearl onions around the pork.

Cook in the preheated Air Fryer at 360 degrees for 15 minutes, turning over halfway through the cooking time.

Bon appétit!

Per serving: 292 Calories; 6.4g Fat; 20.3g Carbs; 36.4g Protein; 3.7g Sugars

119. German-Style Pork with Sauerkraut

(Ready in about 15 minutes | Servings 3)

Ingredients

1 pound pork butt
2 teaspoons olive oil
1 teaspoon dried thyme
Salt and black pepper, to taste
1 tart apple, thinly sliced
1 onion, thinly sliced
2 garlic cloves, minced
1 bay leaf
1/2 teaspoon cayenne pepper
1 pound sauerkraut, drained

Directions

Toss the pork butt with 1 teaspoon of olive oil, thyme, salt and black pepper. Place the pork in the Air Fryer cooking basket.

Cook the pork at 400 degrees F for 7 minutes. Top with apple slices and cook for a further 7 minutes.

Meanwhile, heat the olive oil in a large saucepan over medium-high heat. Now, sauté the onion for 2 to 3 minutes or until just tender and translucent.

Add in the garlic, bay leaf, cayenne pepper and sauerkraut and continue to cook for 10 minutes more or until cooked through.

Slice the pork into 3 portions; top the warm sauerkraut with the pork. Bon appétit!

Per serving: 298 Calories; 12g Fat; 17.5g Carbs; 30.2g Protein; 10.2g Sugars

120. Pineapple Pork Carnitas

(Ready in about 55 minutes | Servings 2)

Ingredients

1/2 pound pork loin
1/2 teaspoon paprika
Kosher salt and ground black pepper, to taste
4 ounces fresh pineapple, crushed
1/4 cup water
1/4 cup tomato paste
1 tablespoon soy sauce
1 teaspoon brown mustard
1 garlic clove, minced
1 shallot, minced
1 green chili pepper, minced
4 (6-inch) corn tortillas, warmed

Directions

Pat the pork loin dry and season it with paprika, salt and black pepper. Then, cook the pork in your Air Fryer at 360 degrees F for 20 minutes; turn it over and cook an additional 25 minutes.

Then, preheat a sauté pan over a moderately high heat. Combine the pineapple, water, tomato paste, soy sauce, mustard, garlic, shallot and green chili, bringing to a rolling boil.

Turn the heat to simmer; continue to cook until the sauce has reduced by half, about 15 minutes.

Let the pork rest for 10 minutes; then, shred the pork with two forks. Spoon the sauce over the pork and serve in corn tortillas. Enjoy!

Per serving: 356 Calories; 7.4g Fat; 43.5g Carbs; 31.1g Protein; 16.5g Sugars

121. Tacos Al Pastor

(Ready in about 50 minutes | Servings 3)

Ingredients

Pork:
1 pound pork loin
1 tablespoon honey
Sea salt and ground black pepper, to taste
1/2 teaspoon cayenne pepper
1/2 teaspoon garlic powder
1/2 teaspoon thyme
1 teaspoon olive oil

Tacos:
1 tablespoon annatto seeds
1 tablespoon olive oil
1/2 teaspoon coriander seeds
1 clove garlic, crushed
1 tablespoon apple cider vinegar
1 dried guajillo chili, deseeded and crushed
3 corn tortillas

Directions

Pat dry pork loin; toss the pork with the remaining ingredients until well coated on all sides.

Cook in the preheated Air Fryer at 360 degrees F for 45 minutes, turning over halfway through the cooking time.

In the meantime, make the achiote paste by mixing the annatto seeds, olive oil, coriander seeds, garlic, apple cider vinegar and dried guajillo chili in your blender.

Slice the pork into bite-sized pieces. Spoon the pork and achiote onto warmed tortillas. Enjoy!

Per serving: 356 Calories; 14.4g Fat; 19.6g Carbs; 36.3g Protein; 6.8g Sugars

122. Italian Nonna's Polpette

(Ready in about 15 minutes | Servings 3)

Ingredients

1 teaspoon olive oil
2 tablespoons green onions, chopped
1/2 teaspoon garlic, pressed
1/2 pound sweet Italian pork sausage, crumbled
1 tablespoon parsley, chopped

1/2 teaspoon cayenne pepper
Sea salt and ground black pepper, to taste
1 egg
2 tablespoons milk
1 crustless bread slice

Directions

Mix the olive oil, green onions, garlic, sausage, parsley, cayenne pepper, salt and black pepper in a bowl.

Whisk the egg and milk until pale and frothy. Soak the bread in the milk mixture. Add the soaked bread to the sausage mixture. Mix again to combine well.

Shape the mixture into 8 meatballs.

Add the meatballs to the cooking basket and cook them at 360 degrees for 5 minutes. Then, turn them and cook the other side for 5 minutes more. You can serve these meatballs over spaghetti. Bon appétit!

Per serving: 356 Calories; 14.4g Fat; 19.6g Carbs; 36.3g Protein; 6.8g Sugars

123. Pork Sausage with Baby Potatoes

(Ready in about 35 minutes | Servings 3)

Ingredients

1 pound pork sausage, uncooked
1 pound baby potatoes
1/4 teaspoon paprika

1/2 teaspoon dried rosemary leaves, crushed
Himalayan salt and black pepper, to taste

Direction

Put the sausage into the Air Fryer cooking basket.

Cook in the preheated Air Fryer at 380 degrees F for 15 minutes; reserve.

Season the baby potatoes with paprika, rosemary, salt and black pepper. Add the baby potatoes to the cooking basket.

Cook the potatoes at 400 degrees F for 15 minutes, shaking the basket once or twice. Serve warm sausages with baby potatoes and enjoy!

Per serving: 640 Calories; 47.5g Fat; 27.4g Carbs; 24.3g Protein; 1.1g Sugars

124. Caprese Pork Chops

(Ready in about 15 minutes + marinating time | Servings 3)

Ingredients

1 pound center-cut pork chops, boneless
1/4 cup balsamic vinegar
1 tablespoon honey
1 tablespoon whole-grain mustard
1/2 teaspoon olive oil
1/2 teaspoon smoked paprika
Salt and black pepper, to taste

1/2 teaspoon shallot powder
1/2 teaspoon porcini powder
1/2 teaspoon granulated garlic
3 slices fresh mozzarella
3 thick slices tomatoes
2 tablespoons fresh basil leaves, chopped

Directions

Place the pork chops, balsamic vinegar, honey, mustard, olive oil and spices in a bowl. Cover and let it marinate in your refrigerator for 1 hour.

Cook in the preheated Air Fryer at 400 degrees F for 7 minutes. Top with cheese and continue to cook for 5 minutes more.

Top with sliced tomato and basil and serve immediately.

Per serving: 345 Calories; 12.9g Fat; 14.7g Carbs; 40.3g Protein; 10.8g Sugars

125. Keto Crispy Pork Chops

(Ready in about 20 minutes | Servings 3)

Ingredients

3 center-cut pork chops, boneless
1/2 teaspoon paprika
Sea salt and ground black pepper, to taste
1/4 cup Romano cheese, grated
1/4 cup crushed pork rinds

1/2 teaspoon garlic powder
1/2 teaspoon mustard seeds
1/2 teaspoon dried marjoram
1 egg, beaten
1 tablespoon buttermilk
1 teaspoon peanut oil

Directions

Pat the pork chops dry with kitchen towels. Season them with paprika, salt and black pepper.

Add the Romano cheese, crushed pork rinds, garlic powder, mustard seeds and marjoram to a rimmed plate.

Beat the egg and buttermilk in another plate. Now, dip the pork chops in the egg, then in the cheese/pork rind mixture.

Drizzle the pork with peanut oil. Cook in the preheated Air Fryer at 400 degrees F for 12 minutes, flipping pork chops halfway through the cooking time.

Serve with keto-friendly sides such as cauliflower rice. Bon appétit!

Per serving: 467 Calories; 26.8g Fat; 2.7g Carbs; 50.3g Protein; 1.3g Sugars

126. The Best BBQ Ribs Ever

(Ready in about 40 minutes | Servings 2)

Ingredients

1/2 pound ribs
Sea salt and black pepper, to taste
1/2 teaspoon red chili flakes
1 tablespoon agave syrup
1/2 teaspoon garlic powder
1/2 cup tomato paste
1 teaspoon brown mustard
1 tablespoon balsamic vinegar
1 tablespoon Worcestershire sauce

Directions

Place the pork ribs, salt, black pepper and red pepper flakes in a Ziplock bag; shake until the ribs are coated on all sides.

Roast in the preheated Air Fryer at 350 degrees F for 35 minutes.

In a saucepan over medium heat, heat all sauce ingredients, bringing to a boil. Turn the heat to a simmer until the sauce has reduced by half.

Spoon the sauce over the ribs and serve warm. Bon appétit!

Per serving: 492 Calories; 33.5g Fat; 26.8g Carbs; 22.5g Protein; 19.7g Sugars

127. Easy Pork Pot Stickers

(Ready in about 10 minutes | Servings 2)

Ingredients

1/2 pound lean ground pork
1/2 teaspoon fresh ginger, freshly grated
1 teaspoon chili garlic sauce
1 tablespoon soy sauce
1 tablespoon rice wine
1/4 teaspoon Szechuan pepper
2 stalks scallions, chopped
1 tablespoon sesame oil
8 (3-inch) round wonton wrappers

Directions

Cook the ground pork in a preheated skillet until no longer pink, crumbling with a fork. Stir in the other ingredients, except for the wonton wrappers; stir to combine well.

Place the wonton wrappers on a clean work surface. Divide the pork filling between the wrappers. Wet the edge of each wrapper with water, fold the top half over the bottom half and pinch the border to seal.

Place the pot stickers in the cooking basket and brush them with a little bit of olive oil. Cook the pot sticker at 400 degrees F for 8 minutes. Serve immediately.

Per serving: 352 Calories; 13.5g Fat; 27.8g Carbs; 31.2g Protein; 2.2g Sugars

128. Chinese Char Siu Pork

(Ready in about 25 minutes + marinating time | Servings 3)

Ingredients

1 pound pork shoulder, cut into long strips
1/2 teaspoon Chinese five-spice powder
1/4 teaspoon Szechuan pepper
1 tablespoon hoisin sauce
2 tablespoons hot water
1 teaspoon sesame oil
1 tablespoon Shaoxing wine
1 tablespoon molasses

Directions

Place all ingredients in a ceramic dish and let it marinate for 2 hours in the refrigerator.

Cook in the preheated Air Fryer at 390 degrees F for 20 minutes, shaking the basket halfway through the cooking time.

Heat the reserved marinade in a wok for about 15 minutes or until the sauce has thickened. Spoon the sauce over the warm pork shoulder and serve with rice if desired. Enjoy!

Per serving: 246 Calories; 10.3g Fat; 7.8g Carbs; 28.6g Protein; 6.7g Sugars

129. Texas Pulled Pork

(Ready in about 1 hour | Servings 3)

Ingredients

1 pound pork shoulder roast
1 teaspoon butter, softened
1 teaspoon Italian seasoning mix
1/2 cup barbecue sauce
1/4 cup apple juice
1 teaspoon garlic paste
2 tablespoons soy sauce
2 hamburger buns, split

Directions

Brush the pork shoulder with butter and sprinkle with Italian seasoning mix on all sides.

Cook in the preheated Air Fryer at 360 degrees F for 1 hour, shaking the basket once or twice.

Meanwhile, warm the barbecue sauce, apple juice, garlic paste and soy sauce in a small saucepan.

Remove the pork shoulder from the basket and shred the meat with two forks. Spoon the sauce over the pork and stir to combine well.

Spoon the pork into the toasted buns and eat warm. Bon appétit!

Per serving: 415 Calories; 10.7g Fat; 39.3g Carbs; 37.9g Protein; 21.7g Sugars

130. Herb-Crusted Pork Roast

(Ready in about 1 hour | Servings 2)

Ingredients

1/2 pound pork loin
Salt and black pepper, to taste
1/2 teaspoon onion powder
1/2 teaspoon parsley flakes
1/2 teaspoon oregano
1/2 teaspoon thyme
1/2 teaspoon grated lemon peel
1 teaspoon garlic, minced
1 teaspoon butter, softened

Directions

Pat the pork loin dry with kitchen towels. Season it with salt and black pepper.

In a bowl, mix the remaining ingredients until well combined.

Coat the pork with the herb rub, pressing to adhere well.

Cook in the preheated Air Fryer at 360 degrees F for 30 minutes; turn it over and cook on the other side for 25 minutes more. Bon appétit!

Per serving: 220 Calories; 11.4g Fat; 3.3g Carbs; 24.9g Protein; 1.7g Sugars

131. Perfect Meatball Hoagies

(Ready in about 15 minutes | Servings 2)

Ingredients

1/2 pound lean ground pork
1 teaspoon fresh garlic, minced
2 tablespoons fresh scallions, chopped
1 teaspoon dried basil
1/2 teaspoon dried oregano
1/2 teaspoon dried parsley flakes
Sea salt and ground black pepper, to taste
1 tablespoon soy sauce
1 egg, beaten
1/4 cup Pecorino Romano cheese, grated
1/2 cup quick-cooking oats
2 hoagie rolls
1 medium-sized tomato, sliced
2 pickled cherry peppers

Directions

In a mixing bowl, thoroughly combine the ground pork, garlic, scallions, basil, oregano, parsley, salt, black pepper, soy sauce, eggs, cheese and quick-cooking oats. Mix until well incorporated.

Shape the mixture into 6 meatballs.

Add the meatballs to the cooking basket and cook them at 360 degrees for 10 minutes. Turn the meatballs halfway through the cooking time.

Cut the hoagie rolls lengthwise almost entirely through. Layer the meatballs onto the bottom of the roll.

Top with the tomato and peppers. Close the rolls, cut in half and serve immediately. Bon appétit!

Per serving: 433 Calories; 16.4g Fat; 33g Carbs; 39.7g Protein; 7g Sugars

132. Balsamic Pork Chops with Asparagus

(Ready in about 15 minutes | Servings 2)

Ingredients

2 pork loin chops
1 pound asparagus spears, cleaned and trimmed
1 teaspoon sesame oil
2 tablespoons balsamic vinegar
1 teaspoon yellow mustard
1/2 teaspoon garlic, minced
1/2 teaspoon smoked pepper
1/4 teaspoon dried dill
Salt and black pepper, to taste

Directions

Toss the pork loin chops and asparagus with the other ingredients until well coated on all sides.

Place the pork in the Air Fryer cooking basket and cook at 400 degrees F for 7 minutes; turn them over, top with the asparagus and continue to cook for a further 5 minutes.

Serve warm with mayo, sriracha sauce, or sour cream if desired. Bon appétit!

Per serving: 308 Calories; 9.4g Fat; 11.9g Carbs; 44.3g Protein; 6.6g Sugars

133. Bacon with Onions Rings and Remoulade Sauce

(Ready in about 15 minutes | Servings 2)

Ingredients

2 thick bacon slices
8 ounces onion rings, frozen
1 teaspoon yellow mustard
2 tablespoons mayonnaise

1/4 teaspoon paprika
1 teaspoon hot sauce
Salt and black pepper, to taste

Directions

Place the slices of bacon and onion rings in the Air Fryer cooking basket.

Cook the bacon and onion rings at 400 degrees F for 4 minutes; shake the basket and cook for a further 4 minutes or until cooked through.

Meanwhile, make the Remoulade sauce by whisking the remaining ingredients. Arrange the bacon and onion rings on plates and garnish with Remoulade sauce. Bon appétit!

Per serving: 371 Calories; 32.7g Fat; 11.2g Carbs; 8.5g Protein; 5.3g Sugars

134. Authentic Greek Pork Gyro

(Ready in about 20 minutes | Servings 2)

Ingredients

3/4 pound pork butt
Sea salt and ground black pepper, to taste
1/2 teaspoon red pepper flakes, crushed
1 teaspoon ground coriander
1/2 teaspoon mustard seeds
1/2 teaspoon granulated garlic
1/2 teaspoon oregano
1/2 teaspoon basil
1 teaspoon olive oil

2 pita bread, warmed
4 lettuce leaves
1 small tomato, diced
2 tablespoons red onion, chopped
Tzatziki:
1/2 cup Greek-style yogurt
1 tablespoon cucumber, minced and drained
1 teaspoon fresh lemon juice
1 teaspoon fresh dill, minced
1/4 teaspoon fresh garlic, pressed

Directions

Toss the pork butt with salt, black pepper, red pepper flakes, coriander, mustard seeds, granulated garlic, oregano, basil and olive oil.

Transfer the pork butt to the Air Fryer cooking basket.

Cook the pork at 400 degrees F for 7 minutes. Turn the pork over and cook for a further 7 minutes. Shred the meat with two forks.

In the meantime, make the Tzatziki sauce by whisking all ingredients until everything is well combined.

Spoon the pork onto each pita bread; top with Tzatziki, lettuce, tomato and red onion. Serve immediately and enjoy!

Per serving: 493 Calories; 26.2g Fat; 26.9g Carbs; 36.2g Protein; 7.5g Sugars

135. Autumn Boston Butt with Acorn Squash

(Ready in about 25 minutes + marinating time | Servings 3)

Ingredients

1 pound Boston butt
1 garlic clove, pressed
1/4 cup rice wine
1 teaspoon molasses
1 tablespoon Hoisin sauce

1/2 teaspoon red pepper flakes
1 teaspoon Sichuan pepper
1/2 teaspoon Himalayan salt
1/2 pound acorn squash, cut into
1/2-inch cubes

Directions

Place the Boston butt, garlic, rice wine, molasses, Hoisin sauce, red pepper flakes, Sichuan pepper and Himalayan salt in a ceramic dish.

Cover and allow it to marinate for 2 hours in your refrigerator.

Cook in the preheated Air Fryer at 400 degrees F for 10 minutes. Turn the Boston butt over and baste with the reserved marinade.

Stir the squash cubes into the cooking basket and cook for 10 minutes on the other side. Taste, adjust seasonings and serve immediately.

Per serving: 396 Calories; 13.3g Fat; 20.9g Carbs; 44.2g Protein; 6.3g Sugars

136. Rustic Pizza with Ground Pork

(Ready in about 30 minutes | Servings 4)

Ingredients

1 (10-count) can refrigerator biscuits
4 tablespoons tomato paste
1 tablespoon tomato ketchup
2 teaspoons brown mustard

1/2 cup ground pork
1/2 cup ground beef sausage
1 red onion, thinly sliced
1/2 cup mozzarella cheese, shredded

Directions

Spritz the sides and bottom of a baking pan with a nonstick cooking spray.

Press five biscuits into the pan. Brush the top of biscuit with 2 tablespoons of tomato paste.

Add 1/2 tablespoon of ketchup, 1 teaspoon of mustard, 1/4 cup of ground pork, 1/4 cup of beef sausage. Top with 1/2 of the red onion slices.

Bake in the preheated Air Fryer at 360 degrees F for 10 minutes. Top with 1/4 cup of mozzarella cheese and bake another 5 minutes.

Repeat the process with the second pizza. Slice the pizza into halves, serve and enjoy!

Per serving: 529 Calories; 9.6g Fat; 65.5g Carbs; 37.9g Protein; 0.9g Sugars

137. Pork Koftas with Yoghurt Sauce

(Ready in about 25 minutes | Servings 4)

Ingredients

2 teaspoons olive oil
1/2 pound ground pork
1/2 pound ground beef
1 egg, whisked
Sea salt and ground black pepper, to taste
1 teaspoon paprika
2 garlic cloves, minced
1 teaspoon dried marjoram
1 teaspoon mustard seeds

1/2 teaspoon celery seeds
Yogurt Sauce:
2 tablespoons olive oil
2 tablespoons fresh lemon juice
Sea salt, to taste
1/4 teaspoon red pepper flakes, crushed
1/2 cup full-fat yogurt
1 teaspoon dried dill weed

Directions

Spritz the sides and bottom of the cooking basket with 2 teaspoons of olive oil.

In a mixing dish, thoroughly combine the ground pork, beef, egg, salt, black pepper, paprika, garlic, marjoram, mustard seeds, and celery seeds.

Form the mixture into kebabs and transfer them to the greased cooking basket. Cook at 365 degrees F for 11 to 12 minutes, turning them over once or twice.

In the meantime, mix all the sauce ingredients and place in the refrigerator until ready to serve. Serve the pork koftas with the yogurt sauce on the side. Enjoy!

Per serving: 407 Calories; 28.5g Fat; 3.4g Carbs; 32.9g Protein; 1.3g Sugars

138. Spicy Bacon-Wrapped Tater Tots

(Ready in about 25 minutes | Servings 5)

Ingredients

10 thin slices of bacon
10 tater tots, frozen
1 teaspoon cayenne pepper

Sauce:
1/4 cup mayo
4 tablespoons ketchup
1 teaspoon rice vinegar
1 teaspoon chili powder

Directions

Lay the slices of bacon on your working surface. Place a tater tot on one end of each slice; sprinkle with cayenne pepper and roll them over.

Cook in the preheated Air Fryer at 390 degrees F for 15 to 16 minutes.

Whisk all ingredients for the sauce in a mixing bowl and store in your refrigerator, covered, until ready to serve.

Serve Bacon-Wrapped Tater Tots with the sauce on the side. Enjoy!

Per serving: 297 Calories; 26.1g Fat; 9.3g Carbs; 7.1g Protein; 3.2g Sugars

139. Pork Cutlets with a Twist

(Ready in about 1 hour 20 minutes | Servings 2)

Ingredients

1 cup water
1 cup red wine
1 tablespoon sea salt
2 pork cutlets
1/2 cup all-purpose flour
1 teaspoon shallot powder
1/2 teaspoon porcini powder

Sea salt and ground black pepper, to taste
1 egg
1/4 cup yogurt
1 teaspoon brown mustard
1 cup tortilla chips, crushed

Directions

In a large ceramic dish, combine the water, wine and salt. Add the pork cutlets and put for 1 hour in the refrigerator.

In a shallow bowl, mix the flour, shallot powder, porcini powder, salt, and ground pepper. In another bowl, whisk the eggs with yogurt and mustard.

In a third bowl, place the crushed tortilla chips.

Dip the pork cutlets in the flour mixture and toss evenly; then, in the egg mixture. Finally, roll them over the crushed tortilla chips.

Spritz the bottom of the cooking basket with cooking oil. Add the breaded pork cutlets and cook at 395 degrees F and for 10 minutes.

Flip and cook for 5 minutes more on the other side. Serve warm.

Per serving: 579 Calories; 19.4g Fat; 50g Carbs; 49.6g Protein; 2.2g Sugars

140. Cheesy Creamy Pork Casserole

(Ready in about 25 minutes | Servings 4)

Ingredients

2 tablespoons olive oil
2 pounds pork tenderloin, cut into serving-size pieces
1 teaspoon coarse sea salt
1/2 teaspoon freshly ground pepper

1/4 teaspoon chili powder
1 teaspoon dried marjoram
1 tablespoon mustard
1 cup Ricotta cheese
1 ½ cups chicken broth

Directions

Start by preheating your Air Fryer to 350 degrees F.

Heat the olive oil in a pan over medium-high heat. Once hot, cook the pork for 6 to 7 minutes, flipping it to ensure even cooking.

Arrange the pork in a lightly greased casserole dish. Season with salt, black pepper, chili powder, and marjoram.

In a mixing dish, thoroughly combine the mustard, cheese, and chicken broth. Pour the mixture over the pork chops in the casserole dish.

Bake for another 15 minutes or until bubbly and heated through. Bon appétit!

Per serving: 433 Calories; 20.4g Fat; 2.6g Carbs; 56.5g Protein; 0.3g Sugars

141. Herbed Pork Loin with Carrot Chips

(Ready in about 1 hour 15 minutes | Servings 4)

Ingredients

1 tablespoon peanut oil
1 ½ pounds pork loin, cut into 4 pieces
Coarse sea salt and ground black pepper, to taste
1/2 teaspoon onion powder
1 teaspoon garlic powder

1/2 teaspoon cayenne pepper
1/2 teaspoon dried rosemary
1/2 teaspoon dried basil
1/2 teaspoon dried oregano
1 pound carrots, cut into matchsticks
1 tablespoon coconut oil, melted

Directions

Drizzle 1 tablespoon of peanut oil all over the pork loin. Season with salt, black pepper, onion powder, garlic powder, cayenne pepper, rosemary, basil, and oregano.

Cook in the preheated Air Fryer at 360 degrees F for 55 minutes; make sure to turn the pork over every 15 minutes to ensure even cooking.

Test for doneness with a meat thermometer.

Toss the carrots with melted coconut oil; season to taste and cook in the preheated Air Fryer at 380 degrees F for 15 minutes.

Serve the warm pork loin with the carrots on the side. Enjoy!

Per serving: 461 Calories; 25.8g Fat; 10.8g Carbs; 44g Protein; 5.3g Sugars

142. Easy Pork & Parmesan Meatballs

(Ready in about 15 minutes | Servings 3)

Ingredients

1 pound ground pork
2 tablespoons tamari sauce
1 teaspoon garlic, minced
2 tablespoons spring onions, finely chopped

1 tablespoon brown sugar
1 tablespoon olive oil
1/2 cup breadcrumbs
2 tablespoons parmesan cheese, preferably freshly grated

Directions

Combine the ground pork, tamari sauce, garlic, onions, and sugar in a mixing dish. Mix until everything is well incorporated.

Form the mixture into small meatballs.

In a shallow bowl, mix the olive oil, breadcrumbs, and parmesan. Roll the meatballs over the parmesan mixture.

Cook at 380 degrees F for 3 minutes; shake the basket and cook an additional 4 minutes or until meatballs are browned on all sides. Bon appétit!

Per serving: 539 Calories; 38.4g Fat; 17.5g Carbs; 29.2g Protein; 4.3g Sugars

143. Italian-Style Honey Roasted Pork

(Ready in about 50 minutes | Servings 3)

Ingredients

1 teaspoon Celtic sea salt
1/2 teaspoon black pepper, freshly cracked
1/4 cup red wine
2 tablespoons mustard

2 tablespoons honey
2 garlic cloves, minced
1 pound pork top loin
1 tablespoon Italian herb seasoning blend

Directions

In a ceramic bowl, mix the salt, black pepper, red wine, mustard, honey, and garlic. Add the pork top loin and let it marinate at least 30 minutes.

Spritz the sides and bottom of the cooking basket with a nonstick cooking spray.

Place the pork top loin in the basket; sprinkle with the Italian herb seasoning blend.

Cook the pork tenderloin at 370 degrees F for 10 minutes. Flip halfway through, spraying with cooking oil and cook for 5 to 6 minutes more. Serve immediately.

Per serving: 314 Calories; 9.8g Fat; 13g Carbs; 41.8g Protein; 11.8g Sugars

144. Ground Pork and Cheese Casserole

(Ready in about 45 minutes | Servings 4)

Ingredients

1 tablespoon olive oil
1 ½ pounds pork, ground
Sea salt and ground black pepper, to taste
1 medium-sized leek, sliced
1 teaspoon fresh garlic, minced
2 carrots, trimmed and sliced
1 (2-ounce) jar pimiento, drained and chopped

1 can (10 ¾-ounces) condensed cream of mushroom soup
1 cup water
1/2 cup ale
1 cup cream cheese
1/2 cup soft fresh breadcrumbs
1 tablespoon fresh cilantro, chopped

Directions

Start by preheating your Air Fryer to 320 degrees F.

Add the olive oil to a baking dish and heat for 1 to 2 minutes. Add the pork, salt, pepper and cook for 6 minutes, crumbling with a fork.

Add the leeks and cook for 4 to 5 minutes, stirring occasionally.

Add the garlic, carrots, pimiento, mushroom soup, water, ale, and cream cheese. Gently stir to combine.

Turn the temperature to 370 degrees F.

Top with the breadcrumbs. Place the baking dish in the cooking basket and cook approximately 30 minutes or until everything is thoroughly cooked. Serve garnished with fresh cilantro. Bon appétit!

Per serving: 561 Calories; 28g Fat; 22.2g Carbs; 52.5g Protein; 7.7g Sugars

145. Mexican-Style Ground Pork with Peppers

(Ready in about 40 minutes | Servings 4)

Ingredients

2 chili peppers
1 red bell pepper
2 tablespoons olive oil
1 large-sized shallot, chopped
1 pound ground pork
2 garlic cloves, minced
2 ripe tomatoes, pureed
1 teaspoon dried marjoram
1/2 teaspoon mustard seeds
1/2 teaspoon celery seeds
1 teaspoon Mexican oregano

1 tablespoon fish sauce
2 tablespoons fresh coriander, chopped
Salt and ground black pepper, to taste
2 cups water
1 tablespoon chicken bouillon granules
2 tablespoons sherry wine
1 cup Mexican cheese blend

Directions

Roast the peppers in the preheated Air Fryer at 395 degrees F for 10 minutes, flipping them halfway through cook time.

Let them steam for 10 minutes; then, peel the skin and discard the stems and seeds. Slice the peppers into halves.

Heat the olive oil in a baking pan at 380 degrees F for 2 minutes; add the shallots and cook for 4 minutes. Add the ground pork and garlic; cook for a further 4 to 5 minutes.

After that, stir in the tomatoes, marjoram, mustard seeds, celery seeds, oregano, fish sauce, coriander, salt, and pepper. Add a layer of sliced peppers to the baking pan.

Mix the water with the chicken bouillon granules and sherry wine. Add the mixture to the baking pan.

Cook in the preheated Air Fryer at 395 degrees F for 10 minutes. Top with cheese and bake an additional 5 minutes until the cheese has melted. Serve immediately.

Per serving: 505 Calories; 39.4g Fat; 9.9g Carbs; 28g Protein; 5.1g Sugars

146. Pork Shoulder with Molasses Sauce

(Ready in about 25 minutes + marinating time | Servings 3)

Ingredients

2 tablespoons molasses
2 tablespoons soy sauce
2 tablespoons Shaoxing wine
2 garlic cloves, minced
1 teaspoon fresh ginger, minced

1 tablespoon cilantro stems and leaves, finely chopped
1 pound boneless pork shoulder
2 tablespoons sesame oil

Directions

In a large-sized ceramic dish, thoroughly combine the molasses, soy sauce, wine, garlic, ginger, and cilantro; add the pork shoulder and allow it to marinate for 2 hours in the refrigerator.

Then, grease the cooking basket with sesame oil. Place the pork shoulder in the cooking basket; reserve the marinade.

Cook in the preheated Air Fryer at 395 degrees F for 14 to 17 minutes, flipping and basting with the marinade halfway through. Let it rest for 5 to 6 minutes before slicing and serving.

While the pork is roasting, cook the marinade in a preheated skillet over medium heat; cook until it has thickened.

Brush the pork shoulder with the sauce and enjoy!

Per serving: 353 Calories; 19.6g Fat; 13.5g Carbs; 29.2g Protein; 12.2g Sugars

147. Tender Spare Ribs

(Ready in about 35 minutes + marinating time | Servings 4)

Ingredients

1 rack pork spareribs, fat trimmed and cut in half
2 tablespoons fajita seasoning
2 tablespoons smoked paprika
Sea salt and pepper, to taste

1 tablespoon prepared brown mustard
3 tablespoons Worcestershire sauce
1/2 cup beer
1 tablespoon peanut oil

Directions

Toss the spareribs with the fajita seasoning, paprika, salt, pepper, mustard, and Worcestershire sauce. Pour in the beer and let it marinate for 1 hour in your refrigerator.

Rub the sides and bottom of the cooking basket with peanut oil.

Cook the spareribs in the preheated Air Fryer at 365 degrees for 17 minutes. Turn the ribs over and cook an additional 14 to 15 minutes. Serve warm. Bon appétit!

Per serving: 443 Calories; 35.2g Fat; 10g Carbs; 20.5g Protein; 3.1g Sugars

148. Pork Belly with New Potatoes

(Ready in about 50 minutes | Servings 4)

Ingredients

1 ½ pounds pork belly, cut into 4 pieces
Kosher salt and ground black pepper, to taste
1 teaspoon smoked paprika

1/2 teaspoon turmeric powder
2 tablespoons oyster sauce
2 tablespoons green onions
4 cloves garlic, sliced
1 pound new potatoes, scrubbed

Directions

Preheat your Air Fryer to 390 degrees F. Pat dry the pork belly and season with all spices listed above.

Add the oyster sauce and spritz with a nonstick cooking spray on all sides. Now, cook in the preheated Air Fryer for 30 minutes. Turn them over every 10 minutes.

Increase the temperature to 400 degrees F. Add the green onions, garlic, and new potatoes.

Cook another 15 minutes, shaking occasionally. Serve warm.

Per serving: 547 Calories; 30.2g Fat; 20.9g Carbs; 45.1g Protein; 1.1g Sugars

149. Smoky Mini Meatloaves with Cheese

(Ready in about 50 minutes | Servings 4)

Ingredients

1 pound ground pork
1/2 pound ground beef
1 package onion soup mix
1/2 cup seasoned bread crumbs
4 tablespoons Romano cheese, grated
2 eggs
1 carrot, grated
1 bell pepper, chopped
1 serrano pepper, minced
2 scallions, chopped

2 cloves garlic, finely chopped
2 tablespoons soy sauce sauce
Sea salt and black pepper, to your liking
Glaze:
1/2 cup tomato paste
2 tablespoons ketchup
1 tablespoon brown mustard
1 teaspoon smoked paprika
1 tablespoon honey

Directions

In a large mixing bowl, thoroughly combine all ingredients for the meatloaf. Mix with your hands until everything is well incorporated.

Then, shape the mixture into four mini loaves. Transfer them to the cooking basket previously generously greased with cooking oil.

Cook in the preheated Air Fryer at 385 degrees F approximately 43 minutes.

Mix all ingredients for the glaze. Spread the glaze over mini meatloaves and cook for another 6 minutes. Bon appétit!

Per serving: 585 Calories; 38.4g Fat; 22.2g Carbs; 38.5g Protein; 14.6g Sugars

150. Asian Sticky Ribs

(Ready in about 40 minutes | Servings 4)

Ingredients

1 teaspoon salt
1 teaspoon cayenne pepper
1/2 teaspoon ground black pepper
2 teaspoons raw honey
2 garlic cloves, minced
1 (1-inch) piece ginger, peeled and grated

1/2 teaspoon onion powder
1/2 teaspoon porcini powder
1 teaspoon mustard seeds
1 tablespoon sweet chili sauce
1 tablespoon balsamic vinegar
1 1/2 pounds pork country-style ribs

Directions

In a mixing bowl, combine the salt, cayenne pepper, black pepper, honey, garlic, ginger, onion powder, porcini powder, mustard seeds, sweet chili sauce, and balsamic vinegar.

Toss and rub the seasoning mixture all over the pork ribs.

Cook the country-style ribs at 360 degrees F for 15 minutes; flip the ribs and cook an additional 20 minutes or until they are tender inside and crisp on the outside.

Serve warm, garnished with fresh chives if desired.

Per serving: 446 Calories; 29.6g Fat; 5.5g Carbs; 45.1g Protein; 4.1g Sugars

151. Smoked Sausage with Sauerkraut

(Ready in about 35 minutes | Servings 4)

Ingredients

4 pork sausages, smoked
2 tablespoons canola oil
2 garlic cloves, minced
1 pound sauerkraut

1 teaspoon cayenne pepper
1/2 teaspoon black peppercorns
2 bay leaves

Directions

Start by preheating your Air Fryer to 360 degrees F.

Prick holes into the sausages using a fork and transfer them to the cooking basket. Cook approximately 14 minutes, shaking the basket a couple of times. Set aside.

Now, heat the canola oil in a baking pan at 380 degrees F. Add the garlic and cook for 1 minute. Immediately stir in the sauerkraut, cayenne pepper, peppercorns, and bay leaves.

Let it cook for 15 minutes, stirring every 5 minutes. Serve in individual bowls with warm sausages on the side!

Per serving: 478 Calories; 42.6g Fat; 6.1g Carbs; 17.2g Protein; 2.1g Sugars

152. Boston Butt with Salsa Verde

(Ready in about 35 minutes | Servings 4)

Ingredients

1 pound Boston butt, thinly sliced across the grain into 2-inch-long strips
1/2 teaspoon red pepper flakes, crushed
Sea salt and ground black pepper, to taste
1/2 pound tomatillos, chopped

1 small-sized onion, chopped
2 chili peppers, chopped
2 cloves garlic
2 tablespoons fresh cilantro, chopped
1 tablespoon olive oil
1 teaspoon sea salt

Directions

Rub the Boston butt with red pepper, salt, and black pepper. Spritz the bottom of the cooking basket with a nonstick cooking spray.

Roast the Boston butt in the preheated Air Fryer at 390 degrees F for 10 minutes. Shake the basket and cook another 10 minutes.

While the pork is roasting, make the salsa.

Blend the remaining ingredients until smooth and uniform. Transfer the mixture to a saucepan and add 1 cup of water.

Bring to a boil; reduce the heat and simmer for 8 to 12 minutes. Serve the roasted pork with the salsa verde on the side. Enjoy!

Per serving: 374 Calories; 24.1g Fat; 8.6g Carbs; 29.9g Protein; 4.7g Sugars

153. Blade Steaks with Butter-Fried Broccoli

(Ready in about 30 minutes | Servings 4)

Ingredients

1 1/2 pounds blade steaks skinless, boneless
Kosher salt and ground black pepper, to taste
2 garlic cloves, crushed
2 tablespoons soy sauce
1 tablespoon oyster sauce

2 tablespoon lemon juice
1 pound broccoli, broken into florets
2 tablespoons butter, melted
1 teaspoon dried dill weed
2 tablespoons sunflower seeds, lightly toasted

Directions

Start by preheating your Air Fryer to 385 degrees F. Spritz the bottom and sides of the cooking basket with cooking spray.

Now, season the pork with salt and black pepper. Add the garlic, soy sauce, oyster sauce, and lemon juice.

Cook for 20 minutes; turning over halfway through the cooking time.

Toss the broccoli with the melted butter and dill. Add the broccoli to the cooking basket and cook at 400 degrees F for 6 minutes, shaking the basket periodically.

Serve the warm pork with broccoli and garnish with sunflower seeds. Bon appétit!

Per serving: 443 Calories; 29.5g Fat; 11.3g Carbs; 34.2g Protein; 2.8g Sugars

154. Authentic Spaghetti Bolognese

(Ready in about 30 minutes | Servings 4)

Ingredients

2 tablespoons olive oil
1 shallot, peeled and chopped
1 teaspoon fresh garlic, minced
1 pound lean ground pork
1 cup tomato puree
2 tablespoons apple cider vinegar

1 teaspoon oregano
1 teaspoon basil
1 teaspoon rosemary
Salt and black pepper, to taste
1 package spaghetti
1 tablespoon fresh parsley

Directions

Heat the oil in a baking pan at 380 degrees F. Then, sauté the shallots until tender about 4 minutes.

Add the garlic and ground pork; cook an additional 6 minutes, stirring and crumbling meat with a spatula.

Add the tomato puree, vinegar, and spices; cook for 4 to 6 minutes longer or until everything is heated through.

Meanwhile, bring a large pot of lightly salted water to a boil. Cook your spaghetti for 10 to 12 minutes; drain and divide between individual plates.

Top with the Bolognese sauce and serve garnished with fresh parsley. Bon appétit!

Per serving: 551 Calories; 25.9g Fat; 50.1g Carbs; 29.1g Protein; 5.5g Sugars

155. Perfect Sloppy Joes

(Ready in about 30 minutes | Servings 4)

Ingredients

1 tablespoon olive oil
1 shallot, chopped
2 garlic cloves, minced
1 bell pepper, chopped
1 pound ground pork
2 ripe medium-sized tomatoes, pureed

1 tablespoon Worcestershire sauce
1 tablespoon poultry seasoning blend
Dash ground allspice
6 hamburger buns

Directions

Start by preheating your Air Fryer to 390 degrees F. Heat the olive oil for a few minutes.

Once hot, sauté the shallots until just tender. Add the garlic and bell pepper; cook for 4 minutes more or until they are aromatic.

Add the ground pork and cook for 5 minutes more, crumbling with a fork. Next step, stir in the pureed tomatoes, Worcestershire sauce, and spices. Decrease the temperature to 365 degrees F and cook another 10 minutes.

Spoon the meat mixture into hamburger buns and transfer them to the cooking basket. Cook for 7 minutes or until thoroughly warmed.

Per serving: 545 Calories; 32g Fat; 38.1g Carbs; 26.1g Protein; 3.9g Sugars

156. Easy Pork Sandwiches

(Ready in about 55 minutes | Servings 3)

Ingredients

2 teaspoons peanut oil
1 ½ pounds pork sirloin
Coarse sea salt and ground black pepper, to taste

1 tablespoon smoked paprika
1/4 cup prepared barbecue sauce
3 hamburger buns, split

Directions

Start by preheating your Air Fryer to 360 degrees F.

Drizzle the oil all over the pork sirloin. Sprinkle with salt, black pepper, and paprika.

Cook for 50 minutes in the preheated Air Fryer.

Remove the roast from the Air Fryer and shred with two forks. Mix in the barbecue sauce. Serve over hamburger buns. Enjoy!

Per serving: 453 Calories; 8.9g Fat; 33.4g Carbs; 56.8g Protein; 11.6g Sugars

157. Egg Noodles with Sausage-Pepper Sauce

(Ready in about 30 minutes | Servings 4)

Ingredients

1 tablespoon lard, at room temperature
2 garlic cloves, smashed
2 scallions, chopped
1 red bell pepper, chopped
1 green bell pepper, chopped
1 pound pork sausages, sliced
2 ripe tomatoes, pureed

2 tablespoons tomato ketchup
1 teaspoon molasses
1 tablespoon flax seed meal
Salt and black pepper, to taste
1 teaspoon basil
1 teaspoon rosemary
1 teaspoon oregano
1 package egg noodles

Directions

Melt the lard in a baking pan at 380 degrees F. Once hot, sauté the garlic, scallions, and peppers until tender about 2 minutes.

Add the sausages and cook an additional 5 minutes, stirring occasionally.

Add the tomato puree, tomato ketchup, molasses, flax seed meal, and spices; cook for 4 to 5 minutes more or until everything is thoroughly warmed and the sauce has thickened.

Meanwhile, bring a large pot of lightly salted water to a boil. Cook the egg noodles for 10 to 12 minutes; drain and divide between individual plates. Top with the warm sauce and serve. Bon appétit!

Per serving: 389 Calories; 32.2g Fat; 11.4g Carbs; 13.6g Protein; 5.7g Sugars

158. Sticky Dijon Pork Chops

(Ready in about 20 minutes | Servings 4)

Ingredients

1/4 cup soy sauce
2 tablespoons brown sugar
1/4 cup rice vinegar
1 pound pork loin center rib chops, bone-in

Celtic salt and ground black pepper, to taste
1 tablespoon Dijon mustard

Directions

Thoroughly combine the soy sauce, brown sugar, and vinegar; add the pork and let it marinate for 1 hour in the refrigerator.

Sprinkle the pork chops with salt and black pepper. Spread the mustard, all over the pork chops.

Cook in the preheated Air Fryer at 400 degrees F for 12 minutes. Serve warm with mashed potatoes if desired.

Per serving: 307 Calories; 14g Fat; 8.3g Carbs; 33.9g Protein; 7.1g Sugars

159. Pork Loin with Mushroom Sauce

(Ready in about 30 minutes | Servings 4)

Ingredients

2 pounds top loin, boneless
1 tablespoon olive oil
1 teaspoon Celtic salt
1/4 teaspoon ground black pepper, or more to taste
2 shallots, sliced

2 garlic cloves, minced
1 cup mushrooms, chopped
2 tablespoons all-purpose flour
3/4 cup cream of mushroom soup
1 teaspoon chili powder
Salt, to taste

Directions

Pat dry the pork and drizzle with olive oil. Season with Celtic salt and pepper. Cook in the preheated Air Fryer at 370 degrees F for 10 minutes.

Top with shallot slices and cook another 10 minutes.

Test the temperature of the meat; it should be around 150 degrees F. Reserve the pork and onion, keeping warm.

Add the cooking juices to a saucepan and preheat over medium-high heat. Cook the garlic and mushrooms until aromatic about 2 minutes.

Combine the flour with the mushroom soup. Add the flour mixture to the pan along with the chili powder and salt. Gradually stir into the pan.

Bring to a boil; immediately turn the heat to medium and cook for 2 to 3 minutes stirring frequently. Spoon the sauce over the reserved pork and onion. Enjoy!

Per serving: 416 Calories; 13.9g Fat; 15.2g Carbs; 55.1g Protein; 4.4g Sugars

160. Sausage and Mushroom Chili

(Ready in about 35 minutes | Servings 4)

Ingredients

1 tablespoon olive oil
1 shallot, chopped
2 garlic cloves, smashed
10 ounces button mushrooms, sliced
1/2 pound pork sausages, chopped
2 cups tomato puree
2 tablespoons tomato ketchup

1 teaspoon yellow mustard
1 cup chicken broth
2 teaspoons ancho chili powder
Salt and ground black pepper, to taste
1 (16-ounce) can pinto beans, rinsed and drained
1/2 cup cream cheese

Directions

Start by preheating your Air Fryer to 360 degrees F. Heat the oil in a baking pan for a few minutes and cook the shallot until tender about 4 minutes.

Add the garlic and mushrooms; cook another 4 minutes or until tender and fragrant.

Next, stir in sausage and cook for a further 9 minutes. Add tomato puree, ketchup, mustard, and broth. Stir to combine and cook another 6 minutes.

Add spices and beans; cook an additional 7 minutes. Divide between individual bowls and top each bowl with cream cheese. Enjoy!

Per serving: 569 Calories; 35.3g Fat; 33.1g Carbs; 33.1g Protein; 10.4g Sugars

161. Easy Keto Pork Rinds

(Ready in about 30 minutes | Servings 10)

Ingredients

2 pounds pork belly, trim the fat layer and cut into cubes
1 teaspoon Celtic salt

1 tablespoon red pepper flakes, crushed

Directions

Add the pork, salt, and red pepper to the baking pan. Bake at 395 degrees F for 10 minutes.

Pat it dry and transfer to your refrigerator to cool for 15 minutes.

Process the pork fat in the blender until it resembles coarse breadcrumbs. Use with your favorite keto creations!

Per serving: 470 Calories; 48g Fat; 0.1g Carbs; 8.4g Protein; 0g Sugars

162. St. Louis-Style Pork Ribs with Roasted Peppers

(Ready in about 55 minutes | Servings 2)

Ingredients

2 pounds St. Louis-style pork spareribs, individually cut
1 teaspoon seasoned salt
1/2 teaspoon ground black pepper

1 tablespoon sweet paprika
1/2 teaspoon mustard powder
2 tablespoons sesame oil
4 bell pepper, seeded

Directions

Toss and rub the spices all over the pork ribs; drizzle with 1 tablespoon of sesame oil.

Cook the pork ribs at 360 degrees F for 15 minutes; flip the ribs and cook an additional 20 minutes or until they are tender inside and crisp on the outside.

Toss the peppers with the remaining 1 tablespoon of oil; season to taste and cook in the preheated Air Fryer at 390 degrees F for 15 minutes.

Serve the warm spareribs with the roasted peppers on the side. Enjoy!

Per serving: 444 Calories; 25.4g Fat; 10g Carbs; 43.3g Protein; 4.9g Sugars

163. Sri Lankan Pork Curry

(Ready in about 35 minutes | Servings 4)

Ingredients

2 cardamom pods, only the seeds, crushed
1 teaspoon fennel seeds
1 teaspoon cumin seeds
1 teaspoon coriander seeds
2 teaspoons peanut oil
2 scallions, chopped
2 garlic cloves, smashed
2 jalapeno peppers, minced

1/2 teaspoon ginger, freshly grated
1 pound pork loin, cut into bite-sized cubes
1 cup coconut milk
1 cup chicken broth
1 teaspoon turmeric powder
1 tablespoon tamarind paste
1 tablespoon fresh lime juice

Directions

Place the cardamom, fennel, cumin, and coriander seeds in a nonstick skillet over medium-high heat. Stir for 6 minutes until the spices become aromatic and start to brown. Stir frequently to prevent the spices from burning. Set aside.

Preheat your Air Fryer to 370 degrees F. Then, in a baking pan, heat the peanut oil for 2 minutes. Once hot, sauté the scallions for 2 to 3 minutes until tender.

Stir in the garlic, peppers, and ginger; cook an additional minute, stirring frequently. Next, cook the pork for 3 to 4 minutes.

Pour in the coconut milk and broth. Add the reserved seeds, turmeric, and tamarind paste. Let it cook for 15 minutes in the preheated Air Fryer.

Divide between individual bowls; drizzle fresh lime juice over the top and serve immediately.

Per serving: 396 Calories; 20.1g Fat; 4.9g Carbs; 44.2g Protein; 3.6g Sugars

164. Herbed and Garlicky Pork Belly

(Ready in about 1 hour 15 minutes + marinating time | Servings 4)

Ingredients

1 pound pork belly
2 garlic cloves, halved
1 teaspoon shallot powder
1 teaspoon sea salt
1 teaspoon dried basil

1 teaspoon dried oregano
1 teaspoon dried thyme
1 teaspoon dried marjoram
1 teaspoon ground black pepper
1 lime, juiced

Directions

Blanch the pork belly in a pot of boiling water for 10 to 13 minutes.

Pat it dry with a kitchen towel. Now, poke holes all over the skin by using a fork.

Then, mix the remaining ingredients to make the rub. Massage the rub all over the pork belly. Drizzle lime juice all over the meat; place the pork belly in the refrigerator for 3 hours.

Preheat your Air Fryer to 320 degrees F. Cook the pork belly for 35 minutes.

Turn up the temperature to 360 degrees F and continue cooking for 20 minutes longer. Serve warm. Bon appétit!

Per serving: 590 Calories; 60.1g Fat; 0.5g Carbs; 10.6g Protein; 0g Sugars

165. Party Pork and Bacon Skewers

(Ready in about 30 minutes + marinating time | Servings 6)

Ingredients

1 cup cream of celery soup
1 (13.5-ounce) can coconut milk, unsweetened
2 tablespoons tamari sauce
1 teaspoon yellow mustard
1 tablespoon honey
Salt and freshly ground white pepper, to taste

1/2 teaspoon cayenne pepper
1/2 teaspoon chili powder
1 teaspoon curry powder
2 pounds pork tenderloin, cut into bite-sized cubes
4 ounces bacon, cut into pieces

12 bamboo skewers, soaked in water Directions

In a large pot, bring the cream of the celery soup, coconut milk, tamari sauce, mustard, honey, salt, white pepper, cayenne pepper, chili powder, and curry powder to a boil.

Then, reduce the heat to simmer; cook until the sauce is heated through, about 13 minutes.

Add the pork, gently stir, and place in your refrigerator for 2 hours.

Thread the pork onto the skewers, alternating the cubes of meat with the pieces of bacon.

Preheat your Air Fryer to 370 degrees F. Cook for 15 minutes, turning over a couple of times. Bon appétit!

Per serving: 572 Calories; 41.1g Fat; 8.9g Carbs; 41.6g Protein; 5.4g Sugars

166. Ranchero Pork Kebabs

(Ready in about 25 minutes | Servings 3)

Ingredients

1 pound lean pork, ground
1 onion, chopped
1 garlic clove, smashed
1 teaspoon mustard

Salt and ground black pepper, to taste
4 tablespoons ranch-flavored tortilla chips, finely crushed

Directions

Mix all ingredients using your hands. Knead until everything is well incorporated.

Shape the meat mixture around flat skewers (sausage shapes).

Cook at 365 degrees F for 11 to 12 minutes, turning them over once or twice. Work in batches. Serve!

Per serving: 394 Calories; 16.7g Fat; 32.9g Carbs; 29.1g Protein; 4.9g Sugars

167. Pork Stuffed Peppers with Cheese

(Ready in about 30 minutes | Servings 3)

Ingredients

3 bell peppers, stems and seeds removed
1 tablespoon olive oil
3 scallions, chopped
1 teaspoon fresh garlic, minced
12 ounces lean pork, ground
1/2 teaspoon sea salt
1/2 teaspoon black pepper
1 tablespoon fish sauce
2 ripe tomatoes, pureed
3 ounces Monterey Jack cheese, grated

Directions

Cook the peppers in boiling salted water for 4 minutes

In a nonstick skillet, heat the olive oil over medium heat. Then, sauté the scallions and garlic until tender and fragrant.

Stir in the ground pork and continue sautéing until the pork has browned; drain off the excess fat.

Add the salt, black pepper, fish sauce, and 1 pureed tomato; give it a good stir.

Divide the filling among the bell peppers. Arrange the peppers in a baking dish lightly greased with cooking oil. Place the remaining tomato puree around the peppers.

Bake in the preheated Air Fryer at 380 degrees F for 13 minutes. Top with grated cheese and bake another 6 minutes. Serve warm and enjoy!

Per serving: 425 Calories; 25.9g Fat; 9.5g Carbs; 38.3g Protein; 5.2g Sugars

168. Enchilada Bake with Corn and Cheese

(Ready in about 30 minutes | Servings 3)

Ingredients

1 tablespoon butter, melted
2 scallions, chopped
1 teaspoon fresh garlic, minced
1 pound ground pork
1 tablespoon California chili powder
1 cup tomato sauce
1 cup chicken stock
1/4 teaspoon ground cumin
2 tablespoons fish sauce
3 corn tortillas
1 cup corn
1 cup Colby cheese, shredded

Directions

Melt the butter in a saucepan over medium heat. Now, add the scallions and garlic and cook for 2 minutes or until tender.

Add the ground pork and cook for a further 3 minutes, crumbling with a spatula.

To make the enchilada sauce, in a mixing bowl, thoroughly combine the chili powder, tomato sauce, chicken stock, cumin, and fish sauce.

Place little sauce on the bottom of a baking pan. Add one tortilla and 1/3 of the tomato sauce; top with 1/3 of the ground pork mixture. Add 1/3 cup of the corn and 1/3 cup of the shredded Colby cheese.

Repeat these steps 2 more times, finishing with cheese.

Cover the top of the casserole with a piece of foil and place in the cooking basket. Cook for 16 minutes at 250 degrees F. Bon appétit!

Per serving: 550 Calories; 24.5g Fat; 39g Carbs; 48.3g Protein; 8.7g Sugars

169. Cracker Pork Chops with Mustard

(Ready in about 20 minutes | Servings 3)

Ingredients

1/4 cup all-purpose flour
1 teaspoon turmeric powder
1 egg
1 teaspoon mustard
Kosher salt, to taste
1/4 teaspoon freshly ground black pepper
2 cups crackers, crushed
1/2 teaspoon porcini powder
1 teaspoon shallot powder
3 center-cut loin pork chops

Directions

Place the flour and turmeric in a shallow bowl. In another bowl, whisk the eggs, mustard, salt, and black pepper.

In the third bowl, mix the crushed crackers with the porcini powder and shallot powder.

Preheat your Air Fryer to 390 degrees F. Dredge the pork chops in the flour mixture, then in the egg, followed by the cracker mixture.

Cook the pork chops for 7 minutes per side, spraying with cooking oil. Bon appétit!

Per serving: 474 Calories; 19.3g Fat; 10.7g Carbs; 60.2g Protein; 0.5g Sugars

170. Festive Pork Fillets with Apples

(Ready in about 20 minutes | Servings 3)

Ingredients

1/4 cup chickpea flour
2 tablespoons Romano cheese, grated
1 teaspoon onion powder
1 teaspoon garlic powder
1/2 teaspoon ground cumin
1 teaspoon cayenne pepper
2 pork fillets (1 pound)
1 Granny Smiths apple, peeled and sliced
1 tablespoon lemon juice
1 ounce butter, cold

Directions

Combine the flour, cheese, onions powder, garlic powder, cumin, and cayenne pepper in a ziploc bag; shake to mix well.

Place the pork fillets in the bag. Shake to coat on all sides. Next, spritz the bottom of the Air Fryer basket with cooking spray.

Cook in the preheated Air Fryer at 370 degrees F for 10 minutes. Add the apples and drizzle with lemon juice; place the cold butter on top and cook an additional 5 minutes. Serve immediately.

Per serving: 485 Calories; 27.3g Fat; 14.7g Carbs; 42.8g Protein; 7.1g Sugars

171. Dijon Ribs with Cherry Tomatoes

(Ready in about 35 minutes | Servings 2)

Ingredients

1 rack ribs, cut in half to fit the Air Fryer
1/4 cup dry white wine
2 tablespoons soy sauce
1 tablespoon Dijon mustard
Sea salt and ground black pepper, to taste
1 cup cherry tomatoes
1 teaspoon dried rosemary

Directions

Toss the pork ribs with wine, soy sauce, mustard, salt, and black pepper.

Add the ribs to the lightly greased cooking basket. Cook in the preheated Air Fryer at 370 degrees F for 25 minutes.

Turn the ribs over, add the cherry tomatoes and rosemary; cook an additional 5 minutes. Serve immediately.

Per serving: 452 Calories; 17.1g Fat; 17.7g Carbs; 55.2g Protein; 13.6g Sugars

172. Pork Cutlets with Plum Sauce

(Ready in about 20 minutes | Servings 4)

Ingredients

4 pork cutlets
2 teaspoosn sesame oil
1/2 teaspoon ground black pepper
Salt, to taste
1 tablespoon Creole seasoning
2 tablespoons aged balsamic vinegar
2 tablespoons soy sauce
6 ripe plums, pitted and diced

Directions

Preheat your Air Fryer to 390 degrees F.

Toss the pork cutlets with the sesame oil, black pepper, salt, Creole seasoning, vinegar, and soy sauce. Transfer them to a lightly greased baking pan; lower the pan onto the cooking basket.

Cook for 13 minutes in the preheated Air Fryer, flipping them halfway through the cooking time. Serve warm.

Per serving: 422 Calories; 23.8g Fat; 20.8g Carbs; 29.4g Protein; 18.3g Sugars

173. Hawaiian Cheesy Meatball Sliders

(Ready in about 20 minutes | Servings 4)

Ingredients

1 pound ground pork
2 tablespoons bacon, chopped
2 garlic cloves, minced
2 tablespoons scallions, chopped
Salt and ground black pepper, to taste

1/2 cup Romano cheese, grated
1 cup tortilla chips, crushed
1 ½ cups marinara sauce
8 Hawaiian rolls
1 cup Cheddar cheese, shredded

Directions

Mix the ground pork with the bacon, garlic, scallions, salt, black pepper, cheese, and tortilla chips. Shape the mixture into 8 meatballs.

Add the meatballs to the lightly greased baking pan. Pour in the marinara sauce and lower the pan onto the cooking basket.

Cook the meatballs in the preheated Air Fryer at 380 degrees for 10 minutes. Check the meatballs halfway through the cooking time.

Place one meatball on top of the bottom half of one roll. Spoon the marinara sauce on top of each meatball. Top with cheese and bake in your Air Fryer at 370 degrees F for 3 to 4 minutes.

Top with the other half of the roll and serve immediately. Bon appétit!

Per serving: 612 Calories; 34.9g Fat; 39.4g Carbs; 33.3g Protein; 10.8g Sugars

174. Country-Style Pork and Mushroom Patties

(Ready in about 30 minutes | Servings 4)

Ingredients

1 tablespoon canola oil
1 onion, chopped
2 garlic cloves, minced
1 pound ground pork
1/2 pound brown mushrooms, chopped

Salt and black pepper, to taste
1 teaspoon cayenne pepper
1/2 teaspoon dried rosemary
1/2 teaspoon dried dill
4 slices Cheddar cheese

Directions

Start by preheating your Air Fryer to 370 degrees F.

In a mixing bowl, thoroughly combine the oil, onions, garlic, ground pork, mushrooms, salt, black pepper, cayenne pepper, rosemary, and dill.

Shape the meat mixture into four patties.

Spritz the bottom of the cooking basket with cooking spray. Cook the meatballs in the preheated Air Fryer at 370 degrees for 20 minutes, flipping them halfway through cooking.

Top the warm patties with cheese and serve. Enjoy!

Per serving: 399 Calories; 29.7g Fat; 8.7g Carbs; 24.3g Protein; 4.6g Sugars

175. Meatloaf Muffins with Sweet Potato Frosting

(Ready in about 1 hour | Servings 4)

Ingredients

Meatloaf Muffins:
1 pound pork sausage, crumbled
1 shallot, chopped
2 garlic cloves, minced
1/2 cup oats
1/2 cup pasta sauce
1 teaspoon dried oregano
1 teaspoon dried basil
Salt and ground black pepper, to taste

1 egg
Sweet Potato Frosting:
1/2 pound sweet potatoes, cut into wedges
1/2 teaspoon garlic powder
1/4 cup coconut milk
1 tablespoon coconut oil
1 teaspoon salt

Directions

Mix all ingredients for the meatloaf muffins until everything is well incorporated.

Place the meat mixture in 4 cupcake liners. Bake at 220 degrees F for 23 minutes. Remove from the cooking basket and reserve keeping warm.

Cook the sweet potatoes at 380 degrees F for 35 minutes, shaking the basket occasionally. When the sweet potatoes are cooled enough to handle, scoop out the flesh into a bowl.

Add the garlic powder, coconut milk, coconut oil, and salt; mix to combine well. Beat with a wire whisk until everything is thoroughly mixed and fluffy.

Pipe the potato mixture onto the sausage muffins using a pastry bag. Enjoy!

Per serving: 408 Calories; 23.4g Fat; 32.7g Carbs; 21.7g Protein; 7.1g Sugars

176. Japanese Ribs (Supearibu no Nikomi)

(Ready in about 25 minutes | Servings 4)

Ingredients

2 pounds pork ribs
1/2 cup tomato puree
1/2 cup ketchup
1 teaspoon orange zest
1 tablespoon Worcestershire sauce

2 tablespoons brown sugar
1 teaspoon garlic powder
1 tablespoon instant dashi
1 tablespoon mirin
1 tablespoon black sesame seeds

Directions

Preheat your Air Fryer to 370 degrees F.

Toss the pork ribs with all ingredients, except the sesame seeds, in a nonstick grill pan.

Grill your ribs approximately 18 minutes at 390 degrees F, turning them periodically.

Serve with the sauce and black sesame seeds and enjoy!

Per serving: 506 Calories; 28.1g Fat; 16.8g Carbs; 45.2g Protein; 12.3g Sugars

177. Elegant Pork Chops with Applesauce

(Ready in about 20 minutes | Servings 4)

Ingredients

4 pork chops, bone-in
Sea salt and ground black pepper, to taste
1/2 teaspoon onion powder
1/2 teaspoon paprika

1/2 teaspoon celery seeds
2 cooking apples, peeled and sliced
1 tablespoon honey
1 tablespoon peanut oil

Directions

Place the pork in a lightly greased baking pan. Season with salt and pepper, and transfer the pan to the cooking basket.

Cook in the preheated Air Fryer at 370 degrees F for 10 minutes.

Meanwhile, in a saucepan, simmer the remaining ingredients over medium heat for about 8 minutes or until the apples are softened.

Pour the applesauce over the prepared pork chops. Add to the Air Fryer and bake for 5 minutes more. Bon appétit!

Per serving: 427 Calories; 21.1g Fat; 17.6g Carbs; 40.7g Protein; 14.3g Sugars

178. Easy Minty Meatballs

(Ready in about 20 minutes | Servings 4)

Ingredients

1/2 pound ground pork
1/2 pound ground beef
1 shallot, chopped
2 garlic cloves, minced
1 tablespoon coriander, chopped
1 teaspoon fresh mint, minced

Sea salt and ground black pepper, to taste
1/2 teaspoon mustard seeds
1 teaspoon fennel seeds
1 teaspoon ground cumin
1 cup mozzarella, sliced

Directions

In a mixing bowl, combine all ingredients, except the mozzarella.

Shape the mixture into balls and transfer them to a lightly greased cooking basket.

Cook the meatballs in the preheated Air Fryer at 380 degrees for 10 minutes. Check the meatballs halfway through the cooking time.

Top with sliced mozzarella and bake for 3 minutes more. To serve, arrange on a nice serving platter. Bon appétit!

Per serving: 311 Calories; 19.5g Fat; 3.5g Carbs; 30.1g Protein; 1.3g Sugars

179. Spanish-Style Pork with Padrón Peppers

(Ready in about 30 minutes | Servings 4)

Ingredients

1 tablespoon olive oil
8 ounces Padrón peppers
2 pounds pork loin, sliced
1 teaspoon Celtic salt
1 teaspoon paprika
1 heaped tablespoon capers, drained
8 green olives, pitted and halved

Directions

Drizzle olive oil all over the Padrón peppers; cook them in the preheated Air Fryer at 400 degrees F for 10 minutes, turning occasionally, until well blistered all over and tender-crisp.

Then, turn the temperature to 360 degrees F.

Season the pork loin with salt and paprika. Add the capers and cook for 16 minutes, turning them over halfway through the cooking time. Serve with olives and the reserved Padrón peppers.

Per serving: 536 Calories; 29.5g Fat; 5.9g Carbs; 59g Protein; 2.9g Sugars

180. Italian Sausage Meatball Casserole

(Ready in about 35 minutes | Servings 4)

Ingredients

1 pound Italian pork sausage, crumbled
1 egg
1 cup regular rolled oat
1 teaspoon cayenne pepper
Sea salt and ground black pepper, to taste
1 tablespoon olive oil
1 leek, chopped
1 teaspoon fresh garlic, minced
1 chili pepper, chopped
1 teaspoon dried oregano
1 teaspoon dried basil
1 teaspoon celery seeds
1 teaspoon brown mustard
2 cups tomato puree

Directions

In a mixing bowl, thoroughly combine the pork sausage with egg, oats, cayenne pepper, salt, and black pepper. Form the sausage mixture into meatballs.

Spritz the Air Fryer basket with cooking oil. Cook the meatballs in the preheated Air Fryer at 380 degrees for 10 minutes, shaking the basket halfway through the cooking time. Reserve.

Meanwhile, heat the olive oil in a pan over medium-high heat. Sauté the leeks until tender and aromatic.

Stir in the garlic, pepper, and seasonings and cook for a further 2 minutes. Add the brown mustard and tomato puree and cook another 5 minutes.

Transfer the tomato sauce to the baking pan. Add the meatballs and cook in the preheated Air Fryer at 350 degrees F for 10 minutes. Serve warm.

Per serving: 534 Calories; 29.7g Fat; 46g Carbs; 23.1g Protein; 8.1g Sugars

181. Omelet with Prosciutto and Ricotta Cheese

(Ready in about 15 minutes | Servings 2)

Ingredients

2 tablespoons olive oil
4 eggs
2 tablespoons scallions, chopped
4 tablespoons Ricotta cheese
1/4 teaspoon black pepper, freshly cracked
Salt, to taste
6 ounces prosciutto, chopped
1 tablespoon Italian parsley, roughly chopped

Directions

Generously grease a baking pan with olive oil.

Then, whisk the eggs, and add the scallions, cheese, black pepper, and salt. Fold in the chopped prosciutto and mix to combine well.

Spoon into the prepared baking pan.

Cook in the preheated Air Fryer at 360 F for 6 minutes. Serve immediately garnished with Italian parsley.

Per serving: 389 Calories; 28.8g Fat; 3.2g Carbs; 29.1g Protein; 0.5g Sugars

182. Pigs in a Blanket with a Twist

(Ready in about 15 minutes | Servings 4)

Ingredients

12 refrigerator biscuits
8 hot dogs, cut into 3 pieces
1 egg yolk
2 tablespoons poppy seeds
1 tablespoon oregano

Directions

Flatten each biscuit slightly; cut in half.

Now, mix the egg yolk with the poppy seeds and oregano.

Wrap the biscuits around the hot dog pieces sealing the edges and brushing with the egg mixture to adhere.

Bake in the preheated Air Fryer at 395 degrees F for 8 minutes, Enjoy!

Per serving: 589 Calories; 40g Fat; 40.1g Carbs; 16.8g Protein; 7g Sugars

183. Tagliatelle al Ragu

(Ready in about 30 minutes | Servings 4)

Ingredients

1 tablespoon olive oil
1 shallot, chopped
2 garlic cloves, minced
2 bell peppers, sliced
1 carrot, trimmed and sliced
1/2 pound ground pork
1/2 pound smoked pork sausage, sliced
2 ripe medium-sized tomatoes, pureed
2 tablespoons ketchup
1/4 cup red wine
2 tablespoons cilantro leaves, chopped
1 teaspoon dried basil
1 teaspoon dried oregano
Salt and ground black pepper, to taste
1 package (16-ounce) tagliatelle

Directions

Heat the oil in the baking pan at 380 degrees F. Then, sauté the shallots until tender about 4 minutes.

Add the garlic, bell pepper, and carrots; cook an additional 2 minutes.

Now, stir in ground pork and sausage and continue cooking for 5 minutes more, crumbling the meat with a spatula.

Add tomato puree, ketchup, red wine, cilantro, basil, oregano, salt, and black pepper. Then, cook for 4 to 6 minutes longer or until everything is heated through.

Meanwhile, bring a large pot of lightly salted water to a boil. Cook your tagliatelle for 10 to 12 minutes; drain.

Top tagliatelle with the sauce and serve. Bon appétit!

Per serving: 522 Calories; 32.2g Fat; 35.8g Carbs; 22.2g Protein; 4.2g Sugars

184. Filipino Pork Adobo

(Ready in about 35 minutes | Servings 4)

Ingredients

1 tablespoon sesame oil
1 ½ pounds Boston butt, boneless and skinless, cut into 2 pieces
Sea salt and ground black pepper, to taste
1 teaspoon paprika
1/2 teaspoon mustard seeds
1 teaspoon sesame oil
3 bell peppers, seeded and sliced

1 jalapeño pepper, seeded and sliced
1 red onion, sliced
2 garlic cloves, smashed
1/2 teaspoon curry
1/2 teaspoon ground bay leaf
1/4 cup soy sauce
1/4 cup apple cider vinegar
1 tablespoon cornstarch plus 2 tablespoons water

Directions

Rub 1 tablespoon of sesame oil all over the Boston butt. Season with salt, pepper, paprika, and mustard seeds.

Roast the Boston butt in the preheated Air Fryer at 390 degrees F for 10 minutes. Turn them over and cook another 10 minutes.

Heat 1 teaspoon of sesame oil in a wok over medium-high heat. Once hot, cook the peppers until tender, about 2 minutes.

Add the onion, garlic, curry, bay leaf, soy sauce, and vinegar. Cook an additional 5 minutes, stirring frequently.

Add the cornstarch slurry and meat. Reduce the temperature to simmer and cook for 2 to 4 minute more or until everything is thoroughly heated. Bon appétit!

Per serving: 334 Calories; 16.8g Fat; 12.8g Carbs; 33.6g Protein; 6.1g Sugars

185. Spanish Pork Skewers (Pinchos Morunos)

(Ready in about 35 minutes + marinating time | Servings 4)

Ingredients

2 pounds center cut loin chop, cut into bite-sized pieces
1 teaspoon oregano
1/2 teaspoon ground turmeric
1/2 teaspoon ground coriander
1 teaspoon ground cumin
2 teaspoons sweet Spanish paprika

Sea salt and freshly ground black pepper, to taste
2 garlic cloves, minced
2 tablespoons extra virgin olive oil
1/4 cup dry red wine
1 lemon, 1/2 juiced 1/2 wedges

Directions

Mix all ingredients, except the lemon wedges, in a large ceramic dish. Allow it to marinate for 2 hours in your refrigerator.

Discard the marinade. Now, thread the pork pieces on to skewers and place them in the cooking basket.

Cook in the preheated Air Fryer at 360 degrees F for 15 to 17 minutes, shaking the basket every 5 minutes. Work in batches.

Serve immediately garnished with lemon wedges. Bon appétit!

Per serving: 432 Calories; 23g Fat; 3.4g Carbs; 49.4g Protein; 0.4g Sugars

186. Greek Pork Loin with Tzatziki

(Ready in about 55 minutes | Servings 4)

Ingredients

Greek Pork:
2 pounds pork sirloin roast
Salt and black pepper, to taste
1 teaspoon smoked paprika
1/2 teaspoon mustard seeds
1/2 teaspoon celery seeds
1 teaspoon fennel seeds
1 teaspoon Ancho chili powder
1 teaspoon turmeric powder
1/2 teaspoon ground ginger
2 tablespoons olive oil

2 cloves garlic, finely chopped
Tzatziki:
1/2 cucumber, finely chopped and squeezed
1 cup full-fat Greek yogurt
1 garlic clove, minced
1 tablespoon extra virgin olive oil
1 teaspoon balsamic vinegar
1 teaspoon minced fresh dill
A pinch of salt

Directions

Toss all ingredients for Greek pork in a large mixing bowl. Toss until the meat is well coated.

Cook in the preheated Air Fryer at 360 degrees F for 30 minutes; turn over and cook another 20 minutes.

Meanwhile, prepare the tzatziki by mixing all the tzatziki ingredients. Place in your refrigerator until ready to use.

Serve the pork sirloin roast with the chilled tzatziki on the side. Enjoy!

Per serving: 560 Calories; 30.1g Fat; 4.9g Carbs; 64.1g Protein; 1.6g Sugars

187. Pork Ragout with Egg Noodles

(Ready in about 50 minutes | Servings 4)

Ingredients

2 pounds country pork ribs
Sea salt, to your liking
1/2 teaspoon freshly cracked black pepper
1/2 teaspoon cayenne pepper
1 tablespoon yellow mustard
2 tablespoons sesame oil
1 shallot, diced

2 ripe tomatoes, pureed
1 cup vegetable broth
1/4 cup red wine
1 tablespoon fish sauce
1 tablespoon fresh lemon juice
1 teaspoon dried thyme
2 bay leaves
8 ounces egg noodles

Directions

Place all ingredients, except the egg noodles, in a ceramic bowl; let it marinate at least 1 hour in your refrigerator.

Discard the marinade and place the pork ribs in the lightly greased cooking basket.

Cook at 365 degrees for 17 minutes. Turn the ribs over and cook an additional 14 to 15 minutes; reserve.

Meanwhile, bring a large pot of lightly salted water to a boil. Cook the egg noodles for 10 to 12 minutes; drain and reserve, keeping warm.

Then, heat the reserved marinade in a large nonstick skillet over a moderate flame; simmer the marinade for 5 to 7 minutes or until it has reduced by half.

Add in the reserved meat and egg noodles; let it simmer an additional 3 to 4 minutes or until thoroughly heated. Bon appétit!

Per serving: 615 Calories; 20.8g Fat; 44.2g Carbs; 59g Protein; 3.2g Sugars

188. Porterhouse Steak for Two

(Ready in about 25 minutes | Servings 2)

Ingredients

1 pound porterhouse steak, cut meat from bone in 2 pieces
1/2 teaspoon ground black pepper
1 teaspoon cayenne pepper
1/2 teaspoon salt

1 teaspoon garlic powder
1/2 teaspoon dried thyme
1/2 teaspoon dried marjoram
1 teaspoon Dijon mustard
1 tablespoon butter, melted

Directions

Sprinkle the porterhouse steak with all the seasonings.

Spread the mustard and butter evenly over the meat.

Cook in the preheated Air Fryer at 390 degrees F for 12 to 14 minutes.

Taste for doneness with a meat thermometer and serve immediately.

Per serving: 402 Calories; 14.6g Fat; 0.1g Carbs; 67.2g Protein; 0g Sugars

189. Pork Leg with Candy Onions

(Ready in about 1 hour | Servings 4)

Ingredients

1 rosemary sprig, chopped
1 thyme sprig, chopped
1 teaspoon dried sage, crushed
Sea salt and ground black pepper, to taste
1 teaspoon cayenne pepper
2 teaspoons sesame oil
2 pounds pork leg roast, scored
1 pound candy onions, peeled
2 chili peppers, minced
4 cloves garlic, finely chopped

Directions

Start by preheating your Air Fryer to 400 degrees F.

Then, mix the seasonings with the sesame oil.

Rub the seasoning mixture all over the pork leg. Cook in the preheated Air Fryer for 40 minutes.

Add the candy onions, peppers and garlic and cook an additional 12 minutes. Slice the pork leg. Afterwards, spoon the pan juices over the meat and serve with the candy onions. Bon appétit!

Per serving: 444 Calories; 12.8g Fat; 11.6g Carbs; 67g Protein; 6.8g Sugars

190. Taco Casserole with Cheese

(Ready in about 25 minutes | Servings 4)

Ingredients

1 pound lean ground pork
1/2 pound ground beef
1/4 cup tomato puree
Sea salt and ground black pepper, to taste
1 teaspoon smoked paprika
1/2 teaspoon dried oregano
1 teaspoon dried basil
1 teaspoon dried rosemary
2 eggs
1 cup Cottage cheese, crumbled, at room temperature
1/2 cup Cotija cheese, shredded

Directions

Lightly grease a casserole dish with a nonstick cooking oil. Add the ground meat to the bottom of your casserole dish.

Add the tomato puree. Sprinkle with salt, black pepper, paprika, oregano, basil, and rosemary.

In a mixing bowl, whisk the egg with cheese. Place on top of the ground meat mixture. Place a piece of foil on top.

Bake in the preheated Air Fryer at 350 degrees F for 10 minutes; remove the foil and cook an additional 6 minutes. Bon appétit!

Per serving: 449 Calories; 23g Fat; 5.6g Carbs; 54g Protein; 3.2g Sugars

BEEF

191. Paprika Porterhouse Steak with Cauliflower

(Ready in about 20 minutes | Servings 4)

Ingredients

1 pound Porterhouse steak, sliced
1 teaspoon butter, room temperature
Coarse sea salt and ground black pepper, to taste
1/2 teaspoon shallot powder

1/2 teaspoon porcini powder
1 teaspoon granulated garlic
1 teaspoon smoked paprika
1 pound cauliflower, torn into florets

Directions

Brush the steak with butter on all sides; season it with all spices. Season the cauliflower with salt and pepper to taste.

Place the steak in the cooking basket and roast at 400 degrees F for 12 minutes; turn over halfway through the cooking time.

Remove the cauliflower from the basket and continue to cook your steak for 2 to 3 minutes if needed.

Serve the steak garnished with the cauliflower. Eat warm.

Per serving: 196 Calories; 7.8g Fat; 7.5g Carbs; 25.4g Protein; 2.8g Sugars

192. Chuck Roast with Sweet 'n' Sticky Sauce

(Ready in about 35 minutes | Servings 3)

Ingredients

1 pound chuck roast
Sea salt and ground black pepper, to taste
2 tablespoons butter, softened
1 tablespoon coriander, chopped

1 tablespoon fresh scallions, chopped
1 teaspoon soy sauce
1 tablespoon fish sauce
2 tablespoons honey

Directions

Season the chuck roast with salt and pepper; spritz a nonstick cooking oil all over the beef.

Air fry at 400 degrees F for 30 to 35 minutes, flipping the chuck roast halfway through the cooking time.

While the roast is cooking, heat the other ingredients in a sauté pan over medium-high heat. Bring to a boil and reduce the heat; let it simmer, partially covered, until the sauce has thickened and reduced.

Slice the chuck roast into thick cuts and serve garnished with sweet 'n' sticky sauce. Bon appétit!

Per serving: 325 Calories; 16.8g Fat; 13.7g Carbs; 31.9g Protein; 12.8g Sugars

193. Italian Sausage Peperonata Pomodoro

(Ready in about 15 minutes | Servings 2)

Ingredients

2 bell peppers, sliced
1 chili pepper
1 yellow onion, sliced
2 smoked beef sausages
1 teaspoon olive oil

2 medium-sized tomatoes, peeled and crushed
1 garlic clove, minced
1 teaspoon Italian spice mix

Directions

Spritz the sides and bottom of the cooking basket with a nonstick cooking oil. Add the peppers, onion and sausage to the cooking basket.

Cook at 390 degrees F for 10 minutes, shaking the basket periodically. Reserve.

Heat the olive oil in a medium-sized saucepan over medium-high flame until sizzling; add in the tomatoes and garlic; let it cook for 2 to 3 minutes.

Stir in the peppers, onion and Italian spice mix. Continue to cook for 1 minute longer or until heated through. Fold in the sausages and serve warm. Bon appétit!

Per serving: 473 Calories; 34.6g Fat; 19.3g Carbs; 22.1g Protein; 9.7g Sugars

194. Flank Steak with Dijon Honey Butter

(Ready in about 15 minutes | Servings 3)

Ingredients

1 pound flank steak
1/2 teaspoon olive oil
Sea salt and red pepper flakes, to taste

3 tablespoons butter
1 teaspoon Dijon mustard
1 teaspoon honey

Directions

Brush the flank steak with olive oil and season with salt and pepper.

Cook at 400 degrees F for 6 minutes. Then, turn the steak halfway through the cooking time and continue to cook for a further 6 minutes.

In the meantime, prepare the Dijon honey butter by whisking the remaining ingredients.

Serve the warm flank steak dolloped with the Dijon honey butter. Bon appétit!

Per serving: 333 Calories; 19.8g Fat; 3.5g Carbs; 32.8g Protein; 3.1g Sugars

195. Easy Homemade Hamburgers

(Ready in about 15 minutes | Servings 2)

Ingredients

3/4 pound lean ground chuck
Kosher salt and ground black pepper, to taste
3 tablespoons onion, minced
1 teaspoon garlic, minced
1 teaspoon soy sauce

1/2 teaspoon smoked paprika
1/4 teaspoon ground cumin
1/2 teaspoon cayenne pepper
1/2 teaspoon mustard seeds
2 burger buns

Directions

Thoroughly combine the ground chuck, salt, black pepper, onion, garlic and soy sauce in a mixing dish.

Season with smoked paprika, ground cumin, cayenne pepper and mustard seeds. Mix to combine well.

Shape the mixture into 2 equal patties.

Spritz your patties with a nonstick cooking spray. Air fry your burgers at 380 degrees F for about 11 minutes or to your desired degree of doneness.

Place your burgers on burger buns and serve with favorite toppings. Devour!

Per serving: 433 Calories; 17.4g Fat; 40g Carbs; 39.2g Protein; 6.4g Sugars

196. Rustic Mini Meatloaves

(Ready in about 20 minutes | Servings 3)

Ingredients

2 slices bacon
1 onion, chopped
1 bell pepper, chopped
3/4 pound lean ground beef
1/2 teaspoon rosemary
1/4 teaspoon basil
1/2 teaspoon oregano

Coarse sea salt and ground black pepper, to taste
1 teaspoon fresh garlic, minced
1 teaspoon mustard
1 egg, beaten
1/2 cup tomato paste

Directions

Het up a frying pan over medium-high heat. Cook the bacon for 2 to 3 minutes, crumbling with a fork or wide spatula; reserve, leaving the bacon fat in the pan.

Now, sauté the onion and pepper until just tender and fragrant.

Add in the ground beef and cook for 2 to 3 minutes longer until no longer pink. Stir in the spices, garlic, mustard, egg and 1/4 of tomato paste.

Add in the reserved bacon. Stir to combine well.

Divide the mixture between three ramekins. Divide the remaining tomato paste between the ramekins.

Then, air fry at 380 degrees F for 10 minutes. Let it rest for a few minutes before serving. Devour!

Per serving: 379 Calories; 21.4g Fat; 15.6g Carbs; 30.2g Protein; 8.8g Sugars

197. Ritzy Cheesy Meatballs

(Ready in about 15 minutes | Servings 2)

Ingredients

1/2 pound ground chuck
1/4 pound ground pork
1/3 cup shallots, chopped
2 tablespoons Italian parsley, chopped
1 teaspoon garlic, minced
1/3 cup parmesan cheese, grated

1 tablespoon flaxseed meal
1/3 cup saltines (e.g. Ritz crackers), crushed
1 tablespoon oyster sauce
1/2 teaspoon cayenne pepper
Kosher salt and ground black pepper, to taste

Directions

In a mixing bowl, thoroughly combine all ingredients until everything is well incorporated.

Shape the mixture into 6 equal meatballs.

Spritz a cooking basket with a nonstick cooking spray. Cook the meatballs at 360 degrees F for 10 to 11 minutes, shaking the basket occasionally to ensure even cooking. An instant thermometer should read 165 degrees F.

Bon appétit!

Per serving: 471 Calories; 28.4g Fat; 14.3g Carbs; 38g Protein; 0.8g Sugars

198. Kansas City-Style Ribs

(Ready in about 35 minutes + marinating time | Servings 3)

Ingredients

1 pound beef ribs
1/4 cup ketchup
1/4 cup rum
1 tablespoon mustard
1 tablespoon olive oil
1 tablespoon brown sugar

1 teaspoon garlic powder
1/2 teaspoon onion powder
1/2 teaspoon chili powder
1 teaspoon liquid smoke
Sea salt and ground black pepper, to season

Directions

Place all ingredients in a ceramic bowl, cover and allow it to marinate for 3 to 4 hours.

Roast in your Air Fryer at 400 degrees F for 10 minutes. Reduce heat to 330 degrees F and cook an additional 20 minutes.

Warm the remaining marinade in a nonstick skillet over a moderate flame to make the sauce. Drizzle the sauce over the beef ribs and eat warm.

Per serving: 327 Calories; 13.4g Fat; 9.2g Carbs; 32.4g Protein; 6.9g Sugars

199. Classic Filet Mignon with Mushrooms

(Ready in about 20 minutes | Servings 2)

Ingredients

1 pound filet mignon
2 garlic cloves, halved
Salt and black pepper, to season
1 bell pepper, sliced

6 ounces button mushrooms, cleaned and halved
1 teaspoon olive oil

Directions

Rub your filet mignon with garlic halves. Season it with the salt and black pepper to taste. Place the filet mignon in a lightly greased cooking basket.

Top with peppers and air fry them at 400 degrees F for 10 minutes. Turn them over. Now, add in the mushrooms. Drizzle olive oil over the mushrooms and continue to cook for 8 minutes more.

Serve warm.

Per serving: 363 Calories; 13.4g Fat; 8.2g Carbs; 55g Protein; 4.4g Sugars

200. Masala Dum Kabab

(Ready in about 20 minutes | Servings 3)

Ingredients

1 ½ pounds ground beef
1/2 cup breadcrumbs
1 teaspoon garam masala
1 teaspoon garlic paste

1/2 teaspoon turmeric powder
1/2 teaspoon coriander powder
Sea salt and ground black pepper, to taste

Directions

In a mixing bowl, combine all ingredients. Divide the mixture into three pieces and roll them into kabab shape.

Spritz each kabab with a nonstick spray and place them in the cooking basket.

Cook in the preheated Air Fryer at 380 degrees F for 10 minutes. Flip them over and cook an additional 5 minutes.

Serve immediately with warm chapati.

Per serving: 313 Calories; 11.5g Fat; 2.8g Carbs; 49g Protein; 0.3g Sugars

201. Greek-Style Roast Beef

(Ready in about 55 minutes | Servings 3)

Ingredients

1 clove garlic, halved
1 ½ pounds beef eye round roast
1 zucchini, sliced lengthwise
2 teaspoons olive oil

1 teaspoon Greek spice mix
Sea salt, to season
1/2 cup Greek-style yogurt

Directions

Rub the beef eye round roast with garlic halves.

Brush the beef eye round roast and zucchini with olive oil. Sprinkle with spices and place the beef in the cooking basket.

Roast in your Air Fryer at 400 degrees F for 40 minutes. Turn the beef over.

Add the zucchini to the cooking basket and continue to cook for 12 minutes more or until cooked through. Serve warm, garnished with Greek-style yogurt. Enjoy!

Per serving: 348 Calories; 16.1g Fat; 1.6g Carbs; 49g Protein; 0.9g Sugars

202. Chuck Roast with Rustic Potatoes

(Ready in about 50 minutes | Servings 3)

Ingredients

1 tablespoon brown mustard
2 tablespoons tomato paste, preferably homemade
2 tablespoons BBQ sauce
1 tablespoon Worcester sauce
1 ½ pounds chuck roast
1 pound medium-sized russet potatoes, quartered

Coarse sea salt and ground black pepper, to taste
1/2 teaspoon cayenne pepper
1 teaspoon shallot powder
1 teaspoon granulated garlic
1 teaspoon dried marjoram

Directions

Mix the mustard, tomato paste, BBQ sauce and Worcester sauce in a small bowl. Rub this mixture all over the chuck roast.

Add spices and place the chuck roast in the Air Fryer cooking basket that is lightly greased with melted butter.

Air fry at 400 degrees F for 30 minutes; turn it over and scatter potato chunks around the beef. Continue to cook an additional 15 minutes. Double check to make sure the beef is cooked thoroughly.

Taste and adjust seasonings. Place the meat on a cutting board. Slice the beef against the grain and eat warm.

Per serving: 438 Calories; 13.1g Fat; 30.8g Carbs; 50g Protein; 2.9g Sugars

203. Marinated London Broil

(Ready in about 25 minutes+ marinating time | Servings 2)

Ingredients

2 tablespoons soy sauce
2 garlic cloves, minced
1 teaspoon mustard
1 tablespoon olive oil
2 tablespoons wine vinegar
1 tablespoon honey
1 pound London broil
1/2 teaspoon paprika
Salt and black pepper, to taste

Directions

In a ceramic dish, mix the soy sauce, garlic, mustard, oil, wine vinegar and honey. Add in the London broil and let it marinate for 2 hours in your refrigerator.

Season the London broil with paprika, salt and pepper.

Cook in the preheated Air Fryer at 400 degrees F for 10 minutes; turn over and continue to cook for a further 10 minutes.

Slice the London broil against the grain and eat warm. Enjoy!

Per serving: 448 Calories; 22.6g Fat; 13.8g Carbs; 48g Protein; 11.7g Sugars

204. Mayo Roasted Sirloin Steak

(Ready in about 20 minutes | Servings 3)

Ingredients

1 pound sirloin steak, cubed
1/2 cup mayonnaise
1 tablespoon red wine vinegar
1/2 teaspoon dried basil
1 teaspoon garlic, minced
1/2 teaspoon cayenne pepper
Kosher salt and ground black pepper, to season

Directions

Pat dry the sirloin steak with paper towels.

In a small mixing dish, thoroughly combine the remaining ingredients until everything is well incorporated.

Toss the cubed steak with the mayonnaise mixture and transfer to the Air Fryer cooking basket.

Cook in the preheated Air Fryer at 400 degrees F for 7 minutes. Shake the basket and continue to cook for a further 7 minutes. Bon appétit!

Per serving: 418 Calories; 31.3g Fat; 0.2g Carbs; 30.1g Protein; 0.2g Sugars

205. Easy Beef Burritos

(Ready in about 25 minutes | Servings 3)

Ingredients

1 pound rump steak
Sea salt and crushed red pepper, to taste
1/2 teaspoon shallot powder
1/2 teaspoon porcini powder
1/2 teaspoon celery seeds
1/2 teaspoon dried Mexican oregano
1 teaspoon piri piri powder
1 teaspoon lard, melted
3 (approx 7-8" dia) whole-wheat tortillas

Directions

Toss the rump steak with the spices and melted lard.

Cook in your Air Fryer at 390 degrees F for 20 minutes, turning it halfway through the cooking time. Place on a cutting board to cool slightly.

Slice against the grain into thin strips.

Spoon the beef strips onto wheat tortillas; top with your favorite fixings, roll them up and serve. Enjoy!

Per serving: 368 Calories; 13g Fat; 20.2g Carbs; 35.1g Protein; 2.7g Sugars

206. Argentinian Beef Empanadas

(Ready in about 20 minutes | Servings 2)

Ingredients

1/2 pound ground chuck
1/2 yellow onion
1 teaspoon fresh garlic, minced
2 tablespoons piri piri sauce
1 tablespoon mustard
6 cubes Cotija cheese
6 Goya discos pastry dough

Directions

Heat a nonstick skillet over medium-high heat. Once hot, cook the ground beef, onion and garlic until tender, about 6 minutes. Crumble with a fork and stir in the piri piri sauce; stir to combine.

Divide the sauce between empanadas. Top with mustard and cheese. Fold each of them in half and seal the edges.

Bake in the preheated Air Fryer at 340 degrees F for about 8 minutes, flipping them halfway through the cooking time. Serve with salsa sauce if desired.

Per serving: 630 Calories; 27.3g Fat; 72g Carbs; 22g Protein; 9.7g Sugars

207. Grandma's Meat Tarts

(Ready in about 20 minutes | Servings 3)

Ingredients

6 ounces refrigerated pie crusts
3/4 pound lean ground beef
1/2 onion
1 clove garlic, finely chopped
Sea salt and ground black pepper, to taste
1/2 cup tomato paste
3 Swiss cheese slices
1 egg white, beaten

Directions

Start by preheating your Air Fryer to 360 degrees F.

Cook the ground beef, onion and garlic in a nonstick skillet until the beef is no longer pink and the onion is translucent. Season with salt and pepper; fold in the tomato paste and stir to combine.

Unroll the pie crust and use a round cookie cutter to make 3 even rounds.

Fill the pie crust rounds with the beef mixture. Top with cheese. Moisten the outside of each round with beaten egg white.

Fold the pie crust rounds in half and use a fork to gently press the edges. Cook at 360 degrees F for about 15 minutes. Serve immediately.

Per serving: 496 Calories; 23.3g Fat; 41.2g Carbs; 32.3g Protein; 7g Sugars

208. Beef Parmigiana Sliders

(Ready in about 15 minutes | Servings 2)

Ingredients

1/2 pound lean ground chuck
1 ounce bacon bits
2 tablespoons tomato paste
3 tablespoons shallots, chopped
1 garlic clove, minced
1/4 cup parmesan cheese, grated
1 teaspoon cayenne pepper
Salt and black pepper, to taste
4 pretzel rolls

Directions

Thoroughly combine the ground chuck, bacon bits, tomato paste, shallots, garlic, parmesan cheese, cayenne pepper, salt, black pepper.

Shape the mixture into 4 equal patties.

Spritz your patties with a nonstick cooking spray. Air fry your burgers at 380 degrees F for about 11 minutes or to your desired degree of doneness.

Place your burgers on pretzel rolls and serve with favorite toppings. Enjoy!

Per serving: 516 Calories; 20.7g Fat; 42g Carbs; 34.3g Protein; 5.1g Sugars

209. Authentic Greek Souvlaki with Sauce

(Ready in about 15 minutes + marinating time | Servings 2)

Ingredients

1/2 pound sirloin steak, cut into bite-sized pieces
1 tablespoon olive oil
2 tablespoons Worcestershire sauce
4 tablespoons wine vinegar
1 tablespoon molasses
1 tablespoon mustard
2 garlic cloves, pressed
1 teaspoon dried oregano
1/4 teaspoon sea salt
1 teaspoon black peppercorns
4 tablespoons Greek-style yogurt
1/2 teaspoon tzatziki spice mix
2 tablespoons mayonnaise
4 wooden skewer sticks, soaked in water

Directions

Place the sirloin steak, olive oil, Worcestershire sauce, vinegar, molasses, mustard, garlic, oregano, salt and black peppercorns in a ceramic dish.

Place in your refrigerator and let it marinate overnight.

Thread the beef cubes onto skewers. Cook in preheated Air Fryer at 395 degrees F for 12 minutes, flipping halfway through the cooking time.

In the meantime, mix the Greek yogurt with the tzatziki spice mix and mayo. Serve the souvlaki with the sauce on the side.

Per serving: 366 Calories; 20.7g Fat; 14.8g Carbs; 26.3g Protein; 10.1g Sugars

210. Dad's Barbecued Ribs

(Ready in about 20 minutes + marinating time | Servings 3)

Ingredients

1 pound beef ribs	1 tablespoon brown sugar
1/4 cup ketchup	2 tablespoons soy sauce
1/4 cup tequila	1/2 red onion, sliced
1 tablespoon brown mustard	2 garlic cloves, pressed

Directions

Cut the ribs into serving size portions and transfer them to a ceramic dish. Add in the remaining ingredients, cover and allow it to marinate in your refrigerator overnight.

Discard the marinade. Grill in the preheated Air Fryer at 400 degrees F for 10 minutes. Turn them over and continue to cook for 10 minutes more.

Meanwhile, make the sauce by warming the marinade ingredients in a nonstick pan. Spoon over the warm ribs and serve immediately.

Per serving: 566 Calories; 45g Fat; 18g Carbs; 25.7g Protein; 10.3g Sugars

211. London Broil with Herb Butter

(Ready in about 30 minutes | Servings 3)

Ingredients

1 pound London broil	1 tablespoon cilantro, chopped
Herb butter:	1 tablespoon chives, chopped
2 tablespoons butter, at room temperature	1 tablespoon lemon juice
1 teaspoon basil, chopped	Coarse sea salt and crushed black peppercorns, to taste

Directions

Pat the London broil dry with paper towels.

Mix all ingredients for the herb butter.

Cook in the preheated Air Fryer at 400 degrees F for 14 minutes; turn over, brush with the herb butter and continue to cook for a further 12 minutes.

Slice the London broil against the grain and serve warm.

Per serving: 378 Calories; 21.3g Fat; 0.4g Carbs; 47g Protein; 0.3g Sugars

212. BBQ Glazed Beef Riblets

(Ready in about 15 minutes + marinating time | Servings 3)

Ingredients

1 pound beef riblets	1 tablespoon oyster sauce
Sea salt and red pepper, to taste	2 tablespoons rice vinegar
1/4 cup tomato paste	1 tablespoon stone-ground mustard
1/4 cup Worcestershire sauce	
2 tablespoons hot sauce	

Directions

Combine all ingredients in a glass dish, cover and marinate at least 2 hours in your refrigerator.

Discard the marinade and place riblets in the Air Fryer cooking basket.

Cook in the preheated Air Fryer at 360 degrees F for 12 minutes, shaking the basket halfway through to ensure even cooking.

Heat the reserved marinade in a small skillet over a moderate flame; spoon the glaze over the riblets and serve immediately.

Per serving: 258 Calories; 9.5g Fat; 10.4g Carbs; 32.7g Protein; 5.3g Sugars

213. American-Style Roast Beef

(Ready in about 30 minutes | Servings 3)

Ingredients

1 pound beef eye of round roast	1/2 teaspoon cumin powder
1 teaspoon sesame oil	Sea salt and black pepper, to taste
1 teaspoon red pepper flakes	1 sprig thyme, crushed
1/4 teaspoon dried bay laurel	

Directions

Simply toss the beef with the remaining ingredients; toss until well coated on all sides.

Cook in the preheated Air Fryer at 390 degrees F for 15 to 20 minutes, flipping the meat halfway through to cook on the other side.

Remove from the cooking basket, cover loosely with foil and let rest for 15 minutes before carving and serving. Bon appétit!

Per serving: 294 Calories; 10.9g Fat; 0.3g Carbs; 45.9g Protein; 0.3g Sugars

214. Porterhouse Steak with Tangy Sauce

(Ready in about 20 minutes | Servings 2)

Ingredients

1/2 pound Porterhouse steak, cut into four thin pieces	1 teaspoon ginger juice
Salt and pepper, to season	1 tablespoon fish sauce
1 teaspoon sesame oil	1 tablespoon soy sauce
1 teaspoon garlic paste	1 habanero pepper, minced
	2 tablespoons brown sugar

Directions

Pat the steak dry and generously season it with salt and black pepper.

Cook in the preheated Air Fryer at 400 degrees F for 7 minutes; turn on the other side and cook an additional 7 to 8 minutes.

To make the sauce, heat the remaining ingredients in a small saucepan over medium-high heat; let it simmer for a few minutes until heated through.

Spoon the sauce over the steak and serve over hot cooked rice or egg noodles. Bon appétit!

Per serving: 309 Calories; 8.1g Fat; 12.3g Carbs; 42.5g Protein; 10.3g Sugars

215. Beef Sausage-Stuffed Zucchini

(Ready in about 30 minutes | Servings 2)

Ingredients

1/2 pound beef sausage, crumbled	2 small-sized zucchini, halved lengthwise and seeds removed
1/2 cup tortilla chips, crushed	1/2 cup sharp cheddar cheese, grated
1/2 teaspoon garlic, pressed	
1/4 cup tomato paste	

Directions

In a mixing bowl, thoroughly combine the beef sausage, tortilla chips, garlic and tomato paste. Divide the sausage mixture between the zucchini halves.

Bake in the preheated Air Fryer at 400 degrees F for 20 minutes.

Top with grated cheddar cheese and cook an additional 5 minutes. Enjoy!

Per serving: 435 Calories; 28g Fat; 19.3g Carbs; 26.5g Protein; 7.7g Sugars

216. Beef and Broccoli Stir-Fry

(Ready in about 20 minutes | Servings 2)

Ingredients

1/2 pound beef stew meat, cut into bite-sized cubes
1/2 pound broccoli, cut into florets
1 small shallot, sliced
1 teaspoon peanut oil
1/2 teaspoon garlic powder
Salt and red pepper, to taste
1 teaspoon Five-spice powder
1 tablespoon fish sauce
1 tablespoon tamari sauce
1 teaspoon sesame seed oil
1 teaspoon Chiu Chow chili sauce

Directions

Toss all ingredients until the beef and veggies are well coated.

Cook in the preheated Air Fryer at 400 degrees F for 6 minutes; shake the basket and continue to air fry for 6 minutes more.

Now, test the meat for doneness, remove the vegetables and cook the meat for 5 minutes more if needed.

Taste and adjust seasonings. Serve immediately.

Per serving: 500 Calories; 23.1g Fat; 9.2g Carbs; 65g Protein; 2.4g Sugars

217. Filet Mignon and Green Bean Salad

(Ready in about 25 minutes | Servings 2)

Ingredients

1/2 pound filet mignon
Salt and ground black pepper, to taste
1/2 pound green beans
1/2 teaspoon butter, melted
1 red bell pepper, sliced
1 green bell pepper, sliced
1 cup mixed greens
1/4 cup walnuts, roughly chopped
1/4 cup feta cheese, crumbled
2 tablespoons tahini
1 tablespoon Dijon mustard
1 tablespoon sesame oil
1 tablespoon balsamic vinegar
2 tablespoons pomegranate seeds

Directions

Season the fillet mignon with salt and pepper to taste. Cook in the preheated Air Fryer at 400 degrees F for 18 minutes, turning them over halfway through the cooking time. Set aside.

Then, add the green beans to the cooking basket and drizzle it with melted butter. Cook at 400 degrees F for 5 minutes, shaking the basket once or twice.

Slice the beef into bite-sized strips and transfer to a nice salad bowl.

Toss the beef and green beans with bell peppers, mixed greens, walnuts and feta cheese.

Then, make the dressing by whisking tahini, mustard, sesame oil and balsamic vinegar; dress your salad and serve garnished with pomegranate seeds. Bon appétit!

Per serving: 500 Calories; 33g Fat; 20.1g Carbs; 33.5g Protein; 8.2g Sugars

218. Cuban Mojo Beef

(Ready in about 15 minutes | Servings 3)

Ingredients

3/4 pound blade steak, cut into cubes
1 teaspoon olive oil
Salt and red pepper flakes, to season
Mojo sauce:
1 teaspoon garlic, smashed
2 tablespoons extra-virgin olive oil
2 tablespoons fresh parsley, chopped
2 tablespoons fresh cilantro, chopped
1/2 lime, freshly squeezed
1 green chili pepper, minced

Directions

Toss the steak with olive oil, salt and red pepper.

Cook in your Air Fryer at 400 degrees F for 12 minutes, turning them over halfway through the cooking time.

Meanwhile, make the sauce by mixing all ingredients in your food processor or blender. Serve the warm blade steak with the Mojo sauce on the side. Enjoy!

Per serving: 263 Calories; 17.4g Fat; 4.1g Carbs; 23.5g Protein; 2g Sugars

219. Italian-Style Steak with Cremini Mushrooms

(Ready in about 15 minutes | Servings 2)

Ingredients

1/2 pound flank steak, cut into bite-sized pieces
8 ounces Cremini mushrooms, sliced
2 tablespoons tamari sauce
1 tablespoon peanut oil
1 teaspoon Italian seasoning blend
Salt and black pepper, to taste

Directions

Toss the steak and mushrooms with tamari sauce, peanut oil, Italian spices, salt and black pepper. Toss until the steak and mushrooms are well coated on all sides.

Transfer the beef to the Air Fryer cooking basket. Cook at 400 degrees F for 7 minutes.

Then, shake the basket and stir in the mushrooms. Continue to cook for 5 minutes longer. Serve immediately.

Per serving: 260 Calories; 12.4g Fat; 7.9g Carbs; 28.4g Protein; 4.7g Sugars

220. Grandma's Roast Beef with Harvest Vegetables

(Ready in about 45 minutes + marinating time | Servings 3)

Ingredients

1 pound beef roast
1 teaspoon brown mustard
1/4 cup apple juice
1 tablespoon fish sauce
1 tablespoon honey
1/2 teaspoon dried dill
1/2 teaspoon dried thyme
2 medium-sized carrots, sliced
1 parsnip, sliced
1 red onion, sliced
Sea salt and ground black pepper, to taste
1 teaspoon paprika

Directions

Toss the beef roast with the mustard, apple juice, fish sauce, honey, dill and thyme in a glass bowl. Cover and let it marinate in your refrigerator overnight.

Add the marinated beef roast to the cooking basket, discarding the marinade.

Roast in your Air Fryer at 400 degrees F for 40 minutes. Turn the beef over and baste with the reserved marinade.

Add the carrots, parsnip and onion to the cooking basket; continue to cook for 12 minutes more. Season the beef and vegetables with salt, black pepper and paprika. Serve warm.

Per serving: 272 Calories; 8.9g Fat; 17.1g Carbs; 32.1g Protein; 10.3g Sugars

221. Chicago-Style Beef Sandwich

(Ready in about 25 minutes | Servings 2)

Ingredients

1/2 pound chuck, boneless
1 tablespoon olive oil
1 tablespoon soy sauce
1/4 teaspoon ground bay laurel
1/2 teaspoon shallot powder
1/4 teaspoon porcini powder
1/2 teaspoon garlic powder
1/2 teaspoon cayenne pepper
Kosher salt and ground black pepper, to taste
1 cup pickled vegetables, chopped
2 ciabatta rolls, sliced in half

Directions

Toss the chuck roast with olive oil, soy sauce and spices until well coated.

Cook in the preheated Air Fryer at 400 degrees F for 20 minutes, turning over halfway through the cooking time.

Shred the meat with two forks and adjust seasonings.

Top the bottom halves of the ciabatta rolls with a generous portion of the meat and pickled vegetables. Place the tops of the ciabatta rolls on the sandwiches. Serve immediately and enjoy!

Per serving: 385 Calories; 17.4g Fat; 28.1g Carbs; 29.8g Protein; 6.2g Sugars

222. Classic Beef Jerky

(Ready in about 4 hours 30 minutes | Servings 4)

Ingredients

6 ounces top round steak, cut into 1/8-inch thick strips
1/2 teaspoon fresh garlic, crushed
1 teaspoon onion powder

2 tablespoons Worcestershire sauce
1/2 tablespoon honey
1 teaspoon liquid smoke
1 teaspoon hot sauce

Directions

Transfer the strips of steak to a large Ziplock bag; add in the other ingredients, seal the bag and shake to combine well.

Refrigerate for at least 30 minutes.

Cook in the preheated Air Fryer at 160 degrees F for about 4 hours, until it is dry and firm.

Refrigerate in an airtight container for up to 1 month. Bon appétit!

Per serving: 77 Calories; 2.4g Fat; 4.1g Carbs; 8.9g Protein; 3.1g Sugars

223. Mediterranean Burgers with Onion Jam

(Ready in about 20 minutes | Servings 2)

Ingredients

1/2 pound ground chuck
2 tablespoons scallions, chopped
1/2 teaspoon garlic, minced
1 teaspoon brown mustard
Kosher salt and ground black pepper, to taste
2 burger buns
2 ounces Haloumi cheese
1 medium tomato, sliced
2 Romaine lettuce leaves

Onion jam:
2 tablespoons butter, at room temperature
2 red onions, sliced
Sea salt and ground black pepper, to taste
1 cup red wine
2 tablespoons honey
1 tablespoon fresh lemon juice

Directions

Mix the ground chuck, scallions, garlic, mustard, salt and black pepper until well combined; shape the mixture into two equal patties.

Spritz a cooking basket with a nonstick cooking spray. Air fry your burgers at 370 degrees F for about 11 minutes or to your desired degree of doneness.

Meanwhile, make the onion jam. In a small saucepan, melt the butter; once hot, cook the onions for about 4 minutes. Turn the heat to simmer, add salt, black pepper and wine and cook until liquid evaporates.

Stir in the honey and continue to simmer until the onions are a jam-like consistency; afterwards, drizzle with freshly squeezed lemon juice.

Top the bottom halves of the burger buns with the warm beef patty. Top with haloumi cheese, tomato, lettuce and onion jam.

Set the bun tops in place and serve right now. Enjoy!

Per serving: 474 Calories; 26.5g Fat; 32.9g Carbs; 29g Protein; 26.1g Sugars

224. Dad's Meatloaf with a Twist

(Ready in about 35 minutes | Servings 2)

Ingredients

1 tablespoon olive oil
1 onion, chopped
1/2 teaspoon garlic, minced
1 Italian pepper, deveined and chopped
1 Serrano pepper, deveined and chopped

1/2 pound ground beef
1 tablespoon soy sauce
1 tablespoon Dijon mustard
1/2 cup crushed corn flakes
4 tablespoons tomato paste
1 teaspoon Italian seasoning mix
1/2 teaspoon liquid smoke

Directions

Start by preheating your Air Fryer to 350 degrees F.

In a mixing bowl, thoroughly combine the onion, garlic, peppers, ground beef, soy sauce, mustard and crushed corn flakes. Salt to taste.

Mix until everything is well incorporated and press into a lightly greased meatloaf pan.

Air fry for about 25 minutes. Whisk the tomato paste with the Italian seasoning mix and liquid smoke; spread the mixture over the top of your meatloaf.

Continue to cook for 3 minutes more. Let it rest for 6 minutes before slicing and serving. Bon appétit!

Per serving: 521 Calories; 25.5g Fat; 42.9g Carbs; 32g Protein; 9.2g Sugars

225. Tex-Mex Taco Pizza

(Ready in about 20 minutes | Servings 1)

Ingredients

1 teaspoon lard, melted
4 ounces ground beef sirloin
4 ounces pizza dough
2 tablespoons jarred salsa
1/4 teaspoon Mexican oregano

1/2 teaspoon basil
1/2 teaspoon granulated garlic
2 ounces cheddar cheese grated
1 plum tomato, sliced

Directions

Melt the lard in a skillet over medium-high heat; once hot, cook the beef until no longer pink, about 5 minutes.

Roll the dough out and transfer it to the Air Fryer cooking basket. Spread the jarred salsa over the dough.

Sprinkle Mexican oregano, basil, garlic and cheese over the salsa. Top with the sautéed beef, then with the sliced tomato.

Bake in your Air Fryer at 375 degrees F for about 11 minutes until the bottom of crust is lightly browned. Bon appétit!

Per serving: 686 Calories; 27.1g Fat; 72.4g Carbs; 40.2g Protein; 21.4g Sugars

226. Italian Piadina Sandwich

(Ready in about 20 minutes | Servings 2)

Ingredients

1/2 pound ribeye steak
1 teaspoon sesame oil
Sea salt and red pepper, to taste

2 medium-sized piadinas
2 ounces Fontina cheese, grated
4 tablespoons Giardiniera

Directions

Brush the ribeye steak with sesame oil and season with salt and red pepper.

Cook at 400 degrees F for 6 minutes. Then, turn the steak halfway through the cooking time and continue to cook for a further 6 minutes.

Slice the ribeye steak into bite-sized strips. Top the piadinas with steak strips and cheese.

Heat the sandwich in your Air Fryer at 380 degrees F for about 3 minutes until the cheese melts. Top with Giardiniera and serve.

Bon appétit!

Per serving: 384 Calories; 24.8g Fat; 11.1g Carbs; 31.1g Protein; 4.9g Sugars

227. Doubly Cheesy Meatballs

(Ready in about 15 minutes | Servings 4)

Ingredients

1 pound ground beef
1/4 cup Grana Padano, grated
2 tablespoons scallion, chopped
2 garlic cloves, minced
2 stale crustless bread slices
1 tablespoon Italian seasoning mix

1 egg, beaten
1/4 cup Mozzarella cheese, shredded
Kosher salt and ground black pepper, to taste

Directions

In a mixing bowl, combine all ingredients. Then, shape the mixture into 8 meatballs.

Cook the meatballs at 370 degrees F for 10 minutes, shaking the basket halfway through the cooking time.

Serve the meatballs in a sandwich if desired.

Per serving: 613 Calories; 35.1g Fat; 16.1g Carbs; 57g Protein; 2g Sugars

228. Traditional Italian Beef Braciole

(Ready in about 15 minutes | Servings 4)

Ingredients

1 pound round steak, pounded 1/4 inch thick
Sea salt and ground black pepper, to taste
1 tablespoon olive oil
1 red onion, sliced
1/4 cup provolone cheese, shredded
2 tablespoons marinara sauce
1 tablespoon fresh cilantro, chopped
1 tablespoon fresh Italian parsley, chopped
1 large Italian pepper, deveined and sliced

Directions

Pat the round steak dry with paper towels and generously season it with salt and black pepper.

Heat the olive oil in a small skillet over a moderate heat; once hot, sauté the onion until just tender and translucent.

Add in the cheese, marinara, cilantro, parsley and pepper; stir to combine well. Spoon the mixture onto the center of the steak.

Roll the steak jelly-roll style and secure with toothpicks.

Cook your Braciole in the preheated Air Fryer at 400 degrees F for about 10 minutes, checking the meat halfway through the cooking time.

Serve with hot cooked orecchiette pasta or polenta. Bon appétit!

Per serving: 243 Calories; 13.1g Fat; 3.1g Carbs; 27g Protein; 1.6g Sugars

229. Sunday Beef Schnitzel

(Ready in about 15 minutes | Servings 2)

Ingredients

2 beef schnitzel
Salt and black pepper, to taste
2 ounces all-purpose flour
1 egg, beaten
1/2 cup breadcrumbs
1/2 teaspoon paprika
1 teaspoon olive oil
1/2 lemon, cut into wedges to serve

Directions

Pat the beef dry and generously season it with salt and black pepper.

Add the flour to a rimmed plate. Place the egg in a shallow bowl and mix the breadcrumbs and paprika in another bowl.

Dip the meat in the flour first, then the egg, then the paprika/breadcrumb mixture. Drizzle olive oil over each beef schnitzel.

Cook in the preheated Air Fryer at 390 degrees F for about 10 minutes, flipping the meat halfway through the cooking time. Bon appétit!

Per serving: 501 Calories; 20.1g Fat; 24.1g Carbs; 54.3g Protein; 2g Sugars

230. Taco Stuffed Avocados

(Ready in about 15 minutes | Servings 3)

Ingredients

1/3 pound ground beef
2 tablespoons shallots, minced
1/2 teaspoon garlic, minced
1 tomato, chopped
1/3 teaspoon Mexican oregano
Salt and black pepper, to taste
1 chipotle pepper in adobo sauce, minced
1/4 cup cilantro
3 avocados, cut into halves and pitted
1/2 cup Cotija cheese, grated

Directions

Preheat a nonstick skillet over medium-high heat. Cook the ground beef and shallot for about 4 minutes.

Stir in the garlic and tomato and continue to sauté for a minute or so. Add in the Mexican oregano, salt, black pepper, chipotle pepper and cilantro.

Then, remove a bit of the pulp from each avocado half and fill them with the taco mixture.

Cook in the preheated Air Fryer at 400 degrees F for 5 minutes. Top with Cotija cheese and continue to cook for 4 minutes more or until cheese is bubbly. Enjoy!

Per serving: 521 Calories; 42.1g Fat; 23.1g Carbs; 20.2g Protein; 4.8g Sugars

231. Dijon Top Chuck with Herbs

(Ready in about 1 hour | Servings 3)

Ingredients

1 ½ pounds top chuck
2 teaspoons olive oil
1 tablespoon Dijon mustard
Sea salt and ground black pepper, to taste
1 teaspoon dried marjoram
1 teaspoon dried thyme
1/2 teaspoon fennel seeds

Directions

Start by preheating your Air Fryer to 380 degrees F

Add all ingredients in a Ziploc bag; shake to mix well. Next, spritz the bottom of the Air Fryer basket with cooking spray.

Place the beef in the cooking basket and cook for 50 minutes, turning every 10 to 15 minutes.

Let it rest for 5 to 7 minutes before slicing and serving. Enjoy!

Per serving: 406 Calories; 24.1g Fat; 0.3g Carbs; 44.1g Protein; 0g Sugars

232. Mediterranean-Style Beef Steak and Zucchini

(Ready in about 20 minutes | Servings 4)

Ingredients

1 ½ pounds beef steak
1 pound zucchini
1 teaspoon dried rosemary
1 teaspoon dried basil
1 teaspoon dried oregano
2 tablespoons extra-virgin olive oil
2 tablespoons fresh chives, chopped

Directions

Start by preheating your Air Fryer to 400 degrees F.

Toss the steak and zucchini with the spices and olive oil. Transfer to the cooking basket and cook for 6 minutes.

Now, shale the basket and cook another 6 minutes. Serve immediately garnished with fresh chives. Enjoy!

Per serving: 396 Calories; 20.4g Fat; 3.5g Carbs; 47.8g Protein; 0.1g Sugars

233. Peperonata with Beef Sausage

(Ready in about 35 minutes | Servings 4)

Ingredients

2 teaspoons canola oil
2 bell peppers, sliced
1 green bell pepper, sliced
1 serrano pepper, sliced
1 shallot, sliced
Sea salt and pepper, to taste
1/2 dried thyme
1 teaspoon dried rosemary
1/2 teaspoon mustard seeds
1 teaspoon fennel seeds
2 pounds thin beef parboiled sausage

Directions

Brush the sides and bottom of the cooking basket with 1 teaspoon of canola oil. Add the peppers and shallot to the cooking basket.

Toss them with the spices and cook at 390 degrees F for 15 minutes, shaking the basket occasionally. Reserve.

Turn the temperature to 380 degrees F

Then, add the remaining 1 teaspoon of oil. Once hot, add the sausage and cook in the preheated Air Frye for 15 minutes, flipping them halfway through the cooking time.

Serve with reserved pepper mixture. Bon appétit!

Per serving: 563 Calories; 41.5g Fat; 10.6g Carbs; 35.6g Protein; 7.9g Sugars

234. New York Strip with Mustard Butter

(Ready in about 20 minutes | Servings 4)

Ingredients

1 tablespoon peanut oil
2 pounds New York Strip
1 teaspoon cayenne pepper
Sea salt and freshly cracked black pepper, to taste
1/2 stick butter, softened
1 teaspoon whole-grain mustard
1/2 teaspoon honey

Directions

Rub the peanut oil all over the steak; season with cayenne pepper, salt, and black pepper.

Cook in the preheated Air Fryer at 400 degrees F for 7 minutes; turn over and cook an additional 7 minutes.

Meanwhile, prepare the mustard butter by whisking the butter, whole-grain mustard, and honey.

Serve the roasted New York Strip dolloped with the mustard butter. Bon appétit!

Per serving: 459 Calories; 27.4g Fat; 2.5g Carbs; 48.3g Protein; 1.4g Sugars

235. Scotch Fillet with Sweet 'n' Sticky Sauce

(Ready in about 40 minutes | Servings 4)

Ingredients

2 pounds scotch fillet, sliced into strips
4 tablespoons tortilla chips, crushed
2 green onions, chopped
Sauce:
1 tablespoon butter

2 garlic cloves, minced
1/2 teaspoon dried rosemary
1/2 teaspoon dried dill
1/2 cup beef broth
1 tablespoons fish sauce
2 tablespoons honey

Directions

Start by preheating your Air Fryer to 390 degrees F.

Coat the beef strips with the crushed tortilla chips on all sides. Spritz with cooking spray on all sides and transfer them to the cooking basket.

Cook for 30 minutes, shaking the basket every 10 minutes.

Meanwhile, heat the sauce ingredient in a saucepan over medium-high heat. Bring to a boil and reduce the heat; cook until the sauce has thickened slightly.

Add the steak to the sauce; let it sit approximately 8 minutes. Serve over the hot egg noodles if desired.

Per serving: 556 Calories; 17.9g Fat; 25.8g Carbs; 60g Protein; 10.4g Sugars

236. Roasted Ribeye with Garlic Mayo

(Ready in about 20 minutes | Servings 3)

Ingredients

1 ½ pounds ribeye, bone-in
1 tablespoon butter, room temperature
Salt, to taste
1/2 teaspoon crushed black pepper
1/2 teaspoon dried dill

1/2 teaspoon cayenne pepper
1/2 teaspoon garlic powder
1/2 teaspoon onion powder
1 teaspoon ground coriander
3 tablespoons mayonnaise
1 teaspoon garlic, minced

Directions

Start by preheating your Air Fryer to 400 degrees F.

Pat dry the ribeye and rub it with softened butter on all sides. Sprinkle with seasonings and transfer to the cooking basket.

Cook in the preheated Air Fryer for 15 minutes, flipping them halfway through the cooking time.

In the meantime, simply mix the mayonnaise with garlic and place in the refrigerator until ready to serve. Bon appétit!

Per serving: 437 Calories; 24.8g Fat; 1.8g Carbs; 51g Protein; 0.1g Sugars

237. Crustless Beef and Cheese Tart

(Ready in about 25 minutes | Servings 4)

Ingredients

1 tablespoon canola oil
1 onion, finely chopped
2 fresh garlic cloves, minced
1/2 pound ground chuck
1/2 pound Chorizo sausage, crumbled
1 cup pasta sauce
Sea salt, to taste

1/4 teaspoon ground black pepper
1/2 teaspoon red pepper flakes, crushed
1 cup cream cheese, room temperature
1/2 cup Swiss cheese, shredded
1 egg
1/2 cup crackers, crushed

Directions

Start by preheating your Air Fryer to 370 degrees F.

Grease a baking pan with canola oil.

Add the onion, garlic, ground chuck, sausage, pasta sauce, salt, black pepper, and red pepper. Cook for 9 minutes.

In the meantime, combine cheese with egg. Place the cheese-egg mixture over the beef mixture.

Sprinkle with crushed crackers and cook for 10 minutes. Serve warm and enjoy!

Per serving: 572 Calories; 44.6g Fat; 16.2g Carbs; 28.1g Protein; 8.9g Sugars

238. Beef Taco Roll-Ups with Cotija Cheese

(Ready in about 25 minutes | Servings 4)

Ingredients

1 tablespoon sesame oil
2 tablespoons scallions, chopped
1 garlic clove, minced
1 bell pepper, chopped
1/2 pound ground beef
1/2 teaspoon Mexican oregano
1/2 teaspoon dried marjoram

1 teaspoon chili powder
1/2 cup refried beans
Sea salt and ground black pepper, to taste
1/2 cup Cotija cheese, shredded
8 roll wrappers

Directions

Start by preheating your Air Fryer to 395 degrees F.

Heat the sesame oil in a nonstick skillet over medium-high heat. Cook the scallions, garlic, and peppers until tender and fragrant.

Add the ground beef, oregano, marjoram, and chili powder. Continue cooking for 3 minutes longer or until it is browned.

Stir in the beans, salt, and pepper. Divide the meat/bean mixture between wrappers that are softened with a little bit of water. Top with cheese.

Roll the wrappers and spritz them with cooking oil on all sides.

Cook in the preheated Air Fryer for 11 to 12 minutes, flipping them halfway through the cooking time. Enjoy!

Per serving: 417 Calories; 15.9g Fat; 41g Carbs; 26.2g Protein; 1.5g Sugars

239. Barbecue Skirt Steak

(Ready in about 20 minutes + marinating time | Servings 5)

Ingredients

2 pounds skirt steak
2 tablespoons tomato paste
1 tablespoon tomato ketchup
1 tablespoon olive oil
1 tablespoon soy sauce
1/4 cup rice vinegar
1 tablespoon fish sauce

Sea salt, to taste
1/2 teaspoon dried dill
1/2 teaspoon dried rosemary
1/4 teaspoon black pepper, freshly cracked
1 tablespoon brown sugar

Directions

Place all ingredients in a large ceramic dish; let it marinate for 3 hours in your refrigerator.

Coat the sides and bottom of the Air Fryer with cooking spray.

Add your steak to the cooking basket; reserve the marinade. Cook the skirt steak in the preheated Air Fryer at 400 degrees F for 12 minutes, turning over a couple of times, basting with the reserved marinade.

Serve warm with roasted new potatoes, if desired.

Per serving: 394 Calories; 19g Fat; 4.4g Carbs; 51.3g Protein; 3.3g Sugars

240. Meatballs with Cranberry Sauce

(Ready in about 40 minutes | Servings 4)

Ingredients

Meatballs:
1 ½ pounds ground chuck
1 egg
1 cup rolled oats
1/2 cup Romano cheese, grated
1/2 teaspoon dried basil
1/2 teaspoon dried oregano

1 teaspoon paprika
2 garlic cloves, minced
2 tablespoons scallions, chopped
Sea salt and cracked black pepper, to taste
Cranberry Sauce:
10 ounces BBQ sauce
8 ounces cranberry sauce

Directions

In a large bowl, mix all ingredients for the meatballs. Mix until everything is well incorporated; then, shape the meat mixture into 2-inch balls using a cookie scoop.

Transfer them to the lightly greased cooking basket and cook at 380 degrees F for 10 minutes. Shake the basket occasionally and work in batches.

Add the BBQ sauce and cranberry sauce to a saucepan and cook over moderate heat until you achieve a glaze-like consistency; it will take about 15 minutes.

Gently stir in the air fried meatballs and cook an additional 3 minutes or until heated through. Enjoy!

Per serving: 520 Calories; 22.4g Fat; 44g Carbs; 45.4g Protein; 25.5g Sugars

241. Kid-Friendly Mini Meatloaves

(Ready in about 30 minutes | Servings 4)

Ingredients

2 tablespoons bacon, chopped
1 small-sized onion, chopped
1 bell pepper, chopped
1 garlic clove, minced
1 pound ground beef
1/2 teaspoon dried basil

1/2 teaspoon dried mustard seeds
1/2 teaspoon dried marjoram
Salt and black pepper, to taste
1/2 cup panko crumbs
4 tablespoons tomato puree

Directions

Heat a nonstick skillet over medium-high heat; cook the bacon for 1 to 2 minutes; add the onion, bell pepper, and garlic and cook another 3 minutes or until fragrant.

Heat off. Stir in the ground beef, spices, and panko crumbs. Stir until well combined. Shape the mixture into four mini meatloaves.

Preheat your Air Fryer to 350 degrees F. Spritz the cooking basket with nonstick spray.

Place the mini meatloaves in the cooking basket and cook for 10 minutes; turn them over, top with the tomato puree and continue to cook for 10 minutes more. Bon appétit!

Per serving: 451 Calories; 27.6g Fat; 15.3g Carbs; 33.4g Protein; 3.7g Sugars

242. Quick Sausage and Veggie Sandwiches

(Ready in about 35 minutes | Servings 4)

Ingredients

4 bell peppers
2 tablespoons canola oil
4 medium-sized tomatoes, halved
4 spring onions

4 beef sausages
4 hot dog buns
1 tablespoon mustard

Directions

Start by preheating your Air Fryer to 400 degrees F.

Add the bell peppers to the cooking basket. Drizzle 1 tablespoon of canola oil all over the bell peppers.

Cook for 5 minutes. Turn the temperature down to 350 degrees F. Add the tomatoes and spring onions to the cooking basket and cook an additional 10 minutes.

Reserve your vegetables.

Then, add the sausages to the cooking basket. Drizzle with the remaining tablespoon of canola oil.

Cook in the preheated Air Fryer at 380 degrees F for 15 minutes, flipping them halfway through the cooking time.

Add the sausage to a hot dog bun; top with the air-fried vegetables and mustard; serve.

Per serving: 627 Calories; 41.9g Fat; 41.3g Carbs; 22.2g Protein; 9.3g Sugars

243. Mayonnaise and Rosemary Grilled Steak

(Ready in about 20 minutes | Servings 4)

Ingredients

1 cup mayonnaise
1 tablespoon fresh rosemary, finely chopped
2 tablespoons Worcestershire sauce

Sea salt, to taste
1/2 teaspoon ground black pepper
1 teaspoon smoked paprika
1 teaspoon garlic, minced
1 ½ pounds short loin steak

Directions

Combine the mayonnaise, rosemary, Worcestershire sauce, salt, pepper, paprika, and garlic; mix to combine well.

Now, brush the mayonnaise mixture over both sides of the steak. Lower the steak onto the grill pan.

Grill in the preheated Air Fryer at 390 degrees F for 8 minutes. Turn the steaks over and grill an additional 7 minutes.

Check for doneness with a meat thermometer. Serve warm and enjoy!

Per serving: 620 Calories; 50g Fat; 2.8g Carbs; 39.7g Protein; 1.3g Sugars

244. Cheesy Beef Burrito

(Ready in about 20 minutes | Servings 4)

Ingredients

1 pound rump steak
1 teaspoon garlic powder
1/2 teaspoon onion powder
1/2 teaspoon cayenne pepper
1 teaspoon piri piri powder
1 teaspoon Mexican oregano

Salt and ground black pepper, to taste
1 cup Mexican cheese blend
4 large whole wheat tortillas
1 cup iceberg lettuce, shredded

Directions

Toss the rump steak with the garlic powder, onion powder, cayenne pepper, piri piri powder, Mexican oregano, salt, and black pepper.

Cook in the preheated Air Fryer at 390 degrees F for 10 minutes. Slice against the grain into thin strips. Add the cheese blend and cook for 2 minutes more.

Spoon the beef mixture onto the wheat tortillas; top with lettuce; roll up burrito-style and serve.

Per serving: 468 Calories; 23.5g Fat; 22.1g Carbs; 42.7g Protein; 2.3g Sugars

245. Tender Marinated Flank Steak

(Ready in about 20 minutes + marinating time | Servings 4)

Ingredients

1 ½ pounds flank steak
1/2 cup red wine
1/2 cup apple cider vinegar
2 tablespoons soy sauce
Salt, to taste

1/2 teaspoon ground black pepper
1/2 teaspoon red pepper flakes, crushed
1/2 teaspoon dried basil
1 teaspoon thyme

Directions

Add all ingredients to a large ceramic bowl. Cover and let it marinate for 3 hours in your refrigerator.

Transfer the flank steak to the Air Fryer basket that is previously greased with nonstick cooking oil.

Cook in the preheated Air Fryer at 400 degrees F for 12 minutes, flipping over halfway through the cooking time. Bon appétit!

Per serving: 312 Calories; 15.5g Fat; 2.5g Carbs; 36.8g Protein; 1.9g Sugars

246. Korean-Style Breakfast Patties

(Ready in about 20 minutes | Servings 4)

Ingredients

1 ½ pounds ground beef
1 teaspoon garlic, minced
2 tablespoons scallions, chopped
Sea salt and cracked black pepper, to taste
1 teaspoon Gochugaru (Korean chili powder)
1/2 teaspoon dried marjoram

1 teaspoon dried thyme
1 teaspoon mustard seeds
1/2 teaspoon shallot powder
1/2 teaspoon cumin powder
1/2 teaspoon paprika
1 tablespoon liquid smoke flavoring

Directions

In a mixing bowl, thoroughly combine all ingredients until well combined.

Shape into four patties and spritz them with cooking oil on both sides. Bake at 357 degrees F for 18 minutes, flipping over halfway through the cooking time.

Serve on hamburger buns if desired. Bon appétit!

Per serving: 377 Calories; 19.3g Fat; 2.4g Carbs; 45.9g Protein; 0.7g Sugars

247. New York Strip with Pearl Onions

(Ready in about 20 minutes + marinating time | Servings 4)

Ingredients

1 ½ pounds New York strip, cut into strips
1 (1-pound) head cauliflower, broken into florets
1 cup pearl onion, sliced
Marinade:

1/4 cup tamari sauce
1 tablespoon olive oil
2 cloves garlic, minced
1 teaspoon of ground ginger
1/4 cup tomato paste
1/4 cup red wine

Directions

Mix all ingredients for the marinade. Add the beef to the marinade and let it sit in your refrigerator for 1 hour.

Preheat your Air Fryer to 400 degrees F. Transfer the meat to the Air Fryer basket. Add the cauliflower and onions.

Drizzle a few tablespoons of marinade all over the meat and vegetables. Cook for 12 minutes, shaking the basket halfway through the cooking time. Serve warm.

Per serving: 445 Calories; 28g Fat; 11.2g Carbs; 36.6g Protein; 5.3g Sugars

248. Beef and Vegetable Stir Fry

(Ready in about 35 minutes + marinating time | Servings 4)

Ingredients

2 pounds top round, cut into bite-sized strips
2 garlic cloves, sliced
1 teaspoon dried marjoram
1/4 cup red wine
1 tablespoon tamari sauce

Salt and black pepper, to taste
1 tablespoon olive oil
1 red onion, sliced
2 bell peppers, sliced
1 carrot, sliced

Directions

Place the top round, garlic, marjoram, red wine, tamari sauce, salt and pepper in a bowl, cover and let it marinate for 1 hour.

Preheat your Air Fryer to 390 degrees F and add the oil.

Once hot, discard the marinade and cook the beef for 15 minutes. Add the onion, peppers, carrot, and garlic and continue cooking until tender about 15 minutes more.

Open the Air Fryer every 5 minutes and baste the meat with the remaining marinade. Serve immediately.

Per serving: 418 Calories; 12.2g Fat; 4.8g Carbs; 68.2g Protein; 2.3g Sugars

249. Grilled London Broil with Mustard

(Ready in about 30 minutes + marinating time | Servings 4)

Ingredients

For the marinade:
2 tablespoons Worcestershire sauce
2 garlic cloves, minced
1 tablespoon oil
2 tablespoons rice vinegar
1 tablespoon molasses

London Broil:
2 pounds London broil
2 tablespoons tomato paste
Sea salt and cracked black pepper, to taste
1 tablespoon mustard

Directions

Combine all the marinade ingredients in a mixing bowl; add the London boil to the bowl. Cover and let it marinate for 3 hours.

Preheat the Air Fryer to 400 degrees F. Spritz the Air Fryer grill pan with cooking oil.

Grill the marinated London broil in the preheated Air Fryer for 18 minutes. Turn London broil over, top with the tomato paste, salt, black pepper, and mustard.

Continue to grill an additional 10 minutes. Serve immediately.

Per serving: 531 Calories; 24.1g Fat; 8.7g Carbs; 70g Protein; 6.2g Sugars

250. Homemade Beef Empanadas

(Ready in about 35 minutes | Servings 5)

Ingredients

1 teaspoon olive oil
1/2 onion, chopped
1 garlic clove, minced
1/2 pound ground beef chuck
1 tablespoon raisins
1/2 teaspoon dried oregano

1/2 cup tomato paste
1/2 cup vegetable broth
Salt and ground pepper, to taste
10 Goya discs pastry dough
2 egg whites, beaten

Directions

Heat the oil in a saucepan over medium-high heat. Once hot, sauté the onion and garlic until tender, about 3 minutes.

Then, add the beef and continue to sauté an additional 4 minutes, crumbling with a fork.

Add the raisins, oregano, tomato paste, vegetable broth, salt, and black pepper. Reduce the heat to low and cook an additional 15 minutes.

Preheat the Air Fryer to 330 degrees F. Brush the Air Fryer basket with cooking oil. Divide the sauce between discs. Fold each of the discs in half and seal the edges. Brush the tops with the beaten eggs.

Bake for 7 to 8 minutes, working with batches. Serve with salsa sauce if desired. Enjoy!

Per serving: 490 Calories; 35.1g Fat; 32g Carbs; 15.1g Protein; 13.2g Sugars

251. Indonesian Beef with Peanut Sauce

(Ready in about 25 minutes + marinating time | Servings 4)

Ingredients

2 pounds filet mignon, sliced into bite-sized strips
1 tablespoon oyster sauce
2 tablespoons sesame oil
2 tablespoons tamari sauce
1 tablespoon ginger-garlic paste
1 tablespoon mustard

1 tablespoon honey
1 teaspoon chili powder
1/4 cup peanut butter
2 tablespoons lime juice
1 teaspoon red pepper flakes
2 tablespoons water

Directions

Place the beef strips, oyster sauce, sesame oil, tamari sauce, ginger-garlic paste, mustard, honey, and chili powder in a large ceramic dish.

Cover and allow it to marinate for 2 hours in your refrigerator.

Cook in the preheated Air Fryer at 400 degrees F for 18 minutes, shaking the basket occasionally.

Mix the peanut butter with lime juice, red pepper flakes, and water. Spoon the sauce onto the air fried beef strips and serve warm.

Per serving: 425 Calories; 20.1g Fat; 11.2g Carbs; 50g Protein; 7.9g Sugars

252. Beef Skewers with Pearl Onions and Eggplant

(Ready in about 1 hour 30 minutes | Servings 4)

Ingredients

1 ½ pounds beef stew meat cubes
1/4 cup mayonnaise
1/4 cup sour cream
1 tablespoon yellow mustard
1 tablespoon Worcestershire sauce

1 cup pearl onions
1 medium-sized eggplant, 1
½-inch cubes
Sea salt and ground black pepper,
to taste

Directions

In a mixing bowl, toss all ingredients until everything is well coated.

Place in your refrigerator, cover, and let it marinate for 1 hour.

Soak wooden skewers in water for 15 minutes

Thread the beef cubes, pearl onions and eggplant onto skewers. Cook in preheated Air Fryer at 395 degrees F for 12 minutes, flipping halfway through the cooking time. Serve warm.

Per serving: 500 Calories; 20.6g Fat; 12.8g Carbs; 63.3g Protein; 6.6g Sugars

253. Sunday Tender Skirt Steak

(Ready in about 20 minutes + marinating time | Servings 4)

Ingredient

1/3 cup soy sauce
4 tablespoon molasses
2 garlic cloves, minced
2 tablespoons champagne vinegar
1 teaspoon shallot powder
1 teaspoon porcini powder

1 teaspoon celery seeds
1 teaspoon paprika
1 ½ pounds skirt steak, cut into
slices
Sea salt and ground black pepper,
to taste

Directions

Place the soy sauce, molasses, garlic, vinegar, shallot powder, porcini powder, celery seeds, paprika, and beef in a large resealable plastic bag. Shake well and let it marinate overnight.

Discard the marinade and place the beef in the Air Fryer basket. Season with salt and black pepper to taste.

Cook in the preheated Air Fryer at 400 degrees F for 12 minutes, flipping and basting with the reserved marinade halfway through the cooking time. Bon appétit!

Per serving: 503 Calories; 24.5g Fat; 21.7g Carbs; 46.2g Protein; 19.2g Sugars

254. Beef with Creamed Mushroom Sauce

(Ready in about 20 minutes | Servings 5)

Ingredients

2 tablespoons butter
2 pounds sirloin, cut into four
pieces
Salt and cracked black pepper, to
taste
1 teaspoon cayenne pepper
1/2 teaspoon dried rosemary

1/2 teaspoon dried dill
1/4 teaspoon dried thyme
1 pound Cremini mushrooms,
sliced
1 cup sour cream
1 teaspoon mustard
1/2 teaspoon curry powder

Directions

Start by preheating your Air Fryer to 396 degrees F. Grease a baking pan with butter.

Add the sirloin, salt, black pepper, cayenne pepper, rosemary, dill, and thyme to the baking pan. Cook for 9 minutes.

Next, stir in the mushrooms, sour cream, mustard, and curry powder. Continue to cook another 5 minutes or until everything is heated through.

Spoon onto individual serving plates. Bon appétit!

Per serving: 349 Calories; 16.2g Fat; 7.4g Carbs; 42.9g Protein; 2.6g Sugars

255. Beef and Sausage Meatloaf with Peppers

(Ready in about 35 minutes | Servings 4)

Ingredients

1/2 pound beef sausage, crumbled
1/2 pound ground beef
1/4 cup pork rinds
2 tablespoons Parmesan,
preferably freshly grated
1 shallot, finely chopped

2 garlic cloves, minced
Sea salt and ground black pepper,
to taste
1 red bell pepper, finely chopped
1 serrano pepper, finely chopped

Directions

Start by preheating your Air Fryer to 390 degrees F.

Mix all ingredients in a bowl. Knead until everything is well incorporated.

Shape the mixture into a meatloaf and place in the baking pan that is previously greased with cooking oil.

Cook for 24 minutes in the preheated Air Fryer.

Let it stand on a cooling rack for 6 minutes before slicing and serving. Enjoy!

Per serving: 415 Calories; 32.2g Fat; 4.4g Carbs; 25.3g Protein; 1.5g Sugars

256. Burgers with Caramelized Onions

(Ready in about 30 minutes | Servings 4)

Ingredients

1 pound ground beef
Salt and ground black pepper, to
taste
1 teaspoon garlic powder
1/2 teaspoon cumin powder
1 tablespoon butter
1 red onion, sliced

1 teaspoon brown sugar
1 tablespoon balsamic vinegar
1 tablespoon vegetable stock
4 hamburger buns
8 tomato slices
4 teaspoons mustard

Directions

Start by preheating your Air Fryer to 370 degrees F. Spritz the cooking basket with nonstick cooking oil.

Mix the ground beef with salt, pepper, garlic powder, and cumin powder. Shape the meat mixture into four patties and transfer them to the preheated Air Fryer.

Cook for 10 minutes; turn them over and cook on the other side for 8 to 10 minutes more.

While the burgers are frying, melt the butter in a pan over medium-high heat. Then, add the red onion and sauté for 4 minutes or until soft.

Add the brown sugar, vinegar, and stock and cook for 2 to 3 minute more.

To assemble your burgers, add the beef patties to the hamburger buns. Top with the caramelized onion, tomato, and mustard. Serve immediately and enjoy!

Per serving: 475 Calories; 21.1g Fat; 33.3g Carbs; 36.2g Protein; 6.1g Sugars

257. Authentic Dum Kebab with Raita Sauce

(Ready in about 25 minutes | Servings 4)

Ingredients

1 ½ pounds ground chuck
1 egg
1 medium-sized leek, chopped
2 garlic cloves, smashed
2 tablespoons fresh parsley,
chopped
1 teaspoon fresh rosemary,
chopped
Sea salt, to taste
1/2 teaspoon ground black pepper
1/2 teaspoon chili powder
1 teaspoon garam masala

1 teaspoon papaya paste
1 teaspoon ginger paste
1/2 teaspoon ground cumin
Raita Sauce:
1 small-sized cucumber, grated
and squeezed
A pinch of salt
1 cup full-fat yogurt
1/4 cup fresh cilantro, coarsely
chopped
1 tablespoon fresh lime juice

Directions

Combine all ingredients until everything is well incorporated. Press the meat mixture into a baking pan.

Cook in the preheated Air Fryer at 360 degrees F for 15 minutes. Taste for doneness with a meat thermometer.

Meanwhile, mix all ingredients for the sauce. Serve the warm meatloaf with the sauce on the side. Enjoy!

Per serving: 530 Calories; 31.1g Fat; 10.3g Carbs; 49.3g Protein; 6.1g Sugars

258. Moroccan-Style Steak Salad

(Ready in about 20 minutes | Servings 4)

Ingredients

2 pounds flank steak
1/4 cup soy sauce
4 tablespoons dry red wine
Salt, to taste
1/2 teaspoon ground black pepper
2 parsnips, peeled and sliced lengthways
1 teaspoon paprika
1 teaspoon onion powder

1 teaspoon garlic powder
1/2 teaspoon ground coriander
1/4 teaspoon ground allspice
2 tablespoons olive oil
2 tablespoons lime juice
1 teaspoon honey
1 cup lettuce leaves, shredded
1/2 cup pomegranate seeds

Directions

Place the flank steak, soy sauce, wine, salt, and black pepper in a ceramic bowl. Let it marinate for 2 hours in your refrigerator.

Transfer the meat to a lightly greased cooking basket. Top with parsnips. Add the paprika, onion powder, garlic powder, coriander, and allspice.

Cook in the preheated Air Fryer at 400 degrees F for 7 minutes; turn over and cook an additional 5 minutes.

In the meantime, make the dressing by mixing olive oil with lime juice and honey.

Put the lettuce leaves and roasted parsnip in a salad bowl; toss with the dressing. Slice the steaks and place on top of the salad. Sprinkle over the pomegranate seeds and serve. Enjoy!

Per serving: 522 Calories; 21.7g Fat; 28.2g Carbs; 51.3g Protein; 13.5g Sugars

259. Easy Asian Gyudon

(Ready in about 20 minutes | Servings 4)

Ingredients

1 shallot, chopped
1/2 cup dashi
1 tablespoon mirin
1 teaspoon agave syrup

2 tablespoons Shoyu sauce
1/2 teaspoon wasabi
1 pound rib eye, sliced

Directions

Add all ingredients to a lightly greased baking pan. Gently stir to combine.

Cook in the preheated Air Fryer at 400 degrees F for 7 minutes. Stir again and cook for a further 7 minutes.

Serve with Japanese ramen noodles if desired. Enjoy!

Per serving: 377 Calories; 32.2g Fat; 3.2g Carbs; 18.5g Protein; 1.9g Sugars

260. Korean Beef Bowl with Rice

(Ready in about 20 minutes | Servings 4)

Ingredients

2 tablespoons bacon, chopped
1 ½ pounds ground chuck
1 leek, chopped
2 garlic cloves, minced
1 tablespoon daenjang (soybean paste)

1 teaspoon kochukaru (chili pepper flakes)
Sea salt and ground black pepper, to taste
2 cups white rice, hot cooked

Directions

Start by preheating your Air Fryer to 360 degrees. Then, add the bacon to the baking pan; cook the bacon just until it starts to get crisp.

Add the ground chuck and cook for 2 minutes more, crumbling with a spatula.

Add the leeks, garlic, and spices. Cook for 12 minutes more. Stir in the hot rice; stir well to combine and serve. Enjoy!

Per serving: 465 Calories; 14.7g Fat; 44.5g Carbs; 37.8g Protein; 1.4g Sugars

261. Best Pretzel Sliders

(Ready in about 40 minutes | Servings 4)

Ingredients

3/4 pound ground beef
1 smoked beef sausage, chopped
4 scallions, chopped
1 garlic clove, minced
2 tablespoons fresh coriander, chopped
4 tablespoons rolled oats

2 tablespoons tomato paste
Himalayan salt and ground black pepper, to taste
8 small pretzel rolls
4 tablespoons mayonnaise
8 thin slices of tomato

Directions

Start by preheating your Air Fryer to 370 degrees F.

In a mixing bowl, thoroughly combine the ground beef, sausage, scallions, garlic, coriander, oats, tomato paste, salt, and black pepper. Knead with your hands until everything is well combined.

Form the mixture into eight patties and cook them for 18 to 20 minutes. Work in batches.

Place the burgers on slider buns; top with mayonnaise and tomato slices. Bon appétit!

Per serving: 553 Calories; 22.1g Fat; 51.1g Carbs; 37.5g Protein; 8.1g Sugars

262. Juicy Strip Steak

(Ready in about 30 minutes | Servings 4)

Ingredients

1 ½ pounds strip steak, sliced
1/4 cup chickpea flour
1/3 cup Shoyu sauce
2 tablespoons honey
1 teaspoon mustard seeds

2 tablespoons champagne vinegar
1 teaspoon ginger-garlic paste
1/2 teaspoon coriander seeds
1 tablespoon cornstarch

Directions

Start by preheating your Air Fryer to 395 degrees F. Spritz the Air Fryer basket with cooking oil.

Toss the strip steak with chickpea flour. Cook the strip steak for 12 minutes; flip them over and cook an additional 10 minutes.

In the meantime, heat the saucepan over medium-high heat. Add the Shoyu sauce, honey, mustard seeds, champagne vinegar, ginger-garlic paste, and coriander seeds.

Reduce the heat and simmer until the sauce is heated through. Make the slurry by whisking the cornstarch with 1 tablespoon of water.

Now, whisk in the cornstarch slurry and continue to simmer until the sauce has thickened. Spoon the sauce over the steak and serve.

Per serving: 417 Calories; 17.9g Fat; 15.6g Carbs; 49.1g Protein; 10.1g Sugars

263. Birthday Party Cheeseburger Pizza

(Ready in about 20 minutes | Servings 4)

Ingredients

Nonstick cooking oil
1 pound ground beef
Kosher salt and ground black pepper, to taste
1/2 teaspoon oregano
1/2 teaspoon basil
1/4 teaspoon red pepper flakes
1/4 cup marinara sauce
2 spring onions, chopped
4 burger buns
1 cup mozzarella cheese, shredded

Directions

Start by preheating your Air Fryer to 370 degrees F. Spritz the Air Fryer basket with cooking oil.

Add the ground beef and cook for 10 minutes, crumbling with a spatula. Season with salt, black pepper, oregano, basil, and red peppers.

Spread the marinara pasta on each half of burger bun. Place the spring onions and ground meat mixture on the buns equally.

Set the temperature to 350 degrees F. Place the burger pizza in the Air Fryer basket. Top with mozzarella cheese.

Bake approximately 4 minutes or until cheese is bubbling. Top with another half of burger bun and serve. Bon appétit!

Per serving: 447 Calories; 16.1g Fat; 29.5g Carbs; 44.5g Protein; 2.7g Sugars

264. Filipino Tortang Giniling

(Ready in about 20 minutes | Servings 3)

Ingredients

1 teaspoon lard
2/3 pound ground beef
1/4 teaspoon chili powder
1/2 teaspoon ground bay leaf
1/2 teaspoon ground pepper
Sea salt, to taste
1 green bell pepper, seeded and chopped
1 red bell pepper, seeded and chopped
6 eggs
1/3 cup double cream
1/2 cup Colby cheese, shredded
1 tomato, sliced

Directions

Melt the lard in a cast-iron skillet over medium-high heat. Add the ground beef and cook for 4 minutes until no longer pink, crumbling with a spatula.

Add the ground beef mixture, along with the spices to the baking pan. Now, add the bell peppers.

In a mixing bowl, whisk the eggs with double cream. Spoon the mixture over the meat and peppers in the pan.

Cook in the preheated Air Fryer at 355 degrees F for 10 minutes.

Top with the cheese and tomato slices. Continue to cook for 5 minutes more or until the eggs are golden and the cheese has melted.

Per serving: 543 Calories; 34.7g Fat; 7.4g Carbs; 48.3g Protein; 4.4g Sugars

265. Pastrami and Cheddar Quiche

(Ready in about 20 minutes | Servings 2)

Ingredients

4 eggs
1 bell pepper, chopped
2 spring onions, chopped
1 cup pastrami, sliced
1/4 cup Greek-style yogurt
1/2 cup Cheddar cheese, grated
Sea salt, to taste
1/4 teaspoon ground black pepper

Directions

Start by preheating your Air Fryer to 330 degrees F. Spritz the baking pan with cooking oil.

Then, thoroughly combine all ingredients and pour the mixture into the prepared baking pan.

Cook for 7 to 9 minutes or until the eggs have set. Place on a cooling rack and let it sit for 10 minutes before slicing and serving.

Per serving: 435 Calories; 31.4g Fat; 6.7g Carbs; 30.4g Protein; 3.8g Sugars

266. Roasted Blade Steak with Green Beans

(Ready in about 25 minutes | Servings 4)

Ingredients

2 garlic cloves, smashed
2 teaspoons sunflower oil
1/2 teaspoon cayenne pepper
1 tablespoon Cajun seasoning
1 ½ pounds blade steak
2 cups green beans
1/2 teaspoon Tabasco pepper sauce
Sea salt and ground black pepper, to taste

Directions

Start by preheating your Air Fryer to 330 degrees F.

Mix the garlic, oil, cayenne pepper, and Cajun seasoning to make a paste. Rub it over both sides of the blade steak.

Cook for 13 minutes in the preheated Air Fryer. Now, flip the steak and cook an additional 8 minutes.

Heat the green beans in a saucepan. Add a few tablespoons of water, Tabasco, salt, and black pepper; heat until it wilts or about 10 minutes.

Serve the roasted blade steak with green beans on the side. Bon appétit!

Per serving: 379 Calories; 18.1g Fat; 5.3g Carbs; 49g Protein; 1.9g Sugars

267. Minty Tender Filet Mignon

(Ready in about 20 minutes + marinating time | Servings 4)

Ingredients

2 tablespoons olive oil
2 tablespoons Worcestershire sauce
1 lemon, juiced
1/4 cup fresh mint leaves, chopped
4 cloves garlic, minced
Sea salt and ground black pepper, to taste
2 pounds filet mignon

Directions

In a ceramic bowl, place the olive oil, Worcestershire sauce, lemon juice, mint leaves, garlic, salt, black pepper, and cayenne pepper.

Add the fillet mignon and let it marinate for 2 hours in the refrigerator.

Roast in the preheated Air Fryer at 400 degrees F for 18 minutes, basting with the reserved marinade and flipping a couple of times. Serve warm. Bon appétit!

Per serving: 389 Calories; 20.4g Fat; 4.6g Carbs; 47.3g Protein; 1.7g Sugars

268. Hungarian Oven Stew (Marha Pörkölt)

(Ready in about 1 hour 10 minutes | Servings 4)

Ingredients

4 tablespoons all-purpose flour
Sea salt and cracked black pepper, to taste
1 teaspoon Hungarian paprika
1 pound beef chuck roast, boneless, cut into bite-sized cubes
2 teaspoons sunflower oil
1 medium-sized leek, chopped
2 garlic cloves, minced
2 bay leaves
1 teaspoon caraway seeds.
2 cups roasted vegetable broth
2 ripe tomatoes, pureed
2 tablespoons red wine
2 bell peppers, chopped
2 medium carrots, sliced
1 celery stalk, peeled and diced

Directions

Add the flour, salt, black pepper, paprika, and beef to a resealable bag; shake to coat well.

Heat the oil in a Dutch oven over medium-high flame; sauté the leeks, garlic, bay leaves, and caraway seeds about 4 minutes or until fragrant. Transfer to a lightly greased baking pan.

Then, brown the beef, stirring occasionally, working in batches. Add to the baking pan.

Add the vegetable broth, tomatoes, and red wine. Lower the pan onto the Air Fryer basket. Bake at 325 degrees F for 40 minutes.

Add the bell peppers, carrots, and celery. Cook an additional 20 minutes. Serve immediately and enjoy!

Per serving: 375 Calories; 16.1g Fat; 16.5g Carbs; 39.6g Protein; 4.6g Sugars

269. Easy Beef Jerky

(Ready in about 1 hour + marinating time | Servings 4)

Ingredients

1 cup beer
1/2 cup tamari sauce
1 teaspoon liquid smoke
2 garlic cloves, minced
Sea salt and ground black pepper

1 teaspoon ancho chili powder
2 tablespoons honey
3/4 pound flank steak, slice into strips

Directions

Place all ingredients in a ceramic dish; let it marinate for 3 hours in the refrigerator. Slice the beef into thin strips

Marinate the beef in the refrigerator overnight.

Now, discard the marinade and hang the meat in the cooking basket by using skewers.

Air Fry at 190 degrees F degrees for 1 hour. Store it in an airtight container for up to 2 weeks.

Per serving: 284 Calories; 13.8g Fat; 16.5g Carbs; 23.1g Protein; 11g Sugars

270. Polish Sausage and Sourdough Kabobs

(Ready in about 20 minutes | Servings 4)

Ingredients

1 pound smoked Polish beef sausage, sliced
1 tablespoon mustard
1 tablespoon olive oil
2 tablespoons Worcestershire sauce

2 bell peppers, sliced
2 cups sourdough bread, cubed
Salt and ground black pepper, to taste

Directions

Toss the sausage with the mustard, olive, and Worcestershire sauce. Thread sausage, peppers, and bread onto skewers.

Sprinkle with salt and black pepper.

Cook in the preheated Air Fryer at 360 degrees F for 11 minutes. Brush the skewers with the reserved marinade. Bon appétit!

Per serving: 284 Calories; 13.8g Fat; 16.5g Carbs; 23.1g Protein; 11g Sugars

271. Ranch Meatloaf with Peppers

(Ready in about 35 minutes | Servings 5)

Ingredients

1 pound beef, ground
1/2 pound veal, ground
1 egg
4 tablespoons vegetable juice
1 cup crackers, crushed
2 bell peppers, chopped
1 onion, chopped
2 garlic cloves, minced
2 tablespoons tomato paste

2 tablespoons soy sauce
1 (1-ounce) package ranch dressing mix
Sea salt, to taste
1/2 teaspoon ground black pepper, to taste
7 ounces tomato paste
1 tablespoon Dijon mustard

Directions

Start by preheating your Air Fryer to 330 degrees F.

In a mixing bowl, thoroughly combine the ground beef, veal, egg, vegetable juice, crackers, bell peppers, onion, garlic, tomato paste, soy sauce, ranch dressing mix, salt, and ground black pepper.

Mix until everything is well incorporated and press into a lightly greased meatloaf pan.

Cook approximately 25 minutes in the preheated Air Fryer. Whisk the tomato paste with the mustard and spread the topping over the top of your meatloaf.

Continue to cook 2 minutes more. Let it stand on a cooling rack for 6 minutes before slicing and serving. Enjoy!

Per serving: 411 Calories; 31.4g Fat; 10g Carbs; 28.2g Protein; 4.3g Sugars

272. Indian Beef Samosas

(Ready in about 35 minutes | Servings 8)

Ingredients

1 tablespoon sesame oil
4 tablespoons shallots, minced
2 cloves garlic, minced
2 tablespoons green chili peppers, chopped
1/2 pound ground chuck
4 ounces bacon, chopped
Salt and ground black pepper, to taste

1 teaspoon cumin powder
1 teaspoon turmeric
1 teaspoon coriander
1 cup frozen peas, thawed
1 (16-ounce) package phyllo dough
1 egg, beaten with 2 tablespoons of water (egg wash)

Directions

Heat the oil in a saucepan over medium-high heat. Once hot, sauté the shallots, garlic, and chili peppers until tender, about 3 minutes.

Then, add the beef and bacon; continue to sauté an additional 4 minutes, crumbling with a fork. Season with the salt, pepper, cumin powder, turmeric, and coriander. Stir in peas.

Then, preheat your Air Fryer to 330 degrees F. Brush the Air Fryer basket with cooking oil.

Place 1 to 2 tablespoons of the mixture onto each phyllo sheet. Fold the sheets into triangles, pressing the edges. Brush the tops with egg wash.

Bake for 7 to 8 minutes, working with batches. Serve with Indian tomato sauce if desired. Enjoy!

Per serving: 266 Calories; 13g Fat; 24.5g Carbs; 12.2g Protein; 1.5g Sugars

273. Grilled Vienna Sausage with Broccoli

(Ready in about 25 minutes | Servings 4)

Ingredients

1 pound beef Vienna sausage
1/2 cup mayonnaise
1 teaspoon yellow mustard
1 tablespoon fresh lemon juice

1 teaspoon garlic powder
1/4 teaspoon black pepper
1 pound broccoli

Directions

Start by preheating your Air Fryer to 380 degrees F. Spritz the grill pan with cooking oil.

Cut the sausages into serving sized pieces. Cook the sausages for 15 minutes, shaking the basket occasionally to get all sides browned. Set aside.

In the meantime, whisk the mayonnaise with mustard, lemon juice, garlic powder, and black pepper. Toss the broccoli with the mayo mixture.

Turn up temperature to 400 degrees F. Cook broccoli for 6 minutes, turning halfway through the cooking time.

Serve the sausage with the grilled broccoli on the side. Bon appétit!

Per serving: 477 Calories; 43.2g Fat; 7.3g Carbs; 15.9g Protein; 0.7g Sugars

274. Aromatic T-Bone Steak with Garlic

(Ready in about 20 minutes | Servings 3)

Ingredients

1 pound T-bone steak
4 garlic cloves, halved
1/4 cup all-purpose flour
2 tablespoons olive oil
1/4 cup tamari sauce
2 teaspoons brown sugar
4 tablespoons tomato paste

1 teaspoon Sriracha sauce
2 tablespoons white vinegar
1 teaspoon dried rosemary
1/2 teaspoon dried basil
2 heaping tablespoons cilantro, chopped

Directions

Rub the garlic halves all over the T-bone steak. Toss the steak with the flour.

Drizzle the oil all over the steak and transfer it to the grill pan; grill the steak in the preheated Air Fryer at 400 degrees F for 10 minutes.

Meanwhile, whisk the tamari sauce, sugar, tomato paste, Sriracha, vinegar, rosemary, and basil. Cook an additional 5 minutes

Serve garnished with fresh cilantro. Bon appétit!

Per serving: 463 Calories; 24.6g Fat; 16.7g Carbs; 44.7g Protein; 5.2g Sugars

275. Sausage Scallion Balls

(Ready in about 20 minutes | Servings 4)

Ingredients

1 ½ pounds beef sausage meat
1 cup rolled oats
4 tablespoons scallions, chopped
1 teaspoon Worcestershire sauce
Flaky sea salt and freshly ground
black pepper, to taste

1 teaspoon paprika
1/2 teaspoon granulated garlic
1 teaspoon dried basil
1/2 teaspoon dried oregano
4 teaspoons mustard
4 pickled cucumbers

Directions

Start by preheating your Air Fryer to 380 degrees F. Spritz the Air Fryer basket with cooking oil.

In a mixing bowl, thoroughly combine the sausage meat, oats, scallions, Worcestershire sauce, salt, black pepper, paprika, garlic, basil, and oregano.

Then, form the mixture into equal sized meatballs using a tablespoon.

Place the meatballs in the Air Fryer basket and cook for 15 minutes, turning halfway through the cooking time.

Serve with mustard and cucumbers. Bon appétit!

Per serving: 560 Calories; 42.2g Fat; 21.5g Carbs; 31.1g Protein; 3.5g Sugars

276. Cube Steak with Cowboy Sauce

(Ready in about 20 minutes | Servings 4)

Ingredients

1 ½ pounds cube steak
Salt, to taste
1/4 teaspoon ground black pepper,
or more to taste
4 ounces butter
2 garlic cloves, finely chopped

2 scallions, finely chopped
2 tablespoon fresh parsley, finely
chopped
1 tablespoon fresh horseradish,
grated
1 teaspoon cayenne pepper

Directions

Pat dry the cube steak and season it with salt and black pepper. Spritz the Air Fryer basket with cooking oil. Add the meat to the basket.

Cook in the preheated Air Fryer at 400 degrees F for 14 minutes.

Meanwhile, melt the butter in a skillet over a moderate heat. Add the remaining ingredients and simmer until the sauce has thickened and reduced slightly.

Top the warm cube steaks with Cowboy sauce and serve immediately.

Per serving: 469 Calories; 30.4g Fat; 0.6g Carbs; 46g Protein; 0g Sugars

277. Steak Fingers with Lime Sauce

(Ready in about 20 minutes + marinating time | Servings 4)

Ingredients

1 ½ pounds sirloin steak
1/4 cup soy sauce
1/4 cup fresh lime juice
1 teaspoon garlic powder
1 teaspoon shallot powder
1 teaspoon celery seeds
1 teaspoon mustard seeds

Coarse sea salt and ground black
pepper, to taste
1 teaspoon red pepper flakes
2 eggs, lightly whisked
1 cup breadcrumbs
1/4 cup parmesan cheese
1 teaspoon paprika

Directions

Place the steak, soy sauce, lime juice, garlic powder, shallot powder, celery seeds, mustard seeds, salt, black pepper, and red pepper in a large ceramic bowl; let it marinate for 3 hours.

Tenderize the cube steak by pounding with a mallet; cut into 1-inch strips.

In a shallow bowl, whisk the eggs. In another bowl, mix the breadcrumbs, parmesan cheese, and paprika.

Dip the beef pieces into the whisked eggs and coat on all sides. Now, dredge the beef pieces in the breadcrumb mixture.

Cook at 400 degrees F for 14 minutes, flipping halfway through the cooking time.

Meanwhile, make the sauce by heating the reserved marinade in a saucepan over medium heat; let it simmer until thoroughly warmed. Serve the steak fingers with the sauce on the side. Enjoy!

Per serving: 471 Calories; 26.3g Fat; 13.9g Carbs; 42.5g Protein; 4.7g Sugars

278. Beef Kofta Sandwich

(Ready in about 30 minutes | Servings 4)

Ingredients

1/2 cup leeks, chopped
2 garlic cloves, smashed
1 pound ground chuck
1 slice of bread, soaked in water
until fully tender
Salt, to taste
1/4 teaspoon ground black pepper,
or more to taste
1 teaspoon cayenne pepper

1/2 teaspoon ground sumac
3 saffron threads
2 tablespoons loosely packed
fresh continental parsley leaves
4 tablespoons tahini sauce
4 warm flatbread
4 ounces baby arugula
2 tomatoes, cut into slices

Directions

In a bowl, mix the chopped leeks, garlic, ground meat, soaked bread, and spices; knead with your hands until everything is well incorporated.

Now, mound the beef mixture around a wooden skewer into a pointed-ended sausage.

Cook in the preheated Air Fryer at 360 degrees F for 25 minutes.

To make the sandwiches, spread the tahini sauce on the flatbread; top with the kofta kebabs, baby arugula and tomatoes. Enjoy!

Per serving: 436 Calories; 20.5g Fat; 32g Carbs; 33.7g Protein; 4.1g Sugars

279. Classic Beef Ribs

(Ready in about 35 minutes | Servings 4)

Ingredients

2 pounds beef back ribs
1 tablespoon sunflower oil
1/2 teaspoon mixed peppercorns,
cracked

1 teaspoon red pepper flakes
1 teaspoon dry mustard
Coarse sea salt, to taste

Directions

Trim the excess fat from the beef ribs. Mix the sunflower oil, cracked peppercorns, red pepper, dry mustard, and salt.

Rub over the ribs.

Cook in the preheated Air Fryer at 395 degrees F for 11 minutes

Turn the heat to 330 degrees F and continue to cook for 18 minutes more. Serve warm.

Per serving: 532 Calories; 39g Fat; 0.4g Carbs; 44.7g Protein; 0g Sugars

280. Spicy Short Ribs with Red Wine Sauce

(Ready in about 20 minutes + marinating time | Servings 4)

Ingredients

1 ½ pounds short ribs
1 cup red wine
1/2 cup tamari sauce
1 lemon, juiced
1 teaspoon fresh ginger, grated
1 teaspoon salt

1 teaspoon black pepper
1 teaspoon paprika
1 teaspoon chipotle chili powder
1 cup ketchup
1 teaspoon garlic powder
1 teaspoon cumin

Directions

In a ceramic bowl, place the beef ribs, wine, tamari sauce, lemon juice, ginger, salt, black pepper, paprika, and chipotle chili powder. Cover and let it marinate for 3 hours in the refrigerator.

Discard the marinade and add the short ribs to the Air Fryer basket. Cook in the preheated Air fry at 380 degrees F for 10 minutes, turning them over halfway through the cooking time.

In the meantime, heat the saucepan over medium heat; add the reserved marinade and stir in the ketchup, garlic powder, and cumin. Cook until the sauce has thickened slightly.

Pour the sauce over the warm ribs and serve immediately. Bon appétit!

Per serving: 505 Calories; 31g Fat; 22.1g Carbs; 35.2g Protein; 15.3g Sugars

281. Beef Schnitzel with Buttermilk Spaetzle

(Ready in about 20 minutes | Servings 2)

Ingredients

1 egg, beaten
1/2 teaspoon ground black pepper
1 teaspoon paprika
1/2 teaspoon coarse sea salt
1 tablespoon ghee, melted
1/2 cup tortilla chips, crushed

2 thin-cut minute steaks
Buttermilk Spaetzle:
2 eggs
1/2 cup buttermilk
1/2 cup all-purpose flour
1/2 teaspoon salt

Directions

Start by preheating your Air Fryer to 360 degrees F.

In a shallow bowl, whisk the egg with black pepper, paprika, and salt.

Thoroughly combine the ghee with the crushed tortilla chips and coarse sea salt in another shallow bowl.

Using a meat mallet, pound the schnitzel to 1/4-inch thick.

Dip the schnitzel into the egg mixture; then, roll the schnitzel over the crumb mixture until coated on all sides.

Cook for 13 minutes in the preheated Air Fryer.

To make the spaetzle, whisk the eggs, buttermilk, flour, and salt in a bowl. Bring a large saucepan of salted water to a boil.

Push the spaetzle mixture through the holes of a potato ricer into the boiling water; slice them off using a table knife. Work in batches.

When the spaetzle float, take them out with a slotted spoon. Repeat with the rest of the spaetzle mixture.

Serve with warm schnitzel. Enjoy!

Per serving: 522 Calories; 20.7g Fat; 17.1g Carbs; 62.2g Protein; 1.8g Sugars

282. Beef Sausage Goulash

(Ready in about 40 minutes | Servings 2)

Ingredients

1 tablespoon lard, melted
1 shallot, chopped
1 bell pepper, chopped
2 red chilies, finely chopped
1 teaspoon ginger-garlic paste
Sea salt, to taste
1/4 teaspoon ground black pepper

4 beef good quality sausages, thinly sliced
2 teaspoons smoked paprika
1 cup beef bone broth
1/2 cup tomato puree
2 handfuls spring greens, shredded

Directions

Melt the lard in a Dutch oven over medium-high flame; sauté the shallots and peppers about 4 minutes or until fragrant.

Add the ginger-garlic paste and cook an additional minute. Season with salt and black pepper and transfer to a lightly greased baking pan.

Then, brown the sausages, stirring occasionally, working in batches. Add to the baking pan.

Add the smoked paprika, broth, and tomato puree. Lower the pan onto the Air Fryer basket. Bake at 325 degrees F for 30 minutes.

Stir in the spring greens and cook for 5 minutes more or until they wilt. Serve over the hot rice if desired. Bon appétit!

Per serving: 565 Calories; 47.1g Fat; 14.3g Carbs; 20.6g Protein; 5.2g Sugars

283. Mom's Toad in the Hole

(Ready in about 45 minutes | Servings 4)

Ingredients

6 beef sausages
1 tablespoon butter, melted
1 cup plain flour

A pinch of salt
2 eggs
1 cup semi-skimmed milk

Directions

Cook the sausages in the preheated Air Fryer at 380 degrees F for 15 minutes, shaking halfway through the cooking time.

Meanwhile, make up the batter mix.

Tip the flour into a bowl with salt; make a well in the middle and crack the eggs into it. Mix with an electric whisk; now, slowly and gradually pour in the milk, whisking all the time.

Place the sausages in a lightly greased baking pan. Pour the prepared batter over the sausages.

Cook in the preheated Air Fryer at 370 degrees F approximately 25 minutes, until golden and risen. Serve with gravy if desired. Bon appétit!

Per serving: 584 Calories; 40.2g Fat; 29.5g Carbs; 23.4g Protein; 3.4g Sugars

284. Beef Nuggets with Cheesy Mushrooms

(Ready in about 25 minutes | Servings 4)

Ingredients

2 eggs, beaten
4 tablespoons yogurt
1 cup tortilla chips, crushed
1 teaspoon dry mesquite flavored seasoning mix
Coarse salt and ground black pepper, to taste

1/2 teaspoon onion powder
1 pound cube steak, cut into bite-size pieces
1 pound button mushrooms
1 cup Swiss cheese, shredded

Directions

In a shallow bowl, beat the eggs and yogurt. In a resealable bag, mix the tortilla chips, mesquite seasoning, salt, pepper, and onion powder.

Dip the steak pieces in the egg mixture; then, place in the bag, and shake to coat on all sides.

Cook at 400 degrees F for 14 minutes, flipping halfway through the cooking time.

Add the mushrooms to the lightly greased cooking basket. Top with shredded Swiss cheese.

Bake in the preheated Air Fryer at 400 degrees F for 5 minutes. Serve with the beef nuggets. Bon appétit!

Per serving: 355 Calories; 15.7g Fat; 13.6g Carbs; 39.8g Protein; 3.4g Sugars

285. Asian-Style Beef Dumplings

(Ready in about 25 minutes | Servings 5)

Ingredients

1/2 pound ground chuck
1/2 pound beef sausage, chopped
1 cup Chinese cabbage, shredded
1 bell pepper, chopped
1 onion, chopped
2 garlic cloves, minced
1 medium-sized egg, beaten
Sea salt and ground black pepper, to taste

20 wonton wrappers
2 tablespoons soy sauce
2 teaspoons sesame oil
2 teaspoons sesame seeds, lightly toasted
2 tablespoons seasoned rice vinegar
1/2 teaspoon chili sauce

Directions

To make the filling, thoroughly combine the ground chuck, sausage, cabbage, bell pepper, onion, garlic, egg, salt, and black pepper.

Place the wrappers on a clean and dry surface. Now, divide the filling among the wrappers.

Then, fold each dumpling in half and pinch to seal.

Transfer the dumplings to the lightly greased cooking basket. Bake at 390 degrees F for 15 minutes, turning over halfway through.

In the meantime, mix the soy sauce, sesame oil, sesame seeds, rice vinegar, and chili sauce. Serve the beef dumplings with the sauce on the side. Enjoy!

Per serving: 353 Calories; 16.7g Fat; 29.5g Carbs; 23.1g Protein; 3.4g Sugars

FISH & SEAFOOD

286. Colorful Salmon and Fennel Salad

(Ready in about 20 minutes | Servings 3)

Ingredients

1 pound salmon
1 fennel, quartered
1 teaspoon olive oil
Sea salt and ground black pepper, to taste
1/2 teaspoon paprika
1 tablespoon balsamic vinegar

1 tablespoon lime juice
1 tablespoon extra-virgin olive oil
1 tomato, sliced
1 cucumber, sliced
1 tablespoon sesame seeds, lightly toasted

Directions

Toss the salmon and fennel with 1 teaspoon of olive oil, salt, black pepper and paprika.

Cook in the preheated Air Fryer at 380 degrees F for 12 minutes; shaking the basket once or twice.

Cut the salmon into bite-sized strips and transfer them to a nice salad bowl. Add in the fennel, balsamic vinegar, lime juice, 1 tablespoon of extra-virgin olive oil, tomato and cucumber.

Toss to combine well and serve garnished with lightly toasted sesame seeds. Enjoy!

Per serving: 306 Calories; 16.3g Fat; 5.6g Carbs; 32.2g Protein; 3g Sugars

287. Parmesan Chip-Crusted Tilapia

(Ready in about 15 minutes | Servings 3)

Ingredients

1 ½ pounds tilapia, slice into 4 portions
Sea salt and ground black pepper, to taste
1/2 teaspoon cayenne pepper
1 teaspoon granulated garlic

1/4 cup almond flour
1/4 cup parmesan cheese, preferably freshly grated
1 egg, beaten
2 tablespoons buttermilk
1 cup tortilla chips, crushed

Directions

Generously season your tilapia with salt, black pepper and cayenne pepper.

Prepare a bread station. Add the granulated garlic, almond flour and parmesan cheese to a rimmed plate.

Whisk the egg and buttermilk in another bowl and place crushed tortilla chips in the third bowl.

Dip the tilapia pieces in the flour mixture, then in the egg/buttermilk mixture and finally roll them in the crushed chips, pressing to adhere well.

Cook in your Air Fryer at 400 degrees F for 10 minutes, flipping halfway through the cooking time. Serve with chips if desired. Bon appétit!

Per serving: 356 Calories; 10.5g Fat; 11.9g Carbs; 52g Protein; 2.1g Sugars

288. Keto Cod Fillets

(Ready in about 15 minutes | Servings 2)

Ingredients

2 cod fish fillets
1 teaspoon butter, melted
1 teaspoon Old Bay seasoning
1 egg, beaten

2 tablespoons coconut milk, unsweetened
1/3 cup coconut flour, unsweetened

Directions

Place the cod fish fillets, butter and Old Bay seasoning in a Ziplock bag; shake until the fish is well coated on all sides.

In a shallow bowl, whisk the egg and coconut milk until frothy.

In another bowl, place the coconut flour. Dip the fish fillets in the egg mixture, then, coat them with coconut flour, pressing to adhere.

Cook the fish at 390 degrees F for 6 minutes; flip them over and cook an additional 6 minutes until your fish flakes easily when tested with a fork. Bon appétit!

Per serving: 218 Calories; 12.5g Fat; 3.5g Carbs; 22g Protein; 1.9g Sugars

289. Easiest Lobster Tails Ever

(Ready in about 10 minutes | Servings 2)

Ingredients

2 (6-ounce) lobster tails
1 teaspoon fresh cilantro, minced
1/2 teaspoon dried rosemary
1/2 teaspoon garlic, pressed

1 teaspoon deli mustard
Sea salt and ground black pepper, to taste
1 teaspoon olive oil

Directions

Toss the lobster tails with the other ingredients until they are well coated on all sides.

Cook the lobster tails at 370 degrees F for 3 minutes. Then, turn them and cook on the other side for 3 to 4 minutes more until they are opaque.

Serve warm and enjoy!

Per serving: 147 Calories; 3.5g Fat; 2.5g Carbs; 25.5g Protein; 1.1g Sugars

290. Salmon Bowl with Lime Drizzle

(Ready in about 15 minutes | Servings 3)

Ingredients

1 pound salmon steak
2 teaspoons sesame oil
Sea salt and Sichuan pepper, to taste
1/2 teaspoon coriander seeds

1 lime, juiced
2 tablespoons reduced-sodium soy sauce
1 teaspoon honey

Directions

Pat the salmon dry and drizzle it with 1 teaspoon of sesame oil.

Season the salmon with salt, pepper and coriander seeds. Transfer the salmon to the Air Fryer cooking basket.

Cook the salmon at 400 degrees F for 5 minutes; turn the salmon over and continue to cook for 5 minutes more or until opaque.

Meanwhile, warm the remaining ingredients in a small saucepan to make the lime drizzle.

Slice the fish into bite-sized strips, drizzle with the sauce and serve immediately. Enjoy!

Per serving: 307 Calories; 15g Fat; 4.5g Carbs; 32.3g Protein; 5g Sugars

291. Famous Tuna Niçoise Salad

(Ready in about 15 minutes | Servings 3)

Ingredients

1 pound tuna steak
Sea salt and ground black pepper, to taste
1/2 teaspoon red pepper flakes, crushed
1/4 teaspoon dried dill weed
1/2 teaspoon garlic paste
1 pound green beans, trimmed
2 handfuls baby spinach
2 handfuls iceberg lettuce, torn into pieces

1/2 red onion, sliced
1 cucumber, sliced
2 tablespoons lemon juice
1 tablespoon olive oil
1 teaspoon Dijon mustard
1 tablespoon balsamic vinegar
1 tablespoon roasted almonds, coarsely chopped
1 tablespoon fresh parsley, coarsely chopped

Directions

Pat the tuna steak dry; toss your tuna with salt, black pepper, red pepper, dill and garlic paste. Spritz your tuna with a nonstick cooking spray.

Cook the tuna steak at 400 degrees F for 5 minutes; turn your tuna steak over and continue to cook for 4 to 5 minutes more.

Then, add the green beans to the cooking basket. Spritz green beans with a nonstick cooking spray. Cook at 400 degrees F for 5 minutes, shaking the basket once or twice.

Cut your tuna into thin strips and transfer to a salad bowl; add in the green beans.

Then, add in the baby spinach, iceberg lettuce, onion and cucumber and toss to combine. In a mixing bowl, whisk the lemon juice, olive oil, mustard and vinegar.

Dress the salad and garnish with roasted almonds and fresh parsley. Bon appétit!

Per serving: 315 Calories; 13g Fat; 11.5g Carbs; 37.3g Protein; 3.9g Sugars

292. Classic Crab Cakes

(Ready in about 15 minutes | Servings 3)

Ingredients

1 egg, beaten
2 tablespoons milk
2 crustless bread slices
1 pound lump crabmeat
2 tablespoons scallions, chopped
1 garlic clove, minced
1 teaspoon deli mustard
1 teaspoon Sriracha sauce
Sea salt and ground black pepper, to taste
4 lemon wedges, for serving

Directions

Whisk the egg and milk until pale and frothy; add in the bread and let it soak for a few minutes.

Stir in the other ingredients, except for the lemon wedges; shape the mixture into 4 equal patties. Place your patties in the Air Fryer cooking basket. Spritz your patties with a nonstick cooking spray.

Cook the crab cakes at 400 degrees F for 5 minutes. Turn them over and cook on the other side for 5 minutes.

Serve warm, garnished with lemon wedges. Bon appétit!

Per serving: 180 Calories; 4.4g Fat; 10.5g Carbs; 24.4g Protein; 3g Sugars

293. Salmon Fillets with Herbs and Garlic

(Ready in about 15 minutes | Servings 3)

Ingredients

1 pound salmon fillets
Sea salt and ground black pepper, to taste
1 tablespoon olive oil
1 sprig thyme
2 sprigs rosemary
2 cloves garlic, minced
1 lemon, sliced

Directions

Pat the salmon fillets dry and season them with salt and pepper; drizzle salmon fillets with olive oil and place in the Air Fryer cooking basket.

Cook the salmon fillets at 380 degrees F for 7 minutes; turn them over, top with thyme, rosemary and garlic and continue to cook for 5 minutes more.

Serve topped with lemon slices and enjoy!

Per serving: 248 Calories; 11.2g Fat; 3.1g Carbs; 31.4g Protein; 1.2g Sugars

294. Grouper with Miso-Honey Sauce

(Ready in about 15 minutes | Servings 2)

Ingredients

3/4 pound grouper fillets
Salt and white pepper, to taste
1 tablespoon sesame oil
1 teaspoon water
1 teaspoon deli mustard or Dijon mustard
1/4 cup white miso
1 tablespoon mirin
1 tablespoon honey
1 tablespoon Shoyu sauce

Directions

Sprinkle the grouper fillets with salt and white pepper; drizzle them with a nonstick cooking oil.

Cook the fish at 400 degrees F for 5 minutes; turn the fish fillets over and cook an additional 5 minutes.

Meanwhile, make the sauce by whisking the remaining ingredients.

Serve the warm fish with the miso-honey sauce on the side. Bon appétit!

Per serving: 331 Calories; 10.7g Fat; 20.7g Carbs; 37.5g Protein; 12.7g Sugars

295. Fish Sticks with Vidalia Onions

(Ready in about 12 minutes | Servings 2)

Ingredients

1/2 pound fish sticks, frozen
1/2 pound Vidalia onions, halved
1 teaspoon sesame oil
Sea salt and ground black pepper, to taste
1/2 teaspoon red pepper flakes
4 tablespoons mayonnaise
4 tablespoons Greek-style yogurt
1/4 teaspoon mustard seeds
1 teaspoon chipotle chili in adobo, minced

Directions

Drizzle the fish sticks and Vidalia onions with sesame oil. Toss them with salt, black pepper and red pepper flakes.

Transfer them to the Air Fryer cooking basket.

Cook the fish sticks and onions at 400 degreed F for 5 minutes. Shake the basket and cook an additional 5 minutes or until cooked through.

Meanwhile, mix the mayonnaise, Greek-style yogurt, mustard seeds and chipotle chili.

Serve the warm fish sticks garnished with Vidalia onions and the sauce on the side. Bon appétit!

Per serving: 571 Calories; 41.7g Fat; 36.2g Carbs; 14.2g Protein; 9.2g Sugars

296. Moroccan Harissa Shrimp

(Ready in about 10 minutes | Servings 3)

Ingredients

1 pound breaded shrimp, frozen
1 teaspoon extra-virgin olive oil
Sea salt and ground black pepper, to taste
1 teaspoon coriander seeds
1 teaspoon caraway seeds
1 teaspoon crushed red pepper
1 teaspoon fresh garlic, minced

Directions

Toss the breaded shrimp with olive oil and transfer to the Air Fryer cooking basket.

Cook in the preheated Air Fryer at 400 degrees F for 5 minutes; shake the basket and cook an additional 4 minutes.

Meanwhile, mix the remaining ingredients until well combined. Taste and adjust seasonings. Toss the warm shrimp with the harissa sauce and serve immediately. Enjoy!

Per serving: 240 Calories; 5.1g Fat; 20.2g Carbs; 25.2g Protein; 2.3g Sugars

297. Ginger-Garlic Swordfish with Mushrooms

(Ready in about 15 minutes | Servings 3)

Ingredients

1 pound swordfish steak
1 teaspoon ginger-garlic paste
Sea salt and ground black pepper, to taste
1/4 teaspoon cayenne pepper
1/4 teaspoon dried dill weed
1/2 pound mushrooms

Directions

Rub the swordfish steak with ginger-garlic paste; season with salt, black pepper, cayenne pepper and dried dill.

Spritz the fish with a nonstick cooking spray and transfer to the Air Fryer cooking basket. Cook at 400 degrees F for 5 minutes.

Now, add the mushrooms to the cooking basket and continue to cook for 5 minutes longer until tender and fragrant. Eat warm.

Per serving: 242 Calories; 10.3g Fat; 4.1g Carbs; 32.4g Protein; 2.2g Sugars

298. Classic Calamari with Mediterranean Sauce

(Ready in about 10 minutes | Servings 2)

Ingredients

1/2 pound calamari tubes cut into rings, cleaned
Sea salt and ground black pepper, to season
1/2 cup almond flour
1/2 cup all-purpose flour
4 tablespoons parmesan cheese, grated
1/2 cup ale beer
1/4 teaspoon cayenne pepper
1/2 cup breadcrumbs
1/4 cup mayonnaise
1/4 cup Greek-style yogurt
1 clove garlic, minced
1 tablespoon fresh lemon juice
1 teaspoon fresh parsley, chopped
1 teaspoon fresh dill, chopped

Directions

Sprinkle the calamari with salt and black pepper.

Mix the flour, cheese and beer in a bowl until well combined. In another bowl, mix cayenne pepper and breadcrumbs

Dip the calamari pieces in the flour mixture, then roll them onto the breadcrumb mixture, pressing to coat on all sides; transfer them to a lightly oiled cooking basket.

Cook at 400 degrees F for 4 minutes, shaking the basket halfway through the cooking time.

Meanwhile, mix the remaining ingredients until everything is well incorporated. Serve warm calamari with the sauce for dipping. Enjoy!

Per serving: 529 Calories; 24.3g Fat; 41g Carbs; 33.2g Protein; 3.2g Sugars

299. Garlic Butter Scallops

(Ready in about 10 minutes | Servings 2)

Ingredients

1/2 pound scallops
Coarse sea salt and ground black pepper, to taste
1/4 teaspoon cayenne pepper
1/4 teaspoon dried oregano
1/4 teaspoon dried basil
2 tablespoons butter pieces, cold
1 teaspoon garlic, minced
1 teaspoon lemon zest

Directions

Sprinkle the scallops with salt, black pepper, cayenne pepper, oregano and basil. Spritz your scallops with a nonstick cooking oil and transfer them to the Air Fryer cooking basket.

Cook the scallops at 400 degrees F for 6 to 7 minutes, shaking the basket halfway through the cooking time.

In the meantime, melt the butter in a small saucepan over medium-high heat. Once hot, add in the garlic and continue to sauté until fragrant, about 1 minute. Add in lemon zest, taste and adjust the seasonings.

Spoon the garlic butter over the warm scallops and serve.

Per serving: 199 Calories; 12.1g Fat; 6.5g Carbs; 14.4g Protein; 1.2g Sugars

300. Baked Sardines with Tangy Dipping Sauce

(Ready in about 45 minutes | Servings 3)

Ingredients

1 pound fresh sardines
Sea salt and ground black pepper, to taste
1 teaspoon Italian seasoning mix
2 cloves garlic, minced
3 tablespoons olive oil
1/2 lemon, freshly squeezed

Directions

Toss your sardines with salt, black pepper and Italian seasoning mix. Cook in your Air Fryer at 325 degrees F for 35 to 40 minutes until skin is crispy.

Meanwhile, make the sauce by whisking the remaining ingredients

Serve warm sardines with the sauce on the side. Bon appétit!

Per serving: 413 Calories; 29.1g Fat; 4g Carbs; 32g Protein; 1.7g Sugars

301. Anchovy and Cheese Wontons

(Ready in about 15 minutes | Servings 2)

Ingredients

1/2 pound anchovies
1/2 cup cheddar cheese, grated
1 cup fresh spinach
2 tablespoons scallions, minced
1 teaspoon garlic, minced
1 tablespoon Shoyu sauce
Himalayan salt and ground black pepper, to taste
1/2 pound wonton wrappers
1 teaspoon sesame oil

Directions

Mash the anchovies and mix with the cheese, spinach, scallions, garlic and Shoyu sauce; season with salt and black pepper and mix to combine well.

Fill your wontons with 1 tablespoon of the filling mixture and fold into triangle shape; brush the side with a bit of oil and water to seal the edges.

Cook in your Air Fryer at 390 degrees F for 10 minutes, flipping the wontons for even cooking. Enjoy!

Per serving: 473 Calories; 25.1g Fat; 19.4g Carbs; 41g Protein; 4.9g Sugars

302. Classic Pancetta-Wrapped Scallops

(Ready in about 10 minutes | Servings 3)

Ingredients

1 pound sea scallops
1 tablespoon deli mustard
2 tablespoons soy sauce
1/4 teaspoon shallot powder
1/4 teaspoon garlic powder
1/2 teaspoon dried dill
Sea salt and ground black pepper, to taste
4 ounces pancetta slices

Directions

Pat dry the sea scallops and transfer them to a mixing bowl. Toss the sea scallops with the deli mustard, soy sauce, shallot powder, garlic powder, dill, salt and black pepper.

Wrap a slice of bacon around each scallop and transfer them to the Air Fryer cooking basket.

Cook in your Air Fryer at 400 degrees F for 4 minutes; turn them over and cook an additional 3 minutes.

Serve with hot sauce for dipping if desired. Bon appétit!

Per serving: 403 Calories; 24.5g Fat; 5.1g Carbs; 40.1g Protein; 3.1g Sugars

303. Fish Cakes with Bell Pepper

(Ready in about 15 minutes | Servings 3)

Ingredients

1 pound haddock
1 egg
2 tablespoons milk
1 bell pepper, deveined and finely chopped
2 stalks fresh scallions, minced
1/2 teaspoon fresh garlic, minced
Sea salt and ground black pepper, to taste
1/2 teaspoon cumin seeds
1/4 teaspoon celery seeds
1/2 cup breadcrumbs
1 teaspoon olive oil

Directions

Thoroughly combine all ingredients, except for the breadcrumbs and olive oil, until everything is blended well.

Then, roll the mixture into 3 patties and coat them with breadcrumbs, pressing to adhere. Drizzle olive oil over the patties and transfer them to the Air Fryer cooking basket.

Cook the fish cakes at 400 degrees F for 5 minutes; turn them over and continue to cook an additional 5 minutes until cooked through.

Bon appétit!

Per serving: 226 Calories; 6.5g Fat; 10.9g Carbs; 31.4g Protein; 2.6g Sugars

304. Greek Sardeles Psites

(Ready in about 40 minutes | Servings 2)

Ingredients

4 sardines, cleaned
1/4 cup all-purpose flour
Sea salt and ground black pepper, to taste
4 tablespoons extra-virgin olive oil
1/2 red onion, chopped

1/2 teaspoon fresh garlic, minced
1/4 cup sweet white wine
1 tablespoon fresh coriander, minced
1/4 cup baby capers, drained
1 tomato, crushed
1/4 teaspoon chili paper flakes

Directions

Coat your sardines with all-purpose flour until well coated on all sides.

Season your sardines with salt and black pepper and arrange them in the cooking basket. Cook in your Air Fryer at 325 degrees F for 35 to 40 minutes until the skin is crispy.

Meanwhile, heat olive oil in a frying pan over a moderate flame. Now, sauté the onion and garlic for 4 to 5 minutes or until tender and aromatic.

Stir in the remaining ingredients, cover and let it simmer, for about 15 minutes or until the sauce has thickened and reduced. Spoon the sauce over the warm sardines and serve immediately. Enjoy!

Per serving: 349 Calories; 17.5g Fat; 19g Carbs; 26.3g Protein; 4.3g Sugars

305. Thai-Style Jumbo Scallops

(Ready in about 40 minutes | Servings 2)

Ingredients

8 jumbo scallops
1 teaspoon sesame oil
Sea salt and red pepper flakes, to season
1 tablespoon coconut oil
1 Thai chili, deveined and minced

1 teaspoon garlic, minced
1 tablespoon oyster sauce
1 tablespoon soy sauce
1/4 cup coconut milk
2 tablespoons fresh lime juice

Directions

Pat the jumbo scallops dry and toss them with 1 teaspoon of sesame oil, salt and red pepper.

Cook the jumbo scallops in your Air Fryer at 400 degrees F for 4 minutes; turn them over and cook an additional 3 minutes.

While your scallops are cooking, make the sauce in a frying pan. Heat the coconut oil in a pan over medium-high heat.

Once hot, cook the Thai chili and garlic for 1 minute or so until just tender and fragrant. Add in the oyster sauce, soy sauce and coconut milk and continue to simmer, partially covered, for 5 minutes longer.

Lastly, stir in fresh lime juice and stir to combine well. Add the warm scallops to the sauce and serve immediately.

Per serving: 200 Calories; 10.5g Fat; 10.2g Carbs; 16.3g Protein; 3.4g Sugars

306. Southwestern Prawns with Asparagus

(Ready in about 10 minutes | Servings 3)

Ingredients

1 pound prawns, deveined
1/2 pound asparagus spears, cut into 1-inch chinks
1 teaspoon butter, melted
1/4 teaspoon oregano

1/2 teaspoon mixed peppercorns, crushed
Salt, to taste
1 ripe avocado
1 lemon, sliced
1/2 cup chunky-style salsa

Directions

Toss your prawns and asparagus with melted butter, oregano, salt and mixed peppercorns.

Cook the prawns and asparagus at 400 degrees F for 5 minutes, shaking the basket halfway through the cooking time.

Divide the prawns and asparagus between serving plates and garnish with avocado and lemon slices. Serve with the salsa on the side. Bon appétit!

Per serving: 280 Calories; 12.1g Fat; 12.8g Carbs; 34.1g Protein; 4g Sugars

307. Halibut Steak with Cremini Mushrooms

(Ready in about 15 minutes | Servings 3)

Ingredients

1 pound halibut steak
1 teaspoon olive oil
Sea salt and ground black pepper, to taste
7 ounces Cremini mushrooms
1 teaspoon butter, melted

1/4 teaspoon onion powder
1/4 teaspoon garlic powder
1/2 teaspoon rosemary
1/2 teaspoon basil
1/2 teaspoon oregano

Directions

Toss the halibut steak with olive oil, salt and black pepper and transfer to the Air Fryer cooking basket.

Toss the Cremini mushrooms with the other ingredients until well coated on all sides.

Cook the halibut steak at 400 degrees F for 5 minutes. Turn the halibut steak over and top with mushrooms.

Continue to cook an additional 5 minutes or until the mushrooms are fragrant. Serve warm and enjoy!

Per serving: 326 Calories; 23.7g Fat; 4.2g Carbs; 23.1g Protein; 1.9g Sugars

308. Marinated Flounder Filets

(Ready in about 15 minutes + marinating time | Servings 3)

Ingredients

1 pound flounder filets
1 teaspoon garlic, minced
2 tablespoons soy sauce
1 teaspoon Dijon mustard
1/4 cup malt vinegar
1 teaspoon granulated sugar

Salt and black pepper, to taste
1/2 cup plain flour
1 egg
2 tablespoons milk
1/2 cup parmesan cheese, grated

Directions

Place the flounder filets, garlic, soy sauce, mustard, vinegar and sugar in a glass bowl; cover and let it marinate in your refrigerator for at least 1 hour.

Transfer the fish to a plate, discarding the marinade. Salt and pepper to taste.

Place the plain flour in a shallow bowl; in another bowl, beat the egg and milk until pale and well combined; add parmesan cheese to the third bowl.

Dip the flounder filets in the flour, then in the egg mixture; repeat the process and coat them with the parmesan cheese, pressing to adhere.

Cook the flounder filets in the preheated Air Fryer at 400 degrees F for 5 minutes; turn the flounder filets over and cook on the other side for 5 minutes more. Enjoy!

Per serving: 376 Calories; 14g Fat; 24.5g Carbs; 34.1g Protein; 4.8g Sugars

309. Herb and Garlic Grouper Filets

(Ready in about 15 minutes | Servings 3)

Ingredients

1 pound grouper filets
1/4 teaspoon shallot powder
1/4 teaspoon porcini powder
1 teaspoon fresh garlic, minced
1/2 teaspoon cayenne pepper
1/2 teaspoon hot paprika

1/4 teaspoon oregano
1/2 teaspoon marjoram
1/2 teaspoon sage
1 tablespoon butter, melted
Sea salt and black pepper, to taste

Directions

Pat dry the grouper filets using kitchen towels.

In a small dish, make the rub by mixing the remaining ingredients until everything is well incorporated.

Rub the fish with the mixture, coating well on all sides.

Cook the grouper filets in the preheated Air Fryer at 400 degrees F for 5 minutes; turn the filets over and cook on the other side for 5 minutes more. Serve over hot rice if desired. Bon appétit!

Per serving: 184 Calories; 5.4g Fat; 2.5g Carbs; 29.8g Protein; 0.9g Sugars

310. Greek-Style Sea Bass

(Ready in about 15 minutes | Servings 2)

Ingredients

1/2 pound sea bass
1 garlic clove, halved
Sea salt and ground black pepper,
to taste
1/2 teaspoon rigani (Greek
oregano)
1/2 teaspoon dried dill weed
1/4 teaspoon ground bay leaf

1/4 teaspoon ground cumin
1/2 teaspoon shallot powder
Greek sauce:
1/2 Greek yogurt
1 teaspoon olive oil
1/2 teaspoon Tzatziki spice mix
1 teaspoon lime juice

Directions

Pat dry the sea bass with paper towels. Rub the fish with garlic halves.

Toss the fish with salt, black pepper, rigani, dill, ground bay leaf, ground cumin and shallot powder.

Cook the sea bass in your Air Fryer at 400 degrees F for 5 minutes; turn the filets over and cook on the other side for 5 to 6 minutes.

In the meantime, make the sauce by simply blending the remaining ingredients. Serve the warm fish dolloped with Greek-style sauce. Enjoy!

Per serving: 174 Calories; 4.8g Fat; 5g Carbs; 25.8g Protein; 2.6g Sugars

311. Melt-in-Your Mouth Salmon with Cilantro Sauce

(Ready in about 15 minutes | Servings 2)

Ingredients

1 pound salmon fillets
1 teaspoon coconut oil
Sea salt and ground black pepper,
to season

2 heaping tablespoons cilantro
1/2 cup Mexican crema
1 tablespoon fresh lime juice

Directions

Rinse and pat your salmon dry using paper towels. Toss the salmon with coconut oil, salt and black pepper.

Cook the salmon filets in your Air Fryer at 380 degrees F for 6 minutes; turn the salmon filets over and cook on the other side for 6 to 7 minutes.

Meanwhile, mix the remaining ingredients in your blender or food processor. Spoon the cilantro sauce over the salmon filets and serve immediately.

Per serving: 419 Calories; 20.2g Fat; 3.2g Carbs; 53.3g Protein; 1.6g Sugars

312. Classic Old Bay Fish with Cherry Tomatoes

(Ready in about 15 minutes | Servings 3)

Ingredients

1 pound swordfish steak
1/2 cup cornflakes, crushed
1 teaspoon Old Bay seasoning

Salt and black pepper, to season
2 teaspoon olive oil
1 pound cherry tomatoes

Directions

Toss the swordfish steak with cornflakes, Old Bay seasoning, salt, black pepper and 1 teaspoon of olive oil.

Cook the swordfish steak in your Air Fryer at 400 degrees F for 6 minutes.

Now, turn the fish over, top with tomatoes and drizzle with the remaining teaspoon of olive oil. Continue to cook for 4 minutes.

Serve with lemon slices if desired. Bon appétit!

Per serving: 291 Calories; 13.5g Fat; 10.4g Carbs; 31.9g Protein; 6.8g Sugars

313. Haddock Steaks with Decadent Mango Salsa

(Ready in about 15 minutes | Servings 2)

Ingredients

2 haddock steaks
1 teaspoon butter, melted
1 tablespoon white wine
Sea salt and ground black pepper,
to taste
Mango salsa:

1/2 mango, diced
1/4 cup red onion, chopped
1 chili pepper, deveined and
minced
1 teaspoon cilantro, chopped
2 tablespoons fresh lemon juice

Directions

Toss the haddock with butter, wine, salt and black pepper.

Cook the haddock in your Air Fryer at 400 degrees F for 5 minutes. Flip the haddock and cook on the other side for 5 minutes more.

Meanwhile, make the mango salsa by mixing all ingredients. Serve the warm haddock with the chilled mango salsa and enjoy!

Per serving: 411 Calories; 25.5g Fat; 18.4g Carbs; 26.3g Protein; 14g Sugars

314. Homemade Fish Fingers

(Ready in about 15 minutes | Servings 2)

Ingredients

3/4 pound tilapia
1 egg
2 tablespoons milk
4 tablespoons chickpea flour
1/4 cup pork rinds

1/2 cup breadcrumbs
1/2 teaspoon red chili flakes
Coarse sea salt and black pepper,
to season

Directions

Rinse the tilapia and pat it dry using kitchen towels. Then, cut the tilapia into strips.

Then, whisk the egg, milk and chickpea flour in a rimmed plate.

Add the pork rinds and breadcrumbs to another plate; stir in red chili flakes, salt and black pepper and stir to combine well.

Dip the fish strips in the egg mixture, then, roll them over the breadcrumb mixture. Transfer the fish fingers to the Air Fryer cooking basket and spritz them with a nonstick cooking spray.

Cook in the preheated Air Fryer at 400 degrees F for 10 minutes, shaking the basket halfway through to ensure even browning. Serve warm and enjoy!

Per serving: 332 Calories; 10.5g Fat; 12.2g Carbs; 46.3g Protein; 2.8g Sugars

315. Ahi Tuna with Peppers and Tartare Sauce

(Ready in about 15 minutes | Servings 2)

Ingredients

2 ahi tuna steaks
2 Spanish peppers, quartered
1 teaspoon olive oil
1/2 teaspoon garlic powder
Salt and freshly ground black
pepper, to taste
Tartare sauce:

4 tablespoons mayonnaise
2 tablespoons sour cream
1 tablespoon baby capers, drained
1 tablespoon gherkins, drained
and chopped
2 tablespoons white onion, minced

Directions

Pat the ahi tuna dry using kitchen towels.

Toss the ahi tuna and Spanish peppers with olive oil, garlic powder, salt and black pepper.

Cook the ahi tuna and peppers in the preheated Air Fryer at 400 degrees F for 10 minutes, flipping them halfway through the cooking time.

Meanwhile, whisk all the sauce ingredients until well combined. Plate the ahi tuna steaks and arrange Spanish peppers around them. Serve with tartare sauce on the side and enjoy!

Per serving: 485 Calories; 24.3g Fat; 7.7g Carbs; 56.3g Protein; 3g Sugars

316. Fried Oysters with Kaffir Lime Sauce

(Ready in about 10 minutes | Servings 2)

Ingredients

8 fresh oysters, shucked
1/3 cup plain flour
1 egg
3/4 cup breadcrumbs
1/2 teaspoon Italian seasoning mix

1 lime, freshly squeezed
1 teaspoon coconut sugar
1 kaffir lime leaf, shredded
1 habanero pepper, minced
1 teaspoon olive oil

Directions

Clean the oysters and set them aside.

Add the flour to a rimmed plate. Whisk the egg in another rimmed plate. Mix the breadcrumbs and Italian seasoning mix in a third plate.

Dip your oysters in the flour, shaking off the excess. Then, dip them in the egg mixture and finally, coat your oysters with the breadcrumb mixture.

Spritz the breaded oysters with a nonstick cooking spray.

Cook your oysters in the preheated Air Fryer at 400 degrees F for 2 to 3 minutes, shaking the basket halfway through the cooking time.

Meanwhile, blend the remaining ingredients to make the sauce. Serve the warm oysters with the kaffir lime sauce on the side. Bon appétit!

Per serving: 295 Calories; 8.7g Fat; 23.4g Carbs; 30g Protein; 3.3g Sugars

317. Mom's Lobster Tails

(Ready in about 10 minutes | Servings 2)

Ingredients

1/2 pound lobster tails
1 teaspoon olive oil
1 teaspoon fresh lime juice
1 bell pepper, sliced
1 jalapeno pepper, sliced
1 carrot, julienned
1 cup green cabbage, shredded

2 tablespoons mayonnaise
2 tablespoons Greek-style yogurt
Sea salt and ground black pepper, to taste
1 teaspoon baby capers, drained
4 leaves butterhead lettuce, for serving

Directions

Drizzle olive oil over the lobster tails and transfer them to the Air Fryer cooking basket.

Cook the lobster tails at 370 degrees F for 3 minutes. Then, turn them over and cook on the other side for 3 to 4 minutes more until they are opaque.

Toss the lobster tails with the other ingredients, except for the lettuce leaves; gently stir until well combined.

Lay the lettuce leaves on a serving platter and top with the lobster salad. Bon appétit!

Per serving: 256 Calories; 13.7g Fat; 12.7g Carbs; 21.5g Protein; 6.3g Sugars

318. Classic Fish Tacos

(Ready in about 15 minutes | Servings 3)

Ingredients

1 pound codfish
1 tablespoon olive oil
1 teaspoon Cajun spice mix
Salt and red pepper, to taste

3 corn tortillas
1/2 avocado, pitted and diced
1 cup purple cabbage
1 jalapeño, minced

Directions

Pat the codfish dry with paper towels; toss the codfish with olive oil, Cajun spice mix, salt and black pepper.

Cook your codfish at 400 degrees F for 5 to 6 minutes. Then, turn the fish over and cook on the other side for 6 minutes until they are opaque.

Let the fish rest for 5 minutes before flaking with a fork.

Assemble the tacos: place the flaked fish over warmed tortillas; top with avocado, purple cabbage and minced jalapeño. Enjoy!

Per serving: 266 Calories; 10.8g Fat; 17.3g Carbs; 25.7g Protein; 2.6g Sugars

319. Dijon Catfish with Eggplant Sauce

(Ready in about 30 minutes | Servings 3)

Ingredients

1 pound catfish fillets
Sea salt and ground black pepper, to taste
1/4 cup Dijon mustard
1 tablespoon honey
1 tablespoon white vinegar

1 pound eggplant, 1 ½-inch cubes
2 tablespoons olive oil
1 tablespoon tahini
1/2 teaspoon garlic, minced
1 tablespoon parsley, chopped

Directions

Pat the catfish dry with paper towels and generously season with salt and black pepper.

In a small mixing bowl, thoroughly combine Dijon mustard, honey and vinegar.

Cook the fish in your Air Fryer at 400 degrees F for 5 minutes. Turn the fish over and brush with the Dijon mixture; continue to cook for a further 5 minutes.

Then, set your Air Fryer to 400 degrees F. Add the eggplant chunks to the cooking basket and cook for 15 minutes, shaking the basket occasionally to ensure even cooking.

Transfer the cooked eggplant to a bowl of your food processor; stir in the remaining ingredients and blitz until everything is well blended and smooth.

Serve the warm catfish with the eggplant sauce on the side. Bon appétit!

Per serving: 336 Calories; 16.9g Fat; 18.6g Carbs; 28.2g Protein; 12.1g Sugars

320. Halibut Steak with Zoodles and Lemon

(Ready in about 15 minutes | Servings 3)

Ingredients

1 pound halibut steak, cut into 3 pieces
1 garlic clove, halved
1 teaspoon avocado oil
Sea salt and black pepper, to taste
1 pound zucchini, julienned

1/2 teaspoon onion powder
1/2 teaspoon granulated garlic
1 tablespoon fresh parsley, minced
1 teaspoon sage, minced
1 lemon, sliced

Directions

Rub the halibut steaks with garlic and toss with avocado oil, salt and black pepper; then, transfer the halibut steaks to the Air Fryer cooking basket.

Cook the halibut steak at 400 degrees F for 5 minutes. Turn the halibut steak over and continue to cook an additional 5 minutes or until it flakes easily when tested with a fork.

Meanwhile, spritz a wok with a nonstick spray; heat the wok over medium-high heat.

Once hot, stir fry the zucchini noodles along with the onion powder and granulated garlic; cook for 2 to 3 minutes or until just tender.

Top your zoodles with the parsley and sage and stir to combine. Serve the hot zoodles with the halibut steaks and lemon slices. Bon appétit!

Per serving: 341 Calories; 23.1g Fat; 8.2g Carbs; 26.3g Protein; 1.2g Sugars

321. Salmon with Baby Bok Choy

(Ready in about 20 minutes | Servings 3)

Ingredients

1 pound salmon filets
1 teaspoon garlic chili paste
1 teaspoon sesame oil
1 tablespoon honey

1 tablespoon soy sauce
1 pound baby Bok choy, bottoms removed
Kosher salt and black pepper, to taste

Directions

Start by preheating your Air Fryer to 380 degrees F.

Toss the salmon fillets with garlic chili paste, sesame oil, honey, soy sauce, salt and black pepper.

Cook the salmon in the preheated Air Fryer for 6 minutes; turn the filets over and cook an additional 6 minutes.

Then, cook the baby Bok choy at 350 degrees F for 3 minutes; shake the basket and cook an additional 3 minutes. Salt and pepper to taste.

Serve the salmon fillets with the roasted baby Bok choy. Enjoy!

Per serving: 308 Calories; 13.6g Fat; 12.2g Carbs; 34.3g Protein; 9.3g Sugars

322. Tuna Steak with Roasted Cherry Tomatoes

(Ready in about 15 minutes | Servings 2)

Ingredients

1 pound tuna steak
1 cup cherry tomatoes
1 teaspoon extra-virgin olive oil
2 sprigs rosemary, leaves picked and crushed

Sea salt and red pepper flakes, to taste
1 teaspoon garlic, finely chopped
1 tablespoon lime juice

Directions

Toss the tuna steaks and cherry tomatoes with olive oil, rosemary leaves, salt, black pepper and garlic.

Place the tuna steaks in a lightly oiled cooking basket; cook tuna steaks at 440 degrees F for about 6 minutes.

Turn the tuna steaks over, add in the cherry tomatoes and continue to cook for 4 minutes more. Drizzle the fish with lime juice and serve warm garnished with roasted cherry tomatoes!

Per serving: 231 Calories; 3.3g Fat; 6.2g Carbs; 45.2g Protein; 3.7g Sugars

323. Seed-Crusted Codfish Fillets

(Ready in about 15 minutes | Servings 2)

Ingredients

2 codfish fillets
1 teaspoon sesame oil
Sea salt and black pepper, to taste

1 teaspoon sesame seeds
1 tablespoon chia seeds

Directions

Start by preheating your Air Fryer to 380 degrees F.

Add the sesame oil, salt, black pepper, sesame seeds and chia seeds to a rimmed plate. Coat the top of the codfish with the seed mixture, pressing it down to adhere.

Lower the codfish fillets, seed side down, into the cooking basket and cook for 6 minutes. Turn the fish fillets over and cook for a further 6 minutes.

Serve warm and enjoy!

Per serving: 263 Calories; 8.3g Fat; 8.2g Carbs; 37.7g Protein; 1.2g Sugars

324. Salmon Filets with Fennel Slaw

(Ready in about 15 minutes | Servings 3)

Ingredients

1 pound salmon filets
1 teaspoon Cajun spice mix
Sea salt and ground black pepper, to taste
Fennel Slaw:
1 pound fennel bulb, thinly sliced

1 Lebanese cucumber, thinly sliced
1/2 red onion, thinly sliced
1/2 ounce tarragon
2 tablespoons tahini
2 tablespoons lemon juice
1 tablespoon soy sauce

Directions

Rinse the salmon filets and pat them dry with a paper towel. Then, toss the salmon filets with the Cajun spice mix, salt and black pepper.

Cook the salmon filets in the preheated Air Fryer at 380 degrees F for 6 minutes; flip the salmon filets and cook for a further 6 minutes.

Meanwhile, make the fennel slaw by stirring fennel, cucumber, red onion and tarragon in a salad bowl. Mix the remaining ingredients to make the dressing.

Dress the salad and transfer to your refrigerator until ready to serve.

Serve the warm fish with chilled fennel slaw. Bon appétit!

Per serving: 337 Calories; 13.6g Fat; 19.3g Carbs; 36.3g Protein; 8.2g Sugars

325. Scallops with Pineapple Salsa and Pickled Onions

(Ready in about 15 minutes | Servings 3)

Ingredients

12 scallops
1 teaspoon sesame oil
1/4 teaspoon dried rosemary
1/2 teaspoon dried tarragon
1/2 teaspoon dried basil
1/4 teaspoon red pepper flakes, crushed
Coarse sea salt and black pepper, to taste
1/2 cup pickled onions, drained
Pineapple Salsa:

1 cup pineapple, diced
2 tablespoons fresh cilantro, roughly chopped
1 jalapeño, deveined and minced
1 small-sized red onion, minced
1 teaspoon ginger root, peeled and grated
1/2 teaspoon coconut sugar
Sea salt and ground black pepper, to taste

Directions

Toss the scallops sesame oil, rosemary, tarragon, basil, red pepper, salt and black pepper.

Cook in the preheated Air Fryer at 400 degrees F for 6 to 7 minutes, shaking the basket once or twice to ensure even cooking.

Meanwhile, process all the salsa ingredients in your blender; cover and place the salsa in your refrigerator until ready to serve.

Serve the warm scallops with pickled onions and pineapple salsa on the side. Bon appétit!

Per serving: 177 Calories; 2.6g Fat; 22.3g Carbs; 15.6g Protein; 15g Sugars

326. Tuna Steaks with Pearl Onions

(Ready in about 20 minutes | Servings 4)

Ingredients

4 tuna steaks
1 pound pearl onions
4 teaspoons olive oil
1 teaspoon dried rosemary
1 teaspoon dried marjoram

1 tablespoon cayenne pepper
1/2 teaspoon sea salt
1/2 teaspoon black pepper, preferably freshly cracked
1 lemon, sliced

Directions

Place the tuna steaks in the lightly greased cooking basket. Top with the pearl onions; add the olive oil, rosemary, marjoram, cayenne pepper, salt, and black pepper.

Bake in the preheated Air Fryer at 400 degrees F for 9 to 10 minutes. Work in two batches.

Serve warm with lemon slices and enjoy!

Per serving: 332 Calories; 5.9g Fat; 10.5g Carbs; 56.1g Protein; 6.1g Sugars

327. Tortilla-Crusted Haddock Fillets

(Ready in about 20 minutes | Servings 2)

Ingredients

2 haddock fillets
1/2 cup tortilla chips, crushed
2 tablespoons parmesan cheese, freshly grated
1 teaspoon dried parsley flakes

1 egg, beaten
1/2 teaspoon coarse sea salt
1/4 teaspoon ground black pepper
1/4 teaspoon cayenne pepper
2 tablespoons olive oil

Directions

Start by preheating your Air Fryer to 360 degrees F. Pat dry the haddock fillets and set aside.

In a shallow bowl, thoroughly combine the crushed tortilla chips with the parmesan and parsley flakes. Mix until everything is well incorporated.

In a separate shallow bowl, whisk the egg with salt, black pepper, and cayenne pepper.

Dip the haddock fillets into the egg. Then, dip the fillets into the tortilla/parmesan mixture until well coated on all sides.

Drizzle the olive oil all over the fish fillets. Lower the coated fillets into the lightly greased Air Fryer basket. Cook for 11 to 13 minutes. Bon appétit!

Per serving: 384 Calories; 21.3g Fat; 7.6g Carbs; 38.4g Protein; 1g Sugars

328. Vermouth and Garlic Shrimp Skewers

(Ready in about 15 minutes + marinating time | Servings 4)

Ingredients

1 ½ pounds shrimp
1/4 cup vermouth
2 cloves garlic, crushed
1 teaspoon dry mango powder
Kosher salt, to taste
1/4 teaspoon black pepper, freshly ground

2 tablespoons olive oil
4 tablespoons flour
8 skewers, soaked in water for 30 minutes
1 lemon, cut into wedges

Directions

Add the shrimp, vermouth, garlic, mango powder, salt, black pepper, and olive oil in a ceramic bowl; let it sit for 1 hour in your refrigerator.

Discard the marinade and toss the shrimp with flour. Thread on to skewers and transfer to the lightly greased cooking basket.

Cook at 400 degrees F for 5 minutes, tossing halfway through. Serve with lemon wedges. Bon appétit!

Per serving: 371 Calories; 12.2g Fat; 30.4g Carbs; 29.5g Protein; 3.2g Sugars

329. Easy Lobster Tails

(Ready in about 20 minutes | Servings 5)

Ingredients

2 pounds fresh lobster tails, cleaned and halved, in shells
2 tablespoons butter, melted
1 teaspoon onion powder
1 teaspoon cayenne pepper

Salt and ground black pepper, to taste
2 garlic cloves, minced
1 cup cornmeal
1 cup green olives

Directions

In a plastic closeable bag, thoroughly combine all ingredients; shake to combine well.

Transfer the coated lobster tails to the greased cooking basket.

Cook in the preheated Air Fryer at 390 degrees for 6 to 7 minutes, shaking the basket halfway through. Work in batches.

Serve with green olives and enjoy!

Per serving: 422 Calories; 7.9g Fat; 49.9g Carbs; 35.4g Protein; 3.1g Sugars

330. Spicy Curried King Prawns

(Ready in about 10 minutes | Servings 2)

Ingredients

12 king prawns, rinsed
1 tablespoon coconut oil
1/2 teaspoon piri piri powder
Salt and ground black pepper, to taste

1 teaspoon garlic paste
1 teaspoon onion powder
1/2 teaspoon cumin powder
1 teaspoon curry powder

Directions

In a mixing bowl, toss all ingredient until the prawns are well coated on all sides.

Cook in the preheated Air Fryer at 360 degrees F for 4 minutes. Shake the basket and cook for 4 minutes more.

Serve over hot rice if desired. Bon appétit!

Per serving: 220 Calories; 9.7g Fat; 15.1g Carbs; 17.6g Protein; 2.2g Sugars

331. Korean-Style Salmon Patties

(Ready in about 15 minutes | Servings 4)

Ingredients

1 pound salmon
1 egg
1 garlic clove, minced
2 green onions, minced
1/2 cup rolled oats
Sauce:

1 teaspoon rice wine
1 ½ tablespoons soy sauce
1 teaspoon honey
A pinch of salt
1 teaspoon gochugaru (Korean red chili pepper flakes)

Directions

Start by preheating your Air Fryer to 380 degrees F. Spritz the Air Fryer basket with cooking oil.

Mix the salmon, egg, garlic, green onions, and rolled oats in a bowl; knead with your hands until everything is well incorporated.

Shape the mixture into equally sized patties. Transfer your patties to the Air Fryer basket.

Cook the fish patties for 10 minutes, turning them over halfway through.

Meanwhile, make the sauce by whisking all ingredients. Serve the warm fish patties with the sauce on the side.

Per serving: 396 Calories; 20.1g Fat; 16.7g Carbs; 35.2g Protein; 3.1g Sugars

332. English-Style Flounder Fillets

(Ready in about 20 minutes | Servings 2)

Ingredients

2 flounder fillets
1/4 cup all-purpose flour
1 egg
1/2 teaspoon Worcestershire sauce

1/2 cup bread crumbs
1/2 teaspoon lemon pepper
1/2 teaspoon coarse sea salt
1/4 teaspoon chili powder

Directions

Rinse and pat dry the flounder fillets.

Place the flour in a large pan.

Whisk the egg and Worcestershire sauce in a shallow bowl. In a separate bowl, mix the bread crumbs with the lemon pepper, salt, and chili powder.

Dredge the fillets in the flour, shaking off the excess. Then, dip them into the egg mixture. Lastly, coat the fish fillets with the breadcrumb mixture until they are coated on all sides.

Spritz with cooking spray and transfer to the Air Fryer basket. Cook at 390 degrees for 7 minutes.

Turn them over, spritz with cooking spray on the other side, and cook another 5 minutes. Bon appétit!

Per serving: 432 Calories; 16.7g Fat; 29g Carbs; 38.4g Protein; 2.7g Sugars

333. Cod and Shallot Frittata

(Ready in about 20 minutes | Servings 3)

Ingredients

2 cod fillets
6 eggs
1/2 cup milk
1 shallot, chopped
2 garlic cloves, minced

Sea salt and ground black pepper, to taste
1/2 teaspoon red pepper flakes, crushed

Directions

Bring a pot of salted water to a boil. Boil the cod fillets for 5 minutes or until it is opaque. Flake the fish into bite-sized pieces.

In a mixing bowl, whisk the eggs and milk. Stir in the shallots, garlic, salt, black pepper, and red pepper flakes. Stir in the reserved fish.

Pour the mixture into the lightly greased baking pan.

Cook in the preheated Air Fryer at 360 degrees F for 9 minutes, flipping over halfway through. Bon appétit!

Per serving: 454 Calories; 30.8g Fat; 10.3g Carbs; 32.4g Protein; 4.1g Sugars

334. Crispy Tilapia Fillets

(Ready in about 20 minutes | Servings 5)

Ingredients

5 tablespoons all-purpose flour
Sea salt and white pepper, to taste
1 teaspoon garlic paste

2 tablespoons extra virgin olive oil
1/2 cup cornmeal
5 tilapia fillets, slice into halves

Directions

Combine the flour, salt, white pepper, garlic paste, olive oil, and cornmeal in a Ziploc bag. Add the fish fillets and shake to coat well.

Spritz the Air Fryer basket with cooking spray. Cook in the preheated Air Fryer at 400 degrees F for 10 minutes; turn them over and cook for 6 minutes more. Work in batches.

Serve with lemon wedges if desired. Enjoy!

Per serving: 315 Calories; 9.1g Fat; 19.4g Carbs; 38.5g Protein; 0.7g Sugars

335. Saucy Garam Masala Fish

(Ready in about 25 minutes | Servings 2)

Ingredients

2 teaspoons olive oil
1/4 cup coconut milk
1/2 teaspoon cayenne pepper
1 teaspoon Garam masala
1/4 teaspoon Kala namak (Indian black salt)
1/2 teaspoon fresh ginger, grated
1 garlic clove, minced
2 catfish fillets
1/4 cup coriander, roughly chopped

Directions

Preheat your Air Fryer to 390 degrees F. Then, spritz the baking dish with a nonstick cooking spray.

In a mixing bowl, whisk the olive oil, milk, cayenne pepper, Garam masala, Kala namak, ginger, and garlic.

Coat the catfish fillets with the Garam masala mixture. Cook the catfish fillets in the preheated Air Fryer approximately 18 minutes, turning over halfway through the cooking time.

Garnish with fresh coriander and serve over hot noodles if desired.

Per serving: 301 Calories; 12.1g Fat; 2.3g Carbs; 43g Protein; 1.6g Sugars

336. Grilled Salmon Steaks

(Ready in about 45 minutes | Servings 4)

Ingredients

2 cloves garlic, minced
4 tablespoons butter, melted
Sea salt and ground black pepper, to taste
1 teaspoon smoked paprika
1/2 teaspoon onion powder
1 tablespoon lime juice
1/4 cup dry white wine
4 salmon steaks

Directions

Place all ingredients in a large ceramic dish. Cover and let it marinate for 30 minutes in the refrigerator.

Arrange the salmon steaks on the grill pan. Bake at 390 degrees for 5 minutes, or until the salmon steaks are easily flaked with a fork.

Flip the fish steaks, baste with the reserved marinade, and cook another 5 minutes. Bon appétit!

Per serving: 420 Calories; 23g Fat; 2.5g Carbs; 48.5g Protein; 0.7g Sugars

337. Cajun Fish Cakes with Cheese

(Ready in about 30 minutes | Servings 4)

Ingredients

2 catfish fillets
1 cup all-purpose flour
3 ounces butter
1 teaspoon baking powder
1 teaspoon baking soda
1/2 cup buttermilk
1 teaspoon Cajun seasoning
1 cup Swiss cheese, shredded

Directions

Bring a pot of salted water to a boil. Boil the fish fillets for 5 minutes or until it is opaque. Flake the fish into small pieces.

Mix the remaining ingredients in a bowl; add the fish and mix until well combined. Shape the fish mixture into 12 patties.

Cook in the preheated Air Fryer at 380 degrees F for 15 minutes. Work in batches. Enjoy!

Per serving: 478 Calories; 30.1g Fat; 27.2g Carbs; 23.8g Protein; 2g Sugars

338. Smoked Halibut and Eggs in Brioche

(Ready in about 25 minutes | Servings 4)

Ingredients

4 brioche rolls
1 pound smoked halibut, chopped
4 eggs
1 teaspoon dried thyme
1 teaspoon dried basil
Salt and black pepper, to taste

Directions

Cut off the top of each brioche; then, scoop out the insides to make the shells.

Lay the prepared brioche shells in the lightly greased cooking basket.

Spritz with cooking oil; add the halibut. Crack an egg into each brioche shell; sprinkle with thyme, basil, salt, and black pepper.

Bake in the preheated Air Fryer at 325 degrees F for 20 minutes. Bon appétit!

Per serving: 372 Calories; 13.1g Fat; 22g Carbs; 38.6g Protein; 3.3g Sugars

339. Crab Cake Burgers

(Ready in about 2 hours 20 minutes | Servings 3)

Ingredients

2 eggs, beaten
1 shallot, chopped
2 garlic cloves, crushed
1 tablespoon olive oil
1 teaspoon yellow mustard
1 teaspoon fresh cilantro, chopped
10 ounces crab meat
1 cup tortilla chips, crushed
1/2 teaspoon cayenne pepper
1/2 teaspoon ground black pepper
Sea salt, to taste
3/4 cup fresh bread crumbs

Directions

In a mixing bowl, thoroughly combine the eggs, shallot, garlic, olive oil, mustard, cilantro, crab meat, tortilla chips, cayenne pepper, black pepper, and salt. Mix until well combined.

Shape the mixture into 6 patties. Dip the crab patties into the fresh breadcrumbs, coating well on all sides. Place in your refrigerator for 2 hours.

Spritz the crab patties with cooking oil on both sides. Cook in the preheated Air Fryer at 360 degrees F for 14 minutes. Serve on dinner rolls if desired. Bon appétit!

Per serving: 500 Calories; 15.1g Fat; 51g Carbs; 44.3g Protein; 1.7g Sugars

340. Coconut Shrimp with Orange Sauce

(Ready in about 1 hour 30 minutes | Servings 3)

Ingredients

1 pound shrimp, cleaned and deveined
Sea salt and white pepper, to taste
1/2 cup all-purpose flour
1 egg
1/4 cup shredded coconut, unsweetened
3/2 cup fresh bread crumbs
2 tablespoons olive oil
1 lemon, cut into wedges
Dipping Sauce:
2 tablespoons butter
1/2 cup orange juice
2 tablespoons soy sauce
A pinch of salt
1/2 teaspoon tapioca starch
2 tablespoons fresh parsley, minced

Directions

Pat dry the shrimp and season them with salt and white pepper.

Place the flour on a large tray; then, whisk the egg in a shallow bowl. In a third shallow bowl, place the shredded coconut and breadcrumbs.

Dip the shrimp in the flour, then, dip in the egg. Lastly, coat the shrimp with the shredded coconut and bread crumbs. Refrigerate for 1 hour.

Then, transfer to the cooking basket. Drizzle with olive oil and cook in the preheated Air Fryer at 370 degrees F for 6 minutes. Work in batches.

Meanwhile, melt the butter in a small saucepan over medium-high heat; add the orange juice and bring it to a boil; reduce the heat and allow it to simmer approximately 7 minutes.

Add the soy sauce, salt, and tapioca; continue simmering until the sauce has thickened and reduced. Spoon the sauce over the shrimp and garnish with lemon wedges and parsley. Serve immediately.

Per serving: 487 Calories; 21.7g Fat; 35.9g Carbs; 37.6g Protein; 8.4g Sugars

341. Monkfish with Sautéed Vegetables and Olives

(Ready in about 20 minutes | Servings 2)

Ingredients

2 teaspoons olive oil
2 carrots, sliced
2 bell peppers, sliced
1 teaspoon dried thyme
1/2 teaspoon dried marjoram
1/2 teaspoon dried rosemary
2 monkfish fillets

1 tablespoon soy sauce
2 tablespoons lime juice
Coarse salt and ground black pepper, to taste
1 teaspoon cayenne pepper
1/2 cup Kalamata olives, pitted and sliced

Directions

In a nonstick skillet, heat the olive oil for 1 minute. Once hot, sauté the carrots and peppers until tender, about 4 minutes. Sprinkle with thyme, marjoram, and rosemary and set aside.

Toss the fish fillets with the soy sauce, lime juice, salt, black pepper, and cayenne pepper. Place the fish fillets in a lightly greased cooking basket and bake at 390 degrees F for 8 minutes.

Turn them over, add the olives, and cook an additional 4 minutes. Serve with the sautéed vegetables on the side. Bon appétit!

Per serving: 310 Calories; 13.3g Fat; 12.7g Carbs; 35.2g Protein; 5.4g Sugars

342. Delicious Snapper en Papillote

(Ready in about 20 minutes | Servings 2)

Ingredients

2 snapper fillets
1 shallot, peeled and sliced
2 garlic cloves, halved
1 bell pepper, sliced
1 small-sized serrano pepper, sliced
1 tomato, sliced

1 tablespoon olive oil
1/4 teaspoon freshly ground black pepper
1/2 teaspoon paprika
Sea salt, to taste
2 bay leaves

Directions

Place two parchment sheets on a working surface. Place the fish in the center of one side of the parchment paper.

Top with the shallot, garlic, peppers, and tomato. Drizzle olive oil over the fish and vegetables. Season with black pepper, paprika, and salt. Add the bay leaves.

Fold over the other half of the parchment. Now, fold the paper around the edges tightly and create a half moon shape, sealing the fish inside.

Cook in the preheated Air Fryer at 390 degrees F for 15 minutes. Serve warm.

Per serving: 329 Calories; 9.8g Fat; 12.7g Carbs; 46.7g Protein; 5.4g Sugars

343. Halibut Cakes with Horseradish Mayo

(Ready in about 20 minutes | Servings 4)

Ingredients

Halibut Cakes:
1 pound halibut
2 tablespoons olive oil
1/2 teaspoon cayenne pepper
1/4 teaspoon black pepper
Salt, to taste
2 tablespoons cilantro, chopped
1 shallot, chopped

2 garlic cloves, minced
1/2 cup Romano cheese, grated
1/2 cup breadcrumbs
1 egg, whisked
1 tablespoon Worcestershire sauce
Mayo Sauce:
1 teaspoon horseradish, grated
1/2 cup mayonnaise

Directions

Start by preheating your Air Fryer to 380 degrees F. Spritz the Air Fryer basket with cooking oil.

Mix all ingredients for the halibut cakes in a bowl; knead with your hands until everything is well incorporated.

Shape the mixture into equally sized patties. Transfer your patties to the Air Fryer basket. Cook the fish patties for 10 minutes, turning them over halfway through.

Mix the horseradish and mayonnaise. Serve the halibut cakes with the horseradish mayo. Bon appétit!

Per serving: 470 Calories; 38.2g Fat; 6.3g Carbs; 24.4g Protein; 1.5g Sugars

344. Dilled and Glazed Salmon Steaks

(Ready in about 20 minutes | Servings 2)

Ingredients

2 salmon steaks
Coarse sea salt, to taste
1/4 teaspoon freshly ground black pepper, or more to taste
2 tablespoons honey
1 tablespoon sesame oil

Zest of 1 lemon
1 tablespoon fresh lemon juice
1 teaspoon garlic, minced
1/2 teaspoon smoked cayenne pepper
1/2 teaspoon dried dill

Directions

Preheat your Air Fryer to 380 degrees F. Pat dry the salmon steaks with a kitchen towel.

In a ceramic dish, combine the remaining ingredients until everything is well whisked.

Add the salmon steaks to the ceramic dish and let them sit in the refrigerator for 1 hour. Now, place the salmon steaks in the cooking basket. Reserve the marinade.

Cook for 12 minutes, flipping halfway through the cooking time.

Meanwhile, cook the marinade in a small sauté pan over a moderate flame. Cook until the sauce has thickened.

Pour the sauce over the steaks and serve with mashed potatoes if desired. Bon appétit!

Per serving: 421 Calories; 16.8g Fat; 19.9g Carbs; 46.7g Protein; 18.1g Sugars

345. Easy Prawns alla Parmigiana

(Ready in about 20 minutes | Servings 4)

Ingredients

2 egg whites
1 cup all-purpose flour
1 cup Parmigiano-Reggiano, grated
1/2 cup fine breadcrumbs
1/2 teaspoon celery seeds
1/2 teaspoon porcini powder

1/2 teaspoon onion powder
1 teaspoon garlic powder
1/2 teaspoon dried rosemary
1/2 teaspoon sea salt
1/2 teaspoon ground black pepper
1 ½ pounds prawns, deveined

Directions

To make a breading station, whisk the egg whites in a shallow dish. In a separate dish, place the all-purpose flour.

In a third dish, thoroughly combine the Parmigiano-Reggiano, breadcrumbs, and seasonings; mix to combine well.

Dip the prawns in the flour, then, into the egg whites; lastly, dip them in the parm/breadcrumb mixture. Roll until they are covered on all sides.

Cook in the preheated Air Fryer at 390 degrees F for 5 to 7 minutes or until golden brown. Work in batches. Serve with lemon wedges if desired.

Per serving: 442 Calories; 10.3g Fat; 40.4g Carbs; 43.7g Protein; 1.2g Sugars

346. Indian Famous Fish Curry

(Ready in about 25 minutes | Servings 4)

Ingredients

2 tablespoons sunflower oil
1/2 pound fish, chopped
2 red chilies, chopped
1 tablespoon coriander powder
1 teaspoon curry paste
1 cup coconut milk

Salt and white pepper, to taste
1/2 teaspoon fenugreek seeds
1 shallot, minced
1 garlic clove, minced
1 ripe tomato, pureed

Directions

Preheat your Air Fryer to 380 degrees F; brush the cooking basket with 1 tablespoon of sunflower oil.

Cook your fish for 10 minutes on both sides. Transfer to the baking pan that is previously greased with the remaining tablespoon of sunflower oil.

Add the remaining ingredients and reduce the heat to 350 degrees F. Continue to cook an additional 10 to 12 minutes or until everything is heated through. Enjoy!

Per serving: 449 Calories; 29.1g Fat; 20.4g Carbs; 27.3g Protein; 13.3g Sugars

347. Cajun Cod Fillets with Avocado Sauce

(Ready in about 20 minutes | Servings 2)

Ingredients

2 cod fish fillets
1 egg
Sea salt, to taste
1/2 cup tortilla chips, crushed
2 teaspoons olive oil
1/2 avocado, peeled, pitted, and mashed
1 tablespoon mayonnaise
3 tablespoons sour cream
1/2 teaspoon yellow mustard
1 teaspoon lemon juice
1 garlic clove, minced
1/4 teaspoon black pepper
1/4 teaspoon salt
1/4 teaspoon hot pepper sauce

Directions

Start by preheating your Air Fryer to 360 degrees F. Spritz the Air Fryer basket with cooking oil.

Pat dry the fish fillets with a kitchen towel. Beat the egg in a shallow bowl.

In a separate bowl, thoroughly combine the salt, crushed tortilla chips, and olive oil.

Dip the fish into the egg, then, into the crumb mixture, making sure to coat thoroughly. Cook in the preheated Air Fryer approximately 12 minutes.

Meanwhile, make the avocado sauce by mixing the remaining ingredients in a bowl. Place in your refrigerator until ready to serve.

Serve the fish fillets with chilled avocado sauce on the side. Bon appétit!

Per serving: 418 Calories; 22.7g Fat; 12.5g Carbs; 40.1g Protein; 0.9g Sugars

348. Old Bay Calamari

(Ready in about 20 minutes + marinating time | Servings 3)

Ingredients

1 cup beer
1 pound squid, cleaned and cut into rings
1 cup all-purpose flour
2 eggs
1/2 cup cornstarch
Sea salt, to taste
1/2 teaspoon ground black pepper
1 tablespoon Old Bay seasoning

Directions

Add the beer and squid in a glass bowl, cover and let it sit in your refrigerator for 1 hour.

Preheat your Air Fryer to 390 degrees F. Rinse the squid and pat it dry.

Place the flour in a shallow bowl. In another bowl, whisk the eggs. Add the cornstarch and seasonings to a third shallow bowl.

Dredge the calamari in the flour. Then, dip them into the egg mixture; finally, coat them with the cornstarch on all sided.

Arrange them in the cooking basket. Spritz with cooking oil and cook for 9 to 12 minutes, depending on the desired level of doneness. Work in batches.

Serve warm with your favorite dipping sauce. Enjoy!

Per serving: 448 Calories; 5.3g Fat; 58.9g Carbs; 31.9g Protein; 0.2g Sugars

349. Crispy Mustardy Fish Fingers

(Ready in about 20 minutes | Servings 4)

Ingredients

1 ½ pounds tilapia pieces (fingers)
1/2 cup all-purpose flour
2 eggs
1 tablespoon yellow mustard
1 cup cornmeal
1 teaspoon garlic powder
1 teaspoon onion powder
Sea salt and ground black pepper, to taste
1/2 teaspoon celery powder
2 tablespoons peanut oil

Directions

Pat dry the fish fingers with a kitchen towel.

To make a breading station, place the all-purpose flour in a shallow dish. In a separate dish, whisk the eggs with mustard.

In a third bowl, mix the remaining ingredients.

Dredge the fish fingers in the flour, shaking the excess into the bowl; dip in the egg mixture and turn to coat evenly; then, dredge in the cornmeal mixture, turning a couple of times to coat evenly.

Cook in the preheated Air Fryer at 390 degrees F for 5 minutes; turn them over and cook another 5 minutes. Enjoy!

Per serving: 468 Calories; 12.7g Fat; 45.6g Carbs; 41.9g Protein; 1.4g Sugars

350. Greek-Style Roast Fish

(Ready in about 20 minutes | Servings 3)

Ingredients

2 tablespoons olive oil
1 red onion, sliced
2 cloves garlic, chopped
1 Florina pepper, deveined and minced
3 pollock fillets, skinless
2 ripe tomatoes, diced
12 Kalamata olives, pitted and chopped
2 tablespoons capers
1 teaspoon oregano
1 teaspoon rosemary
Sea salt, to taste
1/2 cup white wine

Directions

Start by preheating your Air Fryer to 360 degrees F. Heat the oil in a baking pan. Once hot, sauté the onion, garlic, and pepper for 2 to 3 minutes or until fragrant.

Add the fish fillets to the baking pan. Top with the tomatoes, olives, and capers. Sprinkle with the oregano, rosemary, and salt. Pour in white wine and transfer to the cooking basket.

Turn the temperature to 395 degrees F and bake for 10 minutes. Taste for seasoning and serve on individual plates, garnished with some extra Mediterranean herbs if desired. Enjoy!

Per serving: 345 Calories; 32.7g Fat; 8.4g Carbs; 45.9g Protein; 3.5g Sugars

351. Quick-Fix Seafood Breakfast

(Ready in about 30 minutes | Servings 2)

Ingredients

1 tablespoon olive oil
2 garlic cloves, minced
1 small yellow onion, chopped
1/4 pound tilapia pieces
1/4 pound rockfish pieces
1/2 teaspoon dried basil
Salt and white pepper, to taste
4 eggs, lightly beaten
1 tablespoon dry sherry
4 tablespoons cheese, shredded

Directions

Start by preheating your Air Fryer to 350 degrees F; add the olive oil to a baking pan. Once hot, cook the garlic and onion for 2 minutes or until fragrant.

Add the fish, basil, salt, and pepper. In a mixing dish, thoroughly combine the eggs with sherry and cheese. Pour the mixture into the baking pan.

Cook at 360 degrees F approximately 20 minutes. Bon appétit!

Per serving: 414 Calories; 23.4g Fat; 11.6g Carbs; 38.8g Protein; 7.2g Sugars

352. Snapper Casserole with Gruyere Cheese

(Ready in about 25 minutes | Servings 4)

Ingredients

2 tablespoons olive oil
1 shallot, thinly sliced
2 garlic cloves, minced
1 ½ pounds snapper fillets
Sea salt and ground black pepper, to taste
1 teaspoon cayenne pepper
1/2 teaspoon dried basil
1/2 cup tomato puree
1/2 cup white wine
1 cup Gruyere cheese, shredded

Directions

Heat 1 tablespoon of olive oil in a saucepan over medium-high heat. Now cook the shallot and garlic until tender and aromatic.

Preheat your Air Fryer to 370 degrees F.

Grease a casserole dish with 1 tablespoon of olive oil. Place the snapper fillet in the casserole dish. Season with salt, black pepper, and cayenne pepper. Add the sautéed shallot mixture.

Add the basil, tomato puree and wine to the casserole dish. Cook for 10 minutes in the preheated Air Fryer.

Top with the shredded cheese and cook an additional 7 minutes. Serve immediately.

Per serving: 406 Calories; 19.9g Fat; 9.3g Carbs; 46.4g Protein; 4.5g Sugars

353. Monkfish Fillets with Romano Cheese

(Ready in about 15 minutes | Servings 2)

Ingredients

2 monkfish fillets
1 teaspoon garlic paste
2 tablespoons butter, melted
1/2 teaspoon Aleppo chili powder
1/2 teaspoon dried rosemary

1/4 teaspoon cracked black pepper
1/2 teaspoon sea salt
4 tablespoons Romano cheese, grated

Directions

Start by preheating the Air Fryer to 320 degrees F. Spritz the Air Fryer basket with cooking oil.

Spread the garlic paste all over the fish fillets.

Brush the monkfish fillets with the melted butter on both sides. Sprinkle with the chili powder, rosemary, black pepper, and salt. Cook for 7 minutes in the preheated Air Fryer.

Top with the Romano cheese and continue to cook for 2 minutes more or until heated through. Bon appétit!

Per serving: 415 Calories; 22.5g Fat; 3.7g Carbs; 47.4g Protein; 2.3g Sugars

354. Grilled Hake with Garlic Sauce

(Ready in about 20 minutes | Servings 3)

Ingredients

3 hake fillets
6 tablespoons mayonnaise
1 teaspoon Dijon mustard
1 tablespoon fresh lime juice
1 cup panko crumbs
Salt, to taste
1/4 teaspoon ground black pepper, or more to taste

Garlic Sauce
1/4 cup Greek-style yogurt
2 tablespoons olive oil
2 cloves garlic, minced
1/2 teaspoon tarragon leaves, minced

Directions

Pat dry the hake fillets with a kitchen towel.

In a shallow bowl, whisk together the mayo, mustard, and lime juice. In another shallow bowl, thoroughly combine the panko crumbs with salt, and black pepper.

Spritz the Air Fryer grill pan with non-stick cooking spray. Grill in the preheated Air Fry at 395 degrees F for 10 minutes, flipping halfway through the cooking time.

Serve immediately.

Per serving: 479 Calories; 22g Fat; 29.1g Carbs; 39.1g Protein; 3.6g Sugars

355. Grilled Tilapia with Portobello Mushrooms

(Ready in about 20 minutes | Servings 2)

Ingredients

2 tilapia fillets
1 tablespoon avocado oil
1/2 teaspoon red pepper flakes, crushed
1/2 teaspoon dried sage, crushed
1/4 teaspoon lemon pepper

1/2 teaspoon sea salt
1 teaspoon dried parsley flakes
4 medium-sized Portobello mushrooms
A few drizzles of liquid smoke

Directions

Toss all ingredients in a mixing bowl; except for the mushrooms.

Transfer the tilapia fillets to a lightly greased grill pan. Preheat your Air Fryer to 400 degrees F and cook the tilapia fillets for 5 minutes.

Now, turn the fillets over and add the Portobello mushrooms. Continue to cook for 5 minutes longer or until mushrooms are tender and the fish is opaque. Serve immediately.

Per serving: 320 Calories; 11.4g Fat; 29.1g Carbs; 49.3g Protein; 4.2g Sugars

356. Authentic Mediterranean Calamari Salad

(Ready in about 15 minutes | Servings 3)

Ingredients

1 pound squid, cleaned, sliced into rings
2 tablespoons sherry wine
1/2 teaspoon granulated garlic
Salt, to taste
1/2 teaspoon ground black pepper
1/2 teaspoon basil
1/2 teaspoon dried rosemary

1 cup grape tomatoes
1 small red onion, thinly sliced
1/3 cup Kalamata olives, pitted and sliced
1/2 cup mayonnaise
1 teaspoon yellow mustard
1/2 cup fresh flat-leaf parsley leaves, coarsely chopped

Directions

Start by preheating the Air Fryer to 400 degrees F. Spritz the Air Fryer basket with cooking oil.

Toss the squid rings with the sherry wine, garlic, salt, pepper, basil, and rosemary. Cook in the preheated Air Fryer for 5 minutes, shaking the basket halfway through the cooking time.

Work in batches and let it cool to room temperature. When the squid is cool enough, add the remaining ingredients.

Gently stir to combine and serve well chilled. Bon appétit!

Per serving: 457 Calories; 31.3g Fat; 18.4g Carbs; 25.1g Protein; 9.2g Sugars

357. Shrimp Scampi Linguine

(Ready in about 25 minutes | Servings 4)

Ingredients

1 ½ pounds shrimp, shelled and deveined
1/2 tablespoon fresh basil leaves, chopped
2 tablespoons olive oil
2 cloves garlic, minced
1/2 teaspoon fresh ginger, grated

1/4 teaspoon cracked black pepper
1/2 teaspoon sea salt
1/4 cup chicken stock
2 ripe tomatoes, pureed
8 ounces linguine pasta
1/2 cup parmesan cheese, preferably freshly grated

Directions

Start by preheating the Air Fryer to 395 degrees F. Place the shrimp, basil, olive oil, garlic, ginger, black pepper, salt, chicken stock, and tomatoes in the casserole dish.

Transfer the casserole dish to the cooking basket and bake for 10 minutes.

Bring a large pot of lightly salted water to a boil. Cook the linguine for 10 minutes or until al dente; drain.

Divide between four serving plates. Add the shrimp sauce and top with parmesan cheese. Bon appétit!

Per serving: 560 Calories; 15.1g Fat; 47.3g Carbs; 59.3g Protein; 1.6g Sugars

358. Sunday Fish with Sticky Sauce

(Ready in about 20 minutes | Servings 2)

Ingredients

2 pollack fillets
Salt and black pepper, to taste
1 tablespoon olive oil
1 cup chicken broth
2 tablespoons light soy sauce

1 tablespoon brown sugar
2 tablespoons butter, melted
1 teaspoon fresh ginger, minced
1 teaspoon fresh garlic, minced
2 corn tortillas

Directions

Pat dry the pollack fillets and season them with salt and black pepper; drizzle the sesame oil all over the fish fillets.

Preheat the Air Fryer to 380 degrees F and cook your fish for 11 minutes. Slice into bite-sized pieces.

Meanwhile, prepare the sauce. Add the broth to a large saucepan and bring to a boil. Add the soy sauce, sugar, butter, ginger, and garlic. Reduce the heat to simmer and cook until it is reduced slightly.

Add the fish pieces to the warm sauce. Serve on corn tortillas and enjoy!

Per serving: 573 Calories; 38.3g Fat; 31.5g Carbs; 26.2g Protein; 5.7g Sugars

359. Buttermilk Tuna fillets

(Ready in about 50 minutes | Servings 3)

Ingredients

1 pound tuna fillets
1/2 cup buttermilk
1/2 cup tortilla chips, crushed
1/4 cup parmesan cheese, grated
1/4 cup cassava flour

Salt and ground black pepper, to taste
1 teaspoon mustard seeds
1 teaspoon paprika
1 teaspoon garlic powder
1/2 teaspoon onion powder

Directions

Place the tuna fillets and buttermilk in a bowl; cover and let it sit for 30 minutes.

In a shallow bowl, thoroughly combine the remaining ingredients; mix until well combined.

Dip the tuna fillets in the parmesan mixture until they are covered on all sides.

Cook in the preheated Air Fryer at 380 degrees F for 12 minutes, turning halfway through the cooking time. Bon appétit!

Per serving: 266 Calories; 5.7g Fat; 13.6g Carbs; 37.8g Protein; 2.5g Sugars

360. Swordfish with Roasted Peppers and Garlic Sauce

(Ready in about 30 minutes | Servings 3)

Ingredients

3 bell peppers
3 swordfish steaks
1 tablespoon butter, melted
2 garlic cloves, minced

Sea salt and freshly ground black pepper, to taste
1/2 teaspoon cayenne pepper
1/2 teaspoon ginger powder

Directions

Start by preheating your Air Fryer to 400 degrees F. Brush the Air Fryer basket lightly with cooking oil.

Then, roast the bell peppers for 5 minutes. Give the peppers a half turn; place them back in the cooking basket and roast for another 5 minutes.

Turn them one more time and roast until the skin is charred and soft or 5 more minutes. Peel the peppers and set aside.

Then, add the swordfish steaks to the lightly greased cooking basket and cook at 400 degrees F for 10 minutes.

Meanwhile, melt the butter in a small saucepan. Cook the garlic until fragrant and add the salt, pepper, cayenne pepper, and ginger powder. Cook until everything is thoroughly heated.

Plate the peeled peppers and the roasted swordfish; spoon the sauce over them and serve warm.

Per serving: 274 Calories; 14.1g Fat; 5.1g Carbs; 30.5g Protein; 3.2g Sugars

361. Shrimp Scampi Dip with Cheese

(Ready in about 25 minutes | Servings 8)

Ingredients

2 teaspoons butter, melted
8 ounces shrimp, peeled and deveined
2 garlic cloves, minced
1/4 cup chicken stock
2 tablespoons fresh lemon juice
Salt and ground black pepper, to taste

1/2 teaspoon red pepper flakes
4 ounces cream cheese, at room temperature
1/2 cup sour cream
4 tablespoons mayonnaise
1/4 cup mozzarella cheese, shredded

Directions

Start by preheating the Air Fryer to 395 degrees F. Grease the sides and bottom of a baking dish with the melted butter.

Place the shrimp, garlic, chicken stock, lemon juice, salt, black pepper, and red pepper flakes in the baking dish.

Transfer the baking dish to the cooking basket and bake for 10 minutes. Add the mixture to your food processor; pulse until the coarsely is chopped.

Add the cream cheese, sour cream, and mayonnaise. Top with the mozzarella cheese and bake in the preheated Air Fryer at 360 degrees F for 6 to 7 minutes or until the cheese is bubbling.

Serve immediately with breadsticks if desired. Bon appétit!

Per serving: 135 Calories; 9.7g Fat; 3.3g Carbs; 8.7g Protein; 1g Sugars

362. Filet of Flounder Cutlets

(Ready in about 15 minutes | Servings 2)

Ingredients

1 egg
1/2 cup cracker crumbs
1/2 cup Pecorino Romano cheese, grated

Sea salt and white pepper, to taste
1/2 teaspoon cayenne pepper
1 teaspoon dried parsley flakes
2 flounder fillets

Directions

To make a breading station, whisk the egg until frothy.

In another bowl, mix the cracker crumbs, Pecorino Romano cheese, and spices.

Dip the fish in the egg mixture and turn to coat evenly; then, dredge in the cracker crumb mixture, turning a couple of times to coat evenly.

Cook in the preheated Air Fryer at 390 degrees F for 5 minutes; turn them over and cook another 5 minutes. Enjoy!

Per serving: 330 Calories; 20.3g Fat; 12.1g Carbs; 24.8g Protein; 2.3g Sugars

363. King Prawns with Lemon Butter Sauce

(Ready in about 15 minutes | Servings 4)

Ingredients

King Prawns:
1 ½ pounds king prawns, peeled and deveined
2 cloves garlic, minced
1/2 cup Pecorino Romano cheese, grated
Sea salt and ground white pepper, to your liking
1/2 teaspoon onion powder

1 teaspoon garlic powder
1 teaspoon mustard seeds
2 tablespoons olive oil
Sauce:
2 tablespoons butter
2 tablespoons fresh lemon juice
1/2 teaspoon Worcestershire sauce
1/4 teaspoon ground black pepper

Directions

In a plastic closeable bag, thoroughly combine all ingredients for the king prawns; shake to combine well.

Transfer the coated king prawns to the lightly greased Air Fryer basket.

Cook in the preheated Air Fryer at 390 degrees for 6 minutes, shaking the basket halfway through. Work in batches.

In the meantime, heat a small saucepan over a moderate flame; melt the butter and add the remaining ingredients.

Turn the temperature to low and whisk for 2 to 3 minutes until thoroughly heated. Spoon the sauce onto the warm king prawns. Bon appétit!

Per serving: 302 Calories; 17.2g Fat; 3.2g Carbs; 32.2g Protein; 0.2g Sugars

364. Crusty Catfish with Sweet Potato Fries

(Ready in about 50 minutes | Servings 2)

Ingredients

1/2 pound catfish
1/2 cup bran cereal
1/4 cup parmesan cheese, grated
Sea salt and ground black pepper, to taste
1 teaspoon smoked paprika

1 teaspoon garlic powder
1/4 teaspoon ground bay leaf
1 egg
2 tablespoons butter, melted
4 sweet potatoes, cut French fries

Directions

Pat the catfish dry with a kitchen towel.

Combine the bran cereal with the parmesan cheese and all spices in a shallow bowl. Whisk the egg in another shallow bowl.

Dip the fish in the egg mixture and turn to coat evenly; then, dredge in the bran cereal mixture, turning a couple of times to coat evenly.

Spritz the Air Fryer basket with cooking spray. Cook the catfish in the preheated Air Fryer at 390 degrees F for 10 minutes; turn them over and cook for 4 minutes more.

Then, drizzle the melted butter all over the sweet potatoes; cook them in the preheated Air Fryer at 380 degrees F for 30 minutes, shaking occasionally. Serve over the warm fish fillets. Bon appétit!

Per serving: 481 Calories; 25.4g Fat; 37.5g Carbs; 31.3g Protein; 6.6g Sugars

365. Crunchy Topped Fish Bake

(Ready in about 20 minutes | Servings 4)

Ingredients

1 tablespoon butter, melted
1 medium-sized leek, thinly sliced
1 tablespoon chicken stock
1 tablespoon dry white wine
1 pound tuna
1/2 teaspoon red pepper flakes, crushed

Sea salt and ground black pepper, to taste
1/2 teaspoon dried rosemary
1/2 teaspoon dried basil
1/2 teaspoon dried thyme
2 ripe tomatoes, pureed
1/4 cup breadcrumbs
1/4 cup Parmesan cheese, grated

Directions

Melt 1/2 tablespoon of butter in a sauté pan over medium-high heat. Now, cook the leek and garlic until tender and aromatic. Add the stock and wine to deglaze the pan.

Preheat your Air Fryer to 370 degrees F.

Grease a casserole dish with the remaining 1/2 tablespoon of melted butter. Place the fish in the casserole dish. Add the seasonings. Top with the sautéed leek mixture.

Add the tomato puree. Cook for 10 minutes in the preheated Air Fryer. Top with the breadcrumbs and cheese; cook an additional 7 minutes until the crumbs are golden. Bon appétit!

Per serving: 455 Calories; 12.4g Fat; 9.9g Carbs; 73.6g Protein; 3.1g Sugars

366. Creamed Trout Salad

(Ready in about 20 minutes | Servings 2)

Ingredients

1/2 pound trout fillets, skinless
2 tablespoons horseradish, prepared, drained
1/4 cup mayonnaise
1 tablespoon fresh lemon juice
1 teaspoon mustard

Salt and ground white pepper, to taste
6 ounces chickpeas, canned and drained
1 red onion, thinly sliced
1 cup Iceberg lettuce, torn into pieces

Directions

Spritz the Air Fryer basket with cooking spray.

Cook the trout fillets in the preheated Air Fryer at 395 degrees F for 10 minutes or until opaque. Make sure to turn them halfway through the cooking time.

Break the fish into bite-sized chunks and place in the refrigerator to cool. Toss your fish with the remaining ingredients. Bon appétit!

Per serving: 490 Calories; 26.4g Fat; 30.3g Carbs; 33.9g Protein; 7.8g Sugars

367. Roasted Mediterranean Snapper Fillets

(Ready in about 20 minutes + marinating time | Servings 3)

Ingredients

Marinade:
1 tablespoon black olives, chopped
1/4 cup dry white wine
2 tablespoons fresh lemon juice
1/2 teaspoon dried oregano
1/2 teaspoon dried basil

1 tablespoon parsley leaves, chopped
1 tomato, pureed
Roasted Snapper:
1 pound snapper fillets
1/2 cup cassava flour
Salt and white pepper, to taste

Directions

Add all ingredients for the marinade to a large ceramic bowl. Add the snapper fillets and let them marinate for 1 hour in your refrigerator.

Place the cassava flour on a tray; now, coat the snapper fillets with the cassava flour. Season with salt and pepper.

Cook the snapper fillets in the preheated Air Fryer at 395 degrees F for 10 minutes, basting with the marinade and flipping them halfway through the cooking time. Bon appétit!

Per serving: 271 Calories; 4.6g Fat; 21.8g Carbs; 34.9g Protein; 4.9g Sugars

368. Orange Glazed Scallops

(Ready in about 15 minutes | Servings 3)

Ingredients

1 pound jumbo sea scallops
1 tablespoon soy sauce
2 tablespoons orange juice
1 teaspoon orange zest
1/2 teaspoon fresh parsley, minced

1 tablespoon olive oil
Sea salt, to taste
1/2 teaspoon ground black pepper

Directions

Start by preheating your Air Fryer to 400 degrees F.

Toss all ingredients in mixing bowl.

Place the scallops in the lightly greased cooking basket and cook for 7 minutes, shaking the basket halfway through the cooking time. Work in batches.

Taste, adjust the seasonings and serve warm. Bon appétit!

Per serving: 229 Calories; 6.7g Fat; 10.9g Carbs; 31.5g Protein; 2.1g Sugars

369. Beer Battered Fish with Honey Tartar Sauce

(Ready in about 20 minutes | Servings 2)

Ingredients

1/2 pound hoki fillets
Sea salt and black pepper, to taste
1/2 cup flour
1 egg
1 teaspoon paprika
1 (12-ounce) bottle beer

1/4 cup mayonnaise
1/2 teaspoon honey
1 tablespoon fresh lemon juice
1 teaspoon Dijon mustard
1 teaspoon sweet pickle relish

Directions

Rinse the hoki fillets and pat dry.

Combine the flour, egg and paprika in a bowl. Gradually pour in beer until a batter is formed.

Dip the fish fillets into the batter; then, transfer to the lightly greased cooking basket. Cook in the preheated Air Fryer at 380 degrees F for 12 minutes.

In the meantime, whisk the remaining ingredients to make the sauce. Place in the refrigerator until ready to serve. Bon appétit!

Per serving: 424 Calories; 9.7g Fat; 36.5g Carbs; 34.1g Protein; 4.1g Sugars

370. Halibut with Thai Lemongrass Marinade

(Ready in about 45 minutes | Servings 2)

Ingredients

2 tablespoons tamari sauce
2 tablespoons fresh lime juice
2 tablespoons olive oil
1 teaspoon Thai curry paste
1/2 inch lemongrass, finely chopped

1 teaspoon basil
2 cloves garlic, minced
2 tablespoons shallot, minced
Sea salt and ground black pepper, to taste
2 halibut steaks

Directions

Place all ingredients in a ceramic dish; let it marinate for 30 minutes.

Place the halibut steaks in the lightly greased cooking basket.

Bake in the preheated Air Fryer at 400 degrees F for 9 to 10 minutes, basting with the reserved marinade and flipping them halfway through the cooking time. Bon appétit!

Per serving: 359 Calories; 16.7g Fat; 7.8g Carbs; 43.4g Protein; 2.9g Sugars

371. Sea Bass with French Sauce Tartare

(Ready in about 15 minutes | Servings 2)

Ingredients

1 tablespoon olive oil
2 sea bass fillets
Sauce:
1/2 cup mayonnaise
1 tablespoon capers, drained and chopped

1 tablespoon gherkins, drained and chopped
2 tablespoons scallions, finely chopped
2 tablespoons lemon juice

Directions

Start by preheating your Air Fryer to 395 degrees F. Drizzle olive oil all over the fish fillets.

Cook the sea bass in the preheated Air Fryer for 10 minutes, flipping them halfway through the cooking time.

Meanwhile, make the sauce by whisking the remaining ingredients until everything is well incorporated. Place in the refrigerator until ready to serve. Bon appétit!

Per serving: 384 Calories; 28.5g Fat; 3.5g Carbs; 27.6g Protein; 1g Sugars

372. Jamaican-Style Fish and Potato Fritters

(Ready in about 30 minutes | Servings 2)

Ingredients

1/2 pound sole fillets
1/2 pound mashed potatoes
1 egg, well beaten
1/2 cup red onion, chopped
2 garlic cloves, minced
2 tablespoons fresh parsley, chopped

1 bell pepper, finely chopped
1/2 teaspoon scotch bonnet pepper, minced
1 tablespoon olive oil
1 tablespoon coconut aminos
1/2 teaspoon paprika
Salt and white pepper, to taste

Directions

Start by preheating your Air Fryer to 395 degrees F. Spritz the sides and bottom of the cooking basket with cooking spray.

Cook the sole fillets in the preheated Air Fryer for 10 minutes, flipping them halfway through the cooking time.

In a mixing bowl, mash the sole fillets into flakes. Stir in the remaining ingredients. Shape the fish mixture into patties.

Bake in the preheated Air Fryer at 390 degrees F for 14 minutes, flipping them halfway through the cooking time. Bon appétit!

Per serving: 322 Calories; 14g Fat; 27.4g Carbs; 22.1g Protein; 4.2g Sugars

373. Quick Thai Coconut Fish

(Ready in about 20 minutes + marinating time | Servings 2)

Ingredients

1 cup coconut milk
2 tablespoons lime juice
2 tablespoons Shoyu sauce
Salt and white pepper, to taste
1 teaspoon turmeric powder

1/2 teaspoon ginger powder
1/2 Thai Bird's Eye chili, seeded and finely chopped
1 pound tilapia
2 tablespoons olive oil

Directions

In a mixing bowl, thoroughly combine the coconut milk with the lime juice, Shoyu sauce, salt, pepper, turmeric, ginger, and chili pepper. Add tilapia and let it marinate for 1 hour.

Brush the Air Fryer basket with olive oil. Discard the marinade and place the tilapia fillets in the Air Fryer basket.

Cook the tilapia in the preheated Air Fryer at 400 degrees F for 6 minutes; turn them over and cook for 6 minutes more. Work in batches.

Serve with some extra lime wedges if desired. Enjoy!

Per serving: 435 Calories; 21.5g Fat; 11.6g Carbs; 50.2g Protein; 8.7g Sugars

374. Double Cheese Fish Casserole

(Ready in about 30 minutes | Servings 4)

Ingredients

1 tablespoon avocado oil
1 pound hake fillets
1 teaspoon garlic powder
Sea salt and ground white pepper, to taste
2 tablespoons shallots, chopped
1 bell pepper, seeded and chopped

1/2 cup Cottage cheese
1/2 cup sour cream
1 egg, well whisked
1 teaspoon yellow mustard
1 tablespoon lime juice
1/2 cup Swiss cheese, shredded

Directions

Brush the bottom and sides of a casserole dish with avocado oil. Add the hake fillets to the casserole dish and sprinkle with garlic powder, salt, and pepper.

Add the chopped shallots and bell peppers.

In a mixing bowl, thoroughly combine the Cottage cheese, sour cream, egg, mustard, and lime juice. Pour the mixture over fish and spread evenly.

Cook in the preheated Air Fryer at 370 degrees F for 10 minutes.

Top with the Swiss cheese and cook an additional 7 minutes. Let it rest for 10 minutes before slicing and serving. Bon appétit!

Per serving: 456 Calories; 30.1g Fat; 8.8g Carbs; 36.7g Protein; 3g Sugars

375. Rosemary-Infused Butter Scallops

(Ready in about 1 hour 10 minutes | Servings 4)

Ingredients

2 pounds sea scallops
1/2 cup beer
4 tablespoons butter

2 sprigs rosemary, only leaves
Sea salt and freshly cracked black pepper, to taste

Directions

In a ceramic dish, mix the sea scallops with beer; let it marinate for 1 hour.

Meanwhile, preheat your Air Fryer to 400 degrees F. Melt the butter and add the rosemary leaves. Stir for a few minutes.

Discard the marinade and transfer the sea scallops to the Air Fryer basket. Season with salt and black pepper.

Cook the scallops in the preheated Air Fryer for 7 minutes, shaking the basket halfway through the cooking time. Work in batches.

Bon appétit!

376. Shrimp Kabobs with Cherry Tomatoes

(Ready in about 30 minutes | Servings 4)

Per serving: 267 Calories; 6.8g Fat; 18.1g Carbs; 35.4g Protein; 14.5g Sugars

Ingredients

1 ½ pounds jumbo shrimp, cleaned, shelled and deveined
1 pound cherry tomatoes
2 tablespoons butter, melted
1 tablespoons Sriracha sauce
Sea salt and ground black pepper, to taste

1/2 teaspoon dried oregano
1/2 teaspoon dried basil
1 teaspoon dried parsley flakes
1/2 teaspoon marjoram
1/2 teaspoon mustard seeds

Directions

Toss all ingredients in a mixing bowl until the shrimp and tomatoes are covered on all sides.

Soak the wooden skewers in water for 15 minutes.

Thread the jumbo shrimp and cherry tomatoes onto skewers. Cook in the preheated Air Fryer at 400 degrees F for 5 minutes, working with batches. Bon appétit!

Per serving: 317 Calories; 17.3g Fat; 9.2g Carbs; 29.4g Protein; 0.2g Sugars

377. Snapper with Coconut Milk Sauce

(Ready in about 20 minutes + marinating time | Servings 2)

Ingredients

1/2 cup full-fat coconut milk
2 tablespoons lemon juice
1 teaspoon fresh ginger, grated
2 snapper fillets

1 tablespoon olive oil
1 tablespoon cornstarch
Salt and white pepper, to taste

Directions

Place the milk, lemon juice, and ginger in a glass bowl; add fish and let it marinate for 1 hour.

Removed the fish from the milk mixture and place in the Air Fryer basket. Drizzle olive oil all over the fish fillets.

Cook in the preheated Air Fryer at 390 degrees F for 15 minutes.

Meanwhile, heat the milk mixture over medium-high heat; bring to a rapid boil, stirring continuously. Reduce to simmer and add the cornstarch, salt, and pepper; continue to cook 12 minutes more.

Spoon the sauce over the warm snapper fillets and serve immediately. Bon appétit!

Per serving: 431 Calories; 17.3g Fat; 18.5g Carbs; 48.4g Protein; 0.4g Sugars

378. Italian-Style Crab Bruschetta

(Ready in about 15 minutes | Servings 2)

Ingredients

4 slices sourdough bread
2 tablespoons tomato ketchup
4 tablespoons mayonnaise
1 teaspoon fresh rosemary, chopped

8 ounces lump crabmeat
1 teaspoon granulated garlic
2 tablespoons shallots, chopped
4 tablespoons mozzarella cheese, crumbled

Directions

Place the slices of sourdough bread on a flat surface.

In a mixing bowl, thoroughly combine the tomato ketchup, mayo, rosemary, crabmeat, garlic, and shallots.

Divide the crabmeat mixture between the slices of bread. Top with mozzarella cheese.

Bake in the preheated Air Fryer at 370 degrees F for 10 minutes. Bon appétit!

Per serving: 458 Calories; 32.6g Fat; 15.4g Carbs; 25g Protein; 3.3g Sugars

379. Easy Creamy Shrimp Nachos

(Ready in about 15 minutes | Servings 4)

Ingredients

1 pound shrimp, cleaned and deveined
1 tablespoon olive oil
2 tablespoons fresh lemon juice
1 teaspoon paprika
1/4 teaspoon cumin powder
1/2 teaspoon shallot powder

1/2 teaspoon garlic powder
Coarse sea salt and ground black pepper, to taste
1 (9-ounce) bag corn tortilla chips
1/4 cup pickled jalapeño, minced
1 cup Pepper Jack cheese, grated
1/2 cup sour cream

Directions

Toss the shrimp with the olive oil, lemon juice, paprika, cumin powder, shallot powder, garlic powder, salt, and black pepper.

Cook in the preheated Air Fryer at 390 degrees F for 5 minutes.

Place the tortilla chips on the aluminum foil-lined cooking basket. Top with the shrimp mixture, jalapeño and cheese. Cook another 2 minutes or until cheese has melted.

Serve garnished with sour cream and enjoy!

Per serving: 535 Calories; 26.9g Fat; 40g Carbs; 34.7g Protein; 1.5g Sugars

380. Tuna Cake Burgers with Beer Cheese Sauce

(Ready in about 2 hours 20 minutes | Servings 4)

Ingredients

1 pound canned tuna, drained
1 egg, whisked
1 garlic clove, minced
2 tablespoons shallots, minced
1 cup fresh breadcrumbs
Sea salt and ground black pepper, to taste

1 tablespoon sesame oil
Beer Cheese Sauce:
1 tablespoon butter
1 cup beer
1 tablespoon rice flour
2 tablespoons Colby cheese, grated

Directions

In a mixing bowl, thoroughly combine the tuna, egg, garlic, shallots, breadcrumbs, salt, and black pepper. Shape the tuna mixture into four patties and place in your refrigerator for 2 hours.

Brush the patties with sesame oil on both sides. Cook in the preheated Air Fryer at 360 degrees F for 14 minutes.

In the meantime, melt the butter in a pan over a moderate heat. Add the beer and flour and whisk until it starts bubbling.

Now, stir in the grated cheese and cook for 3 to 4 minutes longer or until the cheese has melted. Spoon the sauce over the fish cake burgers and serve immediately.

Per serving: 450 Calories; 22.3g Fat; 28.3g Carbs; 33.6g Protein; 3.8g Sugars

VEGETABLES & SIDE DISHES

381. Roasted Broccoli and Cauliflower with Tahini Sauce

(Ready in about 15 minutes | Servings 3)

Ingredients

1/2 pound broccoli, broken into florets
1/2 pound cauliflower, broken into florets
1 teaspoon onion powder
1/2 teaspoon porcini powder
1/4 teaspoon cumin powder

1/2 teaspoon granulated garlic
1 teaspoon olive oil
3 tablespoons tahini
2 tablespoons soy sauce
1 teaspoon white vinegar
Salt and chili flakes, to taste

Directions

Start by preheating your Air Fryer to 400 degrees F.

Now, toss the vegetables with the onion powder, porcini powder cumin powder, garlic and olive oil. Transfer your vegetables to the lightly greased cooking basket.

Air Fry your veggies in the preheated Air Fryer at 400 degrees F for 6 minutes. Remove the broccoli florets from the cooking basket.

Continue to cook the cauliflower for 5 to 6 minutes more.

Meanwhile, make the tahini sauce by simply whisking the remaining ingredients in a small bowl. Spoon the sauce over the warm vegetables and serve immediately. Bon appétit!

Per serving: 178 Calories; 11.9g Fat; 14.6g Carbs; 6.8g Protein; 4.8g Sugars

382. Green Bean Salad with Goat Cheese and Almonds

(Ready in about 15 minutes | Servings 3)

Ingredients

1 ½ pounds green beans, trimmed and cut into small chunks
Sea salt and ground black pepper, to taste
1 small-sized red onion, sliced
2 bell peppers, deseeded and sliced
1/2 cup goat cheese, crumbled

1/4 cup almonds
Dressing:
1 tablespoon champagne vinegar
1 tablespoon Shoyu sauce
2 tablespoons extra-virgin olive oil
1 teaspoon deli mustard
1 clove garlic, pressed

Directions

Season the green beans with salt and black pepper to your liking. Brush them with a nonstick cooking oil.

Place the green beans in the Air Fryer cooking basket. Cook the green beans at 400 degrees F for 5 minutes and transfer to a salad bowl. Stir in the onion and bell peppers.

Then, add the raw almonds to the cooking basket. Roast the almonds at 350 degrees F for 5 minutes, shaking the basket periodically to ensure even cooking.

In the meantime, make the dressing by blending all ingredients until well incorporated.

Dress your salad and top with goat cheese and roasted almonds. Enjoy!

Per serving: 290 Calories; 17.3g Fat; 25.6g Carbs; 13.8g Protein; 11.5g Sugars

383. Roasted Asparagus with Pecorino Romano Cheese

(Ready in about 10 minutes | Servings 3)

Ingredients

1 pound asparagus spears, trimmed
1 teaspoon sesame oil
1/2 teaspoon garlic powder
1/2 teaspoon shallot powder
1/4 teaspoon cumin powder
1/2 teaspoon dried rosemary

Coarse sea salt and ground black pepper, to taste
4 tablespoons Pecorino Romano cheese, grated
1 tablespoon sesame seeds, toasted

Directions

Start by preheating your Air Fryer to 400 degrees F.

Toss your asparagus with sesame oil, spices and cheese and transfer to the Air Fryer cooking basket.

Cook your asparagus in the preheated Air Fryer for 5 to 6 minutes, shaking the basket halfway through the cooking time to ensure even browning.

Garnish with toasted sesame seeds and serve warm. Bon appétit!

Per serving: 109 Calories; 5.9g Fat; 8.5g Carbs; 7.8g Protein; 3.7g Sugars

384. Mediterranean-Style Roasted Broccoli

(Ready in about 10 minutes | Servings 3)

Ingredients

1 pound broccoli florets
1 teaspoon butter, melted
Sea salt, to taste
1 teaspoon mixed peppercorns, crushed

1/4 cup mayonnaise
1 tablespoon fresh lemon juice
1 teaspoon deli mustard
2 cloves garlic, minced

Directions

Toss the broccoli florets with butter, salt and crushed peppercorns until well coated on all sides.

Cook in the preheated Air Fryer at 400 degrees F for 6 minutes until they've softened.

In the meantime, make your aioli by mixing the mayo, lemon juice, mustard and garlic in a bowl.

Serve the roasted broccoli with the sauce on the side. Enjoy!

Per serving: 199 Calories; 15.6g Fat; 11.3g Carbs; 4.6g Protein; 2.8g Sugars

385. Sweet & Sticky Baby Carrots

(Ready in about 45 minutes | Servings 3)

Ingredients

1 tablespoon coconut oil
1 pound baby carrots
1 teaspoon fresh ginger, peeled and grated

2 lemongrasses, finely chopped
3 tablespoons honey
1 teaspoon lemon thyme

Directions

Toss all ingredients in a mixing bowl and let it stand for 30 minutes.

Transfer the baby carrots to the cooking basket.

Cook the baby carrots at 380 degrees F for 15 minutes, shaking the basket halfway through the cooking time to ensure even cooking.

Serve warm and enjoy!

Per serving: 157 Calories; 4.8g Fat; 29.3g Carbs; 1.2g Protein; 22.4g Sugars

386. Balsamic Brussels Sprouts with Feta Cheese

(Ready in about 15 minutes | Servings 3)

Ingredients

1 pound Brussels sprouts
1 teaspoon olive oil
Sea salt and ground black pepper, to taste
1/4 teaspoon red pepper flakes

1 tablespoon balsamic vinegar
1 tablespoon molasses
1/2 teaspoon dried dill weed
1/2 teaspoon granulated garlic
1/2 cup feta cheese, crumbled

Directions

Toss the Brussels sprouts with olive oil, salt, black pepper, red pepper, balsamic vinegar, molasses, dill and garlic.

Cook the Brussels sprouts in the preheated Air Fryer at 380 degrees F for 15 minutes, shaking the basket halfway through the cooking time to ensure even browning.

Place in a serving platter and serve with feta cheese. Bon appétit!

Per serving: 177 Calories; 7.3g Fat; 22.3g Carbs; 9.1g Protein; 10.1g Sugars

387. Roasted Pepper Salad with Feta Cheese

(Ready in about 15 minutes | Servings 2)

Ingredients

4 bell peppers
1 teaspoon olive oil
1 teaspoon garlic, minced
1 tablespoon champagne vinegar

2 tablespoons fresh parsley, chopped
Kosher salt, to taste
5 ounces feta cheese, crumbled
2 tablespoons pine nuts, toasted

Directions

Brush the peppers with olive oil and place them in the Air Fryer cooking basket.

Roast the peppers at 400 degrees F for 15 minutes, turning your peppers over halfway through the cooking time; roast the peppers until the skin blisters and turns black.

Transfer the peppers to a plastic bag until cool.

Now, the skins should peel away off of the peppers easily. Slice the peppers into strips; stir in the garlic, vinegar, parsley and salt.

Toss to combine well and top with feta cheese and pine nuts. Bon appétit!

Per serving: 249 Calories; 17.6g Fat; 12.3g Carbs; 12.1g Protein; 7.5g Sugars

388. Roasted Acorn Squash with Chèvre

(Ready in about 15 minutes | Servings 3)

Ingredients

1 pound acorn squash, peeled, seeded and cubed
1 teaspoon coconut oil, melted
1 tablespoon honey
1/4 teaspoon grated nutmeg

1/4 teaspoon ground cloves
1/2 teaspoon cinnamon powder
1/4 teaspoon ground white pepper
1/2 teaspoon dread dill weed
1/2 cup chèvre cheese, crumbled

Directions

Toss the acorn squash cubes with coconut oil, honey, nutmeg, cloves, cinnamon, white pepper and dill weed.

Transfer the acorn squash to a lightly greased cooking basket.

Cook the acorn squash in the preheated Air Fryer at 400 degrees F for 6 minutes; shake the basket and cook for a further 6 minutes.

Place the roasted squash on a serving platter, garnish with chèvre cheese and serve. Devour!

Per serving: 189 Calories; 8.4g Fat; 22.3g Carbs; 6.7g Protein; 5.8g Sugars

389. Baby Potatoes and Parsnips with Tahini Sauce

(Ready in about 25 minutes | Servings 3)

Ingredients

2/3 pound baby potatoes
1/3 pound parsnips, sliced lengthwise
1 teaspoon sesame oil
3 tablespoons tahini

2 tablespoons soy sauce
1/2 teaspoon garlic, minced
1 teaspoon white vinegar
Salt and black pepper, to taste

Directions

Brush the baby potatoes and parsnips with sesame oil. Transfer your veggies to the cooking basket.

Cook your veggies in the preheated Air Fryer at 400 degrees F for 20 minutes, shaking the basket halfway through the cooking time to ensure even browning.

Meanwhile, whisk the remaining ingredients for the sauce. Serve the warm potatoes and parsnip with the tahini sauce for dipping. Devour!

Per serving: 259 Calories; 11.7g Fat; 32.3g Carbs; 5.9g Protein; 5.3g Sugars

390. Hot Mexican Corn on the Cob

(Ready in about 10 minutes | Servings 2)

Ingredients

2 ears corn
1/2 cup Mexican crema
1 teaspoon chili powder

2 tablespoons cilantro leaves, minced
1 lime, freshly squeezed

Directions

Husk the corn and pull off the silky threads.

In a shallow dish, mix the Mexican crema, chili powder, cilantro and lime juice.

Cook the corn in the preheated Air Fryer at 390 degrees F for about 4 minutes.

Rub each ear of corn with the Mexican crema mixture and continue to cook for 2 minutes more. Salt to taste and serve immediately.

Per serving: 239 Calories; 9.8g Fat; 30.2g Carbs; 11.5g Protein; 5.4g Sugars

391. Hot Cheesy Roasted Eggplants

(Ready in about 15 minutes | Servings 2)

Ingredients

1 pound eggplants, sliced
1 teaspoon sesame oil
Sea salt and freshly ground black pepper, to taste
1/4 teaspoon chili flakes

1/2 teaspoon parsley flakes
1 teaspoon garlic, pressed
1/2 cup cream cheese, at room temperature

Directions

Brush your eggplants with sesame oil; season your eggplants with salt and black pepper and place them in the Air Fryer cooking basket.

Cook your eggplants at 400 degrees F for 10 minutes.

Meanwhile, mix the remaining ingredients to make the rub. Top your eggplants with the chili cheese mixture and continue to cook for 5 minutes more.

Place your eggplants on a serving platter. Bon appétit!

Per serving: 257 Calories; 19.8g Fat; 16g Carbs; 6.6g Protein; 10.1g Sugars

392. Stuffed and Baked Sweet Potatoes

(Ready in about 35 minutes | Servings 2)

Ingredients

2 medium sweet potatoes
6 ounces canned kidney beans
1/4 cup Cotija cheese, crumbled
1 tablespoon butter, cold

Coarse sea salt and ground black pepper, to taste
2 tablespoons cilantro, chopped

Directions

Poke the sweet potatoes all over using a small knife; transfer them to the Air Fryer cooking basket.

Cook in the preheated Air Fryer at 380 degrees F for 20 to 25 minutes. Then, scrape the sweet potato flesh using a spoon; mix sweet potato flesh with kidney beans, cheese, butter, salt and pepper.

Bake for a further 10 minutes until cooked through.

Place the sweet potatoes on serving plates. Garnish with cilantro and serve.

Per serving: 277 Calories; 13.7g Fat; 31.4g Carbs; 8.1g Protein; 9.9g Sugars

393. Spring Beet and Feta Cheese Salad

(Ready in about 45 minutes | Servings 2)

Ingredients

2 medium beets, scrubbed and trimmed
1 teaspoon olive oil
6 ounces mixed greens
2 scallions stalks, chopped
2 stalks green garlic, finely chopped
1 tablespoon maple syrup
1 tablespoon orange juice concentrate
2 tablespoons white vinegar
2 tablespoons extra-virgin olive oil
1/2 teaspoon Dijon mustard
Salt and black pepper, to taste
1/4 teaspoon ground cumin seeds
2 ounces feta cheese, crumbled

Directions

Toss your beets with 1 teaspoon of olive oil. Cook your beets in the preheated Air Fryer at 400 degrees F for 40 minutes, turning them over once or twice to ensure even cooking.

Let your beets cool completely and then, slice them with a sharp knife. Place the beets in a salad bowl and add in the mixed greens, scallions and garlic.

In a small mixing dish, whisk the maple syrup, orange juice concentrate, vinegar, 2 tablespoons of extra-virgin olive oil, Dijon mustard, salt, black pepper and ground cumin.

Dress your salad, toss to combine and garnish with feta cheese. Bon appétit!

Per serving: 349 Calories; 23.1g Fat; 28.8g Carbs; 11.1g Protein; 15.5g Sugars

394. Roasted Chermoula Parsnip

(Ready in about 20 minutes | Servings 3)

Ingredients

1 pound parsnip, trimmed, peeled and cut into 1/2 inch pieces
1 tablespoon fresh parsley leaves
1 tablespoon fresh cilantro leaves
2 garlic cloves
Salt and black pepper, to taste
1/2 teaspoon cayenne pepper
1 teaspoon ground cumin
1/2 teaspoon ground coriander
1/2 teaspoon saffron strands
4 tablespoons extra-virgin olive oil
1 tablespoon freshly squeezed lemon juice

Directions

Place your parsnips in the Air Fryer cooking basket; spritz the parsnip with a nonstick cooking oil.

Cook the parsnip in the preheated Air Fryer at 380 degrees F for 15 minutes, shaking the basket halfway through the cooking time to ensure even browning.

Add the remaining ingredients to a bowl of your food processor or blender. Blend until smooth and well combined.

Spoon the Chermoula dressing over roasted parsnip and serve. Bon appétit!

Per serving: 201 Calories; 8.7g Fat; 30g Carbs; 2.4g Protein; 8.5g Sugars

395. Roasted Cherry Tomato Pasta

(Ready in about 15 minutes | Servings 3)

Ingredients

1 pound cherry tomatoes
1 teaspoon olive oil
Sea salt and ground black pepper, to taste
1/2 teaspoon oregano
1/2 teaspoon dried basil
1 pound fettucine pasta

Directions

Toss the cherry tomatoes with olive oil, salt, black pepper, oregano and basil.

Cook in the preheated Air Fryer at 400 degrees F for 4 minutes, tossing the basket halfway through the cooking time to ensure even cooking.

Cook the pasta according to the package directions.

Serve the roasted tomatoes over the hot pasta and enjoy!

Per serving: 573 Calories; 3.9g Fat; 90g Carbs; 24g Protein; 4.7g Sugars

396. Pearl Onions with Garlic-Cream Sauce

(Ready in about 10 minutes | Servings 3)

Ingredients

1 pound pearl onions
1 tablespoon butter, softened
1 teaspoon fresh garlic, minced
1/2 cup vegetable broth
1 tablespoon fresh cilantro, chopped
A pinch of freshly grated nutmeg
A pinch of salt
1/2 cup heavy cream

Directions

Start by preheating your Air Fryer to 400 degrees F.

Cook the pearl onions in the preheated Air Fryer for 5 minutes. Shake the basket and continue to cook an additional 5 minutes.

Meanwhile, melt the butter in a saucepan over medium-high heat. Once hot, cook the garlic for a minute or so until aromatic.

Add in the vegetable broth, cilantro, nutmeg, salt and heavy cream and turn the heat to a simmer. Cook for 10 minutes or until heated through.

Spoon the sauce over the pearl onions and serve immediately.

Per serving: 463 Calories; 47.7g Fat; 12.3g Carbs; 1.7g Protein; 8.1g Sugars

397. Roasted Fennel with Pecorino Romano Cheese

(Ready in about 20 minutes | Servings 3)

Ingredients

1 pound fennel bulbs, sliced
1 tablespoon sesame oil
Sea salt and freshly ground black pepper, to taste
1/2 cup Pecorino Romano cheese, shredded
1 tablespoon fresh parsley, chopped

Directions

Toss your fennel with sesame oil, salt and black pepper.

Cook your fennel in the preheated Air Fryer at 370 degrees F for 10 minutes.

Now, top your fennel with Pecorino Romano cheese and cook for a further 5 minutes. Garnish with fresh parsley and serve immediately. Bon appétit!

Per serving: 153 Calories; 9.3g Fat; 11.7g Carbs; 7.2g Protein; 6.1g Sugars

398. Crispy Fried Green Beans

(Ready in about 15 minutes | Servings 3)

Ingredients

1 cup all-purpose flour
2 teaspoons garlic powder, divided
Kosher salt and ground black pepper, to taste
1/2 teaspoon hot paprika
1 large egg
1 pound fresh green beans, cleaned and trimmed

Directions

In a mixing bowl, thoroughly combine the flour, garlic powder, salt, black pepper, hot paprika and egg; mix to combine well.

Dip the green beans in the flour mixture until well coated. Spritz the cooking basket with a nonstick cooking oil and place the green beans in the cooking basket.

Cook the green beans in your Air Fryer at 400 degrees F for 10 minutes, shaking the basket halfway through the cooking time to ensure even cooking. Bon appétit!

Per serving: 217 Calories; 2.7g Fat; 41.6g Carbs; 7.5g Protein; 2.1g Sugars

399. Easy Crispy Button Mushrooms

(Ready in about 10 minutes | Servings 3)

Ingredients

1/2 cup flour
2 tablespoons milk
2 eggs
1 cup fresh breadcrumbs
1/2 teaspoon garlic powder
1/4 teaspoon mustard seeds
1/4 teaspoon cumin powder
1/4 teaspoon ground bay leaf
1/2 teaspoon onion powder
1/2 teaspoon cayenne pepper
Kosher salt and ground pepper, to taste
1 pound button mushrooms, cleaned and cut into half

Directions

Place the flour in a shallow bowl. Then, in another shallow bowl, beat the milk and eggs until pale and frothy.

Then, in a third bowl, thoroughly combine the breadcrumbs with all spices.

Dip the mushrooms into the flour until coated on all sides. Then dip the mushrooms into the egg mixture. Lastly, roll your mushrooms onto the spiced breadcrumb mixture until well coated.

Place the mushrooms in your Air Fryer and spritz them with a nonstick cooking spray. Cook the mushrooms at 380 degrees F for 6 minutes, shaking the basket halfway through the cooking time.

Serve warm with your favorite dipping sauce. Bon appétit!

Per serving: 157 Calories; 1.3g Fat; 28.2g Carbs; 10.4g Protein; 3.2g Sugars

400. Mexican-Style Roasted Zucchini

(Ready in about 15 minutes | Servings 3)

Ingredients

1 pound zucchini, sliced into thick rounds
1 teaspoon chili oil
1/2 teaspoon red pepper flakes, crushed
1/2 teaspoon garlic powder
1/8 teaspoon cayenne pepper

1 teaspoon Mexican oregano
Kosher salt and black pepper, to taste
1/2 cup Cotija cheese, crumbled
1 tablespoon fresh cilantro, roughly chopped

Directions

Toss your zucchini with the chili oil, red pepper flakes, garlic powder, cayenne pepper, Mexican oregano, salt and black pepper.

Transfer your zucchini to the Air Fryer cooking basket.

Cook your zucchini at 400 degrees F for 7 minutes. Turn over the slices of zucchini and top them with crumbled cheese.

Continue to cook for 5 minutes more. Garnish with cilantro and serve.

Per serving: 137 Calories; 8.8g Fat; 6.9g Carbs; 9.9g Protein; 0.9g Sugars

401. Mediterranean Herb-Crusted Cauliflower

(Ready in about 15 minutes | Servings 3)

Ingredients

1 ½ pounds cauliflower, cut into florets
1 teaspoon olive oil
Sea salt and ground black pepper, to taste
1 teaspoon garlic, minced
1 teaspoon lemon zest

1 tablespoon fresh Italian parsley, chopped
1 teaspoon dried rosemary
1/2 teaspoon dried thyme
1/4 cup breadcrumbs
1/4 cup Parmesan cheese, grated
1/4 cup Kalamata olives

Directions

Toss the cauliflower florets with all ingredients, except for the Kalamata olives.

Cook the cauliflower at 400 degrees F for 12 minutes, shaking the basket once or twice to ensure even browning.

Garnish the roasted cauliflower with Kalamata olives and serve immediately. Enjoy!

Per serving: 137 Calories; 5.8g Fat; 16.5g Carbs; 7.4g Protein; 5.3g Sugars

402. Creamed Sweet Potato Casserole

(Ready in about 30 minutes | Servings 3)

Ingredients

1 cup heavy cream
1/2 teaspoon garlic, minced
1 teaspoon rosemary
1/2 teaspoon dried parsley flakes
1 teaspoon basil

A pinch of freshly grated nutmeg
1 ½ ponds sweet potatoes, peeled and thinly sliced
1/2 cup Colby cheese, grated

Direction

Start by preheating your Air Fryer to 330 degrees F. Brush the sides and bottom of a casserole dish with a nonstick cooking oil.

In a bowl, thoroughly combine all ingredients, except for the cheese. Spoon the mixture into the casserole dish.

Bake in the preheated Air Fryer for 25 minutes. Top with the cheese and bake an additional 5 minutes. Bon appétit!

Per serving: 421 Calories; 22g Fat; 46.5g Carbs; 9.6g Protein; 10.7g Sugars

403. Classic Brussels Sprouts with Bacon

(Ready in about 20 minutes | Servings 2)

Ingredients

3/4 pound Brussels sprouts, trimmed and halved
1 teaspoon butter, melted
Sea salt and ground black pepper, to taste
1/2 teaspoon smoked paprika

1 teaspoon garlic, minced
1 teaspoon lemon juice, freshly squeezed
1 tablespoon white wine
3 ounces bacon, sliced

Directions

Toss the Brussels sprouts with butter, salt, black pepper, paprika, garlic, lemon juice and wine. Transfer your Brussels sprouts to the Air Fryer cooking basket.

Top your Brussels sprouts with bacon and cook them at 380 degrees F for 15 minutes, shaking the basket once or twice to ensure even cooking.

Serve warm and enjoy!

Per serving: 277 Calories; 19.2g Fat; 18.7g Carbs; 11.6g Protein; 5.4g Sugars

404. Cauliflower Tater Tots

(Ready in about 20 minutes | Servings 3)

Ingredients

1 ½ pounds cauliflower
1 tablespoon butter
2 tablespoons plain flour
1 tablespoon corn flour
1 teaspoon shallot powder

1/2 teaspoon garlic powder
1 teaspoon dried parsley flakes
1/2 teaspoon dried basil
Sea salt and freshly ground black pepper, to taste

Directions

Blanch the cauliflower in salted boiling water until al dente about 4 minutes. Drain your cauliflower well and pulse in a food processor.

Transfer the cauliflower to a mixing bowl. Stir in the remaining ingredients and mix to combine well. Roll the mixture into bite-sized tots.

Cook in the preheated Air Fryer at 375 degrees F for 16 minutes, shaking the basket halfway through the cooking time to ensure even browning. Bon appétit!

Per serving: 127 Calories; 4.6g Fat; 17.6g Carbs; 5.2g Protein; 4.4g Sugars

405. Double-Cheese Stuffed Mushrooms

(Ready in about 20 minutes | Servings 2)

Ingredients

8 medium-sized button mushrooms, stalks removed
1 teaspoon butter
1 teaspoon garlic, minced
Sea salt and ground black pepper, to taste

4 ounces Ricotta cheese, at room temperature
1/2 cup Romano cheese, grated
1/2 teaspoon ancho chili powder

Directions

Clean your mushrooms and place them on a platter.

Then, mix the remaining ingredients in a bowl. Divide the filling between your mushrooms and transfer them to a lightly greased cooking basket.

Cook the mushrooms in the preheated Air Fryer at 380 degrees for 10 to 12 minutes. Serve warm and enjoy!

Per serving: 267 Calories; 19.6g Fat; 7.2g Carbs; 17.3g Protein; 2.9g Sugars

406. Italian Pitticelle Cucuzze

(Ready in about 20 minutes | Servings 3)

Ingredients

2 medium zucchini, shredded and drained
1 teaspoon Italian seasoning mix
Sea salt and ground black pepper, to taste
1/2 yellow onion, finely chopped
1 teaspoon garlic, finely chopped
1/2 cup plain flour
1 large egg, beaten
1/2 cup Asiago cheese, shredded
1 teaspoon olive oil

Directions

In a mixing bowl, thoroughly combine the zucchini, spices, yellow onion, garlic, flour, egg and Asiago cheese.

Shape the mixture into patties and brush them with olive oil; transfer the patties to a lightly oiled cooking basket.

Cook the patties in the preheated Air Fryer at 380 degrees F for 15 minutes, turning them over once or twice to ensure even cooking.

Garnish with some extra cheese if desired and serve at room temperature. Bon appétit!

Per serving: 227 Calories; 11.5g Fat; 19.2g Carbs; 10.3g Protein; 1.9g Sugars

407. Classic Roasted Potatoes with Scallion Dip

(Ready in about 15 minutes | Servings 2)

Ingredients

4 medium-sized potatoes, peeled and cut into wedges
1 tablespoon olive oil
1/2 teaspoon ancho chili powder
1/2 teaspoon dried marjoram
1/2 teaspoon dried basil
Sea salt and ground black pepper, to taste
1/2 cup cream cheese
3 tablespoons scallions, sliced

Directions

Toss the potatoes with olive oil and spices until well coated.

Transfer them to the Air Fryer basket and cook at 400 degrees F for 6 minutes; shake the basket and cook for a further 6 minutes.

Meanwhile, whisk the cheese with the scallions and place the sauce in your refrigerator until ready to use.

Serve the warm potatoes with the sauce for dipping. Bon appétit!

Per serving: 567 Calories; 27g Fat; 72g Carbs; 11.3g Protein; 8.1g Sugars

408. Mexican-Style Avocado Wedges

(Ready in about 10 minutes | Servings 4)

Ingredients

2 ripe avocados, peeled and cut wedges
1/2 cup plain flour
Himalayan salt and ground white pepper, to taste
1 egg
2 tablespoons milk
1/2 cup tortilla chips, crushed

Directions

Start by preheating your Air Fryer to 395 degrees F.

In a shallow bowl, combine the flour, salt and black pepper. In another shallow dish, whisk the egg and milk until frothy.

Place the crushed tortilla chips in a third shallow dish. Dip the avocado wedges in the flour mixture, shaking off the excess. Then, dip in the egg mixture; lastly, coat the avocado wedges with crushed tortilla chips, pressing to adhere.

Spritz the avocado wedges with cooking oil on all sides.

Cook your avocado in the preheated Air Fryer at 395 degrees F for approximately 8 minutes, turning them over halfway through the cooking time. Bon appétit!

Per serving: 267 Calories; 16.7g Fat; 27g Carbs; 5.9g Protein; 1.9g Sugars

409. Fried Peppers with Roasted Garlic Sauce

(Ready in about 50 minutes | Servings 2)

Ingredients

4 bell peppers
1 teaspoon olive oil
Sea salt and black pepper to taste
1 tablespoon fresh parsley, roughly chopped
Dipping Sauce:
6 cloves garlic
1/4 cup sour cream
1/4 cup mayonnaise
1 teaspoon fresh lime juice
1/4 teaspoon paprika

Directions

Brush the peppers with olive oil and transfer them to the cooking basket.

Roast the peppers at 400 degrees F for 15 minutes, turning your peppers over halfway through the cooking time; roast the peppers until the skin blisters and turns black.

Transfer the peppers to a plastic bag until cool; the skins should peel away off of the peppers easily; season the peppers with salt and pepper and reserve.

To make the sauce, place the garlic on a sheet of aluminum foil and spritz with cooking spray. Wrap the garlic in the foil.

Cook in the preheated Air Fryer at 400 degrees for 12 minutes. Then, open the top of the foil and continue to cook for a further 10 minutes.

Let it cool for about 10 minutes; remove the cloves by squeezing them out of the skins; mash the garlic and combine it with the sour cream, mayonnaise, fresh lime juice and paprika.

Garnish the roasted peppers with parsley and serve with the sauce on the side and enjoy!

Per serving: 307 Calories; 26.2g Fat; 16.3g Carbs; 4.2g Protein; 6.1g Sugars

410. Greek-Style Air Grilled Tomatoes with Feta

(Ready in about 15 minutes | Servings 3)

Ingredients

3 medium tomatoes, quartered, pat dry
1 tablespoon extra-virgin olive oil
1 teaspoon basil
1 teaspoon oregano
1/2 teaspoon rosemary
1 teaspoon parsley
1 teaspoon cilantro
Sea salt and ground black pepper, to season
2 tablespoons Greek black olives, pitted and sliced
3 ounces feta cheese, sliced

Directions

Brush your tomatoes with olive oil. Sprinkle them with spices until well coated on all sides. Now, transfer your tomatoes to the Air Fryer cooking basket

Cook your tomatoes at 350 degrees F for approximately 12 minutes, turning them over halfway through the cooking time.

Garnish with black olives and feta cheese and serve. Enjoy!

Per serving: 147 Calories; 11.2g Fat; 7.6g Carbs; 5.2g Protein; 5.1g Sugars

411. Rainbow Vegetable Croquettes

(Ready in about 15 minutes | Servings 3)

Ingredients

1/3 canned green peas
1/3 sweet corn kernels
1/3 pound zucchini, grated and squeezed
1/4 cup plain flour
1/4 cup chickpea flour
1/2 cup cheddar cheese, grated
1 egg
1 teaspoon fresh coriander, chopped
1 teaspoon fresh parsley, chopped
1/2 teaspoon fresh garlic, pressed
Kosher salt and freshly ground black pepper, to taste
1/2 teaspoon cayenne pepper
1 tablespoon olive oil

Directions

In a mixing bowl, thoroughly combine the vegetables, flour, cheese, egg, coriander, parsley; sprinkle with all spices and stir until everything is well incorporated.

Shape the mixture into small patties and transfer them to the lightly oiled Air Fryer cooking basket.

Cook the vegetable croquettes in the preheated Air Fryer at 365 degrees F for 6 minutes. Turn them over and cook for a further 6 minutes

Serve immediately and enjoy!

Per serving: 234 Calories; 10.8g Fat; 23.4g Carbs; 11.8g Protein; 4g Sugars

412. Sweet Potato Hash Browns

(Ready in about 50 minutes | Servings 3)

Ingredients

1 pound sweet potatoes, grated
1/2 cup scallion, chopped
1 bell pepper, chopped
1/2 teaspoon garlic, finely chopped
Sea salt and ground black pepper, to your liking
1 teaspoon peanut oil
1/4 teaspoon ground allspice
1 tablespoon peanut oil

Directions

Allow your sweet potatoes to soak for 25 minutes in cold water. Drain the water and pat them dry with a paper towel.

Add in the remaining ingredients and stir until everything is well combined.

Cook in the preheated Air Fryer at 395 degrees F for 25 minutes, turning them over halfway through the cooking time. Bon appétit!

Per serving: 188 Calories; 6.2g Fat; 30.4g Carbs; 4g Protein; 3.1g Sugars

413. Authentic Japanese Vegetable Tempura

(Ready in about 15 minutes | Servings 3)

Ingredients

1 cup plain flour
1 egg
1 cup ice-cold water
1 pound green beans
1 white onion, slice into rings
1 teaspoon dashi granules
2 tablespoons soy sauce
1 tablespoon mirin
Himalayan salt, to taste

Directions

Sift the flour in a bowl. In another bowl, whisk the egg until pale and frothy; pour in the water.

Fold the sifted flour into the egg/water mixture and stir to combine.

Dip the green beans and onion in the prepared tempura.

Cook your veggies in the preheated Air Fryer at 400 degrees F for 10 minutes, shaking the basket halfway through the cooking time; work with batches.

Meanwhile, whisk the dashi granules, soy sauce and mirin; salt to taste and set the sauce aside.

Serve the vegetable tempura with the sauce on the side. Serve immediately!

Per serving: 268 Calories; 6.2g Fat; 42.4g Carbs; 9.7g Protein; 5.1g Sugars

414. Greek Kolokythakia Tiganita

(Ready in about 15 minutes | Servings 3)

Ingredients

1 pound zucchini, pat dry
1 cup plain flour
Sea salt and ground black pepper, to taste
1 teaspoon basil
1 teaspoon oregano
1/2 teaspoon granulated garlic
1/2 teaspoon shallot powder
1/2 cup bottled soda water
1/2 cup milk
1/2 cup breadcrumbs

Directions

Slice your zucchini lengthwise into strips about 1/8-inch thick.

Mix the flour and spices in a shallow bowl. Then, add the soda water and milk. Mix again to combine.

Add the breadcrumbs to another bowl.

Dip your zucchini in the batter; then, coat each slice of zucchini with breadcrumbs.

Cook in the preheated Air Fryer at 400 degrees F for 12 minutes, flipping them halfway through the cooking time.

Work with batches until they are crispy and golden brown. Enjoy!

Per serving: 238 Calories; 2.5g Fat; 43g Carbs; 10.5g Protein; 3.1g Sugars

415. Breaded Chipotle Portobellas

(Ready in about 40 minutes | Servings 2)

Ingredients

1 egg, beaten
1/2 cup plain flour
1/4 cup milk
1/4 cup Parmesan cheese, grated
1/4 cup tortilla chips, crushed
Sea salt and ground black pepper, to taste
1/2 teaspoon dried thyme
1/2 teaspoon ground cumin
1 teaspoon chipotle powder
4 Portobello mushrooms, cleaned

Directions

Thoroughly combine the egg, flour and milk in a bowl. In another bowl, thoroughly combine the cheese, tortilla chips and salt, black pepper, thyme, cumin and chipotle powder.

Dip each portobello mushroom in the egg/flour mixture; then, coat them with the spiced cheese mixture.

Allow your mushrooms to sit in the refrigerator for 30 minutes.

Cook the mushrooms in the preheated Air Fryer at 400 degrees for 6 to 7 minutes, tossing the basket halfway through the cooking time.

Serve warm and enjoy!

Per serving: 286 Calories; 7.9g Fat; 40g Carbs; 15.5g Protein; 7.3g Sugars

416. Spanish Patatas Bravas

(Ready in about 15 minutes | Servings 3)

Ingredients

1 pound russet potatoes, cut into 1-inch cubes
2 teaspoons canola oil
Salt and ground black pepper, to taste
1 cup tomatoes, crushed
1/2 teaspoon paprika
1/2 teaspoon chili powder
2 garlic cloves, crushed
A pinch of brown sugar

Directions

Toss the potatoes with 1 teaspoon of oil, salt and black pepper. Transfer the potato chunks to the lightly oiled Air Fryer cooking basket.

Cook the potatoes in your Air Fryer at 400 degrees F for 12 minutes total, shaking the basket halfway through the cooking time.

In the meantime, heat the remaining teaspoon of oil in a saucepan over medium-high heat. Once hot, stir in the other ingredients cook for 8 to 10 minutes until cooked through.

Spoon the sauce over roasted potatoes and serve immediately. Enjoy!

Per serving: 166 Calories; 3.9g Fat; 32g Carbs; 4.5g Protein; 3.3g Sugars

417. Favorite Winter Bliss Bowl

(Ready in about 25 minutes | Servings 3)

Ingredients

1 pound cauliflower florets
9 ounces frozen crab cakes
1 teaspoon olive oil
Sea salt and freshly ground black pepper, to taste
1 cup quinoa
1 cup iceberg lettuce
1 cup baby spinach
1 red bell pepper, deseeded and sliced
2 tablespoons fresh lemon juice
1 tablespoon extra-virgin olive oil
1 teaspoon yellow mustard
2 tablespoons cilantro leaves, chopped

Directions

Brush the cauliflower and crab cakes with olive oil; season them with salt and black pepper and transfer them to the cooking basket.

Cook the cauliflower at 400 degrees F for about 12 minutes total, shaking the basket halfway through the cooking time.

Then, cook the crab cakes at 400 degrees F for about 12 minutes total, flipping them halfway through the cooking time.

In the meantime, rinse your quinoa, drain it and transfer to a soup pot with 2 cups of lightly salted water; bring to a boil.

Turn heat to a simmer and continue to cook, covered, for about 20 minutes; fluff with a fork and transfer to a serving bowl.

Add the cauliflower and crab cakes to the bowl. Add your greens and bell pepper to the bowl. In a small mixing dish, whisk the lemon juice, extra-virgin olive oil and yellow mustard.

Drizzle the dressing over all ingredients, garnish with fresh cilantro and serve immediately. Bon appétit!

Per serving: 166 Calories; 3.9g Fat; 32g Carbs; 4.5g Protein; 3.3g Sugars

418. Vegetable Oatmeal Fritters

(Ready in about 20 minutes | Servings 3)

Ingredients

1 cup rolled oats
1 ½ cups water
2 tablespoons soy sauce
1/2 teaspoon shallot powder
1/2 teaspoon porcini powder
1/2 teaspoon garlic powder
1 cup white mushrooms, chopped
1 carrot, grated
1/2 cup celery, grated
1/2 teaspoon cumin
1/2 teaspoon mustard seeds
2 tablespoons tomato ketchup

Directions

Start by preheating your Air Fryer to 380 degrees F.

Thoroughly combine all ingredients. Shape the batter into equal patties and place them in the cooking basket. Spritz your patties with a nonstick cooking spray.

Cook the fritters in the preheated Air Fryer for 15 minutes, turning them over halfway through the cooking time.

Serve with your favorite dipping sauce. Bon appétit!

Per serving: 263 Calories; 5.9g Fat; 42.8g Carbs; 11.4g Protein; 4.8g Sugars

419. Mexican-Style Roasted Corn Salad

(Ready in about 15 minutes | Servings 2)

Ingredients

2 ears of corn, husked
1 cup Mexican Escabeche
4 ounces Cotija cheese crumbled
1/2 red onion, finely chopped
Fresh juice of 1 lime
2 tablespoons extra-virgin olive oil
1/2 teaspoon Mexican oregano
Kosher salt and freshly ground black pepper, to taste

Directions

Start by preheating your Air Fryer to 390 degrees F.

Place the corn on the cob in the lightly greased cooking basket; cook the corn on the cob for 10 minutes, turning over halfway through the cooking time.

Once the corn has cooled, use a sharp knife to cut off the kernels into a salad bowl.

Toss the corn kernels with the remaining ingredients and serve immediately. Enjoy!

Per serving: 373 Calories; 28.5g Fat; 19.7g Carbs; 13g Protein; 7.7g Sugars

420. Traditional Indian Bhajiya

(Ready in about 20 minutes | Servings 3)

Ingredients

1 cup carrot, grated
1 cup cabbage, shredded
1 small onion, chopped
1 small garlic clove, finely chopped
1/2 cup chickpea flour
Himalayan salt and ground black pepper, to taste
1 teaspoon Chaat masala
1 teaspoon coriander, minced
1 teaspoon olive oil

Directions

In a mixing bowl, combine all ingredients until well combined.

Then, spoon 2 tablespoons of the mixture into the cooking basket and flatten with a wide spatula.

Cook them at 350 degrees F for 7 to 8 minutes; flip them and cook for a further 8 minutes or until golden brown on the top. Eat warm and enjoy!

Per serving: 114 Calories; 2.7g Fat; 18.5g Carbs; 4.8g Protein; 6.3g Sugars

421. Easy Veggie Fried Balls

(Ready in about 30 minutes | Servings 3)

Ingredients

1/2 pound sweet potatoes, grated
1 cup carrots
1 cup corn
2 garlic cloves, minced
1 shallot, chopped
Sea salt and ground black pepper, to taste
2 tablespoons fresh parsley, chopped
1 egg, well beaten
1/2 cup purpose flour
1/2 cup Romano cheese, grated
1/2 cup dried bread flakes
1 tablespoon olive oil

Directions

Mix the veggies, spices, egg, flour, and Romano cheese until everything is well incorporated.

Take 1 tablespoon of the veggie mixture and roll into a ball. Roll the balls onto the dried bread flakes. Brush the veggie balls with olive oil on all sides.

Cook in the preheated Air Fryer at 360 degrees F for 15 minutes or until thoroughly cooked and crispy.

Repeat the process until you run out of ingredients. Bon appétit!

Per serving: 364 Calories; 13.7g Fat; 48.3g Carbs; 14g Protein; 5.3g Sugar

422. Fried Peppers with Sriracha Mayo

(Ready in about 20 minutes | Servings 2)

Ingredients

4 bell peppers, seeded and sliced (1-inch pieces)
1 onion, sliced (1-inch pieces)
1 tablespoon olive oil
1/2 teaspoon dried rosemary
1/2 teaspoon dried basil
Kosher salt, to taste
1/4 teaspoon ground black pepper
1/3 cup mayonnaise
1/3 teaspoon Sriracha

Directions

Toss the bell peppers and onions with the olive oil, rosemary, basil, salt, and black pepper.

Place the peppers and onions on an even layer in the cooking basket. Cook at 400 degrees F for 12 to 14 minutes.

Meanwhile, make the sauce by whisking the mayonnaise and Sriracha. Serve immediately.

Per serving: 346 Calories; 34.1g Fat; 9.5g Carbs; 2.3g Protein; 4.9g Sugars

423. Classic Fried Pickles

(Ready in about 20 minutes | Servings 2)

Ingredients

1 egg, whisked
2 tablespoons buttermilk
1/2 cup fresh breadcrumbs
1/4 cup Romano cheese, grated
1/2 teaspoon onion powder
1 ½ cups dill pickle chips, pressed dry with kitchen towels
1/2 teaspoon garlic powder
Mayo Sauce:
1/4 cup mayonnaise
1/2 tablespoon mustard
1/2 teaspoon molasses
1 tablespoon ketchup
1/4 teaspoon ground black pepper

Directions

In a shallow bowl, whisk the egg with buttermilk.

In another bowl, mix the breadcrumbs, cheese, onion powder, and garlic powder.

Dredge the pickle chips in the egg mixture, then, in the breadcrumb/cheese mixture.

Cook in the preheated Air Fryer at 400 degrees F for 5 minutes; shake the basket and cook for 5 minutes more.

Meanwhile, mix all the sauce ingredients until well combined. Serve the fried pickles with the mayo sauce for dipping.

Per serving: 342 Calories; 28.5g Fat; 12.5g Carbs; 9.1g Protein; 4.9g Sugars

424. Fried Green Beans with Pecorino Romano

(Ready in about 15 minutes | Servings 3)

Ingredients

2 tablespoons buttermilk
1 egg
4 tablespoons cornmeal
4 tablespoons tortilla chips, crushed

4 tablespoons Pecorino Romano cheese, finely grated
Coarse salt and crushed black pepper, to taste
1 teaspoon smoked paprika
12 ounces green beans, trimmed

Directions

In a shallow bowl, whisk together the buttermilk and egg.

In a separate bowl, combine the cornmeal, tortilla chips, Pecorino Romano cheese, salt, black pepper, and paprika.

Dip the green beans in the egg mixture, then, in the cornmeal/cheese mixture. Place the green beans in the lightly greased cooking basket.

Cook in the preheated Air Fryer at 390 degrees F for 4 minutes. Shake the basket and cook for a further 3 minutes.

Taste, adjust the seasonings, and serve with the dipping sauce if desired. Bon appétit!

Per serving: 340 Calories; 9.7g Fat; 50.9g Carbs; 12.8g Protein; 4.7g Sugars

425. Spicy Roasted Potatoes

(Ready in about 15 minutes | Servings 2)

Ingredients

4 potatoes, peeled and cut into wedges
2 tablespoons olive oil

Sea salt and ground black pepper, to taste
1 teaspoon cayenne pepper
1/2 teaspoon ancho chili powder

Directions

Toss all ingredients in a mixing bowl until the potatoes are well covered.

Transfer them to the Air Fryer basket and cook at 400 degrees F for 6 minutes; shake the basket and cook for a further 6 minutes.

Serve warm with your favorite sauce for dipping. Bon appétit!

Per serving: 299 Calories; 13.6g Fat; 40.9g Carbs; 4.8g Protein; 1.4g Sugars

426. Spicy Glazed Carrots

(Ready in about 20 minutes | Servings 3)

Ingredients

1 pound carrots, cut into matchsticks
2 tablespoons peanut oil
1 tablespoon agave syrup

1 jalapeño, seeded and minced
1/4 teaspoon dill
1/2 teaspoon basil
Salt and white pepper to taste

Directions

Start by preheating your Air Fryer to 380 degrees F.

Toss all ingredients together and place them in the Air Fryer basket.

Cook for 15 minutes, shaking the basket halfway through the cooking time. Transfer to a serving platter and enjoy!

Per serving: 162 Calories; 9.3g Fat; 20.1g Carbs; 1.4g Protein; 12.8g Sugars

427. Easy Sweet Potato Bake

(Ready in about 35 minutes | Servings 3)

Ingredients

1 stick butter, melted
1 pound sweet potatoes, mashed
2 tablespoons honey
2 eggs, beaten

1/3 cup coconut milk
1/4 cup flour
1/2 cup fresh breadcrumbs

Directions

Start by preheating your Air Fryer to 325 degrees F.

Spritz a casserole dish with cooking oil.

In a mixing bowl, combine all ingredients, except for the breadcrumbs and 1 tablespoon of butter. Spoon the mixture into the prepared casserole dish.

Top with the breadcrumbs and brush the top with the remaining 1 tablespoon of butter. Bake in the preheated Air Fryer for 30 minutes. Bon appétit!

Per serving: 409 Calories; 26.1g Fat; 38.3g Carbs; 7.2g Protein; 10.9g Sugars

428. Avocado Fries with Roasted Garlic Mayonnaise

(Ready in about 50 minutes | Servings 4)

Ingredients

1/2 head garlic (6-7 cloves)
3/4 cup all-purpose flour
Sea salt and ground black pepper, to taste
2 eggs
1 cup tortilla chips, crushed

3 avocados, cut into wedges
Sauce:
1/2 cup mayonnaise
1 teaspoon lemon juice
1 teaspoon mustard

Directions

Place the garlic on a piece of aluminum foil and spritz with cooking spray. Wrap the garlic in the foil.

Cook in the preheated Air Fryer at 400 degrees for 12 minutes. Check the garlic, open the top of the foil and continue to cook for 10 minutes more.

Let it cool for 10 to 15 minutes; remove the cloves by squeezing them out of the skins; mash the garlic and reserve.

In a shallow bowl, combine the flour, salt, and black pepper. In another shallow dish, whisk the eggs until frothy.

Place the crushed tortilla chips in a third shallow dish. Dredge the avocado wedges in the flour mixture, shaking off the excess. Then, dip in the egg mixture; lastly, dredge in crushed tortilla chips.

Spritz the avocado wedges with cooking oil on all sides.

Cook in the preheated Air Fryer at 395 degrees F approximately 8 minutes, turning them over halfway through the cooking time.

Meanwhile, combine the sauce ingredients with the smashed roasted garlic. To serve, divide the avocado fries between plates and top with the sauce. Enjoy!

Per serving: 351 Calories; 27.7g Fat; 21.5g Carbs; 6.4g Protein; 1.1g Sugars

429. Roasted Broccoli with Sesame Seeds

(Ready in about 15 minutes | Servings 2)

Ingredients

1 pound broccoli florets
2 tablespoons sesame oil
1/2 teaspoon shallot powder
1/2 teaspoon porcini powder
1 teaspoon garlic powder

Sea salt and ground black pepper, to taste
1/2 teaspoon cumin powder
1/4 teaspoon paprika
2 tablespoons sesame seeds

Directions

Start by preheating the Air Fryer to 400 degrees F.

Blanch the broccoli in salted boiling water until al dente, about 3 to 4 minutes. Drain well and transfer to the lightly greased Air Fryer basket.

Add the sesame oil, shallot powder, porcini powder, garlic powder, salt, black pepper, cumin powder, paprika, and sesame seeds.

Cook for 6 minutes, tossing halfway through the cooking time. Bon appétit!

Per serving: 267 Calories; 19.5g Fat; 20.2g Carbs; 8.9g Protein; 5.2g Sugars

430. Corn on the Cob with Herb Butter

(Ready in about 15 minutes | Servings 2)

Ingredients

2 ears fresh corn, shucked and cut into halves
2 tablespoons butter, room temperature
1 teaspoon granulated garlic
1/2 teaspoon fresh ginger, grated
Sea salt and ground black pepper, to taste
1 tablespoon fresh rosemary, chopped
1 tablespoon fresh basil, chopped
2 tablespoons fresh chives, roughly chopped

Directions

Spritz the corn with cooking spray. Cook at 395 degrees F for 6 minutes, turning them over halfway through the cooking time.

In the meantime, mix the butter with the granulated garlic, ginger, salt, black pepper, rosemary, and basil.

Spread the butter mixture all over the corn on the cob. Cook in the preheated Air Fryer an additional 2 minutes. Bon appétit!

Per serving: 239 Calories; 13.3g Fat; 30.2g Carbs; 5.4g Protein; 5.8g Sugars

431. Rainbow Vegetable Fritters

(Ready in about 20 minutes | Servings 2)

Ingredients

1 zucchini, grated and squeezed
1 cup corn kernels
1/2 cup canned green peas
4 tablespoons all-purpose flour
2 tablespoons fresh shallots, minced
1 teaspoon fresh garlic, minced
1 tablespoon peanut oil
Sea salt and ground black pepper, to taste
1 teaspoon cayenne pepper

Directions

In a mixing bowl, thoroughly combine all ingredients until everything is well incorporated.

Shape the mixture into patties. Spritz the Air Fryer basket with cooking spray.

Cook in the preheated Air Fryer at 365 degrees F for 6 minutes. Turn them over and cook for a further 6 minutes

Serve immediately and enjoy!

Per serving: 215 Calories; 8.4g Fat; 31.6g Carbs; 6g Protein; 4.1g Sugars

432. Mediterranean Vegetable Skewers

(Ready in about 30 minutes | Servings 4)

Ingredients

2 medium-sized zucchini, cut into 1-inch pieces
2 red bell peppers, cut into 1-inch pieces
1 green bell pepper, cut into 1-inch pieces
1 red onion, cut into 1-inch pieces
2 tablespoons olive oil
Sea salt, to taste
1/2 teaspoon black pepper, preferably freshly cracked
1/2 teaspoon red pepper flakes

Directions

Soak the wooden skewers in water for 15 minutes.

Thread the vegetables on skewers; drizzle olive oil all over the vegetable skewers; sprinkle with spices.

Cook in the preheated Air Fryer at 400 degrees F for 13 minutes. Serve warm and enjoy!

Per serving: 138 Calories; 10.2g Fat; 10.2g Carbs; 2.2g Protein; 6.6g Sugars

433. Roasted Veggies with Yogurt-Tahini Sauce

(Ready in about 20 minutes | Servings 4)

Ingredients

1 pound Brussels sprouts
1 pound button mushrooms
2 tablespoons olive oil
1/2 teaspoon white pepper
1/2 teaspoon dried dill weed
1/2 teaspoon cayenne pepper
1/2 teaspoon celery seeds
1/2 teaspoon mustard seeds
Salt, to taste
Yogurt Tahini Sauce:
1 cup plain yogurt
2 heaping tablespoons tahini paste
1 tablespoon lemon juice
1 tablespoon extra-virgin olive oil
1/2 teaspoon Aleppo pepper, minced

Directions

Toss the Brussels sprouts and mushrooms with olive oil and spices. Preheat your Air Fryer to 380 degrees F.

Add the Brussels sprouts to the cooking basket and cook for 10 minutes.

Add the mushrooms, turn the temperature to 390 degrees and cook for 6 minutes more.

While the vegetables are cooking, make the sauce by whisking all ingredients. Serve the warm vegetables with the sauce on the side. Bon appétit!

Per serving: 254 Calories; 17.2g Fat; 19.6g Carbs; 11.1g Protein; 8.1g Sugars

434. Swiss Cheese & Vegetable Casserole

(Ready in about 50 minutes | Servings 4)

Ingredients

1 pound potatoes, peeled and sliced (1/4-inch thick)
2 tablespoons olive oil
1/2 teaspoon red pepper flakes, crushed
1/2 teaspoon freshly ground black pepper
Salt, to taste
3 bell peppers, thinly sliced
1 serrano pepper, thinly sliced
2 medium-sized tomatoes, sliced
1 leek, thinly sliced
2 garlic cloves, minced
1 cup Swiss cheese, shredded

Directions

Start by preheating your Air Fryer to 350 degrees F. Spritz a casserole dish with cooking oil.

Place the potatoes in the casserole dish in an even layer; drizzle 1 tablespoon of olive oil over the top. Then, add the red pepper, black pepper, and salt.

Add 2 bell peppers and 1/2 of the leeks. Add the tomatoes and the remaining 1 tablespoon of olive oil.

Add the remaining peppers, leeks, and minced garlic. Top with the cheese.

Cover the casserole with foil and bake for 32 minutes. Remove the foil and increase the temperature to 400 degrees F; bake an additional 16 minutes. Bon appétit!

Per serving: 328 Calories; 16.5g Fat; 33.1g Carbs; 13.1g Protein; 7.6g Sugars

435. Easy Sweet Potato Hash Browns

(Ready in about 50 minutes | Servings 2)

Ingredients

1 pound sweet potatoes, peeled and grated
2 eggs, whisked
1/4 cup scallions, chopped
1 teaspoon fresh garlic, minced
Sea salt and ground black pepper, to taste
1/4 teaspoon ground allspice
1/2 teaspoon cinnamon
1 tablespoon peanut oil

Directions

Allow the sweet potatoes to soak for 25 minutes in cold water. Drain the water; dry the sweet potatoes with a kitchen towel.

Add the remaining ingredients and stir to combine well.

Cook in the preheated Air Fryer at 395 degrees F for 20 minutes. Shake the basket once or twice. Serve with ketchup.

Per serving: 381 Calories; 16.7g Fat; 44.8g Carbs; 14.3g Protein; 3.9g Sugars

436. American-Style Brussel Sprout Salad

(Ready in about 35 minutes | Servings 4)

Ingredients

1 pound Brussels sprouts
1 apple, cored and diced
1/2 cup mozzarella cheese, crumbled
1/2 cup pomegranate seeds
1 small-sized red onion, chopped
4 eggs, hardboiled and sliced

Dressing:
1/4 cup olive oil
2 tablespoons champagne vinegar
1 teaspoon Dijon mustard
1 teaspoon honey
Sea salt and ground black pepper, to taste

Directions

Start by preheating your Air Fryer to 380 degrees F.

Add the Brussels sprouts to the cooking basket. Spritz with cooking spray and cook for 15 minutes. Let it cool to room temperature about 15 minutes.

Toss the Brussels sprouts with the apple, cheese, pomegranate seeds, and red onion.

Mix all ingredients for the dressing and toss to combine well. Serve topped with the hard-boiled eggs. Bon appétit!

Per serving: 319 Calories; 18.5g Fat; 27g Carbs; 14.7g Protein; 14.6g Sugars

437. The Best Cauliflower Tater Tots

(Ready in about 25 minutes | Servings 4)

Ingredients

1 pound cauliflower florets
2 eggs
1 tablespoon olive oil
2 tablespoons scallions, chopped
1 garlic clove, minced
1 cup Colby cheese, shredded

1/2 cup breadcrumbs
Sea salt and ground black pepper, to taste
1/4 teaspoon dried dill weed
1 teaspoon paprika

Directions

Blanch the cauliflower in salted boiling water about 3 to 4 minutes until al dente. Drain well and pulse in a food processor.

Add the remaining ingredients; mix to combine well. Shape the cauliflower mixture into bite-sized tots.

Spritz the Air Fryer basket with cooking spray.

Cook in the preheated Air Fryer at 375 degrees F for 16 minutes, shaking halfway through the cooking time. Serve with your favorite sauce for dipping. Bon appétit!

Per serving: 267 Calories; 19.2g Fat; 9.6g Carbs; 14.9g Protein; 2.9g Sugars

438. Skinny Pumpkin Chips

(Ready in about 20 minutes | Servings 2)

Ingredients

1 pound pumpkin, cut into sticks
1 tablespoon coconut oil
1/2 teaspoon rosemary

1/2 teaspoon basil
Salt and ground black pepper, to taste

Directions

Start by preheating the Air Fryer to 395 degrees F. Brush the pumpkin sticks with coconut oil; add the spices and toss to combine.

Cook for 13 minutes, shaking the basket halfway through the cooking time.

Serve with mayonnaise. Bon appétit!

Per serving: 118 Calories; 7g Fat; 14.7g Carbs; 2.2g Protein; 6.2g Sugars

439. Cheese Stuffed Roasted Peppers

(Ready in about 20 minutes | Servings 2)

Ingredients

2 red bell peppers, tops and seeds removed
2 yellow bell peppers, tops and seeds removed

Salt and pepper, to taste
1 cup cream cheese
4 tablespoons mayonnaise
2 pickles, chopped

Directions

Arrange the peppers in the lightly greased cooking basket. Cook in the preheated Air Fryer at 400 degrees F for 15 minutes, turning them over halfway through the cooking time.

Season with salt and pepper.

Then, in a mixing bowl, combine the cream cheese with the mayonnaise and chopped pickles. Stuff the pepper with the cream cheese mixture and serve. Enjoy!

Per serving: 367 Calories; 21.8g Fat; 21.9g Carbs; 21.5g Protein; 14.1g Sugars

440. Three-Cheese Stuffed Mushrooms

(Ready in about 15 minutes | Servings 3)

Ingredients

9 large button mushrooms, stems removed
1 tablespoon olive oil
Salt and ground black pepper, to taste
1/2 teaspoon dried rosemary
6 tablespoons Swiss cheese shredded

6 tablespoons Romano cheese, shredded
6 tablespoons cream cheese
1 teaspoon soy sauce
1 teaspoon garlic, minced
3 tablespoons green onion, minced

Directions

Brush the mushroom caps with olive oil; sprinkle with salt, pepper, and rosemary.

In a mixing bowl, thoroughly combine the remaining ingredients; mix to combine well and divide the filling mixture among the mushroom caps.

Cook in the preheated Air Fryer at 390 degrees F for 7 minutes.

Let the mushrooms cool slightly before serving. Bon appétit!

Per serving: 345 Calories; 28g Fat; 11.2g Carbs; 14.4g Protein; 8.1g Sugars

441. Sweet Potato Chips with Greek Yogurt Dip

(Ready in about 20 minutes | Servings 2)

Ingredients

4 sweet potatoes, sliced
2 tablespoons olive oil
Coarse sea salt and freshly ground black pepper, to taste
1 teaspoon paprika

Dipping Sauce:
1/2 cup Greek-style yogurt
1 clove garlic, minced
1 tablespoon fresh chives, chopped

Directions

Soak the sweet potato slices in icy cold water for 20 to 30 minutes. Drain the sweet potatoes and pat them dry with kitchen towels.

Toss the sweet potato slices with olive oil, salt, black pepper, and paprika.

Place in the lightly greased cooking basket. Cook in the preheated Air Fryer at 360 degrees F for 14 minutes.

Meanwhile, make the sauce by whisking the remaining ingredients. Serve the sweet potato chips with the sauce for dipping and enjoy!

Per serving: 378 Calories; 13.9g Fat; 55.2g Carbs; 9.4g Protein; 12.6g Sugars

442. Classic Onion Rings

(Ready in about 30 minutes | Servings 2)

Ingredients

1 medium-sized onion, slice into rings
1 cup all-purpose flour
1 teaspoon baking powder
Coarse sea salt and ground black pepper, to your liking
1/2 cup yogurt
2 eggs, beaten
3/4 cup bread crumbs
1 teaspoon onion powder
1 teaspoon garlic powder
1/2 teaspoon celery seeds

Directions

Place the onion rings in the bowl with cold water; let them soak approximately 20 minutes; drain the onion rings and pat dry using a pepper towel.

In a shallow bowl, mix the flour, baking powder, salt, and black pepper. Add the yogurt and eggs and mix well to combine.

In another shallow bowl, mix the bread crumbs, onion powder, garlic powder, and celery seeds. Dip the onion rings in the flour/egg mixture; then, dredge in the breadcrumb mixture.

Spritz the Air Fryer basket with cooking spray; arrange the breaded onion rings in the basket.

Cook in the preheated Air Fryer at 400 degrees F for 4 to 5 minutes, turning them over halfway through the cooking time. Bon appétit!

Per serving: 440 Calories; 12.7g Fat; 60g Carbs; 19.2g Protein; 5.6g Sugars

443. Greek-Style Roasted Tomatoes with Feta

(Ready in about 20 minutes | Servings 2)

Ingredients

3 medium-sized tomatoes, cut into four slices, pat dry
1 teaspoon dried basil
1 teaspoon dried oregano
1/4 teaspoon red pepper flakes, crushed
1/2 teaspoon sea salt
3 slices Feta cheese

Directions

Spritz the tomatoes with cooking oil and transfer them to the Air Fryer basket. Sprinkle with seasonings.

Cook at 350 degrees F approximately 8 minutes turning them over halfway through the cooking time.

Top with the cheese and cook an additional 4 minutes. Bon appétit!

Per serving: 148 Calories; 9.4g Fat; 9.4g Carbs; 7.8g Protein; 6.6g Sugars

444. Sweet Corn Fritters with Avocado

(Ready in about 20 minutes | Servings 3)

Ingredients

2 cups sweet corn kernels
1 small-sized onion, chopped
1 garlic clove, minced
2 eggs, whisked
1 teaspoon baking powder
2 tablespoons fresh cilantro, chopped
Sea salt and ground black pepper, to taste
1 avocado, peeled, pitted and diced
2 tablespoons sweet chili sauce

Directions

In a mixing bowl, thoroughly combine the corn, onion, garlic, eggs, baking powder, cilantro, salt, and black pepper.

Shape the corn mixture into 6 patties and transfer them to the lightly greased Air Fryer basket.

Cook in the preheated Air Fry at 370 degrees for 8 minutes; turn them over and cook for 7 minutes longer.

Serve the fritters with the avocado and chili sauce.

Per serving: 383 Calories; 21.3g Fat; 42.8g Carbs; 12.7g Protein; 9.2g Sugars

445. Cauliflower and Goat Cheese Croquettes

(Ready in about 30 minutes | Servings 2)

Ingredients

1/2 pound cauliflower florets
2 garlic cloves, minced
1 cup goat cheese, shredded
Sea salt and ground black pepper, to taste
1/2 teaspoon shallot powder
1/4 teaspoon cumin powder
1 cup sour cream
1 teaspoon Dijon mustard

Directions

Place the cauliflower florets in a saucepan of water; bring to the boil; reduce the heat and cook for 10 minutes or until tender.

Mash the cauliflower using your blender; add the garlic, cheese, and spices; mix to combine well.

Form the cauliflower mixture into croquettes shapes.

Cook in the preheated Air Fryer at 375 degrees F for 16 minutes, shaking halfway through the cooking time. Serve with the sour cream and mustard. Bon appétit!

Per serving: 297 Calories; 21.7g Fat; 11.7g Carbs; 15.3g Protein; 2.6g Sugars

446. Greek-Style Vegetable Bake

(Ready in about 35 minutes | Servings 4)

Ingredients

1 eggplant, peeled and sliced
2 bell peppers, seeded and sliced
1 red onion, sliced
1 teaspoon fresh garlic, minced
4 tablespoons olive oil
1 teaspoon mustard
1 teaspoon dried oregano
1 teaspoon smoked paprika
Salt and ground black pepper, to taste
1 tomato, sliced
6 ounces halloumi cheese, sliced lengthways

Directions

Start by preheating your Air Fryer to 370 degrees F. Spritz a baking pan with nonstick cooking spray.

Place the eggplant, peppers, onion, and garlic on the bottom of the baking pan. Add the olive oil, mustard, and spices. Transfer to the cooking basket and cook for 14 minutes.

Top with the tomatoes and cheese; increase the temperature to 390 degrees F and cook for 5 minutes more until bubbling. Let it sit on a cooling rack for 10 minutes before serving. Bon appétit!

Per serving: 296 Calories; 22.9g Fat; 16.1g Carbs; 9.3g Protein; 9.9g Sugars

447. Japanese Tempura Bowl

(Ready in about 20 minutes | Servings 3)

Ingredients

1 cup all-purpose flour
Kosher salt and ground black pepper, to taste
1/2 teaspoon paprika
2 eggs
3 tablespoons soda water
1 cup panko crumbs
2 tablespoons olive oil
1 cup green beans
1 onion, cut into rings
1 zucchini, cut into slices
2 tablespoons soy sauce
1 tablespoon mirin
1 teaspoon dashi granules

Directions

In a shallow bowl, mix the flour, salt, black pepper, and paprika. In a separate bowl, whisk the eggs and soda water. In a third shallow bowl, combine the panko crumbs with olive oil.

Dip the vegetables in flour mixture, then in the egg mixture; lastly, roll over the panko mixture to coat evenly.

Cook in the preheated Air Fryer at 400 degrees F for 10 minutes, shaking the basket halfway through the cooking time. Work in batches until the vegetables are crispy and golden brown.

Then, make the sauce by whisking the soy sauce, mirin, and dashi granules. Bon appétit!

Per serving: 446 Calories; 14.7g Fat; 63.5g Carbs; 14.6g Protein; 3.8g Sugars

448. Balsamic Root Vegetables

(Ready in about 25 minutes | Servings 3)

Ingredients

2 potatoes, cut into 1 1/2-inch pieces
2 carrots, cut into 1 1/2-inch pieces
2 parsnips, cut into 1 1/2-inch pieces
1 onion, cut into 1 1/2-inch pieces

Pink Himalayan salt and ground black pepper, to taste
1/4 teaspoon smoked paprika
1 teaspoon garlic powder
1/2 teaspoon dried thyme
1/2 teaspoon dried marjoram
2 tablespoons olive oil
2 tablespoons balsamic vinegar

Directions

Toss all ingredients in a large mixing dish.

Roast in the preheated Air Fryer at 400 degrees F for 10 minutes. Shake the basket and cook for 7 minutes more.

Serve with some extra fresh herbs if desired. Bon appétit!

Per serving: 405 Calories; 9.7g Fat; 74.7g Carbs; 7.7g Protein; 15.2g Sugars

449. Winter Vegetable Braise

(Ready in about 25 minutes | Servings 2)

Ingredients

4 potatoes, peeled and cut into 1-inch pieces
1 celery root, peeled and cut into 1-inch pieces
1 cup winter squash
2 tablespoons unsalted butter, melted

1/2 cup chicken broth
1/4 cup tomato sauce
1 teaspoon parsley
1 teaspoon rosemary
1 teaspoon thyme

Directions

Start by preheating your Air Fryer to 370 degrees F. Add all ingredients in a lightly greased casserole dish. Stir to combine well.

Bake in the preheated Air Fryer for 10 minutes. Gently stir the vegetables with a large spoon and increase temperature to 400 degrees F; cook for 10 minutes more.

Serve in individual bowls with a few drizzles of lemon juice. Bon appétit!

Per serving: 358 Calories; 12.3g Fat; 55.7g Carbs; 7.7g Protein; 7.4g Sugars

450. Family Vegetable Gratin

(Ready in about 35 minutes | Servings 4)

Ingredients

1 pound Chinese cabbage, roughly chopped
2 bell peppers, seeded and sliced
1 jalapeno pepper, seeded and sliced
1 onion, thickly sliced
2 garlic cloves, sliced
1/2 stick butter

4 tablespoons all-purpose flour
1 cup milk
1 cup cream cheese
Sea salt and freshly ground black pepper, to taste
1/2 teaspoon cayenne pepper
1 cup Monterey Jack cheese, shredded

Directions

Heat a pan of salted water and bring to a boil. Boil the Chinese cabbage for 2 to 3 minutes. Transfer the Chinese cabbage to cold water to stop the cooking process.

Place the Chinese cabbage in a lightly greased casserole dish. Add the peppers, onion, and garlic.

Next, melt the butter in a saucepan over a moderate heat. Gradually add the flour and cook for 2 minutes to form a paste.

Slowly pour in the milk, stirring continuously until a thick sauce forms. Add the cream cheese. Season with the salt, black pepper, and cayenne pepper. Add the mixture to the casserole dish.

Top with the shredded Monterey Jack cheese and bake in the preheated Air Fryer at 390 degrees F for 25 minutes. Serve hot.

Per serving: 373 Calories; 26.1g Fat; 17.7g Carbs; 18.7g Protein; 7.7g Sugars

451. Roasted Beet Salad

(Ready in about 20 minutes + chilling time | Servings 2)

Ingredients

2 medium-sized beets, peeled and cut into wedges
2 tablespoons extra virgin olive oil
1 tablespoon balsamic vinegar
1 teaspoon yellow mustard
1 garlic clove, minced

1/4 teaspoon cumin powder
Coarse sea salt and ground black pepper, to taste
1 tablespoon fresh parsley leaves, roughly chopped

Directions

Place the beets in a single layer in the lightly greased cooking basket.

Cook at 370 degrees F for 13 minutes, shaking the basket halfway through the cooking time.

Let it cool to room temperature; toss the beets with the remaining ingredients. Serve well chilled. Enjoy!

Per serving: 149 Calories; 6.5g Fat; 20.6g Carbs; 3.5g Protein; 13.9g Sugars

452. Spicy Ricotta Stuffed Mushrooms

(Ready in about 35 minutes | Servings 4)

Ingredients

1/2 pound small white mushrooms
Sea salt and ground black pepper, to taste
2 tablespoons Ricotta cheese
1/2 teaspoon ancho chili powder

1 teaspoon paprika
4 tablespoons all-purpose flour
1 egg
1/2 cup fresh breadcrumbs

Directions

Remove the stems from the mushroom caps and chop them; mix the chopped mushrooms steams with the salt, black pepper, cheese, chili powder, and paprika.

Stuff the mushroom caps with the cheese filling.

Place the flour in a shallow bowl, and beat the egg in another bowl. Place the breadcrumbs in a third shallow bowl.

Dip the mushrooms in the flour, then, dip in the egg mixture; finally, dredge in the breadcrumbs and press to adhere. Spritz the stuffed mushrooms with cooking spray.

Cook in the preheated Air Fryer at 360 degrees F for 18 minutes. Bon appétit!

Per serving: 214 Calories; 5.6g Fat; 30.4g Carbs; 12.3g Protein; 5g Sugars

453. Baked Cholula Cauliflower

(Ready in about 20 minutes | Servings 4)

Ingredients

1/2 cup all-purpose flour
1/2 cup water
Salt, to taste
1/2 teaspoon ground black pepper
1/2 teaspoon shallot powder
1/2 teaspoon garlic powder

1/2 teaspoon cayenne pepper
2 tablespoons olive oil
1 pound cauliflower, broken into small florets
1/4 cup Cholula sauce

Directions

Start by preheating your Air Fryer to 400 degrees F. Lightly grease a baking pan with cooking spray.

In a mixing bowl, combine the flour, water, spices, and olive oil. Coat the cauliflower with the prepared batter; arrange the cauliflower on the baking pan.

Then, bake in the preheated Air Fryer for 8 minutes or until golden brown.

Brush the Cholula sauce all over the cauliflower florets and bake an additional 4 to 5 minutes. Bon appétit!

Per serving: 153 Calories; 7.3g Fat; 19.3g Carbs; 4.1g Protein; 2.9g Sugars

454. Fall Vegetables with Spiced Yogurt

(Ready in about 25 minutes | Servings 2)

Ingredients

1 pound celeriac, cut into 1 1/2-inch pieces
2 carrots, cut into 1 1/2-inch pieces
2 red onions, cut into 1 1/2-inch pieces
1 tablespoon sesame oil
1/2 teaspoon ground black pepper, to taste
1/2 teaspoon sea salt
Spiced Yogurt:
1/4 cup Greek yogurt
1 tablespoon mayonnaise
1 tablespoon honey
1/2 teaspoon mustard seeds
1/2 teaspoon chili powder

Directions

Place the vegetables in a single layer in the lightly greased cooking basket. Drizzle the sesame oil over vegetables.

Sprinkle with black pepper and sea salt.

Cook at 390 degrees F for 20 minutes, shaking the basket halfway through the cooking time.

Meanwhile, make the sauce by whisking all ingredients. Spoon the sauce over the roasted vegetables. Bon appétit!

Per serving: 319 Calories; 14.1g Fat; 46g Carbs; 6.4g Protein; 20.1g Sugars

455. Sweet-and-Sour Mixed Veggies

(Ready in about 25 minutes | Servings 4)

Ingredients

1/2 pound asparagus, cut into 1 1/2-inch pieces
1/2 pound broccoli, cut into 1 1/2-inch pieces
1/2 pound carrots, cut into 1 1/2-inch pieces
2 tablespoons peanut oil
Some salt and white pepper, to taste
1/2 cup water
4 tablespoons raisins
2 tablespoon honey
2 tablespoons apple cider vinegar

Directions

Place the vegetables in a single layer in the lightly greased cooking basket. Drizzle the peanut oil over the vegetables.

Sprinkle with salt and white pepper.

Cook at 380 degrees F for 15 minutes, shaking the basket halfway through the cooking time.

Add 1/2 cup of water to a saucepan; bring to a rapid boil and add the raisins, honey, and vinegar. Cook for 5 to 7 minutes or until the sauce has reduced by half.

Spoon the sauce over the warm vegetables and serve immediately. Bon appétit!

Per serving: 153 Calories; 7.1g Fat; 21.6g Carbs; 3.6g Protein; 14.2g Sugars

456. Roasted Corn Salad

(Ready in about 15 minutes + chilling time | Servings 3)

Ingredients

2 ears of corn, husked
3 tablespoons sour cream
1/4 cup plain yogurt
1 garlic clove, minced
1 jalapeño pepper, seeded and minced
1 tablespoon fresh lemon juice
Pink salt and white pepper, to your liking
1 shallot, chopped
2 bell peppers, seeded and thinly sliced
2 tablespoons fresh parsley, chopped
1/4 cup Queso Fresco, crumbled

Directions

Start by preheating the Air Fryer to 390 degrees F. Spritz the Air Fryer grill pan with cooking spray.

Place the corn on the grill pan and cook for 10 minutes, turning over halfway through the cooking time. Set aside.

Once the corn has cooled to the touch, use a sharp knife to cut off the kernels into a salad bowl.

While the corn is resting, whisk the sour cream, yogurt, garlic, jalapeño pepper, fresh lemon juice, salt, and white pepper.

Add the shallot, pepper, and parsley to the salad bowl and toss to combine well. Toss with the sauce and serve topped with cheese. Enjoy!

Per serving: 205 Calories; 9.5g Fat; 27g Carbs; 7.5g Protein; 7.9g Sugars

457. Rainbow Vegetable and Parmesan Croquettes

(Ready in about 40 minutes | Servings 4)

Ingredients

1 pound potatoes, peeled
4 tablespoons milk
2 tablespoons butter
Salt and black pepper, to taste
1/2 teaspoon cayenne pepper
1/2 cup mushrooms, chopped
1/4 cup broccoli, chopped
1 carrot, grated
1 clove garlic, minced
3 tablespoons scallions, minced
2 tablespoons olive oil
1/2 cup all-purpose flour
2 eggs
1/2 cup panko bread crumbs
1/2 cup parmesan cheese, grated

Directions

In a large saucepan, boil the potatoes for 17 to 20 minutes. Drain the potatoes and mash with the milk, butter, salt, black pepper, and cayenne pepper.

Add the mushrooms, broccoli, carrots, garlic, scallions, and olive oil; stir to combine well. Shape the mixture into patties.

In a shallow bowl, place the flour; beat the eggs in another bowl; in a third bowl, combine the breadcrumbs with the parmesan cheese.

Dip each patty into the flour, followed by the eggs, and then the breadcrumb mixture; press to adhere.

Cook in the preheated Air Fryer at 375 degrees F for 16 minutes, shaking halfway through the cooking time. Bon appétit!

Per serving: 377 Calories; 19.1g Fat; 40.2g Carbs; 12.1g Protein; 3.9g Sugars

458. Crispy Wax Beans with Almonds and Blue Cheese

(Ready in about 15 minutes | Servings 3)

Ingredients

1 pound wax beans, cleaned
2 tablespoons peanut oil
4 tablespoons seasoned breadcrumbs
Sea salt and ground black pepper, to taste
1/2 teaspoon red pepper flakes, crushed
2 tablespoons almonds, sliced
1/3 cup blue cheese, crumbled

Directions

Toss the wax beans with the peanut oil, breadcrumbs, salt, black pepper, and red pepper.

Place the wax beans in the lightly greased cooking basket.

Cook in the preheated Air Fryer at 400 degrees F for 5 minutes. Shake the basket once or twice.

Add the almonds and cook for 3 minutes more or until lightly toasted. Serve topped with blue cheese and enjoy!

Per serving: 242 Calories; 16.9g Fat; 16.3g Carbs; 6.8g Protein; 3.5g Sugars

459. Indian Malai Kofta

(Ready in about 40 minutes | Servings 4)

Ingredients

Veggie Balls:
1 pound potatoes, peeled and diced
1/2 pound cauliflower, broken into small florets
2 tablespoons olive oil
2 cloves garlic, minced
1 tablespoon Garam masala
1 cup chickpea flour
Himalayan pink salt and ground black pepper, to taste
Sauce:
1 tablespoon sesame oil
1/2 teaspoon cumin seeds
2 cloves garlic, roughly chopped
1 onion, chopped
1 Kashmiri chili pepper, seeded and minced
1 (1-inch) piece ginger, chopped
1 teaspoon paprika
1 teaspoon turmeric powder
2 ripe tomatoes, pureed
1/2 cup vegetable broth
1/4 full fat coconut milk

Directions

Start by preheating your Air Fryer to 400 degrees F. Place the potato and cauliflower in a lightly greased cooking basket.

Cook for 15 minutes, shaking the basket halfway through the cooking time. Mash the cauliflower and potatoes in a mixing bowl.

Add the remaining ingredients for the veggie balls and stir to combine well. Shape the vegetable mixture into small balls and arrange them in the cooking basket.

Cook in the preheated Air Fryer at 360 degrees F for 15 minutes or until thoroughly cooked and crispy. Repeat the process until you run out of ingredients.

Heat the sesame oil in a saucepan over medium heat and add the cumin seeds. Once the cumin seeds turn brown, add the garlic, onions, chili pepper, and ginger. Sauté for 2 to 3 minutes.

Add the paprika, turmeric powder, tomatoes, and broth; let it simmer, covered, for 4 to 5 minutes, stirring occasionally.

Add the coconut milk. Heat off; add the veggie balls and gently stir to combine. Bon appétit!

Per serving: 338 Calories; 13.1g Fat; 46.8g Carbs; 10.9g Protein; 9.2g Sugars

460. Carrot and Oat Balls

(Ready in about 25 minutes | Servings 3)

Ingredients

4 carrots, grated
1 cup rolled oats, ground
1 tablespoon butter, room temperature
1 tablespoon chia seeds
1/2 cup scallions, chopped
2 cloves garlic, minced

2 tablespoons tomato ketchup
1 teaspoon cayenne pepper
1/2 teaspoon sea salt
1/4 teaspoon ground black pepper
1/2 teaspoon ancho chili powder
1/4 cup fresh bread crumbs

Directions

Start by preheating your Air Fryer to 380 degrees F.

In a bowl, mix all ingredients until everything is well incorporated. Shape the batter into bite-sized balls.

Cook the balls for 15 minutes, shaking the basket halfway through the cooking time. Bon appétit!

Per serving: 215 Calories; 4.7g Fat; 37.2g Carbs; 7.5g Protein; 5.6g Sugars

461. Sweet Potato and Chickpea Tacos

(Ready in about 15 minutes | Servings 4)

Ingredients

2 cups sweet potato puree
2 tablespoons butter, melted
14 ounces canned chickpeas, rinsed
1 cup Colby cheese, shredded
1 teaspoon garlic powder
1 teaspoon onion powder

Salt and freshly cracked black pepper, to taste
8 corn tortillas
1/4 cup Pico de gallo
2 tablespoons fresh coriander, chopped

Directions

Mix the sweet potatoes with the butter, chickpeas, cheese, garlic powder, onion powder, salt, black pepper.

Divide the sweet potato mixture between the tortillas. Bake in the preheated Air Fryer at 390 degrees F for 7 minutes.

Garnish with Pico de gallo and coriander. Bon appétit!

Per serving: 427 Calories; 26.6g Fat; 34.4g Carbs; 15.3g Protein; 4.5g Sugars

462. Kid-Friendly Veggie Tots

(Ready in about 20 minutes | Servings 4)

Ingredients

1 zucchini, grated
1 parsnip, grated
1 carrot, grated
1 onion, chopped
1 garlic clove, minced
2 tablespoons ground flax seeds

2 eggs, whisked
1/2 cup tortilla chips, crushed
1/4 cup pork rinds
Sea salt and ground black pepper, to taste

Directions

Start by preheating your Air Fryer to 400 degrees F.

Then, in a mixing bowl, thoroughly combine all ingredients until everything is well combined. Form the mixture into tot shapes and place in the lightly greased cooking basket.

Bake for 9 to 12 minutes, flipping halfway through, until golden brown around the edges. Bon appétit!

Per serving: 222 Calories; 14.2g Fat; 18.3g Carbs; 5.7g Protein; 3.5g Sugars

463. Quick Shrimp and Vegetable Bake

(Ready in about 25 minutes | Servings 4)

Ingredients

1 pound shrimp cleaned and deveined
1 cup broccoli, cut into florets
1 cup cauliflower, cut into florets
1 carrot, sliced

2 bell pepper, sliced
1 shallot, sliced
2 tablespoons sesame oil
1 cup tomato paste

Directions

Start by preheating your Air Fryer to 360 degrees F. Spritz the baking pan with cooking spray.

Now, arrange the shrimp and vegetables in the baking pan. Then, drizzle the sesame oil over the vegetables. Pour the tomato paste over the vegetables.

Cook for 10 minutes in the preheated Air Fryer. Stir with a large spoon and cook for a further 12 minutes. Serve warm.

Per serving: 269 Calories; 8.8g Fat; 21.7g Carbs; 28.2g Protein; 12g Sugars

464. Roasted Brussels Sprout Salad

(Ready in about 35 minutes + chilling time | Servings 2)

Ingredients

1/2 pound Brussels sprouts
1 tablespoon olive oil
Coarse sea salt and ground black pepper, to taste
2 ounces baby arugula
1 shallot, thinly sliced

2 ounces pancetta, chopped
Lemon Vinaigrette:
2 tablespoons extra virgin olive oil
2 tablespoons fresh lemon juice
1 tablespoon honey
1 teaspoon Dijon mustard

Directions

Start by preheating your Air Fryer to 380 degrees F.

Add the Brussels sprouts to the cooking basket. Brush with olive oil and cook for 15 minutes. Let it cool to room temperature about 15 minutes.

Toss the Brussels sprouts with the salt, black pepper, baby arugula, and shallot.

Mix all ingredients for the dressing. Then, dress your salad, garnish with pancetta, and serve well chilled. Bon appétit!

Per serving: 316 Calories; 16.6g Fat; 33.2g Carbs; 13.8g Protein; 17.7g Sugars

465. Winter Bliss Bowl

(Ready in about 45 minutes | Servings 3)

Ingredients

1 cup pearled barley
1 (1-pound) head cauliflower, broken into small florets
Coarse sea salt and ground black pepper, to taste
2 tablespoons champagne vinegar
4 tablespoons mayonnaise
1 teaspoon yellow mustard
4 tablespoons olive oil, divided
10 ounces ounce canned sweet corn, drained
2 tablespoons cilantro leaves, chopped

Directions

Cook the barley in a saucepan with salted water. Bring to a boil and cook approximately 28 minutes. Drain and reserve.

Start by preheating the Air Fryer to 400 degrees F.

Place the cauliflower florets in the lightly greased Air Fryer basket. Season with salt and black pepper; cook for 12 minutes, tossing halfway through the cooking time.

Toss with the reserved barley. Add the champagne vinegar, mayonnaise, mustard, olive oil, and corn. Garnish with fresh cilantro. Bon appétit!

Per serving: 387 Calories; 25.3g Fat; 38.5g Carbs; 6g Protein; 5.8g Sugars

466. Tater Tot Vegetable Casserole

(Ready in about 40 minutes | Servings 6)

Ingredients

1 tablespoon olive oil
1 shallot, sliced
2 cloves garlic, minced
1 red bell pepper, seeded and sliced
1 yellow bell pepper, seeded and sliced
1 ½ cups kale
1 (28-ounce) bag frozen tater tots
6 eggs
1 cup milk
Sea salt and ground black pepper, to your liking
1 cup Swiss cheese, shredded
4 tablespoons seasoned breadcrumbs

Directions

Heat the olive oil in a saucepan over medium-high heat. Sauté the shallot, garlic, and peppers for 2 to 3 minutes. Add the kale and cook until wilted.

Arrange the tater tots evenly over the bottom of a lightly greased casserole dish. Spread the sautéed mixture over the top.

In a mixing bowl, thoroughly combine the eggs, milk, salt, pepper, and shredded cheese. Pour the mixture into the casserole dish.

Lastly, top with the seasoned breadcrumbs. Bake at 330 degrees F for 30 minutes or until top is golden brown. Bon appétit!

Per serving: 493 Calories; 26.1g Fat; 49.6g Carbs; 17.1g Protein; 5.7g Sugars

467. Fried Asparagus with Goat Cheese

(Ready in about 15 minutes | Servings 3)

Ingredients

1 bunch of asparagus, trimmed
1 tablespoon olive oil
1/2 teaspoon kosher salt
1/4 teaspoon cracked black pepper, to taste
1/2 teaspoon dried dill weed
1/2 cup goat cheese, crumbled

Directions

Place the asparagus spears in the lightly greased cooking basket. Toss the asparagus with the olive oil, salt, black pepper, and dill.

Cook in the preheated Air Fryer at 400 degrees F for 9 minutes.

Serve garnished with goat cheese. Bon appétit!

Per serving: 132 Calories; 11.2g Fat; 2.2g Carbs; 6.5g Protein; 1g Sugars

468. Cheesy Crusted Baked Eggplant

(Ready in about 45 minutes | Servings 3)

Ingredients

1 pound eggplant, sliced
1 tablespoon sea salt
1/4 cup Romano cheese, preferably freshly grated
1/3 cup breadcrumbs
Sea salt and cracked black pepper, to taste
1 egg, whisked
4 tablespoons cornmeal
1/4 cup mozzarella cheese, grated
2 tablespoons fresh Italian parsley, roughly chopped

Directions

Toss the eggplant with 1 tablespoon of salt and let it stand for 30 minutes. Drain and rinse.

Mix the cheese, breadcrumbs, salt, and black pepper in a bowl. Then, add the whisked egg and cornmeal.

Dip the eggplant slices in the batter and press to coat on all sides. Transfer to the lightly greased Air Fryer basket.

Cook at 370 degrees F for 7 to 9 minutes. Turn each slice over and top with the mozzarella. Cook an additional 2 minutes or until the cheese melts.

Serve garnished with fresh Italian parsley. Bon appétit!

Per serving: 233 Calories; 7.6g Fat; 29.3g Carbs; 12.9g Protein; 7.4g Sugars

469. Asian Fennel and Noodle Salad

(Ready in about 20 minutes + chilling time | Servings 3)

Ingredients

1 fennel bulb, quartered
Salt and white pepper, to taste
1 clove garlic, finely chopped
1 green onion, thinly sliced
2 cups Chinese cabbage, shredded
2 tablespoons rice wine vinegar
1 tablespoon honey
2 tablespoons sesame oil
1 teaspoon ginger, freshly grated
1 tablespoon soy sauce
1 cup chow mein noodles, for serving

Directions

Start by preheating your Air Fryer to 370 degrees F.

Now, cook the fennel bulb in the lightly greased cooking basket for 15 minutes, shaking the basket once or twice.

Let it cool completely and toss with the remaining ingredients. Serve well chilled.

Per serving: 248 Calories; 13.2g Fat; 29.9g Carbs; 3.7g Protein; 12.7g Sugars

470. Italian Peperonata Classica

(Ready in about 25 minutes | Servings 4)

Ingredients

2 tablespoons olive oil
4 bell peppers, seeded and sliced
1 serrano pepper, seeded and sliced
1/2 cup onion, peeled and sliced
2 garlic cloves, crushed
2 tomatoes, pureed
2 tablespoons tomato ketchup
Sea salt and black pepper
1 teaspoon cayenne pepper
4 fresh basil leaves
10 Sicilian olives green, pitted and sliced
2 Ciabatta rolls

Directions

Brush the sides and bottom of the cooking basket with 1 tablespoon of olive oil. Add the peppers, onions, and garlic to the cooking basket. Cook for 5 minutes or until tender.

Add the tomatoes, ketchup, salt, black pepper, and cayenne pepper; add the remaining tablespoon of olive oil and cook in the preheated Air Fryer at 380 degrees F for 15 minutes, stirring occasionally.

Divide between individual bowls and garnish with basil leaves and olives. Serve with the Ciabatta rolls. Bon appétit!

Per serving: 389 Calories; 18.4g Fat; 49.1g Carbs; 9.3g Protein; 19.8g Sugars

471. Cheesy Scalloped Potatoes

(Ready in about 45 minutes | Servings 4)

Ingredients

4 medium potatoes
2 tablespoons butter
2 tablespoons all-purpose flour
1 cup milk
1 cup half-and-half

Sea salt and red pepper flakes, to taste
1/2 teaspoon shallot powder
1/2 teaspoon garlic powder
1 1/2 cups Colby cheese, shredded

Directions

Bring a large pot of water to a boil. Cook the whole potatoes for about 20 minutes. Drain the potatoes and let sit until cool enough to handle.

Peel your potatoes and slice into 1/8-inch rounds. Melt the butter in a pan over a moderate flame; add the flour and cook for 1 minute. Slowly and gradually, whisk in the milk; cook until the sauce has thickened.

Add the half-and-half, salt, red pepper, shallot powder, and garlic powder.

Place 1/2 of the potatoes overlapping in a single layer in the lightly greased casserole dish. Spoon 1/2 of the cheese sauce on top of the potatoes. Repeat the layers.

Top with the shredded cheese. Bake in the preheated Air Fryer at 325 degrees F for 20 minutes. Serve warm.

Per serving: 470 Calories; 22g Fat; 50.1g Carbs; 18.6g Protein; 8.7g Sugars

472. Twice-Baked Potatoes with Pancetta

(Ready in about 30 minutes | Servings 5)

Ingredients

2 teaspoons canola oil
5 large russet potatoes, peeled
Sea salt and ground black pepper, to taste

5 slices pancetta, chopped
5 tablespoons Swiss cheese, shredded

Directions

Start by preheating your Air Fryer to 360 degrees F.

Drizzle the canola oil all over the potatoes. Place the potatoes in the Air Fryer basket and cook approximately 20 minutes, shaking the basket periodically.

Lightly crush the potatoes to split and season them with salt and ground black pepper. Add the pancetta and cheese.

Place in the preheated Air Fryer and bake an additional 5 minutes or until cheese has melted. Bon appétit!

Per serving: 401 Calories; 7.7g Fat; 69.9g Carbs; 15.2g Protein; 3.8g Sugars

473. Charred Asparagus and Cherry Tomato Salad

(Ready in about 10 minutes + chilling time | Servings 4)

Ingredients

1/4 cup olive oil
1 pound asparagus, trimmed
1 pound cherry tomatoes
1/4 cup balsamic vinegar
2 garlic cloves, minced

2 scallion stalks, chopped
1/2 teaspoon oregano
Coarse sea salt and ground black pepper, to your liking
2 hard-boiled eggs, sliced

Directions

Start by preheating your Air Fryer to 400 degrees F. Brush the cooking basket with 1 tablespoon of olive oil.

Add the asparagus and cherry tomatoes to the cooking basket. Drizzle 1 tablespoon of olive oil all over your veggies.

Cook for 5 minutes, shaking the basket halfway through the cooking time. Let it cool slightly.

Toss with the remaining olive oil, balsamic vinegar, garlic, scallions, oregano, salt, and black pepper.

Afterwards, add the hard-boiled eggs on the top of your salad and serve.

Per serving: 289 Calories; 16.7g Fat; 30.1g Carbs; 8.9g Protein; 19.9g Sugars

474. Skinny Breaded Baby Portabellas

(Ready in about 15 minutes | Servings 4)

Ingredients

1 1/2 pounds baby portabellas
1/2 cup cornmeal
1/2 cup all-purpose flour
2 eggs
2 tablespoons milk
1 cup breadcrumbs

Sea salt and ground black pepper
1/2 teaspoon shallot powder
1 teaspoon garlic powder
1/2 teaspoon cumin powder
1/2 teaspoon cayenne pepper

Directions

Pat the mushrooms dry with a paper towel.

To begin, set up your breading station. Mix the cornmeal and all-purpose flour in a shallow dish. In a separate dish, whisk the eggs with milk.

Finally, place your breadcrumbs and seasonings in the third dish.

Start by dredging the baby portabellas in the flour mixture; then, dip them into the egg wash. Press the baby portabellas into the breadcrumbs, coating evenly.

Spritz the Air Fryer basket with cooking oil. Add the baby portabellas and cook at 400 degrees F for 6 minutes, flipping them halfway through the cooking time. Bon appétit!

Per serving: 260 Calories; 6.4g Fat; 39.2g Carbs; 12.1g Protein; 5.8g Sugars

475. Crispy Parmesan Asparagus

(Ready in about 20 minutes | Servings 4)

Ingredients

2 eggs
1 teaspoon Dijon mustard
1 cup Parmesan cheese, grated
1 cup bread crumbs

Sea salt and ground black pepper, to taste
18 asparagus spears, trimmed
1/2 cup sour cream

Directions

Start by preheating your Air Fryer to 400 degrees F.

In a shallow bowl, whisk the eggs and mustard. In another shallow bowl, combine the Parmesan cheese, breadcrumbs, salt, and black pepper.

Dip the asparagus spears in the egg mixture, then in the parmesan mixture; press to adhere.

Cook for 5 minutes; work in three batches. Serve with sour cream on the side. Enjoy!

Per serving: 207 Calories; 12.4g Fat; 11.7g Carbs; 12.2g Protein; 1.6g Sugars

SNACKS & APPETIZERS

476. Root Vegetable Chips with Dill Mayonnaise

(Ready in about 40 minutes | Servings 4)

Ingredients

1/2 pound red beetroot, julienned
1/2 pound golden beetroot, julienned
1/4 pound carrot, julienned
Sea salt and ground black pepper, to taste
1 teaspoon olive oil
1/2 cup mayonnaise
1 teaspoon garlic, minced
1/4 teaspoon dried dill weed

Directions

Toss your veggies with salt, black pepper and olive oil.

Arrange the veggie chips in a single layer in the Air Fryer cooking basket.

Cook the veggie chips in the preheated Air Fryer at 340 degrees F for 20 minutes; tossing the basket occasionally to ensure even cooking. Work with two batches.

Meanwhile, mix the mayonnaise, garlic and dill until well combined.

Serve the vegetable chips with the mayo sauce on the side. Bon appétit!

Per serving: 187 Calories; 11.2g Fat; 20.1g Carbs; 2.6g Protein; 11.2g Sugars

477. Parmesan Squash Chips

(Ready in about 20 minutes | Servings 3)

Ingredients

3/4 pound butternut squash, cut into thin rounds
1/2 cup Parmesan cheese, grated
Sea salt and ground black pepper, to taste
1 teaspoon butter
1/2 cup ketchup
1 teaspoon Sriracha sauce

Directions

Toss the butternut squash with Parmesan cheese, salt, black pepper and butter.

Transfer the butternut squash rounds to the Air Fryer cooking basket.

Air Fryer at 400 degrees F for 12 minutes. Shake the Air Fryer basket periodically to ensure even cooking. Work with batches.

While the parmesan squash chips are baking, whisk the ketchup and sriracha and set it aside.

Serve the parmesan squash chips with Sriracha ketchup and enjoy!

Per serving: 174 Calories; 6.1g Fat; 26.1g Carbs; 6.4g Protein; 9.3g Sugars

478. Paprika and Cheese French Fries

(Ready in about 15 minutes | Servings 2)

Ingredients

8 ounces French fries, frozen
1/2 cup Monterey-Jack cheese, grated
1 teaspoon paprika
Sea salt, to taste

Directions

Cook the French fries in your Air Fryer at 400 degrees F for about 7 minutes. Shake the basket and continue to cook for a further 6 minutes.

Top the French fries with cheese, paprika and salt cheese. Continue to cook for 1 minute more or until the cheese has melted. Serve warm and enjoy!

Per serving: 368 Calories; 17.1g Fat; 37.2g Carbs; 16.4g Protein; 0.3g Sugars

479. Mexican Crunchy Cheese Straws

(Ready in about 15 minutes | Servings 3)

Ingredients

1/2 cup almond flour
1/4 teaspoon xanthan gum
1/4 teaspoon shallot powder
1/4 teaspoon garlic powder
1/4 teaspoon ground cumin
1 egg yolk, whisked
1 ounce Manchego cheese, grated
2 ounces Cotija cheese, grated

Directions

Mix all ingredients until everything is well incorporated.

Twist the batter into straw strips and place them on a baking mat inside your Air Fryer.

Cook the cheese straws in your Air Fryer at 360 degrees F for 5 minutes; turn them over and cook an additional 5 minutes.

Let the cheese straws cool before serving. Enjoy!

Per serving: 138 Calories; 11g Fat; 0.8g Carbs; 7.8g Protein; 0.2g Sugars

480. Greek-Style Zucchini Rounds

(Ready in about 15 minutes | Servings 3)

Ingredients

1/2 pound zucchini, cut into thin rounds
1 teaspoon extra-virgin olive oil
1/2 teaspoon dried sage, crushed
1/2 teaspoon oregano
1/4 teaspoon ground bay leaf
Coarse sea salt and ground black pepper, to taste
Greek dipping sauce:
1/2 cup Greek yogurt
1/2 teaspoon fresh lemon juice
2 tablespoons mayonnaise
1/2 teaspoon garlic, pressed

Directions

Toss the zucchini rounds with olive oil and spices and place them in the Air Fryer cooking basket.

Cook in the preheated Air Fryer at 400 degrees F for 10 minutes; shaking the basket halfway through the cooking time.

Let it cool slightly and cook an additional minute or so until crispy and golden brown.

Meanwhile, make the sauce by whisking all the sauce ingredients; place the sauce in the refrigerator until ready to serve.

Serve the crispy zucchini rounds with Greek dipping sauce on the side. Enjoy!

Per serving: 128 Calories; 1.2g Fat; 6.2g Carbs; 3.9g Protein; 2.7g Sugars

481. Homemade Ranch Tater Tots

(Ready in about 15 minutes | Servings 2)

Ingredients

1/2 pound potatoes, peeled and shredded
1/2 teaspoon hot paprika
1/2 teaspoon dried marjoram
1 teaspoon Ranch seasoning mix
2 tablespoons Colby cheese, finely grated (about 1/3 cup)
1 teaspoon butter, melted
Sea salt and ground black pepper, to taste

Directions

In a mixing bowl, thoroughly combine all ingredients until everything is well incorporated.

Transfer your tater tots to a lightly greased Air Fryer cooking basket.

Cook your tater tots in the preheated Air Fryer at 400 degrees F for 12 minutes, shaking the basket halfway through the cooking time to ensure even browning.

Bon appétit!

Per serving: 132 Calories; 3.4g Fat; 21.7g Carbs; 3.9g Protein; 1.1g Sugars

482. Beer-Battered Vidalia Onion Rings

(Ready in about 15 minutes | Servings 2)

Ingredients

1/2 cup all-purpose flour
1/2 teaspoon baking powder
1/4 teaspoon cayenne pepper
1/4 teaspoon dried oregano
Kosher salt and ground black pepper, to taste

1 large egg, beaten
1/4 cup beer
1 cup crushed tortilla chips
1/2 pound Vidalia onions, cut into rings

Directions

In a mixing bowl, thoroughly combine the flour, baking powder, cayenne pepper, oregano, salt, black pepper, egg and beer; mix to combine well.

In another shallow bowl, place the crushed tortilla chips.

Dip the Vidalia rings in the beer mixture; then, coat the rings with the crushed tortilla chips, pressing to adhere.

Transfer the onion rings to the Air Fryer cooking basket and spritz them with a nonstick spray.

Cook the onion rings at 380 degrees F for about 8 minutes, shaking the basket halfway through the cooking time to ensure even browning. Bon appétit!

Per serving: 269 Calories; 4.1g Fat; 48.1g Carbs; 7.9g Protein; 7.7g Sugars

483. Italian-Style Tomato Chips

(Ready in about 20 minutes | Servings 2)

Ingredients

2 tomatoes, cut into thick rounds
1 teaspoon extra-virgin olive oil
Sea salt and fresh ground pepper, to taste

1 teaspoon Italian seasoning mix
1/4 cup Romano cheese, grated

Directions

Start by preheating your Air Fryer to 350 degrees F.

Toss the tomato sounds with remaining ingredients. Transfer the tomato rounds to the cooking basket without overlapping.

Cook your tomato rounds in the preheated Air Fryer for 5 minutes. Flip them over and cook an additional 5 minutes. Work with batches. Bon appétit!

Per serving: 119 Calories; 6.5g Fat; 9.1g Carbs; 6.6g Protein; 1.4g Sugars

484. Bacon Chips with Chipotle Dipping Sauce

(Ready in about 15 minutes | Servings 3)

Ingredients

6 ounces bacon, cut into strips
Chipotle Dipping Sauce:

6 tablespoons sour cream
1/2 teaspoon chipotle chili powder

Directions

Place the bacon strips in the Air Fryer cooking basket.

Cook the bacon strips at 360 degrees F for 5 minutes; turn them over and cook for another 5 minutes.

Meanwhile, make the chipotle dipping sauce by whisking the sour cream and chipotle chili powder; reserve.

Serve the bacon chips with the chipotle dipping sauce and enjoy!

Per serving: 265 Calories; 24.5g Fat; 2.4g Carbs; 8.1g Protein; 0.5g Sugars

485. Sea Scallops and Bacon Kabobs

(Ready in about 10 minutes | Servings 2)

Ingredients

10 sea scallops, frozen
4 ounces bacon, diced
1 teaspoon garlic powder

1 teaspoon paprika
Sea salt and ground black pepper, to taste

Directions

Assemble the skewers alternating sea scallops and bacon. Sprinkle the garlic powder, paprika, salt and black pepper all over your kabobs.

Bake your kabobs in the preheated Air Fryer at 400 degrees F for 6 minutes.

Serve warm with your favorite sauce for dipping. Enjoy!

Per serving: 403 Calories; 22g Fat; 4.3g Carbs; 43.6g Protein; 0g Sugars

486. Hot Cheesy Mushrooms Bites

(Ready in about 10 minutes | Servings 3)

Ingredients

1 teaspoon butter, melted
1 teaspoon fresh garlic, finely minced
4 ounces cheddar cheese, grated
4 tablespoons tortilla chips, crushed

1 tablespoon fresh coriander, chopped
1/2 teaspoon hot sauce
12 button mushrooms, stalks removed and chopped
Sea salt and ground black pepper, to taste

Directions

In a mixing bowl, thoroughly combine the butter, garlic, cheddar cheese, tortilla chips, coriander, hot sauce and chopped mushrooms.

Divide the filling among mushroom caps and transfer them to the air Fryer cooking basket; season them with salt and black pepper.

Cook your mushrooms in the preheated Air Fryer at 400 degrees F for 5 minutes.

Transfer the warm mushrooms to a serving platter and serve at room temperature. Bon appétit!

Per serving: 203 Calories; 14.3g Fat; 7.4g Carbs; 13.3g Protein; 1.5g Sugars

487. Avocado Fries with Lime Sauce

(Ready in about 15 minutes | Servings 4)

Ingredients

1/2 cup plain flour
1/2 milk
1/2 cup tortilla chips, crushed
1/2 teaspoon red pepper flakes, crushed
Sea salt and ground black pepper, to taste

2 avocados, peeled, pitted and sliced
1/2 cup Greek yogurt
4 tablespoons mayonnaise
1 teaspoon fresh lime juice
1/2 teaspoon lime chili seasoning salt

Directions

Mix the plain flour and milk in a plate.

Add the crushed tortilla chips, red pepper flakes, salt and black pepper to another rimmed plate.

Dredge the avocado slices in the flour mixture and then, coat them in the crushed tortilla chips.

Cook the avocado at 390 degrees F for about 8 minutes, shaking the basket halfway through the cooking time.

In the meantime, mix the remaining ingredients, until well combined. Serve warm avocado fries with the lime sauce. Bon appétit!

Per serving: 371 Calories; 27.5g Fat; 27.1g Carbs; 6.4g Protein; 4.5g Sugars

488. Hot Paprika Bacon Deviled Eggs

(Ready in about 15 minutes | Servings 4)

Ingredients

4 eggs
2 ounces bacon bits
2 tablespoons mayonnaise
2 tablespoons cream cheese
1 teaspoon hot sauce

1/2 teaspoon garlic, minced
1 tablespoon pickle relish
1/2 teaspoon hot paprika
Salt and ground black pepper, to taste

Directions

Place the wire rack in the Air Fryer basket and lower the eggs onto the rack.

Cook the eggs at 260 degrees F for 15 minutes.

Transfer the eggs to an ice-cold water bath to stop cooking. Peel the eggs under cold running water; slice them into halves, separating the whites and yolks.

Mash the egg yolks; add in the remaining ingredients and stir to combine; spoon the yolk mixture into the egg whites.

Bon appétit!

Per serving: 178 Calories; 14.3g Fat; 3.6g Carbs; 8.6g Protein; 2.3g Sugars

489. Kale Chips with White Horseradish Mayo

(Ready in about 10 minutes | Servings 1)

Ingredients

2 cups loosely packed kale
1 teaspoon sesame oil
Sea salt and ground black pepper, to taste

1 teaspoon sesame seeds, lightly toasted
1 ounce mayonnaise
1 teaspoon prepared white horseradish

Directions

Toss the kale pieces with sesame oil, salt and black pepper.

Cook the kale pieces at 370 degrees F for 2 minutes; shake the basket and continue to cook for 2 minutes more.

Meanwhile, make the horseradish mayo by whisking the mayonnaise and prepared horseradish.

Let cool slightly, kale chips will crisp up as it cools. Sprinkle toasted sesame seeds over the kale chips.

Serve the kale chips with the horseradish mayo. Bon appétit!

Per serving: 291 Calories; 27.3g Fat; 9.2g Carbs; 3.2g Protein; 4.3g Sugars

490. Crunchy Wontons with Sausage and Peppers

(Ready in about 20 minutes | Servings 4)

Ingredients

20 (3-1/2-inch) wonton wrappers
1/2 pound beef sausage crumbled
1 bell pepper, deveined and chopped
1 teaspoon sesame oil
1/2 teaspoon granulated garlic

1 tablespoon soy sauce
1 tablespoon rice wine vinegar
1 tablespoon honey
1 teaspoon Sriracha sauce
1 teaspoon sesame seeds, toasted

Directions

Mix the crumbled sausage with the chopped pepper and set it aside. Place wonton wrappers on a clean work surface.

Divide the sausage filling between the wrappers. Wet the edge of each wrapper with water, fold the top half over the bottom half and pinch the border to seal.

Place the wontons in the cooking basket and brush them with a little bit of olive oil. Cook the wontons at 400 degrees F for 8 minutes. Work with batches.

In the meantime, whisk the sauce ingredients and set it aside. Serve the warm wontons with the sauce for dipping. Enjoy!

Per serving: 295 Calories; 12.3g Fat; 32g Carbs; 13.2g Protein; 7.1g Sugars

491. Easy Toasted Nuts

(Ready in about 10 minutes | Servings 4)

Ingredients

1/2 cup pecans
1 cup almonds
2 tablespoons egg white

1 tablespoon granulated sugar
A pinch of coarse sea salt

Directions

Toss the pecans and almonds with the egg white, granulated sugar and salt until well coated.

Transfer the pecans and almonds to the Air Fryer cooking basket. Roast the pecans and almonds at 360 degrees F for about 6 to 7 minutes, shaking the basket once or twice.

Taste and adjust seasonings. Bon appétit!

Per serving: 304 Calories; 26.7g Fat; 11.4g Carbs; 9.5g Protein; 4.1g Sugars

492. Cinnamon Pear Chips

(Ready in about 10 minutes | Servings 2)

Ingredients

1 large pear, cored and sliced
1 teaspoon apple pie spice blend

1 teaspoon coconut oil
1 teaspoon honey

Directions

Toss the pear slices with the spice blend, coconut oil and honey.

Then, place the pear slices in the Air Fryer cooking basket and cook at 360 degrees F for about 8 minutes.

Shake the basket once or twice to ensure even cooking. Pear chips will crisp up as it cools. Bon appétit!

Per serving: 94 Calories; 2.6g Fat; 18.1g Carbs; 0.7g Protein; 12.6g Sugars

493. Pecorino Romano Meatballs

(Ready in about 15 minutes | Servings 2)

Ingredients

1/2 pound ground turkey
2 tablespoons tomato ketchup
1 teaspoon stone-ground mustard
2 tablespoons scallions, chopped
1 garlic clove, minced
1/4 Pecorino-Romano cheese, grated

1 egg, beaten
1/2 teaspoon red pepper flakes, crushed
Sea salt and ground black pepper, to taste

Directions

In a mixing bowl, thoroughly combine all ingredients.

Shape the mixture into 6 equal meatballs. Transfer the meatballs to the Air Fryer cooking basket that is previously greased with a nonstick cooking spray.

Cook the meatballs at 360 degrees F for 10 to 11 minutes, shaking the basket occasionally to ensure even cooking. An instant thermometer should read 165 degrees F. Bon appétit!

Per serving: 264 Calories; 14.6g Fat; 3.7g Carbs; 29.7g Protein; 1.6g Sugars

494. Crunchy Roasted Chickpeas

(Ready in about 20 minutes | Servings 2)

Ingredients

1 tablespoon extra-virgin olive oil
8 ounces can chickpeas, drained
1/2 teaspoon smoked paprika

1/2 teaspoon ground cumin
1/2 teaspoon garlic powder
Sea salt, to taste

Directions

Drizzle olive oil over the drained chickpeas and transfer them to the Air Fryer cooking basket.

Cook your chickpeas in the preheated Air Fryer at 395 degrees F for 13 minutes. Turn your Air Fryer to 350 degrees F and cook an additional 6 minutes.

Toss the warm chickpeas with smoked paprika, cumin, garlic and salt. Bon appétit!

Per serving: 184 Calories; 6g Fat; 25.5g Carbs; 8.1g Protein; 4.5g Sugars

495. Pork Crackling with Sriracha Dip

(Ready in about 40 minutes | Servings 3)

Ingredients

1/2 pound pork rind
Sea salt and ground black pepper, to taste
1/2 cup tomato sauce
1 teaspoon Sriracha sauce
1/2 teaspoon stone-ground mustard

Directions

Rub sea salt and pepper on the skin side of the pork rind. Allow it to sit for 30 minutes.

Then, cut the pork rind into chunks using kitchen scissors.

Roast the pork rind at 380 degrees F for 8 minutes; turn them over and cook for a further 8 minutes or until blistered.

Meanwhile, mix the tomato sauce with the Sriracha sauce and mustard. Serve the pork crackling with the Sriracha dip and enjoy!

Per serving: 525 Calories; 49.8g Fat; 10.6g Carbs; 6.8g Protein; 5.6g Sugars

496. Fish Sticks with Honey Mustard Sauce

(Ready in about 10 minutes | Servings 3)

Ingredients

10 ounces fish sticks
1/2 cup mayonnaise
2 teaspoons yellow mustard
2 teaspoons honey

Directions

Add the fish sticks to the Air Fryer cooking basket; drizzle the fish sticks with a nonstick cooking spray.

Cook the fish sticks at 400 degrees F for 5 minutes; turn them over and cook for another 5 minutes.

Meanwhile, mix the mayonnaise, yellow mustard and honey until well combined. Serve the fish sticks with the honey mustard sauce for dipping. Enjoy!

Per serving: 315 Calories; 19.8g Fat; 28.5g Carbs; 6.4g Protein; 12.7g Sugars

497. Coconut Banana Chips

(Ready in about 10 minutes | Servings 2)

Ingredients

1 large banana, peeled and sliced
1 teaspoon coconut oil
1/4 teaspoon ground cinnamon
A pinch of coarse salt
2 tablespoons coconut flakes

Directions

Toss the banana slices with the coconut oil, cinnamon and salt. Transfer banana slices to the Air Fryer cooking basket.

Cook the banana slices at 375 degrees F for about 8 minutes, shaking the basket every 2 minutes.

Scatter coconut flakes over the banana slices and let banana chips cool slightly before serving. Bon appétit!

Per serving: 105 Calories; 3.9g Fat; 18.5g Carbs; 0.9g Protein; 10.2g Sugars

498. Sweet Potato Chips with Chili Mayo

(Ready in about 35 minutes | Servings 3)

Ingredients

1 sweet potato, cut into 1/8-inch-thick slices
1 teaspoon olive oil
Sea salt and cracked mixed peppercorns, to taste
1/2 teaspoon turmeric powder
1/3 cup mayonnaise
1 teaspoon granulated garlic
1/2 teaspoon red chili flakes

Directions

Toss the sweet potato slices with olive oil, salt, cracked peppercorns and turmeric powder.

Cook your sweet potatoes at 380 degrees F for 33 to 35 minutes, tossing the basket every 10 minutes to ensure even cooking. Work with batches.

Meanwhile, mix the mayonnaise, garlic and red chili flakes to make the sauce.

The sweet potato chips will crisp up as it cools. Serve the sweet potato chips with the chili mayo on the side.

Per serving: 218 Calories; 19.6g Fat; 9.5g Carbs; 1g Protein; 1.9g Sugars

499. Pepper and Bacon Mini Skewers

(Ready in about 10 minutes | Servings 4)

Ingredients

4 ounces bacon, diced
2 bell peppers, sliced
1/4 cup barbecue sauce
1 teaspoon Ranch seasoning blend
1/2 cup tomato sauce
1 teaspoon jalapeno, minced

Directions

Assemble the skewers alternating bacon and bell pepper. Toss them with barbecue sauce and Ranch seasoning blend.

Cook the mini skewers in the preheated Air Fryer at 400 degrees F for 6 minutes.

Mix the tomato sauce and minced jalapeno. Bon appétit!

Per serving: 198 Calories; 11.5g Fat; 17.1g Carbs; 5.1g Protein; 11.1g Sugars

500. Cheesy Potato Puffs

(Ready in about 15 minutes | Servings 4)

Ingredients

8 ounces potato puffs
1 teaspoon olive oil
4 ounces cheddar cheese, shredded
1/2 cup tomato sauce
1 teaspoon Dijon mustard
1/2 teaspoon Italian seasoning mix

Directions

Brush the potato puffs with olive oil and transfer them to the Air Fryer cooking basket.

Cook the potato puffs at 400 degrees F for 10 minutes, shaking the basket occasionally to ensure even browning. Top them with cheese and continue to cook for 2 minutes more until the cheese melts.

Meanwhile, whisk the tomato sauce with the mustard and Italian seasoning mix. Serve the warm potato puffs with cocktail sticks and the sauce on the side. Bon appétit!

Per serving: 207 Calories; 8.5g Fat; 25.1g Carbs; 5.9g Protein; 5.8g Sugars

501. Southwestern Caprese Bites

(Ready in about 10 minutes | Servings 2)

Ingredients

1/2 pound cherry tomatoes
1 tablespoon extra-virgin olive oil
1/2 pound bocconcini, drained
2 tablespoon fresh basil leaves
1/2 teaspoon chili powder
1/2 teaspoon ground cumin
1/4 teaspoon garlic powder
Sea salt and ground black pepper, to taste

Directions

Brush the cherry tomatoes with olive oil and transfer them to the cooking basket. Bake the cherry tomatoes at 400 degrees F for 4 minutes.

Assemble the bites by using a toothpick and skewer cherry tomatoes, bocconcini and fresh basil leaves.

Season with chili powder, cumin, garlic powder, salt and black pepper. Arrange on a nice serving platter and enjoy!

Per serving: 243 Calories; 7.5g Fat; 8.4g Carbs; 31g Protein; 3.8g Sugars

502. Prosciutto Stuffed Jalapeños

(Ready in about 15 minutes | Servings 2)

Ingredients

8 fresh jalapeño peppers, deseeded and cut in half lengthwise
4 ounces Ricotta cheese, at room temperature
1/4 teaspoon cayenne pepper
1/2 teaspoon granulated garlic
8 slices prosciutto, chopped

Directions

Place the fresh jalapeño peppers on a clean surface.

Mix the remaining ingredients in a bowl; divide the filling between the jalapeño peppers. Transfer the peppers to the Air Fryer cooking basket.

Cook the stuffed peppers at 400 degrees F for 15 minutes. Serve and enjoy!

Per serving: 178 Calories; 8.7g Fat; 11.7g Carbs; 14.3g Protein; 4.6g Sugars

503. Salmon, Cheese and Cucumber Bites

(Ready in about 15 minutes | Servings 3)

Ingredients

1/2 pound salmon
1 teaspoon extra-virgin olive oil
1/2 teaspoon onion powder
1/4 teaspoon cumin powder
1 teaspoon granulated garlic
Sea salt and ground black pepper, to taste
2 ounces cream cheese
1 English cucumber, cut into 1-inch rounds

Directions

Pat the salmon dry and drizzle it with olive oil.

Season the salmon with onion powder, cumin, granulated garlic, salt and black pepper. Transfer the salmon to the Air Fryer cooking basket.

Cook the salmon at 400 degrees F for 5 minutes; turn the salmon over and continue to cook for 5 minutes more or until opaque. Cut the salmon into bite-sized pieces.

Spread 1 teaspoon of cream cheese on top of each cucumber slice; top each slice with a piece of salmon.

Insert a tiny party fork down the center to keep in place. Bon appétit!

Per serving: 184 Calories; 10.6g Fat; 4.3g Carbs; 17.3g Protein; 2.3g Sugars

504. Easy Mexican Elote

(Ready in about 10 minutes | Servings 2)

Ingredients

2 ears of corn, husked
4 tablespoons Mexican crema
4 tablespoons Mexican cheese blend, crumbled
1 teaspoon fresh lime juice
Sea salt and chili powder, to taste
1 tablespoon fresh cilantro, chopped

Directions

Cook the corn in the preheated Air Fryer at 390 degrees F for about 6 minutes.

Mix the Mexican crema, Mexican cheese blend, lime juice, salt and chili powder in a bowl.

Afterwards, insert a wooden stick into the core as a handle. Rub each ear of corn with the topping mixture.

Garnish with fresh chopped cilantro. Serve immediately.

Per serving: 203 Calories; 7.6g Fat; 28.3g Carbs; 11.5g Protein; 4.8g Sugars

505. Classic Jiaozi (Chinese Dumplings)

(Ready in about 15 minutes | Servings 3)

Ingredients

1/2 pound ground pork
1 cup Napa cabbage, shredded
2 scallion stalks, chopped
1 ounce bamboo shoots, shredded
1/2 teaspoon garlic paste
1 teaspoon fresh ginger, peeled and grated
8 ounces round wheat dumpling

Sauce:
2 tablespoons rice vinegar
1/4 cup soy sauce
1 tablespoon ketchup
1 teaspoon deli mustard
1 teaspoon honey
1 teaspoon sesame seeds, lightly toasted

Directions

Cook the pork in a wok that is preheated over medium-high heat; cook until no longer pink and stir in the Napa cabbage, scallions, bamboo shoots, garlic paste and ginger; salt to taste and stir to combine well.

Divide the pork mixture between dumplings. Moisten the edge of each dumpling with water, fold the top half over the bottom half and press together firmly.

Place your dumplings in the Air Fryer cooking basket and spritz them with cooking spray. Cook your dumplings at 400 degrees F for 8 minutes. Work with batches.

While your dumplings are cooking, whisk the sauce ingredients. Serve the warm dumplings with the sauce for dipping. Enjoy!

Per serving: 539 Calories; 23g Fat; 66.2g Carbs; 22.2g Protein; 8.1g Sugars

506. Eggplant Parm Chips

(Ready in about 30 minutes | Servings 2)

Ingredients

1/2 pound eggplant, cut into rounds
Kosher salt and ground black pepper, to taste
1/2 teaspoon shallot powder
1/2 teaspoon porcini powder
1/2 teaspoon garlic powder
1/4 teaspoon cayenne pepper
1/2 cup Parmesan cheese, grated

Directions

Toss the eggplant rounds with the remaining ingredients until well coated on both sides.

Bake the eggplant chips at 400 degrees F for 15 minutes; shake the basket and continue to cook for 15 minutes more.

Let cool slightly, eggplant chips will crisp up as it cools.

Bon appétit!

Per serving: 148 Calories; 7.2g Fat; 13.5g Carbs; 8.2g Protein; 5.1g Sugars

507. Kid-Friendly Mozzarella Sticks

(Ready in about 10 minutes | Servings 3)

Ingredients

2 eggs
1/4 cup corn flour
1/4 cup plain flour
1 cup Italian-style dried breadcrumbs
1 teaspoon Italian seasoning mix
10 ounces mozzarella, cut into 1/2-inch sticks
1 cup marinara sauce

Directions

Beat the eggs in a shallow bowl until pale and frothy. Then, in a second bowl, place both types of flour. In a third bowl, mix breadcrumbs with Italian seasoning mix.

Dip the mozzarella sticks in the beaten eggs and allow the excess egg to drip back into the bowl. Then, dip the mozzarella sticks in the flour mixture. Lastly, roll them over the seasoned breadcrumbs.

Cook the mozzarella sticks in the preheated Air Fryer at 370 degrees F for 4 minutes. Flip them over and continue to cook for 2 to 3 minutes more.

Serve the mozzarella sticks with marinara sauce. Bon appétit!

Per serving: 270 Calories; 3.7g Fat; 23.1g Carbs; 36.2g Protein; 5.7g Sugars

508. Mint Plantain Bites

(Ready in about 10 minutes | Servings 3)

Ingredients

1 pound plantains, peeled and cut into rounds
1 teaspoon coconut oil

A pinch of coarse sea salt
1 tablespoon mint leaves, chopped

Directions

Start by preheating your Air Fryer to 350 degrees F.

Brush the plantain rounds with coconut oil and sprinkle with coarse sea salt.

Cook the plantain rounds in the preheated Air Fryer for 5 minutes; shake the basket and cook for a further 5 minutes or until golden on the top.

Garnish with roughly chopped mint and serve. Enjoy!

Per serving: 198 Calories; 2.1g Fat; 48.1g Carbs; 2g Protein; 22.7g Sugars

509. Chili-Lime French Fries

(Ready in about 20 minutes | Servings 3)

Ingredients

1 pound potatoes, peeled and cut into matchsticks
1 teaspoon olive oil
1 lime, freshly squeezed

1 teaspoon chili powder
Sea salt and ground black pepper, to taste

Directions

Toss your potatoes with the remaining ingredients until well coated.

Transfer your potatoes to the Air Fryer cooking basket.

Cook the French fries at 370 degrees F for 9 minutes. Shake the cooking basket and continue to cook for about 9 minutes. Serve immediately. Bon appétit!

Per serving: 128 Calories; 1.9g Fat; 26.6g Carbs; 2.8g Protein; 2.2g Sugars

510. Hot Roasted Cauliflower Florets

(Ready in about 20 minutes | Servings 3)

Ingredients

1/2 cup plain flour
1/2 teaspoon shallot powder
1 teaspoon garlic powder
1/4 teaspoon dried dill weed
1/2 teaspoon chipotle powder

Sea salt and ground black pepper, to taste
1/2 cup rice milk
2 tablespoons coconut oil, softened
1 pound cauliflower florets

Directions

In a mixing bowl, thoroughly combine the flour, spices, rice milk and coconut oil. Mix to combine well.

Coat the cauliflower florets with the batter and allow the excess batter to drip back into the bowl.

Cook the cauliflower florets at 400 degrees F for 12 minutes, shaking the basket once or twice to ensure even browning.

Serve with some extra hot sauce, if desired. Bon appétit!

Per serving: 218 Calories; 9.9g Fat; 28.6g Carbs; 5.2g Protein; 3.7g Sugars

511. Mustard Brussels Sprout Chips

(Ready in about 25 minutes | Servings 2)

Ingredients

1/2 pound Brussels sprouts, cut into small pieces
1 teaspoon deli mustard
1 teaspoon sesame oil
1 teaspoon champagne vinegar

1/4 teaspoon paprika
1/4 teaspoon cayenne pepper
Coarse sea salt and ground black pepper, to taste

Directions

Start by preheating your Air Fryer to 360 degrees F.

Toss the Brussels sprouts with the other ingredients until well coated. Transfer the Brussels sprouts to the Air Fryer cooking basket.

Cook the Brussels sprout chips in the preheated Air Fryer for about 20 minutes, shaking the basket every 6 to 7 minutes.

Serve with your favorite sauce for dipping. Enjoy!

Per serving: 112 Calories; 7.2g Fat; 10.3g Carbs; 3.9g Protein; 2.5g Sugars

512. Apple Chips with Walnuts

(Ready in about 35 minutes | Servings 2)

Ingredients

2 apples, peeled, cored and sliced
1/2 teaspoon ground cloves

1 teaspoon cinnamon
1/4 cup walnuts

Directions

Toss the apple slices with ground cloves and cinnamon.

Place the apple slices in the Air Fryer cooking basket and cook at 360 degrees F for 10 minutes or until crisp. Reserve.

Then, toast the walnuts at 300 degrees F for 10 minutes; now, shake the basket and cook for another 10 minutes.

Chop the walnuts and scatter them over the apple slices. Bon appétit!

Per serving: 163 Calories; 6.8g Fat; 27.3g Carbs; 2.1g Protein; 19.2g Sugars

513. Sticky Glazed Wings

(Ready in about 30 minutes | Servings 2)

Ingredients

1/2 pound chicken wings
1 tablespoon sesame oil
2 tablespoons brown sugar

1 tablespoon Worcestershire sauce
1 tablespoon hot sauce
1 tablespoon balsamic vinegar

Directions

Brush the chicken wings with sesame oil and transfer them to the Air Fryer cooking basket.

Cook the chicken wings at 370 degrees F for 12 minutes; turn them over and cook for a further 10 minutes.

Meanwhile, bring the other ingredients to a boil in a saucepan; cook for 2 to 3 minutes or until thoroughly cooked.

Toss the warm chicken wings with the sauce and place them on a serving platter. Serve and enjoy!

Per serving: 318 Calories; 19.3g Fat; 11.6g Carbs; 22.1g Protein; 10.2g Sugars

514. Greek-Style Deviled Eggs

(Ready in about 20 minutes | Servings 2)

Ingredients

4 eggs
1 tablespoon chives, chopped
1 tablespoon parsley, chopped
2 tablespoons Kalamata olives, pitted and chopped

1 tablespoon Greek-style yogurt
1 teaspoon habanero pepper, seeded and chopped
Sea salt and crushed red pepper flakes, to taste

Directions

Place the wire rack in the Air Fryer basket and lower the eggs onto the rack.

Cook the eggs at 260 degrees F for 15 minutes.

Transfer the eggs to an ice-cold water bath to stop cooking. Peel the eggs under cold running water; slice them into halves, separating the whites and yolks.

Mash the egg yolks with the remaining ingredients and mix to combine.

Spoon the yolk mixture into the egg whites and serve well chilled. Enjoy!

Per serving: 154 Calories; 9.3g Fat; 3.6g Carbs; 12.1g Protein; 1.9g Sugars

515. Mini Plantain Cups

(Ready in about 10 minutes | Servings 3)

Ingredients

2 blackened plantains, chopped
1/4 cup all-purpose flour
1/2 cup cornmeal
1/2 cup milk
1 tablespoon coconut oil

1 teaspoon fresh ginger, peeled and minced
A pinch of salt
A pinch of ground cinnamon

Directions

In a mixing bowl, thoroughly combine all ingredients until everything is well incorporated.

Spoon the batter into a greased mini muffin tin.

Bake the mini plantain cups in your Air Fryer at 330 degrees F for 6 to 7 minutes or until golden brown.

Bon appétit!

Per serving: 322 Calories; 7.1g Fat; 63g Carbs; 5.5g Protein; 20.1g Sugars

516. Baby Carrots with Asian Flair

(Ready in about 20 minutes | Servings 3)

Ingredients

1 pound baby carrots
2 tablespoons sesame oil
1/2 teaspoon Szechuan pepper
1 teaspoon Wuxiang powder (Five-spice powder)

1 tablespoon honey
1 large garlic clove, crushed
1 (1-inch) piece fresh ginger root, peeled and grated
2 tablespoons tamari sauce

Directions

Start by preheating your Air Fryer to 380 degrees F.

Toss all ingredients together and place them in the Air Fryer basket.

Cook for 15 minutes, shaking the basket halfway through the cooking time. Enjoy!

Per serving: 165 Calories; 9.3g Fat; 20.6g Carbs; 1.6g Protein; 11.8g Sugars

517. Mexican-Style Corn on the Cob with Bacon

(Ready in about 20 minutes | Servings 4)

Ingredients

2 slices bacon
4 ears fresh corn, shucked and cut into halves
1 avocado, pitted, peeled and mashed

1 teaspoon ancho chili powder
2 garlic cloves
2 tablespoons cilantro, chopped
1 teaspoon lime juice
Salt and black pepper, to taste

Directions

Start by preheating your Air Fryer to 400 degrees F. Cook the bacon for 6 to 7 minutes; chop into small chunks and reserve.

Spritz the corn with cooking spray. Cook at 395 degrees F for 8 minutes, turning them over halfway through the cooking time.

Mix the reserved bacon with the remaining ingredients. Spoon the bacon mixture over the corn on the cob and serve immediately. Bon appétit!

Per serving: 261 Calories; 14.2g Fat; 32.5g Carbs; 7.4g Protein; 5.1g Sugars

518. Beer Battered Vidalia Rings

(Ready in about 30 minutes | Servings 4)

Ingredients

1/2 pound Vidalia onions, sliced into rings
1/2 cup all-purpose flour
1/4 cup cornmeal
1/2 teaspoon baking powder
Sea salt and freshly cracked black pepper, to taste

1/4 teaspoon garlic powder
2 eggs, beaten
1/2 cup lager-style beer
1 cup plain breadcrumbs
2 tablespoons peanut oil

Directions

Place the onion rings in the bowl with icy cold water; let them soak approximately 20 minutes; drain the onion rings and pat them dry.

In a shallow bowl, mix the flour, cornmeal, baking powder, salt, and black pepper. Add the garlic powder, eggs and beer; mix well to combine.

In another shallow bowl, mix the breadcrumbs with the peanut oil. Dip the onion rings in the flour/egg mixture; then, dredge in the breadcrumb mixture. Roll to coat them evenly.

Spritz the Air Fryer basket with cooking spray; arrange the breaded onion rings in the basket.

Cook in the preheated Air Fryer at 400 degrees F for 4 to 5 minutes, turning them over halfway through the cooking time. Bon appétit!

Per serving: 318 Calories; 10.7g Fat; 43.9g Carbs; 9.4g Protein; 5.2g Sugars

519. Wonton Sausage Appetizers

(Ready in about 20 minutes | Servings 5)

Ingredients

1/2 pound ground sausage
2 tablespoons scallions, chopped
1 garlic clove, minced
1/2 tablespoon fish sauce

1 teaspoon Sriracha sauce
20 wonton wrappers
1 egg, whisked with 1 tablespoon water

Directions

In a mixing bowl, thoroughly combine the ground sausage, scallions, garlic, fish sauce, and Sriracha.

Divide the mixture between the wonton wrappers. Dip your fingers in the egg wash

Fold the wonton in half. Bring up the 2 ends of the wonton and use the egg wash to stick them together. Pinch the edges and coat each wonton with the egg wash.

Place the folded wontons in the lightly greased cooking basket. Cook at 360 degrees F for 10 minutes. Work in batches and serve warm. Bon appétit!

Per serving: 199 Calories; 5.8g Fat; 19.2g Carbs; 14g Protein; 0.3g Sugars

520. Cocktail Cranberry Meatballs

(Ready in about 15 minutes | Servings 5)

Ingredients

1/2 pound ground beef
1/2 pound ground turkey
1/4 cup Parmesan cheese, grated
1/4 cup breadcrumbs
1 small shallot, chopped
2 eggs, whisked
1/2 teaspoon garlic powder
1/2 teaspoon porcini powder

Sea salt and ground black pepper, to taste
1 teaspoon red pepper flakes, crushed
1 tablespoon soy sauce
1 (8-ounce) can jellied cranberry sauce
6 ounces tomato-based chili sauce

Directions

In a mixing bowl, combine the ground meat together with the cheese, breadcrumbs, shallot, eggs, and spices.

Shape the mixture into 1-inch balls.

Cook the meatballs in the preheated Air Fryer at 380 degrees for 5 minutes. Shake halfway through the cooking time. Work in batches.

Whisk the soy sauce, cranberry sauce, and chili sauce in a mixing bowl. Pour the sauce over the meatballs and bake an additional 2 minutes.

Serve with cocktail sticks. Bon appétit!

Per serving: 365 Calories; 11.6g Fat; 38.1g Carbs; 25.6g Protein; 28.4g Sugars

521. Paprika Potato Chips

(Ready in about 50 minutes | Servings 3)

Ingredients

3 potatoes, thinly sliced
1 teaspoon sea salt
1 teaspoon garlic powder

1 teaspoon paprika
1/4 cup ketchup

Directions

Add the sliced potatoes to a bowl with salted water. Let them soak for 30 minutes. Drain and rinse your potatoes.

Pat dry and toss with salt.

Cook in the preheated Air Fryer at 400 degrees F for 15 minutes, shaking the basket occasionally.

Work in batches. Toss with the garlic powder and paprika. Serve with ketchup. Enjoy!

Per serving: 190 Calories; 0.3g Fat; 43.8g Carbs; 4.7g Protein; 6.1g Sugars

522. Barbecue Little Smokies

(Ready in about 20 minutes | Servings 6)

Ingredients

1 pound beef cocktail wieners

10 ounces barbecue sauce

Directions

Start by preheating your Air Fryer to 380 degrees F.

Prick holes into your sausages using a fork and transfer them to the baking pan.

Cook for 13 minutes. Spoon the barbecue sauce into the pan and cook an additional 2 minutes.

Serve with toothpicks. Bon appétit!

Per serving: 182 Calories; 4.6g Fat; 19.2g Carbs; 15.9g Protein; 15.7g Sugars

523. Sweet Potato Fries with Spicy Dip

(Ready in about 50 minutes | Servings 3)

Ingredients

3 medium sweet potatoes, cut into 1/3-inch sticks
2 tablespoons olive oil
1 teaspoon kosher salt

Spicy Dip:
1/4 cup mayonnaise
1/4 cup Greek yogurt
1/4 teaspoon Dijon mustard
1 teaspoon hot sauce

Directions

Soak the sweet potato in icy cold water for 30 minutes. Drain the sweet potatoes and pat them dry with paper towels.

Toss the sweet potatoes with olive oil and salt.

Place in the lightly greased cooking basket. Cook in the preheated Air Fryer at 360 degrees F for 14 minutes. Wok in batches.

While the sweet potatoes are cooking, make the spicy dip by whisking the remaining ingredients. Place in the refrigerator until ready to serve. Enjoy!

Per serving: 332 Calories; 23.6g Fat; 27.9g Carbs; 3g Protein; 9.8g Sugars

524. Crunchy Broccoli Fries

(Ready in about 15 minutes | Servings 4)

Ingredients

1 pound broccoli florets
1/2 teaspoon onion powder
1 teaspoon granulated garlic
1/2 teaspoon cayenne pepper

Sea salt and ground black pepper, to taste
2 tablespoons sesame oil
4 tablespoons parmesan cheese, preferably freshly grated

Directions

Start by preheating the Air Fryer to 400 degrees F.

Blanch the broccoli in salted boiling water until al dente, about 3 to 4 minutes. Drain well and transfer to the lightly greased Air Fryer basket.

Add the onion powder, garlic, cayenne pepper, salt, black pepper, and sesame oil.

Cook for 6 minutes, tossing halfway through the cooking time. Bon appétit!

Per serving: 127 Calories; 8.6g Fat; 9.9g Carbs; 4.9g Protein; 2.6g Sugars

525. Kale Chips with Tahini Sauce

(Ready in about 15 minutes | Servings 4)

Ingredients

5 cups kale leaves, torn into 1-inch pieces
1 ½ tablespoons sesame oil
1/2 teaspoon shallot powder
1 teaspoon garlic powder
1/4 teaspoon porcini powder

1/2 teaspoon mustard seeds
1 teaspoon salt
1/3 cup tahini (sesame butter)
1 tablespoon fresh lemon juice
2 cloves garlic, minced

Directions

Toss the kale with the sesame oil and seasonings.

Bake in the preheated Air Fryer at 350 degrees F for 10 minutes, shaking the cooking basket occasionally.

Bake until the edges are brown. Work in batches.

Meanwhile, make the sauce by whisking all ingredients in a small mixing bowl. Serve and enjoy!

Per serving: 170 Calories; 15g Fat; 7.1g Carbs; 4.2g Protein; 0.7g Sugars

526. Famous Blooming Onion with Mayo Dip

(Ready in about 25 minutes | Servings 3)

Ingredients

1 large Vidalia onion
1/2 cup all-purpose flour
1 teaspoon salt
1/2 teaspoon ground black pepper
1 teaspoon cayenne pepper
1/2 teaspoon dried thyme
1/2 teaspoon dried oregano
1/2 teaspoon ground cumin

2 eggs
1/4 cup milk
Mayo Dip:
3 tablespoons mayonnaise
3 tablespoons sour cream
1 tablespoon horseradish, drained
Kosher salt and freshly ground black pepper, to taste

Directions

Cut off the top 1/2 inch of the Vidalia onion; peel your onion and place it cut-side down. Starting 1/2 inch from the root, cut the onion in half. Make a second cut that splits each half in two. You will have 4 quarters held together by the root.

Repeat these cuts, splitting the 4 quarters to yield eighths; then, you should split them again until you have 16 evenly spaced cuts. Turn the onion over and gently separate the outer pieces using your fingers.

In a mixing bowl, thoroughly combine the flour and spices. In a separate bowl, whisk the eggs and milk. Dip the onion into the egg mixture, followed by the flour mixture.

Spritz the onion with cooking spray and transfer to the lightly greased cooking basket. Cook for 370 degrees F for 12 to 15 minutes.

Meanwhile, make the mayo dip by whisking the remaining ingredients. Serve and enjoy!

Per serving: 222 Calories; 9.9g Fat; 24.6g Carbs; 8.6g Protein; 3.9g Sugars

527. Thyme-Roasted Sweet Potatoes

(Ready in about 35 minutes | Servings 3)

Ingredients

1 pound sweet potatoes, peeled, cut into bite-sized pieces
2 tablespoons olive oil
1 teaspoon sea salt

1/4 teaspoon freshly ground black pepper
1/2 teaspoon cayenne pepper
2 fresh thyme sprigs

Directions

Arrange the potato slices in a single layer in the lightly greased cooking basket. Add the olive oil, salt, black pepper, and cayenne pepper; toss to coat.

Bake at 380 degrees F for 30 minutes, shaking the cooking basket occasionally.

Bake until tender and slightly browned, working in batches. Serve warm, garnished with thyme sprigs. Bon appétit!

Per serving: 143 Calories; 9.7g Fat; 13.3g Carbs; 3.7g Protein; 0g Sugars

528. Chicken Nuggets with Campfire Sauce

(Ready in about 20 minutes | Servings 6)

Ingredients

1 pound chicken breasts, slice into tenders
1/2 teaspoon cayenne pepper
Salt and black pepper, to taste
1/4 cup cornmeal
1 egg, whisked
1/2 cup seasoned breadcrumbs
1/4 cup mayo
1/4 cup barbecue sauce

Directions

Pat the chicken tenders dry with a kitchen towel. Season with the cayenne pepper, salt, and black pepper.

Dip the chicken tenders into the cornmeal, followed by the egg. Press the chicken tenders into the breadcrumbs, coating evenly.

Place the chicken tenders in the lightly greased Air Fryer basket. Cook at 360 degrees for 9 to 12 minutes, turning them over to cook evenly.

In a mixing bowl, thoroughly combine the mayonnaise with the barbecue sauce. Serve the chicken nuggets with the sauce for dipping. Bon appétit!

Per serving: 211 Calories; 5.4g Fat; 18.4g Carbs; 18.9g Protein; 6.3g Sugars

529. Avocado Fries with Chipotle Sauce

(Ready in about 20 minutes | Servings 3)

Ingredients

2 tablespoons fresh lime juice
1 avocado, pitted, peeled, and sliced
Pink Himalayan salt and ground white pepper, to taste
1/4 cup flour
1 egg
1/2 cup breadcrumbs
1 chipotle chili in adobo sauce
1/4 cup light mayonnaise
1/4 cup plain Greek yogurt

Directions

Drizzle lime juice all over the avocado slices and set aside.

Then, set up your breading station. Mix the salt, pepper, and all-purpose flour in a shallow dish. In a separate dish, whisk the egg.

Finally, place your breadcrumbs in a third dish.

Start by dredging the avocado slices in the flour mixture; then, dip them into the egg. Press the avocado slices into the breadcrumbs, coating evenly.

Cook in the preheating Air Fryer at 380 degrees F for 11 minutes, shaking the cooking basket halfway through the cooking time.

Meanwhile, blend the chipotle chili, mayo, and Greek yogurt in your food processor until the sauce is creamy and uniform.

Serve the warm avocado slices with the sauce on the side. Enjoy!

Per serving: 273 Calories; 18.4g Fat; 23.1g Carbs; 6.7g Protein; 7.7g Sugars

530. Asian Twist Chicken Wings

(Ready in about 20 minutes | Servings 6)

Ingredients

1 ½ pounds chicken wings
2 teaspoons sesame oil
Kosher salt and ground black pepper, to taste
2 tablespoons tamari sauce
1 tablespoon rice vinegar
2 garlic clove, minced
2 tablespoons honey
2 sun-dried tomatoes, minced

Directions

Toss the chicken wings with the sesame oil, salt, and pepper. Add chicken wings to a lightly greased baking pan.

Roast the chicken wings in the preheated Air Fryer at 390 degrees F for 7 minutes. Turn them over once or twice to ensure even cooking.

In a mixing dish, thoroughly combine the tamari sauce, vinegar, garlic, honey, and sun-dried tomatoes.

Pour the sauce all over the chicken wings; bake an additional 5 minutes. Bon appétit!

Per serving: 195 Calories; 5.7g Fat; 9.4g Carbs; 25.5g Protein; 6.4g Sugars

531. Roasted Cauliflower Florets

(Ready in about 20 minutes | Servings 2)

Ingredients

3 cups cauliflower florets
2 teaspoons sesame oil
1 teaspoon onion powder
1 teaspoon garlic powder
Sea salt and cracked black pepper, to taste
1 teaspoon paprika

Directions

Start by preheating your Air Fryer to 400 degrees F.

Toss the cauliflower with the remaining ingredients; toss to coat well.

Cook for 12 minutes, shaking the cooking basket halfway through the cooking time. They will crisp up as they cool. Bon appétit!

Per serving: 80 Calories; 4.9g Fat; 7.9g Carbs; 3.1g Protein; 3.1g Sugars

532. Parsnip Chips with Spicy Citrus Aioli

(Ready in about 20 minutes | Servings 4)

Ingredients

1 pound parsnips, peel long strips
2 tablespoons sesame oil
Sea salt and ground black pepper, to taste
1 teaspoon red pepper flakes, crushed
1/2 teaspoon curry powder
1/2 teaspoon mustard seeds
Spicy Citrus Aioli:
1/4 cup mayonnaise
1 tablespoon fresh lime juice
1 clove garlic, smashed
Salt and black pepper, to taste

Directions

Start by preheating the Air Fryer to 380 degrees F.

Toss the parsnip chips with the sesame oil, salt, black pepper, red pepper, curry powder, and mustard seeds.

Cook for 15 minutes, shaking the Air Fryer basket periodically.

Meanwhile, make the sauce by whisking the mayonnaise, lime juice, garlic, salt, and pepper. Place in the refrigerator until ready to use. Bon appétit!

Per serving: 207 Calories; 12.1g Fat; 23.8g Carbs; 2.8g Protein; 7g Sugars

533. Classic Deviled Eggs

(Ready in about 20 minutes | Servings 3)

Ingredients

5 eggs
2 tablespoons mayonnaise
2 tablespoons sweet pickle relish
Sea salt, to taste
1/2 teaspoon mixed peppercorns, crushed

Directions

Place the wire rack in the Air Fryer basket; lower the eggs onto the wire rack.

Cook at 270 degrees F for 15 minutes.

Transfer them to an ice-cold water bath to stop the cooking. Peel the eggs under cold running water; slice them into halves.

Mash the egg yolks with the mayo, sweet pickle relish, and salt; spoon yolk mixture into egg whites. Arrange on a nice serving platter and garnish with the mixed peppercorns. Bon appétit!

Per serving: 261 Calories; 19.2g Fat; 5.5g Carbs; 15.5g Protein; 4.1g Sugars

534. Cajun Cheese Sticks

(Ready in about 15 minutes | Servings 4)

Ingredients

1/2 cup all-purpose flour
2 eggs
1/2 cup parmesan cheese, grated
1 tablespoon Cajun seasonings
8 cheese sticks, kid-friendly
1/4 cup ketchup

Directions

To begin, set up your breading station. Place the all-purpose flour in a shallow dish. In a separate dish, whisk the eggs.

Finally, mix the parmesan cheese and Cajun seasoning in a third dish.

Start by dredging the cheese sticks in the flour; then, dip them into the egg. Press the cheese sticks into the parmesan mixture, coating evenly.

Place the breaded cheese sticks in the lightly greased Air Fryer basket. Cook at 380 degrees F for 6 minutes.

Serve with ketchup and enjoy!

Per serving: 372 Calories; 22.7g Fat; 19.5g Carbs; 21.8g Protein; 3.8g Sugars

535. Puerto Rican Tostones

(Ready in about 15 minutes | Servings 2)

Ingredients

1 ripe plantain, sliced
1 tablespoon sunflower oil
A pinch of grated nutmeg
A pinch of kosher salt

Directions

Toss the plantains with the oil, nutmeg, and salt in a bowl.

Cook in the preheated Air Fryer at 400 degrees F for 10 minutes, shaking the cooking basket halfway through the cooking time.

Adjust the seasonings to taste and serve immediately.

Per serving: 151 Calories; 7.1g Fat; 23.9g Carbs; 0.6g Protein; 10.7g Sugars

536. The Best Calamari Appetizer

(Ready in about 20 minutes | Servings 6)

Ingredients

1 ½ pounds calamari tubes, cleaned, cut into rings
Sea salt and ground black pepper, to taste
2 tablespoons lemon juice
1 cup cornmeal
1 cup all-purpose flour
1 teaspoon paprika
1 egg, whisked
1/4 cup buttermilk

Directions

Preheat your Air Fryer to 390 degrees F. Rinse the calamari and pat it dry. Season with salt and black pepper. Drizzle lemon juice all over the calamari.

Now, combine the cornmeal, flour, and paprika in a bowl; add the whisked egg and buttermilk.

Dredge the calamari in the egg/flour mixture.

Arrange them in the cooking basket. Spritz with cooking oil and cook for 9 to 12 minutes, shaking the basket occasionally. Work in batches.

Serve with toothpicks. Bon appétit!

Per serving: 274 Calories; 3.3g Fat; 36.8g Carbs; 22.9g Protein; 1.3g Sugars

537. Fried Pickle Chips with Greek Yogurt Dip

(Ready in about 20 minutes | Servings 5)

Ingredients

1/2 cup cornmeal
1/2 cup all-purpose flour
1 teaspoon cayenne pepper
1/2 teaspoon shallot powder
1 teaspoon garlic powder
1/2 teaspoon porcini powder
Kosher salt and ground black pepper, to taste
2 eggs
2 cups pickle chips, pat dry with kitchen towels
Greek Yogurt Dip:
1/2 cup Greek yogurt
1 clove garlic, minced
1/4 teaspoon ground black pepper
1 tablespoon fresh chives, chopped

Directions

In a shallow bowl, mix the cornmeal and flour; add the seasonings and mix to combine well. Beat the eggs in a separate shallow bowl.

Dredge the pickle chips in the flour mixture, then, in the egg mixture. Press the pickle chips into the flour mixture again, coating evenly.

Cook in the preheated Air Fryer at 400 degrees F for 5 minutes; shake the basket and cook for 5 minutes more. Work in batches.

Meanwhile, mix all the sauce ingredients until well combined. Serve the fried pickles with the Greek yogurt dip and enjoy.

Per serving: 138 Calories; 3.2g Fat; 21.8g Carbs; 5.7g Protein; 1.9g Sugars

538. Teriyaki Chicken Drumettes

(Ready in about 40 minutes | Servings 6)

Ingredients

1 ½ pounds chicken drumettes
Sea salt and cracked black pepper, to taste
2 tablespoons fresh chives, roughly chopped
Teriyaki Sauce:
1 tablespoon sesame oil
1/4 cup soy sauce
1/2 cup water
1/4 cup honey
1/2 teaspoon Five-spice powder
2 tablespoons rice wine vinegar
1/2 teaspoon fresh ginger, grated
2 cloves garlic, crushed
1 tablespoon corn starch dissolved in 3 tablespoons of water

Directions

Start by preheating your Air Fryer to 380 degrees F. Rub the chicken drumettes with salt and cracked black pepper.

Cook in the preheated Air Fryer approximately 15 minutes. Turn them over and cook an additional 7 minutes.

While the chicken drumettes are roasting, combine the sesame oil, soy sauce, water, honey, Five-spice powder, vinegar, ginger, and garlic in a pan over medium heat. Cook for 5 minutes, stirring occasionally.

Add the cornstarch slurry, reduce the heat, and let it simmer until the glaze thickens.

After that, brush the glaze all over the chicken drumettes. Air-fry for a further 6 minutes or until the surface is crispy. Serve topped with the remaining glaze and garnished with fresh chives. Bon appétit!

Per serving: 286 Calories; 14.8g Fat; 13.5g Carbs; 23.8g Protein; 12.1g Sugars

539. Baked Cheese Crisps

(Ready in about 15 minutes | Servings 4)

Ingredients

1/2 cup Parmesan cheese, shredded
1 cup Cheddar cheese, shredded
1 teaspoon Italian seasoning
1/2 cup marinara sauce

Directions

Start by preheating your Air Fryer to 350 degrees F. Place a piece of parchment paper in the cooking basket.

Mix the cheese with the Italian seasoning.

Add about 1 tablespoon of the cheese mixture (per crisp) to the basket, making sure they are not touching. Bake for 6 minutes or until browned to your liking.

Work in batches and place them on a large tray to cool slightly. Serve with the marinara sauce. Bon appétit!

Per serving: 198 Calories; 14.7g Fat; 4.7g Carbs; 12g Protein; 1.4g Sugars

540. Mexican Cheesy Zucchini Bites

(Ready in about 25 minutes | Servings 4)

Ingredients

1 large-sized zucchini, thinly sliced
1/2 cup flour
1/4 cup yellow cornmeal
1 egg, whisked
1/2 cup tortilla chips, crushed
1/2 cup Queso Añejo, grated
Salt and cracked pepper, to taste

Directions

Pat dry the zucchini slices with a kitchen towel.

Mix the remaining ingredients in a shallow bowl; mix until everything is well combined. Dip each zucchini slice in the prepared batter.

Cook in the preheated Air Fryer at 400 degrees F for 12 minutes, shaking the basket halfway through the cooking time.

Work in batches until the zucchini slices are crispy and golden brown. Enjoy!

Per serving: 231 Calories; 9g Fat; 29.3g Carbs; 8.4g Protein; 2.3g Sugars

541. Bruschetta with Fresh Tomato and Basil

(Ready in about 15 minutes | Servings 3)

Ingredients

1/2 Italian bread, sliced
2 garlic cloves, peeled
2 tablespoons extra-virgin olive oil
2 ripe tomatoes, chopped

1 teaspoon dried oregano
Salt, to taste
8 fresh basil leaves, roughly chopped

Directions

Place the bread slices on the lightly greased Air Fryer grill pan. Bake at 370 degrees F for 3 minutes.

Cut a clove of garlic in half and rub over one side of the toast; brush with olive oil. Add the chopped tomatoes. Sprinkle with oregano and salt.

Increase the temperature to 380 degrees F. Cook in the preheated Air Fryer for 3 minutes more.

Garnish with fresh basil and serve. Bon appétit!

Per serving: 161 Calories; 5.5g Fat; 23.8g Carbs; 4.4g Protein; 4.5g Sugars

542. Roasted Parsnip Sticks with Salted Caramel

(Ready in about 25 minutes | Servings 4)

Ingredients

1 pound parsnip, trimmed, scrubbed, cut into sticks
2 tablespoon avocado oil
2 tablespoons granulated sugar

2 tablespoons butter
1/4 teaspoon ground allspice
1/2 teaspoon coarse salt

Directions

Toss the parsnip with the avocado oil; bake in the preheated Air Fryer at 380 degrees F for 15 minutes, shaking the cooking basket occasionally to ensure even cooking.

Then, heat the sugar and 1 tablespoon of water in a small pan over medium heat. Cook until the sugar has dissolved; bring to a boil.

Keep swirling the pan around until the sugar reaches a rich caramel color. Pour in 2 tablespoons of cold water. Now, add the butter, allspice, and salt. The mixture should be runny.

Afterwards, drizzle the salted caramel over the roasted parsnip sticks and enjoy!

Per serving: 213 Calories; 13.1g Fat; 24.4g Carbs; 1.4g Protein; 9.3g Sugars

543. Greek-Style Squash Chips

(Ready in about 25 minutes | Servings 4)

Ingredients

1/2 cup seasoned breadcrumbs
1/2 cup Parmesan cheese, grated
Sea salt and ground black pepper, to taste
1/4 teaspoon oregano
2 yellow squash, cut into slices
2 tablespoons grapeseed oil

Sauce:
1/2 cup Greek-style yogurt
1 tablespoon fresh cilantro, chopped
1 garlic clove, minced
Freshly ground black pepper, to your liking

Directions

In a shallow bowl, thoroughly combine the seasoned breadcrumbs, Parmesan, salt, black pepper, and oregano.

Dip the yellow squash slices in the prepared batter, pressing to adhere.

Brush with the grapeseed oil and cook in the preheated Air Fryer at 400 degrees F for 12 minutes. Shake the Air Fryer basket periodically to ensure even cooking. Work in batches.

While the chips are baking, whisk the sauce ingredients; place in your refrigerator until ready to serve. Enjoy!

Per serving: 180 Calories; 10.3g Fat; 13.3g Carbs; 5.8g Protein; 2.8g Sugars

544. Romano Cheese and Broccoli Balls

(Ready in about 25 minutes | Servings 4)

Ingredients

1/2 pound broccoli
1/2 cup Romano cheese, grated
2 garlic cloves, minced
1 shallot, chopped
4 eggs, beaten

2 tablespoons butter, at room temperature
1/2 teaspoon paprika
1/4 teaspoon dried basil
Sea salt and ground black pepper, to taste

Directions

Add the broccoli to your food processor and pulse until the consistency resembles rice.

Stir in the remaining ingredients; mix until everything is well combined. Shape the mixture into bite-sized balls and transfer them to the lightly greased cooking basket.

Cook in the preheated Air Fryer at 375 degrees F for 16 minutes, shaking halfway through the cooking time. Serve with cocktail sticks and tomato ketchup on the side.

Per serving: 192 Calories; 15.2g Fat; 2.9g Carbs; 11.5g Protein; 0.6g Sugars

545. Summer Meatball Skewers

(Ready in about 20 minutes | Servings 6)

Ingredients

1/2 pound ground pork
1/2 pound ground beef
1 teaspoon dried onion flakes
1 teaspoon fresh garlic, minced
1 teaspoon dried parsley flakes

Salt and black pepper, to taste
1 red pepper, 1-inch pieces
1 cup pearl onions
1/2 cup barbecue sauce

Directions

Mix the ground meat with the onion flakes, garlic, parsley flakes, salt, and black pepper. Shape the mixture into 1-inch balls.

Thread the meatballs, pearl onions, and peppers alternately onto skewers.

Microwave the barbecue sauce for 10 seconds.

Cook in the preheated Air Fryer at 380 degrees for 5 minutes. Turn the skewers over halfway through the cooking time. Brush with the sauce and cook for a further 5 minutes. Work in batches.

Serve with the remaining barbecue sauce and enjoy!

Per serving: 218 Calories; 13g Fat; 10.7g Carbs; 14.1g Protein; 8.5g Sugars

546. Italian-Style Tomato-Parmesan Crisps

(Ready in about 20 minutes | Servings 4)

Ingredients

4 Roma tomatoes, sliced
2 tablespoons olive oil
Sea salt and white pepper, to taste

1 teaspoon Italian seasoning mix
4 tablespoons Parmesan cheese, grated

Directions

Start by preheating your Air Fryer to 350 degrees F. Generously grease the Air Fryer basket with nonstick cooking oil.

Toss the sliced tomatoes with the remaining ingredients. Transfer them to the cooking basket without overlapping.

Cook in the preheated Air Fryer for 5 minutes. Shake the cooking basket and cook an additional 5 minutes. Work in batches.

Serve with Mediterranean aioli for dipping, if desired. Bon appétit!

Per serving: 90 Calories; 8.2g Fat; 2.7g Carbs; 1.8g Protein; 1.1g Sugars

547. Green Bean Crisps

(Ready in about 20 minutes | Servings 4)

Ingredients

1 egg, beaten
1/4 cup cornmeal
1/4 cup parmesan, grated
1 teaspoon sea salt

1/2 teaspoon red pepper flakes, crushed
1 pound green beans
2 tablespoons grapeseed oil

Directions

In a mixing bowl, combine together the egg, cornmeal, parmesan, salt, and red pepper flakes; mix to combine well.

Dip the green beans into the batter and transfer them to the cooking basket. Brush with the grapeseed oil.

Cook in the preheated Air Fryer at 390 degrees F for 4 minutes. Shake the basket and cook for a further 3 minutes. Work in batches.

Taste, adjust the seasonings and serve. Bon appétit!

Per serving: 164 Calories; 10.2g Fat; 13.1g Carbs; 6.1g Protein; 1.1g Sugars

548. Spinach Chips with Chili Yogurt Dip

(Ready in about 20 minutes | Servings 3)

Ingredients

3 cups fresh spinach leaves
1 tablespoon extra-virgin olive oil
1 teaspoon sea salt
1/2 teaspoon cayenne pepper
1 teaspoon garlic powder

Chili Yogurt Dip:
1/4 cup yogurt
2 tablespoons mayonnaise
1/2 teaspoon chili powder

Directions

Toss the spinach leaves with the olive oil and seasonings.

Bake in the preheated Air Fryer at 350 degrees F for 10 minutes, shaking the cooking basket occasionally.

Bake until the edges brown, working in batches.

In the meantime, make the sauce by whisking all ingredients in a mixing dish. Serve immediately.

Per serving: 128 Calories; 12.3g Fat; 3.1g Carbs; 1.8g Protein; 1.2g Sugars

549. Cheesy Zucchini Sticks

(Ready in about 20 minutes | Servings 2)

Ingredients

1 zucchini, slice into strips
2 tablespoons mayonnaise
1/4 cup tortilla chips, crushed
1/4 cup Romano cheese, shredded

Sea salt and black pepper, to your liking
1 tablespoon garlic powder
1/2 teaspoon red pepper flakes

Directions

Coat the zucchini with mayonnaise.

Mix the crushed tortilla chips, cheese and spices in a shallow dish.

Then, coat the zucchini sticks with the cheese/chips mixture.

Cook in the preheated Air Fryer at 400 degrees F for 12 minutes, shaking the basket halfway through the cooking time.

Work in batches until the sticks are crispy and golden brown. Bon appétit!

Per serving: 197 Calories; 16.6g Fat; 8.7g Carbs; 4.4g Protein; 0.3g Sugars

550. Party Greek Keftedes

(Ready in about 20 minutes | Servings 6)

Ingredients

Greek Keftedes:
1/2 pound mushrooms, chopped
1/2 pound pork sausage, chopped
1 teaspoon shallot powder
1 teaspoon granulated garlic
1 teaspoon dried rosemary
1 teaspoon dried basil
1 teaspoon dried oregano
2 eggs

2 tablespoons cornbread crumbs
Tzatziki Dip:
1 Lebanese cucumbers, grated, juice squeezed out
1 cup full-fat Greek yogurt
1 tablespoon fresh lemon juice
1 garlic clove, minced
1 tablespoon extra-virgin olive oil
1/2 teaspoon salt

Directions

In a mixing bowl, thoroughly combine all ingredients for the Greek keftedes.

Shape the meat mixture into bite-sized balls.

Cook in the preheated Air Fryer at 380 degrees for 10 minutes, shaking the cooking basket once or twice to ensure even cooking.

Meanwhile, make the tzatziki dip by mixing all ingredients. Serve the keftedes with cocktail sticks and tzatziki dip on the side. Enjoy!

Per serving: 208 Calories; 15.8g Fat; 6.1g Carbs; 10.3g Protein; 3.3g Sugars

551. Loaded Tater Tot Bites

(Ready in about 20 minutes | Servings 6)

Ingredients

24 tater tots, frozen
1 cup Swiss cheese, grated

6 tablespoons Canadian bacon, cooked and chopped
1/4 cup Ranch dressing

Directions

Spritz the silicone muffin cups with non-stick cooking spray. Now, press the tater tots down into each cup.

Divide the cheese, bacon, and Ranch dressing between tater tot cups.

Cook in the preheated Air Fryer at 395 degrees for 10 minutes. Serve in paper cake cups. Bon appétit!

Per serving: 164 Calories; 9.7g Fat; 9.2g Carbs; 9.3g Protein; 0.8g Sugars

552. Southern Cheese Straws

(Ready in about 30 minutes | Servings 6)

Ingredients

1 cup all-purpose flour
Sea salt and ground black pepper, to taste
1/4 teaspoon smoked paprika

1/2 teaspoon celery seeds
4 ounces mature Cheddar, cold, freshly grated
1 sticks butter

Directions

Start by preheating your air Fryer to 330 degrees F. Line the Air Fryer basket with parchment paper.

In a mixing bowl, thoroughly combine the flour, salt, black pepper, paprika, and celery seeds.

Then, combine the cheese and butter in the bowl of a stand mixer. Slowly stir in the flour mixture and mix to combine well.

Then, pack the dough into a cookie press fitted with a star disk. Pipe the long ribbons of dough across the parchment paper. Then cut into six-inch lengths.

Bake in the preheated Air Fryer for 15 minutes.

Repeat with the remaining dough. Let the cheese straws cool on a rack. You can store them between sheets of parchment in an airtight container. Bon appétit!

Per serving: 269 Calories; 19.3g Fat; 16.6g Carbs; 7.4g Protein; 0.1g Sugars

553. Sea Scallops and Bacon Skewers

(Ready in about 50 minutes | Servings 6)

Ingredients

1/2 pound sea scallops
1/2 cup coconut milk
6 ounces orange juice
1 tablespoon vermouth
Sea salt and ground black pepper, to taste

1/2 pound bacon, diced
1 shallot, diced
1 teaspoon garlic powder
1 teaspoon paprika

Directions

In a ceramic bowl, place the sea scallops, coconut milk, orange juice, vermouth, salt, and black pepper; let it marinate for 30 minutes.

Assemble the skewers alternating the scallops, bacon, and shallots. Sprinkle garlic powder and paprika all over the skewers.

Bake in the preheated air Fryer at 400 degrees F for 6 minutes. Serve warm and enjoy!

Per serving: 138 Calories; 3.6g Fat; 8.3g Carbs; 17.6g Protein; 5.5g Sugars

554. Blue Cheesy Potato Wedges

(Ready in about 20 minutes | Servings 4)

Ingredients

2 Yukon Gold potatoes, peeled
and cut into wedges
2 tablespoons ranch seasoning

Kosher salt, to taste
1/2 cup blue cheese, crumbled

Directions

Sprinkle the potato wedges with the ranch seasoning and salt. Grease generously the Air Fryer basket.

Place the potatoes in the cooking basket.

Roast in the preheated Air Fryer at 400 degrees for 12 minutes. Top with the cheese and roast an additional 3 minutes or until cheese begins to melt. Bon appétit!

Per serving: 157 Calories; 4.9g Fat; 22.1g Carbs; 6g Protein; 1.2g Sugars

555. Cocktail Sausage and Veggies on a Stick

(Ready in about 25 minutes | Servings 4)

Ingredients

16 cocktail sausages, halved
16 pearl onions
1 red bell pepper, cut into 1
½-inch pieces

1 green bell pepper, cut into 1
½-inch pieces
Salt and cracked black pepper, to
taste
1/2 cup tomato chili sauce

Directions

Thread the cocktail sausages, pearl onions, and peppers alternately onto skewers. Sprinkle with salt and black pepper.

Cook in the preheated Air Fryer at 380 degrees for 15 minutes, turning the skewers over once or twice to ensure even cooking.

Serve with the tomato chili sauce on the side. Enjoy!

Per serving: 190 Calories; 6.8g Fat; 18.5g Carbs; 13.3g Protein; 10.3g Sugars

556. Yakitori (Japanese Chicken Skewers)

(Ready in about 2 hours 15 minutes | Servings 4)

Ingredients

1/2 pound chicken tenders, cut
bite-sized pieces
1 clove garlic, minced
1 teaspoon coriander seeds
Sea salt and ground pepper, to
taste

2 tablespoons Shoyu sauce
2 tablespoons sake
1 tablespoon fresh lemon juice
1 teaspoon sesame oil

Directions

Place the chicken tenders, garlic, coriander, salt, black pepper, Shoyu sauce, sake, and lemon juice in a ceramic dish; cover and let it marinate for 2 hours.

Then, discard the marinade and tread the chicken tenders onto bamboo skewers.

Place the skewered chicken in the lightly greased Air Fryer basket. Drizzle sesame oil all over the skewered chicken.

Cook at 360 degrees for 6 minutes. Turn the skewered chicken over; brush with the reserved marinade and cook for a further 6 minutes. Enjoy!

Per serving: 93 Calories; 2.7g Fat; 2.7g Carbs; 12.1g Protein; 1g Sugars

557. Spicy Korean Short Ribs

(Ready in about 35 minutes | Servings 4)

Ingredients

1 pound meaty short ribs
1/2 rice vinegar
1/2 cup soy sauce
1 tablespoon brown sugar
1 tablespoons Sriracha sauce
2 garlic cloves, minced
1 tablespoon daenjang (soybean
paste)

1 teaspoon kochukaru (chili
pepper flakes)
Sea salt and ground black pepper,
to taste
1 tablespoon sesame oil
1/4 cup green onions, roughly
chopped

Directions

Place the short ribs, vinegar, soy sauce, sugar, Sriracha, garlic, and spices in Ziploc bag; let it marinate overnight.

Rub the sides and bottom of the Air Fryer basket with sesame oil. Discard the marinade and transfer the ribs to the prepared cooking basket.

Cook the marinated ribs in the preheated Air Fryer at 365 degrees for 17 minutes. Turn the ribs over, brush with the reserved marinade, and cook an additional 15 minutes.

Garnish with green onions. Bon appétit!

Per serving: 328 Calories; 19.6g Fat; 12.5g Carbs; 26g Protein; 9.1g Sugars

558. Crunchy Roasted Pepitas

(Ready in about 20 minutes | Servings 4)

Ingredients

2 cups fresh pumpkin seeds with
shells
1 tablespoon olive oil

1 teaspoon sea salt
1 teaspoon ground coriander
1 teaspoon cayenne pepper

Directions

Toss the pumpkin seeds with the olive oil.

Spread in an even layer in the Air Fryer basket; roast the seeds at 350 degrees F for 15 minutes, shaking the basket every 5 minutes.

Immediately toss the seeds with the salt, coriander, salt, and cayenne pepper. Enjoy!

Per serving: 199 Calories; 17.8g Fat; 4.3g Carbs; 8.8g Protein; 0.3g Sugars

559. Quick and Easy Popcorn

(Ready in about 20 minutes | Servings 4)

Ingredients

2 tablespoons dried corn kernels
1 teaspoon safflower oil
Kosher salt, to taste

1 teaspoon red pepper flakes,
crushed

Directions

Add the dried corn kernels to the Air Fryer basket; brush with safflower oil.

Cook at 395 degrees F for 15 minutes, shaking the basket every 5 minutes.

Sprinkle with salt and red pepper flakes. Bon appétit!

Per serving: 41 Calories; 1.9g Fat; 4.9g Carbs; 1g Protein; 0.6g Sugars

560. Cheddar Cheese Lumpia Rolls

(Ready in about 20 minutes | Servings 5)

Ingredients

5 ounces mature cheddar cheese,
cut into 15 sticks

15 pieces spring roll lumpia
wrappers
2 tablespoons sesame oil

Directions

Wrap the cheese sticks in the lumpia wrappers. Transfer to the Air Fryer basket. Brush with sesame oil.

Bake in the preheated Air Fryer at 395 degrees for 10 minutes or until the lumpia wrappers turn golden brown. Work in batches.

Shake the Air Fryer basket occasionally to ensure even cooking. Bon appétit!

Per serving: 128 Calories; 6.2g Fat; 14g Carbs; 3.7g Protein; 0g Sugars

561. Easy and Delicious Pizza Puffs

(Ready in about 15 minutes | Servings 6)

Ingredients

6 ounces crescent roll dough
1/2 cup mozzarella cheese,
shredded
3 ounces pepperoni

3 ounces mushrooms, chopped
1 teaspoon oregano
1 teaspoon garlic powder
1/4 cup Marina sauce, for dipping

Directions

Unroll the crescent dough. Roll out the dough using a rolling pin; cut into 6 pieces.

Place the cheese, pepperoni, and mushrooms in the center of each pizza puff. Sprinkle with oregano and garlic powder.

Fold each corner over the filling using wet hands. Press together to cover the filling entirely and seal the edges.

Now, spritz the bottom of the Air Fryer basket with cooking oil. Lay the pizza puffs in a single layer in the cooking basket. Work in batches.

Bake at 370 degrees F for 5 to 6 minutes or until golden brown. Serve with the marinara sauce for dipping.

Per serving: 186 Calories; 12g Fat; 12.4g Carbs; 6.5g Protein; 3.6g Sugars

562. Red Beet Chips with Pizza Sauce

(Ready in about 30 minutes | Servings 4)

Ingredients

2 red beets, thinly sliced	1/2 teaspoon ground black pepper
1 tablespoon grapeseed oil	1/4 teaspoon cumin powder
1 teaspoon seasoned salt	1/2 cup pizza sauce

Directions

Toss the red beets with the oil, salt, black pepper, and cumin powder.

Arrange the beet slices in a single layer in the Air Fryer basket.

Cook in the preheated Air Fryer at 330 degrees F for 13 minutes. Serve with the pizza sauce and enjoy!

Per serving: 66 Calories; 3.7g Fat; 7.7g Carbs; 1.2g Protein; 3.8g Sugars

563. Paprika Zucchini Bombs with Goat Cheese

(Ready in about 20 minutes | Servings 4)

Ingredients

1 cup zucchini, grated, juice squeezed out	1/2 cup cornbread crumbs
1 egg	1/2 cup parmesan cheese, grated
1 garlic clove, minced	1/2 cup goat cheese, grated
1/2 cup all-purpose flour	Salt and black pepper, to taste
	1 teaspoon paprika

Directions

Start by preheating your Air Fryer to 330 degrees F. Spritz the cooking basket with nonstick cooking oil.

Mix all ingredients until everything is well incorporated. Shape the zucchini mixture into golf sized balls and place them in the cooking basket.

Cook in the preheated Air Fryer for 15 to 18 minutes, shaking the basket periodically to ensure even cooking.

Garnish with some extra paprika if desired and serve at room temperature. Bon appétit!

Per serving: 201 Calories; 9.5g Fat; 16.5g Carbs; 12.7g Protein; 1.2g Sugars

564. The Best Party Mix Ever

(Ready in about 15 minutes | Servings 10)

Ingredients

2 cups mini pretzels	1 tablespoon Creole seasoning
1 cup mini crackers	2 tablespoons butter, melted
1 cup peanuts	

Directions

Toss all ingredients in the Air Fryer basket.

Cook in the preheated Air Fryer at 360 degrees F approximately 9 minutes until lightly toasted. Shake the basket periodically. Enjoy!

Per serving: 228 Calories; 12.2g Fat; 24.7g Carbs; 5.9g Protein; 0.6g Sugars

565. Cauliflower Bombs with Sweet & Sour Sauce

(Ready in about 25 minutes | Servings 4)

Ingredients

Cauliflower Bombs:	1 red bell pepper, jarred
1/2 pound cauliflower	1 clove garlic, minced
2 ounces Ricotta cheese	1 teaspoon sherry vinegar
1/3 cup Swiss cheese	1 tablespoon tomato puree
1 egg	2 tablespoons olive oil
1 tablespoon Italian seasoning mix	Salt and black pepper, to taste
Sweet & Sour Sauce:	

Directions

Blanch the cauliflower in salted boiling water about 3 to 4 minutes until al dente. Drain well and pulse in a food processor.

Add the remaining ingredients for the cauliflower bombs; mix to combine well.

Bake in the preheated Air Fryer at 375 degrees F for 16 minutes, shaking halfway through the cooking time.

In the meantime, pulse all ingredients for the sauce in your food processor until combined. Season to taste. Serve the cauliflower bombs with the Sweet & Sour Sauce on the side. Bon appétit!

Per serving: 156 Calories; 11.9g Fat; 7.2g Carbs; 6.9g Protein; 3.3g Sugars

566. Crunchy Roasted Chickpeas

(Ready in about 25 minutes | Servings 4)

Ingredients

1 (15-ounce) can chickpeas, drained and patted dry	1/2 teaspoon garlic powder
1 tablespoon sesame oil	1 teaspoon coriander, minced
1/8 cup Romano cheese, grated	1/2 teaspoon red pepper flakes, crushed
1/4 teaspoon mustard powder	Coarse sea salt and ground black pepper, to taste
1/2 teaspoon shallot powder	

Directions

Toss all ingredients in a mixing bowl.

Roast in the preheated Air Fryer at 380 degrees F for 10 minutes, shaking the basket halfway through the cooking time.

Work in batches. Bon appétit!

Per serving: 226 Calories; 7.7g Fat; 28.4g Carbs; 11.1g Protein; 5g Sugars

567. Homemade Apple Chips

(Ready in about 20 minutes | Servings 4)

Ingredients

2 cooking apples, cored and thinly sliced	1/4 teaspoon ground cloves
1 teaspoon peanut oil	1/4 teaspoon ground cinnamon
	1 tablespoon smooth peanut butter

Directions

Toss the apple slices with the peanut oil.

Bake at 350 degrees F for 5 minutes; shake the basket to ensure even cooking and continue to cook an additional 5 minutes.

Spread each apple slice with a little peanut butter and sprinkle with ground cloves and cinnamon. Bon appétit!

Per serving: 92 Calories; 3.4g Fat; 16.4g Carbs; 1.3g Protein; 12g Sugars

568. Mini Turkey and Corn Burritos

(Ready in about 25 minutes | Servings 6)

Ingredients

1 tablespoon olive oil
1/2 pound ground turkey
2 tablespoons shallot, minced
1 garlic clove, smashed
1 red bell pepper, seeded and chopped
1 ancho chili pepper, seeded and minced

1/2 teaspoon ground cumin
Sea salt and freshly ground black pepper, to taste
1/3 cup salsa
6 ounces sweet corn kernels
12 (8-inch) tortilla shells
1 tablespoon butter, melted
1/2 cup sour cream, for serving

Directions

Heat the olive oil in a sauté pan over medium-high heat. Cook the ground meat and shallots for 3 to 4 minutes.

Add the garlic and peppers and cook an additional 3 minutes or until fragrant. After that, add the spices, salsa, and corn. Stir until everything is well combined.

Place about 2 tablespoons of the meat mixture in the center of each tortilla. Roll your tortillas to seal the edges and make the burritos.

Brush each burrito with melted butter and place them in the lightly greased cooking basket. Bake at 395 degrees F for 10 minutes, turning them over halfway through the cooking time.

Garnish each burrito with a dollop of sour cream and serve.

Per serving: 242 Calories; 13.6g Fat; 19.9g Carbs; 13.7g Protein; 2.1g Sugars

569. Crunchy Asparagus with Mediterranean Aioli

(Ready in about 50 minutes | Servings 4)

Ingredients

Crunchy Asparagus:
2 eggs
3/4 cup breadcrumbs
2 tablespoons Parmesan cheese
Sea salt and ground white pepper, to taste
1/2 pound asparagus, cleaned and trimmed

Cooking spray
Mediterranean Aioli:
4 garlic cloves, minced
4 tablespoons olive oil mayonnaise
1 tablespoons lemon juice, freshly squeezed

Directions

Start by preheating your Air Fryer to 400 degrees F.

In a shallow bowl, thoroughly combine the eggs, breadcrumbs, Parmesan cheese, salt, and white pepper.

Dip the asparagus spears in the egg mixture; roll to coat well. Cook in the preheated Air Fryer for 5 to 6 minutes; work in two batches.

Place the garlic on a piece of aluminum foil and spritz with cooking spray. Wrap the garlic in the foil.

Cook in the preheated Air Fryer at 400 degrees for 12 minutes. Check the garlic, open the top of the foil and continue to cook for 10 minutes more.

Let it cool for 10 to 15 minutes; remove the cloves by squeezing them out of the skins; mash the garlic and add the mayo and fresh lemon juice; whisk until everything is well combined.

Serve the asparagus with the chilled aioli on the side. Bon appétit!

Per serving: 222 Calories; 13.6g Fat; 18.2g Carbs; 7.1g Protein; 1.3g Sugars

570. Party Chicken Pillows

(Ready in about 20 minutes | Servings 4)

Ingredients

1 teaspoon olive oil
1 cup ground chicken
1 (8-ounces) can Pillsbury Crescent Roll dough
Sea salt and ground black pepper, to taste

1 teaspoon onion powder
1/2 teaspoon garlic powder
4 tablespoons tomato paste
4 ounces cream cheese, at room temperature
2 tablespoons butter, melted

Directions

Heat the olive oil in a pan over medium-high heat. Then, cook the ground chicken until browned or about 4 minutes.

Unroll the crescent dough. Roll out the dough using a rolling pin; cut into 8 pieces.

Place the browned chicken, salt, black pepper, onion powder, garlic powder, tomato paste, and cheese in the center of each piece.

Fold each corner over the filling using wet hands. Press together to cover the filling entirely and seal the edges.

Now, spritz the bottom of the Air Fryer basket with cooking oil. Lay the chicken pillows in a single layer in the cooking basket. Drizzle the melted butter all over chicken pillows.

Bake at 370 degrees F for 6 minutes or until golden brown. Work in batches. Bon appétit!

Per serving: 245 Calories; 16.6g Fat; 10.1g Carbs; 14.8g Protein; 3.5g Sugars

RICE & GRAINS

571. Mom's Favorite Wontons

(Ready in about 10 minutes | Servings 2)

Ingredients

1/2 pound ground turkey
1 teaspoon shallot powder
1 teaspoon instant dashi granules
1 teaspoon fish sauce
1 tablespoon tomato paste

1 teaspoon soy sauce
1 teaspoon sesame oil
Seas salt and ground black pepper, to taste
20 wonton wrappers, defrosted

Directions

Brush a nonstick skillet with cooking spray. Once hot, cook the ground turkey until no longer pink, crumbling with a fork. Stir in the other ingredients, except for the wonton wrappers; stir to combine well.

Place the wonton wrappers on a clean work surface. Divide the filling between wrappers. Wet the edge of each wrapper with water, fold top half over bottom half and pinch border to seal.

Cook your wontons at 400 degrees F for 8 minutes; working in batches. Bon appétit!

Per serving: 445 Calories; 12.7g Fat; 50.8g Carbs; 32g Protein; 2.8g Sugars

572. Classic Honey Muffins

(Ready in about 20 minutes | Servings 3)

Ingredients

2 ½ ounces all-purpose flour
1 teaspoon baking powder
A pinch of ground cloves
A pinch of coarse salt
1/2 teaspoon vanilla extract

2 tablespoons honey
1 egg
2 ounces milk
2 tablespoons butter, melted

Directions

In a mixing bowl, combine the ingredients in the order listed above. Spritz a silicone muffin tin with a nonstick cooking spray.

Divide the batter between cups.

Bake in the preheated Air Fryer at 330 degrees F for 12 to 15 minutes. Rotate the muffin tin halfway through the cooking time.

Bon appétit!

Per serving: 345 Calories; 14.7g Fat; 43.2g Carbs; 10.8g Protein; 16.9g Sugars

573. Old-Fashioned Greek Tiganites

(Ready in about 50 minutes | Servings 3)

Ingredients

1/2 cup plain flour
1/2 cup barley flour
1 teaspoon baking powder
A pinch of salt
A pinch of sugar
A pinch of cinnamon
1 egg

1/2 cup milk
1/2 cup carbonated water
1 tablespoon butter, melted
3 tablespoons honey
3 tablespoons walnuts, chopped
3 tablespoons Greek yogurt

Directions

Thoroughly combine the flour, baking powder, salt, sugar and cinnamon in a large bowl. Fold in the egg and mix again.

Gradually pour in the milk, water and melted butter, whisking continuously, until well combined.

Let the batter stand for about 30 minutes.

Spritz the Air Fryer baking pan with a cooking spray. Pour the batter into the pan using a measuring cup.

Cook at 230 degrees F for 6 to 8 minutes or until golden brown. Repeat with the remaining batter.

Serve your tiganites with the honey, walnuts and Greek yogurt. Enjoy!

Per serving: 384 Calories; 14.1g Fat; 55.2g Carbs; 11.8g Protein; 20.5g Sugars

574. Easy Tortilla Chips

(Ready in about 15 minutes | Servings 3)

Ingredients

1/2 (12-ounce) package corn tortillas
1 teaspoon olive oil

1 teaspoon lime juice
1/2 teaspoon chili powder
Coarse sea salt, to taste

Directions

Cut the tortillas into chip-sized wedges using a cookie cutter.

Brush your chips with olive oil, lime juice, chili powder and sea salt.

Transfer the tortilla chips to the lightly greased Air Fryer basket and bake at 360 degrees F for 5 minutes, shaking the basket halfway through; work with batches.

Serve with salsa or guacamole. Enjoy!

Per serving: 139 Calories; 6.1g Fat; 25.6g Carbs; 3.8g Protein; 0.5g Sugars

575. Classic Fried Rice

(Ready in about 40 minutes | Servings 2)

Ingredients

1 cup white rice
1 tablespoon sesame oil
Himalayan sea salt and ground black pepper, to taste

1 teaspoon hot paprika
2 tablespoons vegetable broth
2 tablespoons tamari sauce
1 egg, whisked

Directions

Bring 2 cups of a lightly salted water to a boil in a medium saucepan over medium-high heat. Add in the rice, turn to a simmer and cook, covered, for about 18 minutes until water is absorbed.

Let your rice stand, covered, for 5 to 7 minutes; fluff with a fork and transfer to a lightly greased Air Fryer safe pan.

Stir in the sesame oil, salt, black pepper, paprika and broth; stir until everything is well incorporated.

Cook the rice at 350 degrees F for about 10 minutes. Stir in the tamari sauce and egg and continue to cook for a further 5 minutes. Serve hot.

Per serving: 451 Calories; 9.6g Fat; 79.6g Carbs; 9.9g Protein; 2g Sugars

576. Cinnamon French Toast with Neufchâtel cheese

(Ready in about 10 minutes | Servings 2)

Ingredients

2 tablespoons butter
1/2 teaspoon ground cinnamon
1/4 teaspoon ground anise
A pinch of ground cloves
2 tablespoons brown sugar

A pinch of sea salt
3 tablespoons milk
2 slices bread, about 1-inch thick
2 ounces Neufchâtel cheese, softened

Directions

Thoroughly combine the butter, cinnamon, anise, cloves, brown sugar, salt and milk. Spread the cinnamon butter on both sides of the bread slices.

Arrange the bread slices in the cooking basket and cook them at 390 degrees F for 2 minutes; flip and cook on the other side for 2 to 3 minutes more.

Serve with Neufchâtel cheese. Bon appétit!

Per serving: 326 Calories; 23g Fat; 25.6g Carbs; 5.2g Protein; 11.5g Sugars

577. Quick and Easy Cornbread

(Ready in about 20 minutes | Servings 4)

Ingredients

1/2 cup self-rising cornmeal mix
A dash of salt
A dash of grated nutmeg
A dash of granulated sugar
1 tablespoon honey
4 tablespoons butter, melted
1/2 cup full-fat milk

Directions

In a mixing bowl, thoroughly combine the dry ingredients. In another bowl, mix the wet ingredients.

Then, stir the wet mixture into the dry mixture.

Pour the batter into a lightly buttered baking pan. Now, bake your cornbread at 340 degrees F for about 15 minutes.

Check for doneness and transfer to a wire rack to cool slightly before cutting and serving. Bon appétit!

Per serving: 196 Calories; 12.4g Fat; 18.6g Carbs; 2.5g Protein; 5.8g Sugars

578. Everyday Mac and Cheese

(Ready in about 25 minutes | Servings 2)

Ingredients

3/4 cup cavatappi
1/4 cup double cream
4 ounces Colby cheese, shredded
1/2 teaspoon granulated garlic
Sea salt and ground black pepper, to taste
1/4 teaspoon cayenne pepper

Direction

Bring a pot of salted water to a boil over high heat; turn the heat down to medium and add the cavatappi.

Let it simmer about 8 minutes. Drain cavatappi, reserving 1/4 cup of the cooking water; add them to a lightly greased baking pan.

Add in 1/4 cup of the cooking water, double cream, cheese and spices to the baking pan; gently stir to combine.

Bake your mac and cheese in the preheated Air Fryer at 360 degrees F for 15 minutes. Garnish with fresh basil leaves if desired. Bon appétit!

Per serving: 439 Calories; 24.4g Fat; 34.4g Carbs; 19.5g Protein; 3.6g Sugars

579. Chocolate Chip Bread Pudding Squares

(Ready in about 20 minutes | Servings 3)

Ingredients

3 thick slices bread, cut into cubes
1 egg
1 cup heavy cream
1 tablespoon agave nectar
1/4 teaspoon ground cinnamon
1/4 teaspoon ground cloves
2 tablespoons chocolate chips
2 tablespoons icing sugar

Directions

Add the bread chunks to a lightly oiled baking dish.

In a mixing dish, whisk the egg, heavy cream, agave nectar, cinnamon and cloves. Pour the custard over the bread chunks and press to soak well.

Fold in the chocolate chips.

Cook in the preheated Air Fryer at 370 degrees F for about 13 minutes.

Place the bread pudding in the refrigerator until it is chilled completely; cut into 1 ½-inch squares.

Bake the squares at 330 degrees F for 2 minutes until golden on the top. Dust with icing sugar and serve. Bon appétit!

Per serving: 339 Calories; 18.4g Fat; 34.6g Carbs; 6.5g Protein; 21.2g Sugars

580. Old-Fashioned Burritos

(Ready in about 20 minutes | Servings 3)

Ingredients

1/2 pound ground turkey
1 teaspoon taco seasoning blend
1 teaspoon deli mustard
8 ounces canned black beans
1/2 red onion, sliced
Sea salt and ground black pepper, to taste
3 (12-inch) whole-wheat tortillas, warmed
1/2 cup Cotija cheese, crumbled
1 cup butterhead lettuce, torn into pieces
1 teaspoon olive oil

Directions

Cook the ground turkey in a nonstick skillet for about 4 minutes, crumbling with a fork. Stir the taco seasoning blend, mustard, beans, onion, salt and pepper into the skillet.

Place the meat mixture in the center of each tortilla. Top with cheese and lettuce. Roll your tortillas to make burritos.

Brush each burrito with olive oil and place them in the lightly greased cooking basket. Bake your burritos at 395 degrees F for 10 minutes, turning them over halfway through the cooking time.

Serve immediately with salsa on the side, if desired.

Per serving: 580 Calories; 21.3g Fat; 65.6g Carbs; 31g Protein; 5.7g Sugars

581. Classic Rizzi Bizzi

(Ready in about 35 minutes | Servings 2)

Ingredients

1 cup long-grain brown rice, soaked overnight
1 carrot, grated
1 cup green peas, fresh or thawed
1/4 cup Shoyu sauce
1 teaspoon sesame oil

Directions

Add the brown rice and 2 cups of water to a saucepan. Bring to a boil.

Cover and reduce the heat to a slow simmer. Cook your rice for 30 minutes, then, fluff it with a fork.

Combine your rice with the remaining ingredients and transfer it to the cooking basket.

Cook your rizzi bizzi at 340 degrees F for about 13 minutes, stirring halfway through the cooking time. Serve immediately!

Per serving: 444 Calories; 5.7g Fat; 86g Carbs; 12.1g Protein; 6.3g Sugars

582. Chinese Spring Rolls

(Ready in about 15 minutes | Servings 2)

Ingredients

1 tablespoon sesame oil, divided
1 cup Chinese cabbage, shredded
1 bell pepper, deveined and cut into sticks
3 ounces prawns, deveined and chopped
1 garlic clove, minced
1 teaspoon fresh coriander, minced
1 tablespoon rice vinegar
2 tablespoons soy sauce
4 (8-inch-square) spring roll wrappers
1/2 cup hot sauce

Directions

In a wok, heat the sesame oil over medium-high heat. Then, sauté the Chinese cabbage and bell pepper for 2 to 3 minutes.

Add in the prawns and garlic and continue to sauté an additional minute or so until aromatic. Remove from heat and add in coriander, vinegar and soy sauce.

Divide the filling between spring roll wrappers. Fold the top corner over the filling; fold in the two side corners; brush with water to seal the edges.

Place the spring rolls in the cooking basket and brush them with nonstick cooking oil.

Cook the spring rolls at 380 degrees F for 5 minutes; turn them over and continue to cook for a further 2 to 3 minutes until they are crisped and lightly browned.

Serve with hot sauce. Enjoy!

Per serving: 227 Calories; 10.3g Fat; 21.5g Carbs; 13.2g Protein; 7.3g Sugars

583. Aromatic Seafood Pilaf

(Ready in about 45 minutes | Servings 2)

Ingredients

1 cup jasmine rice
Salt and black pepper, to taste
1 bay leaf
1 small yellow onion, chopped
1 small garlic clove, finely chopped
1 teaspoon butter, melted
4 tablespoons cream of mushroom soup
1/2 pound shrimp, divined and sliced

Directions

Bring 2 cups of a lightly salted water to a boil in a medium saucepan over medium-high heat. Add in the jasmine rice, turn to a simmer and cook, covered, for about 18 minutes until water is absorbed.

Let the jasmine rice stand covered for 5 to 6 minutes; fluff with a fork and transfer to a lightly greased Air Fryer safe pan.

Stir in the salt, black pepper, bay leaf, yellow onion, garlic, butter and cream of mushroom soup; stir until everything is well incorporated.

Cook the rice at 350 degrees F for about 13 minutes. Stir in the shrimp and continue to cook for a further 5 minutes.

Check the rice for softness. If necessary, cook for a few minutes more. Bon appétit!

Per serving: 481 Calories; 3.1g Fat; 81.5g Carbs; 29.9g Protein; 3.3g Sugars

584. Easy Pizza Margherita

(Ready in about 15 minutes | Servings 1)

Ingredients

6-inch dough
2 tablespoons tomato sauce
2 ounces mozzarella
1 teaspoon extra-virgin olive oil
Coarse sea salt, to taste
2-3 fresh basil leaves

Directions

Start by preheating your Air Fryer to 380 degrees F.

Stretch the dough on a pizza peel lightly dusted with flour. Spread with a layer of tomato sauce.

Add mozzarella to the crust and drizzle with olive oil. Salt to taste.

Bake in the preheated Air Fryer for 4 minutes. Rotate the baking tray and bake for a further 4 minutes. Garnish with fresh basil leaves and serve immediately. Bon appétit!

Per serving: 531 Calories; 24.1g Fat; 57.7g Carbs; 20.9g Protein; 7.1g Sugars

585. Famous Greek Tyrompiskota

(Ready in about 45 minutes | Servings 3)

Ingredients

1 cup all-purpose flour
1 tablespoon flaxseed meal
1 teaspoon baking powder
1/2 stick butter
1/2 cup halloumi cheese, grated
1 egg
1 teaspoon Greek spice blend
Salt to taste

Directions

In a mixing bowl, combine the flour, flaxseed meal and baking powder. In another bowl, mix the butter, cheese and egg. Add the cheese mixture to the dry flour mixture.

Mix with your hands and stir in the Greek spice blend; salt to taste and stir again to combine well.

Shape the batter into a log, wrap in cling film and refrigerate for about 30 minutes.

Cut the chilled log into thin slices using a sharp knife. Cook your biscuits in the preheated Air Fryer at 360 degrees F for 15 minutes. Work with batches.

Bon appétit!

Per serving: 301 Calories; 18.9g Fat; 25.7g Carbs; 9.2g Protein; 0.2g Sugars

586. Bacon and Cheese Sandwich

(Ready in about 15 minutes | Servings 1)

Ingredients

2 slices whole-wheat bread
1 tablespoon ketchup
1/2 teaspoon Dijon mustard
2 ounces bacon, sliced
1 ounce cheddar cheese, sliced

Directions

Spread the ketchup and mustard on a slice of bread. Add the bacon and cheese and top with another slice of bread.

Place your sandwich in the lightly buttered Air Fryer cooking basket.

Now, bake your sandwich at 380 degrees F for 10 minutes or until the cheese has melted. Make sure to turn it over halfway through the cooking time. Bon appétit!

Per serving: 406 Calories; 26.2g Fat; 27g Carbs; 14.2g Protein; 8.3g Sugars

587. Autumn Pear Beignets

(Ready in about 15 minutes | Servings 3)

Ingredients

1 medium-sized pear, peeled, cored and chopped
1/4 cup powdered sugar
2 tablespoons walnuts, ground
1/4 teaspoon ground cloves
1/2 teaspoon vanilla paste
1/4 teaspoon ground cinnamon
5 ounces refrigerated buttermilk biscuits
2 tablespoons coconut oil, at room temperature

Directions

In a mixing bowl, thoroughly combine the pear, sugar, walnuts, cloves, vanilla and cinnamon.

Separate the dough into 3 biscuits and then, divide each of them into 2 layers. Shape the biscuits into rounds.

Divide the pear mixture between the biscuits and roll them up. Brush the biscuits with coconut oil and transfer them to the Air Fryer cooking basket.

Cook your beignets at 330 degrees F for about 13 minutes, turning them over halfway through the cooking time. Serve with some extra powdered sugar if desired. Bon appétit!

Per serving: 336 Calories; 17.5g Fat; 41.3g Carbs; 4.6g Protein; 17.9g Sugars

588. Mexicana Air Grilled Fish Tacos

(Ready in about 15 minutes | Servings 3)

Ingredients

1 pound tilapia filets
1 teaspoon chipotle powder
1 teaspoon fresh coriander, finely chopped
1 teaspoon fresh garlic, minced
1 teaspoon extra-virgin olive oil
1 teaspoon taco seasoning mix
1 cup pickled cabbage, drained and shredded
6 mini taco shells

Directions

Toss the tilapia filets with the chipotle powder, coriander, garlic, olive oil and taco seasoning mix.

Cook the fish in your Air Fryer at 400 degrees F for 10 minutes, flipping halfway through the cooking time.

Remove the tilapia filets to a cutting board then flake into pieces.

To assemble the tacos, divide the fish and pickled cabbage between taco shells. Roll them up and transfer to the Air Fryer cooking basket.

Bake your tacos at 360 degrees F for 5 minutes until thoroughly warmed. Bon appétit!

Per serving: 422 Calories; 11.5g Fat; 41.3g Carbs; 39g Protein; 3.3g Sugars

589. Festive Crescent Ring

(Ready in about 25 minutes | Servings 3)

Ingredients

1/2 (8-ounce) can crescent dough sheet
3 slices Colby cheese, cut into half
2 ounces bacon, sliced
2 ounces capocollo, sliced
4 tablespoons tomato sauce
1/3 teaspoon dried rosemary
1/2 teaspoon dried basil
1 teaspoon dried oregano

Directions

Separate the crescent dough sheet into 8 triangles. Then, arrange the triangles in a sunburst pattern so it should look like the sun.

Place the cheese, bacon, capocollo and tomato sauce on the bottom of each triangle. Sprinkle with dried herbs.

Now, fold the triangle tips over the filling and tuck under the base to secure.

Bake the ring at 360 degrees F for 20 minutes until the dough is golden and the cheese has melted. Bon appétit!

Per serving: 370 Calories; 23.7g Fat; 23.6g Carbs; 15.1g Protein; 2.7g Sugars

590. Mediterranean Mini Monkey Bread

(Ready in about 15 minutes | Servings 3)

Ingredients

6 ounces refrigerated crescent rolls
1/4 cup ketchup
1/4 cup pesto sauce
1/2 cup provolone cheese, shredded
2 cloves garlic, minced
1/2 teaspoon dried oregano
1/2 teaspoon dried basil
1/2 teaspoon dried parsley flakes

Directions

Start by preheating your Air Fryer to 350 degrees F.

Roll out crescent rolls. Divide the ingredients between crescent rolls and roll them up. Using your fingertips, gently press them to seal the edges.

Bake the mini monkey bread for 12 minutes or until the top is golden brown. Bon appétit!

Per serving: 270 Calories; 9.5g Fat; 33.6g Carbs; 11.2g Protein; 6.1g Sugars

591. Oatmeal Pizza Cups

(Ready in about 25 minutes | Servings 3)

Ingredients

1 egg
1/2 cup oat milk
1 cup rolled oats
1/2 teaspoon baking soda
1/4 teaspoon salt
1/8 teaspoon ground black pepper
2 tablespoons butter, melted
3 ounces smoked ham, chopped
3 ounces mozzarella cheese, shredded
4 tablespoons ketchup

Directions

In a mixing bowl, beat the egg and milk until pale and frothy.

In a separate bowl, mix the rolled oats, baking soda, salt, pepper and butter; mix to combine well.

Fold in the smoked ham and mozzarella; gently stir to combine and top with ketchup.

Spoon the mixture into a lightly greased muffin tin.

Bake in the preheated Air Fryer at 330 degrees F for 20 minutes until a toothpick inserted comes out clean. Bon appétit!

Per serving: 305 Calories; 15.5g Fat; 30.6g Carbs; 21.2g Protein; 7.9g Sugars

592. Traditional Italian Arancini

(Ready in about 35 minutes | Servings 3)

Ingredients

3 cups vegetable broth
1 cup white rice
2 ounces Colby cheese, grated
1 ounce Ricotta cheese, at room temperature
1 tablespoon fresh cilantro, chopped
Sea salt and ground black pepper to taste
1 large egg
1/2 cup Italian seasoned breadcrumbs

Directions

Bring the vegetable broth to a boil in a saucepan over medium-high heat. Stir in the rice and reduce the heat to simmer; cook about 20 minutes.

Add in the cheese and cilantro. Season with salt and pepper and shape the mixture into bite-sized balls.

Beat the egg in a shallow bowl; in another shallow bowl, place the seasoned breadcrumbs.

Dip each rice ball into the beaten egg, then, roll in the seasoned breadcrumbs, gently pressing to coat well.

Bake the rice balls in the preheated Air Fryer at 350 degrees F for about 10 minutes, shaking the basket halfway through the cooking time to ensure even browning. Bon appétit!

Per serving: 365 Calories; 9.5g Fat; 56g Carbs; 12.6g Protein; 1.2g Sugars

593. Basic Air Grilled Granola

(Ready in about 20 minutes | Servings 3)

Ingredients

1 cup rolled oats
A pinch of salt
A pinch of grated nutmeg
1/4 teaspoon ground cinnamon
1 tablespoon honey
1 tablespoon coconut oil
1/4 cup walnuts, chopped
1 tablespoon sunflower seeds
1 tablespoon pumpkin seeds

Directions

In a mixing bowl, thoroughly combine the rolled oats, salt, nutmeg, cinnamon, honey and coconut oil.

Spread the mixture into an Air Fryer baking pan and bake at 330 degrees F for about 15 minutes.

Stir in the walnuts, sunflower seeds and pumpkin seeds. Continue to cook for a further 5 minutes.

Store your granola in an airtight container for up to 2 weeks. Enjoy!

Per serving: 255 Calories; 14.3g Fat; 26.2g Carbs; 7.1g Protein; 6.2g Sugars

594. Spanish-Style Chorizo and Cheese Casserole

(Ready in about 20 minutes | Servings 3)

Ingredients

8 slices white bread, cubed
1 tablespoon butter, softened
3 ounces chorizo sausage, crumbled
1 Spanish pepper, deveined and chopped
1 habanero pepper, deveined and chopped
1 cup Mexican cheese blend, shredded
2 tablespoons fresh cilantro, chopped
3 eggs
1 cup double cream
1/4 teaspoon cayenne pepper
1/4 teaspoon Mexican oregano
Sea salt and freshly ground black pepper

Directions

Add the bread chunks to a greased Air Fryer safe dish. Add in the butter, sausage, peppers, cheese and cilantro; stir to combine well.

In a mixing dish, thoroughly combine the remaining ingredients and stir to combine well. Spoon the custard into the baking dish and press with a spatula to soak.

Cook in the preheated Air Fryer at 370 degrees F for about 15 minutes until golden on the top. Bon appétit!

Per serving: 548 Calories; 43g Fat; 16.3g Carbs; 22g Protein; 2.2g Sugar

595. Honey Cornbread Muffins

(Ready in about 20 minutes | Servings 3)

Ingredients

1/2 cup cornmeal
1/2 cup plain flour
1 tablespoon flaxseed meal
1 teaspoon baking powder
3 tablespoons honey
A pinch of coarse sea salt

A pinch of grated nutmeg
1/2 teaspoon ground cinnamon
1 egg, whisked
3/4 cup milk
2 tablespoons butter, melted

Directions

In a mixing bowl, thoroughly combine the dry ingredients. In another bowl, mix the wet ingredients.

Then, stir the wet mixture into the dry mixture.

Pour the batter into a lightly buttered muffin tin. Now, bake your cornbread muffins at 350 degrees F for about 20 minutes.

Check for doneness with a toothpick and transfer to a wire rack to cool slightly before serving. Bon appétit!

Per serving: 382 Calories; 13.1g Fat; 53g Carbs; 8.5g Protein; 20.9g Sugars

596. Easy 5-Ingredient Pizza

(Ready in about 10 minutes | Servings 1)

Ingredients

1 (6-inch) flatbread
1 tablespoon marinara sauce
2 ounces cheddar cheese, freshly grated

1 ounce pepperoni, sliced
1/2 teaspoon dried oregano

Directions

Spread the marinara sauce over your flatbread. Add the cheese and pepperoni; sprinkle with dried oregano.

Cook your pizza at 350 degrees for 6 to 7 minutes.

Slide your pizza onto a serving plate and serve warm. Bon appétit!

Per serving: 412 Calories; 18.1g Fat; 41g Carbs; 19.8g Protein; 5.5g Sugars

597. Authentic Tortilla Española

(Ready in about 20 minutes | Servings 2)

Ingredients

1/2 pound medium-starch potatoes, peeled and cut into wedges
1/3 cup shallots
1/4 teaspoon cayenne pepper
Kosher salt and black pepper, to season

1 clove garlic, minced
3 large eggs
1/2 cup heavy cream
4 ounces Cotija cheese, shredded
1 teaspoon olive oil

Directions

Cook your potatoes in a saucepan for about 10 minutes; drain and transfer to a bowl of your food processor.

Add in the shallots and process them until smooth. Transfer the mixture to a mixing bowl; add in the other ingredients and mix to combine.

Spoon the pancake batter into an Air Fryer baking pan.

Cook the Spanish tortilla at 370 degrees for 5 minutes; turn over and cook for a further 5 minutes. Repeat until you run out of the pancake batter. Serve warm and enjoy!

Per serving: 512 Calories; 35.1g Fat; 26.8g Carbs; 22.3g Protein; 4.9g Sugars

598. Fluffy Pancake Cups with Sultanas

(Ready in about 30 minutes | Servings 3)

Ingredients

1/2 cup all-purpose flour
1/2 cup coconut flour
1/3 cup carbonated water
1/3 cup coconut milk
1 tablespoon dark rum

2 eggs
1/2 teaspoon vanilla
1/4 teaspoon cardamom
1/2 cup Sultanas, soaked for 15 minutes

Directions

In a mixing bowl, thoroughly combine the dry ingredients; in another bowl, mix the wet ingredients.

Then, stir the wet mixture into the dry mixture and stir again to combine well. Let the batter sit for 20 minutes in your refrigerator. Spoon the batter into a greased muffin tin.

Bake the pancake cups in your Air Fryer at 330 degrees F for 6 to 7 minutes or until golden brown. Repeat with the remaining batter.

Bon appétit!

Per serving: 261 Calories; 7.7g Fat; 38g Carbs; 10g Protein; 17.2g Sugars

599. Apple Cinnamon Rolls

(Ready in about 20 minutes | Servings 4)

Ingredients

1 (10-ounces) can buttermilk biscuits
1 apple, cored and chopped

1/4 cup powdered sugar
1 teaspoon cinnamon
1 tablespoon coconut oil, melted

Directions

Line the bottom of the Air Fryer cooking basket with a parchment paper.

Separate the dough into biscuits and cut each of them into 2 layers. Mix the remaining ingredients in a bowl.

Divide the apple/cinnamon mixture between biscuits and roll them up. Brush the biscuits with coconut oil and transfer them to the Air Fryer cooking basket.

Cook the rolls at 330 degrees F for about 13 minutes, turning them over halfway through the cooking time. Bon appétit!

Per serving: 268 Calories; 5.7g Fat; 50.1g Carbs; 5.2g Protein; 14.4g Sugars

600. Healthy Oatmeal Cups

(Ready in about 15 minutes | Servings 2)

Ingredients

1 large banana, mashed
1 cup quick-cooking steel cut oats
1 tablespoon agave syrup

1 egg, well beaten
1 cup coconut milk
3 ounces mixed berries

Directions

In a mixing bowl, thoroughly combine the banana, oats, agave syrup, beaten egg and coconut milk.

Spoon the mixture into an Air Fryer safe baking dish.

Bake in the preheated Air Fryer at 395 degrees F for about 7 minutes. Top with berries and continue to bake an additional 2 minutes.

Spoon into individual bowls and serve with a splash of coconut milk if desired. Bon appétit!

Per serving: 294 Calories; 8.5g Fat; 47.2g Carbs; 10.2g Protein; 25.4g Sugars

601. Traditional Japanese Onigiri

(Ready in about 30 minutes | Servings 3)

Ingredients

3 cups water
1 cup white Japanese rice
1 teaspoon dashi granules
1 egg, beaten
1/2 cup cheddar cheese, grated
1/2 teaspoon kinako

1 tablespoon fish sauce
1/2 teaspoon coriander seeds
1/2 teaspoon cumin seeds
1 teaspoon sesame oil
1/4 cup shallots, chopped
Sea salt, to taste

Directions

Bring the vegetable broth to a boil in a saucepan over medium-high heat. Stir in the rice and reduce the heat to simmer; cook about 20 minutes and fluff with a fork.

Mix the cooked rice with the remaining ingredients and stir until everything is well incorporated.

Then, shape and press the mixture into triangle-shape cakes.

Bake the rice cakes in the preheated Air Fryer at 350 degrees F for about 10 minutes, turning them over halfway through the cooking time.

Serve with seasoned nori, if desired. Bon appétit!

Per serving: 374 Calories; 11.5g Fat; 53.2g Carbs; 12.2g Protein; 1.9g Sugars

602. Italian-Style Fried Polenta Slices

(Ready in about 35 minutes | Servings 3)

Ingredients

9 ounces pre-cooked polenta roll
1 teaspoon sesame oil

2 ounces prosciutto, chopped
1 teaspoon Italian seasoning blend

Directions

Cut the pre-cooked polenta roll into nine equal slices. Brush them with sesame oil on all sides. Then, transfer the polenta slices to the lightly oiled Air Fryer cooking basket.

Cook the polenta slices at 395 degrees F for about 30 minutes; then, top them with chopped prosciutto and Italian seasoning blend.

Continue to cook for another 5 minutes until cooked through. Serve with marinara sauce, if desired. Bon appétit!

Per serving: 451 Calories; 4.4g Fat; 91g Carbs; 11.2g Protein; 0g Sugars

603. Sun-Dried Tomato and Herb Pull-Apart Bread

(Ready in about 20 minutes | Servings 6)

Ingredients

1 (16-ounce) can refrigerated buttermilk biscuits
1/2 cup stick butter, melted
1/3 cup parmesan cheese, grated
1/4 cup sun-dried tomatoes
1 teaspoon rosemary

1 teaspoon basil
1 teaspoon oregano
1/2 teaspoon sage
1 teaspoon parsley
2 garlic cloves very finely minced

Directions

Separate your dough into the biscuits and cut each of them in half; roll them into balls. Dip each ball into the butter and begin layering in a nonstick Bundt pan.

Cover the bottom of the pan with one layer of dough balls; then, top the dough balls with half of the cheese and half of the sun-dried tomatoes. Repeat for another layer.

In a small mixing bowl, thoroughly combine the garlic with herbs.

Finish with a third layer of dough and top it with the herb/garlic mixture.

Cook the pull-apart bread in the Air Fryer at 320 degrees for 13 to 16 minutes. Bon appétit!

Per serving: 412 Calories; 24.4g Fat; 39.1g Carbs; 7.2g Protein; 7g Sugars

604. Honey Raisin French Toast

(Ready in about 5 minutes | Servings 2)

Ingredients

2 eggs
1/4 cup full-fat milk
1/4 teaspoon ground cloves
1/2 teaspoon ground cinnamon

4 tablespoons honey
2 tablespoons coconut oil, melted
4 slices sweet raisin bread

Directions

Thoroughly combine the eggs, mink, ground cloves, cinnamon, honey and coconut oil. Spread the mixture on both sides of the bread slices.

Arrange the bread slices in the cooking basket and cook them at 390 degrees F for 2 minutes; flip and cook on the other side for 2 to 3 minutes more.

Serve with some extra honey if desired. Bon appétit!

Per serving: 492 Calories; 24g Fat; 57.1g Carbs; 13.2g Protein; 38.7g Sugars

605. Authentic Prosciutto Bruschetta

(Ready in about 10 minutes | Servings 3)

Ingredients

3 slices sourdough bread
1/2 cup marinara sauce
3 slices mozzarella

6 slices prosciutto
6 fresh basil leaves

Directions

Using a rolling pin, flatten the bread slightly.

Spread the marinara sauce on top of each slice of bread, then, top with mozzarella and prosciutto.

Now, bake your bruschetta at 360 degrees F for about 8 minutes until the cheese is melted and golden.

Garnish with basil leaves and serve. Bon appétit!

Per serving: 269 Calories; 12.4g Fat; 20.5g Carbs; 18.9g Protein; 3.7g Sugars

606. Air Grilled Cheese Roll-Ups

(Ready in about 10 minutes | Servings 3)

Ingredients

6 slices bread
2 tablespoons butter

6 slices Colby cheese
A pinch of ground black pepper

Directions

Flatten the bread slices to 1/4-inch thickness using a rolling pin. Spread the melted butter on top of each slice of bread.

Place a cheese slice on top of each slice of bread; sprinkle with black pepper and roll them up tightly.

Bake the cheese roll-ups at 390 degrees F for about 8 minutes. Bon appétit!

Per serving: 395 Calories; 26.4g Fat; 21.1g Carbs; 16.9g Protein; 2.5g Sugars

607. Double Cheese Risotto Balls with Arrabbiata Sauce

(Ready in about 35 minutes | Servings 3)

Ingredients

1 cup Arborio rice
2 tablespoons butter
2 ounces Provolone cheese, grated
2 ounces Asiago cheese, grated
1 egg, whisked
1/3 cup seasoned breadcrumbs, passed through a sieve
1 tablespoon olive oil
1/4 cup leeks, chopped

9 ounces canned San Marzano tomatoes
1 teaspoon red pepper flakes, crushed
2 tablespoons fresh basil leaves, roughly chopped
Sea salt and freshly cracked black pepper, to taste

Directions

Bring 3 cups of water to a boil in a saucepan over medium-high heat. Stir in the rice and reduce the heat to simmer; cook for about 20 minutes.

Fluff your rice in a mixing bowl; stir in the butter and cheese. Salt and pepper to taste; shape the mixture into equal balls.

Beat the egg in a shallow bowl; in another shallow bowl, place the seasoned breadcrumbs.

Dip each rice ball into the beaten egg, then, roll in the seasoned breadcrumbs, gently pressing to adhere.

Bake the rice balls in the preheated Air Fryer at 350 degrees F for about 10 minutes, shaking the basket halfway through the cooking time to ensure even cooking.

Meanwhile, heat the olive oil in a saucepan over a moderate flame. Once hot, sauté the leeks until just tender and fragrant.

Now, add in the tomatoes and spices and let it simmer for about 25 minutes, breaking your tomatoes with a spatula. Serve the warm risotto balls with Arrabbiata sauce for dipping.

Bon appétit!

Per serving: 505 Calories; 21.4g Fat; 60g Carbs; 13.9g Protein; 4.8g Sugars

608. Last Minute German Franzbrötchen

(Ready in about 15 minutes | Servings 6)

Ingredients

6 slices white bread
1 tablespoon butter, melted
1/4 cup brown sugar
1 tablespoon ground cinnamon

Glaze:
1/2 cup icing sugar
1/2 teaspoon vanilla paste
1 tablespoon milk

Directions

Flatten the bread slices to 1/4-inch thickness using a rolling pin. In a small mixing bowl, thoroughly combine the butter, brown sugar and ground cinnamon.

Spread the butter mixture on top of each slice of bread; roll them up.

Bake the rolls at 350 degrees F for 10 minutes, flipping them halfway through the cooking time.

Meanwhile, whisk the icing sugar, vanilla paste and milk until everything is well incorporated. Drizzle the glaze over the top of the slightly cooled rolls.

Let the glaze set before serving. Bon appétit!

Per serving: 157 Calories; 2.4g Fat; 30g Carbs; 3.1g Protein; 18.6g Sugars

609. Mexican-Style Bubble Loaf

(Ready in about 20 minutes | Servings 4)

Ingredients

1 (16-ounce) can flaky buttermilk biscuits
4 tablespoons olive oil, melted
1/2 cup Manchego cheese, grated
1/2 teaspoon granulated garlic

1 tablespoon fresh cilantro, chopped
1/2 teaspoon Mexican oregano
1 teaspoon chili pepper flakes
Kosher salt and ground black pepper, to taste

Directions

Open a can of biscuits and cut each biscuit into quarters. Brush each piece of biscuit with the olive oil and begin layering in a lightly greased Bundt pan.

Cover the bottom of the pan with one layer of biscuits.

Next, top the first layer with half of the cheese, spices and granulated garlic. Repeat for another layer.

Finish with a third layer of dough.

Cook your bubble loaf in the Air Fryer at 330 degrees for about 15 minutes until the cheese is bubbly. Bon appétit!

Per serving: 382 Calories; 17.5g Fat; 50.8g Carbs; 7.1g Protein; 6g Sugars

610. Mediterranean Monkey Bread

(Ready in about 20 minutes | Servings 6)

Ingredients

1 (16-ounce) can refrigerated buttermilk biscuits
3 tablespoons olive oil
1 cup Provolone cheese, grated
1/4 cup black olives, pitted and chopped

4 tablespoons basil pesto
1/4 cup pine nuts, chopped
1 tablespoon Mediterranean herb mix

Directions

Separate your dough into the biscuits and cut each of them in half; roll them into balls. Dip each ball into the olive oil and begin layering in a nonstick Bundt pan.

Cover the bottom of the pan with one layer of dough balls.

Prepare the coating mixtures. In a shallow bowl, place the provolone cheese and olives, add the basil pesto to a second bowl and add the pine nuts to a third bowl.

Roll the dough balls in the coating mixtures; then, arrange them in the Bundt pan so the various coatings are alternated. Top with Mediterranean herb mix

Cook the monkey bread in the Air Fryer at 320 degrees for 13 to 16 minutes. Bon appétit!

Per serving: 427 Calories; 25.4g Fat; 38.1g Carbs; 11.6g Protein; 6.5g Sugars

611. Cinnamon Breakfast Muffins

(Ready in about 20 minutes | Servings 4)

Ingredients

1 cup all-purpose flour
1 teaspoon baking powder
1 tablespoon brown sugar
2 eggs

1 teaspoon cinnamon powder
1 teaspoon vanilla paste
1/4 cup milk
4 tablespoons butter, melted

Directions

Start by preheating your Air Fryer to 330 degrees F. Now, spritz the silicone muffin tins with cooking spray.

Thoroughly combine all ingredients in a mixing dish. Fill the muffin cups with batter.

Cook in the preheated Air Fryer approximately 13 minutes. Check with a toothpick; when the toothpick comes out clean, your muffins are done.

Place on a rack to cool slightly before removing from the muffin tins. Enjoy!

Per serving: 302 Calories; 17.1g Fat; 27.7g Carbs; 8.3g Protein; 3.3g Sugars

612. Hibachi-Style Fried Rice

(Ready in about 30 minutes | Servings 2)

Ingredients

1 ¾ cups leftover jasmine rice
2 teaspoons butter, melted
Sea salt and freshly ground black pepper, to your liking
2 eggs, beaten
2 scallions, white and green parts separated, chopped

1 cup snow peas
1 tablespoon Shoyu sauce
1 tablespoon sake
2 tablespoons Kewpie Japanese mayonnaise

Directions

Thoroughly combine the rice, butter, salt, and pepper in a baking dish.

Cook at 340 degrees F about 13 minutes, stirring halfway through the cooking time.

Pour the eggs over the rice and continue to cook about 5 minutes. Next, add the scallions and snow peas and stir to combine. Continue to cook 2 to 3 minutes longer or until everything is heated through.

Meanwhile, make the sauce by whisking the Shoyu sauce, sake, and Japanese mayonnaise in a mixing bowl.

Divide the fried rice between individual bowls and serve with the prepared sauce. Enjoy!

Per serving: 428 Calories; 13.4g Fat; 58.9g Carbs; 14.4g Protein; 4.7g Sugars

613. Italian Panettone Bread Pudding

(Ready in about 45 minutes | Servings 3)

Ingredients

4 slices of panettone bread, crusts trimmed, bread cut into 1-inch cubes
4 tablespoons dried cranberries
2 tablespoons amaretto liqueur
1 cup coconut milk

1/2 cup whipping cream
2 eggs
1 tablespoon agave syrup
1/2 vanilla extract
1/2 teaspoon ground cloves
1/2 teaspoon ground cinnamon

Directions

Place the panettone bread cubes in a lightly greased baking dish. Scatter the dried cranberry over the top. In a mixing bowl, thoroughly combine the remaining ingredients.

Pour the custard over the bread cubes. Let it stand for 30 minutes, occasionally pressing with a wide spatula to submerge.

Cook in the preheated Air Fryer at 370 degrees F degrees for 7 minutes; check to ensure even cooking and cook an additional 5 to 6 minutes. Bon appétit!

Per serving: 279 Calories; 8.7g Fat; 37.9g Carbs; 8.9g Protein; 23.1g Sugars

614. Classic Italian Arancini

(Ready in about 35 minutes | Servings 2)

Ingredients

1 ½ cups chicken broth
1/2 cup white rice
2 tablespoons parmesan cheese, grated
Sea salt and cracked black pepper, to your liking

2 eggs
1 cup fresh bread crumbs
1/2 teaspoon oregano
1 teaspoon basil

Directions

Bring the chicken broth to a boil in a saucepan over medium-high heat. Stir in the rice and reduce the heat to simmer; cook about 20 minutes. Drain the rice and allow it to cool completely.

Add the parmesan, salt, and black pepper. Shape the mixture into bite-sized balls.

In a shallow bowl, beat the eggs; in another shallow bowl, mix bread crumbs with oregano and basil.

Dip each rice ball into the beaten eggs, then, roll in the breadcrumb mixture, gently pressing to adhere.

Bake in the preheated Air Fryer at 350 degrees F for 10 to 12 minutes, flipping them halfway through the cooking time. Bon appétit!

Per serving: 348 Calories; 7.5g Fat; 52.2g Carbs; 15.8g Protein; 2.4g Sugars

615. Smoked Salmon and Rice Rollups

(Ready in about 25 minutes | Servings 3)

Ingredients

1 tablespoon fresh lemon juice
6 slices smoked salmon
1 tablespoon extra-virgin olive oil
1/2 cup cooked rice
1 tablespoon whole-grain mustard
3 tablespoons shallots, chopped

1 garlic clove, minced
1 teaspoon capers, rinsed and chopped
Sea salt and ground black pepper, to taste
3 ounces sour cream

Directions

Drizzle the lemon juice all over the smoked salmon.

Then, spread each salmon strip with olive oil. In a mixing bowl, thoroughly combine the cooked rice, mustard, shallots, garlic, and capers.

Spread the rice mixture over the olive oil. Roll the slices into individual rollups and secure with a toothpick. Season with salt and black pepper.

Place in the lightly greased Air Fryer basket. Bake at 370 degrees F for 16 minutes, turning them over halfway through the cooking time. Serve with sour cream and enjoy!

Per serving: 226 Calories; 11.6g Fat; 15.1g Carbs; 15.2g Protein; 1.9g Sugars

616. Spicy Seafood Risotto

(Ready in about 25 minutes | Servings 3)

Ingredients

1 ½ cups cooked rice, cold
3 tablespoons shallots, minced
2 garlic cloves, minced
1 tablespoon oyster sauce
2 tablespoons dry white wine
2 tablespoons sesame oil

Salt and ground black pepper, to taste
2 eggs
4 ounces lump crab meat
1 teaspoon ancho chili powder
2 tablespoons fresh parsley, roughly chopped

Directions

Mix the cold rice, shallots, garlic, oyster sauce, dry white wine, sesame oil, salt, and black pepper in a lightly greased baking pan. Stir in the whisked eggs.

Cook in the preheated Air Fryer at 370 degrees for 13 to 16 minutes.

Add the crab and ancho chili powder to the baking dish; stir until everything is well combined. Cook for 6 minutes more.

Serve at room temperature, garnished with fresh parsley. Bon appétit!

Per serving: 445 Calories; 17.7g Fat; 48.8g Carbs; 24.4g Protein; 2.5g Sugars

617. Polenta Fries with Sriracha Sauce

(Ready in about 45 minutes + chilling time | Servings 3)

Ingredients

Polenta Fries:
1 ½ cups water
1 teaspoon sea salt
1/2 cup polenta
1 tablespoon butter, room temperature
A pinch of grated nutmeg

1 teaspoon dried Italian herb mix
Sriracha Sauce:
1 red jalapeno pepper, minced
1 garlic clove, minced
1 tablespoon cider vinegar
2 tablespoons tomato paste
1 tablespoon honey

Directions

Bring the water and 1 teaspoon sea salt to a boil in a saucepan; slowly and gradually stir in the polenta, whisking continuously until there are no lumps.

Reduce the heat to simmer and cook for 5 to 6 minutes until the polenta starts to thicken. Cover and continue to simmer for 25 minutes or until you have a thick mixture, whisking periodically.

Stir in the butter, nutmeg, and Italian herbs.

Pour your polenta into a parchment-lined rimmed baking tray, spreading the mixture evenly. Cover with plastic wrap; let it stand in your refrigerator for about 2 hours to firm up.

Then, slice the polenta into strips and place them in the greased Air Fryer basket. Cook in the preheated Air Fryer at 395 degrees F for about 11 minutes.

Meanwhile, make the Sriracha sauce by whisking all ingredients. Serve the warm polenta fries with the Sriracha sauce on the side. Enjoy!

Per serving: 247 Calories; 6.5g Fat; 43.8g Carbs; 3.7g Protein; 11.5g Sugars

618. Basic Air Fryer Granola

(Ready in about 45 minutes | Servings 12)

Ingredients

1/2 cup rolled oats
1 cup walnuts, chopped
3 tablespoons sunflower seeds

3 tablespoons pumpkin seeds
1 teaspoon coarse sea salt
2 tablespoons honey

Directions

Thoroughly combine all ingredients and spread the mixture onto the Air Fryer trays. Spritz with nonstick cooking spray.

Bake at 230 degrees F for 25 minutes; rotate the trays and bake 10 to 15 minutes more.

This granola can be kept in an airtight container for up to 2 weeks. Enjoy

Per serving: 103 Calories; 6.8g Fat; 8.8g Carbs; 3.1g Protein; 3.1g Suga

619. Taco Stuffed Bread

(Ready in about 15 minutes | Servings 4)

Ingredients

1 loaf French bread
1/2 pound ground beef
1 onion, chopped
1 teaspoon garlic, minced
1 package taco seasoning
1 ½ cups Queso Panela, sliced

Salt and ground black pepper, to taste
3 tablespoons tomato paste
2 tablespoons fresh cilantro leaves, chopped

Directions

Cut the top off of the loaf of bread; remove some of the bread from the middle creating a well and reserve.

In a large skillet, cook the ground beef with the onion and garlic until the beef is no longer pink and the onion is translucent.

Add the taco seasoning, cheese, salt, black pepper, and tomato paste. Place the taco mixture into your bread.

Bake in the preheated Air Fryer at 380 degrees F for 5 minutes. Garnish with fresh cilantro leaves. Enjoy!

Per serving: 472 Calories; 21.9g Fat; 37.6g Carbs; 30.5g Protein; 6.6g Sugars

620. New York-Style Pizza

(Ready in about 15 minutes | Servings 4)

Ingredients

1 pizza dough
1 cup tomato sauce

14 ounces mozzarella cheese, freshly grated
2 ounces parmesan, freshly grated

Directions

Stretch your dough on a pizza peel lightly dusted with flour. Spread with a layer of tomato sauce.

Top with cheese. Place on the baking tray.

Bake in the preheated Air Fryer at 395 degrees F for 5 minutes. Rotate the baking tray and bake for a further 5 minutes. Serve immediately.

Per serving: 308 Calories; 4.1g Fat; 25.7g Carbs; 42.7g Protein; 6.1g Sugars

621. Favorite Cheese Biscuits

(Ready in about 30 minutes | Servings 4)

Ingredients

1 ½ cups all-purpose flour
1/3 cup butter, room temperature
1 teaspoon baking powder
1 teaspoon baking soda

1/2 cup buttermilk
2 eggs, beaten
1 cup Swiss cheese, shredded

Directions

In a mixing bowl, thoroughly combine the flour and butter. Gradually stir in the remaining ingredients.

Divide the mixture into 12 balls.

Bake in the preheated Air Fryer at 360 degrees F for 15 minutes. Work in two batches.

Serve at room temperature. Bon appétit!

Per serving: 462 Calories; 25.8g Fat; 39.1g Carbs; 17.6g Protein; 2.1g Sugars

622. Pretzel Knots with Cumin Seeds

(Ready in about 25 minutes | Servings 6)

Ingredients

1 package crescent refrigerator rolls

2 eggs, whisked with 4 tablespoons of water
1 teaspoon cumin seeds

Directions

Roll the dough out into a rectangle. Slice the dough into 6 pieces.

Roll each piece into a log and tie each rope into a knot. Cover and let it rest for 10 minutes.

Brush the top of the pretzel knots with the egg wash; sprinkle with the cumin seeds. Arrange the pretzel knots in the lightly greased Air Fryer basket.

Bake in the preheated Air Fryer at 340 degrees for 7 minutes until golden brown. Bon appétit!

Per serving: 121 Calories; 6.5g Fat; 11.1g Carbs; 3.9g Protein; 3.1g Sugars

623. Delicious Turkey Sammies

(Ready in about 50 minutes | Servings 4)

Ingredients

1/2 pound turkey tenderloins
1 tablespoon olive oil
Salt and ground black pepper, to your liking
4 slices bread

1/4 cup tomato paste
1/4 cup pesto sauce
1 yellow onion, thinly sliced
1 cup mozzarella cheese, shredded

Directions

Brush the turkey tenderloins with olive oil. Season with salt and black pepper.

Cook the turkey tenderloins at 350 degrees F for 30 minutes, flipping them over halfway through. Let them rest for 5 to 9 minutes before slicing.

Cut the turkey tenderloins into thin slices. Make your sandwiches with bread, tomato paste, pesto, and onion. Place the turkey slices on top. Add the cheese and place the sandwiches in the Air Fryer basket.

Then, preheat your Air Fryer to 390 degrees F. Bake for 7 minutes or until cheese is melted. Serve immediately.

Per serving: 452 Calories; 24.8g Fat; 22.9g Carbs; 38.5g Protein; 9.1g Sugars

624. Mexican-Style Brown Rice Casserole

(Ready in about 50 minutes | Servings 4)

Ingredients

1 tablespoon olive oil
1 shallot, chopped
2 cloves garlic, minced
1 habanero pepper, minced
2 cups brown rice
3 cups chicken broth
1 cup water
2 ripe tomatoes, pureed

Sea salt and ground black pepper, to taste
1/2 teaspoon dried Mexican oregano
1 teaspoon red pepper flakes
1 cup Mexican Cotija cheese, crumbled

Directions

In a nonstick skillet, heat the olive oil over a moderate flame. Once hot, cook the shallot, garlic, and habanero pepper until tender and fragrant; reserve.

Heat the brown rice, vegetable broth and water in a pot over high heat. Bring it to a boil; turn the stove down to simmer and cook for 35 minutes.

Grease a baking pan with nonstick cooking spray.

Spoon the cooked rice into the baking pan. Add the sautéed mixture. Spoon the tomato puree over the sautéed mixture. Sprinkle with salt, black pepper, oregano, and red pepper.

Cook in the preheated Air Fryer at 380 degrees F for 8 minutes. Top with the Cotija cheese and bake for 5 minutes longer or until cheese is melted. Enjoy!

Per serving: 433 Calories; 7.4g Fat; 79.6g Carbs; 12.1g Protein; 2.8g Sugars

625. Japanese Chicken and Rice Salad

(Ready in about 45 minutes + chilling time | Servings 4)

Ingredients

1 pound chicken tenderloins
2 tablespoons shallots, chopped
1 garlic clove, minced
1 red bell pepper, chopped
1 ½ cups brown rice
1 cup baby spinach
1/2 cup snow peas
2 tablespoons soy sauce
1 teaspoon yellow mustard

1 tablespoon rice vinegar
1 tablespoon liquid from pickled ginger
1 teaspoon agave syrup
2 tablespoons black sesame seeds, to serve
1/4 cup Mandarin orange segments

Directions

Start by preheating your Air Fryer to 380 degrees F. Then, add the chicken tenderloins to the baking pan and cook until it starts to get crisp or about 6 minutes.

Add the shallots, garlic, and bell pepper. Cook for 6 minutes more. Wait for the chicken mixture to cool down completely and transfer to a salad bowl.

Bring 3 cups of water and 1 teaspoon of salt to a boil in a saucepan over medium-high heat. Stir in the rice and reduce the heat to simmer; cook about 20 minutes.

Let your rice sit in the covered saucepan for another 10 minutes. Drain the rice and allow it to cool completely.

Stir the cold rice into the salad bowl; add the baby spinach and snow peas. In a small mixing dish, whisk the soy sauce, mustard, rice vinegar, liquid from pickled ginger, and agave syrup.

Dress the salad and stir well to combine. Garnish with black sesame seeds and Mandarin orange. Enjoy!

Per serving: 387 Calories; 4.7g Fat; 63.9g Carbs; 22.4g Protein; 3.9g Sugars

626. Risotto Balls with Bacon and Corn

(Ready in about 30 minutes + chilling time | Servings 6)

Ingredients

4 slices Canadian bacon
1 tablespoon olive oil
1/2 medium-sized leek, chopped
1 teaspoon fresh garlic, minced
Sea salt and freshly ground
pepper, to taste
1 cup white rice
4 cups vegetable broth
1/3 cup dry white wine

2 tablespoons tamari sauce
1 tablespoon oyster sauce
1 tablespoon butter
1 cup sweet corn kernels
1 bell pepper, seeded and chopped
2 eggs lightly beaten
1 cup bread crumbs
1 cup parmesan cheese, preferably
freshly grated

Directions

Cook the Canadian bacon in a nonstick skillet over medium-high heat. Let it cool, finely chop and reserve.

Heat the olive oil in a saucepan over medium heat. Now, sauté the leeks and garlic, stirring occasionally, about 5 minutes. Add the salt and pepper.

Stir in the white rice. Continue to cook approximately 3 minutes or until translucent. Add the warm broth, wine, tamari sauce, and oyster sauce; cook until the liquid is absorbed.

Remove the saucepan from the heat; stir in the butter, corn, bell pepper, and reserved Canadian bacon. Let it cool completely. Then, shape the mixture into small balls.

In a shallow bowl, combine the eggs with the breadcrumbs and parmesan cheese. Dip each ball in the eggs/crumb mixture.

Cook in the preheated Air Fryer at 395 degrees F for 10 to 12 minutes, shaking the basket periodically. Serve warm.

Per serving: 435 Calories; 15.6g Fat; 47.4g Carbs; 23.3g Protein; 4.1g Sugars

627. Ciabatta Bread Pudding with Walnuts

(Ready in about 45 minutes | Servings 4)

Ingredients

4 cups ciabatta bread cubes
2 eggs, slightly beaten
1 cup milk
2 tablespoons butter
4 tablespoons honey
1 teaspoon vanilla extract

1/2 teaspoon ground cloves
1/2 teaspoon ground cinnamon
A pinch of salt
A pinch of grated nutmeg
1/3 cup walnuts, chopped

Directions

Place the ciabatta bread cubes in a lightly greased baking dish. In a mixing bowl, thoroughly combine the eggs, milk, butter, honey, vanilla, ground cloves, cinnamon, salt, and nutmeg.

Pour the custard over the bread cubes. Scatter the chopped walnuts over the top of your bread pudding.

Let stand for 30 minutes, occasionally pressing with a wide spatula to submerge.

Cook in the preheated Air Fryer at 370 degrees F degrees for 7 minutes; check to ensure even cooking and cook an additional 5 to 6 minutes. Bon appétit!

Per serving: 454 Calories; 18.2g Fat; 56.7g Carbs; 18.3g Protein; 25.1g Sugars

628. Sunday Glazed Cinnamon Rolls

(Ready in about 15 minutes | Servings 4)

Ingredients

1 can cinnamon rolls
2 tablespoons butter
1 cup powdered sugar

1 teaspoon vanilla extract
3 tablespoons hot water

Directions

Place the cinnamon rolls in the Air Fryer basket.

Bake at 300 degrees F for 10 minutes, flipping them halfway through the cooking time.

Meanwhile, mix the butter, sugar, and vanilla. Pour in water, 1 tablespoon at a time, until the glaze reaches desired consistency.

Spread over the slightly cooled cinnamon rolls. Bon appétit!

Per serving: 313 Calories; 10.8g Fat; 52.9g Carbs; 2.1g Protein; 39.4g Sugars

629. Rich Couscous Salad with Goat Cheese

(Ready in about 45 minutes | Servings 4)

Ingredients

1/2 cup couscous
4 teaspoons olive oil
1/2 lemon, juiced, zested
1 tablespoon honey
Sea salt and freshly ground black
pepper, to your liking
2 tomatoes, sliced
1 red onion, thinly sliced

1/2 English cucumber, thinly
sliced
2 ounces goat cheese, crumbled
1 teaspoon ghee
2 tablespoons pine nuts
1/2 cup loosely packed Italian
parsley, finely chopped

Directions

Put the couscous in a bowl; now, pour the boiling water over it. Cover and set aside for 5 to 8 minutes; fluff with a fork.

Place the couscous in a cake pan. Transfer the pan to the Air Fryer basket and cook at 360 digress F about 20 minutes. Make sure to stir every 5 minutes to ensure even cooking.

Meanwhile, in a small mixing bowl, whisk the olive oil, lemon juice and zest, honey, salt, and black pepper. Toss the couscous with this dressing.

Add the tomatoes, red onion, English cucumber, and goat cheese; gently stir to combine.

Rub the ghee in the pine nuts, using your hands and place them in the Air Fryer basket. Roast for 4 minutes; give the nuts a good toss. Put the cooking basket back again and roast for a further 3 to 4 minutes.

Scatter the toasted nuts over your salad and garnish with parsley. Enjoy!

Per serving: 258 Calories; 13g Fat; 28.3g Carbs; 8.8g Protein; 8.2g Sugars

630. The Best Fish Tacos Ever

(Ready in about 25 minutes | Servings 3)

Ingredients

1 tablespoon mayonnaise
1 teaspoon Dijon mustard
1 tablespoon sour cream
1/2 teaspoon fresh garlic, minced
1/4 teaspoon red pepper flakes
Sea salt, to taste
2 bell peppers, seeded and sliced
1 shallot, thinly sliced
1 egg

1 tablespoon water
1 tablespoon taco seasoning mix
1/3 cup tortilla chips, crushed
1/4 cup parmesan cheese, grated
1 halibut fillets, cut into 1-inch
strips
6 mini flour taco shells
6 lime wedges, for serving

Directions

Thoroughly combine the mayonnaise, mustard, sour cream, garlic, red pepper flakes, and salt. Add the bell peppers and shallots; toss to coat well. Place in your refrigerator until ready to serve.

Line the Air Fryer basket with a piece of parchment paper.

In a shallow bowl, mix the egg, water, and taco seasoning mix. In a separate shallow bowl, mix the crushed tortilla chips and parmesan.

Dip the fish into the egg mixture, then coat with the parmesan mixture, pressing to adhere.

Bake in the preheated Air Fryer at 380 degrees F for 13 minutes, flipping halfway through the cooking time.

Divide the creamed pepper mixture among the taco shells. Top with the fish, and serve with lime wedges. Enjoy!

Per serving: 493 Calories; 19.2g Fat; 48.4g Carbs; 30.8g Protein; 5.8g Sugars

631. Savory Cheese and Herb Biscuits

(Ready in about 30 minutes | Servings 3)

Ingredients

1 cup self-rising flour
1/2 teaspoon baking powder
1/2 teaspoon honey
1/2 stick butter, melted
1/2 cup Colby cheese, grated

1/2 cup buttermilk
1/4 teaspoon kosher salt
1 teaspoon dried parsley
1 teaspoon dried rosemary

Directions

Preheat your Air Fryer to 360 degrees F. Line the cooking basket with a piece of parchment paper.

In a mixing bowl, thoroughly combine the flour, baking powder, honey, and butter. Gradually stir in the remaining ingredients.

Bake in the preheated Air Fryer for 15 minutes.

Work in batches. Serve at room temperature. Bon appétit!

Per serving: 382 Calories; 22.1g Fat; 35.6g Carbs; 10.3g Protein; 3.1g Sugars

632. Favorite Spinach Cheese Pie

(Ready in about 30 minutes | Servings 4)

Ingredients

1 (16-ounce) refrigerated rolled pie crusts
4 eggs, beaten
1/2 cup buttermilk
1/2 teaspoon salt
1/2 teaspoon garlic powder
1/4 teaspoon cayenne pepper
2 cups spinach, torn into pieces
1 cup Swiss cheese, shredded
2 tablespoons scallions, chopped

Directions

Unroll the pie crust and press it into a cake pan, crimping the top edges if desired.

In a mixing dish, whisk together the eggs, buttermilk, salt, garlic, powder, and cayenne pepper.

Add the spinach, 1/2 of Swiss cheese, and scallions into the pie crust; pour the egg mixture over the top. Sprinkle the remaining 1/2 cup of Swiss cheese on top of the egg mixture.

Bake in the preheated Air Fryer at 350 degrees F for 10 minutes. Rotate the cake pan and bake an additional 10 minutes.

Transfer to a wire rack to cool for 5 to 10 minutes. Serve warm.

Per serving: 521 Calories; 33.9g Fat; 36.1g Carbs; 17.9g Protein; 5.2g Sugars

633. Greek-Style Pizza with Spinach and Feta

(Ready in about 20 minutes | Servings 2)

Ingredients

2 ounces frozen chopped spinach
Coarse sea salt, to taste
2 personal pizza crusts
1 tablespoon olive oil
1/4 cup tomato sauce
2 tablespoons fresh basil, roughly chopped
1/2 teaspoon dried oregano
1/2 feta cheese, crumbled

Directions

Add the frozen spinach to the saucepan and cook until all the liquid has evaporated, about 6 minutes. Season with sea salt to taste.

Preheat the Air Fryer to 395 degrees F.

Unroll the pizza dough on the Air Fryer baking tray; brush with olive oil.

Spread the tomato sauce over the pizza crust. Add the sautéed spinach, basil, and oregano. Sprinkle the feta cheese, covering the pizza crust to the edges.

Cook for 10 minutes, rotating your pizza halfway through the cooking time. Repeat with another pizza and serve warm.

Per serving: 502 Calories; 29.5g Fat; 53.6g Carbs; 14.8g Protein; 17.3g Sugars

634. Cheese and Bacon Crescent Ring

(Ready in about 25 minutes | Servings 4)

Ingredients

1 (8-ounce) can crescent dough sheet
1 ½ cups Monterey Jack cheese, shredded
4 slices bacon, cut chopped
4 tablespoons tomato sauce
1 teaspoon dried oregano

Directions

Unroll the crescent dough sheet and separate into 8 triangles. Arrange the triangles on a piece of parchment paper; place the triangles in the ring so it should look like the sun.

Place the shredded Monterey Jack cheese, bacon, and tomato sauce on the half of each triangle, at the center of the ring. Sprinkle with oregano.

Bring each triangle up over the filling. Press the overlapping dough to flatten. Transfer the parchment paper with the crescent ring to the Air Fryer basket.

Bake at 355 degrees F for 20 minutes or until the ring is golden brown. Bon appétit!

Per serving: 506 Calories; 30.8g Fat; 33.6g Carbs; 21.7g Protein; 6.9g Sugars

635. Crème Brûlée French Toast

(Ready in about 10 minutes | Servings 2)

Ingredients

4 slices bread, about 1-inch thick
2 tablespoons butter, softened
1 teaspoon ground cinnamon
2 ounces brown sugar
1/2 teaspoon vanilla paste
A pinch of sea salt
2 ounces Neufchâtel cheese, softened

Directions

In a mixing dish, combine the butter, cinnamon, brown sugar, vanilla, and salt. Spread the cinnamon butter on both sides of the bread slices.

Arrange in the cooking basket. Cook at 390 degrees F for 2 minutes; turn over and cook an additional 2 minutes.

Serve with softened Neufchâtel cheese on individual plates. Bon appétit!

Per serving: 407 Calories; 18.8g Fat; 51.7g Carbs; 8.3g Protein; 32.2g Sugars

636. Puff Pastry Meat Strudel

(Ready in about 40 minutes | Servings 8)

Ingredients

1 tablespoon olive oil
1 small onion, chopped
2 garlic cloves, minced
1/3 pound ground beef
1/3 pound ground pork
2 tablespoons tomato puree
2 tablespoons matzo meal
Sea salt and ground black pepper, to taste
1/2 teaspoon cayenne pepper
1/4 teaspoon dried marjoram
2 cans (8-ounces) refrigerated crescent rolls
1 egg, whisked with 1 tablespoon of water
2 tablespoons sesame seeds
1/2 cup marinara sauce
1 cup sour cream

Directions

Heat the oil in a heavy skillet over medium flame. Sauté the onion just until soft and translucent. Add the garlic and sauté for 1 minute more.

Add the ground beef and pork and continue to cook for 3 minutes more or until the meat is no longer pink. Remove from the heat.

Add the tomato puree and matzo meal.

Roll out the puff pastry and spread the meat mixture lengthwise on the dough. Sprinkle with salt, black pepper, cayenne pepper, and marjoram.

Fold in the sides of the dough over the meat mixture. Pinch the edges to seal.

Place the strudel on the parchment lined Air Fryer basket. Brush the strudel with the egg wash; sprinkle with sesame seeds.

Bake in the preheated Air Fryer at 330 degrees F for 18 to 20 minutes or until the pastry is puffed and golden and the filling is thoroughly cooked.

Allow your strudel to rest for 5 to 10 minutes before cutting and serving. Serve with the marinara sauce and sour cream on the side. Bon appétit!

Per serving: 356 Calories; 16g Fat; 35.6g Carbs; 16.5g Protein; 1.7g Sugars

637. Paella-Style Spanish Rice

(Ready in about 35 minutes | Servings 2)

Ingredients

2 cups water
1 cup white rice, rinsed and drained
1 cube vegetable stock
1 chorizo, sliced
2 cups brown mushrooms, cleaned and sliced
2 cloves garlic, finely chopped

1/2 teaspoon fresh ginger, ground
1 long red chili, minced
1/4 cup dry white wine
1/2 cup tomato sauce
1 teaspoon smoked paprika
Kosher salt and ground black pepper, to taste
1 cup green beans

Directions

In a medium saucepan, bring the water to a boil. Add the rice and vegetable stock cube. Stir and reduce the heat. Cover and let it simmer for 20 minutes.

Then, place the chorizo, mushrooms, garlic, ginger, and red chili in the baking pan. Cook at 380 degrees F for 6 minutes, stirring periodically.

Add the prepared rice to the casserole dish. Add the remaining ingredients and gently stir to combine.

Cook for 6 minutes, checking periodically to ensure even cooking. Serve in individual bowls and enjoy!

Per serving: 546 Calories; 12.4g Fat; 90.7g Carbs; 17.6g Protein; 4.5g Sugars

638. Beef and Wild Rice Casserole

(Ready in about 50 minutes | Servings 3)

Ingredients

3 cups beef stock
1 cup wild rice, rinsed well
1 tablespoon olive oil
1/2 pound steak, cut into strips
1 carrot, chopped

1 medium-sized leek, chopped
2 garlic cloves, minced
1 chili pepper, minced
Kosher salt and ground black pepper, to your liking

Directions

Place beef stock and rice in a saucepan over medium-high heat.

Cover and bring it to a boil. Reduce the heat and let it simmer about 40 minutes. Drain the excess liquid and reserve.

Heat the olive oil in a heavy skillet over moderate heat. Cook the steak until no longer pink; place in the lightly greased baking pan.

Add carrot, leek, garlic, chili pepper, salt, and black pepper. Stir in the reserved wild rice. Stir to combine well.

Cook in the preheated Air Fryer at 360 degrees for 9 to 10 minutes. Serve immediately and enjoy!

Per serving: 444 Calories; 13.1g Fat; 49.6g Carbs; 34.3g Protein; 4.7g Sugars

639. Baked Tortilla Chips

(Ready in about 15 minutes | Servings 3)

Ingredients

1/2 (12-ounce) package corn tortillas
1 tablespoon canola oil

1/2 teaspoon chili powder
1 teaspoon salt

Directions

Cut the tortillas into small rounds using a cookie cutter.

Brush the rounds with canola oil. Sprinkle them with chili powder and salt.

Transfer to the lightly greased Air Fryer basket and bake at 360 degrees F for 5 minutes, shaking the basket halfway through. Bake until the chips are crisp, working in batches.

Serve with salsa or guacamole. Enjoy!

Per serving: 167 Calories; 6.1g Fat; 26.4g Carbs; 3.2g Protein; 0.5g Sugars

640. Classic Air Fryer Cornbread

(Ready in about 30 minutes | Servings 4)

Ingredients

3/4 cup cornmeal
1 cup flour
2 teaspoons baking powder
1/2 tablespoon brown sugar

1/2 teaspoon salt
5 tablespoons butter, melted
3 eggs, beaten
1 cup full-fat milk

Directions

Start by preheating your Air Fryer to 370 degrees F. Then, spritz a baking pan with cooking oil.

In a mixing bowl, combine the flour, cornmeal, baking powder, brown sugar, and salt. In a separate bowl, mix the butter, eggs, and milk.

Pour the egg mixture into the dry cornmeal mixture; mix to combine well.

Pour the batter into the baking pan; cover with aluminum foil and poke tiny little holes all over the foil. Now, bake for 15 minutes.

Remove the foil and bake for 10 minutes more. Transfer to a wire rack to cool slightly before cutting and serving. Bon appétit!

Per serving: 455 Calories; 23.9g Fat; 46.1g Carbs; 13.9g Protein; 4.7g Sugars

641. Delicious Sultana Muffins

(Ready in about 20 minutes | Servings 4)

Ingredients

1 cup flour
1 teaspoon baking powder
1 tablespoon honey 1 egg
1/2 teaspoon star anise, ground
1 teaspoon vanilla extract

1 egg
1/2 cup milk
2 tablespoons melted butter
1 cup dried Sultanas, soaked in 2 tablespoons of rum

Directions

Mix all the ingredients until everything is well incorporated. Spritz a silicone muffin tin with cooking spray.

Pour the batter into the silicone muffin tin.

Bake in the preheated Air Fryer at 330 degrees F for 12 to 15 minutes. Rotate the silicone muffin tin halfway through the cooking time to ensure even cooking.

Bon appétit!

Per serving: 288 Calories; 9.5g Fat; 44.3g Carbs; 6.7g Protein; 18.5g Sugars

642. Easy Mexican Burritos

(Ready in about 25 minutes | Servings 4)

Ingredients

1 tablespoon olive oil
1 cup ground beef
1 teaspoon fresh garlic, minced
2 tablespoons scallions, chopped
1 habanero pepper, seeded and chopped

2 (8-ounce) cans refrigerated crescent dinner rolls
1/2 cup canned pinto beans, rinsed and drained
1 tablespoon taco seasoning mix
1 cup Colby cheese, shredded

Directions

Heat the olive oil in a skillet over medium heat. Now, cook the ground beef, garlic, scallions, and habanero pepper until the beef is no longer pink and the onion is translucent and fragrant.

Separate the crescent dinner rolls into 8 rectangles.

Divide the beef mixture between rectangles; add the pinto beans and taco seasoning mix; top with the shredded cheese. Roll up and pinch the edge to seal.

Place the seam side down on the parchment-lined Air Fryer basket. Bake in the preheated Air Fryer at 355 degrees F for 20 minutes. Bon appétit!

Per serving: 377 Calories; 20.3g Fat; 25.1g Carbs; 22.7g Protein; 1.8g Sugars

643. Beef Taquito Casserole

(Ready in about 20 minutes | Servings 4)

Ingredients

1/2 (15-ounce) can black beans, drained and rinsed well
1 tablespoon taco seasoning mix
4 ounces mild enchilada sauce
1 cup Mexican cheese blend, shredded

1/2 (20-ounce) box frozen taquitos (chicken and cheese in tortillas)
2 tablespoons fresh chives, roughly chopped

Directions

Start by preheating your Air Fryer to 350 degrees F. Spritz the baking pan with cooking spray.

Mix the beans, taco seasoning mix, enchilada sauce and 1/2 cups of shredded cheese in the baking dish.

Top the mixture with taquitos. Bake for 15 minutes. Top with the remaining 1/2 cup of shredded cheese and bake for a further 15 minutes.

Serve garnished with chopped chives. Enjoy!

Per serving: 364 Calories; 19g Fat; 32.8g Carbs; 16g Protein; 2.8g Sugars

644. Fried Bread Pudding Squares

(Ready in about 40 minutes | Servings 4)

Ingredients

6 slices bread, cubed
1 cup sugar
2 cups milk
2 large eggs, beaten

1/2 teaspoon vanilla extract
1/2 teaspoon ground cinnamon
2 tablespoons dark rum
2 tablespoons icing sugar

Directions

Place the bread cubes in a lightly greased baking dish. In a mixing bowl, thoroughly combine the sugar, milk, eggs, vanilla, cinnamon, and rum.

Pour the custard over the bread cubes. Let stand for 30 minutes, occasionally pressing with a wide spatula to submerge.

Cook in the preheated Air Fryer at 370 degrees F degrees for 7 minutes; check to ensure even cooking and cook an additional 5 to 6 minutes.

Place your bread pudding in the refrigerator to cool completely; cut into 1 ½-inch squares. Bake at 330 degrees F for 2 minutes in the lightly buttered Air Fryer basket.

Dust with icing sugar and serve. Bon appétit!

Per serving: 313 Calories; 7.2g Fat; 50.2g Carbs; 7.8g Protein; 36.3g Sugars

645. Golden Cornbread Muffins

(Ready in about 30 minutes | Servings 4)

Ingredients

1/2 cup sorghum flour
1/2 cup yellow cornmeal
1/4 cup white sugar
2 teaspoons baking powder
A pinch of salt

A pinch of grated nutmeg
2 eggs, beaten
1/2 cup milk
4 tablespoons butter, melted
4 tablespoons honey

Directions

Start by preheating your Air Fryer to 370 degrees F. Then, line the muffin cups with the paper baking cups.

In a mixing bowl, combine the flour, cornmeal, sugar, baking powder, salt, and nutmeg. In a separate bowl, mix the eggs, milk, and butter.

Pour the egg mixture into the dry cornmeal mixture; mix to combine well.

Pour the batter into the prepared muffin cups. Bake for 15 minutes. Rotate the pan and bake for 10 minutes more.

Transfer to a wire rack to cool slightly before cutting and serving. Serve with honey and enjoy!

Per serving: 383 Calories; 18.3g Fat; 48.8g Carbs; 8.1g Protein; 25.6g Sugars

646. Cheese and Bacon Ciabatta Sandwich

(Ready in about 10 minutes | Servings 2)

Ingredients

2 ciabatta sandwich buns, split
2 tablespoons butter
2 teaspoons Dijon mustard

4 slices Canadian bacon
4 slices Monterey Jack cheese

Directions

Place the bottom halves of buns, cut sides up in the parchment lined Air Fryer basket.

Spread the butter and mustard on the buns. Top with the bacon and cheese.

Bake in the preheated Air Fryer at 400 degrees F for 3 minutes. Flip the sandwiches over and cook for 3 minutes longer or until the cheese has melted.

Serve with some extra ketchup or salsa sauce. Bon appétit!

Per serving: 504 Calories; 31.4g Fat; 28.5g Carbs; 26.8g Protein; 3.8g Sugars

647. Caprese Mac and Cheese

(Ready in about 25 minutes | Servings 3)

Ingredients

1/2 pound cavatappi
1 cup cauliflower florets
1 cup milk
2 cups mozzarella cheese, grated
1/2 teaspoon Italian seasoning

Salt and ground black pepper, to taste
2 tomatoes, sliced
1 cup Parmesan cheese, grated
1 tablespoon fresh basil leaves

Directions

Bring a pot of salted water to a boil over high heat; turn the heat down to medium and add the cavatappi and cauliflower.

Let it simmer about 8 minutes. Drain the cavatappi and cauliflower; place them in a lightly greased baking pan.

Add the milk and mozzarella cheese to the baking pan; gently stir to combine. Add the Italian seasoning, salt, and black pepper.

Top with the tomatoes and parmesan cheese.

Bake in the preheated Air Fryer at 360 degrees F for 15 minutes. Serve garnished with fresh basil leaves. Bon appétit!

Per serving: 587 Calories; 13.2g Fat; 69.7g Carbs; 46.5g Protein; 8.2g Sugars

648. Buckwheat and Potato Flat Bread

(Ready in about 20 minutes | Servings 4)

Ingredients

4 potatoes, medium-sized
1 cup buckwheat flour
1/2 teaspoon salt

1/2 teaspoon red chili powder
1/4 cup honey

Directions

Put the potatoes into a large saucepan; add water to cover by about 1 inch. Bring to a boil. Then, lower the heat, and let your potatoes simmer about 8 minutes until they are fork tender.

Mash the potatoes and add the flour, salt, and chili powder. Create 4 balls and flatten them with a rolling pin

Bake in the preheated Air Fryer at 390 degrees F for 6 minutes. Serve warm with honey.

Per serving: 334 Calories; 1.2g Fat; 77.3g Carbs; 8.4g Protein; 19.5g Sugars

649. Couscous and Black Bean Bowl

(Ready in about 35 minutes | Servings 4)

Ingredients

1 cup couscous
1 cup canned black beans, drained and rinsed
1 tablespoon fresh cilantro, chopped
1 bell pepper, sliced
2 tomatoes, sliced
2 cups baby spinach

1 red onion, sliced
Sea salt and ground black pepper, to taste
1 teaspoon lemon juice
1 teaspoon lemon zest
1 tablespoon olive oil
4 tablespoons tahini

Directions

Put the couscous in a bowl; pour the boiling water to cover by about 1 inch. Cover and set aside for 5 to 8 minutes; fluff with a fork.

Place the couscous in a lightly greased cake pan. Transfer the pan to the Air Fryer basket and cook at 360 digress F about 20 minutes. Make sure to stir every 5 minutes to ensure even cooking.

Transfer the prepared couscous to a mixing bowl. Add the remaining ingredients; gently stir to combine. Bon appétit!

Per serving: 352 Calories; 12g Fat; 49.9g Carbs; 12.6g Protein; 1.7g Sugars

650. Delicious Coconut Granola

(Ready in about 40 minutes | Servings 12)

Ingredients

2 cups rolled oats
2 tablespoons butter
1 cup honey
1/2 teaspoon coconut extract

1/2 teaspoon vanilla extract
1/4 cup sesame seeds
1/4 cup pumpkin seeds
1/2 cup coconut flakes

Directions

Thoroughly combine all ingredients, except the coconut flakes; mix well.

Spread the mixture onto the Air Fryer trays. Spritz with nonstick cooking spray.

Bake at 230 degrees F for 25 minutes; rotate the trays, add the coconut flakes, and bake for a further 10 to 15 minutes.

This granola can be stored in an airtight container for up to 3 weeks. Enjoy!

Per serving: 192 Calories; 7.1g Fat; 36.2g Carbs; 4.3g Protein; 24.8g Sugars

651. Savory Cheesy Cornmeal Biscuits

(Ready in about 35 minutes | Servings 6)

Ingredients

2 cups all-purpose flour
1 teaspoon baking soda
1 teaspoon baking powder
1 teaspoon granulated sugar
1/4 teaspoon ground chipotle
Sea salt, to taste
A pinch of grated nutmeg

1 stick butter, cold
6 ounces canned whole corn kernels
1 cup Colby cheese, shredded
2 tablespoons sour cream
2 eggs, beaten

Directions

In a mixing bowl, combine the flour, baking soda, baking powder, sugar, ground chipotle, salt, and a pinch of nutmeg.

Cut in the butter until the mixture resembles coarse crumbs. Stir in the corn, Colby cheese, sour cream, and eggs; stir until everything is well incorporated.

Turn the dough out onto a floured surface. Knead the dough with your hands and roll it out to 1-inch thickness. Using 3-inch round cutter, cut out the biscuits.

Transfer the cornmeal biscuits to the lightly greased Air Fryer basket. Brush the biscuits with cooking oil.

Bake in the preheated Air Fryer at 400 degrees F for 17 minutes. Continue cooking until all the batter is used. Bon appétit!

Per serving: 444 Calories; 26.7g Fat; 37.6g Carbs; 13.4g Protein; 1.6g Sugars

652. Asian-Style Shrimp Pilaf

(Ready in about 45 minutes | Servings 3)

Ingredients

1 cup koshihikari rice, rinsed
1 yellow onion, chopped
2 garlic cloves, minced
1/2 teaspoon fresh ginger, grated
1 tablespoon Shoyu sauce
2 tablespoons rice wine

1 tablespoon sushi seasoning
1 tablespoon caster sugar
1/2 teaspoon sea salt
5 ounces frozen shrimp, thawed
2 tablespoons katsuobushi flakes, for serving

Directions

Place the koshihikari rice and 2 cups of water in a large saucepan and bring to a boil. Cover, turn the heat down to low, and continue cooking for 15 minutes more. Set aside for 10 minutes.

Mix the rice, onion, garlic, ginger, Shoyu sauce, wine, sushi seasoning, sugar, and salt in a lightly greased baking dish.

Cook in the preheated Air Fryer at 370 degrees for 13 to 16 minutes.

Add the shrimp to the baking dish and gently stir until everything is well combined. Cook for 6 minutes more.

Serve at room temperature, garnished with katsuobushi flakes. Enjoy!

Per serving: 368 Calories; 5.3g Fat; 68.4g Carbs; 9.9g Protein; 13.9g Sugars

653. Classic Pancakes with Blueberries

(Ready in about 30 minutes | Servings 4)

Ingredients

1 cup flour
1 teaspoon baking powder
1 teaspoon baking soda
1/2 teaspoon salt
1 teaspoon granulated sugar

2 eggs, beaten
1/2 cup milk
2 tablespoons butter melted
4 tablespoons maple syrup
1/2 cup fresh blueberries

Directions

Mix the flour, baking powder, baking soda, salt, sugar, and eggs in a large bowl. Gradually add the milk and the melted butter, whisking continuously, until well combined.

Let it stand for 20 minutes.

Spritz the Air Fryer baking pan with cooking spray. Pour the batter into the pan using a measuring cup.

Cook at 230 degrees F for 4 to 5 minutes or until golden brown. Repeat with the remaining batter.

Serve with maple syrup and fresh blueberries. Bon appétit!

Per serving: 331 Calories; 12g Fat; 46.9g Carbs; 8.9g Protein; 21.2g Sugars

654. Mediterranean Pita Pockets

(Ready in about 25 minutes | Servings 4)

Ingredients

1 teaspoon olive oil
1 onion
2 garlic cloves, minced
3/4 pound ground turkey
Salt and ground black pepper, to taste
1/2 teaspoon mustard seeds
4 small pitas

Tzatziki
1/2 cup Greek-style yogurt
1/2 cucumber, peeled
1 clove garlic, minced
2 tablespoons fresh lemon juice
Sea salt, to taste
1/4 teaspoon dried oregano

Directions

Mix the olive oil, onion, garlic, turkey, salt, black pepper, and mustard seeds; shape the mixture into four patties.

Cook in the preheated Air Fryer at 370 degrees F for 10 minutes, turning them over once or twice.

Meanwhile, mix all ingredients for the tzatziki and place in the refrigerator until ready to use.

Warm the pita pockets in the preheated Air Fryer at 360 degrees F for 4 to 5 minutes or until thoroughly heated.

Spread the tzatziki in pita pockets and add the turkey patties. Enjoy!

Per serving: 350 Calories; 10.5g Fat; 42.1g Carbs; 24.9g Protein; 4.2g Sugars

655. Grilled Garlic and Avocado Toast

(Ready in about 15 minutes | Servings 2)

Ingredients

4 slices artisan bread
1 garlic clove, halved
2 tablespoons olive oil

1 avocado, seeded, peeled and mashed
1/2 teaspoon sea salt
1/4 teaspoon ground black pepper

Directions

Rub 1 side of each bread slice with garlic. Brush with olive oil.

Place the bread slices on the Air Fryer grill pan. Bake in the preheated Air Fryer at 400 degrees F for 3 to 4 minutes.

Slather the mashed avocado on top of the toast and season with salt and pepper. Enjoy!

Per serving: 389 Calories; 29.5g Fat; 28.8g Carbs; 5.6g Protein; 2.9g Sugars

656. Stuffed French Toast

(Ready in about 15 minutes | Servings 3)

Ingredients

3 slices of challah bread, without crusts
1/4 cup Mascarpone cheese
3 tablespoons fig jam
1 egg
3 tablespoons milk

1/2 teaspoon grated nutmeg
1 teaspoon ground cinnamon
1/2 teaspoon vanilla paste
1/4 cup butter, melted
1/2 cup brown sugar

Directions

Spread the three slices of bread with the mascarpone cheese, leaving 1/2-inch border at the edges.

Spread the three slices of bread with 1/2 tablespoon of fig jam; then, invert them onto the slices with the cheese in order to make sandwiches.

Mix the egg, milk, nutmeg, cinnamon, and vanilla in a shallow dish. Dip your sandwiches in the egg mixture.

Cook in the preheated Air Fryer at 340 degrees F for 4 minutes. Dip in the melted butter, then, roll in the brown sugar. Serve warm.

Per serving: 430 Calories; 24.1g Fat; 44.1g Carbs; 10.3g Protein; 24g Sugars

657. Almost Famous Four-Cheese Pizza

(Ready in about 15 minutes | Servings 4)

Ingredients

1 (11-ounce) can refrigerated thin pizza crust
1/2 cup tomato pasta sauce
2 tablespoons scallions, chopped
1/4 cup Parmesan cheese, grated

1 cup provolone cheese, shredded
1 cup mozzarella cheese. sliced
4 slices cheddar cheese
1 tablespoon olive oil

Directions

Stretch the dough on a work surface lightly dusted with flour. Spread with a layer of tomato pasta sauce.

Top with the scallions and cheese. Place on the baking tray that is previously greased with olive oil.

Bake in the preheated Air Fryer at 395 degrees F for 5 minutes. Rotate the baking tray and bake for a further 5 minutes. Serve immediately.

Per serving: 551 Calories; 34.3g Fat; 32.7g Carbs; 26.6g Protein; 6.2g Sugars

658. Crispy Pork Wontons

(Ready in about 20 minutes | Servings 3)

Ingredients

1 tablespoon olive oil
3/4 pound ground pork
1 red bell pepper, seeded and chopped
1 green bell pepper, seeded and chopped
1 habanero pepper, minced

3 tablespoons onion, finely chopped
Salt and ground black pepper, to taste
1/2 teaspoon dried parsley flakes
1 teaspoon dried thyme
6 wonton wrappers

Directions

Heat the olive oil in a heavy skillet over medium heat. Cook the ground pork, peppers, and onion until tender and fragrant or about 4 minutes.

Add the seasonings and stir to combine.

Lay a piece of the wonton wrapper on your palm; add the filling in the middle of the wrapper. Then, fold it up to form a triangle; pinch the edges to seal tight.

Place the folded wontons in the lightly greased cooking basket. Cook at 360 degrees F for 10 minutes. Work in batches and serve warm. Bon appétit!

Per serving: 296 Calories; 14.5g Fat; 21.8g Carbs; 18.3g Protein; 1.7g Sugars

659. Japanese Yaki Onigiri

(Ready in about 50 minutes | Servings 2)

Ingredients

1/2 cup sushi rice, cooked
1 cup canned green peas, drained
1/4 cup cream cheese
1/4 cup Colby cheese, shredded
2 tablespoons dashi

Salt and cracked black pepper, to taste
2 tablespoons scallions, chopped
1 cup all-purpose flour
1 egg, whisked
2 tablespoons soy sauce (unagi)

Directions

In a bowl, combine the rice, green peas, cheese, dashi, salt, black pepper, and scallions. Add the flour and egg and mix to combine well.

Refrigerate for 20 to 40 minutes.

Then, put some salt in your hands and rub to spread all around. Form the rice mixture into triangles.

Cook in the preheated Air Fryer at 370 degrees F for 7 to 10 minutes. Brush with the unagi sauce and serve immediately. Enjoy!

Per serving: 603 Calories; 13.3g Fat; 95.8g Carbs; 23.3g Protein; 4.4g Sugars

660. Mexican Taco Bake

(Ready in about 40 minutes | Servings 4)

Ingredients

1 tablespoon olive oil
1/4 pound ground beef
1/2 pound ground pork
1 shallot, minced
1 garlic, minced
1/2 cup beef broth
1 bell pepper, seeded and chopped

1 Mexican chili pepper, seeded and minced
1 ½ cups tomato sauce
4 flour tortillas for fajitas
1 cup Mexican cheese blend, shredded

Directions

Heat the olive oil in a heavy skillet over a moderate flame. Cook the ground meat with the shallots and garlic until no longer pink.

Then, add the beef broth, peppers, and tomato sauce to the skillet. Continue to cook on low heat for 3 minutes, stirring continuously.

Spritz a baking dish with nonstick cooking spray. Cut the tortillas in half; place 2 tortilla halves in the bottom of the baking dish.

Top with half of the meat mixture. Sprinkle with 1/2 cup of the cheese and the remaining tortilla halves. Top with the remaining meat mixture and cheese.

Cover with a piece of aluminum foil and bake in the preheated Air Fryer at 330 degrees F for 20 minutes. Remove the foil and bake for a further 12 minutes or until thoroughly heated. Enjoy!

Per serving: 540 Calories; 29.5g Fat; 33.3g Carbs; 34.8g Protein; 7.2g Sugars

661. Broccoli Bruschetta with Romano Cheese

(Ready in about 20 minutes | Servings 3)

Ingredients

6 slices of panini bread
1 teaspoon garlic puree
3 tablespoons extra-virgin olive oil

6 tablespoons passata di pomodoro (tomato passata)
1 cup small broccoli florets
1/2 cup Romano cheese, grated

Directions

Place the slices of panini bread on a flat surface.

In a small mixing bowl, combine together the garlic puree and extra-virgin olive oil. Brush one side of each bread slice with the garlic/oil mixture.

Place in the Air Fryer grill pan. Add the tomato passata, broccoli, and cheese.

Cook in the preheated Air Fryer at 370 degrees F for 10 minutes. Bon appétit!

Per serving: 264 Calories; 14.2g Fat; 24.3g Carbs; 10.4g Protein; 4.9g Sugars

662. Polenta Bites with Wild Mushroom Ragout

(Ready in about 50 minutes | Servings 3)

Ingredients

2 cups water
1 teaspoon salt
1/2 cup polenta
2 tablespoons butter, melted
1 tablespoon olive oil
6 ounces wild mushrooms, sliced

1/2 red onion, chopped
1/2 teaspoon fresh garlic, minced
Sea salt and freshly ground black pepper, to taste
1 teaspoon cayenne pepper
1/2 cup dry white wine

Directions

Bring 2 cups of water and 1 teaspoon salt to a boil in a saucepan over medium-high heat. Slowly and gradually, stir in the polenta, whisking constantly.

Reduce the heat to medium-low and continue to cook for 5 to 6 minutes more. Stir in the butter and mix to combine. Pour the prepared polenta into a parchment-lined baking pan, cover and let stand for 15 to 20 minutes or until set.

In the meantime, preheat your Air Fryer to 360 degrees F. Heat the olive oil until sizzling. Then, add the mushrooms, onion, and garlic to the baking pan.

Cook for 5 minutes, stirring occasionally. Season with salt, black pepper, cayenne pepper, and wine; cook an additional 5 minutes and reserve.

Cut the polenta into 18 squares. Transfer to the lightly greased cooking basket. Cook in the preheated Air Fryer at 395 degrees F for about 8 minutes.

Top with the wild mushroom ragout and bake an additional 3 minutes. Serve warm.

Per serving: 220 Calories; 16.6g Fat; 12.4g Carbs; 6.8g Protein; 2.2g Sugars

663. Cornmeal Crusted Okra

(Ready in about 30 minutes | Servings 2)

Ingredients

3/4 cup cornmeal
1/4 cup parmesan cheese, grated
Sea salt and ground black pepper, to taste
1 teaspoon cayenne pepper

1 teaspoon garlic powder
1/2 teaspoon cumin seeds
1/2 pound of okra, cut into small chunks
2 teaspoons sesame oil

Directions

In a mixing bowl, thoroughly combine the cornmeal, parmesan, salt, black pepper, cayenne pepper, garlic powder, and cumin seeds. Stir well to combine.

Roll the okra pods over the cornmeal mixture, pressing to adhere. Drizzle with sesame oil.

Cook in the preheated Air Fryer at 370 digress F for 20 minutes, shaking the basket periodically to ensure even cooking. Bon appétit!

Per serving: 314 Calories; 10.1g Fat; 49.3g Carbs; 10.3g Protein; 3.2g Sugars

664. Tex Mex Pasta Bake

(Ready in about 40 minutes | Servings 4)

Ingredients

3/4 pound pasta noodles
1 tablespoon olive oil
3/4 pound ground beef
1 medium-sized onion, chopped
1 teaspoon fresh garlic, minced
1 bell pepper, seeded and sliced
1 jalapeno, seeded and minced
Sea salt and cracked black pepper, to taste

1 ½ cups enchilada sauce
1 cup Mexican cheese blend, shredded
1/3 cup tomato paste
1/2 teaspoon Mexican oregano
1/2 cup nacho chips
2 tablespoons fresh coriander, chopped

Directions

Boil the pasta noodles for 3 minutes less than mentioned on the package; drain, rinse and place in the lightly greased casserole dish.

In a saucepan, heat the olive oil until sizzling. Add the ground beef and cook for 2 to 3 minutes or until slightly brown.

Now, add the onion, garlic, and peppers and continue to cook until tender and fragrant or about 2 minutes. Season with salt and black pepper.

Add the enchilada sauce to the casserole dish. Add the beef mixture and 1/2 cup of the Mexican cheese blend. Gently stir to combine.

Add the tomato paste, Mexican oregano, nacho chips, and the remaining 1/2 cup of cheese blend. Cover with foil.

Bake in the preheated Air Fryer at 350 degrees F for 20 minutes; remove the foil and bake for a further 10 to 12 minutes. Serve garnished with fresh coriander and enjoy!

Per serving: 666 Calories; 27.7g Fat; 72.2g Carbs; 42.3g Protein; 4.3g Sugars

665. Tyrolean Kaiserschmarrn (Austrian Pancakes)

(Ready in about 30 minutes | Servings 4)

Ingredients

1/2 cup flour
A pinch of salt
A pinch of sugar
1/2 cup whole milk
3 eggs

1 shot of rum
4 tablespoons raisins
1/2 cup icing sugar
1/2 cup stewed plums

Directions

Mix the flour, salt, sugar, and milk in a bowl until the batter becomes semi-solid.

Fold in the eggs; add the rum and whisk to combine well. Let it stand for 20 minutes.

Spritz the Air Fryer baking pan with cooking spray. Pour the batter into the pan using a measuring cup. Scatter the raisins over the top.

Cook at 230 degrees F for 4 to 5 minutes or until golden brown. Repeat with the remaining batter.

Cut the pancake into pieces, sprinkle over the icing sugar, and serve with the stewed plums. Bon appétit!

Per serving: 370 Calories; 5.8g Fat; 72.3g Carbs; 10.2g Protein; 48.2g Sugars

VEGAN

666. Air Grilled Tofu

(Ready in about 15 minutes | Servings 3)

Ingredients

8 ounces firm tofu, pressed and cut into bite-sized cubes
1 tablespoon tamari sauce
1 teaspoon peanut oil
1/2 teaspoon garlic powder
1/2 teaspoon onion powder

Directions

Toss the tofu cubes with tamari sauce, peanut oil, garlic powder and onion powder.

Cook your tofu in the preheated Air Fryer at 380 degrees F for about 13 minutes, shaking the basket once or twice to ensure even browning. Bon appétit!

Per serving: 112 Calories; 6.6g Fat; 3.6g Carbs; 12.1g Protein; 0.2g Sugars

667. Golden Beet Salad with Tahini Sauce

(Ready in about 40 minutes | Servings 2)

Ingredients

2 golden beets
1 tablespoon sesame oil
Sea salt and ground black pepper, to taste
2 cups baby spinach
2 tablespoons tahini
2 tablespoons soy sauce
1 tablespoon white vinegar
1 clove garlic, pressed
1/2 jalapeno pepper, chopped
1/4 teaspoon ground cumin

Directions

Toss the golden beets with sesame oil. Cook the golden beets in the preheated Air Fryer at 400 degrees F for 40 minutes, turning them over once or twice to ensure even cooking.

Let your beets cool completely and then, slice them with a sharp knife. Place the beets in a salad bowl and add in salt, pepper and baby spinach.

In a small mixing dish, whisk the remaining ingredients until well combined.

Spoon the sauce over your beets, toss to combine and serve immediately. Bon appétit!

Per serving: 253 Calories; 18.1g Fat; 19.1g Carbs; 6.4g Protein; 10.1g Sugars

668. Easy Roasted Fennel

(Ready in about 25 minutes | Servings 3)

Ingredients

1 pound fennel bulbs, sliced
1 tablespoon olive oil
1/2 teaspoon dried basil
1/2 teaspoon dried marjoram
Sea salt and ground black pepper, to taste
1/4 cup vegan mayonnaise

Directions

Toss the fennel slices with the olive oil and spices and transfer them to the Air Fryer cooking basket.

Roast the fennel at 370 degrees F for about 20 minutes, shaking the basket once or twice to promote even cooking.

Serve the fennel slice with mayonnaise and enjoy!

Per serving: 158 Calories; 11.2g Fat; 13.1g Carbs; 3.4g Protein; 6.8g Sugars

669. Asian-Style Brussels Sprouts

(Ready in about 20 minutes | Servings 3)

Ingredients

1 pound Brussels sprouts, trimmed and halved
1 teaspoon coconut oil
2 tablespoons Shoyu sauce
1 tablespoon agave syrup
1 teaspoon rice vinegar
1/2 teaspoon Gochujang paste
1 clove garlic, minced
2 scallion stalks, chopped
1 tablespoon sesame seeds, toasted

Directions

Toss the Brussels sprouts with coconut oil, Shoyu sauce, agave syrup, rice vinegar, Gochujang paste and garlic.

Cook the Brussels sprouts in the preheated Air Fryer at 380 degrees F for 15 minutes, shaking the basket halfway through the cooking time.

Place the roasted Brussels sprouts on a serving platter and garnish with scallions and sesame seeds. Serve immediately!

Per serving: 124 Calories; 3.6g Fat; 21.1g Carbs; 5.9g Protein; 9.7g Sugars

670. Korean-Style Broccoli

(Ready in about 12 minutes | Servings 2)

Ingredients

1/2 pound broccoli florets
1 tablespoon sesame oil
1 tablespoon soy sauce
1/4 teaspoon coriander seeds
1/2 teaspoon garlic powder
1 tablespoon brown sugar
1/2 teaspoon gochukaru (Korean red chili powder)
Sea salt and ground black pepper, to taste

Directions

Toss the broccoli florets with the other ingredients until well coated.

Air fry your broccoli at 390 degrees F for about 10 minutes, shaking the basket halfway through the cooking time.

Serve with your favorite vegan dip. Enjoy!

Per serving: 141 Calories; 8.6g Fat; 14.2g Carbs; 3.9g Protein; 7.4g Sugars

671. Sweet Potato Croquettes

(Ready in about 20 minutes | Servings 3)

Ingredients

1/2 pound sweet potatoes
1/4 cup wheat flour
1/4 cup glutinous rice flour
1 teaspoon baking powder
1 tablespoon brown sugar
1/4 teaspoon cayenne pepper
A pinch of grated nutmeg
Kosher salt and ground black pepper, to taste

Directions

Mix all ingredients in a bowl; stir until everything is well combined.

Transfer the sweet potato balls to the Air Fryer cooking basket and spritz them with a nonstick cooking oil.

Bake the sweet potato balls in the preheated Air Fryer at 360 degrees F for 15 minutes or until thoroughly cooked and crispy.

Bon appétit!

Per serving: 171 Calories; 0.2g Fat; 38.2g Carbs; 3.3g Protein; 5.8g Sugars

672. Cajun Celery Sticks

(Ready in about 20 minutes | Servings 3)

Ingredients

1/2 pound celery root, peeled and cut into 1/2-inch sticks
1 teaspoon Cajun seasoning mix
Salt and white pepper, to taste
Sauce:
1/3 cup tofu mayonnaise
1 teaspoon lime juice
1 teaspoon deli mustard
1 teaspoon agave nectar

Directions

Toss the celery sticks with the Cajun seasoning mix, salt and white pepper and place them in the Air Fryer cooking basket.

Now, cook the celery sticks at 400 degrees F for about 17 minutes, shaking the basket halfway through the cooking time.

In the meantime, mix the mayonnaise with the lime juice, deli mustard and agave nectar.

Serve the celery sticks with the mayo sauce on the side. Bon appétit!

Per serving: 108 Calories; 8.6g Fat; 5.2g Carbs; 2.4g Protein; 2.4g Sugars

673. Roasted Asparagus Salad

(Ready in about 10 minutes | Servings 4)

Ingredients

1 pound asparagus spears, trimmed and sliced into 1-inch chunks
1/2 teaspoon turmeric powder
1 cup canned chickpeas, drained
1/2 cup canned white beans, drained
1/4 cup shallots, chopped

1 clove garlic, pressed
2 tablespoons champagne vinegar
2 tablespoons extra-virgin olive oil
1/4 teaspoon cayenne pepper
Kosher salt and freshly ground black pepper, to taste

Directions

Toss the asparagus with turmeric powder and brush with a nonstick cooking spray.

Air fry your asparagus at 400 degrees F for 5 minutes, tossing halfway through the cooking time to promote even cooking.

Allow your asparagus to cool slightly and transfer to a salad bowl. Toss your asparagus with the chickpeas, white beans, shallots and garlic.

In a small bowl, whisk the remaining ingredients to make the dressing. Dress the salad and serve at room temperature. Bon appétit!

Per serving: 188 Calories; 11.1g Fat; 17g Carbs; 6.9g Protein; 3.4g Sugars

674. Corn on the Cob with Mediterranean Sauce

(Ready in about 10 minutes | Servings 2)

Ingredients

2 ears corn, husked
1/3 cup raw cashews, soaked
2 cloves garlic, minced
1/2 teaspoon nutritional yeast
1/2 teaspoon Dijon mustard
4 tablespoons oat milk

1 tablespoon extra-virgin olive oil
1 teaspoon freshly squeezed lemon juice
Sea salt and ground black pepper, to taste

Directions

Cook your corn in the preheated Air Fryer at 390 degrees F for about 6 minutes.

Meanwhile, blitz the remaining ingredients in your food processor or blender until smooth, creamy and uniform.

Rub each ear of corn with the Mediterranean spread and serve immediately. Bon appétit!

Per serving: 434 Calories; 27.4g Fat; 45.1g Carbs; 10.8g Protein; 5.4g Sugars

675. Decadent Carrot Salad with Sultanas

(Ready in about 20 minutes | Servings 3)

Ingredients

1 pound carrots, cut into 1/2-inch slices
1/4 teaspoon dried dill
1/2 teaspoon dried parsley flakes
2 tablespoons maple syrup
2 tablespoons Sultanas

1/2 cup orange juice
1 tablespoon champagne vinegar
6 ounces baby spinach
1/4 cup pine nuts, roughly chopped

Directions

Toss your carrots with dried dill and dried parsley flakes; brush them with a nonstick cooking spray.

Cook your carrots in the preheated Air Fryer at 380 degrees F for about 15 minutes, shaking the basket halfway through the cooking time.

Meanwhile, add the maple syrup, Sultanas, orange juice and champagne vinegar to a saucepan; let it simmer over a moderate heat until the sauce has thickened.

Spoon the sauce over the roasted carrots and stir in the baby spinach. Top with chopped pine nuts and serve at room temperature. Bon appétit!

Per serving: 208 Calories; 8.3g Fat; 32.1g Carbs; 4.8g Protein; 19.4g Sugars

676. Cauliflower Oatmeal Fritters

(Ready in about 20 minutes | Servings 3)

Ingredients

1/2 pound cauliflower florets
1 cup rolled oats
2 tablespoons flaxseed meal
2 tablespoons sunflower seeds
2 tablespoons hemp hearts
4 tablespoons pumpkin seeds butter

1 glove garlic, chopped
1 small yellow onion
1/2 teaspoon smoked paprika
Kosher salt and freshly ground black pepper, to taste
1 tablespoon canola oil

Directions

Place all ingredients in the bowl of your food processor or blender; mix until well combined. Then, shape the mixture into small patties and transfer them to the Air Fryer cooking basket.

Cook the cauliflower patties in the preheated Air Fryer at 375 degrees F for 16 minutes, shaking the basket halfway through the cooking time to ensure even browning.

Bon appétit!

Per serving: 408 Calories; 18.3g Fat; 45.5g Carbs; 16.1g Protein; 2.8g Sugars

677. Louisiana-Style Eggplant Cutlets

(Ready in about 45 minutes | Servings 3)

Ingredients

1 pound eggplant, cut lengthwise into 1/2-inch thick slices
1/4 cup plain flour
1/4 cup almond milk
1 cup fresh bread crumbs
1 teaspoon Cajun seasoning mix

Sea salt and ground black pepper, to taste
1 cup tomato sauce
1 teaspoon brown mustard
1/2 teaspoon chili powder

Directions

Toss your eggplant with 1 teaspoon of salt and leave it for 30 minutes; drain and rinse the eggplant and set it aside.

In a shallow bowl, mix the flour with almond milk until well combined. In a separate bowl, mix the breadcrumbs with Cajun seasoning mix, salt and black pepper.

Dip your eggplant in the flour mixture, then, coat each slice with the breadcrumb mixture, pressing to adhere.

Cook the breaded eggplant at 400 degrees F for 10 minutes, flipping them halfway through the cooking time to ensure even browning.

In the meantime, mix the remaining ingredients for the sauce. Divide the tomato mixture between eggplant cutlets and continue to cook for another 5 minutes or until thoroughly cooked.

Transfer the warm eggplant cutlets to a wire rack to stay crispy. Bon appétit!

Per serving: 214 Calories; 1.3g Fat; 43g Carbs; 6.1g Protein; 16.8g Sugars

678. Fried Green Beans

(Ready in about 10 minutes | Servings 2)

Ingredients

1/2 pound green beans, cleaned and trimmed
1 teaspoon extra-virgin olive oil
1/2 teaspoon onion powder
1/2 teaspoon shallot powder
1/4 teaspoon cumin powder
1/2 teaspoon cayenne pepper

1/2 teaspoon garlic powder
Himalayan salt and freshly ground black pepper, to taste
1 tablespoon lime juice
1 tablespoon soy sauce
1/4 cup pecans, roughly chopped

Directions

Toss the green beans with olive oil, spices and lime juice.

Cook the green beans in your Air Fryer at 400 degrees F for 5 minutes, shaking the basket halfway through the cooking time to promote even cooking.

Toss the green beans with soy sauce and serve garnished with chopped pecans. Bon appétit!

Per serving: 162 Calories; 11.3g Fat; 13g Carbs; 4.1g Protein; 6g Sugars

679. Famous Everything Bagel Kale Chips

(Ready in about 12 minutes | Servings 1)

Ingredients

2 cups loosely packed kale leaves, stems removed
1 teaspoon olive oil
1 tablespoon nutritional yeast flakes
Coarse salt and ground black pepper, to taste

1 teaspoon sesame seeds, lightly toasted
1/2 teaspoon poppy seeds, lightly toasted
1/4 teaspoon garlic powder

Directions

Toss the kale leaves with olive oil, nutritional yeast, salt and black pepper.

Cook your kale at 250 degrees F for 12 minutes, shaking the basket every 4 minutes to promote even cooking.

Place the kale leaves on a platter and sprinkle evenly with sesame seeds, poppy seeds and garlic powder while still hot. Enjoy!

Per serving: 134 Calories; 7.3g Fat; 12.1g Carbs; 7.5g Protein; 3.4g Sugars

680. Portobello Mushroom Schnitzel

(Ready in about 10 minutes | Servings 2)

Ingredients

7 ounces Portobello mushrooms
1/4 cup chickpea flour
1/4 cup plain flour
1/3 cup beer
1 cup breadcrumbs
1/2 teaspoon porcini powder
1/2 teaspoon dried basil

1/4 teaspoon dried oregano
1/4 teaspoon ground cumin
1/4 teaspoon ground bay leaf
1/2 teaspoon garlic powder
1/2 teaspoon shallot powder
Kosher salt and ground black pepper, to taste

Directions

Pat dry the Portobello mushrooms and set them aside.

Then, add the flour and beer to a rimmed plate and mix to combine well. In another bowl, mix the breadcrumbs with spices.

Dip your mushrooms in the flour mixture, then, coat them with the breadcrumb mixture.

Cook the breaded mushrooms in the preheated Air Fryer at 380 degrees F for 6 to 7 minutes, flipping them over halfway through the cooking time. Eat warm.

Per serving: 156 Calories; 1.4g Fat; 27.1g Carbs; 7.2g Protein; 5g Sugars

681. Pearl Onions with Tahini Sauce

(Ready in about 10 minutes | Servings 2)

Ingredients

3/4 pound pearl onions
1 teaspoon olive oil
Sea salt and ground black pepper, to taste

1/2 teaspoon thyme
2 tablespoons tahini
2 tablespoons soy sauce
1 tablespoon balsamic vinegar

Directions

Toss the pearl onions with olive oil, salt, black pepper and thyme.

Cook the pearl onions in the preheated Air Fryer at 400 degrees F for 5 minutes. Shake the basket and continue to cook for another 5 minutes.

Meanwhile, make the tahini sauce by whisking the remaining ingredients; whisk to combine well. Spoon the tahini sauce over the pearl onions and enjoy!

Per serving: 226 Calories; 3.3g Fat; 23.5g Carbs; 5.5g Protein; 14.1g Sugars

682. Fried Parsnip with Mint Yogurt Sauce

(Ready in about 10 minutes | Servings 2)

Ingredients

1/2 parsnip, peeled and sliced into sticks
1 teaspoon olive oil
Sea salt and ground black pepper, to taste

3 ounces Greek-style dairy-free yogurt, unsweetened
1 teaspoon juice
1/2 teaspoon fresh garlic, pressed
1 teaspoon fresh mint, chopped

Directions

Toss your parsnip with olive oil, salt and black pepper.

Cook the parsnip in the preheated Air Fryer at 390 degrees F for 15 minutes, shaking the basket halfway through the cooking time.

In the meantime, mix the remaining ingredients until well combined. Serve the warm parsnip with the mint yogurt for dipping. Bon appétit!

Per serving: 141 Calories; 2.8g Fat; 24.6g Carbs; 6.2g Protein; 8.2g Sugars

683. Authentic Vegan Ratatouille

(Ready in about 15 minutes | Servings 2)

Ingredients

4 ounces courgette, sliced
4 ounces eggplant, sliced
1 bell pepper, sliced
4 ounces tomatoes, peeled and quartered
1 yellow onion, peeled and sliced

1 teaspoon fresh garlic, minced
1/2 teaspoon oregano
1/2 teaspoon basil
Coarse sea salt and ground black pepper, to taste
1 tablespoon olive oil

Directions

Place the sliced veggies in the Air Fryer cooking basket. Season your veggies with oregano, basil, salt and black pepper. Drizzle olive oil over the top.

Cook your veggies at 400 degrees F for about 15 minutes, shaking the basket halfway through the cooking time to promote even cooking.

Arrange the sliced veggies in alternating patterns and serve warm. Bon appétit!

Per serving: 136 Calories; 7.4g Fat; 16g Carbs; 3.7g Protein; 8.3g Sugars

684. Peppers Provençal with Garbanzo Beans

(Ready in about 25 minutes | Servings 3)

Ingredients

1 pound bell peppers, deseeded and sliced
2 teaspoons olive oil
1 teaspoon Herbs de Provence

1 onion, chopped
10 ounces canned tomato sauce
1 teaspoon red wine vinegar
9 ounces canned garbanzo beans

Directions

Drizzle the bell peppers with 1 teaspoon of olive oil; sprinkle them with Herbs de Provence and transfer to the Air Fryer cooking basket.

Cook the peppers in the preheated Air Fryer at 400 degrees F for 15 minutes, shaking the basket halfway through the cooking time.

Meanwhile, heat the remaining teaspoon of olive oil in a saucepan over medium-high heat. Once hot, sauté the onion until just tender and translucent.

Then, add in the tomato sauce and let it simmer, partially covered, for about 10 minutes until the sauce has thickened. Remove from the heat and add in the vinegar and garbanzo beans; stir to combine.

Serve the roasted peppers with the saucy garbanzo beans. Bon appétit!

Per serving: 236 Calories; 5.9g Fat; 40.1g Carbs; 10.1g Protein; 15.1g Sugars

685. Crispy Garlic Tofu with Brussels Sprouts

(Ready in about 20 minutes | Servings 2)

Ingredients

8 ounces firm tofu, pressed and cut into bite-sized cubes
1 teaspoon garlic paste
1 tablespoons arrowroot powder
1 teaspoon peanut oil

1/2 pound Brussels sprouts, halved
Sea salt and ground black pepper, to taste

Directions

Toss the tofu cubes with the garlic paste, arrowroot powder and peanut oil.

Transfer your tofu to the Air Fryer cooking basket; add in the Brussels sprouts and season everything with salt and black pepper.

Cook the tofu cubes and Brussels sprouts at 380 degrees F for 15 minutes, shaking the basket halfway through the cooking time. Bon appétit!

Per serving: 256 Calories; 12.5g Fat; 21.1g Carbs; 22.8g Protein; 3.6g Sugars

686. Baby Potatoes with Garlic-Rosemary Sauce

(Ready in about 50 minutes | Servings 3)

Ingredients

1 pound baby potatoes, scrubbed
1 tablespoon olive oil
1/2 garlic bulb, slice the top 1/4-inch off the garlic head
1 tablespoon fresh rosemary leaves, chopped

1 teaspoon sherry vinegar
1/2 cup white wine
Salt and freshly ground black pepper

Directions

Brush the baby potatoes with olive oil and transfer them to the air Fryer cooking basket. Cook the baby potatoes at 400 degrees F for 12 minutes, shaking the basket halfway through the cooking time.

Place the garlic bulb into the center of a piece of aluminum foil. Drizzle the garlic bulb with a nonstick cooking spray and wrap tightly in foil.

Cook the garlic at 390 degrees F for about 25 minutes or until the cloves are tender.

Let it cool for about 10 minutes; remove the cloves by squeezing them out of the skins; mash the garlic and add it to a saucepan.

Stir the remaining ingredients into the saucepan and let it simmer for 10 to 15 minutes until the sauce has reduced by half. Spoon the sauce over the baby potatoes and serve warm. Bon appétit!

Per serving: 166 Calories; 4.6g Fat; 28.1g Carbs; 3.5g Protein; 1.6g Sugars

687. Quinoa-Stuffed Winter Squash

(Ready in about 30 minutes | Servings 2)

Ingredients

1/2 cup quinoa
1 cup loosely mixed greens, torn into small pieces
1 teaspoon sesame oil
1 clove garlic, pressed

1 small winter squash, halved lengthwise, seeds removed
Sea salt and ground black pepper, to taste
1 tablespoon fresh parsley, roughly chopped

Directions

Rinse your quinoa, drain it and transfer to a pot with 1 cup of lightly salted water; bring to a boil.

Turn the heat to a simmer and continue to cook, covered, for about 10 minutes; add in the mixed greens and continue to cook for 5 minutes longer.

Stir in the sesame oil and garlic and stir to combine. Divide the quinoa mixture between the winter squash halves and sprinkle it with the salt and pepper.

Cook your squash in the preheated Air Fryer at 400 degrees F for about 12 minutes.

Place the stuffed squash on individual plates, garnish with fresh parsley and serve. Bon appétit!

Per serving: 279 Calories; 5.1g Fat; 53.1g Carbs; 8.7g Protein; 1.3g Sugars

688. Italian-Style Tomato Cutlets

(Ready in about 10 minutes | Servings 2)

Ingredients

1 beefsteak tomato – sliced into halves
1/2 cup all-purpose flour

1/2 cup almond milk
1/2 cup breadcrumbs
1 teaspoon Italian seasoning mix

Directions

Pat the beefsteak tomato dry and set it aside.

In a shallow bowl, mix the all-purpose flour with almond milk. In another bowl, mix breadcrumbs with Italian seasoning mix.

Dip the beefsteak tomatoes in the flour mixture; then, coat the beefsteak tomatoes with the breadcrumb mixture, pressing to adhere to both sides.

Cook your tomatoes at 360 degrees F for about 5 minutes; turn them over and cook on the other side for 5 minutes longer. Serve at room temperature and enjoy!

Per serving: 181 Calories; 2.6g Fat; 32.2g Carbs; 6.1g Protein; 4.1g Sugars

689. Paprika Squash Fries

(Ready in about 15 minutes | Servings 3)

Ingredients

1/4 cup rice milk
1/4 cup almond flour
2 tablespoons nutritional yeast
1/4 teaspoon shallot powder
1/2 teaspoon garlic powder
1/2 teaspoon paprika

Sea salt and ground black pepper to taste
1 pound butternut squash, peeled and into sticks
1 cup tortilla chips, crushed

Directions

In a bowl, thoroughly combine the milk flour, nutritional yeast and spices. In another shallow bowl, place the crushed tortilla chips.

Dip the butternut squash sticks into the batter and then, roll them over the crushed tortilla chips until well coated.

Arrange the squash pieces in the Air Fryer cooking basket. Cook the squash fries at 400 degrees F for about 12 minutes, shaking the basket once or twice. Bon appétit!

Per serving: 202 Calories; 5.8g Fat; 30.2g Carbs; 8.1g Protein; 2.9g Sugars

690. Authentic Platanos Maduros

(Ready in about 15 minutes | Servings 2)

Ingredients

1 very ripe, sweet plantain
1 teaspoon Caribbean Sorrel Rum Spice Mix

1 teaspoon coconut oil, melted

Directions

Cut your plantain into slices.

Toss your plantain with Caribbean Sorrel Rum Spice Mix and coconut oil

Cook your plantain in the preheated Air Fryer at 400 degrees F for 10 minutes, shaking the cooking basket halfway through the cooking time.

Serve immediately and enjoy!

Per serving: 129 Calories; 2.5g Fat; 28.2g Carbs; 1.1g Protein; 13.4g Sugars

691. Southwestern Fried Apples

(Ready in about 10 minutes | Servings 3)

Ingredients

2 granny smith apples, peeled, cored and sliced
1 tablespoon coconut oil
1 teaspoon fresh lemon juice

1/4 cup brown sugar
1 teaspoon apple pie seasoning mix

Directions

Toss the apple slices with the coconut oil, lemon juice, brown sugar and apple pie seasoning mix.

Place the apple slices in the Air Fryer cooking basket and cook them at 360 degrees F for about 8 minutes, shaking the cooking basket halfway through the cooking time.

Bon appétit!

Per serving: 140 Calories; 4.7g Fat; 24.2g Carbs; 0.5g Protein; 18.4g Sugars

692. Buffalo Cauliflower Bites

(Ready in about 35 minutes | Servings 2)

Ingredients

1/2 pound cauliflower florets
1/2 cup all-purpose flour
1/2 cup rice milk
1/2 teaspoon chili powder

1 teaspoon garlic powder
Sea salt and ground black pepper, to taste

Directions

Pat the cauliflower florets dry and reserve.

In a mixing bowl, thoroughly combine the flour, rice milk, chili powder, garlic powder, salt and black pepper.

Dip the cauliflower florets in the batter until well coated on all sides. Place the cauliflower florets in your freezer for 15 minutes.

Cook the cauliflower in the preheated Air Fryer at 390 degrees F for about 10 minutes; turn them over and cook for another 10 minutes.

Taste, adjust the seasonings and serve warm. Bon appétit!

Per serving: 195 Calories; 2.7g Fat; 36g Carbs; 8.1g Protein; 6.5g Sugars

693. Green Potato Croquettes

(Ready in about 45 minutes | Servings 2)

Ingredients

1/2 pound cup russet potatoes
1 teaspoon olive oil
1/2 teaspoon garlic, pressed
2 cups loosely packed mixed greens, torn into pieces

2 tablespoons oat milk
Sea salt and ground black pepper, to taste
1/4 teaspoon red pepper flakes, crushed

Directions

Cook your potatoes for about 30 minutes until they are fork-tender; peel the potatoes and add them to a mixing bowl.

Mash your potatoes and stir in the remaining ingredients.

Shape the mixture into bite-sized balls and place them in the cooking basket; sprits the balls with a nonstick cooking oil.

Cook the croquettes at 390 degrees F for about 13 minutes, shaking the cooking basket halfway through the cooking time.

Serve with tomato ketchup if desired. Bon appétit!

Per serving: 137 Calories; 2.9g Fat; 25.2g Carbs; 4.1g Protein; 2.8g Sugars

694. Old-Fashioned Potato Wedges

(Ready in about 15 minutes | Servings 2)

Ingredients

2 medium potatoes, scrubbed and cut into wedges
1 teaspoon olive oil
1 teaspoon garlic powder

1 teaspoon shallot powder
1/4 teaspoon cayenne pepper
Kosher salt and ground black pepper, to season

Directions

Toss the potato wedges with olive oil and spices and transfer them to the Air Fryer cooking basket.

Cook the potato wedges at 400 degrees F for 6 minutes; shake the basket and cook for another 6 to 8 minutes.

Serve with your favorite vegan dip. Bon appétit!

Per serving: 184 Calories; 2.4g Fat; 37.2g Carbs; 4.3g Protein; 1.6g Sugars

695. Easy Homemade Falafel

(Ready in about 15 minutes | Servings 3)

Ingredients

1 cup dry chickpeas, soaked overnight
1 small onion, sliced
2 tablespoons fresh cilantro
2 tablespoons fresh parsley

2 cloves garlic
1/2 teaspoon cayenne pepper
Sea salt and ground black pepper, to taste
1/2 teaspoon ground cumin

Directions

Drain and rinse your chickpeas and place them in a bowl of a food processor.

Add in the remaining ingredients and blitz until the ingredients form a coarse meal. Roll the mixture into small balls with oiled hands.

Cook your falafel in the preheated Air Fryer at 395 degrees F for 5 minutes; turn them over and cook for another 5 to 6 minutes. Bon appétit!

Per serving: 274 Calories; 4.2g Fat; 46.7g Carbs; 14.3g Protein; 8.9g Sugars

696. Italian-Style Pasta Chips

(Ready in about 15 minutes | Servings 2)

Ingredients

1 cup dry rice pasta
1 teaspoon olive oil
1 tablespoon nutritional yeast
1/2 teaspoon dried oregano

1/2 teaspoon dried basil
1 teaspoon dried parsley flakes
Kosher salt and ground black pepper, to taste

Directions

Cook the pasta according to the manufacturer's instructions. Drain your pasta and toss it with the remaining ingredients.

Cook the pasta chips at 390 degrees F for about 10 minutes, shaking the cooking basket halfway through the cooking time.

The pasta chips will crisp up as it cools.

Serve with tomato ketchup if desired. Bon appétit!

Per serving: 224 Calories; 3.4g Fat; 43.4g Carbs; 6.1g Protein; 0.1g Sugars

697. Shawarma Roasted Chickpeas

(Ready in about 20 minutes | Servings 2)

Ingredients

8 ounces canned chickpeas
1/4 teaspoon turmeric powder
1/4 teaspoon cinnamon
1/4 teaspoon allspice
1/2 teaspoon ground coriander

1/4 teaspoon ground ginger
1/4 teaspoon smoked paprika
Coarse sea salt and freshly ground black pepper, to taste

Directions

Rinse your chickpeas with cold running water and pat it dry using kitchen towels.

Place the spices in a plastic bag; add in the chickpeas and shake until all the chickpeas are coated with the spices.

Spritz the spiced chickpeas with a nonstick cooking oil and transfer them to the Air Fryer cooking basket.

Cook your chickpeas in the preheated Air Fryer at 395 degrees F for 13 minutes. Turn your Air Fryer to 350 degrees F and cook an additional 6 minutes. Bon appétit!

Per serving: 217 Calories; 9.4g Fat; 25.4g Carbs; 8g Protein; 4.5g Sugars

698. Spicy Sesame Cauliflower Steaks

(Ready in about 25 minutes | Servings 2)

Ingredients

1/2 pound cauliflower, cut into 2 slabs
1/2 cup plain flour
1/4 cup cornstarch
1/2 cup ale
1/2 teaspoon hot sauce
1/4 teaspoon onion powder
1/2 teaspoon garlic powder
1/2 teaspoon smoked paprika
1 tablespoon sesame seeds
Kosher salt and ground black pepper, to taste
1/4 cup buffalo sauce

Directions

Parboil the cauliflower in the pot with a lightly salted water for about 15 minutes.

In a mixing bowl, combine the remaining ingredients, except for the buffalo sauce, until everything is well incorporated. Then, dip the cauliflower steaks into the batter.

Cook the cauliflower steaks at 400 degrees F for 10 minutes, flipping them over halfway through the cooking time to promote even cooking.

Serve the warm cauliflower steaks with buffalo sauce and enjoy!

Per serving: 247 Calories; 0.8g Fat; 54.4g Carbs; 6.6g Protein; 10.1g Sugars

699. Perfect Shallot Rings

(Ready in about 15 minutes | Servings 2)

Ingredients

1/2 cup all-purpose flour
1/4 cup cornflour
1/2 cup rice milk
1/4 cup fizzy water
1/4 teaspoon turmeric powder
Sea salt and red pepper, to taste
1/2 cup seasoned breadcrumbs
2 shallots, sliced into rings

Directions

In a shallow bowl, thoroughly combine the flour, milk, fizzy water, turmeric, salt and pepper. In another bowl, place seasoned breadcrumbs.

Dip the shallot rings in the flour mixture; then, coat the rings with the seasoned breadcrumbs, pressing to adhere.

Transfer the shallot rings to the Air Fryer cooking basket and spritz them with a nonstick spray.

Cook the shallot rings at 380 degrees F for about 10 minutes, shaking the basket halfway through the cooking time to ensure even browning. Bon appétit!

Per serving: 347 Calories; 4.3g Fat; 66.1g Carbs; 11g Protein; 8.8g Sugars

700. Spicy Bean Burgers

(Ready in about 15 minutes | Servings 3)

Ingredients

1/2 cup old-fashioned oats
2 tablespoons red onions, finely chopped
2 garlic cloves, finely chopped
8 ounces canned beans
1/3 cup marinara sauce
1 teaspoon tamari sauce
A few drops of liquid smoke
Kosher salt and ground black pepper, to taste
1/4 teaspoon ancho chile powder

Directions

Pulse all ingredients in your food processor leaving some larger chunks of beans.

Now, form the mixture into patties and place them in the Air Fryer cooking basket. Brush the patties with a nonstick cooking oil.

Cook your burgers at 380 degrees F for about 15 minutes, flipping them halfway through the cooking time.

Serve on burger buns garnished with your favorite fixings. Bon appétit!

Per serving: 227 Calories; 2.3g Fat; 40.1g Carbs; 12.1g Protein; 2.2g Sugars

701. The Best Potato Fritters Ever

(Ready in about 55 minutes | Servings 3)

Ingredients

3 medium-sized potatoes, peeled
1 tablespoon flax seeds, ground
1/2 cup plain flour
1/2 teaspoon cayenne pepper
1/4 teaspoon dried dill weed
Sea salt and ground black pepper, to taste
1 tablespoon olive oil
1 tablespoon fresh chives, chopped

Directions

Place your potatoes in the Air Fryer cooking basket and cook them at 400 degrees F for about 40 minutes, shaking the basket occasionally to promote even cooking. Mash your potatoes with a fork or potato masher.

Make a vegan egg by mixing 1 tablespoon of ground flax seeds with 1 ½ tablespoons of water. Let it stand for 5 minutes.

Stir in the mashed potatoes, flour and spices; form the mixture into equal patties and brush them with olive oil.

Cook your fritters at 390 degrees F for about 10 minutes, flipping them halfway through the cooking time.

Garnish with fresh, chopped chives and serve warm. Bon appétit!

Per serving: 304 Calories; 6.5g Fat; 55.1g Carbs; 7.4g Protein; 2.6g Sugars

702. Bell Pepper Fries

(Ready in about 15 minutes | Servings 2)

Ingredients

1 cup flour
1 cup oat milk
1/2 teaspoon dried marjoram
1/2 teaspoon turmeric powder
Sea salt and ground black pepper, to taste
1 cup seasoned breadcrumbs
2 large bell peppers

Directions

In a shallow bowl, thoroughly combine the flour, milk, marjoram, turmeric, salt and black pepper. In another bowl, place seasoned breadcrumbs.

Dip the pepper rings in the flour mixture; then, coat the rings with the seasoned breadcrumbs, pressing to adhere.

Transfer the pepper rings to the Air Fryer cooking basket and spritz them with a nonstick spray.

Cook the pepper rings at 380 degrees F for about 10 minutes, shaking the basket halfway through the cooking time to promote even cooking. Bon appétit!

Per serving: 392 Calories; 5.5g Fat; 71.1g Carbs; 13.4g Protein; 11.1g Sugars

703. Polish Placki Ziemniaczan

(Ready in about 10 minutes | Servings 2)

Ingredients

1/2 pound potatoes, peeled and finely grated
1/2 small white onion, finely chopped
1/4 cup all-purpose flour
1/2 teaspoon turmeric powder
2 tablespoons breadcrumbs
Kosher salt and freshly ground black pepper, to taste
2 tablespoons granulated sugar
2 ounces sour cream

Directions

Place the grated potatoes in a triple layer of cheesecloth; now, twist and squeeze the potatoes until no more liquid comes out of them.

Place the potatoes in a mixing bowl; stir in the onion, flour, turmeric powder, breadcrumbs, salt and black pepper.

Cook them at 380 degrees for about 10 minutes, turning over after 5 minutes. Serve with granulated sugar and sour cream. Enjoy!

Per serving: 262 Calories; 3.7g Fat; 50.1g Carbs; 6.4g Protein; 10.3g Sugars

704. Favorite Lentil Burgers

(Ready in about 15 minutes | Servings 3)

Ingredients

1/2 cup wild rice, cooked
1 cup red lentils, cooked
1/2 small onion, quartered
1/2 small beet, peeled and quartered
1 garlic clove
1/4 cup walnuts

2 tablespoons breadcrumbs
1/2 teaspoon cayenne pepper
Sea salt and ground black pepper, to taste
1 tablespoon vegan barbecue sauce

Directions

In your food processor, pulse all ingredients until a moldable dough forms.

Shape the mixture into equal patties and place them in the lightly oiled Air Fryer cooking basket.

Cook your burgers at 380 degrees F for about 15 minutes, flipping them halfway through the cooking time.

Serve on burger buns and enjoy!

Per serving: 195 Calories; 4.8g Fat; 31.1g Carbs; 8.9g Protein; 9.8g Sugars

705. Traditional Indian Pakora

(Ready in about 35 minutes | Servings 2)

Ingredients

1 large zucchini, grated
1/2 cup besan flour
1/2 teaspoon baking powder
2 scallion stalks, chopped
1/2 teaspoon paprika

1/4 teaspoon curry powder
14 teaspoon ginger-garlic paste
Sea salt and ground black pepper, to taste
1 teaspoon olive oil

Directions

Sprinkle the salt over the grated zucchini and leave it for 20 minutes. Then, squeeze the zucchini and drain off the excess liquid.

Mix the grated zucchini with the flour, baking powder, scallions, paprika, curry powder and ginger-garlic paste. Salt and pepper to taste.

Shape the mixture into patties and transfer them to the Air Fryer cooking basket. Brush the zucchini patties with 1 teaspoon of olive oil.

Cook the pakora at 380 degrees F for about 12 minutes, flipping them halfway through the cooking time.

Serve on dinner rolls and enjoy!

Per serving: 175 Calories; 4.4g Fat; 24.6g Carbs; 9.5g Protein; 3.9g Sugars

706. The Best Crispy Tofu

(Ready in about 55 minutes | Servings 4)

Ingredients

16 ounces firm tofu, pressed and cubed
1 tablespoon vegan oyster sauce
1 tablespoon tamari sauce
1 teaspoon cider vinegar
1 teaspoon pure maple syrup

1 teaspoon sriracha
1/2 teaspoon shallot powder
1/2 teaspoon porcini powder
1 teaspoon garlic powder
1 tablespoon sesame oil
5 tablespoons cornstarch

Directions

Toss the tofu with the oyster sauce, tamari sauce, vinegar, maple syrup, sriracha, shallot powder, porcini powder, garlic powder, and sesame oil. Let it marinate for 30 minutes.

Toss the marinated tofu with the cornstarch.

Cook at 360 degrees F for 10 minutes; turn them over and cook for 12 minutes more. Bon appétit!

Per serving: 245 Calories; 13.3g Fat; 16.7g Carbs; 18.2g Protein; 1.2g Sugars

707. Rainbow Roasted Vegetables

(Ready in about 25 minutes | Servings 4)

Ingredients

1 red bell pepper, seeded and cut into 1/2-inch chunks
1 cup squash, peeled and cut into 1/2-inch chunks
1 yellow bell pepper, seeded and cut into 1/2-inch chunks
1 yellow onion, quartered
1 green bell pepper, seeded and cut into 1/2-inch chunks
1 cup broccoli, broken into 1/2-inch florets

2 parsnips, trimmed and cut into 1/2-inch chunks
2 garlic cloves, minced
Pink Himalayan salt and ground black pepper, to taste
1/2 teaspoon marjoram
1/2 teaspoon dried oregano
1/4 cup dry white wine
1/4 cup vegetable broth
1/2 cup Kalamata olives, pitted and sliced

Directions

Arrange your vegetables in a single layer in the baking pan in the order of the rainbow (red, orange, yellow, and green). Scatter the minced garlic around the vegetables.

Season with salt, black pepper, marjoram, and oregano. Drizzle the white wine and vegetable broth over the vegetables.

Roast in the preheated Air Fryer at 390 degrees F for 15 minutes, rotating the pan once or twice.

Scatter the Kalamata olives all over your vegetables and serve warm. Bon appétit!

Per serving: 333 Calories; 23.4g Fat; 25.9g Carbs; 8.7g Protein; 8g Sugars

708. Crispy Butternut Squash Fries

(Ready in about 25 minutes | Servings 4)

Ingredients

1 cup all-purpose flour
Salt and ground black pepper, to taste
3 tablespoons nutritional yeast flakes
1/2 cup almond milk

1/2 cup almond meal
1/2 cup bread crumbs
1 tablespoon herbs (oregano, basil, rosemary), chopped
1 pound butternut squash, peeled and cut into French fry shapes

Directions

In a shallow bowl, combine the flour, salt, and black pepper. In another shallow dish, mix the nutritional yeast flakes with the almond milk until well combined.

Mix the almond meal, breadcrumbs, and herbs in a third shallow dish. Dredge the butternut squash in the flour mixture, shaking off the excess. Then, dip in the milk mixture; lastly, dredge in the breadcrumb mixture.

Spritz the butternut squash fries with cooking oil on all sides.

Cook in the preheated Air Fryer at 400 degrees F approximately 12 minutes, turning them over halfway through the cooking time.

Serve with your favorite sauce for dipping. Bon appétit!

Per serving: 288 Calories; 7.6g Fat; 45.6g Carbs; 11.4g Protein; 3.1g Sugars

709. Easy Crispy Shawarma Chickpeas

(Ready in about 25 minutes | Servings 4)

Ingredients

1 (12-ounce) can chickpeas, drained and rinsed
2 tablespoons canola oil
1 teaspoon cayenne pepper

1 teaspoon sea salt
1 tablespoon Shawarma spice blend

Directions

Toss all ingredients in a mixing bowl.

Roast in the preheated Air Fryer at 380 degrees F for 10 minutes, shaking the basket halfway through the cooking time.

Work in batches. Bon appétit!

Per serving: 150 Calories; 8.7g Fat; 14.2g Carbs; 4.4g Protein; 2.5g Sugars

710. Caribbean-Style Fried Plantains

(Ready in about 20 minutes | Servings 2)

Ingredients

2 plantains, peeled and cut into slices
2 tablespoons avocado oil
2 teaspoons Caribbean Sorrel Rum Spice Mix

Directions

Toss the plantains with the avocado oil and spice mix.

Cook in the preheated Air Fryer at 400 degrees F for 10 minutes, shaking the cooking basket halfway through the cooking time.

Adjust the seasonings to taste and enjoy!

Per serving: 302 Calories; 14.2g Fat; 47.9g Carbs; 1.2g Protein; 21.6g Sugars

711. Famous Buffalo Cauliflower

(Ready in about 30 minutes | Servings 4)

Ingredients

1 pound cauliflower florets
1/2 cup all-purpose flour
1/2 cup rice flour
Sea salt and cracked black pepper, to taste
1/2 teaspoon cayenne pepper
1/2 teaspoon chili powder
1/2 cup soy milk
2 tablespoons soy sauce
2 tablespoons tahini
1 teaspoon vegetable oil
2 cloves garlic, minced
6 scotch bonnet peppers, seeded and sliced
1 small-sized onion, minced
1/2 teaspoon salt
1 cup water
2 tablespoons white vinegar
1 tablespoon granulated sugar

Directions

Rinse the cauliflower florets and pat them dry. Spritz the Air Fryer basket with cooking spray.

In a mixing bowl, combine the all purpose flour and rice flour; add the salt, black pepper, cayenne pepper, and chili powder.

Add the soy milk, soy sauce, and tahini. Stir until a thick batter is formed. Dip the cauliflower florets in the batter.

Cook the cauliflower at 400 degrees F for 16 minutes, turning them over halfway through the cooking time.

Meanwhile, heat the vegetable oil in a saucepan over medium-high heat; then, sauté the garlic, peppers, and onion for a minute or so or until they are fragrant.

Add the remaining ingredients and bring the mixture to a rapid boil. Now, reduce the heat to simmer, and continue cooking for 10 minutes more or until the sauce has reduced by half.

Pour the sauce over the prepared cauliflower and serve. Bon appétit!

Per serving: 306 Calories; 8.6g Fat; 50.3g Carbs; 9.7g Protein; 12.1g Sugars

712. Crunchy Eggplant Rounds

(Ready in about 45 minutes | Servings 4)

Ingredients

1 (1-pound) eggplant, sliced
1/2 cup flax meal
1/2 cup rice flour
Coarse sea salt and ground black pepper, to taste
1 teaspoon paprika
1 cup water
1 cup cornbread crumbs, crushed
1/2 cup vegan parmesan

Directions

Toss the eggplant with 1 tablespoon of salt and let it stand for 30 minutes. Drain and rinse well.

Mix the flax meal, rice flour, salt, black pepper, and paprika in a bowl. Then, pour in the water and whisk to combine well.

In another shallow bowl, mix the cornbread crumbs and vegan parmesan.

Dip the eggplant slices in the flour mixture, then in the crumb mixture; press to coat on all sides. Transfer to the lightly greased Air Fryer basket.

Cook at 370 degrees F for 6 minutes. Turn each slice over and cook an additional 5 minutes.

Serve garnished with spicy ketchup if desired. Bon appétit!

Per serving: 327 Calories; 8.5g Fat; 51.9g Carbs; 12.5g Protein; 7.3g Sugars

713. Classic Vegan Chili

(Ready in about 40 minutes | Servings 3)

Ingredients

1 tablespoon olive oil
1/2 yellow onion, chopped
2 garlic cloves, minced
2 red bell peppers, seeded and chopped
1 red chili pepper, seeded and minced
Sea salt and ground black pepper, to taste
1 teaspoon ground cumin
1 teaspoon cayenne pepper
1 teaspoon Mexican oregano
1/2 teaspoon mustard seeds
1/2 teaspoon celery seeds
1 can (28-ounces) diced tomatoes with juice
1 cup vegetable broth
1 (15-ounce) can black beans, rinsed and drained
1 bay leaf
1 teaspoon cider vinegar
1 avocado, sliced

Directions

Start by preheating your Air Fryer to 365 degrees F.

Heat the olive oil in a baking pan until sizzling. Then, sauté the onion, garlic, and peppers in the baking pan. Cook for 4 to 6 minutes.

Now, add the salt, black pepper, cumin, cayenne pepper, oregano, mustard seeds, celery seeds, tomatoes, and broth. Cook for 20 minutes, stirring every 4 minutes.

Stir in the canned beans, bay leaf, cider vinegar; let it cook for a further 8 minutes, stirring halfway through the cooking time.

Serve in individual bowls garnished with the avocado slices. Enjoy!

Per serving: 335 Calories; 17.6g Fat; 37.3g Carbs; 11.5g Protein; 6.1g Sugars

714. Dad's Roasted Pepper Salad

(Ready in about 25 minutes + chilling time | Servings 4)

Ingredients

2 yellow bell peppers
2 red bell peppers
2 green bell peppers
1 Serrano pepper
4 tablespoons olive oil
2 tablespoons cider vinegar
2 garlic cloves, peeled and pressed
1 teaspoon cayenne pepper
Sea salt, to taste
1/2 teaspoon mixed peppercorns, freshly crushed
1/2 cup pine nuts
1/4 cup loosely packed fresh Italian parsley leaves, roughly chopped

Directions

Start by preheating your Air Fryer to 400 degrees F. Brush the Air Fryer basket lightly with cooking oil.

Then, roast the peppers for 5 minutes. Give the peppers a half turn; place them back in the cooking basket and roast for another 5 minutes.

Turn them one more time and roast until the skin is charred and soft or 5 more minutes. Peel the peppers and let them cool to room temperature.

In a small mixing dish, whisk the olive oil, vinegar, garlic, cayenne pepper, salt, and crushed peppercorns. Dress the salad and set aside.

Add the pine nuts to the cooking basket. Roast at 360 degrees F for 4 minutes; give the nuts a good toss. Put the cooking basket back again and roast for a further 3 to 4 minutes.

Scatter the toasted nuts over the peppers and garnish with parsley. Bon appétit!

Per serving: 296 Calories; 25.6g Fat; 15.6g Carbs; 4.6g Protein; 4.7g Sugars

715. Cinnamon Pear Chips

(Ready in about 25 minutes | Servings 1)

Ingredients

1 medium pear, cored and thinly sliced
2 tablespoons cinnamon & sugar mixture

Directions

Toss the pear slices with the cinnamon & sugar mixture. Transfer them to the lightly greased Air Fryer basket.

Bake in the preheated Air Fryer at 380 degrees F for 8 minutes, turning them over halfway through the cooking time.

Transfer to wire rack to cool. Bon appétit!

Per serving: 133 Calories; 0.2g Fat; 35g Carbs; 0.6g Protein; 25.2g Sugars

716. Swiss Chard and Potato Fritters

(Ready in about 35 minutes | Servings 4)

Ingredients

8 baby potatoes
2 tablespoons olive oil
1 garlic clove, pressed
1/2 cup leeks, chopped
1 cup Swiss chard, torn into small pieces

Sea salt and ground black pepper, to your liking
1 tablespoon flax seed, soaked in 3 tablespoon water (vegan egg)
1 cup vegan cheese, shredded
1/4 cup chickpea flour

Directions

Start by preheating your Air Fryer to 400 degrees F.

Drizzle olive oil all over the potatoes. Place the potatoes in the Air Fryer basket and cook approximately 15 minutes, shaking the basket periodically.

Lightly crush the potatoes to split; mash the potatoes with the other ingredients.

Form the potato mixture into patties.

Bake in the preheated Air Fryer at 380 degrees F for 14 minutes, flipping them halfway through the cooking time. Bon appétit!

Per serving: 492 Calories; 18.5g Fat; 66.7g Carbs; 16.9g Protein; 4.8g Sugars

717. Veggie Fajitas with Simple Guacamole

(Ready in about 25 minutes | Servings 4)

Ingredients

1 tablespoon canola oil
1/2 cup scallions, thinly sliced
2 bell peppers, seeded and sliced into strips
1 habanero pepper, seeded and minced
1 garlic clove, minced
4 large Portobello mushrooms, thinly sliced
1/4 cup salsa
1 tablespoon yellow mustard

Kosher salt and ground black pepper, to taste
1/2 teaspoon Mexican oregano
1 medium ripe avocado, peeled, pitted and mashed
1 tablespoon fresh lemon juice
1/2 teaspoon onion powder
1/2 teaspoon garlic powder
1 teaspoon red pepper flakes
4 (8-inch) flour tortillas

Directions

Brush the sides and bottom of the cooking basket with canola oil. Add the scallions and cook for 1 to 2 minutes or until aromatic.

Then, add the peppers, garlic, and mushrooms to the cooking basket. Cook for 2 to 3 minutes or until tender.

Stir in the salsa, mustard, salt, black pepper, and oregano. Cook in the preheated Air Fryer at 380 degrees F for 15 minutes, stirring occasionally.

In the meantime, make your guacamole by mixing mashed avocado together with the lemon juice, garlic powder, onion powder, and red pepper flakes.

Divide between the tortillas and garnish with guacamole. Roll up your tortillas and enjoy!

Per serving: 307 Calories; 14.3g Fat; 40.2g Carbs; 8.2g Protein; 7.5g Sugars

718. Authentic Churros with Hot Chocolate

(Ready in about 25 minutes | Servings 3)

Ingredients

1/2 cup water
2 tablespoons granulated sugar
1/4 teaspoon sea salt
1 teaspoon lemon zest
1 tablespoon canola oil
1 cup all-purpose flour

2 ounces dark chocolate
1 cup milk
1 tablespoon cornstarch
1/3 cup sugar
1 teaspoon ground cinnamon

Directions

To make the churro dough, boil the water in a pan over medium-high heat; now, add the sugar, salt and lemon zest; cook until dissolved.

Add the canola oil and remove the pan from the heat. Gradually stir in the flour, whisking continuously until the mixture forms a ball.

Pour the mixture into a piping bag with a large star tip. Squeeze 4-inch strips of dough into the greased Air Fryer pan.

Cook at 410 degrees F for 6 minutes.

Meanwhile, prepare the hot chocolate for dipping. Melt the chocolate and 1/2 cup of milk in a pan over low heat.

Dissolve the cornstarch in the remaining 1/2 cup of milk; stir into the hot chocolate mixture. Cook on low heat approximately 5 minutes.

Mix the sugar and cinnamon; roll the churros in this mixture. Serve with the hot chocolate on the side. Enjoy!

Per serving: 432 Calories; 15.8g Fat; 63.9g Carbs; 8.4g Protein; 24.7g Sugars

719. Ooey-Gooey Dessert Quesadilla

(Ready in about 25 minutes | Servings 2)

Ingredients

1/4 cup blueberries
1/4 cup fresh orange juice
1/2 tablespoon maple syrup
1/2 cup vegan cream cheese

1 teaspoon vanilla extract
2 (6-inch) tortillas
2 teaspoons coconut oil
1/4 cup vegan dark chocolate

Directions

Bring the blueberries, orange juice, and maple syrup to a boil in a saucepan. Reduce the heat and let it simmer until the sauce thickens, about 10 minutes.

In a mixing dish, combine the cream cheese with the vanilla extract; spread on the tortillas. Add the blueberry filling on top. Fold in half.

Place the quesadillas in the greased Air Fryer basket. Cook at 390 degrees F for 10 minutes, until tortillas are golden brown and filling is melted. Make sure to turn them over halfway through the cooking.

Heat the coconut oil in a small pan and add the chocolate; whisk to combine well. Drizzle the chocolate sauce over the quesadilla and serve. Enjoy!

Per serving: 476 Calories; 28.8g Fat; 45g Carbs; 9.2g Protein; 18.5g Sugars

720. Couscous with Sun-Dried Tomatoes

(Ready in about 30 minutes | Servings 4)

Ingredients

1 cup couscous
1 cup boiled water
2 garlic cloves, pressed
1/3 cup coriander, chopped
1 cup shallots, chopped
4 ounces sun-dried tomato strips in oil

1 cup arugula lettuce, torn into pieces
2 tablespoons apple cider vinegar
Sea salt and ground black pepper, to taste

Directions

Put the couscous in a bowl; pour the boiling water, cover and set aside for 5 to 8 minutes; fluff with a fork.

Place the couscous in a lightly greased cake pan. Transfer the pan to the Air Fryer basket and cook at 360 digress F about 20 minutes. Make sure to stir every 5 minutes to ensure even cooking.

Transfer the prepared couscous to a nice salad bowl. Add the remaining ingredients; stir to combine and enjoy!

Per serving: 230 Calories; 4.3g Fat; 41.3g Carbs; 7.2g Protein; 0.3g Sugars

721. Thai Sweet Potato Balls

(Ready in about 50 minutes | Servings 4)

Ingredients

1 pound sweet potatoes
1 cup brown sugar
1 tablespoon orange juice
2 teaspoons orange zest
1/2 teaspoon ground cinnamon
1/4 teaspoon ground cloves
1/2 cup almond meal
1 teaspoon baking powder
1 cup coconut flakes

Directions

Bake the sweet potatoes at 380 degrees F for 30 to 35 minutes until tender; peel and mash them.

Add the brown sugar, orange juice, orange zest, ground cinnamon, cloves, almond meal, and baking powder; mix to combine well.

Roll the balls in the coconut flakes.

Bake in the preheated Air Fryer at 360 degrees F for 15 minutes or until thoroughly cooked and crispy.

Repeat the process until you run out of ingredients. Bon appétit!

Per serving: 286 Calories; 6.1g Fat; 56.8g Carbs; 3.1g Protein; 33.7g Sugars

722. Easy Granola with Raisins and Nuts

(Ready in about 40 minutes | Servings 8)

Ingredients

2 cups rolled oats
1/2 cup walnuts, chopped
1/3 cup almonds chopped
1/4 cup raisins
1/4 cup whole wheat pastry flour
1/2 teaspoon cinnamon
1/4 teaspoon nutmeg, preferably freshly grated
1/2 teaspoon salt
1/3 cup coconut oil, melted
1/3 cup agave nectar
1/2 teaspoon coconut extract
1/2 teaspoon vanilla extract

Directions

Thoroughly combine all ingredients. Then, spread the mixture onto the Air Fryer trays. Spritz with cooking spray.

Bake at 230 degrees F for 25 minutes; rotate the trays and bake 10 to 15 minutes more.

This granola can be stored in an airtight container for up to 2 weeks. Enjoy!

Per serving: 222 Calories; 14g Fat; 29.9g Carbs; 5.3g Protein; 11.3g Sugars

723. Indian Plantain Chips (Kerala Neenthram)

(Ready in about 30 minutes | Servings 2)

Ingredients

1 pound plantain, thinly sliced
1 tablespoon turmeric
2 tablespoons coconut oil

Directions

Fill a large enough cup with water and add the turmeric to the water.

Soak the plantain slices in the turmeric water for 15 minutes. Brush with coconut oil and transfer to the Air Fryer basket.

Cook in the preheated Air Fryer at 400 degrees F for 10 minutes, shaking the cooking basket halfway through the cooking time.

Serve at room temperature. Enjoy!

Per serving: 263 Calories; 9.4g Fat; 49.2g Carbs; 1.5g Protein; 21.3g Sugars

724. Aromatic Baked Potatoes with Chives

(Ready in about 45 minutes | Servings 2)

Ingredients

4 medium baking potatoes, peeled
2 tablespoons olive oil
1/4 teaspoon red pepper flakes
1/4 teaspoon smoked paprika
1 tablespoon sea salt
2 garlic cloves, minced
2 tablespoons chives, chopped

Directions

Toss the potatoes with the olive oil, seasoning, and garlic.

Place them in the Air Fryer basket. Cook in the preheated Air Fryer at 400 degrees F for 40 minutes or until fork tender.

Garnish with fresh chopped chives. Bon appétit!

Per serving: 434 Calories; 14.1g Fat; 69g Carbs; 8.2g Protein; 5.1g Sugars

725. Classic Baked Banana

(Ready in about 20 minutes | Servings 2)

Ingredients

2 just-ripe bananas
2 teaspoons lime juice
2 tablespoons honey
1/4 teaspoon grated nutmeg
1/2 teaspoon ground cinnamon
A pinch of salt

Directions

Toss the banana with all ingredients until well coated. Transfer your bananas to the parchment-lined cooking basket.

Bake in the preheated Air Fryer at 370 degrees F for 12 minutes, turning them over halfway through the cooking time. Enjoy!

Per serving: 202 Calories; 5.9g Fat; 40.2g Carbs; 1.1g Protein; 29g Sugars

726. Garlic-Roasted Brussels Sprouts with Mustard

(Ready in about 20 minutes | Servings 3)

Ingredients

1 pound Brussels sprouts, halved
2 tablespoons olive oil
Sea salt and freshly ground black pepper, to taste
2 garlic cloves, minced
1 tablespoon Dijon mustard

Directions

Toss the Brussels sprouts with the olive oil, salt, black pepper, and garlic.

Roast in the preheated Air Fryer at 380 degrees F for 15 minutes, shaking the basket occasionally.

Serve with Dijon mustard and enjoy!

Per serving: 151 Calories; 9.6g Fat; 14.5g Carbs; 5.4g Protein; 3.4g Sugars

727. Italian-Style Risi e Bisi

(Ready in about 20 minutes | Servings 4)

Ingredients

2 cups brown rice
4 cups water
1/2 cup frozen green peas
3 tablespoons soy sauce
1 tablespoon olive oil
1 cup brown mushrooms, sliced
2 garlic cloves, minced
1 small-sized onion, chopped
1 tablespoon fresh parsley, chopped

Directions

Heat the brown rice and water in a pot over high heat. Bring it to a boil; turn the stove down to simmer and cook for 35 minutes. Allow your rice to cool completely.

Transfer the cold cooked rice to the lightly greased Air Fryer pan. Add the remaining ingredients and stir to combine.

Cook in the preheated Air Fryer at 360 degrees F for 18 to 22 minutes. Serve warm.

Per serving: 434 Calories; 8.3g Fat; 79.8g Carbs; 9.9g Protein; 5g Sugars

728. Tofu in Sweet & Sour Sauce

(Ready in about 25 minutes | Servings 3)

Ingredients

2 tablespoons Shoyu sauce
16 ounces extra-firm tofu, drained, pressed and cubed
1/2 cup water
1/4 cup pineapple juice
2 garlic cloves, minced
1/2 teaspoon fresh ginger, grated
1 teaspoon cayenne pepper
1/4 teaspoon ground black pepper
1/2 teaspoon salt
1 teaspoon honey
1 tablespoon arrowroot powder

Directions

Drizzle the Shoyu sauce all over the tofu cubes. Cook in the preheated Air Fryer at 380 degrees F for 6 minutes; shake the basket and cook for a further 5 minutes.

Meanwhile, cook the remaining ingredients in a heavy skillet over medium heat for 10 minutes, until the sauce has slightly thickened.

Stir the fried tofu into the sauce and continue cooking for 4 minutes more or until the tofu is thoroughly heated.

Serve warm and enjoy!

Per serving: 171 Calories; 7.1g Fat; 13.2g Carbs; 14.4g Protein; 6.2g Sugars

729. Gourmet Wasabi Popcorn

(Ready in about 30 minutes | Servings 2)

Ingredients

1/2 teaspoon brown sugar
1 teaspoon salt
1/2 teaspoon wasabi powder, sifted

1 tablespoon avocado oil
3 tablespoons popcorn kernels

Directions

Add the dried corn kernels to the Air Fryer basket; toss with the remaining ingredients.

Cook at 395 degrees F for 15 minutes, shaking the basket every 5 minutes. Work in two batches.

Taste, adjust the seasonings and serve immediately. Bon appétit!

Per serving: 149 Calories; 11.7g Fat; 9.7g Carbs; 1.3g Protein; 0.6g Sugars

730. Baked Oatmeal with Berries

(Ready in about 30 minutes | Servings 4)

Ingredients

1 cup fresh strawberries
1/2 cup dried cranberries
1 ½ cups rolled oats
1/2 teaspoon baking powder
A pinch of sea salt

A pinch of grated nutmeg
1/2 teaspoon ground cinnamon
1/2 teaspoon vanilla extract
4 tablespoons agave syrup
1 ½ cups coconut milk

Directions

Spritz a baking pan with cooking spray.

Place 1/2 cup of strawberries on the bottom of the pan; place the cranberries over that.

In a mixing bowl, thoroughly combine the rolled oats, baking powder, salt, nutmeg, cinnamon, vanilla, agave syrup, and milk.

Pour the oatmeal mixtures over the fruits; allow it to soak for 15 minutes. Top with the remaining fruits.

Bake at 330 degrees F for 12 minutes. Serve warm or at room temperature. Enjoy!

Per serving: 387 Calories; 24.1g Fat; 52.5g Carbs; 8.4g Protein; 25.9g Sugars

731. Green Beans with Oyster Mushrooms

(Ready in about 20 minutes | Servings 3)

Ingredients

1 tablespoon extra-virgin olive oil
2 garlic cloves, minced
1/2 cup scallions, chopped
2 cups oyster mushrooms, sliced

12 ounces fresh green beans, trimmed
1 tablespoon soy sauce
Sea salt and ground black pepper, to taste

Directions

Start by preheating your Air Fryer to 390 degrees F. Heat the oil and sauté the garlic and scallions until tender and fragrant, about 5 minutes.

Add the remaining ingredients and stir to combine well.

Increase the temperature to 400 degrees F and cook for a further 5 minutes. Serve warm.

Per serving: 109 Calories; 6.4g Fat; 11.6g Carbs; 3.9g Protein; 2.9g Sugars

732. Hoisin-Glazed Bok Choy

(Ready in about 10 minutes | Servings 4)

Ingredients

1 pound baby Bok choy, bottoms removed, leaves separated
2 garlic cloves, minced
1 teaspoon onion powder

1/2 teaspoon sage
2 tablespoons hoisin sauce
2 tablespoons sesame oil
1 tablespoon all-purpose flour

Directions

Place the Bok choy, garlic, onion powder, and sage in the lightly greased Air Fryer basket.

Cook in the preheated Air Fryer at 350 degrees F for 3 minutes.

In a small mixing dish, whisk the hoisin sauce, sesame oil, and flour. Drizzle the sauce over the Bok choy. Cook for a further 3 minutes. Bon appétit!

Per serving: 235 Calories; 11.2g Fat; 6g Carbs; 25.7g Protein; 2.2g Sugars

733. Herb Roasted Potatoes and Peppers

(Ready in about 30 minutes | Servings 4)

Ingredients

1 pound russet potatoes, cut into 1-inch chunks
2 bell peppers, seeded and cut into 1-inch chunks
2 tablespoons olive oil
1 teaspoon dried rosemary

1 teaspoon dried basil
1 teaspoon dried oregano
1 teaspoon dried parsley flakes
Sea salt and ground black pepper, to taste
1/2 teaspoon smoked paprika

Directions

Toss all ingredients in the Air Fryer basket.

Roast at 400 degrees F for 15 minutes, tossing the basket occasionally. Work in batches.

Serve warm and enjoy!

Per serving: 158 Calories; 6.8g Fat; 22.6g Carbs; 1.8g Protein; 2.2g Sugars

734. Corn on the Cob with Spicy Avocado Spread

(Ready in about 15 minutes | Servings 4)

Ingredients

4 corn cobs
1 avocado, pitted, peeled and mashed
1 clove garlic, pressed
1 tablespoon fresh lime juice
1 tablespoon soy sauce
4 teaspoons nutritional yeast

1/2 teaspoon cayenne pepper
1/2 teaspoon dried dill
Sea salt and ground black pepper, to taste
1 teaspoon hot sauce
2 heaping tablespoons fresh cilantro leaves, roughly chopped

Directions

Spritz the corn with cooking spray. Cook at 390 degrees F for 6 minutes, turning them over halfway through the cooking time.

In the meantime, mix the avocado, lime juice, soy sauce, nutritional yeast, cayenne pepper, dill, salt, black pepper, and hot sauce.

Spread the avocado mixture all over the corn on the cob. Garnish with fresh cilantro leaves. Bon appétit!

Per serving: 234 Calories; 9.2g Fat; 37.9g Carbs; 7.2g Protein; 1.9g Sugars

735. Delicious Asparagus and Mushroom Fritters

(Ready in about 15 minutes | Servings 4)

Ingredients

1 pound asparagus spears
1 tablespoon canola oil
1 teaspoon paprika
Sea salt and freshly ground black pepper, to taste
1 teaspoon garlic powder
3 tablespoons scallions, chopped

1 cup button mushrooms, chopped
1/2 cup fresh breadcrumbs
1 tablespoon flax seeds, soaked in 2 tablespoons of water (vegan "egg")
4 tablespoons sun-dried tomato hummus

Directions

Place the asparagus spears in the lightly greased cooking basket. Toss the asparagus with the canola oil, paprika, salt, and black pepper.

Cook in the preheated Air Fryer at 400 degrees F for 5 minutes. Chop the asparagus spears and add the garlic powder, scallions, mushrooms, breadcrumbs, and vegan "egg".

Mix until everything is well incorporated and form the asparagus mixture into patties.

Cook in the preheated Air Fryer at 400 degrees F for 5 minutes, flipping halfway through the cooking time. Serve with sun-dried tomato hummus. Bon appétit!

Per serving: 231 Calories; 12.7g Fat; 24g Carbs; 10.2g Protein; 6.3g Sugars

736. Greek-Style Roasted Vegetables

(Ready in about 25 minutes | Servings 3)

Ingredients

1/2 pound butternut squash, peeled and cut into 1-inch chunks
1/2 pound cauliflower, cut into 1-inch florets
1/2 pound zucchini, cut into 1-inch chunks
1 red onion, sliced
2 bell peppers, cut into 1-inch chunks

2 tablespoons extra-virgin olive oil
1 cup dry white wine
1 teaspoon dried rosemary
Sea salt and freshly cracked black pepper, to taste
1/2 teaspoon dried basil
1 (28-ounce) canned diced tomatoes with juice
1/2 cup Kalamata olives, pitted

Directions

Toss the vegetables with the olive oil, wine, rosemary, salt, black pepper, and basil until well coated.

Pour 1/2 of the canned diced tomatoes into a lightly greased baking dish; spread to cover the bottom of the baking dish.

Add the vegetables and top with the remaining diced tomatoes. Scatter the Kalamata olives over the top.

Bake in the preheated Air Fryer at 390 degrees F for 20 minutes, rotating the dish halfway through the cooking time. Serve warm and enjoy!

Per serving: 299 Calories; 12.9g Fat; 30.4g Carbs; 5.8g Protein; 12.5g Sugars

737. Warm Farro Salad with Roasted Tomatoes

(Ready in about 40 minutes | Servings 2)

Ingredients

3/4 cup farro
3 cups water
1 tablespoon sea salt
1 pound cherry tomatoes
2 spring onions, chopped
2 carrots, grated

2 heaping tablespoons fresh parsley leaves
2 tablespoons champagne vinegar
2 tablespoons white wine
2 tablespoons extra-virgin olive oil
1 teaspoon red pepper flakes

Directions

Place the farro, water, and salt in a saucepan and bring it to a rapid boil. Turn the heat down to medium-low, and simmer, covered, for 30 minutes or until the farro has softened.

Drain well and transfer to an air fryer-safe pan.

Meanwhile, place the cherry tomatoes in the lightly greased Air Fryer basket. Roast at 400 degrees F for 4 minutes.

Add the roasted tomatoes to the pan with the cooked farro, Toss the salad ingredients with the spring onions, carrots, parsley, vinegar, white wine, and olive oil.

Bake at 360 degrees F an additional 5 minutes. Serve garnished with red pepper flakes and enjoy!

Per serving: 452 Calories; 14.5g Fat; 72.9g Carbs; 7.7g Protein; 9.5g Sugars

738. Winter Squash and Tomato Bake

(Ready in about 30 minutes | Servings 4)

Ingredients

Cashew Cream:
1/2 cup sunflower seeds, soaked overnight, rinsed and drained
1/4 cup lime juice
Sea salt, to taste
2 teaspoons nutritional yeast
1 tablespoon tahini
1/2 cup water
Squash:
1 pound winter squash, peeled and sliced
2 tablespoons olive oil

Sea salt and ground black pepper, to taste
Sauce:
2 tablespoons olive oil
2 ripe tomatoes, crushed
6 ounces spinach, torn into small pieces
2 garlic cloves, minced
1 cup vegetable broth
1/2 teaspoon dried rosemary
1/2 teaspoon dried basil

Directions

Mix the ingredients for the cashew cream in your food processor until creamy and uniform. Reserve.

Place the squash slices in the lightly greased casserole dish. Add the olive oil, salt, and black pepper.

Mix all the ingredients for the sauce. Pour the sauce over the vegetables. Bake in the preheated Air Fryer at 390 degrees F for 15 minutes.

Top with the cashew cream and bake an additional 5 minutes or until everything is thoroughly heated.

Transfer to a wire rack to cool slightly before sling and serving.

Per serving: 330 Calories; 25.3g Fat; 23.2g Carbs; 8.5g Protein; 3.2g Sugars

739. Mashed Potatoes with Roasted Peppers

(Ready in about 1 hour | Servings 4)

Ingredients

4 potatoes
1 tablespoon vegan margarine
1 teaspoon garlic powder
1 pound bell peppers, seeded and quartered lengthwise
2 Fresno peppers, seeded and halved lengthwise

4 tablespoons olive oil
2 tablespoons cider vinegar
4 garlic cloves, pressed
Kosher salt, to taste
1/2 teaspoon freshly ground black pepper
1/2 teaspoon dried dill

Directions

Place the potatoes in the Air Fryer basket and cook at 400 degrees F for 40 minutes. Discard the skin and mash the potatoes with the vegan margarine and garlic powder.

Then, roast the peppers at 400 degrees F for 5 minutes. Give the peppers a half turn; place them back in the cooking basket and roast for another 5 minutes.

Turn them one more time and roast until the skin is charred and soft or 5 more minutes. Peel the peppers and let them cool to room temperature.

Toss your peppers with the remaining ingredients and serve with the mashed potatoes. Bon appétit!

Per serving: 490 Calories; 17g Fat; 79.1g Carbs; 10.5g Protein; 9.8g Sugars

740. Hungarian Mushroom Pilaf

(Ready in about 50 minutes | Servings 4)

Ingredients

1 ½ cups white rice
3 cups vegetable broth
2 tablespoons olive oil
1 pound fresh porcini mushrooms, sliced
2 tablespoons olive oil
2 garlic cloves

1 onion, chopped
1/4 cup dry vermouth
1 teaspoon dried thyme
1/2 teaspoon dried tarragon
1 teaspoon sweet Hungarian paprika

Directions

Place the rice and broth in a large saucepan, add water; and bring to a boil. Cover, turn the heat down to low, and continue cooking for 16 to 18 minutes more. Set aside for 5 to 10 minutes.

Now, stir the hot cooked rice with the remaining ingredients in a lightly greased baking dish.

Cook in the preheated Air Fryer at 370 degrees for 20 minutes, checking periodically to ensure even cooking.

Serve in individual bowls. Bon appétit!

Per serving: 566 Calories; 19.1g Fat; 72.8g Carbs; 24.6g Protein; 7.2g Sugars

741. Rosemary Au Gratin Potatoes

(Ready in about 45 minutes | Servings 4)

Ingredients
2 pounds potatoes
1/4 cup sunflower kernels, soaked overnight
1/2 cup almonds, soaked overnight
1 cup unsweetened almond milk
2 tablespoons nutritional yeast

1 teaspoon shallot powder
2 fresh garlic cloves, minced
1/2 cup water
Kosher salt and ground black pepper, to taste
1 teaspoon cayenne pepper
1 tablespoon fresh rosemary

Directions

Bring a large pan of water to a boil. Cook the whole potatoes for about 20 minutes. Drain the potatoes and let sit until cool enough to handle.

Peel your potatoes and slice into 1/8-inch rounds.

Add the sunflower kernels, almonds, almond milk, nutritional yeast, shallot powder, and garlic to your food processor; blend until uniform, smooth, and creamy. Add the water and blend for 30 seconds more.

Place 1/2 of the potatoes overlapping in a single layer in the lightly greased casserole dish. Spoon 1/2 of the sauce on top of the potatoes. Repeat the layers, ending with the sauce.

Top with salt, black pepper, cayenne pepper, and fresh rosemary. Bake in the preheated Air Fryer at 325 degrees F for 20 minutes. Serve warm.

Per serving: 386 Calories; 15.7g Fat; 50.5g Carbs; 14.3g Protein; 6.1g Sugars

742. Kid-Friendly Vegetable Fritters

(Ready in about 20 minutes | Servings 4)

Ingredients

1 pound broccoli florets
1 tablespoon ground flaxseeds
1 yellow onion, finely chopped
1 sweet pepper, seeded and chopped
1 carrot, grated
2 garlic cloves, pressed

1 teaspoon turmeric powder
1/2 teaspoon ground cumin
1/2 cup all-purpose flour
1/2 cup cornmeal
Salt and ground black pepper, to taste
2 tablespoons olive oil

Directions

Blanch the broccoli in salted boiling water until al dente, about 3 to 4 minutes. Drain well and transfer to a mixing bowl; mash the broccoli florets with the remaining ingredients.

Form the mixture into patties and place them in the lightly greased Air Fryer basket.

Cook at 400 degrees F for 6 minutes, turning them over halfway through the cooking time; work in batches.

Serve warm with your favorite Vegenaise. Enjoy!

Per serving: 299 Calories; 11.3g Fat; 44.1g Carbs; 7.9g Protein; 4.6g Sugars

743. Marinated Tofu Bowl with Pearl Onions

(Ready in about 1 hour 20 minutes | Servings 4)

Ingredients

16 ounces firm tofu, pressed and cut into 1-inch pieces
2 tablespoons vegan Worcestershire sauce
1 tablespoon apple cider vinegar
1 tablespoon maple syrup

1/2 teaspoon shallot powder
1/2 teaspoon porcini powder
1/2 teaspoon garlic powder
2 tablespoons peanut oil
1 cup pearl onions, peeled

Directions

Place the tofu, Worcestershire sauce, vinegar, maple syrup, shallot powder, porcini powder, and garlic powder in a ceramic dish. Let it marinate in your refrigerator for 1 hour.

Transfer the tofu to the lightly greased Air Fryer basket. Add the peanut oil and pearl onions; toss to combine.

Cook the tofu with the pearl onions in the preheated Air Fryer at 380 degrees F for 6 minutes; pause and brush with the reserved marinade; cook for a further 5 minutes.

Serve immediately. Bon appétit!

Per serving: 296 Calories; 16.7g Fat; 23.2g Carbs; 18.1g Protein; 14.1g Sugars

744. Easy Vegan "Chicken"

(Ready in about 20 minutes | Servings 4)

Ingredients

8 ounces soy chunks
1/2 cup cornmeal
1/4 cup all-purpose flour
1 teaspoon cayenne pepper

1/2 teaspoon mustard powder
1 teaspoon celery seeds
Sea salt and ground black pepper, to taste

Directions

Boil the soya chunks in lots of water in a saucepan over medium-high heat. Remove from the heat and let them soak for 10 minutes.

Drain, rinse, and squeeze off the excess water.

Mix the remaining ingredients in a bowl. Roll the soy chunks over the breading mixture, pressing to adhere.

Arrange the soy chunks in the lightly greased Air Fryer basket.

Cook in the preheated Air Fryer at 390 degrees for 10 minutes, turning them over halfway through the cooking time; work in batches. Bon appétit!

Per serving: 348 Calories; 12.1g Fat; 41.5g Carbs; 21.7g Protein; 4.5g Sugars

745. The Best Falafel Ever

(Ready in about 20 minutes | Servings 2)

Ingredients

1 cup dried chickpeas, soaked overnight
1 small-sized onion, chopped
2 cloves garlic, minced
2 tablespoons fresh cilantro leaves, chopped

1 tablespoon flour
1/2 teaspoon baking powder
1 teaspoon cumin powder
A pinch of ground cardamom
Sea salt and ground black pepper, to taste

Directions

Pulse all the ingredients in your food processor until the chickpeas are ground.

Form the falafel mixture into balls and place them in the lightly greased Air Fryer basket.

Cook at 380 degrees F for about 15 minutes, shaking the basket occasionally to ensure even cooking.

Serve in pita bread with toppings of your choice. Enjoy!

Per serving: 411 Calories; 6.1g Fat; 70.2g Carbs; 21.4g Protein; 12.2g Sugars

746. Onion Rings with Spicy Ketchup

(Ready in about 30 minutes | Servings 2)

Ingredients

1 onion, sliced into rings
1/3 cup all-purpose flour
1/2 cup oat milk
1 teaspoon curry powder
1 teaspoon cayenne pepper

Salt and ground black pepper, to your liking
1/2 cup cornmeal
4 tablespoons vegan parmesan
1/4 cup spicy ketchup

Directions

Place the onion rings in the bowl with cold water; let them soak approximately 20 minutes; drain the onion rings and pat dry using a kitchen towel.

In a shallow bowl, mix the flour, milk, curry powder, cayenne pepper, salt, and black pepper. Mix to combine well.

Mix the cornmeal and vegan parmesan in another shallow bowl. Dip the onion rings in the flour/milk mixture; then, dredge in the cornmeal mixture.

Spritz the Air Fryer basket with cooking spray; arrange the breaded onion rings in the Air Fryer basket.

Cook in the preheated Air Fryer at 400 degrees F for 4 to 5 minutes, turning them over halfway through the cooking time. Serve with spicy ketchup. Bon appétit!

Per serving: 361 Calories; 4.5g Fat; 67.5g Carbs; 12.1g Protein; 10.5g Sugars

747. Spicy Roasted Cashew Nuts

(Ready in about 20 minutes | Servings 4)

Ingredients

1 cup whole cashews
1 teaspoon olive oil
Salt and ground black pepper, to taste

1/2 teaspoon smoked paprika
1/2 teaspoon ancho chili powder

Directions

Toss all ingredients in the mixing bowl.

Line the Air Fryer basket with baking parchment. Spread out the spiced cashews in a single layer in the basket.

Roast at 350 degrees F for 6 to 8 minutes, shaking the basket once or twice. Work in batches. Enjoy!

Per serving: 400 Calories; 35.1g Fat; 19.3g Carbs; 7.7g Protein; 5.8g Sugars

748. Barbecue Tofu with Green Beans

(Ready in about 1 hour | Servings 3)

Ingredients

12 ounces super firm tofu, pressed and cubed
1/4 cup ketchup
1 tablespoon white vinegar
1 tablespoon coconut sugar
1 tablespoon mustard
1/4 teaspoon ground black pepper

1/2 teaspoon sea salt
1/4 teaspoon smoked paprika
1/2 teaspoon freshly grated ginger
2 cloves garlic, minced
2 tablespoons olive oil
1 pound green beans

Directions

Toss the tofu with the ketchup, white vinegar, coconut sugar, mustard, black pepper, sea salt, paprika, ginger, garlic, and olive oil. Let it marinate for 30 minutes.

Cook at 360 degrees F for 10 minutes; turn them over and cook for 12 minutes more. Reserve.

Place the green beans in the lightly greased Air Fryer basket. Roast at 400 degrees F for 5 minutes. Bon appétit!

Per serving: 316 Calories; 19.8g Fat; 20.8g Carbs; 20.1g Protein; 8.1g Sugars

749. Cinnamon Sugar Tortilla Chips

(Ready in about 20 minutes | Servings 4)

Ingredients

4 (10-inch) flour tortillas
1/4 cup vegan margarine, melted

1 ½ tablespoons ground cinnamon
1/4 cup caster sugar

Directions

Slice each tortilla into eight slices. Brush the tortilla pieces with the melted margarine.

In a mixing bowl, thoroughly combine the cinnamon and sugar. Toss the cinnamon mixture with the tortillas.

Transfer to the cooking basket and cook at 360 degrees F for 8 minutes or until lightly golden. Work in batches.

They will crisp up as they cool. Serve and enjoy!

Per serving: 270 Calories; 14.1g Fat; 32.7g Carbs; 3.8g Protein; 7.7g Sugars

750. Tofu and Brown Rice Bake

(Ready in about 55 minutes + marinating time| Servings 4)

Ingredients

1 cup brown rice
16 ounces extra firm tofu, pressed, drained, and cut into bite-sized cubes
Marinade:
2 tablespoons sesame oil

1/2 cup tamari sauce
2 tablespoons maple syrup
1 tablespoon white vinegar
1 teaspoon hot sauce
4 tablespoons cornstarch
Salt and black pepper, to taste

Directions

Heat the brown rice and 2 ½ cups of water in a saucepan over high heat. Bring it to a boil; turn the stove down to simmer and cook for 35 minutes.

Place the tofu in a ceramic dish; add the remaining ingredients for the marinade and whisk to combine well. Allow it to marinate for 1 hour in your refrigerator.

Grease a baking pan with nonstick cooking spray. Add the hot rice and place the tofu on the top. Stir in the reserved marinade.

Cook at 370 degrees F for 15 minutes, checking occasionally to ensure even cooking. Enjoy!

Per serving: 402 Calories; 14.7g Fat; 54.7g Carbs; 15.3g Protein; 8.3g Sugars

751. Healthy Mac and Cheese

(Ready in about 30 minutes | Servings 4)

Ingredients

12 ounces elbow pasta
2 garlic cloves, minced
1/3 cup vegan margarine
1/3 cup chickpea flour
3/4 cup unsweetened almond milk
2 heaping tablespoons nutritional yeast
1/2 teaspoon curry powder

1/2 teaspoon mustard powder
1/2 teaspoon celery seeds
Sea salt and white pepper, to taste
1 ½ cups pasta water
1/2 cup seasoned breadcrumbs
1 heaping tablespoon Italian parsley, roughly chopped

Directions

Bring a pot of salted water to a boil over high heat; turn the heat down to medium and add the elbow pasta.

Let it cook approximately 8 minutes. Drain and transfer to the lightly greased baking pan.

In a mixing dish, thoroughly combine the garlic, margarine, chickpea flour, milk, nutritional yeast, and spices. Add the pasta water and mix to combine well.

Pour the milk mixture into the baking pan; gently stir to combine. Top with the seasoned breadcrumbs.

Bake in the preheated Air Fryer at 360 degrees F for 15 minutes. Serve garnished with fresh parsley leaves. Bon appétit!

Per serving: 449 Calories; 18.3g Fat; 55.5g Carbs; 14.2g Protein; 9.7g Sugars

752. Cauliflower, Broccoli and Chickpea Salad

(Ready in about 20 minutes + chilling time | Servings 4)

Ingredients

1/2 pound cauliflower florets
1/2 pound broccoli florets
Sea salt, to taste
1/2 teaspoon red pepper flakes
2 tablespoons soy sauce
2 tablespoons cider vinegar
1 teaspoon Dijon mustard
2 tablespoons extra-virgin olive oil

1 cup canned or cooked chickpeas, drained
1 avocado, pitted, peeled and sliced
1 small sized onion, peeled and sliced
1 garlic clove, minced
2 cups arugula
2 tablespoons sesame seeds, lightly toasted

Directions

Start by preheating your Air Fryer to 400 degrees F.

Brush the cauliflower and broccoli florets with cooking spray.

Cook for 12 minutes, shaking the cooking basket halfway through the cooking time. Season with salt and red pepper.

In a mixing dish, whisk the soy sauce, cider vinegar, Dijon mustard, and olive oil. Dress the salad. Add the chickpeas, avocado, onion, garlic, and arugula. Top with sesame seeds.

Bon appétit!

Per serving: 263 Calories; 15.8g Fat; 24.8g Carbs; 9.4g Protein; 6.1g Sugars

753. Butternut Squash Chili

(Ready in about 35 minutes | Servings 4)

Ingredients

2 tablespoons canola oil
1 cup leeks, chopped
2 garlic cloves, crushed
2 ripe tomatoes, pureed
2 chipotle peppers in adobo, chopped
1 teaspoon ground cumin
1 teaspoon chili powder

Kosher salt and ground black pepper, to your liking
1 cup vegetable broth
1 pound butternut squash, peeled and diced into 1/2-inch chunks
16 ounces canned kidney beans, drained and rinsed
1 avocado, pitted, peeled and diced

Directions

Start by preheating your Air Fryer to 365 degrees F.

Heat the oil in a baking pan until sizzling. Then, sauté the leeks and garlic in the baking pan. Cook for 4 to 6 minutes.

Now, add the tomatoes, chipotle peppers, cumin, chili powder, salt, pepper, and vegetable broth. Cook for 15 minutes, stirring every 5 minutes.

Stir in the the butternut squash and canned beans; let it cook for a further 8 minutes, stirring halfway through the cooking time.

Serve in individual bowls, garnished with the avocado. Enjoy!

Per serving: 295 Calories; 18.9g Fat; 29.3g Carbs; 7g Protein; 4.6g Sugars

754. Ultimate Vegan Calzone

(Ready in about 25 minutes | Servings 1)

Ingredients

1 teaspoon olive oil
1/2 small onion, chopped
2 sweet peppers, seeded and sliced
Sea salt, to taste
1/4 teaspoon ground black pepper
1/4 teaspoon dried oregano

4 ounces prepared Italian pizza dough
1/4 cup marinara sauce
2 ounces plant-based cheese Mozzarella-style, shredded

Directions

Heat the olive oil in a nonstick skillet. Once hot, cook the onion and peppers until tender and fragrant, about 5 minutes. Add salt, black pepper, and oregano.

Sprinkle some flour on a kitchen counter and roll out the pizza dough.

Spoon the marinara sauce over half of the dough; add the sautéed mixture and sprinkle with the vegan cheese. Now, gently fold over the dough to create a pocket; make sure to seal the edges.

Use a fork to poke the dough in a few spots. Add a few drizzles of olive oil and place in the lightly greased cooking basket.

Bake in the preheated Air Fryer at 330 degrees F for 12 minutes, turning the calzones over halfway through the cooking time. Bon appétit!

Per serving: 535 Calories; 14g Fat; 88.2g Carbs; 16g Protein; 19g Sugars

755. Mediterranean-Style Potato Chips with Vegveeta Dip

(Ready in about 1 hour | Servings 4)

Ingredients

1 large potato, cut into 1/8 inch thick slices
1 tablespoon olive oil
Sea salt, to taste
1/2 teaspoon red pepper flakes, crushed
1 teaspoon fresh rosemary
1/2 teaspoon fresh sage

1/2 teaspoon fresh basil
Dipping Sauce:
1/3 cup raw cashews
1 tablespoon tahini
1 ½ tablespoons olive oil
1/4 cup raw almonds
1/4 teaspoon prepared yellow mustard

Directions

Soak the potatoes in a large bowl of cold water for 20 to 30 minutes. Drain the potatoes and pat them dry with a kitchen towel.

Toss with olive oil and seasonings.

Place in the lightly greased cooking basket and cook at 380 degrees F for 30 minutes. Work in batches.

Meanwhile, puree the sauce ingredients in your food processor until smooth. Serve the potato chips with the Vegveeta sauce for dipping. Bon appétit!

Per serving: 244 Calories; 18g Fat; 19.4g Carbs; 4g Protein; 1.7g Sugars

756. Sunday Potato Fritters

(Ready in about 30 minutes | Servings 3)

Ingredients

1 tablespoon olive oil
1/2 pound potatoes, peeled and cut into chunks
1/2 cup cashew cream
1/2 cup chickpea flour
1/2 teaspoon baking powder

1/2 onion, chopped
1 garlic clove, minced
Sea salt and ground black pepper, to your liking
1 cup tortilla chips, crushed

Directions

Start by preheating your Air Fryer to 400 degrees F.

Drizzle the olive oil all over the potatoes. Place the potatoes in the Air Fryer basket and cook approximately 15 minutes, shaking the basket periodically.

Lightly crush the potatoes to split; mash the potatoes and combine with the other ingredients. Form the potato mixture into patties.

Bake in the preheated Air Fryer at 380 degrees F for 14 minutes, flipping them halfway through the cooking time to ensure even cooking. Bon appétit!

Per serving: 367 Calories; 8.9g Fat; 60.6g Carbs; 12.8g Protein; 7.5g Sugars

757. Paprika Brussels Sprout Chips

(Ready in about 20 minutes | Servings 2)

Ingredients

10 Brussels sprouts
1 teaspoon canola oil
1 teaspoon coarse sea salt
1 teaspoon paprika

Directions

Toss all ingredients in the lightly greased Air Fryer basket.

Bake at 380 degrees F for 15 minutes, shaking the basket halfway through the cooking time to ensure even cooking.

Serve and enjoy!

Per serving: 64 Calories; 2.6g Fat; 9.1g Carbs; 3.3g Protein; 2.2g Sugars

758. Vegetable Kabobs with Simple Peanut Sauce

(Ready in about 30 minutes | Servings 4)

Ingredients

8 whole baby potatoes, diced into 1-inch pieces
2 bell peppers, diced into 1-inch pieces
8 pearl onions, halved
8 small button mushrooms, cleaned
2 tablespoons extra-virgin olive oil
Sea salt and ground black pepper, to taste
1 teaspoon red pepper flakes, crushed
1 teaspoon dried rosemary, crushed
1/3 teaspoon granulated garlic
Peanut Sauce:
2 tablespoons peanut butter
1 tablespoon balsamic vinegar
1 tablespoon soy sauce
1/2 teaspoon garlic salt

Directions

Soak the wooden skewers in water for 15 minutes.

Thread the vegetables on skewers; drizzle the olive oil all over the vegetable skewers; sprinkle with spices.

Cook in the preheated Air Fryer at 400 degrees F for 13 minutes.

Meanwhile, in a small dish, whisk the peanut butter with the balsamic vinegar, soy sauce, and garlic salt. Serve your kabobs with the peanut sauce on the side. Enjoy!

Per serving: 323 Calories; 8.8g Fat; 56g Carbs; 7.6g Protein; 11.5g Sugars

759. Baked Spicy Tortilla Chips

(Ready in about 20 minutes | Servings 3)

Ingredients

6 (6-inch) corn tortillas
1 teaspoon canola oil
1 teaspoon salt
1/4 teaspoon ground white pepper
1/2 teaspoon ground cumin
1/2 teaspoon ancho chili powder

Directions

Slice the tortillas into quarters. Brush the tortilla pieces with the canola oil until well coated.

Toss with the spices and transfer to the Air Fryer basket.

Bake at 360 degrees F for 8 minutes or until lightly golden. Work in batches. Bon appétit!

Per serving: 189 Calories; 5.1g Fat; 30.7g Carbs; 4.7g Protein; 2g Sugars

760. Barbecue Roasted Almonds

(Ready in about 20 minutes | Servings 6)

Ingredients

1 ½ cups raw almonds
Sea salt and ground black pepper, to taste
1/4 teaspoon garlic powder
1/4 teaspoon mustard powder
1/2 teaspoon cumin powder
1/4 teaspoon smoked paprika
1 tablespoon olive oil

Directions

Toss all ingredients in a mixing bowl.

Line the Air Fryer basket with baking parchment. Spread out the coated almonds in a single layer in the basket.

Roast at 350 degrees F for 6 to 8 minutes, shaking the basket once or twice. Work in batches. Enjoy!

Per serving: 340 Calories; 30.1g Fat; 11.5g Carbs; 11.3g Protein; 2.3g Sugars

DESSERTS

761. Homemade Chelsea Currant Buns

(Ready in about 50 minutes | Servings 4)

Ingredients

1/2 pound cake flour
1 teaspoon dry yeast
2 tablespoons granulated sugar
A pinch of sea salt
1/2 cup milk, warm

1 egg, whisked
4 tablespoons butter
1/2 cup dried currants
1 ounce icing sugar

Directions

Mix the flour, yeast, sugar and salt in a bowl; add in milk, egg and 2 tablespoons of butter and mix to combine well. Add lukewarm water as necessary to form a smooth dough.

Knead the dough until it is elastic; then, leave it in a warm place to rise for 30 minutes.

Roll out your dough and spread the remaining 2 tablespoons of butter onto the dough; scatter dried currants over the dough.

Cut into 8 equal slices and roll them up. Brush each bun with a nonstick cooking oil and transfer them to the Air Fryer cooking basket.

Cook your buns at 330 degrees F for about 20 minutes, turning them over halfway through the cooking time.

Dust with icing sugar before serving. Bon appétit!

Per serving: 395 Calories; 14g Fat; 56.1g Carbs; 7.6g Protein; 13.6g Sugars

762. Old-Fashioned Pinch-Me Cake with Walnuts

(Ready in about 20 minutes | Servings 4)

Ingredients

1 (10-ounces) can crescent rolls
1/2 stick butter
1/2 cup caster sugar

1 teaspoon pumpkin pie spice blend
1 tablespoon dark rum
1/2 cup walnuts, chopped

Directions

Start by preheating your Air Fryer to 350 degrees F.

Roll out the crescent rolls. Spread the butter onto the crescent rolls; scatter the sugar, spices and walnuts over the rolls. Drizzle with rum and roll them up.

Using your fingertips, gently press them to seal the edges.

Bake your cake for about 13 minutes or until the top is golden brown. Bon appétit!

Per serving: 455 Calories; 25.4g Fat; 52.1g Carbs; 6.1g Protein; 15g Sugars

763. Authentic Swedish Kärleksmums

(Ready in about 20 minutes | Servings 3)

Ingredients

2 tablespoons Swedish butter, at room temperature
4 tablespoons brown sugar
1 egg
1 tablespoon lingonberry jam

5 tablespoons all-purpose flour
1/2 teaspoon baking powder
2 tablespoons cocoa powder
A pinch of grated nutmeg
A pinch of coarse sea salt

Directions

Cream the butter and sugar using an electric mixer. Fold in the egg and lingonberry jam and mix to combine well.

Stir in the flour, baking powder, cocoa powder, grated nutmeg and salt; mix again to combine well. Pour the batter into a lightly buttered baking pan.

Bake your cake at 330 degrees F for about 15 minutes until a tester inserted into the center of the cake comes out dry and clean. Bon appétit!

Per serving: 256 Calories; 11.5g Fat; 27.6g Carbs; 5.1g Protein; 13.9g Sugars

764. Air Grilled Peaches with Cinnamon-Sugar Butter

(Ready in about 25 minutes | Servings 2)

Ingredients

2 fresh peaches, pitted and halved
1 tablespoon butter

2 tablespoons caster sugar
1/4 teaspoon ground cinnamon

Directions

Mix the butter, sugar and cinnamon. Spread the butter mixture onto the peaches and transfer them to the Air Fryer cooking basket.

Cook your peaches at 320 degrees F for about 25 minutes or until the top is golden.

Serve with vanilla ice cream, if desired. Bon appétit!

Per serving: 146 Calories; 6.1g Fat; 22.6g Carbs; 1.4g Protein; 20.4g Sugars

765. Chocolate Mug Cake

(Ready in about 10 minutes | Servings 2)

Ingredients

1/2 cup self-rising flour
6 tablespoons brown sugar
5 tablespoons coconut milk
4 tablespoons coconut oil

4 tablespoons unsweetened cocoa powder
2 eggs
A pinch of grated nutmeg
A pinch of salt

Directions

Mix all the ingredients together; divide the batter between two mugs.

Place the mugs in the Air Fryer cooking basket and cook at 390 degrees F for about 10 minutes. Bon appétit!

Per serving: 546 Calories; 34.1g Fat; 55.4g Carbs; 11.4g Protein; 25.7g Sugars

766. Easy Plantain Cupcakes

(Ready in about 10 minutes | Servings 4)

Ingredients

1 cup all-purpose flour
1 teaspoon baking powder
1/4 teaspoon ground cloves
1/4 teaspoon ground cinnamon
A pinch of salt
2 ripe plantains, peeled and mashed with a fork

4 tablespoons coconut oil, room temperature
1/4 cup brown sugar
1 egg, whisked
4 tablespoons pecans, roughly chopped
2 tablespoons raisins, soaked

Directions

In a mixing bowl, thoroughly combine all ingredients until everything is well incorporated.

Spoon the batter into a greased muffin tin.

Bake the plantain cupcakes in your Air Fryer at 350 degrees F for about 10 minutes or until golden brown on the top. Bon appétit!

Per serving: 471 Calories; 22.5g Fat; 65.8g Carbs; 6.9g Protein; 24.2g Sugars

767. Strawberry Dessert Dumplings

(Ready in about 10 minutes | Servings 3)

Ingredients

9 wonton wrappers
1/3 strawberry jam

2 ounces icing sugar

Directions

Start by laying out the wonton wrappers.

Divide the strawberry jam between the wonton wrappers. Fold the wonton wrapper over the jam; now, seal the edges with wet fingers.

Cook your wontons at 400 degrees F for 8 minutes; working in batches. Bon appétit!

Per serving: 471 Calories; 22.5g Fat; 65.8g Carbs; 6.9g Protein; 24.2g Sugars

768. Crunchy French Toast Sticks

(Ready in about 10 minutes | Servings 3)

Ingredients

1 egg
1/4 cup double cream
1/4 cup milk
1 tablespoon brown sugar
1/4 teaspoon ground cloves
1/4 teaspoon ground cinnamon
1/4 vanilla paste
3 thick slices of brioche bread, cut into thirds
1 cup crispy rice cereal

Directions

Thoroughly combine the egg, cream, milk, sugar, ground cloves, cinnamon and vanilla.

Dip each piece of bread into the cream mixture and then, press gently into the cereal, pressing to coat all sides.

Arrange the pieces of bread in the Air Fryer cooking basket and cook them at 380 degrees F for 2 minutes; flip and cook on the other side for 2 to 3 minutes longer.

Bon appétit!

Per serving: 188 Calories; 8.3g Fat; 21.9g Carbs; 6.2g Protein; 6.1g Sugars

769. Old-Fashioned Apple Crumble

(Ready in about 35 minutes | Servings 4)

Ingredients

2 baking apples, peeled, cored and diced
2 tablespoons brown sugar
1 tablespoon cornstarch
1/4 teaspoon grated nutmeg
1/4 teaspoon ground cloves
1/2 teaspoon ground cinnamon
1/2 teaspoon vanilla essence
1/4 cup apple juice
1/2 cup quick-cooking oats
1/4 cup self-rising flour
1/4 cup brown sugar
1/2 teaspoon baking powder
1/4 cup coconut oil

Directions

Toss the apples with 2 tablespoons of brown sugar and cornstarch. Place the apples in a baking pan that is previously lightly greased with a nonstick cooking spray.

In a mixing dish, thoroughly combine the remaining topping ingredients. Sprinkle the topping ingredients over the apple layer.

Bake your apple crumble in the preheated Air Fryer at 330 degrees F for 35 minutes. Bon appétit!

Per serving: 261 Calories; 14.1g Fat; 35.7g Carbs; 1.9g Protein; 21.1g Sugars

770. Blueberry Fritters with Cinnamon Sugar

(Ready in about 20 minutes | Servings 4)

Ingredients

1/2 cup plain flour
1/2 teaspoon baking powder
1 teaspoon brown sugar
A pinch of grated nutmeg
1/4 teaspoon ground star anise
A pinch of salt
1 egg
1/4 cup coconut milk
1 cup fresh blueberries
1 tablespoon coconut oil, melted
4 tablespoons cinnamon sugar

Directions

Combine the flour, baking powder, brown sugar, nutmeg, star anise and salt.

In another bowl, whisk the eggs and milk until frothy. Add the wet mixture to the dry mixture and mix to combine well. Fold in the fresh blueberries.

Carefully place spoonfuls of batter into the Air Fryer cooking basket. Brush them with melted coconut oil.

Cook your fritters in the preheated Air Fryer at 370 degrees for 10 minutes, flipping them halfway through the cooking time. Repeat with the remaining batter.

Dust your fritters with the cinnamon sugar and serve at room temperature. Bon appétit!

Per serving: 218 Calories; 6.6g Fat; 35.6g Carbs; 4.7g Protein; 22.5g Sugars

771. Summer Fruit Pie

(Ready in about 35 minutes | Servings 4)

Ingredients

2 (8-ounce) refrigerated pie crusts
2 cups fresh blackberries
1/4 cup caster sugar
2 teaspoons cornstarch
A pinch of sea salt
1/4 teaspoon ground nutmeg
1/4 teaspoon ground cinnamon
1/4 teaspoon vanilla extract

Directions

Start by preheating your Air Fryer to 350 degrees F.

Place the pie crust in a lightly greased pie plate.

In a bowl, combine the fresh blackberries with caster sugar, cornstarch, salt, nutmeg, cinnamon and vanilla extract. Spoon the blackberry filling into the prepared pie crust.

Top the blackberry filling with second crust and cut slits in pastry.

Bake your pie in the preheated Air Fryer for 35 minutes or until the top is golden brown. Bon appétit!

Per serving: 318 Calories; 14.6g Fat; 43.5g Carbs; 2.7g Protein; 9.6g Sugars

772. Banana and Pecan Muffins

(Ready in about 25 minutes | Servings 4)

Ingredients

1 extra-large ripe banana, mashed
1/4 cup coconut oil
1 egg
1/4 cup brown sugar
1/2 teaspoon vanilla essence
1/2 teaspoon ground cinnamon
4 tablespoons pecans, chopped
1/2 cup self-rising flour

Directions

Start by preheating your Air Fryer to 330 degrees F.

In a mixing bowl, combine the banana, coconut oil, egg, brown sugar, vanilla and cinnamon.

Add in the chopped pecans and flour and stir again to combine well.

Spoon the mixture into a lightly greased muffin tin and transfer to the Air Fryer cooking basket.

Bake your muffins in the preheated Air Fryer for 15 to 17 minutes or until a tester comes out dry and clean.

Sprinkle some extra icing sugar over the top of each muffin if desired. Serve and enjoy!

Per serving: 315 Calories; 21.4g Fat; 27.9g Carbs; 4.8g Protein; 11.3g Sugars

773. Sweet Potato Boats

(Ready in about 35 minutes | Servings 2)

Ingredients

2 sweet potatoes, pierce several times with a fork
1/4 cup quick-cooking oats
2 tablespoons peanut butter
1 tablespoon agave nectar
1/2 teaspoon vanilla essence
1/4 teaspoon ground cloves
1/2 teaspoon ground cinnamon
A pinch of salt

Directions

Cook the sweet potatoes in the preheated Air Fryer at 380 degrees F for 20 to 25 minutes.

Then, scrape the sweet potato flesh using a spoon; mix the sweet potato flesh with the remaining ingredients. Stuff the potatoes and place them in the Air Fryer cooking basket.

Bake the sweet potatoes for a further 10 minutes or until cooked through. Bon appétit!

Per serving: 148 Calories; 3.1g Fat; 27.8g Carbs; 3.6g Protein; 7.4g Sugars

774. Mini Apple and Cranberry Crisp Cakes

(Ready in about 40 minutes | Servings 3)

Ingredients

2 Bramley cooking apples, peeled, cored and chopped
1/4 cup dried cranberries
1 teaspoon fresh lemon juice
1 tablespoon golden caster sugar
1 teaspoon apple pie spice mix
A pinch of coarse salt
1/2 cup rolled oats
1/3 cup brown bread crumbs
1/4 cup butter, diced

Directions

Divide the apples and cranberries between three lightly greased ramekins. Drizzle your fruits with lemon juice and sprinkle with caster sugar, spice mix and salt.

Then, make the streusel by mixing the remaining ingredients in a bowl. Spread the streusel batter on top of the filling.

Bake the mini crisp cakes in the preheated Air Fryer at 330 degrees F for 35 minutes or until they're a dark golden brown around the edges.

Bon appétit!

Per serving: 338 Calories; 17.5g Fat; 41.9g Carbs; 5.2g Protein; 18.1g Sugars

775. Cinnamon-Streusel Coffeecake

(Ready in about 30 minutes | Servings 4)

Ingredients

Cake:
1/2 cup unbleached white flour
1/4 cup yellow cornmeal
1 teaspoon baking powder
3 tablespoons white sugar
1 tablespoon unsweetened cocoa powder
A pinch of kosher salt
3 tablespoons coconut oil
1/4 cup milk
1 egg
Topping:
2 tablespoons polenta
1/4 cup brown sugar
1 teaspoon ground cinnamon
1/4 cup pecans, chopped
2 tablespoons coconut oil

Directions

In a large bowl, combine together the cake ingredients. Spoon the mixture into a lightly greased baking pan.

Then, in another bowl, combine the topping ingredients. Spread the topping ingredients over your cake.

Bake the cake at 330 degrees F for 12 to 15 minutes until a tester comes out dry and clean.

Allow your cake to cool for about 15 minutes before cutting and serving. Bon appétit!

Per serving: 364 Calories; 23.9g Fat; 35.1g Carbs; 5.1g Protein; 13.3g Sugars

776. Air Grilled Apricots with Mascarpone

(Ready in about 30 minutes | Servings 2)

Ingredients

6 apricots, halved and pitted
1 teaspoon coconut oil, melted
2 ounces mascarpone cheese
1/2 teaspoon vanilla extract
1 tablespoon confectioners' sugar
A pinch of sea salt

Directions

Place the apricots in the Air Fryer cooking basket. Drizzle the apricots with melted coconut oil.

Cook the apricots at 320 degrees F for about 25 minutes or until the top is golden.

In a bowl, whisk the mascarpone, vanilla extract, confectioners' sugar by hand until soft and creamy.

Remove the apricots from the cooking basket. Spoon the whipped mascarpone into the cavity of each apricot.

Sprinkle with coarse sea salt and enjoy!

Per serving: 244 Calories; 10.9g Fat; 30.1g Carbs; 7.5g Protein; 28.1g Sugars

777. Chocolate Chip Banana Crepes

(Ready in about 30 minutes | Servings 2)

Ingredients

1 small ripe banana
1/8 teaspoon baking powder
1/4 cup chocolate chips
1 egg, whisked

Directions

Mix all ingredients until creamy and fluffy. Let it stand for about 20 minutes.

Spritz the Air Fryer baking pan with cooking spray. Pour 1/2 of the batter into the pan using a measuring cup.

Cook at 230 degrees F for 4 to 5 minutes or until golden brown. Repeat with another crepe. Bon appétit!

Per serving: 214 Calories; 5.4g Fat; 36.4g Carbs; 5.8g Protein; 25.1g Sugars

778. Classic Flourless Cake

(Ready in about 2 hours | Servings 4)

Ingredients

Crust:
1 teaspoon butter
1/3 cup almond meal
1 tablespoon flaxseed meal
1 teaspoon pumpkin pie spice
1 teaspoon caster sugar
Filling:
6 ounces cream cheese
1 egg
1/2 teaspoon pure vanilla extract
2 tablespoons powdered sugar

Directions

Mix all the ingredients for the crust and then, press the mixture into the bottom of a lightly greased baking pan.

Bake the crust at 350 degrees F for 18 minutes. Transfer the crust to the freezer for about 25 minutes.

Now, make the cheesecake topping by mixing the remaining ingredients. Spread the prepared topping over the cooled crust.

Bake your cheesecake in the preheated Air Fryer at 320 degrees F for about 30 minutes; leave it in the Air Fryer to keep warm for another 30 minutes.

Serve well chilled. Bon appétit!

Per serving: 254 Calories; 21.4g Fat; 9.4g Carbs; 6.1g Protein; 6.4g Sugars

779. Old-Fashioned Baked Pears

(Ready in about 10 minutes | Servings 2)

Ingredients

2 large pears, halved and cored
1 teaspoon lemon juice
2 teaspoons coconut oil
1/2 cup rolled oats
1/4 cup walnuts, chopped
1/4 cup brown sugar
1 teaspoon apple pie spice mix

Directions

Drizzle the pear halves with lemon juice and coconut oil. In a mixing bowl, thoroughly combine the rolled oats, walnuts, brown sugar and apple pie spice mix.

Cook in the preheated Air Fryer at 360 degrees for 8 minutes, checking them halfway through the cooking time.

Dust with powdered sugar if desired. Bon appétit!

Per serving: 445 Calories; 14g Fat; 89g Carbs; 9g Protein; 49.1g Sugars

780. Sweet Dough Dippers

(Ready in about 10 minutes | Servings 4)

Ingredients

8 ounces bread dough
2 tablespoons butter, melted
2 ounces powdered sugar

Directions

Cut the dough into strips and twist them together 3 to 4 times. Then, brush the dough twists with melted butter and sprinkle sugar over them.

Cook the dough twists at 350 degrees F for 8 minutes, tossing the basket halfway through the cooking time.

Serve with your favorite dip. Bon appétit!

Per serving: 255 Calories; 7.6g Fat; 42.1g Carbs; 5g Protein; 17.1g Sugars

781. Mini Molten Lava Cakes

(Ready in about 12 minutes | Servings 2)

Ingredients

1/2 cup dark chocolate chunks
3 tablespoons butter
1 egg
1 ounce granulated sugar
1 tablespoon self-rising flour
2 tablespoons almonds, chopped

Directions

Microwave the chocolate chunks and butter for 30 to 40 seconds until the mixture is smooth.

Then, beat the eggs and sugar; stir in the egg mixture into the chocolate mixture. Now, stir in the flour and almonds.

Pour the batter into two ramekins.

Bake your cakes at 370 degrees for about 10 minutes and serve at room temperature. Bon appétit!

Per serving: 405 Calories; 29.5g Fat; 30.1g Carbs; 5.1g Protein; 23.1g Sugars

782. Baked Banana with Chocolate Glaze

(Ready in about 15 minutes | Servings 2)

Ingredients

2 bananas, peeled and cut in half lengthwise
1 tablespoon coconut oil, melted
1 tablespoon cocoa powder
1 tablespoon agave syrup

Directions

Bake your bananas in the preheated Air Fryer at 370 degrees F for 12 minutes, turning them over halfway through the cooking time.

In the meantime, microwave the coconut oil for 30 seconds; stir in the cocoa powder and agave syrup.

Serve the baked bananas with a few drizzles of the chocolate glaze. Bon appétit!

Per serving: 201 Calories; 7.5g Fat; 36.9g Carbs; 1.7g Protein; 23g Sugars

783. Chocolate Peppermint Cream Pie

(Ready in about 40 minutes + chilling time | Servings 4)

Ingredients

12 cookies, crushed into fine crumbs
2 ounces butter, melted
2 ounces dark chocolate chunks
1/2 cup heavy whipping cream
4 tablespoons brown sugar
2 drops peppermint extract
1/4 teaspoon ground cinnamon
1/4 teaspoon ground cloves

Directions

In a mixing bowl, thoroughly combine crushed cookies and butter to make the crust. Press the crust into the bottom of a lightly oiled baking dish.

Bake the crust at 350 degrees F for 18 minutes. Transfer it to your freezer for 20 minutes.

Then, microwave the chocolate chunks for 30 seconds; stir in the heavy whipping cream, brown sugar, peppermint extract, cinnamon and cloves.

Spread the mousse evenly over the crust. Refrigerate until firm for about 3 hours. Bon appétit!

Per serving: 417 Calories; 28.2g Fat; 39g Carbs; 3.3g Protein; 23g Sugars

784. Lemon-Glazed Crescent Ring

(Ready in about 25 minutes | Servings 6)

Ingredients

8 ounces refrigerated crescent dough
2 ounces mascarpone cheese, at room temperature
1/2 teaspoon vanilla paste
1 tablespoon coconut oil, at room temperature
2 ounces caster sugar
Glaze:
1/3 cup powdered sugar
1 tablespoon fresh lemon juice
1 tablespoon full-fat coconut milk

Directions

Separate the crescent dough sheet into 8 triangles. Then, arrange the triangles in a sunburst pattern so it should look like the sun.

Mix the mascarpone cheese, vanilla, coconut oil and caster sugar in a bowl

Place the mixture on the bottom of each triangle; fold triangle tips over filling and tuck under base to secure.

Bake the ring at 360 degrees F for 20 minutes until dough is golden.

In small mixing dish, whisk the powdered sugar, lemon juice and coconut milk. Drizzle over warm crescent ring and garnish with grated lemon peel. Bon appétit!

Per serving: 227 Calories; 6.7g Fat; 35.4g Carbs; 5.3g Protein; 15g Sugars

785. Fluffy Chocolate Chip Cookies

(Ready in about 20 minutes | Servings 6)

Ingredients

1/2 cup butter, softened
1/2 cup granulated sugar
1 large egg
1/2 teaspoon coconut extract
1/2 teaspoon vanilla paste
1 cup quick-cooking oats
1/2 cup all-purpose flour
1/2 teaspoon baking powder
6 ounces dark chocolate chips

Directions

Start by preheating your Air Fryer to 330 degrees F.

In a mixing bowl, beat the butter and sugar until fluffy. Beat in the egg, coconut extract and vanilla paste.

In a second mixing bowl, whisk the oats, flour and baking powder. Add the flour mixture to the egg mixture. Fold in the chocolate chips and gently stir to combine.

Drop 2-tablespoon scoops of the dough onto the parchment paper and transfer it to the Air Fryer cooking basket. Gently flatten each scoop to make a cookie shape.

Cook in the preheated Air Fryer for about 10 minutes. Work in batches. Bon appétit!

Per serving: 490 Calories; 30.1g Fat; 45.4g Carbs; 8.8g Protein; 15g Sugars

786. Authentic Spanish Churros

(Ready in about 20 minutes | Servings 4)

Ingredients

1/2 cup water
1/4 cup butter, cut into cubes
1 tablespoon granulated sugar
A pinch of ground cinnamon
A pinch of salt
1/2 teaspoon lemon zest
1/2 cup plain flour
1 egg
Chocolate Dip:
2 ounces dark chocolate
1/2 cup milk
1 teaspoon ground cinnamon

Directions

Boil the water in a saucepan over medium-high heat; now, add the butter, sugar, cinnamon, salt and lemon zest; cook until the sugar has dissolved.

Next, remove the pan from the heat. Gradually stir in the flour, whisking continuously until the mixture forms a ball; let it cool slightly.

Fold in the egg and continue to beat using an electric mixer until everything comes together.

Pour the dough into a piping bag with a large star tip. Squeeze 4-inch strips of dough into the greased Air Fryer pan.

Cook your churros at 380 degrees F for about 10 minutes, shaking the basket halfway through the cooking time.

In the meantime, melt the chocolate and milk in a saucepan over low heat. Add in the cinnamon and cook on low heat for about 5 minutes. Serve the warm churros with the chocolate dip and enjoy!

Per serving: 287 Calories; 19.7g Fat; 22.5g Carbs; 5.2g Protein; 7.1g Sugars

787. Classic Brownie Cupcakes

(Ready in about 25 minutes | Servings 3)

Ingredients

1/3 cup all-purpose flour	1 large egg
1/4 teaspoon baking powder	1/2 teaspoon rum extract
3 tablespoons cocoa powder	A pinch of ground cinnamon
1/3 cup caster sugar	A pinch of salt
2 ounces butter, room temperature	

Directions

Mix the dry ingredients in a bowl. In another bowl, mix the wet ingredients. Gradually, stir in the wet ingredients into the dry mixture.

Divide the batter among muffin cups and transfer them to the Air Fryer cooking basket.

Bake your cupcakes at 330 degrees for 15 minuets until a tester comes out dry and clean. Transfer to a wire rack and let your cupcakes sit for 10 minutes before unmolding. Bon appétit!

Per serving: 264 Calories; 17.7g Fat; 24.4g Carbs; 4.6g Protein; 10.9g Sugars

788. Baked Fruit Salad

(Ready in about 15 minutes | Servings 2)

Ingredients

1 banana, peeled	1/2 teaspoon ground star anise
1 cooking pear, cored	1/4 teaspoon ground cinnamon
1 cooking apple, cored	1/2 teaspoon granulated ginger
1 tablespoon freshly squeezed lemon juice	1/4 cup brown sugar
	1 tablespoon coconut oil, melted

Directions

Toss your fruits with lemon juice, star anise, cinnamon, ginger, sugar and coconut oil.

Transfer the fruits to the Air Fryer cooking basket.

Bake the fruit salad in the preheated Air Fryer at 330 degrees F for 15 minutes.

Serve in individual bowls, garnished with vanilla ice cream. Bon appétit!

Per serving: 263 Calories; 7.3g Fat; 53.2g Carbs; 1.3g Protein; 37.7g Sugars

789. Indian-Style Donuts (Gulgulas)

(Ready in about 10 minutes | Servings 2)

Ingredients

1/3 cup whole wheat flour	1 tablespoon Indian dahi
1/3 cup sugar	1 tablespoon apple juice
1 teaspoon ghee	

Directions

Mix the ingredients until everything is well incorporated.

Drop a spoonful of batter onto the greased Air Fryer pan. Cook Indian gulgulas at 360 degrees F for 5 minutes or until golden brown, flipping them halfway through the cooking time.

Repeat with the remaining batter. Serve with hot Indian tea and enjoy!

Per serving: 160 Calories; 2.9g Fat; 31.9g Carbs; 2.9g Protein; 16.7g Sugars

790. Honey-Drizzled Banana Fritters

(Ready in about 15 minutes | Servings 3)

Ingredients

3 ripe bananas, peeled	1/2 teaspoon baking powder
1 egg, whisked	1 teaspoon canola oil
1/4 cup almond flour	1 tablespoon honey
1/4 cup plain flour	

Directions

Mash your bananas in a bowl. Now, stir in the egg, almond flour, plain flour and baking powder.

Drop spoonfuls of the batter into the preheated Air Fryer cooking basket. Brush the fritters with canola oil.

Cook the banana fritters at 360 degrees F for 10 minutes, flipping them halfway through the cooking time.

Drizzle with some honey just before serving. Bon appétit!

Per serving: 247 Calories; 7.3g Fat; 42.5g Carbs; 5.9g Protein; 20.6g Sugars

791. Chocolate Puff Pastry Sticks

(Ready in about 15 minutes | Servings 3)

Ingredients

8 ounces frozen puff pastry, thawed, cut into strips	1/2 teaspoon ground cinnamon
1/2 stick butter, melted	1/2 cup chocolate hazelnut spread

Directions

Brush the strips of the puff pastry with melted butter.

Arrange the strips in the Air Fryer cooking basket and bake them at 380 degrees F for 2 minutes; flip and cook on the other side for 2 to 3 minutes longer.

Top the pastry sticks with cinnamon and chocolate hazelnut spread. Bon appétit!

Per serving: 407 Calories; 21.2g Fat; 46.1g Carbs; 6.9g Protein; 5.5g Sugars

792. Old-Fashioned Donuts

(Ready in about 15 minutes | Servings 4)

Ingredients

8 ounces refrigerated buttermilk biscuits	4 tablespoons caster sugar
2 tablespoons butter, unsalted and melted	A pinch of salt
	A pinch of grated nutmeg
1/2 tablespoon cinnamon	

Directions

Separate the biscuits and cut holes out of the center of each biscuit using a 1-inch round biscuit cutter; place them on a parchment paper.

Lower your biscuits into the Air Fryer cooking basket. Brush them with 1 tablespoon of melted butter.

Air fry your biscuits at 340 degrees F for about 8 minutes or until golden brown, flipping them halfway through the cooking time.

Meanwhile, mix the sugar with cinnamon, salt and nutmeg.

Brush your donuts with remaining 1 tablespoon of melted butter; roll them in the cinnamon-sugar and serve. Bon appétit!

Per serving: 268 Calories; 12.2g Fat; 36.1g Carbs; 3.9g Protein; 12.4g Sugars

793. Perfect English-Style Scones

(Ready in about 15 minutes | Servings 4)

Ingredients

1 ½ cups cake flour	1/2 teaspoon vanilla essence
1/4 cup caster sugar	1/2 stick butter
1 teaspoon baking powder	1 egg, beaten
1 teaspoon baking soda	1/2 cup almond milk
1/4 teaspoon salt	

Directions

Start by preheating your Air Fryer to 360 degrees F.

Thoroughly combine all dry ingredients. In another bowl, combine all wet ingredients. Then, add the wet mixture to the dry ingredients and stir to combine well.

Roll your dough out into a circle and cut into wedges.

Bake the scones in the preheated Air Fryer for about 11 minutes, flipping them halfway through the cooking time. Bon appétit!

Per serving: 458 Calories; 25g Fat; 47.1g Carbs; 6.8g Protein; 7.9g Sugars

794. Red Velvet Pancakes

(Ready in about 35 minutes | Servings 3)

Ingredients

1 cup all-purpose flour
1/2 teaspoon baking soda
1 teaspoon granulated sugar
1/8 teaspoon sea salt
1/8 teaspoon freshly grated nutmeg
2 tablespoons ghee, melted

1 small-sized egg, beaten
1/2 cup milk
1 teaspoon red paste food color
2 ounces cream cheese, softened
1 tablespoon butter, softened
1/2 cup powdered sugar

Directions

Thoroughly combine the flour, baking soda, granulated sugar, salt and nutmeg in a large bowl.

Gradually add in the melted ghee, egg, milk and red paste food color, stirring into the flour mixture until moistened. Allow your batter to rest for about 30 minutes.

Spritz the Air Fryer baking pan with cooking spray. Pour the batter into the pan using a measuring cup. Set the pan into the Air Fryer cooking basket.

Cook at 330 degrees F for about 5 minutes or until golden brown. Repeat with the other pancakes.

Meanwhile, mix the remaining ingredients until creamy and fluffy. Decorate your pancakes with cream cheese topping. Bon appétit!

Per serving: 422 Calories; 19g Fat; 52.1g Carbs; 8.6g Protein; 20.3g Sugars

795. Apricot and Almond Crumble

(Ready in about 35 minutes | Servings 3)

Ingredients

1 cup apricots, pitted and diced
1/4 cup flaked almonds
1/3 cup self-raising flour
4 tablespoons granulated sugar

1/2 teaspoon ground cinnamon
1 teaspoon crystallized ginger
1/2 teaspoon ground cardamom
2 tablespoons butter

Directions

Place the sliced apricots and almonds in a baking pan that is lightly greased with a nonstick cooking spray.

In a mixing bowl, thoroughly combine the remaining ingredients. Sprinkle this topping over the apricot layer.

Bake your crumble in the preheated Air Fryer at 330 degrees F for 35 minutes. Bon appétit!

Per serving: 192 Calories; 7.9g Fat; 29.1g Carbs; 1.7g Protein; 17.7g Sugars

796. Easy Monkey Rolls

(Ready in about 25 minutes | Servings 4)

Ingredients

8 ounces refrigerated buttermilk biscuit dough
1/2 cup brown sugar
4 ounces butter, melted

1/4 teaspoon grated nutmeg
1/2 teaspoon ground cinnamon
1/4 teaspoon ground cardamom

Directions

Spritz 4 standard-size muffin cups with a nonstick spray. Thoroughly combine the brown sugar with the melted butter, nutmeg, cinnamon and cardamom.

Spoon the butter mixture into muffins cups.

Separate the dough into biscuits and divide your biscuits between muffin cups.

Bake the Monkey rolls at 340 degrees F for about 15 minutes or until golden brown. Turn upside down just before serving. Bon appétit!

Per serving: 432 Calories; 29.3g Fat; 40.1g Carbs; 4.1g Protein; 16.8g Sugars

797. Sherry Roasted Sweet Cherries

(Ready in about 35 minutes | Servings 4)

Ingredients

2 cups dark cherries
1/4 cup granulated sugar
1 tablespoon honey

3 tablespoons sherry
A pinch of sea salt
A pinch of grated nutmeg

Directions

Arrange your cherries in the bottom of a lightly greased baking dish.

Whisk the remaining ingredients; spoon this mixture into the baking dish.

Air fry your cherries at 370 degrees F for 35 minutes. Bon appétit!

Per serving: 53 Calories; 0.3g Fat; 11.1g Carbs; 0.1g Protein; 11.2g Sugars

798. Greek Roasted Figs with Yiaourti me Meli

(Ready in about 20 minutes | Servings 3)

Ingredients

1 teaspoon coconut oil, melted
6 medium-sized figs
1/4 teaspoon ground cardamom
1/4 teaspoon ground cloves

1/4 teaspoon ground cinnamon
3 tablespoon honey
1/2 cup Greek yogurt

Directions

Drizzle the melted coconut oil all over your figs.

Sprinkle cardamom, cloves and cinnamon over your figs.

Roast your figs in the preheated Air Fryer at 330 degrees F for 15 to 16 minutes, shaking the basket occasionally to promote even cooking.

In the meantime, thoroughly combine the honey with the Greek yogurt to make the yiaourti me meli.

Divide the roasted figs between 3 serving bowls and serve with a dollop of yiaourti me meli. Enjoy!

Per serving: 169 Calories; 1.9g Fat; 37.1g Carbs; 3.7g Protein; 34.3g Sugars

799. Apple Fries with Snickerdoodle Dip

(Ready in about 10 minutes | Servings 2)

Ingredients

1 Gala apple, cored and sliced
1 teaspoon peanut oil
1 teaspoon butter, room temperature

2 ounces cream cheese, room temperature
2 ounces Greek yogurt
2 ounces caster sugar
1 teaspoon ground cinnamon

Directions

Drizzle peanut oil all over the apple slices; transfer the apple slices to the Air Fryer.

Bake the apple slices at 350 degrees F for 5 minutes; shake the basket and continue cooking an additional 5 minutes.

In the meantime, mix the remaining ingredients until everything is well incorporated.

Serve the apple fries with Snickerdoodle dip on the side. Bon appétit!

Per serving: 309 Calories; 14.1g Fat; 43g Carbs; 4.7g Protein; 39g Sugars

800. Panettone Pudding Tart

(Ready in about 45 minutes | Servings 3)

Ingredients

3 cups panettone bread, crusts trimmed, bread cut into 1-inch cubes
1/2 cup creme fraiche
1/2 cup coconut milk
2 tablespoons orange marmalade
1 tablespoon butter

2 tablespoons amaretto liqueur
1/2 teaspoon vanilla extract
1/4 cup sugar
A pinch of grated nutmeg
A pinch of sea salt
1 egg, whisked

Directions

Put the panettone bread cubes into a lightly greased baking pan.

Then, make the custard by mixing the remaining ingredients.

Pour the custard over your panettone. Let it rest for 30 minutes, pressing with a wide spatula to submerge.

Cook the panettone pudding in the preheated Air Fryer at 370 degrees F degrees for 7 minutes; rotate the pan and cook an additional 5 to 6 minutes. Bon appétit!

Per serving: 326 Calories; 13.6g Fat; 37.3g Carbs; 8.7g Protein; 17.8g Sugars

801. Dessert French Toast with Blackberries

(Ready in about 20 minutes | Servings 2)

Ingredients

2 tablespoons butter, at room temperature
1 egg
2 tablespoons granulated sugar
1/4 teaspoon ground cinnamon
1/4 teaspoon vanilla extract
6 slices French baguette
1 cup fresh blackberries
2 tablespoons powdered sugar

Direction

Start by preheating your Air Fryer to 375 degrees F.

In a mixing dish, whisk the butter, egg, granulated sugar, cinnamon and vanilla.

Dip all the slices of the French baguette in this mixture. Transfer the French toast to the baking pan.

Bake in the preheated Air Fryer for 8 minutes, turning them over halfway through the cooking time to ensure even cooking.

To serve, divide the French toast between two warm plates. Arrange the blackberries on top of each slice. Dust with powdered sugar and serve immediately. Enjoy!

Per serving: 324 Calories; 14.9g Fat; 42.2g Carbs; 6.5g Protein; 24.9g Sugars

802. Chocolate Lava Cake

(Ready in about 20 minutes | Servings 4)

Ingredients

4 ounces butter, melted
4 ounces dark chocolate
2 eggs, lightly whisked
4 tablespoons granulated sugar
2 tablespoons cake flour
1 teaspoon baking powder
1/2 teaspoon ground cinnamon
1/4 teaspoon ground star anise

Directions

Begin by preheating your Air Fryer to 370 degrees F. Spritz the sides and bottom of a baking pan with nonstick cooking spray.

Melt the butter and dark chocolate in a microwave-safe bowl. Mix the eggs and sugar until frothy.

Pour the butter/chocolate mixture into the egg mixture. Stir in the flour, baking powder, cinnamon, and star anise. Mix until everything is well incorporated.

Scrape the batter into the prepared pan. Bake in the preheated Air Fryer for 9 to 11 minutes.

Let stand for 2 minutes. Invert on a plate while warm and serve. Bon appétit!

Per serving: 450 Calories; 37.2g Fat; 24.2g Carbs; 5.6g Protein; 14.7g Sugars

803. Banana Chips with Chocolate Glaze

(Ready in about 20 minutes | Servings 2)

Ingredients

2 banana, cut into slices
1/4 teaspoon lemon zest
1 tablespoon agave syrup
1 tablespoon cocoa powder
1 tablespoon coconut oil, melted

Directions

Toss the bananas with the lemon zest and agave syrup. Transfer your bananas to the parchment-lined cooking basket.

Bake in the preheated Air Fryer at 370 degrees F for 12 minutes, turning them over halfway through the cooking time.

In the meantime, melt the coconut oil in your microwave; add the cocoa powder and whisk to combine well.

Serve the baked banana chips with a few drizzles of the chocolate glaze. Enjoy!

Per serving: 201 Calories; 7.5g Fat; 37.1g Carbs; 1.8g Protein; 22.9g Sugars

804. Grandma's Butter Cookies

(Ready in about 25 minutes | Servings 4)

Ingredients

8 ounces all-purpose flour
2 ½ ounces sugar
1 teaspoon baking powder
A pinch of grated nutmeg
A pinch of coarse salt
1 large egg, room temperature.
1 stick butter, room temperature
1 teaspoon vanilla extract

Directions

Mix the flour, sugar, baking powder, grated nutmeg, and salt in a bowl. In a separate bowl, whisk the egg, butter, and vanilla extract.

Stir the egg mixture into the flour mixture; mix to combine well or until it forms a nice, soft dough.

Roll your dough out and cut out with a cookie cutter of your choice.

Bake in the preheated Air Fryer at 350 degrees F for 10 minutes. Decrease the temperature to 330 degrees F and cook for 10 minutes longer. Bon appétit!

Per serving: 492 Calories; 24.7g Fat; 61.1g Carbs; 6.7g Protein; 17.5g Sugars

805. Cinnamon Dough Dippers

(Ready in about 20 minutes | Servings 6)

Ingredients

1/2 pound bread dough
1/4 cup butter, melted
1/2 cup caster sugar
1 tablespoon cinnamon
1/2 cup cream cheese, softened
1 cup powdered sugar
1/2 teaspoon vanilla
2 tablespoons milk

Directions

Roll the dough into a log; cut into 1-1/2 inch strips using a pizza cutter.

Mix the butter, sugar, and cinnamon in a small bowl. Use a rubber spatula to spread the butter mixture over the tops of the dough dippers.

Bake at 360 degrees F for 7 to 8 minutes, turning them over halfway through the cooking time. Work in batches.

Meanwhile, make the glaze dip by whisking the remaining ingredients with a hand mixer. Beat until a smooth consistency is reached.

Serve at room temperature and enjoy!

Per serving: 332 Calories; 14.8g Fat; 45.6g Carbs; 5.1g Protein; 27.6g Sugars

806. Chocolate Apple Chips

(Ready in about 15 minutes | Servings 2)

Ingredients

1 large Pink Lady apple, cored and sliced
1 tablespoon light brown sugar
A pinch of kosher salt
2 tablespoons lemon juice
2 teaspoons cocoa powder

Directions

Toss the apple slices with the other ingredients.

Bake at 350 degrees F for 5 minutes; shake the basket to ensure even cooking and continue to cook an additional 5 minutes.

Bon appétit!

Per serving: 81 Calories; 0.5g Fat; 21.5g Carbs; 0.7g Protein; 15.9g Sugars

807. Favorite Apple Crisp

(Ready in about 40 minutes | Servings 4)

Ingredients

4 cups apples, peeled, cored and sliced
1/2 cup brown sugar
1 tablespoon honey
1 tablespoon cornmeal
1/4 teaspoon ground cloves
1/2 teaspoon ground cinnamon
1/4 cup water
1/2 cup quick-cooking oats
1/2 cup all-purpose flour
1/2 cup caster sugar
1/2 teaspoon baking powder
1/3 cup coconut oil, melted

Directions

Toss the sliced apples with the brown sugar, honey, cornmeal, cloves, and cinnamon. Divide between four custard cups coated with cooking spray.

In a mixing dish, thoroughly combine the remaining ingredients. Sprinkle over the apple mixture.

Bake in the preheated Air Fryer at 330 degrees F for 35 minutes. Bon appétit!

Per serving: 403 Calories; 18.6g Fat; 61.5g Carbs; 2.9g Protein; 40.2g Sugars

808. Peppermint Chocolate Cheesecake

(Ready in about 40 minutes | Servings 6)

Ingredients

1 cup powdered sugar
1/2 cup all-purpose flour
1/2 cup butter
1 cup mascarpone cheese, at room temperature
4 ounces semisweet chocolate, melted
1 teaspoon vanilla extract
2 drops peppermint extract

Directions

Beat the sugar, flour, and butter in a mixing bowl. Press the mixture into the bottom of a lightly greased baking pan.

Bake at 350 degrees F for 18 minutes. Place it in your freezer for 20 minutes.

Then, make the cheesecake topping by mixing the remaining ingredients. Place this topping over the crust and allow it to cool in your freezer for a further 15 minutes. Serve well chilled.

Per serving: 484 Calories; 36.7g Fat; 38.8g Carbs; 5g Protein; 22.2g Sugars

809. Baked Coconut Doughnuts

(Ready in about 20 minutes | Servings 6)

Ingredients

1 ½ cups all-purpose flour
1 teaspoon baking powder
A pinch of kosher salt
A pinch of freshly grated nutmeg
1/2 cup white sugar
2 eggs
2 tablespoons full-fat coconut milk
2 tablespoons coconut oil, melted
1/4 teaspoon ground cardamom
1/4 teaspoon ground cinnamon
1 teaspoon coconut essence
1/2 teaspoon vanilla essence
1 cup coconut flakes

Directions

In a mixing bowl, thoroughly combine the all-purpose flour with the baking powder, salt, nutmeg, and sugar.

In a separate bowl, beat the eggs until frothy using a hand mixer; add the coconut milk and oil and beat again; lastly, stir in the spices and mix again until everything is well combined.

Then, stir the egg mixture into the flour mixture and continue mixing until a dough ball forms. Try not to over-mix your dough. Transfer to a lightly floured surface.

Roll out your dough to a 1/4-inch thickness using a rolling pin. Cut out the doughnuts using a 3-inch round cutter; now, use a 1-inch round cutter to remove the center.

Bake in the preheated Air Fryer at 340 degrees F approximately 5 minutes or until golden. Repeat with remaining doughnuts. Decorate with coconut flakes and serve.

Per serving: 305 Calories; 13.2g Fat; 40.1g Carbs; 6.7g Protein; 13.8g Sugars

810. Classic Vanilla Mini Cheesecakes

(Ready in about 40 minutes + chilling time | Servings 6)

Ingredients

1/2 cup almond flour
1 ½ tablespoons unsalted butter, melted
1 tablespoon white sugar
1 (8-ounce) package cream cheese, softened
1/4 cup powdered sugar
1/2 teaspoon vanilla paste
1 egg, at room temperature
Topping:
1 ½ cups sour cream
3 tablespoons white sugar
1 teaspoon vanilla extract
1/4 cup maraschino cherries

Directions

Thoroughly combine the almond flour, butter, and sugar in a mixing bowl. Press the mixture into the bottom of lightly greased custard cups.

Then, mix the cream cheese, 1/4 cup of powdered sugar, vanilla, and egg using an electric mixer on low speed. Pour the batter into the pan, covering the crust.

Bake in the preheated Air Fryer at 330 degrees F for 35 minutes until edges are puffed and the surface is firm.

Mix the sour cream, 3 tablespoons of white sugar, and vanilla for the topping; spread over the crust and allow it to cool to room temperature.

Transfer to your refrigerator for 6 to 8 hours. Decorate with maraschino cherries and serve well chilled.

Per serving: 321 Calories; 25g Fat; 17.1g Carbs; 8.1g Protein; 11.4g Sugars

811. Bakery-Style Hazelnut Cookies

(Ready in about 20 minutes | Servings 6)

Ingredients

1 ½ cups all-purpose flour
1 teaspoon baking soda
1 teaspoon fine sea salt
1 stick butter
1 cup brown sugar
2 teaspoons vanilla
2 eggs, at room temperature
1 cup hazelnuts, coarsely chopped

Directions

Begin by preheating your Air Fryer to 350 degrees F.

Mix the flour with the baking soda, and sea salt.

In the bowl of an electric mixer, beat the butter, brown sugar, and vanilla until creamy. Fold in the eggs, one at a time, and mix until well combined.

Slowly and gradually, stir in the flour mixture. Finally, fold in the coarsely chopped hazelnuts.

Divide the dough into small balls using a large cookie scoop; drop onto the prepared cookie sheets. Bake for 10 minutes or until golden brown, rotating the pan once or twice through the cooking time.

Work in batches and cool for a couple of minutes before removing to wire racks. Enjoy!

Per serving: 450 Calories; 28.6g Fat; 43.9g Carbs; 8.1g Protein; 17.5g Sugars

812. Chocolate Biscuit Sandwich Cookies

(Ready in about 20 minutes | Servings 10)

Ingredients

2 ½ cups self-rising flour
4 ounces brown sugar
1 ounce honey
5 ounces butter, softened
1 egg, beaten
1 teaspoon vanilla essence
4 ounces double cream
3 ounces dark chocolate
1 teaspoon cardamom seeds, finely crushed

Directions

Start by preheating your Air Fryer to 350 degrees F.

In a mixing bowl, thoroughly combine the flour, brown sugar, honey, and butter. Mix until your mixture resembles breadcrumbs.

Gradually, add the egg and vanilla essence. Shape your dough into small balls and place in the parchment-lined Air Fryer basket.

Bake in the preheated Air Fryer for 10 minutes. Rotate the pan and bake for another 5 minutes. Transfer the freshly baked cookies to a cooling rack.

As the biscuits are cooling, melt the double cream and dark chocolate in an air-fryer safe bowl at 350 degrees F. Add the cardamom seeds and stir well.

Spread the filling over the cooled biscuits and sandwich together. Bon appétit!

Per serving: 353 Calories; 18.6g Fat; 41.4g Carbs; 5.1g Protein; 16.1g Sugars

813. Easy Chocolate Brownies

(Ready in about 30 minutes | Servings 8)

Ingredients

1 stick butter, melted
1/2 cup caster sugar
1/2 cup white sugar
1 egg
1 teaspoon vanilla essence

1/2 cup all-purpose flour
1 teaspoon baking powder
1/2 cup cocoa powder
A pinch of salt
A pinch of ground cardamom

Directions

Start by preheating your Air Fryer to 350 degrees F. Now, spritz the sides and bottom of a baking pan with cooking spray.

In a mixing dish, beat the melted butter with sugar until fluffy. Next, fold in the egg and beat again.

After that, add the vanilla, flour, baking powder, cocoa, salt, and ground cardamom. Mix until everything is well combined.

Bake in the preheated Air Fryer for 20 to 22 minutes. Enjoy!

Per serving: 200 Calories; 12.7g Fat; 21.7g Carbs; 2.5g Protein; 12.4g Sugars

814. Light and Fluffy Chocolate Cake

(Ready in about 20 minutes | Servings 6)

Ingredients

1/2 stick butter, at room temperature
1/2 cup chocolate chips
2 tablespoons honey

2/3 cup almond flour
A pinch of fine sea salt
1 egg, whisked
1/2 teaspoon vanilla extract

Directions

Begin by preheating your Air Fryer to 330 degrees F.

In a microwave-safe bowl, melt the butter, chocolate, and honey.

Add the other ingredients to the cooled chocolate mixture; stir to combine well. Scrape the batter into a lightly greased baking pan.

Bake in the preheated Air Fryer for 15 minutes or until the center is springy and a toothpick comes out dry. Enjoy!

Per serving: 242 Calories; 19.5g Fat; 13.6g Carbs; 4.7g Protein; 9.2g Sugars

815. Cinnamon and Sugar Sweet Potato Fries

(Ready in about 30 minutes | Servings 2)

Ingredients

1 large sweet potato, peeled and sliced into sticks
1 teaspoon ghee
1 tablespoon cornstarch

1/4 teaspoon ground cardamom
1/4 cup sugar
1 tablespoon ground cinnamon

Directions

Toss the sweet potato sticks with the melted ghee and cornstarch.

Cook in the preheated Air Fryer at 380 degrees F for 20 minutes, shaking the basket halfway through the cooking time.

Sprinkle the cardamom, sugar, and cinnamon all over the sweet potato fries and serve. Bon appétit!

Per serving: 162 Calories; 2.1g Fat; 34.9g Carbs; 1.8g Protein; 18.1g Sugars

816. Easy Blueberry Muffins

(Ready in about 20 minutes | Servings 10)

Ingredients

1 ½ cups all-purpose flour
1/2 teaspoon baking soda
1 teaspoon baking powder
1/4 teaspoon kosher salt
1/2 cup granulated sugar

2 eggs, whisked
1/2 cup milk
1/4 cup coconut oil, melted
1/2 teaspoon vanilla paste
1 cup fresh blueberries

Directions

In a mixing bowl, combine the flour, baking soda, baking powder, sugar, and salt. Whisk to combine well.

In another mixing bowl, mix the eggs, milk, coconut oil, and vanilla.

Now, add the wet egg mixture to dry the flour mixture. Then, carefully fold in the fresh blueberries; gently stir to combine.

Scrape the batter mixture into the muffin cups. Bake your muffins at 350 degrees F for 12 minutes or until the tops are golden brown.

Sprinkle some extra icing sugar over the top of each muffin if desired. Serve and enjoy!

Per serving: 191 Calories; 8g Fat; 25.7g Carbs; 4.3g Protein; 10.9g Sugars

817. Chocolate Raspberry Wontons

(Ready in about 15 minutes | Servings 6)

Ingredients

1 (12-ounce) package wonton wrappers
6 ounces chocolate chips
1/2 cup raspberries, mashed

1 egg, lightly whisked + 1 tablespoon of water (egg wash)
1/4 cup caster sugar

Directions

Divide the chocolate chips and raspberries among the wonton wrappers. Now, fold the wrappers diagonally in half over the filling; press the edges with a fork.

Brush with the egg wash and seal the edges.

Bake at 370 degrees F for 8 minutes, flipping them halfway through the cooking time.

Work in batches. Sprinkle the caster sugar over your wontons and enjoy!

Per serving: 356 Calories; 13g Fat; 51.2g Carbs; 7.9g Protein; 11.3g Sugars

818. Country Pie with Walnuts

(Ready in about 20 minutes | Servings 6)

Ingredients

1 cup coconut milk
2 eggs
1/2 stick butter, at room temperature
1 teaspoon vanilla essence

1/4 teaspoon ground cardamom
1/4 teaspoon ground cloves
1/2 cup walnuts, ground
1/2 cup sugar
1/3 cup almond flour

Directions

Begin by preheating your Air Fryer to 360 degrees F. Spritz the sides and bottom of a baking pan with nonstick cooking spray.

Mix all ingredients until well combined. Scrape the batter into the prepared baking pan.

Bake approximately 13 minutes; use a toothpick to test for doneness. Bon appétit!

Per serving: 244 Calories; 19.1g Fat; 12.7g Carbs; 6.5g Protein; 10.9g Sugars

819. Cocktail Party Fruit Kabobs

(Ready in about 10 minutes | Servings 6)

Ingredients

2 pears, diced into bite-sized chunks
2 apples, diced into bite-sized chunks
2 mangos, diced into bite-sized chunks

1 tablespoon fresh lemon juice
1 teaspoon vanilla essence
2 tablespoons maple syrup
1 teaspoon ground cinnamon
1/2 teaspoon ground cloves

Directions

Toss all ingredients in a mixing dish.

Tread the fruit pieces on skewers.

Cook at 350 degrees F for 5 minutes. Bon appétit!

Per serving: 165 Calories; 0.7g Fat; 41.8g Carbs; 1.6g Protein; 33.6g Sugars

820. Sunday Banana Chocolate Cookies

(Ready in about 20 minutes | Servings 8)

Ingredients

1 stick butter, at room temperature
1 ¼ cups caster sugar
2 ripe bananas, mashed
1 teaspoon vanilla paste
1 2/3 cups all-purpose flour
1/3 cup cocoa powder
1 ½ teaspoons baking powder
1/4 teaspoon ground cinnamon
1/4 teaspoon crystallized ginger
1 ½ cups chocolate chips

Directions

In a mixing dish, beat the butter and sugar until creamy and uniform. Stir in the mashed bananas and vanilla.

In another mixing dish, thoroughly combine the flour, cocoa powder, baking powder, cinnamon, and crystallized ginger.

Add the flour mixture to the banana mixture; mix to combine well. Afterwards, fold in the chocolate chips.

Drop by large spoonfuls onto a parchment-lined Air Fryer basket. Bake at 365 degrees F for 11 minutes or until golden brown on the top. Bon appétit!

Per serving: 298 Calories; 12.3g Fat; 45.9g Carbs; 3.8g Protein; 19.6g Sugars

821. Rustic Baked Apples

(Ready in about 25 minutes | Servings 4)

Ingredients

4 Gala apples
1/4 cup rolled oats
1/4 cup sugar
2 tablespoons honey
1/3 cup walnuts, chopped
1 teaspoon cinnamon powder
1/2 teaspoon ground cardamom
1/2 teaspoon ground cloves
2/3 cup water

Directions

Use a paring knife to remove the stem and seeds from the apples, making deep holes.

In a mixing bowl, combine together the rolled oats, sugar, honey, walnuts, cinnamon, cardamom, and cloves.

Pour the water into an Air Fryer safe dish. Place the apples in the dish.

Bake at 340 degrees F for 17 minutes. Serve at room temperature. Bon appétit!

Per serving: 211 Calories; 5.1g Fat; 45.5g Carbs; 2.6g Protein; 33.9g Sugars

822. The Ultimate Berry Crumble

(Ready in about 40 minutes | Servings 6)

Ingredients

18 ounces cherries
1/2 cup granulated sugar
2 tablespoons cornmeal
1/4 teaspoon ground star anise
1/2 teaspoon ground cinnamon
2/3 cup all-purpose flour
1 cup demerara sugar
1/2 teaspoon baking powder
1/3 cup rolled oats
1/2 stick butter, cut into small pieces

Directions

Toss the cherries with the granulated sugar, cornmeal, star anise, and cinnamon. Divide between six custard cups coated with cooking spray.

In a mixing dish, thoroughly combine the remaining ingredients. Sprinkle over the berry mixture.

Bake in the preheated Air Fryer at 330 degrees F for 35 minutes. Bon appétit!

Per serving: 272 Calories; 8.3g Fat; 49.5g Carbs; 3.3g Protein; 31g Sugars

823. Mocha Chocolate Espresso Cake

(Ready in about 40 minutes | Servings 8)

Ingredients

1 ½ cups flour
2/3 cup sugar
1 teaspoon baking powder
1/4 teaspoon salt
1 stick butter, melted
1/2 cup hot strongly brewed coffee
1/2 teaspoon vanilla
1 egg
Topping:
1/4 cup flour
1/2 cup sugar
1/2 teaspoon ground cardamom
1 teaspoon ground cinnamon
3 tablespoons coconut oil

Directions

Mix all dry ingredients for your cake; then, mix in the wet ingredients. Mix until everything is well incorporated.

Spritz a baking pan with cooking spray. Scrape the batter into the baking pan.

Then make the topping by mixing all ingredients. Place on top of the cake. Smooth the top with a spatula.

Bake at 330 degrees F for 30 minutes or until the top of the cake springs back when gently pressed with your fingers. Serve with your favorite hot beverage. Bon appétit!

Per serving: 320 Calories; 18.1g Fat; 35.9g Carbs; 4.1g Protein; 14.5g Sugars

824. Chocolate and Peanut Butter Brownies

(Ready in about 30 minutes | Servings 10)

Ingredients

1 cup peanut butter
1 ¼ cups sugar
3 eggs
1 cup all-purpose flour
1 teaspoon baking powder
1/4 teaspoon kosher salt
1 cup dark chocolate, broken into chunks

Directions

Start by preheating your Air Fryer to 350 degrees F. Now, spritz the sides and bottom of a baking pan with cooking spray.

In a mixing dish, thoroughly combine the peanut butter with the sugar until creamy. Next, fold in the egg and beat until fluffy.

After that, stir in the flour, baking powder, salt, and chocolate. Mix until everything is well combined.

Bake in the preheated Air Fryer for 20 to 22 minutes. Transfer to a wire rack to cool before slicing and serving. Bon appétit!

Per serving: 291 Calories; 7.9g Fat; 48.2g Carbs; 6.4g Protein; 32.3g Sugars

825. Coconut Chip Cookies

(Ready in about 20 minutes | Servings 12)

Ingredients

1 cup butter, melted
1 ¾ cups granulated sugar
3 eggs
2 tablespoons coconut milk
1 teaspoon coconut extract
1 teaspoon vanilla extract
2 ¼ cups all-purpose flour
1/2 teaspoon baking powder
1/2 teaspoon baking soda
1/2 teaspoon fine table salt
2 cups coconut chips

Directions

Begin by preheating your Air Fryer to 350 degrees F.

In the bowl of an electric mixer, beat the butter and sugar until well combined. Now, add the eggs one at a time, and mix well; add the coconut milk, coconut extract, and vanilla; beat until creamy and uniform.

Mix the flour with baking powder, baking soda, and salt. Then, stir the flour mixture into the butter mixture and stir until everything is well incorporated.

Finally, fold in the coconut chips and mix again. Scoop out 1 tablespoon size balls of the batter on a cookie pan, leaving 2 inches between each cookie.

Bake for 10 minutes or until golden brown, rotating the pan once or twice through the cooking time.

Let your cookies cool on wire racks. Bon appétit!

Per serving: 304 Calories; 16.7g Fat; 34.2g Carbs; 4.3g Protein; 15.6g Sugars

826. Easy Chocolate and Coconut Cake

(Ready in about 20 minutes | Servings 10)

Ingredients

1 stick butter
1 ¼ cups dark chocolate, broken into chunks
1/4 cup tablespoon agave syrup

1/4 cup sugar
2 tablespoons milk
2 eggs, beaten
1/3 cup coconut, shredded

Directions

Begin by preheating your Air Fryer to 330 degrees F.

In a microwave-safe bowl, melt the butter, chocolate, and agave syrup. Allow it to cool to room temperature.

Add the remaining ingredients to the chocolate mixture; stir to combine well. Scrape the batter into a lightly greased baking pan.

Bake in the preheated Air Fryer for 15 minutes or until a toothpick comes out dry and clean. Enjoy!

Per serving: 252 Calories; 18.9g Fat; 17.9g Carbs; 3.4g Protein; 13.8g Sugars

827. Grilled Banana Boats

(Ready in about 15 minutes | Servings 3)

Ingredients

3 large bananas
1 tablespoon ginger snaps
2 tablespoons mini chocolate chips

3 tablespoons mini marshmallows
3 tablespoons crushed vanilla wafers

Directions

In the peel, slice your banana lengthwise; make sure not to slice all the way through the banana. Divide the remaining ingredients between the banana pockets.

Place in the Air Fryer grill pan. Cook at 395 degrees F for 7 minutes.

Let the banana boats cool for 5 to 6 minutes, and then eat with a spoon. Bon appétit!

Per serving: 269 Calories; 5.9g Fat; 47.9g Carbs; 2.6g Protein; 28.3g Sugars

828. Chocolate Birthday Cake

(Ready in about 35 minutes + chilling time | Servings 6)

Ingredients

2 eggs, beaten
2/3 cup sour cream
1 cup flour
1/2 cup sugar
1/4 cup honey
1/3 cup coconut oil, softened
1/4 cup cocoa powder
2 tablespoons chocolate chips

1 ½ teaspoons baking powder
1 teaspoon vanilla extract
1/2 teaspoon pure rum extract
Chocolate Frosting:
1/2 cup butter, softened
1/4 cup cocoa powder
2 cups powdered sugar
2 tablespoons milk

Directions

Mix all ingredients for the chocolate cake with a hand mixer on low speed. Scrape the batter into a cake pan.

Bake at 330 degrees F for 25 to 30 minutes. Transfer the cake to a wire rack

Meanwhile, whip the butter and cocoa until smooth. Stir in the powdered sugar. Slowly and gradually, pour in the milk until your frosting reaches desired consistency.

Whip until smooth and fluffy; then, frost the cooled cake. Place in your refrigerator for a couple of hours. Serve well chilled.

Per serving: 689 Calories; 43.4g Fat; 76.1g Carbs; 6.5g Protein; 55.6g Sugars

829. Favorite New York Cheesecake

(Ready in about 40 minutes + chilling time | Servings 8)

Ingredients

1 ½ cups digestive biscuits crumbs
2 ounces white sugar
1 ounce demerara sugar
1/2 stick butter, melted
32 ounces full-fat cream cheese

1/2 cup heavy cream
1 ¼ cups caster sugar
3 eggs, at room temperature
1 tablespoon vanilla essence
1 teaspoon grated lemon zest

Directions

Coat the sides and bottom of a baking pan with a little flour.

In a mixing bowl, combine the digestive biscuits, white sugar, and demerara sugar. Add the melted butter and mix until your mixture looks like breadcrumbs.

Press the mixture into the bottom of the prepared pan to form an even layer. Bake at 330 degrees F for 7 minutes until golden brown. Allow it to cool completely on a wire rack.

Meanwhile, in a mixer fitted with the paddle attachment, prepare the filling by mixing the soft cheese, heavy cream, and caster sugar; beat until creamy and fluffy.

Crack the eggs into the mixing bowl, one at a time; add the vanilla and lemon zest and continue to mix until fully combined.

Pour the prepared topping over the cooled crust and spread evenly.

Bake in the preheated Air Fryer at 330 degrees F for 25 to 30 minutes; leave it in the Air Fryer to keep warm for another 30 minutes.

Cover your cheesecake with plastic wrap. Place in your refrigerator and allow it to cool at least 6 hours or overnight. Serve well chilled.

Per serving: 477 Calories; 30.2g Fat; 39.5g Carbs; 12.8g Protein; 32.9g Sugars

830. English-Style Scones with Raisins

(Ready in about 20 minutes | Servings 6)

Ingredients

1 ½ cups all-purpose flour
1/4 cup brown sugar
1 teaspoon baking powder
1/4 teaspoon sea salt
1/4 teaspoon ground cloves
1/2 teaspoon ground cardamom
1 teaspoon ground cinnamon

1/2 cup raisins
6 tablespoons butter, cooled and sliced
1/2 cup double cream
2 eggs, lightly whisked
1/2 teaspoon vanilla essence

Directions

In a mixing bowl, thoroughly combine the flour, sugar, baking powder, salt, cloves, cardamom cinnamon, and raisins. Mix until everything is combined well.

Add the butter and mix again.

In another mixing bowl, combine the double cream with the eggs and vanilla; beat until creamy and smooth.

Stir the wet ingredients into the dry mixture. Roll your dough out into a circle and cut into wedges.

Bake in the preheated Air Fryer at 360 degrees for 11 minutes, rotating the pan halfway through the cooking time. Bon appétit!

Per serving: 317 Calories; 18.9g Fat; 29.5g Carbs; 6.9g Protein; 5.2g Sugars

831. Baked Peaches with Oatmeal Pecan Streusel

(Ready in about 20 minutes | Servings 3)

Ingredients

2 tablespoons old-fashioned rolled oats
3 tablespoons golden caster sugar
1/2 teaspoon ground cinnamon
1 egg

2 tablespoons cold salted butter, cut into pieces
3 tablespoons pecans, chopped
3 large ripe freestone peaches, halved and pitted

Directions

Mix the rolled oats, sugar, cinnamon, egg, and butter until well combined.

Add a big spoonful of prepared topping to the center of each peach. Pour 1/2 cup of water into an Air Fryer safe dish. Place the peaches in the dish.

Top the peaches with the roughly chopped pecans. Bake at 340 degrees F for 17 minutes. Serve at room temperature. Bon appétit!

Per serving: 247 Calories; 14.1g Fat; 28.8g Carbs; 5.9g Protein; 23.1g Sugars

832. Red Velvet Pancakes

(Ready in about 35 minutes | Servings 3)

Ingredients

1/2 cup flour
1 teaspoon baking powder
1/4 teaspoon salt
2 tablespoons white sugar
1/2 teaspoon cinnamon
1 teaspoon red paste food color
1 egg

1/2 cup milk
1 teaspoon vanilla
Topping:
2 ounces cream cheese, softened
2 tablespoons butter, softened
3/4 cup powdered sugar

Directions

Mix the flour, baking powder, salt, sugar, cinnamon, red paste food color in a large bowl.

Gradually add the egg and milk, whisking continuously, until well combined. Let it stand for 20 minutes.

Spritz the Air Fryer baking pan with cooking spray. Pour the batter into the pan using a measuring cup.

Cook at 230 degrees F for 4 to 5 minutes or until golden brown. Repeat with the remaining batter.

Meanwhile, make your topping by mixing the ingredients until creamy and fluffy. Decorate your pancakes with topping. Bon appétit!

Per serving: 392 Calories; 17.8g Fat; 50g Carbs; 7.8g Protein; 33.2g Sugars

833. Spanish-Style Doughnut Tejeringos

(Ready in about 20 minutes | Servings 4)

Ingredients

3/4 cup water
1 tablespoon sugar
1/4 teaspoon sea salt
1/4 teaspoon grated nutmeg

1/4 teaspoon ground cloves
6 tablespoons butter
3/4 cup all-purpose flour
2 eggs

Directions

To make the dough, boil the water in a pan over medium-high heat; now, add the sugar, salt, nutmeg, and cloves; cook until dissolved.

Add the butter and turn the heat to low. Gradually stir in the flour, whisking continuously, until the mixture forms a ball.

Remove from the heat; fold in the eggs one at a time, stirring to combine well.

Pour the mixture into a piping bag with a large star tip. Squeeze 4-inch strips of dough into the greased Air Fryer pan.

Cook at 410 degrees F for 6 minutes, working in batches. Bon appétit!

Per serving: 311 Calories; 22.3g Fat; 20.5g Carbs; 7.1g Protein; 2.4g Sugars

834. Baked Fruit Compote with Coconut Chip

(Ready in about 25 minutes | Servings 6)

Ingredients

1 tablespoon butter
8 ounces canned apricot halves, drained
8 ounces canned pear halves, drained
16 ounces pineapple slices, undrained

1/3 cup packed brown sugar
1/4 teaspoon grated nutmeg
1/4 teaspoon ground cloves
1/2 teaspoon ground cinnamon
1 teaspoon pure vanilla extract
1/2 cup coconut chips

Directions

Start by preheating your Air Fryer to 330 degrees F. Grease a baking pan with butter.

Place all ingredients, except for the coconut chips, in a baking pan. Bake in the preheated Air Fryer for 20 minutes.

Serve in individual bowls, garnished with coconut chips. Bon appétit!

Per serving: 215 Calories; 7.5g Fat; 38.2g Carbs; 1.2g Protein; 29.6g Sugars

835. Summer Peach Crisp

(Ready in about 40 minutes | Servings 4)

Per serving: 330 Calories; 16.6g Fat; 48.2g Carbs; 4.2g Protein; 30.8g Sugars

Ingredients

2 cups fresh peaches, pitted and sliced
1/4 cup cornmeal
1/4 cup brown sugar
1 teaspoon pure vanilla extract

1/2 teaspoon ground cinnamon
A pinch of fine sea salt
1 stick cold butter
1/2 cup rolled oats

Directions

Toss the sliced peaches with the cornmeal, brown sugar, vanilla extract, cinnamon, and sea salt. Place in a baking pan coated with cooking spray.

In a mixing dish, thoroughly combine the cold butter and rolled oats. Sprinkle the mixture over each peach.

Bake in the preheated Air Fryer at 330 degrees F for 35 minutes. Bon appétit!

836. Greek-Style Griddle Cakes

(Ready in about 15 minutes | Servings 4)

Ingredients

3/4 cup self-raising flour
1/4 teaspoon fine sea salt
2 tablespoons sugar
1/2 cup milk
2 eggs, lightly beaten

1 tablespoon butter
Topping:
1 cup Greek-style yogurt
1 banana, mashed
2 tablespoons honey

Directions

Mix the flour, salt, and sugar in a bowl. Then, stir in the milk, eggs, and butter. Mix until smooth and uniform.

Drop tablespoons of the batter into the Air Fryer pan.

Cook at 300 degrees F for 4 to 5 minutes or until bubbles form on top of the griddle cakes. Repeat with the remaining batter.

Meanwhile, mix all ingredients for the topping. Place in your refrigerator until ready to serve. Serve the griddle cakes with the chilled topping. Enjoy!

Per serving: 276 Calories; 8.5g Fat; 40.2g Carbs; 10.4g Protein; 19.4g Sugars

837. Nana's Famous Apple Fritters

(Ready in about 20 minutes | Servings 4)

Ingredients

2/3 cup all-purpose flour
3 tablespoons granulated sugar
A pinch of sea salt
A pinch of freshly grated nutmeg
1 teaspoon baking powder

2 eggs, whisked
1/4 cup milk
2 apples, peeled, cored and diced
1/2 cup powdered sugar

Directions

Mix the flour, sugar, salt, nutmeg and baking powder.

In a separate bowl whisk the eggs with the milk; add this wet mixture into the dry ingredients; mix to combine well.

Add the apple pieces and mix again.

Cook in the preheated Air Fryer at 370 degrees for 3 minutes, flipping them halfway through the cooking time. Repeat with the remaining batter.

Dust with powdered sugar and serve at room temperature. Bon appétit!

Per serving: 280 Calories; 5.7g Fat; 51.1g Carbs; 7.4g Protein; 30.8g Sugars

838. Authentic Indian Gulgulas

(Ready in about 20 minutes | Servings 3)

Ingredients

1 banana, mashed
1/4 cup sugar
1 egg
1/2 teaspoon vanilla essence
1/4 teaspoon ground cardamom
1/4 teaspoon cinnamon
1/2 milk
3/4 cup all-purpose flour
1 teaspoon baking powder

Directions

In a mixing bowl, whisk the mashed banana with the sugar and egg; add the vanilla, cardamom, and cinnamon and mix to combine well.

Gradually pour in the milk and mix again. Stir in the flour and baking powder. Mix until everything is well incorporated.

Drop a spoonful of batter onto the greased Air Fryer pan. Cook in the preheated Air Fryer at 360 degrees F for 5 minutes, flipping them halfway through the cooking time.

Repeat with the remaining batter and serve warm. Enjoy!

Per serving: 252 Calories; 4.9g Fat; 43.8g Carbs; 7.9g Protein; 15.4g Sugars

839. Coconut Pancake Cups

(Ready in about 30 minutes | Servings 4)

Ingredients

1/2 cup flour
1/3 cup coconut milk
2 eggs
1 tablespoon coconut oil, melted
1 teaspoon vanilla
A pinch of ground cardamom
1/2 cup coconut chips

Directions

Mix the flour, coconut milk, eggs, coconut oil, vanilla, and cardamom in a large bowl.

Let it stand for 20 minutes. Spoon the batter into a greased muffin tin.

Cook at 230 degrees F for 4 to 5 minutes or until golden brown. Repeat with the remaining batter.

Decorate your pancakes with coconut chips. Bon appétit!

Per serving: 274 Calories; 17.3g Fat; 21.6g Carbs; 7.7g Protein; 1.5g Sugars

840. Salted Caramel Cheesecake

(Ready in about 1 hour + chilling time | Servings 10)

Ingredients

1 cup granulated sugar
1/3 cup water
3/4 cup heavy cream
2 tablespoons butter
1 teaspoon vanilla extract
1/2 teaspoon coarse sea salt
Crust:
1 ½ cups graham cracker crumbs
1/3 cup salted butter, melted
2 tablespoons brown sugar
Topping:
20 ounces cream cheese, softened
1 cup sour cream
1 cup granulated sugar
1 teaspoon vanilla essence
1/4 teaspoon ground star anise
3 eggs

Directions

To make the caramel sauce, cook the sugar in a saucepan over medium heat; shake it to form a flat layer.

Add the water and cook until the sugar dissolves. Raise the heat to medium-high, and continue to cook your caramel for a further 10 minutes until it turns amber colored.

Turn the heat off; immediately stir in the heavy cream, butter, vanilla extract, and salt. Stir to combine well.

Let the salted caramel sauce cool to room temperature.

Beat all ingredients for the crust in a mixing bowl. Press the mixture into the bottom of a lightly greased baking pan.

Bake at 350 degrees F for 18 minutes. Place it in your freezer for 20 minutes.

Then, make the cheesecake topping by mixing the remaining ingredients. Pour the prepared topping over the cooled crust and spread evenly.

Bake in the preheated Air Fryer at 330 degrees F for 25 to 30 minutes; leave it in the Air Fryer to keep warm for another 30 minutes.

Refrigerate your cheesecake until completely cool and firm or overnight. Prior to serving, pour the salted caramel sauce over the cheesecake. Bon appétit!

Per serving: 501 Calories; 36.3g Fat; 35.6g Carbs; 9.1g Protein; 24.2g Sugars

841. Banana Crepes with Apple Topping

(Ready in about 40 minutes | Servings 2)

Ingredients

Banana Crepes:
1 large banana, mashed
2 eggs, beaten
1/4 teaspoon baking powder
1 shot dark rum
1/2 teaspoon vanilla extract
1 teaspoon butter, melted
2 tablespoons brown sugar
Topping:
2 apples, peeled, cored, and chopped
2 tablespoons sugar
1/2 teaspoon cinnamon
3 tablespoons water

Directions

Mix all ingredients for the banana crepes until creamy and fluffy. Let it stand for 15 to 20 minutes.

Spritz the Air Fryer baking pan with cooking spray. Pour the batter into the pan using a measuring cup.

Cook at 230 degrees F for 4 to 5 minutes or until golden brown. Repeat with the remaining batter.

To make the pancake topping, place all ingredients in a heavy-bottomed skillet over medium heat. Cook for 10 minutes, stirring occasionally. Spoon on top of the banana crepes and enjoy!

Per serving: 367 Calories; 12.1g Fat; 57.7g Carbs; 10.2g Protein; 43.6g Sugars

842. Apricot and Walnut Crumble

(Ready in about 40 minutes | Servings 8)

Ingredients

2 pounds apricots, pitted and sliced
1 cup brown sugar
2 tablespoons cornstarch
Topping:
1 ½ cups old-fashioned rolled oats
1/2 cup brown sugar
2 tablespoons agave nectar
1 teaspoon crystallized ginger
1/2 teaspoon ground cardamom
A pinch of salt
1 stick butter, cut into pieces
1/2 cup walnuts, chopped
1/2 cup dried cranberries

Directions

Toss the sliced apricots with the brown sugar and cornstarch. Place in a baking pan lightly greased with nonstick cooking spray.

In a mixing dish, thoroughly combine all the topping ingredients. Sprinkle the topping ingredients over the apricot layer.

Bake in the preheated Air Fryer at 330 degrees F for 35 minutes. Bon appétit!

Per serving: 404 Calories; 16.4g Fat; 69.2g Carbs; 5.6g Protein; 52.1g Sugars

843. Butter Rum Cookies with Walnuts

(Ready in about 35 minutes | Servings 6)

Ingredients

1 cup all-purpose flour
1/2 teaspoon baking powder
1/4 teaspoon fine sea salt
1 stick butter, unsalted and softened

1/2 cup sugar
1 egg
1/2 teaspoon vanilla
1 teaspoon butter rum flavoring
3 ounces walnuts, finely chopped

Directions

Begin by preheating the Air Fryer to 360 degrees F.

In a mixing dish, thoroughly combine the flour with baking powder and salt.

Beat the butter and sugar with a hand mixer until pale and fluffy; add the whisked egg, vanilla, and butter rum flavoring; mix again to combine well. Now, stir in the dry ingredients.

Fold in the chopped walnuts and mix to combine. Divide the mixture into small balls; flatten each ball with a fork and transfer them to a foil-lined baking pan.

Bake in the preheated Air Fryer for 14 minutes. Work in a few batches and transfer to wire racks to cool completely. Bon appétit!

Per serving: 364 Calories; 26.9g Fat; 26.3g Carbs; 5.9g Protein; 8.7g Sugars

844. Classic Butter Cake

(Ready in about 35 minutes | Servings 8)

Ingredients

1 stick butter, at room temperature
1 cup sugar
2 eggs
1 cup all-purpose flour
1 teaspoon baking powder
1/2 teaspoon baking soda

1/4 teaspoon salt
A pinch of freshly grated nutmeg
A pinch of ground star anise
1/4 cup buttermilk
1 teaspoon vanilla essence

Directions

Begin by preheating your Air Fryer to 320 degrees F. Spritz the bottom and sides of a baking pan with cooking spray.

Beat the butter and sugar with a hand mixer until creamy. Then, fold in the eggs, one at a time, and mix well until fluffy.

Stir in the flour along with the remaining ingredients. Mix to combine well. Scrape the batter into the prepared baking pan.

Bake for 15 minutes; rotate the pan and bake an additional 15 minutes, until the top of the cake springs back when gently pressed with your fingers. Bon appétit!

Per serving: 244 Calories; 14.2g Fat; 25.1g Carbs; 4.2g Protein; 12.8g Sugars

845. Pecan Fudge Brownies

(Ready in about 30 minutes | Servings 6)

Ingredients

1/2 cup butter, melted
1/2 cup sugar
1 teaspoon vanilla essence
1 egg
1/2 cup flour
1/2 teaspoon baking powder

1/4 cup cocoa powder
1/2 teaspoon ground cinnamon
1/4 teaspoon fine sea salt
1 ounce semisweet chocolate, coarsely chopped
1/4 cup pecans, finely chopped

Directions

Start by preheating your Air Fryer to 350 degrees F. Now, lightly grease six silicone molds.

In a mixing dish, beat the melted butter with the sugar until fluffy. Next, stir in the vanilla and egg and beat again.

After that, add the flour, baking powder, cocoa powder, cinnamon, and salt. Mix until everything is well combined.

Fold in the chocolate and pecans; mix to combine. Bake in the preheated Air Fryer for 20 to 22 minutes. Enjoy!

Per serving: 341 Calories; 23.5g Fat; 31.3g Carbs; 4.2g Protein; 19.2g Sugars

846. Fried Honey Banana

(Ready in about 20 minutes | Servings 2)

Ingredients

2 ripe bananas, peeled and sliced
2 tablespoons honey
3 tablespoons rice flour
3 tablespoons desiccated coconut

A pinch of fine sea salt
1/2 teaspoon baking powder
1/4 teaspoon cardamom powder

Directions

Preheat the Air Fryer to 390 degrees F.

Drizzle honey over the banana slices.

In a mixing dish, thoroughly combine the rice flour, coconut, salt, baking powder, and cardamom powder. Roll each slice of banana over the flour mixture.

Bake in the preheated Air Fryer approximately 13 minutes, flipping them halfway through the cooking time. Bon appétit!

Per serving: 363 Calories; 14.3g Fat; 61.1g Carbs; 3.7g Protein; 33.3g Sugars

847. Pop Tarts with Homemade Strawberry Jam

(Ready in about 45 minutes | Servings 8)

Ingredients

1 cup strawberries, sliced
1 tablespoon fresh lemon juice
1 teaspoon maple syrup
2 tablespoons chia seeds

1 (14-ounce) box refrigerated pie crust
1 egg, whisked with 1 tablespoon of water (egg wash)
1/2 cup powdered sugar

Directions

In a saucepan, heat the strawberries until they start to get syrupy. Mash them and add the lemon juice and maple syrup.

Remove from the heat and stir in the chia seeds. Let it stand for 30 minutes or until it thickens up.

Unroll the pie crusts and cut them into small rectangles. Spoon the strawberry jam in the center of a rectangle; top with another piece of crust.

Repeat until you run out of ingredients. Line the Air Fryer basket with parchment paper.

Brush the pop tarts with the egg wash and bake at 400 degrees F for 6 minutes or until slightly brown. Work in batches and transfer to cooling racks.

Dust with powdered sugar and enjoy!

Per serving: 173 Calories; 8.9g Fat; 20.1g Carbs; 3.6g Protein; 7.7g Sugars

848. Fall Harvest Apple Cinnamon Buns

(Ready in about 1 hour 20 minutes | Servings 6)

Ingredients

1/2 cup milk
1/2 cup granulated sugar
1 tablespoon yeast
1/2 stick butter, at room temperature
1 egg, at room temperature
1/4 teaspoon salt
2 ¼ cups all-purpose flour
Filling:

3 tablespoons butter, at room temperature
1/4 cup brown sugar
1/2 teaspoon ground cardamom
1/2 teaspoon ground cloves
1 teaspoon ground cinnamon
1 apple, peeled, cored, and chopped
1/2 cup powdered sugar

Directions

Heat the milk in a microwave safe bowl and transfer the warm milk to the bowl of a stand electric mixer. Add the granulated sugar and yeast, and mix to combine well. Cover and let sit until the yeast is foamy.

Then, beat the butter on low speed. Fold in the the egg and mix again. Add the salt and flour. Mix on medium speed until a soft dough forms.

Knead the dough on a lightly floured surface. Cover it loosely and let sit in a warm place about 1 hour or until doubled in size. Then, spritz the bottom and sides of a baking pan with cooking oil (butter flavored).

Roll your dough out into a rectangle.

Spread 3 tablespoons of butter all over the dough. In a mixing dish, combine the brown sugar, cardamom, cloves, and cinnamon; sprinkle evenly over the dough.

Top with the chopped apples. Then, roll up your dough to form a log. Cut into 6 equal rolls and place them in the parchment-lined Air Fryer basket.

Bake at 350 degrees for 12 minutes, turning them halfway through the cooking time. Dust with powdered sugar. Bon appétit!

Per serving: 430 Calories; 16.3g Fat; 63.1g Carbs; 8g Protein; 25g Sugars

849. Pear Fritters with Cinnamon and Ginger

(Ready in about 20 minutes | Servings 4)

Ingredients

2 pears, peeled, cored and sliced
1 tablespoon coconut oil, melted
1 ½ cups all-purpose flour
1 teaspoon baking powder
A pinch of fine sea salt

A pinch of freshly grated nutmeg
1/2 teaspoon ginger
1 teaspoon cinnamon
2 eggs
4 tablespoons milk

Directions

Mix all ingredients, except for the pears, in a shallow bowl. Dip each slice of the pears in the batter until well coated.

Cook in the preheated Air Fryer at 360 degrees for 4 minutes, flipping them halfway through the cooking time. Repeat with the remaining ingredients.

Dust with powdered sugar if desired. Bon appétit!

Per serving: 333 Calories; 9.5g Fat; 52.2g Carbs; 10.5g Protein; 10.9g Sugars

850. Old-Fashioned Plum Dumplings

(Ready in about 40 minutes | Servings 4)

Ingredients

1 (14-ounce) box pie crusts
2 cups plums, pitted
2 tablespoons granulated sugar
2 tablespoons coconut oil

1/4 teaspoon ground cardamom
1/2 teaspoon ground cinnamon
1 egg white, slightly beaten

Directions

Place the pie crust on a work surface. Roll into a circle and cut into quarters.

Place 1 plum on each crust piece. Add the sugar, coconut oil, cardamom, and cinnamon. Roll up the sides into a circular shape around the plums.

Repeat with the remaining ingredients. Brush the edges with the egg white. Place in the lightly greased Air Fryer basket.

Bake in the preheated Air Fryer at 360 degrees F for 20 minutes, flipping them halfway through the cooking time. Work in two batches, decorate and serve at room temperature. Bon appétit!

Per serving: 395 Calories; 19.2g Fat; 54.5g Carbs; 4.1g Protein; 32.7g Sugars

851. Almond Chocolate Cupcakes

(Ready in about 20 minutes | Servings 6)

Ingredients

3/4 cup self-raising flour
1 cup powdered sugar
1/4 teaspoon salt
1/4 teaspoon nutmeg, preferably freshly grated
1 tablespoon cocoa powder

2 ounces butter, softened
1 egg, whisked
2 tablespoons almond milk
1/2 teaspoon vanilla extract
1 ½ ounces dark chocolate chunks
1/2 cup almonds, chopped

Directions

In a mixing bowl, combine the flour, sugar, salt, nutmeg, and cocoa powder. Mix to combine well.

In another mixing bowl, whisk the butter, egg, almond milk, and vanilla.

Now, add the wet egg mixture to the dry ingredients. Then, carefully fold in the chocolate chunks and almonds; gently stir to combine.

Scrape the batter mixture into muffin cups. Bake your cupcakes at 350 degrees F for 12 minutes until a toothpick comes out clean.

Decorate with chocolate sprinkles if desired. Serve and enjoy!

Per serving: 288 Calories; 14.7g Fat; 35.1g Carbs; 5.1g Protein; 20g Sugars

852. White Chocolate Rum Molten Cake

(Ready in about 20 minutes | Servings 4)

Ingredients

2 ½ ounces butter, at room temperature
3 ounces white chocolate
2 eggs, beaten

1/2 cup powdered sugar
1/3 cup self-rising flour
1 teaspoon rum extract
1 teaspoon vanilla extract

Directions

Begin by preheating your Air Fryer to 370 degrees F. Spritz the sides and bottom of four ramekins with cooking spray.

Melt the butter and white chocolate in a microwave-safe bowl. Mix the eggs and sugar until frothy.

Pour the butter/chocolate mixture into the egg mixture. Stir in the flour, rum extract, and vanilla extract. Mix until everything is well incorporated.

Scrape the batter into the prepared ramekins. Bake in the preheated Air Fryer for 9 to 11 minutes.

Let stand for 2 to 3 minutes. Invert on a plate while warm and serve. Bon appétit!

Per serving: 336 Calories; 19.5g Fat; 34.5g Carbs; 6.1g Protein; 23.1g Sugars

853. Summer Fruit Pie with Cinnamon Streusel

(Ready in about 40 minutes | Servings 4)

Ingredients

1 (14-ounce) box pie crusts
Filling:
1/3 cup caster sugar
1/3 cup all-purpose flour
1/4 teaspoon ground cardamom
1/2 teaspoon ground cinnamon
1 teaspoon pure vanilla extract
2 cups apricots, pitted and sliced peeled

2 cups peaches, pitted and sliced peeled
Streusel:
1 cup all-purpose flour
1/2 cup brown sugar
1 teaspoon ground cinnamon
1/3 cup cold salted butter

Directions

Place the pie crust in a lightly greased pie plate.

In a mixing bowl, thoroughly combine the caster sugar, 1/3 cup of flour, cardamom, cinnamon, and vanilla extract. Add the apricots and peaches and mix until coated. Spoon into the prepared pie crust.

Make the streusel by mixing 1 cup of flour, brown sugar, and cinnamon. Cut in the cold butter and continue to mix until the mixture looks like coarse crumbs. Sprinkle over the filling.

Bake at 350 degrees F for 35 minutes or until topping is golden brown. Bon appétit!

Per serving: 582 Calories; 23.1g Fat; 86.5g Carbs; 8.5g Protein; 31.6g Sugars

854. Mom's Orange Rolls

(Ready in about 1 hour 20 minutes | Servings 6)

Ingredients

1/2 cup milk
1/4 cup granulated sugar
1 tablespoon yeast
1/2 stick butter, at room temperature
1 egg, at room temperature
1/4 teaspoon salt
2 cups all-purpose flour

2 tablespoons fresh orange juice
Filling:
2 tablespoons butter
4 tablespoons white sugar
1 teaspoon ground star anise
1/4 teaspoon ground cinnamon
1 teaspoon vanilla paste
1/2 cup confectioners' sugar

Directions

Heat the milk in a microwave safe bowl and transfer the warm milk to the bowl of a stand electric mixer. Add the granulated sugar and yeast, and mix to combine well. Cover and let it sit until the yeast is foamy.

Then, beat the butter on low speed. Fold in the egg and mix again. Add salt and flour. Add the orange juice and mix on medium speed until a soft dough forms.

Knead the dough on a lightly floured surface. Cover it loosely and let it sit in a warm place about 1 hour or until doubled in size. Then, spritz the bottom and sides of a baking pan with cooking oil (butter flavored).

Roll your dough out into a rectangle.

Spread 2 tablespoons of butter all over the dough. In a mixing dish, combine the white sugar, ground star anise, cinnamon, and vanilla; sprinkle evenly over the dough.

Then, roll up your dough to form a log. Cut into 6 equal rolls and place them in the parchment-lined Air Fryer basket.

Bake at 350 degrees for 12 minutes, turning them halfway through the cooking time. Dust with confectioners' sugar and enjoy!

Per serving: 365 Calories; 14.1g Fat; 51.9g Carbs; 7.3g Protein; 19.1g Sugars

855. Coconut Cheesecake Bites

(Ready in about 25 minutes + chilling time | Servings 8)

Ingredients

1 ½ cups Oreo cookies, crushed
4 ounces granulated sugar
4 tablespoons butter, softened
12 ounces cream cheese
4 ounces double cream

2 eggs, lightly whisked
1 teaspoon pure vanilla extract
1 teaspoon pure coconut extract
1 cup toasted coconut

Directions

Start by preheating your Air Fryer to 350 degrees F.

Mix the crushed Oreos with sugar and butter; press the crust into silicone cupcake molds. Bake for 5 minutes and allow them to cool on wire racks.

Using an electric mixer, whip the cream cheese and double cream until fluffy; add one egg at a time and continue to beat until creamy. Finally, add the vanilla and coconut extract.

Pour the topping mixture on top of the crust. Bake at 320 degrees F for 13 to 15 minutes.

Afterwards, top with the toasted coconut. Allow the mini cheesecakes to chill in your refrigerator before serving. Bon appétit!

Per serving: 415 Calories; 32.3g Fat; 26.4g Carbs; 6.8g Protein; 17.1g Sugars

OTHER AIR FRYER FAVORITES

856. Traditional Greek Revithokeftedes

(Ready in about 20 minutes | Servings 4)

Ingredients

2 cups chickpeas, soaked overnight
1 teaspoon fresh garlic, minced
1 red onion, chopped

2 boiled potatoes, peeled and mashed
2 tablespoons all-purpose flour
1 teaspoon Greek spice mix
1 teaspoon olive oil

Directions

In a mixing bowl, thoroughly combine all ingredients until everything is well incorporated. Shape the mixture into equal patties.

Then, transfer the patties to the Air Fryer cooking basket.

Cook the patties at 380 degrees F for about 15 minutes, turning them over halfway through the cooking time.

Serve your revithokeftedes in pita bread with toppings of your choice. Enjoy!

Per serving: 474 Calories; 7.3g Fat; 82g Carbs; 22.4g Protein; 12.5g Sugars

857. Greek Fried Cheese Balls (Tirokroketes)

(Ready in about 40 minutes | Servings 3)

Ingredients

4 ounces smoked gouda cheese, shredded
2 ounces feta cheese, crumbled
1 tablespoon all-purpose flour

1 egg, whisked
1 tablespoon full-fat milk
1/2 cup bread crumbs

Directions

In a bowl, mix all ingredients, except for the bread crumbs; cover the bowl with plastic wrap and transfer it to your refrigerator for 30 minutes.

Use about a spoonful of the mixture and roll it into a ball. Roll your balls into breadcrumbs and transfer them to a lightly greased cooking basket.

Cook cheese balls at 390 degrees F for about 7 minutes, shaking the basket halfway through the cooking time. Eat warm.

Per serving: 274 Calories; 17.3g Fat; 7.2g Carbs; 16.1g Protein; 2.4g Sugars

858. Spanish Bolitas de Queso

(Ready in about 15 minutes | Servings 3)

Ingredients

1/2 cup plain flour
2 tablespoons cornstarch
2 eggs
1 garlic clove minced

1/2 teaspoon red pepper flakes, crushed
1/2 teaspoon pimentón
6 ounces goat cheese, shredded
1 cup tortilla chips, crushed

Directions

In a mixing bowl, thoroughly combine all ingredients, except for the crushed tortilla chips.

Shape the mixture into bite-sized balls. Roll your balls into the crushed tortilla chips and transfer them to a lightly greased cooking basket.

Cook the balls at 390 degrees F for about 8 minutes, shaking the basket halfway through the cooking time to promote even cooking. Enjoy!

Per serving: 444 Calories; 24.1g Fat; 30.2g Carbs; 24.6g Protein; 1.9g Sugars

859. Chocolate Apple Chips

(Ready in about 40 minutes | Servings 2)

Ingredients

1 Honeycrisp apple, cored and sliced
1/4 teaspoon ground cloves
1/4 teaspoon crystalized ginger

1/4 teaspoon ground cinnamon
1 teaspoon avocado oil
2 tablespoons almond butter
2 ounces chocolate chips

Directions

Toss the apple slices with the spices and avocado oil all; transfer the apple slices to the Air Fryer.

Bake the apple slices at 350 degrees F for 5 minutes; shake the basket and continue cooking an additional 5 minutes.

In the meantime, microwave the almond butter and chocolate chips to make the chocolate glaze. Drizzle the warm apple slices with the chocolate glaze and let it cool for 30 minutes before serving.

Per serving: 249 Calories; 14.1g Fat; 31.3g Carbs; 0.9g Protein; 23.5g Sugars

860. Malaysian Sweet Potato Balls

(Ready in about 30 minutes | Servings 3)

Ingredients

1/2 pound sweet potatoes
1/2 cup rice flour
1 tablespoon milk

2 tablespoons honey
1/2 teaspoon vanilla extract
1/2 cup icing sugar, for dusting

Directions

Steam the sweet potatoes until fork-tender and mash them in a bowl. Add in the rice flour, milk, honey and vanilla.

Then, shape the mixture into bite-sized balls.

Bake the sweet potato balls in the preheated Air Fryer at 360 degrees F for 15 minutes or until thoroughly cooked and crispy.

Dust the sweet potato balls with icing sugar. Bon appétit!

Per serving: 274 Calories; 0.5g Fat; 64.3g Carbs; 2.9g Protein; 31.3g Sugars

861. Pumpkin Griddle Cake

(Ready in about 20 minutes | Servings 3)

Ingredients

1/3 cup almond butter
2/3 cup pumpkin puree
1/2 cup all-purpose flour
1/2 teaspoon baking powder

2 eggs, beaten
1/2 teaspoon crystalized ginger
1 teaspoon pumpkin pie spice
4 tablespoons honey

Directions

Start by preheating your Air Fryer to 340 degrees F.

In a mixing bowl, thoroughly combine all ingredients.

Working in batches, drop batter, 1/2 cup at a time, into a lightly oiled baking dish.

Cook the griddle cake for about 8 minutes or until golden brown. Repeat with the other cake and serve with some extra honey, if desired. Bon appétit!

Per serving: 437 Calories; 22.1g Fat; 49.1g Carbs; 14.6g Protein; 27.1g Sugars

862. Easy Spicy Deviled Eggs

(Ready in about 20 minutes | Servings 3)

Ingredients

6 large eggs
1 teaspoon prepared white horseradish
1/4 cup mayonnaise

1/4 teaspoon hot sauce
Sea salt and ground black pepper, to taste

Directions

Place the wire rack in the Air Fryer basket and lower the eggs onto the rack.

Cook the eggs at 260 degrees F for 15 minutes.

Transfer the eggs to an ice-cold water bath to stop cooking. Peel the eggs under cold running water; slice them into halves, separating the whites and yolks.

Mash the egg yolks; add in the remaining ingredients and stir to combine; spoon the yolk mixture into the egg whites. Bon appétit!

Per serving: 237 Calories; 22.7g Fat; 1.5g Carbs; 5.6g Protein; 0.4g Sugars

863. Broccoli and Ham Croquettes

(Ready in about 12 minutes | Servings 3)

Ingredients

1/2 pound broccoli florets, grated
1 teaspoon olive oil
2 tablespoons shallot, chopped
2 ounces ham, chopped
1/2 teaspoon garlic, pressed
1/2 cup all-purpose flour
1 egg
Sea salt and ground black pepper, to taste

Directions

In a mixing bowl, thoroughly combine all ingredients.

Shape the mixture into small patties and transfer them to the lightly oiled Air Fryer cooking basket.

Cook your croquettes in the preheated Air Fryer at 365 degrees F for 6 minutes. Turn them over and cook for a further 6 minutes

Serve immediately and enjoy!

Per serving: 189 Calories; 5.8g Fat; 24.1g Carbs; 10.6g Protein; 2.8g Sugars

864. Coconut Chip Cookies

(Ready in about 40 minutes | Servings 3)

Ingredients

1/4 cup almond flour
1/2 cup plain flour
1/2 teaspoon baking powder
1/3 cup granulated sugar
1/8 teaspoon coarse sea slat
1 tablespoon butter, melted
1 egg, beaten
1/2 teaspoon vanilla extract
1/2 teaspoon coconut extract
1/4 cup coconut chips

Directions

Begin by preheating your Air Fryer to 350 degrees F.

In a mixing bowl, combine the flour, baking powder, sugar and salt. Add in the butter and egg and continue stirring into the flour mixture until moistened.

Stir in the vanilla and coconut extract. Lastly, fold in the coconut chips and mix again. Allow your batter to rest for about 30 minutes.

Scoop out 1 tablespoon size balls of the batter on a cookie pan, leaving 2 inches between each cookie.

Bake for 10 minutes or until golden brown, rotating the pan once or twice through the cooking time. Bon appétit!

Per serving: 202 Calories; 7.3g Fat; 28.1g Carbs; 5.3g Protein; 11.6g Sugars

865. Rustic Air Grilled Pears

(Ready in about 10 minutes | Servings 2)

Ingredients

2 pears, cored and halved
2 teaspoons coconut oil, melted
2 teaspoons honey
1/2 teaspoon pure vanilla extract
1/2 teaspoon ground cinnamon
1/4 teaspoon ground cardamom
1 tablespoon rum
2 ounces walnuts

Directions

Drizzle pear halves with the coconut oil and honey.

Sprinkle vanilla, cinnamon, cardamom and rum over your pears. Top them with chopped walnuts.

Air fry your pears at 360 degrees for 8 minutes, checking them halfway through the cooking time.

Drizzle with some extra honey, if desired. Bon appétit!

Per serving: 313 Calories; 23.1g Fat; 22.7g Carbs; 4.7g Protein; 17.5g Sugars

866. Apple Oatmeal Cups

(Ready in about 10 minutes | Servings 3)

Ingredients

1 cup rolled oats
1/4 teaspoon ground cardamom
1/4 teaspoon ground cinnamon
1/2 teaspoon baking powder
1/4 teaspoon sea salt
1/2 cup milk
2 tablespoons honey
1/2 teaspoon vanilla extract
1 apple, peeled, cored and diced
2 tablespoons peanut butter

Directions

In a mixing bowl, thoroughly combine the rolled oats, cardamom, cinnamon, baking powder, sea salt, milk, honey and vanilla.

Lastly, fold in the apple and spoon the mixture into an Air Fryer safe baking dish.

Bake in the preheated Air Fryer at 395 degrees F for about 9 minutes.

Spoon into individual bowls and serve with peanut butter. Bon appétit!

Per serving: 367 Calories; 9.1g Fat; 60.7g Carbs; 13.7g Protein; 21g Sugars

867. Mexican Chorizo and Egg Cups

(Ready in about 15 minutes | Servings 3)

Ingredients

1/2 pound Chorizo sausage
5 eggs, whisked
1 cup Mexican cheese blend, shredded
1/4 teaspoon Mexican oregano
Sea salt and ground black pepper, to taste
1/2 teaspoon paprika
1 tablespoon fresh cilantro leaves, roughly chopped

Directions

Start by preheating your Air Fryer to 360 degrees F. Cook the sausage in the preheated Air Fryer for about 5 minutes.

Spritz the sides and bottom of a muffin tin with a cooking oil. Chop the cooked sausage and divide the sausage between the muffin cups.

Thoroughly combine the eggs, Mexican cheese blend, Mexican oregano, salt, black pepper and paprika.

Pour the mixture over the sausages. Cook your muffins in the preheated Air Fryer at 360 degrees F for 6 to 7 minutes.

Top with fresh cilantro leaves and eat warm. Bon appétit!

Per serving: 507 Calories; 41g Fat; 3.4g Carbs; 29g Protein; 1.5g Sugars

868. Grilled Milano Ciabatta Sandwich

(Ready in about 15 minutes | Servings 1)

Ingredients

1 ciabatta roll
1 teaspoon butter
1 tablespoon kalamata olive tapenade
2 leaves romaine lettuce
1 slice provolone cheese
2 slices tomato

Directions

Cut the ciabatta roll horizontally in half. Spread the butter and tapenade over the bottom half of the roll; top with romaine lettuce.

Layer the provolone cheese and tomatoes on the lettuce leaves. Add the top of the ciabatta roll.

Air fry your sandwich at 380 degrees F for 10 minutes or until the cheese has melted, turning it over halfway through the cooking time. Bon appétit!

Per serving: 267 Calories; 13.8g Fat; 23.4g Carbs; 11.6g Protein; 3.6g Sugars

869. Easy Fluffy Flapjacks

(Ready in about 15 minutes | Servings 4)

Ingredients

1/2 cup all-purpose flour
1/2 cup quick-cooking oats
1/2 teaspoon baking powder
1/2 teaspoon baking soda
A pinch of granulated sugar
A pinch of sea salt
1/2 teaspoon lemon zest
1 egg, whisked
1/2 cup milk

Directions

In a mixing bowl, thoroughly combine the dry ingredients; in another bowl, mix the wet ingredients.

Then, stir the wet mixture into the dry mixture and stir again to combine well. Allow your batter to rest for 20 minutes in the refrigerator. Spoon the batter into a greased muffin tin.

Bake your flapjacks in the Air Fryer at 330 degrees F for 6 to 7 minutes or until golden brown. Repeat with the remaining batter. Bon appétit!

Per serving: 167 Calories; 3.8g Fat; 26.4g Carbs; 7.2g Protein; 1.6g Sugars

870. Tropical Sunrise Pudding

(Ready in about 30 minutes | Servings 3)

Ingredients

cup water
cup coconut milk
cup jasmine rice, rinsed and
drained
tablespoon coconut oil
tablespoons brown sugar

1 tablespoon agave nectar
1/4 teaspoon ground cardamom
1/4 teaspoon ground star anise
1/4 teaspoon ground cinnamon
1/4 cup pineapple chunks
2 teaspoons toasted coconut flakes

Directions

In a medium saucepan, bring the water and coconut milk to a boil. Add the rice, stir and reduce the heat. Cover and let it simmer for 20 minutes.

Grease the sides and bottoms of three ramekins with the coconut oil.

Add the prepared rice to the ramekins. Add in sugar, agave nectar, cardamom, star anise and cinnamon and gently stir to combine.

Air fry the rice pudding for 6 to 7 minutes, checking periodically to ensure even cooking. Spoon your pudding into individual bowls and garnish with the pineapple chunks and toasted coconut flakes. Enjoy!

Per serving: 507 Calories; 24.3g Fat; 64g Carbs; 6.2g Protein; 14.8g Sugars

871. Mini Banana Bread Loaves

(Ready in about 40 minutes | Servings 4)

Ingredients

cup all-purpose flour
1/2 teaspoon baking powder
A pinch of salt
teaspoon apple spice

2 bananas, peeled
3 tablespoons date syrup
4 tablespoons coconut oil
2 eggs, whisked

Directions

Start by preheating your Air Fryer to 320 degrees F. Then, grease bottoms of mini loaf pans with a nonstick cooking spray.

In a mixing bowl, combine the flour with baking powder, salt and apple spice.

In another bowl, mash your bananas with date syrup, coconut oil and eggs until everything is well incorporated. Fold the banana mixture into the flour mixture.

Spoon the mixture into prepared mini loaf pans and transfer them to the Air Fryer cooking basket.

Bake your loaves in the preheated Air Fryer for 35 minutes or until a tester comes out dry and clean.

Sprinkle some extra icing sugar over the top of banana bread, if desired. Devour!

Per serving: 367 Calories; 16.2g Fat; 50.4g Carbs; 6.6g Protein; 20.3g Sugars

872. Air-Fried Popcorn

(Ready in about 15 minutes | Servings 1)

Ingredients

tablespoons corn kernels
teaspoon butter, melted

Sea salt, to taste

Directions

Start by preheating your Air Fryer to 390 degrees F.

Now, line the bottom and sides of the cooking basket with aluminum foil. Add the kernels to the Air Fryer cooking basket.

Air fry your popcorn in the preheated Air Fryer for 15 minutes, shaking the basket every 5 minutes to ensure the kernels are not burning.

Toss your popcorn with melted butter and sea salt. Devour!

Per serving: 149 Calories; 5.2g Fat; 22.4g Carbs; 3.6g Protein; 1.6g Sugars

873. Quick and Easy Pita Bread Pizza

(Ready in about 10 minutes | Servings 1)

Ingredients

1 (6-inch) pita bread
1/2 teaspoon yellow mustard
2 tablespoons tomato sauce
1 scallion stalk, sliced
1 bell pepper, sliced

2 ounces mozzarella cheese (part-skim milk), shredded
Salt and ground black pepper, to taste

Directions

Start by preheating your Air Fryer to 360 degrees F.

Spread yellow mustard and tomato sauce on top of the pita bread. Top with the scallion and pepper; lastly, top with mozzarella cheese. Season with the salt and pepper to taste.

Bake your pizza in the preheated Air Fryer for 6 minutes. Bon appétit!

Per serving: 399 Calories; 10.2g Fat; 52.4g Carbs; 24.6g Protein; 7.3g Sugars

874. Classic Potato Latkes

(Ready in about 20 minutes | Servings 3)

Ingredients

1/2 cup all-purpose flour
2 tablespoons matzo meal
1 potato, scrubbed and grated
1 small-sized sweet onion, finely chopped

1 egg, beaten
Coarse sea salt and ground black pepper, to taste
1 teaspoon chicken schmaltz, melted

Directions

Thoroughly combine the flour, matzo meal, potato, onion and egg in a mixing bowl. Season with the salt and pepper to taste.

Drop the mixture in 2-tablespoon dollops into the cooking basket, flattening the tops with a wide spatula.

Drizzle each patty with the melted chicken schmaltz.

Cook your latkes in the preheated Air Fryer at 370 degrees F for 15 minutes or until thoroughly cooked and crispy.

Bon appétit!

Per serving: 279 Calories; 5.2g Fat; 48.4g Carbs; 9.1g Protein; 7.5g Sugars

875. Chicken and Cheese Pita Pockets

(Ready in about 20 minutes | Servings 2)

Ingredients

1/2 pound chicken breasts, boneless skinless
1 teaspoon avocado oil
Sea salt and ground black pepper, to taste

1/2 teaspoon paprika
1/2 teaspoon garlic powder
2 whole-wheat pita pockets
3 ounces cheddar cheese, shredded

Directions

Brush the chicken breasts with avocado oil.

Cook the chicken breasts in the preheated Air Fryer at 380 degrees F for 12 minutes. Transfer to a cutting board to cool slightly before slicing.

Cut the chicken breast into bite-sized strips. Toss the chicken strips with spices.

Fill the pitas with chicken and cheese and transfer them to the preheated Air Fryer.

Bake your pita pockets at 370 degrees F for 5 to 6 minutes until cheese has melted. Serve warm and enjoy!

Per serving: 571 Calories; 25.2g Fat; 38.4g Carbs; 40.1g Protein; 1.8g Sugars

876. Air-Fried Guacamole Balls

(Ready in about 20 minutes | Servings 4)

Ingredients

2 avocados, pitted, peeled and mashed
2 tablespoons shallots, finely chopped
2 tablespoons fresh cilantro, chopped

2 eggs, whisked
1/2 teaspoon paprika
Himalayan salt and ground black pepper, to taste
1 cup tortilla chips, crushed

Directions

In a mixing bowl, thoroughly combine the avocado, shallots, cilantro, eggs, paprika, salt and black pepper.

Scoop the mixture onto a parchment-lined cookie sheet; freeze for about 3 hours or until hardened.

Shape the mixture into balls and roll them in crushed tortilla chips.

Cook the guacamole balls in the preheated Air Fryer at 400 degrees F for about 4 minutes; shake the basket and continue to cook an additional 3 minutes. Work in batches.

Bon appétit!

Per serving: 236 Calories; 17.5g Fat; 16.4g Carbs; 6.1g Protein; 2.4g Sugars

877. Pancake and Banana Kabobs

(Ready in about 30 minutes | Servings 4)

Ingredients

Mini Pancakes:
3 eggs
1/2 cup whole milk
1/2 cup all-purpose flour
A pinch of salt
A pinch of granulated sugar

A pinch of ground cinnamon
1/2 teaspoon fresh lemon juice
Baked Banana:
1 banana, cut into 1-inch rounds
1 teaspoon coconut oil

Directions

Beat all ingredients for the pancakes using an electric mixer. Allow the batter to rest for about 20 minutes.

Spritz the Air Fryer baking pan with a nonstick cooking spray. Drop the pancake batter on the pan with a small spoon.

Cook the mini pancakes at 380 degrees F for 4 minutes or until golden brown.

Drizzle the banana with the melted coconut oil. Bake the banana rounds in the preheated Air Fryer at 370 degrees F for 6 minutes, turning them over halfway through the cooking time.

Tread the mini pancakes and banana rounds onto bamboo skewers. Enjoy!

Per serving: 168 Calories; 5.5g Fat; 22.8g Carbs; 6.9g Protein; 7.7g Sugars

878. Air-Grilled Fruit Skewers

(Ready in about 10 minutes | Servings 2)

Ingredients

2 ounces pear chunks
2 ounces apple chunks
2 ounces peach chunks
2 ounces pineapple chunks

1 teaspoon fresh lemon juice
1/2 teaspoon apple pie spice
1 teaspoon coconut oil, melted

Directions

Toss your fruit with the fresh lemon juice, apple pie spice and coconut oil. Then, thread the pieces of fruit onto bamboo skewers.

Bake the fruit skewers in the preheated Air Fryer at 330 degrees F for 10 minutes.

Serve with vanilla ice cream, if desired. Bon appétit!

Per serving: 92 Calories; 2.5g Fat; 19.1g Carbs; 0.4g Protein; 16.2g Sugars

879. Spicy Polenta Fries

(Ready in about 35 minutes | Servings 2)

Ingredients

8 ounces pre-cooked polenta
1 teaspoon canola oil

1/2 teaspoon red chili flakes
Salt and black pepper, to taste

Directions

Pour the polenta onto a large lined baking tray; now, let it cool and firm up. Using a sharp knife, cut chilled polenta into sticks.

Sprinkle canola oil, red chili flakes, salt and black pepper onto polenta sticks.

Air fry the polenta fries at 400 degrees F for about 30 minutes, turning them over once or twice. Enjoy!

Per serving: 126 Calories; 2.7g Fat; 22.8g Carbs; 2g Protein; 0.4g Sugars

880. Lentil and Mushroom Burgers

(Ready in about 35 minutes | Servings 2)

Ingredients

1/2 cup dried red lentils, soaked overnight
2 eggs, beaten
1 teaspoon garlic, minced
1/2 shallot, finely chopped
4 ounces brown mushrooms, chopped
1/4 teaspoon cumin powder

1/4 teaspoon ground bay leaf
1/2 teaspoon cayenne pepper
Kosher salt and ground black pepper, to taste
2 tablespoons breadcrumbs
1 teaspoon olive oil
2 hamburger buns

Directions

Drain and rinse your lentils.

Cook your lentils in a large saucepan of lightly salted water until tender o about 15 minutes.

Add in the eggs, garlic, shallot, mushrooms and spices and mix to combine well. Shape the mixture into equal patties.

Roll the patties into breadcrumbs. Brush the lentil patties with olive oil and transfer them to the cooking basket.

Cook the lentil burgers at 390 degrees F for about 20 minutes, turning them over halfway through the cooking time.

Serve on burger buns, garnished with toppings of choice. Devour!

Per serving: 399 Calories; 9.3g Fat; 57.5g Carbs; 23.2g Protein; 5.4g Sugars

881. Salted Pretzel Croissants

(Ready in about 20 minutes | Servings 3)

Ingredients

1 (8-ounce) can refrigerated crescent rolls
1/2 cup baking soda

1 egg, whisked with 1 tablespoon of water
2 tablespoons sesame seed
1 teaspoon coarse sea salt

Directions

Unroll the dough and separate it into triangles. Roll them up to make a croissan shape.

Bring 6 cups of water and the baking soda to a boil in a medium saucepa

Cook each croissant for 30 seconds and carefully remove from the water with a slotted spoon; pat dry with a kitchen towel.

Now, brush the tops of your croissants with the egg wash; sprinkle each roll with sesame seed and coarse sea salt. Allow them to rest for about 10 minutes.

Now, place your croissants in the lightly greased Air Fryer cooking basket.

Bake your croissants in the preheated Air Fryer at 330 degrees for about minutes or until golden brown. Bon appétit!

Per serving: 269 Calories; 7.5g Fat; 38.6g Carbs; 10.3g Protein; 4.9g Sugars

882. Air Grilled Yam Skewers

(Ready in about 35 minutes | Servings 3)

Ingredients

1 pound yams, peeled and cut into bite-sized chunks
1 teaspoon olive oil
1/4 teaspoon cayenne pepper
Kosher salt and ground white pepper, to taste

Directions

Toss the pieces of yams with olive oil, cayenne pepper, salt and white pepper.

Thread the pieces of yams onto bamboo skewers and transfer them to the Air Fryer cooking basket.

Air fry your skewers at 380 degrees F for 15 minutes; turn them over and continue to cook an additional 15 minutes. Enjoy!

Per serving: 192 Calories; 1.7g Fat; 42.1g Carbs; 2.3g Protein; 0.7g Sugars

883. Air-Grilled Sweet English Muffin

(Ready in about 10 minutes | Servings 1)

Ingredients

1 English muffin, split in half
1 teaspoon butter
2 egg
1 ounce milk
1 ounce double cream
1 tablespoon brown sugar
1/4 teaspoon ground cinnamon
1 tablespoon icing sugar

Directions

Spread the butter onto the bottom half of the English muffin.

In a mixing bowl, beat the eggs with milk, double cream, brown sugar and cinnamon.

Dip the English muffin into the egg/cream mixture and place it in the lightly greased Air Fryer cooking basket.

Cook the English muffin in the preheated Air Fryer at 380 degrees F for 5 minutes, turning it over halfway through the cooking time.

Dust with icing sugar and serve immediately.

Per serving: 423 Calories; 19.7g Fat; 45.1g Carbs; 17.7g Protein; 19.3g Sugars

884. Mediterranean Keto Bread

(Ready in about 10 minutes | Servings 1)

Ingredients

1/2 cup provolone cheese, shredded
1 egg, whisked
1/2 teaspoon oregano
1/4 teaspoon basil
1/2 teaspoon garlic powder

Directions

Thoroughly combine all ingredients in a mixing bowl.

Press the batter into a round circle on a piece of parchment paper. Transfer it to the Air Fryer cooking basket.

Bake the keto bread at 350 degrees F for 9 to 10 minutes. Eat warm and enjoy!

Per serving: 361 Calories; 27g Fat; 2.4g Carbs; 25.7g Protein; 1.3g Sugars

885. Kid-Friendly Crescent Dogs

(Ready in about 10 minutes | Servings 4)

Ingredients

8 ounces crescent rolls
1 tablespoon deli mustard
8 cocktail-size hot dogs

Directions

Unroll the crescents rolls and separate them into triangles.

Lay a triangle on a working surface and spread the mustard on it. Place a hot dog over it and roll it up. Repeat with the remaining triangles.

Bake the crescent dogs at 390 degrees F for 8 to 9 minutes, turning them over every 3 minutes to promote even cooking. Work in batches.

Bon appétit!

Per serving: 461 Calories; 30.1g Fat; 30g Carbs; 16.2g Protein; 0.1g Sugars

886. Greek-Style Frittata

(Ready in about 15 minutes | Servings 1)

Ingredients

1/2 teaspoon olive oil
2 eggs
4 tablespoons Greek-style yogurt
1 scallion stalk, chopped
1 bell pepper, divined and chopped
1/4 teaspoon oregano
Coarse sea salt and ground black pepper, to season
1 small tomato, sliced
2 ounces feta cheese, crumbled
1 tablespoon fresh basil leaves

Directions

Brush the sides and bottoms of a baking dish with olive oil.

In a mixing dish, beat the eggs until frothy; then, stir in Greek yogurt, scallion, bell pepper, oregano, salt and black pepper.

Cook your frittata at 350 degrees for 10 minutes; top with tomatoes and continue to cook for 5 minutes more; check for doneness.

Garnish with feta cheese and fresh basil leaves, serve warm. Enjoy!

Per serving: 384 Calories; 23.4g Fat; 19.2g Carbs; 27.2g Protein; 8.5g Sugars

887. Baked Eggs in Dinner Rolls

(Ready in about 15 minutes | Servings 2)

Ingredients

4 dinner rolls
2 tablespoons butter
4 eggs
1/4 teaspoon cayenne pepper
Sea salt and ground black pepper, to taste

Directions

Scoop out the insides of dinner rolls to make the shells. Brush them with melted butter on all sides.

Crack an egg into each roll shell; sprinkle with cayenne pepper, salt and black pepper.

Bake your rolls in the preheated Air Fryer at 330 degrees F for about 10 minutes until eggs are set. Cook for a few more minutes to achieve your desired level of doneness, if needed.

Bon appétit!

Per serving: 444 Calories; 24.4g Fat; 36.7g Carbs; 19.2g Protein; 6.7g Sugars

888. Cornbread Muffins with Raisins

(Ready in about 25 minutes | Servings 3)

Ingredients

1/2 cup yellow cornmeal
1/2 cup plain flour
1 teaspoon baking powder
1/3 cup brown sugar
1/2 teaspoon salt
A pinch of grated nutmeg
A pinch of ground cinnamon
1/2 cup whole milk
1 egg, beaten
2 ounces butter, melted
1/2 cup raisins

Directions

In a mixing bowl, thoroughly combine the dry ingredients. In another bowl, mix the wet ingredients.

Then, stir the wet mixture into the dry mixture.

Pour the batter into a lightly buttered muffin tin. Now, bake your cornbread muffins at 350 degrees F for about 20 minutes.

Check for doneness and transfer to a wire rack to cool slightly before serving. Enjoy!

Per serving: 408 Calories; 20.7g Fat; 48.7g Carbs; 8.1g Protein; 16.4g Sugars

889. Homemade Party Mix

(Ready in about 10 minutes | Servings 4)

Ingredients

1 cup cheese squares
1 cup Rice Chex
1/2 cup pistachios
1/4 cup sunflower seeds
1/2 cup cheddar-flavored mini pretzel twists
3 tablespoons melted butter

1/2 teaspoon salt
1/4 teaspoon ground black pepper
1/2 teaspoon paprika
1/2 teaspoon shallot powder
1/2 teaspoon porcini powder
1/2 teaspoon garlic powder

Directions

Thoroughly combine all ingredients in a bowl.

Place the mixture in a single layer in the parchment-lined cooking basket.

Bake in the preheated Air Fryer at 330 degrees F for 7 minutes. Allow the mixture to cool completely. Bon appétit!

Per serving: 358 Calories; 8.7g Fat; 36.1g Carbs; 21.2g Protein; 2.4g Sugars

890. Mini Espresso Brownies

(Ready in about 30 minutes | Servings 3)

Ingredients

1/3 cup granulated sugar
1/3 cup cocoa powder
1 tablespoon instant espresso powder
1/3 cup cake flour
1/2 teaspoon baking powder

1/4 teaspoon ground cinnamon
A pinch of grated nutmeg
A pinch of kosher salt
1/2 teaspoon lime zest
1 egg
1/3 cup butter, melted

Directions

Brush a muffin tin with a nonstick cooking spray. In a bowl, thoroughly combine the sugar, cocoa powder, instant espresso powder, cake flour, baking powder, cinnamon, nutmeg, salt and lime zest.

In another bowl, beat the egg with the melted butter until smooth. Then, stir the egg/butter mixture into the dry flour mixture and stir until everything is well combined.

Divide the brownie batter between muffin cups and smooth top with a spatula. Cook your brownies at 350 degrees F for about 17 minutes.

Allow your brownies to cool for 8 to 10 minutes before unmolding and serving. Bon appétit!

Per serving: 315 Calories; 23.1g Fat; 27.1g Carbs; 5.2g Protein; 11.1g Sugars

891. Classic French Potato Galette

(Ready in about 40 minutes | Servings 2)

Ingredients

1/2 pound potatoes, thinly sliced
3 tablespoons butter, melted
2 tablespoons white onion, finely chopped

Kosher salt and freshly ground black pepper, to season
1/4 teaspoon rosemary
1/4 teaspoon allspices
4 ounces goat cheese

Directions

Toss the potato slices with melted butter, onion, salt, black pepper, rosemary and allspice. Place 1/2 of the potato mixture on a foil-lined cooking basket.

Top with 2 ounces of goat cheese. Then, cover it with a layer of the potato slices. Top with goat cheese and fold the foil loosely over it.

Bake your galette at 380 degrees F for 25 to 30 minutes. Now, turn the temperature to 340 degrees F, open the foil and continue to cook for 5 to 7 minutes more until the potatoes are tender.

Cut your galette into wedges and serve warm. Enjoy!

Per serving: 501 Calories; 37.1g Fat; 22.1g Carbs; 19.9g Protein; 2.5g Sugars

892. German Blueberry Dessert with Pecan Streusel

(Ready in about 20 minutes | Servings 3)

Ingredients

2 cups fresh blueberries
1 teaspoon fresh lemon juice
1/4 teaspoon lemon zest
1/2 teaspoon crystallized ginger
2 ounces brown sugar

1/2 cup pecans, chopped
2 tablespoons honey
1/2 teaspoon ground cinnamon
2 tablespoons cold salted butter, cut into pieces

Directions

Place the fresh blueberries on the bottom of a lightly buttered Air Fryer-safe dish.

In a mixing bowl, thoroughly combine the remaining ingredients for the topping.

Top your blueberries with the prepared topping.

Bake your dessert at 340 degrees F for about 17 minutes. Serve at room temperature and enjoy!

Per serving: 331 Calories; 17.3g Fat; 47.5g Carbs; 2.3g Protein; 40.5g Sugars

893. Mini Raspberry Pies

(Ready in about 20 minutes | Servings 4)

Ingredients

11 ounces flaky-style biscuit dough

8 ounces canned raspberry pie filling
1/2 cup powdered sugar

Directions

Roll each section of the biscuit dough into a round circle. Divide the raspberry pie filling among the circles.

Roll them up and transfer to the Air Fryer cooking basket. Brush the rolls with a nonstick cooking oil.

Air fry your pies at 330 degrees F for about 12 minutes, work in batches. Roll the warm pies in powdered sugar until well coated on all sides.

Transfer them to a wire rack to cool before serving. Bon appétit!

Per serving: 358 Calories; 8.8g Fat; 60.5g Carbs; 5.3g Protein; 26.4g Sugars

894. Taco Rolls with A Twist

(Ready in about 15 minutes | Servings 3)

Ingredients

1/2 pound ground turkey
2 cloves garlic, minced
1 teaspoon jalapeno pepper, chopped
1 small-sized shallot, finely chopped

1 tablespoon taco seasoning
6 ounces refrigerated crescent rolls
2 ounces Cotija cheese, shredded
1 tablespoon butter, melted
1/2 cup salsa

Directions

Cook the ground turkey in a frying pan for about 3 minutes until no longer pink. Now, add in the garlic, jalapeno and shallot and cook for a minute or so until fragrant.

Stir the taco seasoning into the cooked taco meat.

Lay the crescent rolls flat on a piece of parchment paper; divide the cooked taco meat between the crescent rolls. Top with the shredded cheese and roll them up.

Brush the top of each roll with melted butter and transfer them to the Air Fryer cooking basket.

Air fry your taco rolls at 370 degrees F for about 7 minutes, checking them for doneness. Serve with salsa and enjoy!

Per serving: 394 Calories; 17g Fat; 33.1g Carbs; 24g Protein; 2.5g Sugars

895. Mixed Berry Crumble Pots

(Ready in about 20 minutes | Servings 2)

Ingredients

cup fresh mixed berries	2 ounces almond meal
tablespoons granulated sugar	1 ounce walnuts, chopped
/2 apple pie spice	1 ounce coconut oil, room
/2 teaspoon lemon zest	temperature

Directions

Toss the fresh mixed berries with the granulated sugar, apple pie spice and lemon zest. Divide the mixture between two custard cups.

Then, thoroughly combine the almond meal, walnuts and coconut oil. Sprinkle the mixture over the berry mixture.

Bake the crumble pots in the preheated Air Fryer at 350 degrees F for about 16 minutes. Bon appétit!

Per serving: 453 Calories; 37.3g Fat; 26.5g Carbs; 8.7g Protein; 16.8g Sugars

896. Farmer's Breakfast Deviled Eggs

(Ready in about 25 minutes | Servings 3)

Ingredients

eggs	2 tablespoons green onions,
slices bacon	chopped
tablespoons mayonnaise	1 tablespoon pickle relish
teaspoon hot sauce	Salt and ground black pepper, to
/2 teaspoon Worcestershire sauce	taste
	1 teaspoon smoked paprika

Directions

Place the wire rack in the Air Fryer basket; lower the eggs onto the wire rack.

Cook at 270 degrees F for 15 minutes.

Transfer them to an ice-cold water bath to stop the cooking. Peel the eggs under cold running water; slice them into halves.

Cook the bacon at 400 degrees F for 3 minutes; flip the bacon over and cook an additional 3 minutes; chop the bacon and reserve.

Mash the egg yolks with the mayo, hot sauce, Worcestershire sauce, green onions, pickle relish, salt, and black pepper; add the reserved bacon and spoon the yolk mixture into the egg whites.

Garnish with smoked paprika. Bon appétit!

Per serving: 512 Calories; 42.9g Fat; 5.1g Carbs; 25.2g Protein; 3.6g Sugars

897. Easy Greek Revithokeftedes

(Ready in about 30 minutes | Servings 3)

Ingredients

2 ounces canned chickpeas,	2 tablespoons all-purpose flour
drained	1/2 teaspoon cayenne pepper
red onion, sliced	Sea salt and freshly ground
cloves garlic	pepper, to taste
chili pepper	3 large (6 ½ -inch) pita bread
tablespoon fresh coriander	

Directions

Pulse the chickpeas, onion, garlic, chili pepper and coriander in your food processor until the chickpeas are ground.

Add the all-purpose flour, cayenne pepper, salt, and black pepper; stir to combine well.

Form the chickpea mixture into balls and place them in the lightly greased Air Fryer basket.

Cook at 380 degrees F for about 15 minutes, shaking the basket occasionally to ensure even cooking.

Warm the pita bread in your Air Fryer at 390 degrees F for around 6 minutes.

Serve the revithokeftedes in pita bread with tzatziki or your favorite Greek topping. Enjoy!

Per serving: 353 Calories; 4.1g Fat; 65.5g Carbs; 14.5g Protein; 6.3g Sugars

898. Philadelphia Mushroom Omelet

(Ready in about 20 minutes | Servings 2)

Ingredients

1 tablespoon olive oil	4 eggs
1/2 cup scallions, chopped	2 tablespoons milk
1 bell pepper, seeded and thinly	Sea salt and freshly ground black
sliced	pepper, to taste
6 ounces button mushrooms,	1 tablespoon fresh chives, for
thinly sliced	serving

Directions

Heat the olive oil in a skillet over medium-high heat. Now, sauté the scallions and peppers until aromatic.

Add the mushrooms and continue to cook an additional 3 minutes or until tender. Reserve.

Generously grease a baking pan with nonstick cooking spray.

Then, whisk the eggs, milk, salt, and black pepper. Spoon into the prepared baking pan.

Cook in the preheated Air Fryer at 360 F for 4 minutes. Flip and cook for a further 3 minutes.

Place the reserved mushroom filling on one side of the omelet. Fold your omelet in half and slide onto a serving plate. Serve immediately garnished with fresh chives. Bon appétit!

Per serving: 272 Calories; 19.1g Fat; 8.1g Carbs; 18.3g Protein; 4.5g Sugars

899. Rosemary Roasted Mixed Nuts

(Ready in about 20 minutes | Servings 6)

Ingredients

2 tablespoons butter, at room	1/2 teaspoon paprika
temperature	1/2 cup pine nuts
1 tablespoon dried rosemary	1 cup pecans
1 teaspoon coarse sea salt	1/2 cup hazelnuts

Directions

Toss all the ingredients in the mixing bowl.

Line the Air Fryer basket with baking parchment. Spread out the coated nuts in a single layer in the basket.

Roast at 350 degrees F for 6 to 8 minutes, shaking the basket once or twice. Work in batches. Enjoy!

Per serving: 295 Calories; 30.2g Fat; 5.8g Carbs; 4.8g Protein; 1.6g Sugars

900. Fingerling Potatoes with Cashew Sauce

(Ready in about 20 minutes | Servings 4)

Ingredients

1 pound fingerling potatoes	1/2 cup raw cashews
1 tablespoon butter, melted	1 teaspoon cayenne pepper
Sea salt and ground black pepper,	3 tablespoons nutritional yeast
to your liking	2 teaspoons white vinegar
1 teaspoon shallot powder	4 tablespoons water
1 teaspoon garlic powder	1/4 teaspoon dried rosemary
Cashew Sauce:	1/4 teaspoon dried dill

Directions

Toss the potatoes with the butter, salt, black pepper, shallot powder, and garlic powder.

Place the fingerling potatoes in the lightly greased Air Fryer basket and cook at 400 degrees F for 6 minutes; shake the basket and cook for a further 6 minutes.

Meanwhile, make the sauce by mixing all ingredients in your food processor or high-speed blender.

Drizzle the cashew sauce over the potato wedges. Bake at 400 degrees F for 2 more minutes or until everything is heated through. Enjoy!

Per serving: 341 Calories; 20.2g Fat; 34.2g Carbs; 9.8g Protein; 4.6g Sugars

901. Brown Rice Bowl

(Ready in about 55 minutes | Servings 4)

Ingredients

1 cup brown rice
1 tablespoon peanut oil
2 tablespoons soy sauce
1/2 cup scallions, chopped
2 bell pepper, chopped

2 eggs, beaten
Sea salt and ground black pepper, to taste
1/2 teaspoon granulated garlic

Directions

Heat the brown rice and 2 ½ cups of water in a saucepan over high heat. Bring it to a boil; turn the stove down to simmer and cook for 35 minutes.

Grease a baking pan with nonstick cooking spray. Add the hot rice and the other ingredients.

Cook at 370 degrees F for 15 minutes, checking occasionally to ensure even cooking. Enjoy!

Per serving: 302 Calories; 11g Fat; 41.2g Carbs; 9.4g Protein; 3.7g Sugars

902. Fruit Skewers with a Greek Flair

(Ready in about 10 minutes | Servings 2)

Ingredients

6 strawberries, halved
1 banana, peeled and sliced
1/4 pineapple, peeled and cubed
1 teaspoon fresh lemon juice

1/4 cup Greek-Style yoghurt, optional
2 tablespoons honey
1 teaspoon vanilla

Directions

Toss the fruits with lemon juice in a mixing dish. Tread the fruit pieces on skewers.

Cook at 340 degrees F for 5 minutes.

Meanwhile, whisk the Greek yogurt with the honey and vanilla. Serve the fruit skewers with the Greek sauce on the side. Bon appétit!

Per serving: 194 Calories; 0.5g Fat; 49.2g Carbs; 3.1g Protein; 37.9g Sugars

903. Delicious Hot Fruit Bake

(Ready in about 40 minutes | Servings 4)

Ingredients

2 cups blueberries
2 cups raspberries
1 tablespoon cornstarch
3 tablespoons maple syrup
2 tablespoons coconut oil, melted

A pinch of freshly grated nutmeg
A pinch of salt
1 cinnamon stick
1 vanilla bean

Directions

Place your berries in a lightly greased baking dish. Sprinkle the cornstarch onto the fruit.

Whisk the maple syrup, coconut oil, nutmeg, and salt in a mixing dish; add this mixture to the berries and gently stir to combine.

Add the cinnamon and vanilla. Bake in the preheated Air Fryer at 370 degrees F for 35 minutes. Serve warm or at room temperature. Enjoy!

Per serving: 334 Calories; 7.4g Fat; 70g Carbs; 1.9g Protein; 60.9g Sugars

904. Jamaican Cornmeal Pudding

(Ready in about 1 hour + chilling time | Servings 6)

Ingredients

3 cups coconut milk
2 ounces butter, softened
1 teaspoon cinnamon
1/2 teaspoon grated nutmeg
1 cup sugar
1/2 teaspoon fine sea salt
1 ½ cups yellow cornmeal
1/4 cup all-purpose flour
1/2 cup water

1/2 cup raisins
1 teaspoon rum extract
1 teaspoon vanilla extract
Custard:
1/2 cup full-fat coconut milk
1 ounce butter
1/4 cup honey
1 dash vanilla

Directions

Place the coconut milk, butter, cinnamon, nutmeg, sugar, and salt in a large saucepan; bring to a rapid boil. Heat off.

In a mixing bowl, thoroughly combine the cornmeal, flour and water; mix to combine well.

Add the milk/butter mixture to the cornmeal mixture; mix to combine. Bring the cornmeal mixture to boil; then, reduce the heat and simmer approximately 7 minutes, whisking continuously.

Remove from the heat. Now, add the raisins, rum extract, and vanilla.

Place the mixture into a lightly greased baking pan and bake at 325 degrees F for 12 minutes.

In a saucepan, whisk the coconut milk, butter, honey, and vanilla; let it simmer for 2 to 3 minutes. Now, prick your pudding with a fork and top with the prepared custard.

Return to your Air Fryer and bake for about 35 minutes more or until a toothpick inserted comes out dry and clean. Place in your refrigerator until ready to serve. Bon appétit!

Per serving: 538 Calories; 21.5g Fat; 82.4g Carbs; 8.2g Protein; 49.4g Sugars

905. Easy Frittata with Mozzarella and Kale

(Ready in about 20 minutes | Servings 3)

Ingredients

1 yellow onion, finely chopped
6 ounces wild mushrooms, sliced
6 eggs
1/4 cup double cream
1/2 teaspoon cayenne pepper
Sea salt and ground black pepper, to taste

1 tablespoon butter, melted
2 tablespoons fresh Italian parsley chopped
2 cups kale, chopped
1/2 cup mozzarella, shredded

Directions

Begin by preheating the Air Fryer to 360 degrees F. Spritz the sides and bottom of a baking pan with cooking oil.

Add the onions and wild mushrooms, and cook in the preheated Air Fryer at 360 degrees F for 4 to 5 minutes.

In a mixing dish, whisk the eggs and double cream until pale. Add the spices, butter, parsley, and kale; stir until everything is well incorporated.

Pour the mixture into the baking pan with the mushrooms.

Top with the cheese. Cook in the preheated Air Fryer for 10 minutes. Serve immediately and enjoy!

Per serving: 289 Calories; 19.6g Fat; 9.2g Carbs; 19.9g Protein; 5g Sugars

906. Mother's Day Pudding

(Ready in about 45 minutes | Servings 6)

Ingredients

1 pound French baguette bread, cubed
4 eggs, beaten
1/4 cup chocolate liqueur
1 cup granulated sugar
2 tablespoons honey

2 cups whole milk
1/2 cup heavy cream
1 teaspoon vanilla extract
1/4 teaspoon ground cloves
2 ounces milk chocolate chips

Directions

Place the bread cubes in a lightly greased baking dish. In a mixing bowl, thoroughly combine the eggs, chocolate liqueur, sugar, honey, milk, heavy cream, vanilla, and ground cloves.

Pour the custard over the bread cubes. Scatter the milk chocolate chips over the top of your bread pudding.

Let stand for 30 minutes, occasionally pressing with a wide spatula to submerge.

Cook in the preheated Air Fryer at 370 degrees F degrees for 7 minutes; check to ensure even cooking and cook an additional 5 to 6 minutes. Bon appétit!

Per serving: 548 Calories; 11.8g Fat; 92.2g Carbs; 14.9g Protein; 57.4g Sugars

907. Traditional Onion Bhaji

(Ready in about 40 minutes | Servings 3)

Ingredients

1 egg, beaten
2 tablespoons olive oil
2 onions, sliced
1 green chili, deseeded and finely chopped
2 ounces chickpea flour
1 ounce all-purpose flour
Salt and black pepper, to taste
1 teaspoon cumin seeds
1/2 teaspoon ground turmeric

Directions

Place all ingredients, except for the onions, in a mixing dish; mix to combine well, adding a little water to the mixture.

Once you've got a thick batter, add the onions; stir to coat well.

Cook in the preheated Air Fryer at 370 degrees F for 20 minutes flipping them halfway through the cooking time.

Work in batches and transfer to a serving platter. Enjoy!

Per serving: 243 Calories; 13.8g Fat; 21.2g Carbs; 8.6g Protein; 3.6g Sugars

908. Savory Italian Crespelle

(Ready in about 35 minutes | Servings 3)

Ingredients

3/4 cup all-purpose flour
2 eggs, beaten
1/4 teaspoon allspice
1/2 teaspoon salt
3/4 cup milk
1 cup ricotta cheese
1/2 cup Parmigiano-Reggiano cheese, preferably freshly grated
1 cup marinara sauce

Directions

Mix the flour, eggs, allspice, and salt in a large bowl. Gradually add the milk, whisking continuously, until well combined.

Let it stand for 20 minutes.

Spritz the Air Fryer baking pan with cooking spray. Pour the batter into the prepared pan.

Cook at 230 degrees F for 3 minutes. Flip and cook until browned in spots, 2 to 3 minutes longer.

Repeat with the remaining batter. Serve with the cheese and marinara sauce. Bon appétit!

Per serving: 451 Calories; 22.9g Fat; 36.1g Carbs; 25.1g Protein; 7.2g Sugars

909. Country-Style Apple Fries

(Ready in about 20 minutes | Servings 4)

Ingredients

1/2 cup milk
1 egg
1/2 all-purpose flour
1 teaspoon baking powder
4 tablespoons brown sugar
1 teaspoon vanilla extract
1/2 teaspoon ground cloves
A pinch of kosher salt
A pinch of grated nutmeg
1 tablespoon coconut oil, melted
2 Pink Lady apples, cored, peeled, slice into pieces (shape and size of French fries)
1/3 cup granulated sugar
1 teaspoon ground cinnamon

Directions

In a mixing bowl, whisk the milk and eggs; gradually stir in the flour; add the baking powder, brown sugar, vanilla, cloves, salt, nutmeg, and melted coconut oil. Mix to combine well.

Dip each apple slice into the batter, coating on all sides. Spritz the bottom of the cooking basket with cooking oil.

Cook the apple fries in the preheated Air Fryer at 395 degrees F approximately 8 minutes, turning them over halfway through the cooking time.

Cook in small batches to ensure even cooking.

In the meantime, mix the granulated sugar with the ground cinnamon; sprinkle the cinnamon sugar over the apple fries. Serve warm.

Per serving: 219 Calories; 7.1g Fat; 34.3g Carbs; 5.1g Protein; 19.2g Sugars

910. Grilled Cheese Sandwich

(Ready in about 15 minutes | Servings 1)

Ingredients

2 slices artisan bread
1 tablespoon butter, softened
1 tablespoon tomato ketchup
1/2 teaspoon dried oregano
2 slices Cheddar cheese

Directions

Brush one side of each slice of the bread with melted butter.

Add the tomato ketchup, oregano, and cheese. Make the sandwich and grill at 360 degrees F for 9 minutes or until cheese is melted. Bon appétit!

Per serving: 446 Calories; 31.9g Fat; 22.7g Carbs; 17.6g Protein; 3.7g Sugars

911. Green Pea Fritters with Parsley Yogurt Dip

(Ready in about 20 minutes | Servings 4)

Ingredients

Pea Fritters:
1 ½ cups frozen green peas
1 tablespoon sesame oil
1/2 cup scallions, chopped
2 garlic cloves, minced
1 cup chickpea flour
1 teaspoon baking powder
1/2 teaspoon sea salt
1/2 teaspoon ground black pepper
1/4 teaspoon dried dill
1/2 teaspoon dried basil
Parsley Yogurt Dip:
1/2 cup Greek-Style yoghurt
2 tablespoons mayonnaise
2 tablespoons fresh parsley, chopped
1 tablespoon fresh lemon juice
1/2 teaspoon garlic, smashed

Directions

Place the thawed green peas in a mixing dish; pour in hot water. Drain and rinse well.

Mash the green peas; add the remaining ingredients for the pea fritters and mix to combine well. Shape the mixture into patties and transfer them to the lightly greased cooking basket.

Bake at 330 degrees F for 14 minutes or until thoroughly heated.

Meanwhile, make your dipping sauce by whisking the remaining ingredients. Place in your refrigerator until ready to serve.

Serve the green pea fritters with the chilled dip on the side. Enjoy!

Per serving: 233 Calories; 11.3g Fat; 23.8g Carbs; 9.4g Protein; 6.9g Sugars

912. Baked Eggs Florentine

(Ready in about 20 minutes | Servings 2)

Ingredients

1 tablespoon ghee, melted
2 cups baby spinach, torn into small pieces
2 tablespoons shallots, chopped
1/4 teaspoon red pepper flakes
Salt, to taste
1 tablespoon fresh thyme leaves, roughly chopped
4 eggs

Directions

Start by preheating your Air Fryer to 350 degrees F. Brush the sides and bottom of a gratin dish with the melted ghee.

Put the spinach and shallots into the bottom of the gratin dish. Season with red pepper, salt, and fresh thyme.

Make four indents for the eggs; crack one egg into each indent. Bake for 12 minutes, rotating the pan once or twice to ensure even cooking. Enjoy!

Per serving: 325 Calories; 25.1g Fat; 5.1g Carbs; 19.1g Protein; 2.2g Sugars

913. Bagel 'n' Egg Melts

(Ready in about 25 minutes | Servings 3)

Ingredients

3 eggs
3 slices smoked ham, chopped
1 teaspoon Dijon mustard
1/4 cup mayonnaise
Salt and white pepper, to taste
3 bagels
3 ounces Colby cheese, shredded

Directions

Place the wire rack in the Air Fryer basket; lower the eggs onto the wire rack.

Cook at 270 degrees F for 15 minutes.

Transfer them to an ice-cold water bath to stop the cooking. Peel the eggs under cold running water; coarsely chop them and set aside.

Combine the chopped eggs, ham, mustard, mayonnaise, salt, and pepper in a mixing bowl.

Slice the bagels in half. Spread the egg mixture on top and sprinkle with the shredded cheese.

Grill in the preheated Air Fryer at 360 degrees F for 7 minutes or until cheese is melted. Bon appétit!

Per serving: 575 Calories; 29.4g Fat; 50.8g Carbs; 26.6g Protein; 7.5g Sugars

914. Italian Sausage and Veggie Bake

(Ready in about 20 minutes | Servings 4)

Ingredients

1 pound Italian sausage
2 red peppers, seeded and sliced
2 green peppers, seeded and sliced
1 cup mushrooms, sliced
1 shallot, sliced
4 cloves garlic
1 teaspoon dried basil
1 teaspoon dried oregano
1/4 teaspoon black pepper
1/4 teaspoon cayenne pepper
Sea salt, to taste
2 tablespoons Dijon mustard
1 cup chicken broth

Directions

Toss all ingredients in a lightly greased baking pan. Make sure the sausages and vegetables are coated with the oil and seasonings.

Bake in the preheated Air Fryer at 380 degrees F for 15 minutes.

Divide between individual bowls and serve warm. Bon appétit!

Per serving: 537 Calories; 35.6g Fat; 16.3g Carbs; 37.2g Protein; 5.9g Sugars

915. Greek-Style Roasted Figs

(Ready in about 20 minutes | Servings 4)

Ingredients

2 teaspoons butter, melted
8 figs, halved
2 tablespoons brown sugar
1/2 teaspoon cinnamon
1 teaspoon lemon zest
1 cup Greek yogurt
4 tablespoons honey

Directions

Drizzle the melted butter all over the fig halves.

Sprinkle brown sugar, cinnamon, and lemon zest on the fig slices. Meanwhile, mix the Greek yogurt with the honey.

Roast in the preheated Air Fryer at 330 degrees F for 16 minutes.

To serve, divide the figs among 4 bowls and serve with a dollop of the yogurt sauce. Enjoy!

Per serving: 209 Calories; 4.2g Fat; 43.6g Carbs; 2.9g Protein; 40.3g Sugars

916. Classic Egg Salad

(Ready in about 20 minutes + chilling time | Servings 3)

Ingredients

6 eggs
1 teaspoon mustard
1/2 cup mayonnaise
1 tablespoons white vinegar
2 carrots, trimmed and sliced
1 red bell pepper, seeded and sliced
1 green bell pepper, seeded and sliced
1 shallot, sliced
Sea salt and ground black pepper, to taste

Directions

Place the wire rack in the Air Fryer basket; lower the eggs onto the wire rack.

Cook at 270 degrees F for 15 minutes.

Transfer them to an ice-cold water bath to stop the cooking. Peel the eggs under cold running water; coarsely chop the hard-boiled eggs and set aside.

Toss with the remaining ingredients and serve well chilled. Bon appétit!

Per serving: 294 Calories; 21.2g Fat; 10.5g Carbs; 14.9g Protein; 4.9g Sugars

917. Breakfast Muffins with Mushrooms and Goat Cheese

(Ready in about 25 minutes | Servings 6)

Ingredients

2 tablespoons butter, melted
1 yellow onion, chopped
2 garlic cloves, minced
1 cup brown mushrooms, sliced
Sea salt and ground black pepper, to taste
1 teaspoon fresh basil
8 eggs, lightly whisked
6 tablespoons goat cheese, crumbled

Directions

Start by preheating your Air Fryer to 330 degrees F. Now, spritz a 6-tin muffin tin with cooking spray.

Melt the butter in a heavy-bottomed skillet over medium-high heat. Sauté the onions, garlic, and mushrooms until just tender and fragrant.

Add the salt, black pepper, and basil and remove from heat. Divide out the sautéed mixture into the muffin tin.

Pour the whisked eggs on top and top with the goat cheese. Bake for 20 minutes rotating the pan halfway through the cooking time. Bon appétit!

Per serving: 278 Calories; 21.5g Fat; 5.5g Carbs; 15.2g Protein; 3.3g Sugars

918. Scrambled Eggs with Sausage

(Ready in about 25 minutes | Servings 6)

Ingredients

1 teaspoon lard
1/2 pound turkey sausage
6 eggs
1 scallion, chopped
1 garlic clove, minced
1 sweet pepper, seeded and chopped
1 chili pepper, seeded and chopped
Sea salt and ground black pepper, to taste
1/2 cup Swiss cheese, shredded

Directions

Start by preheating your Air Fryer to 330 degrees F. Now, spritz 6 silicone molds with cooking spray.

Melt the lard in a saucepan over medium-high heat. Now, cook the sausage for 5 minutes or until no longer pink.

Coarsely chop the sausage; add the eggs, scallions, garlic, peppers, salt, and black pepper. Divide the egg mixture between the silicone molds. Top with the shredded cheese.

Bake in the preheated Air Fryer at 340 degrees F for 15 minutes, checking halfway through the cooking time to ensure even cooking. Enjoy!

Per serving: 204 Calories; 11.5g Fat; 8.7g Carbs; 15.6g Protein; 1.1g Sugars

919. Southwest Bean Potpie

(Ready in about 30 minutes | Servings 5)

Ingredients

1 tablespoon olive oil
2 sweet peppers, seeded and sliced
1 carrot, chopped
1 onion, chopped
2 garlic cloves, minced
1 cup cooked bacon, diced
1 ½ cups beef bone broth

20 ounces canned red kidney beans, drained
Sea salt and freshly ground black pepper, to taste
1 package (8 1/2-ounce) cornbread mix
1/2 cup milk
2 tablespoons butter, melted

Directions

Heat the olive oil in a saucepan over medium-high heat. Now, cook the peppers, carrot, onion, and garlic until they have softened, about 7 minutes

Add the bacon and broth. Bring to a boil and cook for 2 minutes more. Stir in the kidney beans, salt and black pepper; continue to cook until everything is heated through.

Transfer the mixture to the lightly greased baking pan.

In a small bowl, combine the muffin mix, milk, and melted butter. Stir until well mixed and spoon evenly over the bean mixture. Smooth it with a spatula and transfer to the Air Fryer cooking basket.

Bake in the preheated Air Fryer at 400 degrees F for 12 minutes. Place on a wire rack to cool slightly before slicing and serving. Bon appétit!

Per serving: 459 Calories; 26.3g Fat; 47.9g Carbs; 10.4g Protein; 12.5g Sugars

920. Veggie Casserole with Ham and Baked Eggs

(Ready in about 30 minutes | Servings 4)

Ingredients

2 tablespoons butter, melted
1 zucchini, diced
1 bell pepper, seeded and sliced
1 red chili pepper, seeded and minced
1 medium-sized leek, sliced
3/4 pound ham, cooked and diced

5 eggs
1 teaspoon cayenne pepper
Sea salt, to taste
1/2 teaspoon ground black pepper
1 tablespoon fresh cilantro, chopped

Directions

Start by preheating the Air Fryer to 380 degrees F. Grease the sides and bottom of a baking pan with the melted butter.

Place the zucchini, peppers, leeks and ham in the baking pan. Bake in the preheated Air Fryer for 6 minutes.

Crack the eggs on top of ham and vegetables; season with the cayenne pepper, salt, and black pepper. Bake for a further 20 minutes or until the whites are completely set.

Garnish with fresh cilantro and serve. Bon appétit!

Per serving: 325 Calories; 20.9g Fat; 7.9g Carbs; 26.6g Protein; 2.8g Sugars

921. French Toast with Blueberries and Honey

(Ready in about 20 minutes | Servings 6)

Ingredients

1/4 cup milk
2 eggs
2 tablespoons butter, melted
1/2 teaspoon ground cinnamon
1/4 teaspoon ground cloves

1 teaspoon vanilla extract
6 slices day-old French baguette
2 tablespoons honey
1/2 cup blueberries

Directions

In a mixing bowl, whisk the milk eggs, butter, cinnamon, cloves, and vanilla extract.

Dip each piece of the baguette into the egg mixture and place in the parchment-lined Air Fryer basket.

Cook in the preheated Air Fryer at 360 degrees F for 6 to 7 minutes, turning them over halfway through the cooking time to ensure even cooking.

Serve garnished with honey and blueberries. Enjoy!

Per serving: 275 Calories; 14.4g Fat; 27.8g Carbs; 8.5g Protein; 10.9g Sugars

922. Carrot Fries with Romano Cheese

(Ready in about 20 minutes | Servings 3)

Ingredients

3 carrots, sliced into sticks
1 tablespoon coconut oil
1/3 cup Romano cheese, preferably freshly grated

2 teaspoons granulated garlic
Sea salt and ground black pepper, to taste

Directions

Toss all ingredients in a mixing bowl until the carrots are coated on all sides.

Cook at 380 degrees F for 15 minutes, shaking the basket halfway through the cooking time.

Serve with your favorite dipping sauce. Bon appétit!

Per serving: 122 Calories; 10g Fat; 4.2g Carbs; 4.1g Protein; 0.4g Sugars

923. Quinoa with Baked Eggs and Bacon

(Ready in about 40 minutes | Servings 4)

Ingredients

1/2 cup quinoa
1/2 pound potatoes, diced
1 onion, diced
6 slices bacon, precooked

1 tablespoon butter, melted
Sea salt and ground black pepper, to taste
6 eggs

Directions

Rinse the quinoa under cold running water. Place the rinsed quinoa in a pan and add 1 cup of water.

Bring it to the boil. Turn the heat down and let it simmer for 13 to 15 minutes or until tender; reserve.

Place the diced potatoes and onion in a lightly greased casserole dish. Add the bacon and the reserved quinoa. Drizzle the melted butter over the quinoa and sprinkle with salt and pepper.

Bake in the preheated Air Fryer at 390 degrees F for 10 minutes.

Turn the temperature down to 350 degrees F.

Make six indents for the eggs; crack one egg into each indent. Bake for 12 minutes, rotating the pan once or twice to ensure even cooking. Enjoy!

Per serving: 416 Calories; 25.8g Fat; 27.9g Carbs; 17.8g Protein; 2.7g Sugars

924. Famous Western Eggs

(Ready in about 20 minutes | Servings 6)

Ingredients

6 eggs
3/4 cup milk
1 ounce cream cheese, softened
Sea salt, to your liking
1/4 teaspoon ground black pepper

1/4 teaspoon paprika
6 ounces cooked ham, diced
1 onion, chopped
1/3 cup cheddar cheese, shredded

Directions

Begin by preheating the Air Fryer to 360 degrees F. Spritz the sides and bottom of a baking pan with cooking oil.

In a mixing dish, whisk the eggs, milk, and cream cheese until pale. Add the spices, ham, and onion; stir until everything is well incorporated.

Pour the mixture into the baking pan; top with the cheddar cheese.

Bake in the preheated Air Fryer for 12 minutes. Serve warm and enjoy!

Per serving: 336 Calories; 22.6g Fat; 7.2g Carbs; 25.1g Protein; 4.7g Sugars

925. Celery Fries with Harissa Mayo

(Ready in about 30 minutes | Servings 3)

Ingredients

1/2 pound celery root
2 tablespoons olive oil
Sea salt and ground black pepper, to taste
Harissa Mayo
1/4 cup mayonnaise
2 tablespoons sour cream
1/2 tablespoon harissa paste
1/4 teaspoon ground cumin
Salt, to taste

Directions

Cut the celery root into desired size and shape.

Then, preheat your Air Fryer to 400 degrees F. Now, spritz the Air Fryer basket with cooking spray.

Toss the celery fries with the olive oil, salt, and black pepper. Bake in the preheated Air Fryer for 25 to 30 minutes, turning them over every 10 minutes to promote even cooking.

Meanwhile, mix all ingredients for the harissa mayo. Place in your refrigerator until ready to serve. Bon appétit!

Per serving: 233 Calories; 23.7g Fat; 4.3g Carbs; 1.3g Protein; 1.9g Sugars

926. English Muffins with a Twist

(Ready in about 15 minutes | Servings 4)

Ingredients

4 English muffins, split in half
2 eggs
1/3 cup milk
1/4 cup heavy cream
2 tablespoons honey
1 teaspoon pure vanilla extract
1/4 cup confectioners' sugar

Directions

Cut the muffins crosswise into strips.

In a mixing bowl, whisk the eggs, milk, heavy cream, honey, and vanilla extract.

Dip each piece of muffins into the egg mixture and place in the parchment-lined Air Fryer basket.

Cook in the preheated Air Fryer at 360 degrees F for 6 to 7 minutes, turning them over halfway through the cooking time to ensure even cooking.

Dust with confectioners' sugar and serve warm.

Per serving: 289 Calories; 9.3g Fat; 42.2g Carbs; 10.2g Protein; 17.3g Sugars

927. Easy Roasted Hot Dogs

(Ready in about 25 minutes | Servings 6)

Ingredients

6 hot dogs
6 hot dog buns
1 tablespoon mustard
6 tablespoons ketchup
6 lettuce leaves

Directions

Place the hot dogs in the lightly greased Air Fryer basket.

Bake at 380 degrees F for 15 minutes, turning them over halfway through the cooking time to promote even cooking.

Place on the bun and add the mustard, ketchup, and lettuce leaves. Enjoy!

Per serving: 415 Calories; 15.2g Fat; 41.4g Carbs; 28.1g Protein; 11.8g Sugars

928. Rum Roasted Cherries

(Ready in about 40 minutes | Servings 3)

Ingredients

9 ounces dark sweet cherries
2 tablespoons brown sugar
1 tablespoon honey
3 tablespoons rum
A pinch of grated nutmeg
1/4 teaspoon ground cloves
1/4 teaspoon ground cardamom
1 teaspoon vanilla

Directions

Place the cherries in a lightly greased baking dish.

Whisk the remaining ingredients until everything is well combined; add this mixture to the baking dish and gently stir to combine.

Bake in the preheated Air Fryer at 370 degrees F for 35 minutes. Serve at room temperature. Bon appétit!

Per serving: 128 Calories; 0.2g Fat; 24.7g Carbs; 0.9g Protein; 21.8g Sugars

929. Mediterranean Roasted Vegetable and Bean Salad

(Ready in about 20 minutes | Servings 4)

Ingredients

1 red onion, sliced
1 pound cherry tomatoes
1/2 pound asparagus
1 cucumber, sliced
2 cups baby spinach
2 tablespoons white vinegar
1/4 cup extra-virgin olive oil
2 tablespoons fresh parsley
Sea salt and pepper to taste
8 ounces canned red kidney bean rinsed
1/2 cup Kalamata olives, pitted and sliced

Directions

Begin by preheating your Air Fryer to 400 degrees F.

Place the onion, cherry tomatoes, and asparagus in the lightly greased Air Fryer basket. Bake for 5 to 6 minutes, tossing the basket occasionally.

Transfer to a salad bowl. Add the cucumber and baby spinach.

Then, whisk the vinegar, olive oil, parsley, salt, and black pepper in a small mixing bowl. Dress your salad; add the beans and olives.

Toss to combine well and serve.

Per serving: 209 Calories; 17.6g Fat; 11.3g Carbs; 4.1g Protein; 4.8g Sugars

930. Easiest Vegan Burrito Ever

(Ready in about 35 minutes | Servings 6)

Ingredients

2 tablespoons olive oil
1 small onion, chopped
2 sweet peppers, seeded and chopped
1 chili pepper, seeded and minced
Sea salt and ground black pepper, to taste
1 teaspoon red pepper flakes, crushed
1 teaspoon dried parsley flakes
10 ounces cooked pinto beans
12 ounces canned sweet corn, drained
6 large corn tortillas
1/2 cup vegan sour cream

Directions

Begin by preheating your Air Frye to 400 degrees F.

Heat the olive oil in a baking pan. Once hot, cook the onion and peppers until they are tender and fragrant, about 15 minutes.

Stir in the salt, black pepper, red pepper, parsley, beans, and sweet corn; stir to combine well.

Divide the bean mixture between the corn tortillas. Roll up your tortillas and place them on the parchment-lined Air Fryer basket.

Bake in the preheated Air Fryer at 350 degrees F for 15 minutes. Serve garnished with sour cream. Bon appétit!

Per serving: 344 Calories; 8g Fat; 57.1g Carbs; 15.2g Protein; 4.4g Sugars

931. Bourbon Glazed Mango with Walnuts

(Ready in about 20 minutes | Servings 4)

Ingredients

2 ripe mangos, peeled and diced
2 tablespoons bourbon whiskey
2 tablespoons sugar
2 tablespoons coconut oil, melted
1/4 teaspoon ground cardamom
1 teaspoon vanilla essence
1/4 teaspoon pure coconut extract
1/2 cup walnuts, coarsely chopped

Directions

Start by preheating your Air Fryer to 400 degrees F.

Toss all ingredients in a baking dish and transfer to the Air fryer basket.

Now, bake for 10 minutes, or until browned on top. Serve with whipped cream if desired. Bon appétit!

Per serving: 251 Calories; 13.9g Fat; 32.5g Carbs; 2.9g Protein; 29g Sugars

932. Baked Apples with Crisp Topping

(Ready in about 25 minutes | Servings 3)

Ingredients

3 Granny Smith apples, cored
2/3 cup rolled oats
3 tablespoons honey
1 tablespoon fresh orange juice
1/2 teaspoon ground cardamom
1/2 teaspoon ground cinnamon
1/4 teaspoon ground cloves
1/4 teaspoon ground star anise
2 tablespoons butter, cut in pieces
3 tablespoons cranberries

Directions

Use a paring knife to remove the stem and seeds from the apples, making deep holes.

In a mixing bowl, combine together the rolled oats, honey, orange juice, cardamom, cinnamon, cloves, anise, butter, and cranberries.

Pour enough water into an Air Fryer safe dish. Place the apples in the dish.

Bake at 340 degrees F for 16 to 18 minutes. Serve at room temperature. Bon appétit!

Per serving: 294 Calories; 9.5g Fat; 57.3g Carbs; 4.6g Protein; 35.8g Sugars

933. Crunch-Crunch Party Mix

(Ready in about 25 minutes | Servings 8)

Ingredients

1 cup whole-grain Rice Chex
2 cups cheese squares
1 cup pistachios
1/2 cup almonds
1 cup cheddar-flavored mini pretzel twists
2 tablespoons butter, melted
1/4 cup poppy seeds
1/2 cup sunflower seeds
1 tablespoon coarse sea salt
1 tablespoon garlic powder
1 tablespoon paprika

Directions

Mix all ingredients in a large bowl. Toss to combine well.

Place in a single layer in the parchment-lined cooking basket.

Bake in the preheated Air Fryer at 310 degrees F for 13 to 16 minutes. Allow it to cool completely before serving.

Store in an airtight container for up to 3 months. Bon appétit!

Per serving: 409 Calories; 27.1g Fat; 28.2g Carbs; 17.1g Protein; 1.8g Sugars

934. Homemade Pork Scratchings

(Ready in about 50 minutes | Servings 10)

Ingredients

1 pound pork rind raw, scored by the butcher
1 tablespoon sea salt
2 tablespoon smoked paprika

Directions

Sprinkle and rub salt on the skin side of the pork rind. Allow it to sit for 30 minutes.

Roast at 380 degrees F for 8 minutes; turn them over and cook for a further 8 minutes or until blistered.

Sprinkle the smoked paprika all over the pork scratchings and serve. Bon appétit!

Per serving: 245 Calories; 14.1g Fat; 0g Carbs; 27.6g Protein; 0g Sugars

935. Salted Pretzel Crescents

(Ready in about 20 minutes | Servings 4)

Ingredients

1 can crescent rolls
10 cups water
1/2 cup baking soda
1 egg, whisked with 1 tablespoon water
1 tablespoon poppy seeds
2 tablespoons sesame seed
1 teaspoon coarse sea salt

Directions

Unroll the dough onto your work surface; separate into 8 triangles.

In a large saucepan, bring the water and baking soda to a boil over high heat.

Cook each roll for 30 seconds. Remove from the water using a slotted spoon; place on a kitchen towel to drain.

Repeat with the remaining rolls. Now, brush the tops with the egg wash; sprinkle each roll with the poppy seeds, sesame seed and coarse sea salt. Cover and let rest for 10 minutes.

Arrange the pretzels in the lightly greased Air Fryer basket.

Bake in the preheated Air Fryer at 340 degrees for 7 minutes or until golden brown. Bon appétit!

Per serving: 273 Calories; 16.3g Fat; 23.7g Carbs; 6.6g Protein; 4.4g Sugars

936. Mozzarella Stick Nachos

(Ready in about 40 minutes | Servings 4)

Ingredients

1 (16-ounce) package mozzarella cheese sticks
2 eggs
1/2 cup flour
1/2 (7 12-ounce) bag multigrain tortilla chips, crushed
1 teaspoon garlic powder
1 teaspoon dried oregano
1/2 cup salsa, preferably homemade

Directions

Set up your breading station. Put the flour into a shallow bowl; beat the eggs in another shallow bowl; in a third bowl, mix the crushed tortilla chips, garlic powder, and oregano.

Coat the mozzarella sticks lightly with flour, followed by the egg, and then the tortilla chips mixture. Place in your freezer for 30 minutes.

Place the breaded cheese sticks in the lightly greased Air Fryer basket. Cook at 380 degrees F for 6 minutes.

Serve with salsa on the side and enjoy!

Per serving: 551 Calories; 28.7g Fat; 36.3g Carbs; 39.1g Protein; 1.7g Sugars

937. Easy Fried Button Mushrooms

(Ready in about 15 minutes | Servings 4)

Ingredients

1 pound button mushrooms
1 cup cornstarch
1 cup all-purpose flour
1/2 teaspoon baking powder
2 eggs, whisked
2 cups seasoned breadcrumbs
1/2 teaspoon salt
2 tablespoons fresh parsley leaves, roughly chopped

Directions

Pat the mushrooms dry with a paper towel.

To begin, set up your breading station. Mix the cornstarch, flour, and baking powder in a shallow dish. In a separate dish, whisk the eggs.

Finally, place your breadcrumbs and salt in a third dish.

Start by dredging the mushrooms in the flour mixture; then, dip them into the eggs. Press your mushrooms into the breadcrumbs, coating evenly.

Spritz the Air Fryer basket with cooking oil. Add the mushrooms and cook at 400 degrees F for 6 minutes, flipping them halfway through the cooking time.

Serve garnished with fresh parsley leaves. Bon appétit!

Per serving: 259 Calories; 4.3g Fat; 47.5g Carbs; 8.7g Protein; 2.4g Sugars

938. Party Pancake Kabobs

(Ready in about 40 minutes | Servings 4)

Ingredients

Pancakes:
1 cup all-purpose flour
1 teaspoon baking powder
1 tablespoon sugar
1/4 teaspoon salt
1 large egg, beaten
1/2 cup milk

1/2 teaspoon vanilla extract
2 tablespoons unsalted butter,
melted
Kabobs:
1 banana, diced
1 Granny Smith apples, diced
1/4 cup maple syrup, for serving

Directions

Mix all ingredients for the pancakes until creamy and fluffy. Let it stand for 20 minutes.

Spritz the Air Fryer baking pan with cooking spray. Drop the pancake batter on the pan with a small spoon.

Cook at 230 degrees F for 4 minutes or until golden brown. Repeat with the remaining batter.

Tread the mini pancakes and the fruit onto bamboo skewers, alternating between the mini pancakes and fruit.

Drizzle maple syrup all over the kabobs and serve immediately.

Per serving: 292 Calories; 6.5g Fat; 53.1g Carbs; 5.6g Protein;
23.1g Sugars

939. Mini Bread Puddings with Cinnamon Glaze

(Ready in about 50 minutes | Servings 5)

Ingredients

5 tablespoons butter
1/2 pound cinnamon-raisin bread,
cubed
1 cup milk
1/2 cup double cream
2/3 cup sugar
1 tablespoon honey

1 teaspoon pure vanilla extract
2 eggs, lightly beaten
Cinnamon Glaze:
1/4 cup powdered sugar
1 teaspoon ground cinnamon
1 tablespoon milk
1/2 teaspoon vanilla

Directions

Begin by preheating your Air Fryer to 370 degrees F. Lightly butter five ramekins.

Place the bread cubes in the greased ramekins. In a mixing bowl, thoroughly combine the milk, double cream, sugar, honey, vanilla, and eggs.

Pour the custard over the bread cubes. Let it stand for 30 minutes, occasionally pressing with a wide spatula to submerge.

Cook in the preheated Air Fryer at 370 degrees F degrees for 7 minutes; check to ensure even cooking and cook an additional 5 to 6 minutes.

Meanwhile, prepare the glaze by whisking the powdered sugar, cinnamon, milk, and vanilla until smooth. Top the bread puddings with the glaze and serve at room temperature. Bon appétit!

Per serving: 435 Calories; 23.1g Fat; 49.6g Carbs; 9g Protein;
28.1g Sugars

940. Easy Zucchini Chips

(Ready in about 20 minutes | Servings 4)

Ingredients

3/4 pound zucchini, peeled and
sliced
1 egg, lightly beaten

1/2 cup seasoned breadcrumbs
1/2 cup parmesan cheese,
preferably freshly grated

Directions

Pat the zucchini dry with a kitchen towel.

In a mixing dish, thoroughly combine the egg, breadcrumbs, and cheese. Then, coat the zucchini slices with the breadcrumb mixture.

Cook in the preheated Air Fryer at 400 degrees F for 9 minutes, shaking the basket halfway through the cooking time.

Work in batches until the chips is golden brown. Bon appétit!

Per serving: 154 Calories; 5.9g Fat; 14.7g Carbs; 8.5g Protein;
2.2g Sugars

941. Creamed Asparagus and Egg Salad

(Ready in about 25 minutes + chilling time | Servings 4)

Ingredients

2 eggs
1 pound asparagus, chopped
2 cup baby spinach
1/2 cup mayonnaise

1 teaspoon mustard
1 teaspoon fresh lemon juice
Sea salt and ground black pepper,
to taste

Directions

Place the wire rack in the Air Fryer basket; lower the eggs onto the wire rack.

Cook at 270 degrees F for 15 minutes.

Transfer them to an ice-cold water bath to stop the cooking. Peel the eggs under cold running water; coarsely chop the hard-boiled eggs and set aside.

Increase the temperature to 400 degrees F. Place your asparagus in the lightly greased Air Fryer basket.

Cook for 5 minutes or until tender. Place in a nice salad bowl. Add the baby spinach.

In a mixing dish, thoroughly combine the remaining ingredients. Drizzle this dressing over the asparagus in the salad bowl and top with the chopped eggs. Bon appétit!

Per serving: 245 Calories; 22.9g Fat; 5.3g Carbs; 6g Protein; 2.4g Sugars

942. Roasted Green Bean Salad with Goat Cheese

(Ready in about 10 minutes + chilling time | Servings 4)

Ingredients

1 pound trimmed green beans, cut
into bite-sized pieces
Salt and freshly cracked mixed
pepper, to taste
1 shallot, thinly sliced
1 tablespoon lime juice
1 tablespoon champagne vinegar

1/4 cup extra-virgin olive oil
1/2 teaspoon mustard seeds
1/2 teaspoon celery seeds
1 tablespoon fresh basil leaves,
chopped
1 tablespoon fresh parsley leaves
1 cup goat cheese, crumbled

Directions

Toss the green beans with salt and pepper in a lightly greased Air Fryer basket.

Cook in the preheated Air Fryer at 400 degrees F for 5 minutes or until tender.

Add the shallots and gently stir to combine.

In a mixing bowl, whisk the lime juice, vinegar, olive oil, and spices. Dress the salad and top with the goat cheese. Serve at room temperature or chilled. Enjoy!

Per serving: 296 Calories; 24.3g Fat; 11.1g Carbs; 10.3g Protein;
3.9g Sugars

943. Red Currant Cupcakes

(Ready in about 20 minutes | Servings 3)

Ingredients

1 cup all-purpose flour
1/2 cup sugar
1 teaspoon baking powder
A pinch of kosher salt
A pinch of grated nutmeg
1/4 cup coconut, oil melted

1 egg
1/4 cup full-fat coconut milk
1/4 teaspoon ground cardamom
1/4 teaspoon ground cinnamon
1 teaspoon vanilla extract
6 ounces red currants

Directions

Mix the flour with the sugar, baking powder, salt, and nutmeg. In a separate bowl, whisk the coconut oil, egg, milk, cardamom, cinnamon, and vanilla.

Add the egg mixture to the dry ingredients; mix to combine well.

Now, fold in the red currants; gently stir to combine. Scrape the batter into lightly greased 6 standard-size muffin cups.

Bake your cupcakes at 360 degrees F for 12 minutes or until the tops are golden brown. Sprinkle some extra icing sugar over the top of each muffin if desired. Enjoy!

Per serving: 346 Calories; 8.5g Fat; 58.9g Carbs; 8.7g Protein;
22.2g Sugars

944. Scrambled Egg Muffins with Cheese

(Ready in about 20 minutes | Servings 6)

Ingredients

ounces smoked turkey sausage, chopped

eggs, lightly beaten

tablespoons shallots, finely chopped

garlic cloves, minced

Sea salt and ground black pepper, to taste

1 teaspoon cayenne pepper

6 ounces Monterey Jack cheese, shredded

Directions

Simply combine the sausage, eggs, shallots, garlic, salt, black pepper, and cayenne pepper in a mixing dish. Mix to combine well.

Spoon the mixture into 6 standard-size muffin cups with paper liners.

Bake in the preheated Air Fryer at 340 degrees F for 8 minutes. Top with the cheese and bake an additional 8 minutes. Enjoy!

Per serving: 286 Calories; 19.9g Fat; 6.8g Carbs; 19.6g Protein; 2.4g Sugars

945. Spring Chocolate Doughnuts

(Ready in about 20 minutes | Servings 6)

Ingredients

can (16-ounce) can buttermilk biscuits

Chocolate Glaze:

cup powdered sugar

4 tablespoons unsweetened baking cocoa

2 tablespoon butter, melted

2 tablespoons milk

Directions

Bake your biscuits in the preheated Air Fryer at 350 degrees F for 8 minutes, flipping them halfway through the cooking time.

While the biscuits are baking, make the glaze.

Beat the ingredients with whisk until smooth, adding enough milk for the desired consistency; set aside.

Dip your doughnuts into the chocolate glaze and transfer to a cooling rack to set. Bon appétit!

Per serving: 345 Calories; 11.6g Fat; 56g Carbs; 6.1g Protein; 22.8g Sugars

946. Sweet Mini Monkey Rolls

(Ready in about 25 minutes | Servings 6)

Ingredients

/4 cup brown sugar

stick butter, melted

/4 cup granulated sugar

teaspoon ground cinnamon

1/4 teaspoon ground cardamom

1 (16-ounce) can refrigerated buttermilk biscuit dough

Directions

Spritz 6 standard-size muffin cups with nonstick spray. Mix the brown sugar and butter; divide the mixture between muffin cups.

Mix the granulated sugar with cinnamon and cardamom. Separate the dough into 16 biscuits; cut each in 6 pieces. Roll the pieces over the cinnamon sugar mixture to coat. Divide between muffin cups.

Bake at 340 degrees F for about 20 minutes or until golden brown. Turn upside down and serve.

Per serving: 446 Calories; 23.7g Fat; 54.1g Carbs; 5.3g Protein; 22.5g Sugars

947. Cranberry Cornbread Muffins

(Ready in about 35 minutes | Servings 4)

Ingredients

/4 cup all-purpose flour

/4 cup cornmeal

teaspoon baking powder

/2 teaspoon baking soda

/2 teaspoon salt

tablespoons honey

1 egg, well whisked

1/4 cup olive oil

3/4 cup milk

1/2 cup fresh cranberries, roughly chopped

Directions

In a mixing dish, thoroughly combine the flour, cornmeal, baking powder, baking soda, and salt. In a separate bowl, mix the honey, egg, olive oil, and milk.

Next, stir the liquid mixture into the dry ingredients; mix to combine well. Fold in the fresh cranberries and stir to combine well.

Pour the batter into a lightly greased muffin tin; cover with aluminum foil and poke tiny little holes all over the foil. Now, bake for 15 minutes.

Remove the foil and bake for 10 minutes more. Transfer to a wire rack to cool slightly before cutting and serving. Bon appétit!

Per serving: 439 Calories; 18.2g Fat; 60.9g Carbs; 8.2g Protein; 19.7g Sugars

948. Hanukkah Latkes (Jewish Potato Pancakes)

(Ready in about 20 minutes | Servings 4)

Ingredients

6 potatoes

4 onions

2 eggs, beaten

Sea salt and ground black pepper, to taste

1/2 teaspoon smoked paprika

1/2 cup all-purpose flour

Directions

Pulse the potatoes and onions in your food processor until smooth. Drain the mixture well and stir in the other ingredients. Mix to combine well.

Drop the pancake batter on the baking pan with a small spoon. Flatten them slightly so the center can cook.

Cook at 370 degrees for 5 minutes; turn over and cook for a further 5 minutes. Repeat with the additional batter.

Serve with sour cream if desired.

Per serving: 384 Calories; 2.7g Fat; 79g Carbs; 12.3g Protein; 7.8g Sugars

949. Crispy Wontons with Asian Dipping Sauce

(Ready in about 20 minutes | Servings 4)

Ingredients

1 teaspoon sesame oil

3/4 pound ground beef

Sea salt, to taste

1/4 teaspoon Sichuan pepper

20 wonton wrappers

Dipping Sauce:

2 tablespoons low-sodium soy sauce

1 tablespoon honey

1 teaspoon Gochujang

1 teaspoon rice wine vinegar

1/2 teaspoon sesame oil

Directions

Heat 1 teaspoon of sesame oil in a wok over medium-high heat. Cook the ground beef until no longer pink. Season with salt and Sichuan pepper.

Lay a piece of the wonton wrapper on your palm; add the beef mixture in the middle of the wrapper. Then, fold it up to form a triangle; pinch the edges to seal tightly.

Place your wontons in the lightly greased Air Fryer basket. Cook in the preheated Air Fryer at 360 degrees F for 10 minutes. Work in batches.

Meanwhile, mix all ingredients for the sauce. Serve warm.

Per serving: 335 Calories; 11.7g Fat; 28.1g Carbs; 27.2g Protein; 4.5g Sugars

950. Oatmeal Pizza Cups

(Ready in about 30 minutes | Servings 4)

Ingredients

1 cup rolled oats
1 teaspoon baking powder
1/4 teaspoon ground black pepper
Salt, to taste
2 tablespoons butter, melted

1 cup milk
4 slices smoked ham, chopped
4 ounces mozzarella cheese, shredded
4 tablespoons ketchup

Directions

Start by preheating your Air Fryer to 350 degrees F. Now, lightly grease a muffin tin with nonstick spray.

Pulse the rolled oats, baking powder, pepper, and salt in your food processor until the mixture looks like coarse meal.

Add the remaining ingredients and stir to combine well. Spoon the mixture into the prepared muffin tin.

Bake in the preheated Air Fryer for 20 minutes until a toothpick inserted comes out clean. Bon appétit!

Per serving: 343 Calories; 12.8g Fat; 35.6g Carbs; 22.4g Protein; 7.2g Sugars

951. Scrambled Eggs with Spinach and Tomato

(Ready in about 15 minutes | Servings 2)

Ingredients

2 tablespoons olive oil, melted
4 eggs, whisked
5 ounces fresh spinach, chopped
1 medium-sized tomato, chopped
1 teaspoon fresh lemon juice

1/2 teaspoon coarse salt
1/2 teaspoon ground black pepper
1/2 cup of fresh basil, roughly chopped

Directions

Add the olive oil to an Air Fryer baking pan. Make sure to tilt the pan to spread the oil evenly.

Simply combine the remaining ingredients, except for the basil leaves; whisk well until everything is well incorporated.

Cook in the preheated Air Fryer for 8 to 12 minutes at 280 degrees F. Garnish with fresh basil leaves. Serve warm with a dollop of sour cream if desired.

Per serving: 274 Calories; 23.2g Fat; 5.7g Carbs; 13.7g Protein; 2.6g Sugars

952. Colby Potato Patties

(Ready in about 15 minutes | Servings 8)

Ingredients

2 pounds white potatoes, peeled and grated
1/2 cup scallions, finely chopped
1/2 teaspoon freshly ground black pepper, or more to taste

1 tablespoon fine sea salt
1/2 teaspoon hot paprika
2 cups Colby cheese, shredded
1/4 cup canola oil
1 cup crushed crackers

Directions

Firstly, boil the potatoes until fork tender. Drain, peel and mash your potatoes.

Thoroughly mix the mashed potatoes with scallions, pepper, salt, paprika, and cheese. Then, shape the balls using your hands. Now, flatten the balls to make the patties.

In a shallow bowl, mix canola oil with crushed crackers. Roll the patties over the crumb mixture.

Next, cook your patties at 360 degrees F approximately 10 minutes, working in batches. Serve with tabasco mayo if desired. Bon appétit!

Per serving: 291 Calories; 18.0g Fat; 23.7g Carbs; 9.3g Protein; 1.7g Sugars

953. Zesty Broccoli Bites with Hot Sauce

(Ready in about 20 minutes | Servings 6)

Ingredients

For the Broccoli Bites:
1 medium-sized head broccoli, broken into florets
1/2 teaspoon lemon zest, freshly grated
1/3 teaspoon fine sea salt
1/2 teaspoon hot paprika
1 teaspoon shallot powder
1 teaspoon porcini powder

1/2 teaspoon granulated garlic
1/3 teaspoon celery seeds
1 ½ tablespoons olive oil
For the Hot Sauce:
1/2 cup tomato sauce
3 tablespoons brown sugar
1 tablespoon balsamic vinegar
½ teaspoon ground allspice

Directions

Toss all the ingredients for the broccoli bites in a mixing bowl, covering the broccoli florets on all sides.

Cook them in the preheated Air Fryer at 360 degrees for 13 to 15 minutes. In the meantime, mix all ingredients for the hot sauce.

Pause your Air Fryer, mix the broccoli with the prepared sauce and cook for further 3 minutes. Bon appétit!

Per serving: 80 Calories; 3.8g Fat; 10.8g Carbs; 2.5g Protein; 6.6g Sugars

954. Sweet Corn and Kernel Fritters

(Ready in about 20 minutes | Servings 4)

Ingredients

1 medium-sized carrot, grated
1 yellow onion, finely chopped
4 ounces canned sweet corn kernels, drained
1 teaspoon sea salt flakes
1 heaping tablespoon fresh cilantro, chopped

1 medium-sized egg, whisked
2 tablespoons plain milk
1 cup of Parmesan cheese, grated
1/4 cup of self-rising flour
1/3 teaspoon baking powder
1/3 teaspoon brown sugar

Directions

Press down the grated carrot in the colander to remove excess liquid. Then, spread the grated carrot between several sheets of kitchen towels and pat it dry.

Then, mix the carrots with the remaining ingredients in the order listed above.

Roll 1 tablespoon of the mixture into a ball; gently flatten it using the back of a spoon or your hand. Now, repeat with the remaining ingredients.

Spitz the balls with a nonstick cooking oil. Cook in a single layer at 350 degrees for 8 to 11 minutes or until they're firm to touch in the center. Serve warm and enjoy!

Per serving: 275 Calories; 8.4g Fat; 40.5g Carbs; 15.7g Protein; 7.3g Sugars

955. Gorgonzola Stuffed Mushrooms with Horseradish Mayo

(Ready in about 15 minutes | Servings 5)

Ingredients

1/2 cup of breadcrumbs
2 cloves garlic, pressed
2 tablespoons fresh coriander, chopped
1/3 teaspoon kosher salt
1/2 teaspoon crushed red pepper flakes
1 ½ tablespoons olive oil

20 medium-sized mushrooms, cut off the stems
1/2 cup Gorgonzola cheese, grated
1/4 cup low-fat mayonnaise
1 teaspoon prepared horseradish, well-drained
1 tablespoon fresh parsley, finely chopped

Directions

Mix the breadcrumbs together with the garlic, coriander, salt, red pepper, and the olive oil; mix to combine well.

Stuff the mushroom caps with the breadcrumb filling. Top with grated Gorgonzola.

Place the mushrooms in the Air Fryer grill pan and slide them into the machine. Grill them at 380 degrees F for 8 to 12 minutes or until the stuffing is warmed through.

Meanwhile, prepare the horseradish mayo by mixing the mayonnaise, horseradish and parsley. Serve with the warm fried mushrooms. Enjoy!

Per serving: 210 Calories; 15.2g Fat; 13.6g Carbs; 7.6g Protein; 2.7g Sugars

956. Potato Appetizer with Garlic-Mayo Sauce

(Ready in about 19 minutes | Servings 4)

Ingredients

2 tablespoons vegetable oil of choice
Kosher salt and freshly ground black pepper, to taste
3 Russet potatoes, cut into wedges

For the Dipping Sauce:
2 teaspoons dried rosemary, crushed
3 garlic cloves, minced
1/3 teaspoon dried marjoram, crushed
1/4 cup sour cream
1/3 cup mayonnaise

Per serving: 277 Calories; 7.2g Fat; 50g Carbs; 6g Protein; 1.7g Sugars

Directions

Lightly grease your potatoes with a thin layer of vegetable oil. Season with salt and ground black pepper.

Arrange the seasoned potato wedges in an air fryer cooking basket. Bake at 395 degrees F for 15 minutes, shaking once or twice.

In the meantime, prepare the dipping sauce by mixing all the sauce ingredients. Serve the potatoes with the dipping sauce and enjoy!

957. The Best Sweet Potato Fries Ever

(Ready in about 20 minutes | Servings 4)

Ingredients

1 1/2 tablespoons olive oil
1/2 teaspoon smoked cayenne pepper
3 sweet potatoes, peeled and cut into 1/4-inch long slices

1/2 teaspoon shallot powder
1/3 teaspoon freshly ground black pepper, or more to taste
3/4 teaspoon garlic salt

Directions

Firstly, preheat your air fryer to 360 degrees F.

Then, add the sweet potatoes to a mixing dish; toss them with the other ingredients.

Cook the sweet potatoes approximately 14 minutes. Serve with a dipping sauce of choice.

Per serving: 180 Calories; 5.4g Fat; 31.8g Carbs; 1.8g Protein; 0.7g Sugars

958. Spicy Cheesy Risotto Balls

(Ready in about 26 minutes | Servings 4)

Ingredients

3 ounces cooked rice
1 /2 cup roasted vegetable stock
1 egg, beaten
1 cup white mushrooms, finely chopped
1/2 cup seasoned breadcrumbs
3 garlic cloves, peeled and minced
1/2 yellow onion, finely chopped

1/3 teaspoon ground black pepper, or more to taste
1 ½ bell peppers, seeded minced
1/2 chipotle pepper, seeded and minced
1/2 tablespoon Colby cheese, grated
1 ½ tablespoons canola oil
Sea salt, to savor

Directions

Heat a saucepan over a moderate heat; now, heat the oil and sweat the garlic, onions, bell pepper and chipotle pepper until tender. Throw in the mushrooms and fry until they are fragrant and the liquid has almost evaporated.

Throw in the cooked rice and stock; boil for 18 minutes. Now, add the cheese and spices; mix to combine.

Allow the mixture to cool completely. Shape the risotto mixture into balls. Dip the risotto balls in the beaten egg; then, roll them over the breadcrumbs.

Air-fry risotto balls for 6 minutes at 400 degrees F. Serve with marinara sauce and enjoy!

Per serving: 176 Calories; 9.1g Fat; 16.9g Carbs; 4.7g Protein; 5.2g Sugars

959. Easy Cheesy Broccoli

(Ready in about 25 minutes | Servings 4)

Ingredients

1/3 cup grated yellow cheese
1 large-sized head broccoli, stemmed and cut small florets
2 1/2 tablespoons canola oil

2 teaspoons dried rosemary
2 teaspoons dried basil
Salt and ground black pepper, to taste

Directions

Bring a medium pan filled with a lightly salted water to a boil. Then, boil the broccoli florets for about 3 minutes.

Then, drain the broccoli florets well; toss them with the canola oil, rosemary, basil, salt and black pepper.

Set your air fryer to 390 degrees F; arrange the seasoned broccoli in the cooking basket; set the timer for 17 minutes. Toss the broccoli halfway through the cooking process.

Serve warm topped with grated cheese and enjoy!

Per serving: 103 Calories; 9.1g Fat; 4.9g Carbs; 1.9g Protein; 1.2g Sugars

960. Potato and Kale Croquettes

(Ready in about 9 minutes | Servings 6)

Ingredients

4 eggs, slightly beaten
1/3 cup flour
1/3 cup goat cheese, crumbled
1 ½ teaspoons fine sea salt
4 garlic cloves, minced

1 cup kale, steamed
1/3 cup breadcrumbs
1/3teaspoon red pepper flakes
3 potatoes, peeled and quartered
1/3 teaspoon dried dill weed

Directions

Firstly, boil the potatoes in salted water. Once the potatoes are cooked, mash them; add the kale, goat cheese, minced garlic, sea salt, red pepper flakes, dill and one egg; stir to combine well.

Now, roll the mixture to form small croquettes.

Grab three shallow bowls. Place the flour in the first shallow bowl.

Beat the remaining 3 eggs in the second bowl. After that, throw the breadcrumbs into the third shallow bowl.

Dip each croquette in the flour; then, dip them in the eggs bowl; lastly, roll each croquette in the breadcrumbs.

Air fry at 335 degrees F for 7 minutes or until golden. Tate, adjust for seasonings and serve warm.

Per serving: 309 Calories; 6.9g Fat; 49.8g Carbs; 12.1g Protein; 2g Sugars

961. Spicy Potato Wedges

(Ready in about 23 minutes | Servings 4)

Ingredients

1 ½ tablespoons melted butter
1 teaspoon dried parsley flakes
1 teaspoon ground coriander
1 teaspoon seasoned salt

3 large-sized red potatoes, cut into wedges
1/2 teaspoon chili powder
1/3 teaspoon garlic pepper

Directions

Dump the potato wedges into the air fryer cooking basket. Drizzle with melted butter and cook for 20 minutes at 380 degrees F. Make sure to shake them a couple of times during the cooking process.

Add the remaining ingredients; toss to coat potato wedges on all sides. Bon appétit!

Per serving: 288 Calories; 4.7g Fat; 44.5g Carbs; 5.4g Protein; 3.7g Sugars

962. Family Favorite Stuffed Mushrooms

(Ready in about 16 minutes | Servings 2)

Ingredients

2 teaspoons cumin powder
4 garlic cloves, peeled and minced
1 small onion, peeled and chopped
2 tablespoons bran cereal, crushed
18 medium-sized white mushrooms

Fine sea salt and freshly ground black pepper, to your liking
A pinch ground allspice
2 tablespoons olive oil

Directions

First, clean the mushrooms; remove the middle stalks from the mushrooms to prepare the "shells".

Grab a mixing dish and thoroughly combine the remaining items. Fill the mushrooms with the prepared mixture.

Cook the mushrooms at 345 degrees F heat for 12 minutes. Enjoy!

Per serving: 176 Calories; 14.7g Fat; 10.5g Carbs; 6g Protein; 4g Sugars

963. Cheese and Chive Stuffed Chicken Rolls

(Ready in about 20 minutes | Servings 6)

Ingredients

2 eggs, well-whisked
Tortilla chips, crushed
1 1/2 tablespoons extra-virgin olive oil
1 ½ tablespoons fresh chives, chopped
3 chicken breasts, halved lengthwise

1 ½ cup soft cheese
2 teaspoons sweet paprika
1/2 teaspoon whole grain mustard
1/2 teaspoon cumin powder
1/3 teaspoon fine sea salt
1/3 cup fresh cilantro, chopped
1/3 teaspoon freshly ground black pepper, or more to taste

Directions

Flatten out each piece of the chicken breast using a rolling pin. Then, grab three mixing dishes.

In the first one, combine the soft cheese with the cilantro, fresh chives, cumin, and mustard.

In another mixing dish, whisk the eggs together with the sweet paprika. In the third dish, combine the salt, black pepper, and crushed tortilla chips.

Spread the cheese mixture over each piece of chicken. Repeat with the remaining pieces of the chicken breasts; now, roll them up.

Coat each chicken roll with the whisked egg; dredge each chicken roll into the tortilla chips mixture. Lower the rolls onto the air fryer cooking basket. Drizzle extra-virgin olive oil over all rolls.

Air fry at 345 degrees F for 28 minutes, working in batches. Serve warm, garnished with sour cream if desired.

Per serving: 311 Calories; 18.3g Fat; 1.3g Carbs; 33.4g Protein; 0.3 g Sugars

964. Chicken Drumsticks with Ketchup-Lemon Sauce

(Ready in about 20 minutes + marinating time | Servings 6)

Ingredients

3 tablespoons lemon juice
1 cup tomato ketchup
1 ½ tablespoons fresh rosemary, chopped
6 skin-on chicken drumsticks, boneless

1/2 teaspoon ground black pepper
2 teaspoons lemon zest, grated
1/3 cup honey
3 cloves garlic, minced

Directions

Dump the chicken drumsticks into a mixing dish. Now, add the other items and give it a good stir; let it marinate overnight in your refrigerator.

Discard the marinade; roast the chicken legs in your air fryer at 375 degrees F for 22 minutes, turning once.

Now, add the marinade and cook an additional 6 minutes or until everything is warmed through.

Per serving: 274 Calories; 12g Fat; 17.3g Carbs; 23.3g Protein; 16.2g Sugars

965. Creamed Cajun Chicken

(Ready in about 10 minutes | Servings 6)

Ingredients

3 green onions, thinly sliced
½ tablespoon Cajun seasoning
1 ½ cup buttermilk
2 large-sized chicken breasts, cut into strips
1/2 teaspoon garlic powder

1 teaspoon salt
1 cup cornmeal mix
1 teaspoon shallot powder
1 ½ cup flour
1 teaspoon ground black pepper, or to taste

Directions

Prepare three mixing bowls. Combine 1/2 cup of the plain flour together with the cornmeal and Cajun seasoning in your bowl. In another bowl, place the buttermilk.

Pour the remaining 1 cup of flour into the third bowl.

Sprinkle the chicken strips with all the seasonings. Then, dip each chicken strip in the 1 cup of flour, then in the buttermilk; finally, dredge them in the cornmeal mixture.

Cook the chicken strips in the air fryer baking pan for 16 minutes at 365 degrees F. Serve garnished with green onions. Bon appétit!

Per serving: 400 Calories; 10.2g Fat; 48.2g Carbs; 27.3g Protein; 3.5g Sugars

966. Chive, Feta and Chicken Frittata

(Ready in about 10 minutes | Servings 4)

Ingredients

1/3 cup Feta cheese, crumbled
1 teaspoon dried rosemary
½ teaspoon brown sugar
2 tablespoons fish sauce
1 ½ cup cooked chicken breasts, boneless and shredded
1/2 teaspoon coriander sprig, finely chopped

3 medium-sized whisked eggs
1/3 teaspoon ground white pepper
1 cup fresh chives, chopped
1/2 teaspoon garlic paste
Fine sea salt, to taste
Nonstick cooking spray

Directions

Grab a baking dish that fit in your air fryer.

Lightly coat the inside of the baking dish with a nonstick cooking spray of choice. Stir in all ingredients, minus Feta cheese. Stir to combine well.

Set your machine to cook at 335 degrees for 8 minutes; check for doneness. Scatter crumbled Feta over the top and eat immediately!

Per serving: 176 Calories; 7.7g Fat; 2.4g Carbs; 22.8g Protein; 1.5g Sugars

967. Grilled Chicken Tikka Masala

(Ready in about 35 minutes + marinating time | Servings 4)

Ingredients

1 teaspoon Tikka Masala
1 teaspoon fine sea salt
2 heaping teaspoons whole grain mustard
2 teaspoons coriander, ground
2 tablespoon olive oil

2 large-sized chicken breasts, skinless and halved lengthwise
2 teaspoons onion powder
1 ½ tablespoons cider vinegar
Basmati rice, steamed
1/3 teaspoon red pepper flakes, crushed

Directions

Preheat the air fryer to 335 degrees for 4 minutes.

Toss your chicken together with the other ingredients, minus basmati rice. Let it stand at least 3 hours.

Cook for 25 minutes in your air fryer; check for doneness because the time depending on the size of the piece of chicken.

Serve immediately over warm basmati rice. Enjoy!

Per serving: 319 Calories; 20.1g Fat; 1.9g Carbs; 30.5g Protein; 0.1g Sugars

968. Award Winning Breaded Chicken

(Ready in about 10 minutes + marinating time | Servings 4)

Ingredients

For the Marinade:
- 1/2 teaspoons olive oil
- teaspoon red pepper flakes, crushed
- /3 teaspoon chicken bouillon granules
- /3 teaspoon shallot powder
- 1/2 tablespoons tamari soy sauce
- /3 teaspoon cumin powder

- 1 ½ tablespoons mayo
- 1 teaspoon kosher salt

For the chicken:
- 2 beaten eggs
- Breadcrumbs
- 1 ½ chicken breasts, boneless and skinless
- 1 ½ tablespoons plain flour

Directions

Butterfly the chicken breasts, and then, marinate them for at least 55 minutes.

Coat the chicken with plain flour; then, coat with the beaten eggs; finally, roll them in the breadcrumbs.

Lightly grease the cooking basket. Air-fry the breaded chicken at 345 degrees F for 12 minutes, flipping them halfway.

Per serving: 262 Calories; 14.9g Fat; 2.7g Carbs; 27.5g Protein; 0.3g Sugars

969. Cheese and Garlic Stuffed Chicken Breasts

(Ready in about 20 minutes | Servings 2)

Ingredients

- /2 cup Cottage cheese
- eggs, beaten
- medium-sized chicken breasts, halved
- tablespoons fresh coriander, chopped

- 1 teaspoon fine sea salt
- Seasoned breadcrumbs
- 1/3 teaspoon freshly ground black pepper, to savor
- 3 cloves garlic, finely minced

Directions

Firstly, flatten out the chicken breast using a meat tenderizer.

In a medium-sized mixing dish, combine the Cottage cheese with the garlic, coriander, salt, and black pepper.

Spread 1/3 of the mixture over the first chicken breast. Repeat with the remaining ingredients. Roll the chicken around the filling; make sure to secure with toothpicks.

Now, whisk the egg in a shallow bowl. In another shallow bowl, combine the salt, ground black pepper, and seasoned breadcrumbs.

Coat the chicken breasts with the whisked egg; now, roll them in the breadcrumbs.

Cook in the air fryer cooking basket at 365 degrees F for 22 minutes. Serve immediately.

Per serving: 424 Calories; 24.5g Fat; 7.5g Carbs; 43.4g Protein; 5.3g Sugars

970. Dinner Avocado Chicken Sliders

(Ready in about 10 minutes | Servings 4)

Ingredients

- /2 pounds ground chicken meat
- burger buns
- /2 cup Romaine lettuce, loosely packed
- teaspoon dried parsley flakes
- /3 teaspoon mustard seeds
- teaspoon onion powder
- ripe fresh avocado, mashed

- 1 teaspoon garlic powder
- 1 ½ tablespoon extra-virgin olive oil
- 1 cloves garlic, minced
- Nonstick cooking spray
- Salt and cracked black pepper (peppercorns), to taste

Directions

Firstly, spritz an air fryer cooking basket with a nonstick cooking spray.

Mix ground chicken meat, mustard seeds, garlic powder, onion powder, parsley, salt, and black pepper until everything is thoroughly combined. Make sure not to overwork the meat to avoid tough chicken burgers.

Shape the meat mixture into patties and roll them in breadcrumbs; transfer your burgers to the prepared cooking basket. Brush the patties with the cooking spray.

Air-fry at 355 F for 9 minutes, working in batches. Slice burger buns into halves. In the meantime, combine olive oil with mashed avocado and pressed garlic.

To finish, lay Romaine lettuce and avocado spread on bun bottoms; now, add burgers and bun tops. Bon appétit!

Per serving: 321 Calories; 18.7g Fat; 15.8g Carbs; 23.5g Protein; 1.2g Sugars

971. Peanut Butter and Chicken Bites

(Ready in about 10 minutes | Servings 8)

Ingredients

- 1 ½ tablespoons soy sauce
- 1/2 teaspoon smoked cayenne pepper
- 8 ounces soft cheese
- 1 1/2 tablespoons peanut butter
- 1/3 leftover chicken

- 1 teaspoon sea salt
- 32 wonton wrappers
- 1/3 teaspoon freshly cracked mixed peppercorns
- 1/2 tablespoon pear cider vinegar

Directions

Combine all of the above ingredients, minus the wonton wrappers, in a mixing dish.

Lay out the wrappers on a clean surface. Now, spread the wonton wrappers with the prepared chicken filling.

Fold the outside corners to the center over the filling; after that, roll up the wrappers tightly; you can moisten the edges with a little water.

Set the air fryer to cook at 360 degrees F. Air fry the rolls for 6 minutes, working in batches. Serve with marinara sauce. Bon appétit!

Per serving: 150 Calories; 9.7g Fat; 2.1g Carbs; 12.9g Protein; 1.6g Sugars

972. Tangy Paprika Chicken

(Ready in about 30 minutes | Servings 4)

Ingredients

- 1 ½ tablespoons freshly squeezed lemon juice
- 2 small-sized chicken breasts, boneless
- 1/2 teaspoon ground cumin
- 1 teaspoon dry mustard powder

- 1 teaspoon paprika
- 2 teaspoons cup pear cider vinegar
- 1 tablespoon olive oil
- 2 garlic cloves, minced
- Kosher salt and freshly ground mixed peppercorns, to savor

Directions

Warm the olive oil in a nonstick pan over a moderate flame. Sauté the garlic for just 1 minutes.

Remove your pan from the heat; add cider vinegar, lemon juice, paprika, cumin, mustard powder, kosher salt, and black pepper. Pour this paprika sauce into a baking dish.

Pat the chicken breasts dry; transfer them to the prepared sauce. Bake in the preheated air fryer for about 28 minutes at 335 degrees F; check for doneness using a thermometer or a fork.

Allow to rest for 8 to 9 minutes before slicing and serving. Serve with dressing.

Per serving: 312 Calories; 17.6g Fat; 2.6g Carbs; 30.4g Protein; 1.2g Sugars

973. Super-Easy Chicken with Tomato Sauce

(Ready in about 20 minutes + marinating time | Servings 4)

Ingredients

1 tablespoon balsamic vinegar
½ teaspoon red pepper flakes, crushed
1 fresh garlic, roughly chopped
2 ½ large-sized chicken breasts, cut into halves
1/3 handful fresh cilantro, roughly chopped

2 tablespoons olive oil
4 Roma tomatoes, diced
1 ½ tablespoons butter
1/3 handful fresh basil, loosely packed, sniped
1 teaspoon kosher salt
2 cloves garlic, minced
Cooked bucatini, to serve

Directions

Place the first seven ingredients in a medium-sized bowl; let it marinate for a couple of hours.

Preheat the air fryer to 325 degrees F. Air-fry your chicken for 32 minutes and serve warm.

In the meantime, prepare the tomato sauce by preheating a deep saucepan. Simmer the tomatoes until you make a chunky mixture. Throw in the garlic, basil, and butter; give it a good stir.

Serve the cooked chicken breasts with the tomato sauce and the cooked bucatini. Bon appétit!

Per serving: 377 Calories; 24.8g Fat; 6.5g Carbs; 31.6g Protein; 4.1g Sugars

974. Cheesy Pasilla Turkey

(Ready in about 30 minutes | Servings 2)

Ingredients

1/3 cup Parmesan cheese, shredded
2 turkey breasts, cut into four pieces
1/3 cup mayonnaise
1 ½ tablespoons sour cream

1/2 cup crushed crackers
1 dried Pasilla peppers
1 teaspoon onion salt
1/3 teaspoon mixed peppercorns, freshly cracked

Directions

In a shallow bowl, mix the crushed crackers, Parmesan cheese, onion salt, and the cracked mixed peppercorns together.

In a food processor, blitz the mayonnaise, along with the cream and dried Pasilla peppers until there are no lumps.

Coat the turkey breasts with this mixture, ensuring that all sides are covered.

Then, coat each piece of turkey in the Parmesan/cracker mix.

Now, preheat the air fryer to 365 degrees F; cook for 28 minutes until thoroughly cooked.

Per serving: 259 Calories; 19.1g Fat; 7.6g Carbs; 14g Protein; 1.5g Sugars

975. Festive Turkey Drumsticks with Gala Apples

(Ready in about 30 minutes + marinating time | Servings 6)

Ingredients

3 Gala apples, cored and diced
1/2 tablespoon Dijon mustard
2 sprigs rosemary, chopped
3 turkey drumsticks
1/3 cup cider vinegar
2 teaspoons olive oil

1/2 cup tamari sauce
1/2 teaspoon smoked cayenne pepper
Kosher salt and ground black pepper, to taste

Directions

Dump drumsticks, along with cider vinegar, tamari, and olive oil, into a mixing dish. Let it marinate overnight or at least 3 hours.

Set your air fryer to cook at 355 degrees F. Spread turkey drumsticks with Dijon mustard.

Season turkey drumsticks with salt, black pepper, smoked cayenne pepper, and rosemary;

Place the prepared drumstick in a lightly greased baking dish; scatter diced apples over them; work in batches, one drumstick at a time.

Pause the machine after 13 minutes; flip turkey drumstick and continue to cook for a further 10 minutes. Bon appétit!

Per serving: 100 Calories; 3.6g Fat; 14.7g Carbs; 4.9g Protein; 10.4g Sugars

976. Roasted Turkey Sausage with Potatoes

(Ready in about 40 minutes | Servings 6)

Ingredients

1/2 pound red potatoes, peeled and diced
1/2 teaspoon onion salt
1/2 teaspoon dried sage
1/2 pound ground turkey
1/3 teaspoon ginger, ground

1 sprig rosemary, chopped
1 ½ tablespoons olive oil
1/2 teaspoon paprika
2 sprigs thyme, chopped
1 teaspoon ground black pepper

Directions

In a bowl, mix the first six ingredients; give it a good stir. Heat a thin layer of vegetable oil in a nonstick skillet that is placed over a moderate flame.

Form the mixture into patties; fry until they're browned on all sides, or about 12 minutes.

Arrange the potatoes at the bottom of a baking dish. Sprinkle with the rosemary and thyme; add a drizzle of olive oil. Top with the turkey.

Roast for 32 minutes at 365 degrees F, turning once halfway through. Eat warm.

Per serving: 212 Calories; 17.1g Fat; 6.3g Carbs; 8g Protein; 0.5g Sugar

977. Dinner Turkey Sandwiches

(Ready in about 4 hours 30 minutes | Servings 4)

Ingredients

1/2 pound turkey breast
1 teaspoon garlic powder
7 ounces condensed cream of onion soup

1/3 teaspoon ground allspice
BBQ sauce, to savor

Directions

Simply dump the cream of onion soup and turkey breast into your crock-pot. Cook on HIGH heat setting for 3 hours.

Then, shred the meat and transfer to a lightly greased baking dish.

Pour in your favorite BBQ sauce. Sprinkle with ground allspice and garlic powder. Air-fry an additional 28 minutes.

To finish, assemble the sandwiches; add toppings such as pickled or fresh salad, mustard, etc.

Per serving: 114 Calories; 5.6g Fat; 3.6g Carbs; 13.1g Protein; 0.2g Sugars

978. Dijon and Curry Turkey Cutlets

(Ready in about 30 minutes + marinating time | Servings 4)

Ingredients

1/2 tablespoon Dijon mustard
1/2 teaspoon curry powder
Sea salt flakes and freshly cracked black peppercorns, to savor

1/3 pound turkey cutlets
1/2 cup fresh lemon juice
1/2 tablespoons tamari sauce

Directions

Set the air fryer to cook at 375 degrees. Then, put the turkey cutlets into a mixing dish; add fresh lemon juice, tamari, and mustard; let it marinate at least 2 hours.

Coat each turkey cutlet with the curry powder, salt, and freshly cracked black peppercorns; roast for 28 minutes; work in batches. Bon appétit!

Per serving: 190 Calories; 16.8g Fat; 2.5g Carbs; 7.4g Protein; 0.8g Sugars

979. Super Easy Sage and Lime Wings

(Ready in about 30 minutes + marinating time | Servings 4)

Ingredients

1 teaspoon onion powder
1/3 cup fresh lime juice
1/2 tablespoon corn flour
1/2 heaping tablespoon fresh chopped parsley
1/3 teaspoon mustard powder
1/2 pound turkey wings, cut into smaller pieces

2 heaping tablespoons fresh chopped sage
1/2 teaspoon garlic powder
1/2 teaspoon seasoned salt
1 teaspoon freshly cracked black or white peppercorns

Directions

Simply dump all of the above ingredients into a mixing dish; cover and let it marinate for about 1 hours in your refrigerator.

Air-fry turkey wings for 28 minutes at 355 degrees F. Bon appétit!

Per serving: 127 Calories; 7.6g Fat; 3.7g Carbs; 11.9g Protein; 0.2g Sugars

980. Creamy Lemon Turkey

(Ready in about 2 hours 25 minutes | Servings 4)

Ingredients

1/3 cup sour cream	1 teaspoon fresh marjoram, chopped
2 cloves garlic, finely minced	
1/3 teaspoon lemon zest	Salt and freshly cracked mixed peppercorns, to taste
2 small-sized turkey breasts, skinless and cubed	
1/3 cup thickened cream	1/2 cup scallion, chopped
2 tablespoons lemon juice	1/2 can tomatoes, diced
	1 ½ tablespoons canola oil

Directions

Firstly, pat dry the turkey breast. Mix the remaining items; marinate the turkey for 2 hours.

Set the air fryer to cook at 355 degrees F. Brush the turkey with a nonstick spray; cook for 23 minutes, turning once. Serve with naan and enjoy!

Per serving: 260 Calories; 15.3g Fat; 8.9g Carbs; 28.6g Protein; 1.9g Sugars

981. Turkey Wontons with Garlic-Parmesan Sauce

(Ready in about 15 minutes | Servings 8)

Ingredients

8 ounces cooked turkey breasts, shredded	8 ounces Asiago cheese, shredded
16 wonton wrappers	3 tablespoons Parmesan cheese, grated
1 ½ tablespoons butter, melted	1 teaspoon garlic powder
1/3 cup cream cheese, room temperature	Fine sea salt and freshly ground black pepper, to taste

Directions

In a small-sized bowl, mix the butter, Parmesan, garlic powder, salt, and black pepper; give it a good stir.

Lightly grease a mini muffin pan; lay 1 wonton wrapper in each mini muffin cup. Fill each cup with the cream cheese and turkey mixture.

Air-fry for 8 minutes at 335 degrees F. Immediately top with Asiago cheese and serve warm. Bon appétit!

Per serving: 362 Calories; 13.5g Fat; 40.4g Carbs; 18.5g Protein; 1.2g Sugars

982. Cajun Turkey Meatloaf

(Ready in about 45 minutes | Servings 6)

Ingredients

1 1/3 pounds turkey breasts, ground	2 tablespoons butter, room temperature
½ cup vegetable stock	1/2 cup scallions, chopped
2 eggs, lightly beaten	1/3 teaspoon ground nutmeg
1/2 sprig thyme, chopped	1/3 cup tomato ketchup
1/2 teaspoon Cajun seasonings	1/2 teaspoon table salt
1/2 sprig coriander, chopped	2 teaspoons whole grain mustard
½ cup seasoned breadcrumbs	1/3 teaspoon mixed peppercorns, freshly cracked

Directions

Firstly, warm the butter in a medium-sized saucepan that is placed over a moderate heat; sauté the scallions together with the chopped thyme and coriander leaves until just tender.

While the scallions are sautéing, set your air fryer to cook at 365 degrees F.

Combine all the ingredients, minus the ketchup, in a mixing dish; fold in the sautéed mixture and mix again.

Shape into a meatloaf and top with the tomato ketchup. Air-fry for 50 minutes. Bon appétit!

Per serving: 429 Calories; 31.6g Fat; 8.3g Carbs; 25.3g Protein; 2.2g Sugars

983. Wine-Braised Turkey Breasts

(Ready in about 30 minutes + marinating time | Servings 4)

Ingredients

1/3 cup dry white wine	1/2 cup plain flour
1½ tablespoon sesame oil	2 tablespoons oyster sauce
1/2 pound turkey breasts, boneless, skinless and sliced	Sea salt flakes and cracked black peppercorns, to taste
1/2 tablespoon honey	

Directions

Set the air fryer to cook at 385 degrees. Pat the turkey slices dry and season with the sea salt flakes and the cracked peppercorns.

In a bowl, mix the other ingredients together, minus the flour; rub your turkey with this mixture. Set aside to marinate for at least 55 minutes.

Coat each turkey slice with the plain flour. Cook for 27 minutes; make sure to flip once or twice and work in batches. Bon appétit!

Per serving: 230 Calories; 11.6g Fat; 15.2g Carbs; 16.1g Protein; 2.2g Sugars

984. Peppery Roasted Potatoes with Smoked Bacon

(Ready in about 15 minutes | Servings 2)

Ingredients

5 small rashers smoked bacon	1/3 teaspoon ground black pepper
1/3 teaspoon garlic powder	1 bell pepper, seeded and sliced
1 teaspoon sea salt	1 teaspoon mustard
2 teaspoons paprika	2 habanero peppers, halved

Directions

Simply toss all the ingredients in a mixing dish; then, transfer them to your air fryer's basket.

Air-fry at 375 degrees F for 10 minutes. Serve warm.

Per serving: 242 Calories; 11.6g Fat; 15,4g Carbs; 14.9g Protein; 5.7g Sugars

985. Cornbread with Pulled Pork

(Ready in about 24 minutes | Servings 2)

Ingredients

2 ½ cups pulled pork, leftover works well too	1/2 recipe cornbread
1 teaspoon dried rosemary	1/2 tablespoon brown sugar
1/2 teaspoon chili powder	1/3 cup scallions, thinly sliced
3 cloves garlic, peeled and pressed	1 teaspoon sea salt

Directions

Preheat a large-sized nonstick skillet over medium heat; now, cook the scallions together with the garlic and pulled pork.

Next, add the sugar, chili powder, rosemary, and salt. Cook, stirring occasionally, until the mixture is thickened.

Preheat your air fryer to 335 degrees F. Now, coat two mini loaf pans with a cooking spray. Add the pulled pork mixture and spread over the bottom using a spatula.

Spread the previously prepared cornbread batter over top of the spiced pulled pork mixture.

Bake this cornbread in the preheated air fryer until a tester inserted into the center of it comes out clean, or for 18 minutes. Bon appétit!

Per serving: 239 Calories; 7.6g Fat; 6.3g Carbs; 34.6g Protein; 4g Sugars

986. Famous Cheese and Bacon Rolls

(Ready in about 10 minutes | Servings 6)

Ingredients

1/3 cup Swiss cheese, shredded
10 slices of bacon
10 ounces canned crescent rolls
2 tablespoons yellow mustard 6

Directions

Start by preheating your air fryer to 325 degrees F.

Then, form the crescent rolls into "sheets". Spread mustard over the sheets. Place the chopped Swiss cheese and bacon in the middle of each dough sheet.

Create the rolls and bake them for about 9 minutes.

Then, set the machine to 385 degrees F; bake for an additional 4 minutes in the preheated air fryer. Eat warm with some extra yellow mustard.

Per serving: 386 Calories; 16.2g Fat; 29.7g Carbs; 14.7g Protein; 4g Sugars

987. Baked Eggs with Kale and Ham

(Ready in about 15 minutes | Servings 2)

Ingredients

2 eggs
1/4 teaspoon dried or fresh marjoram
2 teaspoons chili powder
1/3 teaspoon kosher salt
½ cup steamed kale
1/4 teaspoon dried or fresh rosemary
4 pork ham slices
1/3 teaspoon ground black pepper, or more to taste

Directions

Divide the kale and ham among 2 ramekins; crack an egg into each ramekin. Sprinkle with seasonings.

Cook for 15 minutes at 335 degrees F or until your eggs reach desired texture.

Serve warm with spicy tomato ketchup and pickles. Bon appétit!

Per serving: 417 Calories; 17.8g Fat; 3g Carbs; 61g Protein; 0.9g Sugars

988. Easiest Pork Chops Ever

(Ready in about 22 minutes | Servings 6)

Ingredients

1/3 cup Italian breadcrumbs
Roughly chopped fresh cilantro, to taste
2 teaspoons Cajun seasonings
Nonstick cooking spray
2 eggs, beaten
3 tablespoons white flour
1 teaspoon seasoned salt
Garlic & onion spice blend, to taste
6 pork chops
1/3 teaspoon freshly cracked black pepper

Directions

Coat the pork chops with Cajun seasonings, salt, pepper, and the spice blend on all sides.

Then, add the flour to a plate. In a shallow dish, whisk the egg until pale and smooth. Place the Italian breadcrumbs in the third bowl.

Dredge each pork piece in the flour; then, coat them with the egg; finally, coat them with the breadcrumbs. Spritz them with cooking spray on both sides.

Now, air-fry pork chops for about 18 minutes at 345 degrees F; make sure to taste for doneness after first 12 minutes of cooking. Lastly, garnish with fresh cilantro. Bon appétit!

Per serving: 398 Calories; 21g Fat; 4.7g Carbs; 44.2g Protein; 0.5g Sugars

989. Onion Rings Wrapped in Bacon

(Ready in about 25 minutes | Servings 4)

Ingredients

12 rashers back bacon
1/2 teaspoon ground black pepper
Chopped fresh parsley, to taste
1/2 teaspoon paprika
1/2 teaspoon chili powder
1/2 tablespoon soy sauce
½ teaspoon salt

Directions

Start by preheating your air fryer to 355 degrees F.

Season the onion rings with paprika, salt, black pepper, and chili powder. Simply wrap the bacon around the onion rings; drizzle with soy sauce.

Bake for 17 minutes, garnish with fresh parsley and serve. Bon appétit!

Per serving: 317 Calories; 16.8g Fat; 22.7g Carbs; 20.2g Protein; 2.7g Sugars

990. Easy Pork Burgers with Blue Cheese

(Ready in about 44 minutes | Servings 6)

Ingredients

1/3 cup blue cheese, crumbled
6 hamburger buns, toasted
2 teaspoons dried basil
1/3 teaspoon smoked paprika
1 pound ground pork
2 tablespoons tomato puree
2 small-sized onions, peeled and chopped
1/2 teaspoon ground black pepper
3 garlic cloves, minced
1 teaspoon fine sea salt

Directions

Start by preheating your air fryer to 385 degrees F.

In a mixing dish, combine the pork, onion, garlic, tomato puree, and seasonings; mix to combine well.

Form the pork mixture into six patties; cook the burgers for 23 minutes. Pause the machine, turn the temperature to 365 degrees F and cook for 18 more minutes.

Place the prepared burger on the bottom bun; top with blue cheese; assemble the burgers and serve warm.

Per serving: 383 Calories; 19.5g Fat; 24.7g Carbs; 25.7g Protein; 4g Sugars

991. Sausage, Pepper and Fontina Frittata

(Ready in about 14 minutes | Servings 5)

Ingredients

3 pork sausages, chopped
5 well-beaten eggs
1 ½ bell peppers, seeded and chopped
1 teaspoon smoked cayenne pepper
2 tablespoons Fontina cheese
1/2 teaspoon tarragon
1/2 teaspoon ground black pepper
1 teaspoon salt

Directions

In a cast-iron skillet, sweat the bell peppers together with the chopped pork sausages until the peppers are fragrant and the sausage begins to release liquid.

Lightly grease the inside of a baking dish with pan spray.

Throw all of the above ingredients into the prepared baking dish, including the sautéed mixture; stir to combine.

Bake at 345 degrees F approximately 9 minutes. Serve right away with the salad of choice.

Per serving: 420 Calories; 19.6g Fat; 3.7g Carbs; 41g Protein; 2g Sugars

992. Country-Style Pork Meatloaf

(Ready in about 25 minutes | Servings 4)

Ingredients

1/2 pound lean minced pork
1/3 cup breadcrumbs
1/2 tablespoons minced green garlic
1½ tablespoon fresh cilantro, minced
1/2 tablespoon fish sauce
1/3 teaspoon dried basil
2 leeks, chopped
2 tablespoons tomato puree
1/2 teaspoons dried thyme
Salt and ground black pepper, to taste

Directions

Add all ingredients, except for breadcrumbs, to a large-sized mixing dish and combine everything using your hands.

Lastly, add the breadcrumbs to form a meatloaf.

Bake for 23 minutes at 365 degrees F. Afterward, allow your meatloaf to rest for 10 minutes before slicing and serving. Bon appétit!

Per serving: 460 Calories; 26.6g Fat; 3.9g Carbs; 48.9g Protein; 2g Sugars

993. Grilled Lemony Pork Chops

(Ready in about 34 minutes | Servings 5)

Ingredients

pork chops	1 teaspoon garlic salt½ lemon, cut
/3 cup vermouth	into wedges
/2 teaspoon paprika	1 teaspoon freshly cracked black
sprigs thyme, only leaves,	pepper
rushed	3 tablespoons lemon juice
/2 teaspoon dried oregano	3 cloves garlic, minced
Fresh parsley, to serve	2 tablespoons canola oil

Directions

Firstly, heat the canola oil in a sauté pan over a moderate heat. Now, sweat the garlic until just fragrant.

Remove the pan from the heat and pour in the lemon juice and vermouth. Now, throw in the seasonings. Dump the sauce into a baking dish, along with the pork chops.

Tuck the lemon wedges among the pork chops and air-fry for 27 minutes at 345 degrees F. Bon appétit!

Per serving: 400 Calories; 23g Fat; 4.1g Carbs; 40.5g Protein; 1.5g Sugars

994. Herbed Crumbed Filet Mignon

(Ready in about 20 minutes | Servings 4)

Ingredients

/2 pound filet mignon	1 teaspoon dried rosemary
Sea salt and ground black pepper,	1 teaspoon dried thyme
o your liking	1 tablespoon sesame oil
/2 teaspoon cayenne pepper	1 small-sized egg, well-whisked
teaspoon dried basil	1/2 cup seasoned breadcrumbs

Directions

Season the filet mignon with salt, black pepper, cayenne pepper, basil, rosemary, and thyme. Brush with sesame oil.

Put the egg in a shallow plate. Now, place the breadcrumbs in another plate.

Coat the filet mignon with the egg; then, lay it into the crumbs. Set your Air Fryer to cook at 360 degrees F.

Cook for 10 to 13 minutes or until golden. Serve with mixed salad leaves and enjoy!

Per serving: 268 Calories; 14.5g Fat; 1.0g Carbs; 32.0g Protein; 0.0g Sugars

995. The Best London Broil Ever

(Ready in about 30 minutes + marinating time | Servings 8)

Ingredients

pounds London broil	2 tablespoons olive oil
large garlic cloves, minced	Sea salt and ground black pepper,
tablespoons balsamic vinegar	to taste
tablespoons whole-grain	1/2 teaspoon dried hot red pepper
mustard	flakes

Directions

Score both sides of the cleaned London broil.

Thoroughly combine the remaining ingredients; massage this mixture into the meat to coat it on all sides. Let it marinate for at least 3 hours.

Set the Air Fryer to cook at 400 degrees F; Then cook the London broil for 15 minutes. Flip it over and cook another 10 to 12 minutes. Bon appétit!

Per serving: 257 Calories; 9.2g Fat; 0.1g Carbs; 41.0g Protein; 0.4g Sugars

996. Old-Fashioned Beef Stroganoff

(Ready in about 20 minutes | Servings 4)

Ingredients

3/4 pound beef sirloin steak, cut	1 cup leek, chopped
into small-sized strips	2 cloves garlic, crushed
1/4 cup balsamic vinegar	1 teaspoon cayenne pepper
1 tablespoon brown mustard	Sea salt flakes and crushed red
2 tablespoons all-purpose flour	pepper, to taste
1 tablespoon butter	1 cup sour cream
1 cup beef broth	2 ½ tablespoons tomato paste

Directions

Place the beef along with the balsamic vinegar and the mustard in a mixing dish; cover and marinate in your refrigerator for about 1 hour.

Then, coat the beef strips with the flour; butter the inside of a baking dish and put the beef into the dish.

Add the broth, leeks and garlic. Cook at 380 degrees for 8 minutes. Pause the machine and add the cayenne pepper, salt, red pepper, sour cream and tomato paste; cook for additional 7 minutes.

Check for doneness and serve with warm egg noodles, if desired. Bon appétit!

Per serving: 352 Calories; 20.8g Fat; 10.0g Carbs; 29.8g Protein; 1.4g Sugars

997. Tender Beef Chuck with Brussels Sprouts

(Ready in about 25 minutes + marinating time | Servings 4)

Ingredients

1 pound beef chuck shoulder steak	1/2 teaspoon garlic powder
2 tablespoons vegetable oil	1/2 pound Brussels sprouts,
1 tablespoon red wine vinegar	cleaned and halved
1 teaspoon fine sea salt	1/2 teaspoon fennel seeds
1/2 teaspoon ground black pepper	1 teaspoon dried basil
1 teaspoon smoked paprika	1 teaspoon dried sage
1 teaspoon onion powder	

Directions

Firstly, marinate the beef with vegetable oil, wine vinegar, salt, black pepper, paprika, onion powder, and garlic powder. Rub the marinade into the meat and let it stay at least for 3 hours.

Air fry at 390 degrees F for 10 minutes. Pause the machine and add the prepared Brussels sprouts; sprinkle them with fennel seeds, basil, and sage.

Turn the machine to 380 degrees F; press the power button and cook for 5 more minutes. Pause the machine, stir and cook for further 10 minutes.

Next, remove the meat from the cooking basket and cook the vegetables a few minutes more if needed and according to your taste. Serve with your favorite mayo sauce.

Per serving: 302 Calories; 14.2g Fat; 6.5g Carbs; 36.6g Protein; 1.6g Sugars

998. All-In-One Spicy Spaghetti with Beef

(Ready in about 30 minutes | Servings 4)

Ingredients

3/4 pound ground chuck
1 onion, peeled and finely chopped
1 teaspoon garlic paste
1 bell pepper, chopped
1 small-sized habanero pepper, deveined and finely minced
1/2 teaspoon dried rosemary

1/2 teaspoon dried marjoram
1 ¼ cups crushed tomatoes, fresh or canned
1/2 teaspoon sea salt flakes
1/4 teaspoon ground black pepper, or more to taste
1 package cooked spaghetti, to serve

Directions

In the Air Fryer baking dish, place the ground meat, onion, garlic paste, bell pepper, habanero pepper, rosemary, and the marjoram.

Air-fry, uncovered, for 10 to 11 minutes. Next step, stir in the tomatoes along with salt and pepper; cook 17 to 20 minutes. Serve over cooked spaghetti. Bon appétit!

Per serving: 359 Calories; 5.5g Fat; 59.9g Carbs; 16.9g Protein; 2.7g Sugars

999. Beer-Braised Short Loin

(Ready in about 15 minutes | Servings 4)

Ingredients

1 ½ pounds short loin
2 tablespoons olive oil
1 bottle beer

2-3 cloves garlic, finely minced
2 Turkish bay leaves

Directions

Pat the beef dry; then, tenderize the beef with a meat mallet to soften the fibers. Place it in a large-sized mixing dish.

Add the remaining ingredients; toss to coat well and let it marinate for at least 1 hour.

Cook about 7 minutes at 395 degrees F; after that, pause the Air Fryer. Flip the meat over and cook for another 8 minutes, or until it's done.

Per serving: 379 Calories; 16.4g Fat; 3.7g Carbs; 46.0g Protein; 0.0g Sugars

1000. Beef and Kale Omelet

(Ready in about 20 minutes | Servings 4)

Ingredients

Non-stick cooking spray
1/2 pound leftover beef, coarsely chopped
2 garlic cloves, pressed
1 cup kale, torn into pieces and wilted
1 tomato, chopped

1/4 teaspoon brown sugar
4 eggs, beaten
4 tablespoons heavy cream
1/2 teaspoon turmeric powder
Salt and ground black pepper, to your liking
1/8 teaspoon ground allspice

Directions

Spritz the inside of four ramekins with a cooking spray.

Divide all of the above ingredients among the prepared ramekins. Stir until everything is well combined.

Air-fry at 360 degrees F for 16 minutes; check with a wooden stick and return the eggs to the Air Fryer for a few more minutes as needed. Serve immediately.

Per serving: 236 Calories; 13.7g Fat; 4.0g Carbs; 23.8g Protein; 1.0g Sugars

Made in the USA
Las Vegas, NV
10 July 2022

51333435R00103